1968 • McCarthy • New Hampshire

To John + Pat
Holland –
the keeper of the
campaign purse --
I'm still solvent as
a result. Best
Dick

1968 • McCarthy • New Hampshire

I Hear America Singing

David Charles Hoeh

Lone Oak Press, Ltd.

1968 • McCarthy • New Hampshire
David Charles Hoeh

10987654321 Library of Congress Catalog Card Number: 94-73145

ISBN 883477-00-X

Set in Galliard and Stone Sans by Montgomery Media, Inc.
Cover design by Montgomery Media, Inc.
Printed and bound by BookCrafters, Inc.

Printed in the United States of America.

  Printed on acid-free recycled paper.

Published
by
Lone Oak Press, Ltd.
304 Eleventh Avenue Southeast
Rochester, Minnesota 55904
507-280-6557 Fax 507-280-6260

To my family

The reason
Then and now

To inspirations

William L. Dunfey
Allard K. Lowenstein

Eugene J. McCarthy

Contents

Acknowledgments

The draft of this book was written between 1973 and 1978 using then contemporary sources based in that time. It is a story about an event that is now political history of twenty five years ago. The story has been edited only modestly to reflect changes in usage and especially gender reference from the early 1970s. If some usage seems dated, it is deliberately retained to reflect what we were then.

The preparation of this book from the material written earlier was delayed until both time and technology made it possible. The problem of time is easily explained—time from other things to be able to work on the story. Technology which was not available when the draft was written now provides the ability to turn the typewritten text into copy that could be reviewed, manipulated, edited and printed. The technology of personal computing made it possible to scan rough copy and turn it into laser printed text in my own office—a miracle of our era. Without this technology, returning to the 1970s text would have been an overwhelming task.

Technology takes the process so far but to make a book, which is, hopey, useful and interesting, there needs to be an editor. Kate Reed accepted this task with unusual skill and sensitivity to the topic. She took a massive text and shaped it into a story which now achieves the twin objectives of being interesting reading and a faithful account of an important political event. Her sensitivity comes from having lived the era as a McCarthy supporter who did not venture to New Hampshire but shared the experience as it happened. She now feels as if she knows the people of the story and the events are of her time then and now. It is to her that the credit goes if this book comes alive for the reader.

Montgomery Media took the copy and created the book. Susan Montgomery and Barbara Capstran's encouragement, and the book development talent of Mary Beth Nilles made text into a book design. Their commitment to the project has been exceptional and one which kept the goal always in focus.

To all of those who participated in what made this political event happen—named and unnamed in this book—without you, and what brought you to New Hampshire and to the candidacy of Senator Eugene J. McCarthy in 1968, none of this story would exist. To that courageous band of people, the New Hampshire Steering Committee, you made it happen by being there at the beginning and being the energy which became the political conscience of 1968.

There are people of particular importance to me, to what brought me to the political event of 1968, and to the enduring commitment to tell the story. William L. "Bud" Dunfey opened the New Hampshire political door to me in 1959 and continued as my friend and political mentor. My personal regret is that Bud died before this book was finished.

From my academic life, my writing professor at the University of New Hampshire, author Thomas Williams, challenged me to write, keep writing, and work at writing. The second political scientist, John Fenton of the University of Massachusetts–Amherst, encouraged me to write about my 1968 experience. He persisted until the University generously acknowledged my effort, in 1978, with a doctoral degree.

The explorers of the political wilderness leading to 1968 were Allard K. Lowenstein and Curtis Gans. Their vision, energy, and personal sacrifice blazed a trail which we then followed. Allard the Pied Piper, and Curtis the pragmatist, took to the air and roads as Johnny Appleseed had once done, and found the places across the nation where the seed of questioning might flourish. Without their talent for connecting and then energizing individuals, little but noise at the fringes would be remembered of this political challenge.

Gerry Studds, now a distinguished and long-term Congressman from the State of Massachusetts, helped put the New Hampshire campaign pieces in place. Without him on the telephone, at the meetings, and then in the headquarters during those early 1968 winter days, McCarthy would not have come to New Hampshire nor would the effort have succeeded.

The details of the 1968 McCarthy campaign are collected at the Lauinger Library of Georgetown University, which houses the product of the McCarthy Historical Project. Oral history tapes, personal files, and the materials of the entire campaign have been collected. I relieved an attic of my collection some years ago and gave it to the library. To help with this book I needed the assistance of George Barringer, special collections librarian, and research librarian Nicole Wallace. Their counterpart in New Hampshire is Charles Brereton, political writer and resident chronologist of the New Hampshire presidential primary—past, present, and future. To Chuck special thanks for more than twenty-five years of infrequent but always stimulating contact.

Brigid Sullivan, my spouse, gave me the time, the patience, and the nudge to assemble this book from the pieces of prior work. She recognized how important achieving this goal was for me and let me devote my energy to it when the opportunity opened in 1992 and early 1993. Now I am back at work grateful to her for sustaining me during the months of translating scanned text and edited pages.

The final acknowledgment is to the genius of those who put the New Hampshire presidential primary into the political landscape of this nation. The New Hampshire Presidential Primary is a modest door to the political system which opens by time lock every four years. It offers a neutral process, available to any one to use, but is clearly one of those safety valves in the political system which allows the energy of change to be expressed, tested, proven, or released with little or no threat to the entire construction of the republic.

I sincerely hope this book does credit to all those who were part of *1968 • McCarthy • New Hampshire,* and that it will endure as a record of how one generation of patriotic Americans fought to keep this democracy alive.

The message is, when it needs to be done again, be sure to do it—that is our legacy.

David Charles Hoeh
December 1993

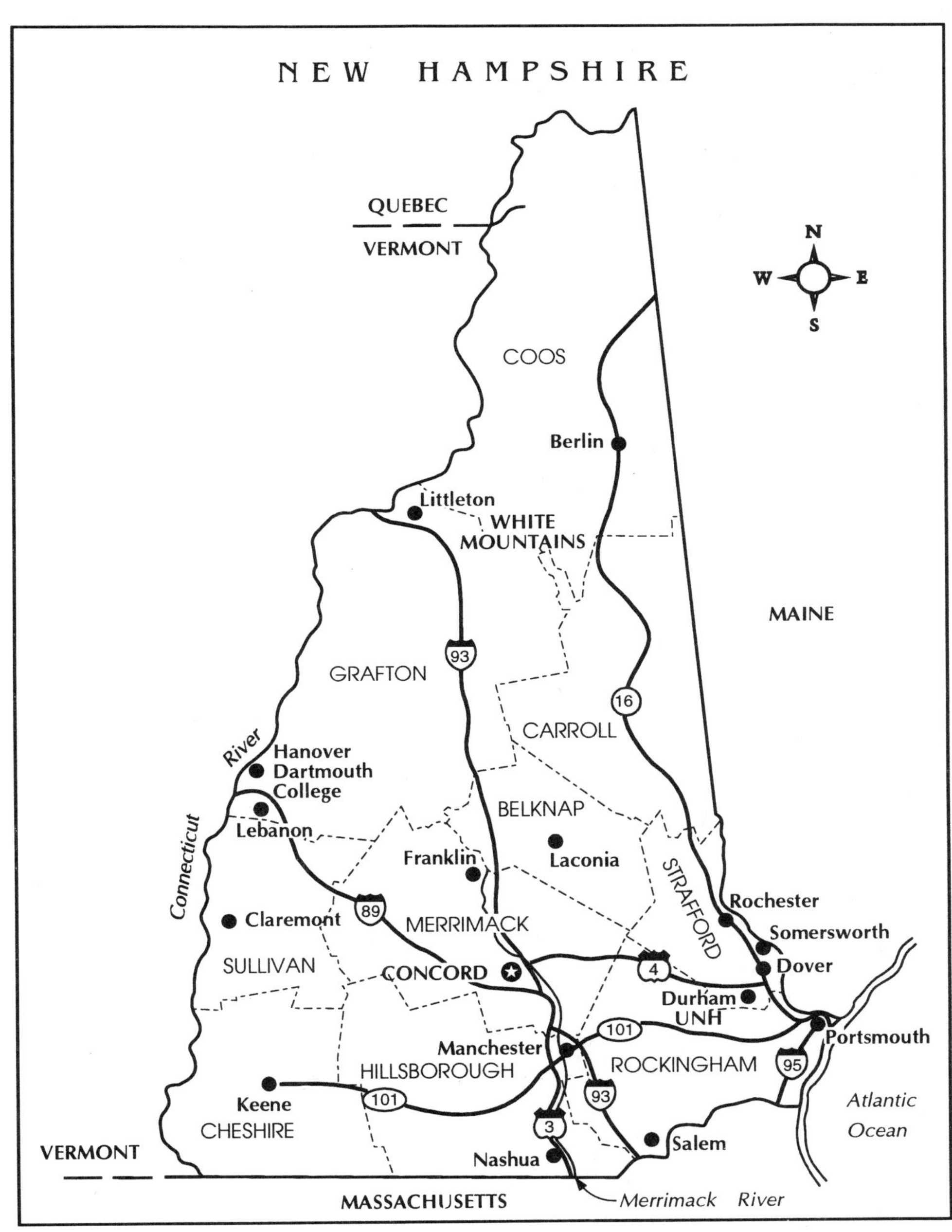
NEW HAMPSHIRE
QUEBEC
VERMONT
N
W
E
S
COOS
Berlin
Littleton
WHITE MOUNTAINS
MAINE
93
GRAFTON
16
CARROLL
River
Hanover
Dartmouth College
Lebanon
BELKNAP
Laconia
Connecticut
Franklin
STRAFFORD
Rochester
Somersworth
Claremont
89
MERRIMACK
Dover
SULLIVAN
CONCORD
4
Durham
UNH
101
Manchester
Portsmouth
HILLSBOROUGH
ROCKINGHAM
95
93
Keene
101
Atlantic Ocean
CHESHIRE
3
Salem
VERMONT
Nashua
MASSACHUSETTS
Merrimack River

Introduction

A BEGINNING

A political event like the McCarthy campaign in New Hampshire has many perhaps even thousands of beginnings, as many in fact as the individuals who became involved in the campaign. This book begins with a personal account. It has been said that many were caught up in the events and were moved by changing conditions to join the movement, but in the early stages what was to become the McCarthy campaign, and even later the New Politics movement, was made up of persons who deliberately took a different direction from that of their friends, neighbors, colleagues, and even families.

At the time these personal decisions were made, the goals seemed unobtainable. No incumbent president had been denied a nomination in modern times, and no essential policy embodied by an incumbent president had been changed as a result of renomination challenges. The objective for those who were concerned about the state of national affairs in 1967—to get the president to change Vietnam policy or to replace the incumbent as the nominee of the Democratic Party—was not considered to be politically realistic. The personal decision to oppose, politically, the policy and/or the president became a decision of personal vindication, almost an act of private absolution. Instead of hand-wringing frustration and, perhaps, implied complicity with contemporary events and policies, people sought methods to absolve themselves, to clean their hands, not only by expressing their opposition to policies and actions they did not like but also by actually creating organizations through which they might act.

In the back of many minds were the questions that our children would ask: Where were you during 1967 and 1968 when the war in Vietnam was being escalated? Where did you stand on that war? What did you do to affirm yourself as an American capable of speaking out and working to change such policies?

Was it arrogance, selfishness, fear, cowardice, or self-preservation that motivated you, as critics of the McCarthy effort charged, or was it vindication, concern, a sense of destiny that drove you to each of these decisions? The individual substance of those decisions has not been recorded, qualified, or quantified. We know who voted, where, when, and to some extent even why, but how they got the chance to vote, to make a choice, and to ponder alternatives is a different story. The voters be praised; the politicians be damned. The movement be praised; the workers be forgotten. The beginning is lost; only the ending is pondered. To regain some of these events and to tie them to happenings requires blending time, space, perspective, perception, image, personalities, and experience within a defined period. That is the challenge of this book.

NEW HAMPSHIRE DEMOCRATS

I gradually became involved in New Hampshire politics and became a leader of the 1968 McCarthy campaign in that state. Born in Boston, brought up in Newton, Massachusetts, I enrolled as an undergraduate at the University of New Hampshire in 1956. My interest in politics had been spurred by an attraction to Adlai E. Stevenson, and, through Stevenson, to the Democratic Party.

Small states offer openings to be involved politically that larger, more politically structured states do not. New Hampshire, during the late 1950s, offered unique opportunities to get involved in the Democratic Party. The few leaders with statewide political interests were young, aggressive, needed helpers and were, above all, open to having young people become active. My first campaign experience came as part of a course assignment at the university. Each student was to participate, as best they could, in the gubernatorial campaign. I chose to help the candidacy of the then Democratic mayor of Laconia, New Hampshire, Bernard L. Boutin.

The Boutin candidacy was the first serious attempt by the young leadership of the Democratic Party to challenge Republican dominance in the postwar era. The reform-minded wing of the party had succeeded in nominating a respectable candidate who was both energetic and capable. In 1958, Boutin came within five thousand votes of being elected governor as the result of both a severe split in the Republican Party and the aggressive new organization of the Democratic Party.

A leader in the revitalization of the New Hampshire Democrats was William L. Dunfey, who had organized the Young Democrats of New Hampshire. Out of that political venture and its contacts an organization developed that would eventually overpower an entrenched and resistant senior party.

In the course of the Boutin campaign, Dunfey became acquainted with John F. Kennedy, then the junior U.S. senator from Massachusetts, and was included in Kennedy's presidential campaign planning. John Kennedy saw to it that Bill Dunfey was appointed as a regional representative.

Dunfey's domain included the six New England states and New York. His job was to find Democrats, create party organizations, generate political energy, stimulate candidates, placate those involved in intraparty conflicts, and assist in managing the revival of a Democratic Party that had been out of the White House for eight hungry years.

Dunfey critically absorbed the experiences of the skilled and advised the unskilled. Nothing was to be left to chance; each state had its important role; each state would have its say; each Democratic organization would feel the presence of the ambassador from the national party. It was unquestionably a unique effort and one that paved the way for the reemergence of the Democratic Party nationally and particularly in states such as New Hampshire and Vermont that felt the presence of Bill Dunfey.

Out of that frustratingly close Boutin campaign of 1958, I became acquainted with the Dunfey family. During the summer of 1960, I helped Bill Dunfey with various projects for the Democratic Party in New Hampshire. A solid block of New England state delegations had been assembled in support of the nomination of John F. Kennedy. Dunfey's role with the National Committee shifted to that of assisting Kennedy. Dunfey was the convention contact for the delegations of his region and, as a result, he became a recognized political power in his own right.

The political structure of New Hampshire, during that time, can be described as a truncated pyramid. That is, virtually anyone willing and able to become involved in Democratic politics could become a part of the upper hierarchy of the party. The simple act of sticking one's neck out and being available to work was often sufficient to gain recognition.

The party had long suffered from both a lack of an active hierarchy and the disloyalty of those holding office in the name of the party. For more than a generation, the only reason to be a Democratic Party official was to gain sufficient party identity to qualify for those jobs and commissions requiring minority representation. The crumbs were regularly swept from the ruling Republican Party tables into the mouths of waiting Democrats. Such party officers were not interested in gambling away a sure reward system for the long shot of actually electing a Democrat to major office. Nominations were filled by those only marginally interested in making a vigorous run for the actual office. It was often more valuable to run a tidy race and wait for the minority appointment, or be rewarded with a federal appointment during the years of Democratic administrations in Washington than it was to wage a vigorous campaign.

In order for John Kennedy to have a reasonable chance for the 1960 presidential nomination, he had to assemble votes in the convention that would be fully reliable and in numbers large enough to constitute a block. Although the process of assembling the New England delegations into one voting block could be relatively manageable, there was one flaw in the strategy. In all of the states but New Hampshire, manageable delegation selection processes were available. Delegates were selected through party-controlled conventions, caucuses, or a combination of these, or by direct appointment. Only in New Hampshire were delegates selected directly by the voters in a delegate selection primary. Not only did New Hampshire present a much less manageable political situation, it also was a state that was in the early throes of party reorganization.

Dunfey's analysis showed the state party organization was dominated by delegations from the two largest cities, Manchester and Nashua, both within the state's most populous county, Hillsborough. Inside those cities and within that county, the Democratic Party was the majority party to the extent of practically excluding the

Republicans in the cities. The Democrats functioned in the urban enclaves it dominated much as the Republicans did in the statewide context. The urban Democratic Party tended to be hierarchical; leadership was difficult to challenge; the rules were well known and observed by most; and the scope of interest and the operation of the party were confined to protecting the territory and powers that were secure. The urban Democrats did not venture far from their domains nor did the outside Republicans attempt to disrupt or seriously contest the urban fiefdoms.

Outside of Hillsborough County, and with the exception of several concentrations of Democrats in the state's other twelve cities, Democrats almost did not exist. Where they did, the idea of party organization and political efficacy was remote, if not actually farcical. In many towns there was not a sufficient number of registered Democrats to staff the minority offices required by law for election supervision. In others, local Republicans actively repressed anyone's desire to register in the minority party. Social and even economic ostracism could be the consequence for those who dared to insist on becoming a Democrat.

The combination of one-party repression, both Republican and Democratic, and conservative one-party politics made the New Hampshire political environment a narrow-minded and intolerant place for those who espoused liberal political philosophies. Political security and social respectability were ensured by maintaining a stance in the mainstream of New Hampshire's right-of-center conservatism.

This, then, was the political situation Dunfey and his reform-minded associates had to confront when they sought to revive the New Hampshire Democratic Party. The first victory was won in 1956. The Dunfey forces were able to elect their own state Democratic Party chair, Robert Branch, in spite of their small numbers. Much of the energy of the reformers came from the Democrats in the smaller cities and larger towns of the state. Matched in a coalition with the excluded liberals of the urban centers, the reform effort was well underway when Bernard Boutin came within a whisker of gaining an upset victory in 1958. His loss was attributed to a smaller than normal plurality from the conservative Democrats of the state's largest city, Manchester. This will be seen again in 1968.

New Hampshire's presidential politics duplicates its state traditions. Political credits have often been amassed through working for the right candidate in the presidential primary. These credits are cashed in for jobs or favors should the candidate actually win. To maximize this strategy, New Hampshire created, on purpose or by accident, its presidential primary which, by its very existence, gave New Hampshire politicos the chance for direct contact with candidates. Through this contact and appropriate political work, a political career could be established. Since the better debt payoffs are the federal rewards, such as postal jobs, judgeships, contracts, and access, those who wanted such jobs or rewards went with the perceived winner. Under these circumstances ideology is an inconvenience. The appropriate role is that of the broker or facilitator. The local political operative puts oneself in the position of delivering votes.

Since Dunfey-Boutin and their allies had maneuvered close to the fortunes of John F. Kennedy, the wounded Old Guard of the party was left without an option in the upcoming presidential primary. Since no other prominent Democrat intended to challenge John Kennedy on home turf, the Old Guard was left to act the spoiler role in the delegate selection portion of the March 1960 event.

KENNEDY DELEGATE STRATEGY: 1960

The Kennedy-Dunfey-Boutin strategy for New Hampshire was to begin assembling Kennedy's New England bloc with as tight delegate-to-candidate ties as possible. This meant that a carefully selected slate of ten "pledged" to Kennedy possible delegate candidates would have to be placed on the ballot and then elected. Those seeking the "spoiler" or broker role contended that to be pledged was antithetical to the concept of a self-nominated, freely elected, and voter-selected delegation. A pledged delegation to the Los Angeles Convention would have no room to maneuver and, therefore, could not effectively barter for the interests of the state. On the other hand, a delegation composed of representatives elected as favorable to the nomination of John F. Kennedy would have room to maneuver should the Kennedy candidacy weaken as the convention approached.

The 1960 Kennedy primary was not the automatic victory that it appeared once the votes were counted. The problem of turning out a significant vote when almost no contest existed was the first test. The second test was to put life into the New England delegate bloc strategy by electing the full slate of ten pledged Kennedy delegates. On both counts the Kennedy-Dunfey-Boutin forces were successful. An unprecedented forty thousand votes were cast for John F. Kennedy and the total pledged slate of Kennedy delegates was elected. The Kennedy candidacy had passed through the exceedingly hazardous waters of the New Hampshire presidential primary not only unharmed but battle-wise and confident as well.

Working with William Dunfey during the weeks just prior to the Los Angeles convention and after John Kennedy's nomination, I was offered a rare experience in the presidential campaign and with the significant races for that year in New Hampshire. I was asked by Dunfey to help with the arrangements for a presidential candidate's New Hampshire visit, by organizing party meetings, and participating in gubernatorial and congressional campaign planning. Such participation had seemed only a dream as recently as a few months before it happened.

The relatively few people in the new Democratic Party leadership meant that all willing persons, regardless of age or experience, would be quickly pressed into service. Foreshadowing the 1968 youthful volunteers, we became the substitute for the paid workers of the past, workers who could only deliver those votes that they had delivered over and over again through the years. The new New Hampshire Democratic Party had, as its goal, to elect a governor and to become the majority party. While this goal was ambitious, it was the era of the New Frontier and New Hampshire Democrats were determined not to be left behind.

Before the fall 1960 election I left New Hampshire for graduate school in Boston. By that time I could name the ten counties, their Democratic party chairs, the major cities and towns of the state, and I was acquainted with at least one person in each of these population centers.

I had organized meetings, written press releases, published a newsletter, helped with fund-raising, prepared agendas for campaign strategy sessions, helped plan the State Democratic Convention, helped draft planks of the party platform, worked with candidate advertising agencies, assisted in the preparation of campaign materials, and advised on the operation of public opinion survey. In three short months I had become intimately familiar with the New Hampshire Democratic Party, its past, and its 1960 present.

As the principal guide in this educational process, Bill Dunfey served as an effective model for involving persons in political activity. For him the political system, and especially the Democratic Party, should be wide open and willing to welcome any and all who wished to work. The objective of a campaign was not to build exclusive groups, organizations, or cabals, but to get votes and to elect good candidates to public office.

To Dunfey each campaign had its own life. The Kennedy campaign of 1960 symbolized youth, embodied vigor, sought to release new national energies, and expressed a new openness and desire for activity. For Dunfey a political campaign was a continuum extending from the candidate to the organization to the voter. The response that a campaign and a candidate elicit in terms of campaign resources, principally workers and money, makes possible the ultimate objective of sufficient votes to elect the candidate. Since the thread connecting these aspects is essential to a successful political venture, each aspect and the interaction between them must be understood. From Dunfey I learned that the consistency of this mixture differs from political situation to political situation. Politicians who are successful, not just in being elected but in having influence over events, understand the complexity of these assessments and are capable of managing changing political situations.

The Dunfey style was the Kennedy style, and he adapted that style to the political environment of New Hampshire. As with the national Kennedy style, the New Hampshire version appealed to the young, the forward looking, the vigorous, and the intellectual. Kennedy's Catholicism was not expected to be a problem for New Hampshire Democrats as election day approached. What did cause the most concern for the youthful Kennedy campaigners and for the Democratic in-state candidates was the apparent unwillingness of the New Hampshire voter to respond to campaigns or candidates that promised change.

The status quo in northern New England was not paradise, but it is a known condition. Change as a political promise is only attractive in New Hampshire when the status quo has become uncertain. Hard work is perceived to ensure not only survival but a modicum of prosperity. Sudden riches are not part of the northern New England experience. Conservative governments, churches, schools, and philosophies have dominated New Hampshire for too long to respond to a sudden call for change. In 1960, political change for its own sake was not seen as a virtue in New Hampshire. Whatever desire there was for change was not strong enough to overcome the habit of voting a straight party ticket, nor was it strong enough to overcome a resistance to electing a Boston Irish Catholic president of the United States.

That year, 1960, Richard Nixon carried New Hampshire by a wide margin while H. Styles Bridges for U.S. Senate smothered his opponent, Dartmouth professor Herbert Hill. Wesley Powell, governor, proceeded to swamp even the spunky candidacy of Bernard L. Boutin.

What, throughout the summer of 1960, had appeared to be an exceptionally well-developed and contagiously optimistic campaign, had by November crashed against New Hampshire's fundamental resistance to change. Although the results were unsatisfactory, the experience of the campaigns for those who participated was not diminished as a consequence of the result.

Dunfey was elected to the Democratic National Committee by New Hampshire's pledged Kennedy delegation to the Los Angeles convention, and Bernard Boutin was appointed assistant administrator, the second highest office in the General Services Administration. Other New Hampshire Kennedy supporters were appointed to various federal positions both in Washington and New Hampshire. The possibility of building a strong Democratic Party from this new base became Bill Dunfey's goal for the future. With John Kennedy's national victory, the New Hampshire Democratic Party began to emerge. Once again, it was desirable to be a Democrat. A Democrat occupied the White House, and New Hampshire was well connected to the new President through Kennedy loyalists such as Dunfey and Boutin.

Democrats began to attend meetings, identify with the Kennedy postelection popularity, become interested in contesting local offices, and participate in what now appeared to be a powerful state party. The party quickly paid its campaign debts, established a state office with staff, and began planning organizational and funding activities. Even without the election of a major Democratic state official, a political revolution was beginning in New Hampshire.

The experiences of the 1960 campaign tied closely with my graduate studies on voting behavior, campaign tactics, voter characteristics, information cost theory, and political institutions. This academic work, the 1960 campaign experience, and 1961 summer work for the New Hampshire Democratic State Committee led to campaign assignments in the senatorial candidacy of Thomas J. McIntyre and as coordinator for then State Representative John W. King's gubernatorial campaign in 1962.

Assignments that I had filled as a novice in the 1960 campaigns were now repeated with the assumption that I was an experienced campaign manager. Again, availability and low cost were substitutes for professional competence, but William Dunfey's training helped me to withstand the test. That year McIntyre was elected to the U.S. Senate and John W. King was elected governor of New Hampshire.

DEMOCRATS WIN ELECTIONS: 1962–1964

The 1962 election completed my emergence in the New Hampshire Democratic Party. I was identified as a member of the group of new liberals, willing to work, willing to open the party, and closely allied with the Dunfey-Boutin-Kennedy leadership prevalent during those days. The Old Guard had joined the efforts to win the elections and found new places in the party of the 1960s through appointments from the new governor and the new senator. Party leadership began to shift from the activist managerial role of Dunfey to an officeholder protection and preservation leadership that would respond to the leadership needs of high officeholders—a less activist leadership that made officeholders feel more comfortable as reelection came closer.

Whether the coalition that had elected King and McIntyre would survive beyond the actual election was a critical question, especially for John W. King. He would be facing the voters again in two short years. As a result of this situation Governor King, for one, would take few chances or adopt few policies that appeared to be in opposition to those voters with the potential for disaffection—even though King's stance would put him in opposition to policies of the Kennedy administration and the nationally oriented reformist leadership of New Hampshire Democrats like William Dunfey and Bernard Boutin.

Although a semblance of the power and unity in the New Hampshire Democratic Party continued to prevail during the middle 1960s, the effort to build a progressive, nationally oriented party from the 1960 election activity deteriorated. With the assassination of John F. Kennedy, November 22, 1963, the ties to Washington that reinforced Democratic liberals such as Dunfey and Boutin began to weaken as New Hampshire Kennedy loyalists drifted from federal government positions and lost the access they once had.

Governor King was reelected in 1964 by a ninety thousand vote plurality, a figure that exceeded Lyndon Johnson's New Hampshire total by approximately twenty thousand votes. King's political strategy had worked for him. The 1962 coalition held and was supplemented by other voters who were afraid that by splitting their party column ballot they would invalidate their vote. Generations of voting "the straight Republican ticket" meant that when the same voters were frightened by the Republicans' presidential candidate, Barry Goldwater, they did to the Democratic ballot what they had always done to their own, voted a straight party ballot, but this time it was a Democratic ballot.

During that unique political year of 1964, Lyndon Johnson made an historic campaign swing through New England that concluded with a speech in Manchester. The pivotal issues in the Johnson-Goldwater contest had by then been narrowed to the war in Vietnam.

In President Johnson's Manchester speech, I heard the peace candidate of 1964 say, "I have no intention of sending American boys to do in Vietnam what Asian boys should do for themselves." The tone of his speech and the clarity of its principal lines assured me and the one thousand plus others in the audience that they were supporting sane and responsible political leadership—leadership that would keep out of further Vietnam involvement. On the other hand, Barry Goldwater was assumed to be an irresponsible reactionary who was likely to find enemies of the United States under every bed and in every closet, to say nothing of in the forests and villages of South Vietnam. Large numbers of Americans and especially large numbers of Democratic Party activists voted for Lyndon B. Johnson in 1964 because he assured his supporters that his policies were the policies of John F. Kennedy, that is, of restraint and of peace.

During that same election year, I left a position as a planner with the New Hampshire State Planning Project to become the campaign manager for the 2nd Congressional District candidacy of Charles B. Officer. Officer's candidacy was premised on issues such as developing sensible limitations to the testing and proliferation of nuclear weapons, a liberal noninterventionist foreign policy, and the continuation of the Kennedy-Johnson tradition in domestic affairs.

The campaign was well organized, had adequate financing, effective media, and was challenging the incumbent in all of the cities and most of the towns of the district. It drew responses that were a combination of positive reaction and nostalgia for the vanishing spirit of the Kennedy presidency. Officer came within 450 votes of winning the congressional seat on election evening out of a total 120,000 votes cast. The Officer campaign added an important additional facet to my New Hampshire political experience.

With the majority of New Hampshire's Democratic Party statewide voting strength concentrated in Hillsborough County, centered in the southernmost portion of the state, there was little reason for Democratic candidates to spend much time outside of that area. The two congressional districts divide the state along a line that extends north from the Massachusetts border to the southern boundary of northernmost Coos County, where it then turns east to the Maine border. (All of New Hampshire west and north of that line, including the length of the Connecticut River; the cities of Nashua, on the Massachusetts border; Concord, the state capital, and north to the Canadian border constitute the 2nd Congressional District.)

The entire state was not dominated by Manchester or the Manchester media as many Democratic Party leaders presumed. Substantial population concentrations existed in the 2nd District; politics was more open and susceptible to rational arguments. The cross-pressured politics of Manchester, focused on combustible issues by the *Manchester Union Leader*, had little impact on the independent thinking of the 2nd District residents. The population mix was also different from that of the lst District. Smaller cities meant that urban and ethnic conflicts were less pronounced than in the urban centers of Hillsborough County. Also, the scattered urban and rural Yankees had a stronger influence.

The northern communities, whose resource-based economics depended on forest products, paper manufacturing, and recreation services, were experiencing declining urban and rural populations. The southern cities and towns of the 2nd Congressional District reflected a variety of growth patterns. Some were growing as the result of in-migrating new industries; others were becoming suburbs for expanding manufacturing and marketing centers; while still others were becoming bedroom communities for those employed in Massachusetts.

Not only were the more densely populated southern and southeastern parts of the state under the information umbrella of the *Manchester Union Leader*, but they were also heavily dependent on Massachusetts media sources that gave little attention to New Hampshire politics or events.

The western and northwestern cities and towns of the 2nd Congressional District are dispersed over a much larger geographical area and tend to be more isolated than those of the more dense lst District. The economic ties and media sources of the 2nd District are less linked to Boston and more to their own regions. Vermont, New York state, Maine, and even Canada provide the external media that supplements the coverage of the radio and the district's daily and weekly press.

Although New Hampshire is a small state with an estimated 1968 population of seven hundred thousand persons, the distribution of that population and the diversity of its information sources makes it politically unique. To many political observers that very diversity is a microcosm that reflects and represents the political dynamics of the United States.

By working this peculiar political state, and gaining experience with the variety of its political and voting populations, I came to know the breadth and limitation of each political situation and the extent to which a political situation was elastic. I learned that rules and constraints for each electoral event were distinct, and that each campaign, each office, and each election contained a particular political ethos that had to be understood.

DISILLUSIONED WITH JOHNSON: 1965–1967

Elected to congress with Lyndon Johnson in 1964 were approximately forty Democrats who had replaced Republican predecessors.

Johnson and Congress enacted legislation that included civil rights and voting rights guarantees, a war on poverty, Medicare, new assistance for education, natural resources protection laws, and numerous other measures that sought to make the Johnson administration's dream for America a reality.

To many observers and political activists alike, Lyndon Johnson was omnipotent. His political skills and his legislative acumen led many to believe that he was capable of directing the destiny not only of the nation but also of his political party.

However, a creeping cancer was beginning to nibble at the facade of Johnson's leadership. Early in 1965 the military buildup in South Vietnam had began. As the casualties increased, draft quotas grew, and war expenditures cut the funding of the Great Society programs. The credibility of the administration began to decline. Those who had worked for the election of Lyndon Johnson as the "peace" candidate in 1964 questioned the wisdom of their loyalty.

Through the spring, summer, and fall of 1966, many of the congressional class of 1964 maintained their loyalty to the administration that they had supported during the previous two years, expecting that some change would occur in Vietnam policy.

In New Hampshire, the rising insecurity among politicians and the public took several significant forms. The first was that in the 2nd Congressional District, Eugene S. Daniell, a former Franklin mayor, state senator, state representative, and 1960 congressional candidate, announced his candidacy for Congress. The unusual part of his announcement was that he would run in opposition to the continuation of the war policy in Vietnam.

In addition to the two congressional seats to be filled in the 1966 election, Governor King would be seeking an unprecedented third term, and Thomas McIntyre (elected to a short-term U.S. Senate seat in 1962) would be up for election to a full term. Daniell's candidacy and possible nomination would be an embarrassment to the unity thrust of the New Hampshire Democratic incumbents.

At that stage the opponents to the war in Vietnam were mostly viewed as a ragged fringe of antisocial malcontents who had little faith in the capacity of Lyndon Johnson to control the Vietnam situation and to manage U.S. involvement. This was the case in New Hampshire. With the exception of Daniell, who had an extensive though controversial political history, the scattering of dissidents were, for the most part, nonpolitical, politically inexperienced, without party ties, and with limited organizational interest or capacity. From the perspective of the Democratic Party organization they could not be allowed to disrupt the party's drive to consolidate the 1964 electoral gains and, especially, could not be allowed to jeopardize the reelection of Senator McIntyre.

McIntyre had become the special target of William Loeb and the editorial page of the *Manchester Union Leader.* Loeb had found an about-to-be-retired U.S. Army general named Harrison W. Thyng, whom Loeb anointed as his candidate against McIntyre. While McIntyre had been a staunch supporter of the Johnson administration on domestic matters, to the infuriation of Loeb, he was also a member of the Armed Services Committee and a supporter of the administration in its Vietnam policy. Contrasted with Loeb and his political puppet, General Thyng (who wanted to totally unshackle the military in Vietnam), McIntyre seemed reasonable and restrained.

An impossible political situation began to evolve. The Daniell candidacy posed a direct threat to party unity, support for President Johnson and, thereby, the Democratic reelection strategy in New Hampshire. Without unity, it was argued, Senator McIntyre would be especially vulnerable to attack by Loeb and Thyng. In all probability this would lead to McIntyre's defeat. Although some Democrats were becoming uncomfortable with the Johnson Vietnam policy, there appeared to be little choice except to support the administration for the sake of maintaining Democrats in hard won offices.

Expecting that President Johnson would do something in Vietnam before the election to save his majority in Congress, an opponent to Eugene Daniell was found. William Barry, a Nashua lawyer, son of a former Nashua mayor and clerk of federal court, and well regarded in his home city, was persuaded to run. Since Nashua provided the bulk of the primary vote in the 2nd District, his candidacy ensured that Eugene Daniell would be eliminated from the 1966 Democratic ticket.

For those like myself who supported the unity strategy but harbored serious questions about the Vietnam policy, the several months prior to the primary election were difficult. Daniell challenged Barry to a series of debates on the Vietnam issue. A successful orator, Daniell outlined the case against continued U.S. involvement in Southeast Asia. It was a factual, well-argued case that would be repeated time and again as the dissent against the war grew during the remainder of 1966 and on through 1967.

Although the Daniell candidacy generated interest and attracted a somewhat larger following of dissenters, it suffered the predictable result. Barry carried Nashua by a significant margin and won the Democratic nomination handily.

After the Officer campaign in 1964, I had returned to state planning assignments for the state government and did not participate actively in the 1966 congressional contest. Sandra Hoeh, my spouse, served as Senator McIntyre's Concord chair and campaign organizer. McIntyre unexpectedly carried the city on his way to reelection.

On election night King was reelected governor by his Manchester friends and neighbors. McIntyre was reelected by approximately the same margin as the governor, but his vote was assembled from voters outside of Manchester who were outraged by the insult of the Loeb-Thyng challenge. The Barry contest in the 2nd Congressional District never got beyond the blush of primary victory. Lacking resources and a sufficiently clear image, Barry lost by more than two to one.

Election eve 1966 produced a quantum increase in the depth and breadth of the Vietnam dissenters. Lyndon Johnson had not succeeded in producing the Vietnam miracle that might have saved at least some of the more outstanding members of the congressional class of 1964. During the last weeks of the fall campaign, Lyndon Johnson seemed to be running away from those congressional loyalists who had delivered the immense legislative calendar of the 89th Congress. Instead of staying to help with the fight or to produce the Vietnam policy change, the man who had appeared omnipotent, the consummate politician, the creator of the 1964 landslide, vanished from the political stage. In fact, during those final weeks of the campaign, he seemed to retreat inside the White House and toward the end, actually left the country on a tour of the Pacific. When his power was needed most at home, and in the face of a preelection faith in his ability to make politically right the gloomy international situation, Lyndon Johnson, by his withdrawal, jumped ship. He was leaving the sinking class of 1964 alone while he, the skipper, fled to safe ground.

For those like Sandra and myself who had accepted the notion that Lyndon Johnson could manage Vietnam with restraint and that he would protect the political fortress of the Democratic Party, election eve 1966 was a major blow. Those who supported William Barry against Eugene Daniell, those who accepted the party unity strategy for the reelection of Tom McIntyre, began to feel that they had been duped. Not only had they been taken in by the idea of the strategy, but even more by the argument that those who were reelected in New Hampshire reflected the state's support of the administration's war policy. An added consequence was the fear that those who were reelected, King and McIntyre, would interpret their success as the result of their unquestioning support of the administration's policies in Southeast Asia. To bring them back to that happier political day in 1964 when they joined Lyndon Johnson on the platform in Manchester and applauded their president's commitment to keep our boys out of Vietnam, would be a difficult, even impossible, task.

The chronicle of the escalation of the U.S. involvement in Vietnam from late 1966 through 1967 has been recounted, examined, and dissected in numerous accounts. Those accounts do not need to be restated except as specific recollections of events that influenced my decision to actively oppose the war and the leadership of the New Hampshire Democratic Party.

During the 1966 election year the war rhetoric increased. Deliberate allusions to the memories of a period of national unity that had accompanied U.S. participation in World War II were used to cloud the public consciousness of the Vietnam War. However, growing draft quotas, escalating war costs, increasing casualties, and a growing uncertainty as to the utility of that war policy countered almost point by point the administration's attempts to wrap U.S. involvement in a blanket of patriotism. Skepticism, distrust, and disillusionment were remanufactured with each full-color television evening news report from Vietnam. A steady rise of protest was also being broadcast from the nation's universities and colleges as student protests increased.

An increasing number of opinion leaders were questioning the relationship between our involvement in Vietnam and the nation's purpose. When Martin Luther King Jr., recent recipient of the Nobel Peace Prize, joined the ranks of opposition and added both his prestige and eloquence to the protest, the cause gained an important advocate.

Violations of protesters' civil rights increased as the intensity of the protest grew. Repression was often an acceptable community ethic that prompted excesses in the streets, meeting halls, police stations, jails, and courts. Often a community standard of good behavior, as articulated by the veterans' groups, patriotic organizations, and the police, was imposed on the protesters with little or no attention being given to the protesters' constitutional rights and guarantees of liberties. Although not yet an active protester, I, like others with a strong sense of the civil libertarian principles of the constitution, was disturbed by the number of violations, the intensity of the violations, and the sanctions that seemed to sustain the authorities in continuing to violate the protesters' civil liberties.

During the months following the 1966 elections, it was clear that the high watermark of the Democratic Party in New Hampshire and the Great Society programs of the Johnson administration had passed. Unable to respond to the promise of the Dunfey-Boutin revival of the New Hampshire Democrats, John King was left with Republican control of both houses of the General Court and the governor's council. Without the revitalizing congressional output of new programs and funding, little opportunity remained in New Hampshire state government to create an effective state administration. The drift away from the Democratic Party began in New Hampshire as well as nationally.

A NEW SCENE

As the bright prospects of the early 1960s faded into a frustrating Democratic decline, and as disillusionment with Vietnam policies became deeper, I concluded that continuing to work for New Hampshire state government would not be fulfilling and began looking for a new position. Two possibilities developed. The first was as the New Hampshire coordinator for the Economic Development Administration. The position offered a sizable increase in salary and what appeared to be an opportunity to continue my interest in New Hampshire planning and economic development. The second possibility was as the associate director of the Public Affairs Center at Dartmouth College.

Although both positions were attractive, the offer from Dartmouth College seemed to open a wider range of choices while maintaining contacts with the state and federal agencies with program interests in New Hampshire. An underlying consideration was my desire participate in the political life of the state. As a state employee from 1963 until my resignation in March 1967, I had not been able to hold political office or to be directly active in party or campaign affairs. With the exception of the time when I left state government in 1964 to manage the Officer congressional candidacy, I had been more an observer and casual advisor than a full participant. If I had accepted the job with the Economic Development Administration, I would have been "hatched" or subject to the federal law that limits the participation of federal employees and of state and local employees whose salaries are paid in part out of federal funds in partisan activity. I accepted the Dartmouth College appointment, and we moved to Hanover.

DARTMOUTH COLLEGE: SPRING 1967

A vigil of students, faculty, and area residents stood by the flagpole on the Dartmouth College Green in protest against the war, regardless of the weather, each Wednesday noon. Although not usually a large crowd and often subject to curious stares and heckling, the group maintained its vigil for almost two years.

That March, the warrant of the Hanover town meeting contained an article condemning the war in Vietnam. Sufficient signatures had been secured to place the article on the warrant. By parliamentary maneuver, however, the article was tabled before either lengthy debate or a vote.

The town and the campus remained alive with controversy toward the war. Several times resolutions were introduced in faculty meetings to place the college on record in opposition to the war. Another issue was the relationship between the college and the student. The Selective Service Administration had advised its local boards that students who did not maintain high class placement or academic averages would be subject to the draft. The system required student records be reported to the local Selective Service Boards, an action that was held by some members of the faculty as aiding and abetting the conduct of the war.

The issue of the appropriateness of releasing confidential records to government agencies became a basis for calling the roll of the faculty regarding its position on the war. Between the several meetings that it took to consider the issue, student antagonism increased. Supporters of the Johnson administration's policy called for a show of strength to demonstrate once and for all that the opponents were a small minority of the campus and, presumably, also across the country. The supporters the ROTC department on the campus took the lead with help from the Dartmouth College Athletics Council. The showdown was to be in the middle of the Dartmouth College Green, where all could see. The day was a Wednesday toward the middle of May 1967. The confrontation was one of numbers. Ranks of supporters and opponents faced each other stretching east, across the Dartmouth College Green from the flagpole on its western boarder.

Much to the surprise of all concerned, and especially to those opposing the war policies, the lines were almost even. Perhaps as much as half the student body, faculty, and staff, with some area residents, made up those two facing lines. Although no one was injured, arrested, mauled, or even insulted, that matched rank across the Dartmouth College Green indicated that substantial opposition to the war now existed. Not only was that opposition demonstrated, the individual decisions that led those to stand there, willing to protest in public, had to be considered more than a casual display of obstinacy on a sunny spring day.

As a political observer, I appreciated the powerful national lineage reflected by the students assembled on that Green and the sincerity with which that concern was manifested. I could not mistake the tremor that was about to shake the system.

CONTROVERSY AND POLITICS IN NEW HAMPSHIRE

If there is one prevalent characteristic in New Hampshire politics, it is opposition to controversy. In basic terms, if someone is said to be "controversial" and then behaves in a controversial manner, the level of public uncertainty increases and the credibility of the person or issue represented by the person declines. New Hampshire's media situation is such that its politics tend to be highly personalized. Personality becomes far more important to the New Hampshire body politic than do the issues the person espouses. To a considerable extent this condition is attributable to the small size of the state and the inconvenience that issue polarity presents to the conduct of daily affairs within small communities.

Once a public person is identified as controversial and likely to upset tranquillity, that person begins to lose credibility. Presidential candidates, at least in New Hampshire, have to look like presidents, speak like presidents, behave like presidents, and earn the respect due a president. With almost complete disregard for what is actually said or for what the candidate represents, an instinctive, almost physical response to personality prevails.

What had appeared as fringe dissent on Vietnam during the pre-1966 election period had, by the spring of 1967, the appearance of a commitment to see Vietnam policy changed. Political action groups that had long sought to change national policy on issues of nuclear weapons control, military influence on foreign policy, and the expansion of the military establishment, now shifted their emphasis toward stopping the war in Vietnam. Coalitions of political action groups were formed of religious leaders, college and university professors, and even some business and corporate leaders.

They did so with the objective of bringing about changes in U.S. policy. The process of converting fringe dissent into valid political force was underway.

Essential to this conversion was speculation as to what avenues protest should take to be effective. Petitions were circulated, advertisements placed, solicitations for funds and supporters conducted, and mailings to groups and influential persons prepared and distributed. Drives to send letters to Congress were organized, and other tactics, all designed to demonstrate the concern of the public, were tried. Vigils, marches, teach-ins, debates, forums, articles, books, and prayers were conducted, written, and sent forth. Even as desperation led to raids on Selective Service records, draft avoidance, desertion, exile, and even personal injury, the impenetrability of the policy makers, the ambivalence of Congress, and the steady escalation of the war by the administration was frustratingly evident.

Throughout 1967 the dissenters, now fully qualified by size and diversity to be called the "peace movement," flailed at the political system without notable impact. Strategies were confused. Options were unclear. Leadership was scarce and usually limited in appeal. None of the leaders with national constituencies had expressed their opposition to the point where a break with the administration on Vietnam was conceivable. Vice President Hubert H. Humphrey was an enthusiastic apologist for the administration. Senator Robert Kennedy, though critical, would not adopt the full-confrontation posture true commitment required. Few others had sufficient stature to make a difference. It was too early in the maturation process to expect a coalition of elected officials to confront the president. To be effective, such a coalition would have had to arise from within the president's own party. From the point of view of an incumbent senator, the power of the president and his administration is considerable. For a senator anticipating reelection campaign in the fall of 1968, keeping things in order within one's own house and party was of utmost importance. But from the perspective of a member of Congress, who must face the voters every two years, the power of the presidency is awesome and the necessity to express and maintain loyalty is of the highest order. To have an impact on the mutually reinforcing sequences that shape the dynamics of the political system, wedges had to be driven between Congress, the president, the party, and the electorate. The firm structure of rewards and favors, confidences and reenforcements that supported the scheme of mutual reliances had to be cracked.

By the end of 1967, the foundations had begun to shake. Elected officials, who as recently as one year before hadn't been concerned with the war as an issue, sensed the shifting sands not only under their own feet but especially under those close associates they relied upon to do their fund-raising, election, and reelection work.

Below the high officials are those individuals who through their political skills, hard work, money, and considerable time, support and sustain those who do hold the offices. These are the workers, the friends, the professional colleagues, the law partners, the business associates, the bankers, the union leaders, the industrialists, and the many others who have access to those holding public office. When the sands of public opinion shift, they shift first and with the strongest effect upon those diverse individuals who are the interpreters, the translators of the political mood. From trusted voices are heard the first hints of political trouble. It is in these circles that the discussion of options becomes meaningful. These are the individuals who are likely to know the options, understand the risks, contemplate the possibilities, and organize within the constraints of the political system.

Toward the middle of 1967, an increasing number of these politically sensitive individuals, such as Richard Goodwin, Bill Moyers, John Gardner, and Roger Hillsman, began to consider the options offered in the political system and to speak out against the continuation of the Johnson administration's Vietnam policy. What prompted them was the result of not being able to convince their elected friends to come out against the war policies; or conversely, the result of pleas from their elected friends to demonstrate that there was antiwar support in the home state or district, or personal frustration over a Vietnam loss or the sting of generation gap conflict over the war issues.

At this stage in the movement, many had come to the conclusion that the use of pressure against individual members of Congress was not particularly effective. A bloc of committed war opponents in Congress capable of attracting converts and having an impact on policy did not exist. The likelihood of a bloc forming in Congress from within the party of the president was small especially since the election year of 1968 loomed ahead. Congress felt that the president held all of the essential power with respect to the conduct of the war. Many were in awe of that power and also vulnerable should they assert opposition to the president's handling of the war. A change in policy, a victory in Vietnam, or a major intervention by China or Russia, they perceived, would seriously undercut their election prospects. Getting too far away from the pack is an unsettling experience—especially when the pack is led by a president of one's own party.

Recognizing how difficult it would be to change a large congressional bloc by internal pressure or even by organizing at the state or district level, those considering political options directed their attention to the upcoming presidential election. Organizing to take hold of the political machinery in accord with the rules and the laws of the respective states had promise. In many states, even before the nominating process reforms of the 1970s, the political party structures and the electoral processes were open and reasonably penetrable by those who wanted to be involved in politics. In others, as would be discovered, the party structures were not protected by law and had become closed, impenetrable, or so atrophied as to be almost unusable.

In either case, whether moving into an accessible party organization or developing new organizational vehicles, an acceptable and legally reinforced system was available. To go outside this system, or to neglect to examine this system as the vehicle for political action, meant one would have to not only create new organizations, but to subject them to tests of legality and community acceptance. Using the same organizations and political structures that had produced the members of Congress and the president, and then putting these structures to a different purpose was at least legally acceptable.

Even in 1968, there were openings in the political system with many legally set time locks opening and closing political system doors that led to party organizations and candidate nominations. All those in opposition had to do was learn the laws, determine the sequence and schedule of political events, and organize to participate.

Through the fall of 1967, Lyndon Johnson appeared uninfluenced by the arguments of the opponents of the war. Those few members of Johnson's party in high office, such as John Gardner, who were staunch opponents were being systematically excluded from either their offices or prerogatives of office. Opposition within the administration was not wise if officials wished to retain their jobs. Opposition to the war policy anywhere in the political structure of the Democratic Party was viewed as disloyal, divisive, and even traitorous.

Lyndon Johnson had one Achilles' heel: The election of 1968 was drawing closer. Johnson had a lengthy history of political quicksteps. He had survived and prospered through years of legislative offices where his skill at balancing the needs of his Texas constituency with the requirements of congressional leadership had made him a legend. It appeared that the peace movement had tried all of its tactics except those that would strike the only exposed political nerve of his system. If votes could be cast that would show disapproval for his administration's handling of the war, and at least have some of these votes counted directly against him as the responsible policymaker of his administration, then Lyndon Johnson could be made to react. To work, those votes had to have clear meaning. They had to be cast in a political context that Lyndon Johnson would understand and assembled in a manner that could not be discounted. As a political animal, with roots close to the people, Lyndon Johnson understood votes.

OPTIONS AND ALTERNATIVES

A look at the options led immediately to the presidential primaries that would be conducted in fifteen states. The problem with a primary election is that, in order to make the system work, there must be a candidate. Although the procedure varied from state to state, it was difficult if not impossible to register protest in a presidential primary. Only one state in 1968, Wisconsin, offered the voter the option of voting "no" to the names listed on the ballot. A vote of "no" would be a rejection of all of the candidates listed.

Early in 1967, antiwar groups in Wisconsin organized with the objective of identifying the "no" option as a protest vehicle for those opposing the war. The option met all the requirements of a political protest; it did not, however, represent an alternative. A significant "no" vote would show the size of the opposition to the war. What it would not show was commitment to a viable political alternative. The possibility that such a vote would be disregarded or only peripherally considered by the president and Congress was high.

The movement, however, lent a sense of political responsibility to those considering protest options within the political system. Those organizing the Wisconsin effort received a great deal of publicity on the possible impact of a large "no" vote. This speculation was the 1967 genesis of most reporters' preoccupation throughout the presidential primary season with vote size and significance. In each event, in each primary, a magic number had to be determined—how many votes would have to be cast for the "no" option or for candidate "X" in order to be large enough to be considered significant opposition to President Johnson. Playing the numbers was a strange but ultimately important part of the 1968 political game. It made possible the less-than-majority win that gave the opposition an important advantage.

In New Hampshire, the site of the nation's first presidential primary, the search for alternatives was underway early in 1967. Eugene S. Daniell, the defeated 1966 primary contestant for the 2nd district congressional nomination, had renewed his antiwar activities shortly after the first of the year. He announced the formation of a committee to draft Senator Robert F. Kennedy.

Daniell had been contacted by a New York City group headed by Dr. Martin Shepard. Without contact with Robert Kennedy or any close Kennedy family supporters, Shepard was on his own. The effort had the distinct ring of an amateur venture. Shepard had heard of Daniell as the result of the antiwar position he had taken in 1966, and sought him out to organize the Draft Kennedy drive in New Hampshire. Daniell was not particularly concerned about the reality of a political action that was based on trying to draft an unwilling subject. In fact, both Shepard and Daniell lacked a sense of what was required to organize effectively. They were content to issue press releases, raise a few dollars, meet with others of like interest, and rely on the coverage their respective press releases generated for impact.

In the early stages of any political year, the media is hungry for something even half solid to report. Especially in a year when it was taken for granted that Lyndon B. Johnson would seek renomination and would not be seriously opposed in that quest, anything that sparked of a variation on the set theme was attractive. At the same time, much of what would eventually become politically interesting in the Republican Party was in the formative stages. Shepard and Daniell gave the hungry reporters some political hard news to report.

If Robert Kennedy had any intention of sparking or subtly approving a primary-oriented draft movement, that thought was quickly snuffed out by the activities of Shepard and Daniell. Repeated letters and press statements calling for Robert Kennedy's candidacy were set aside. Eventually the irritation of the press prompted by the nondenials forced Robert Kennedy's hand. He wrote to both Shepard and Daniell disavowing their activities and stated that he would not be a candidate, drafted or otherwise, in 1968. A political option which, perhaps, Kennedy would have liked to have kept open in order to apply greater pressure on the administration from the inside, had to be closed. The timing and the auspices of the draft venture forced Kennedy to reveal his position long before it was advisable.

Even with the Kennedy denial, Daniell still had several options open. Since his mission was to express protest against the war, the availability of a popular name was enough. He stated early in his effort that his objective was to manifest dissent on the administration's war policies. Without a "no" option like Wisconsin's, Daniell needed a name. He said he would file a slate of delegate candidates favorable to the nomination of Robert Kennedy.

SPECULATING ON OTHER NEW HAMPSHIRE OPTIONS

Late in January 1967 I received a telephone call from Charles B. Officer. He surprised me by saying that something had to be done about the war and the president's war policies. His conclusions were based on his analysis of the administration's preoccupation with Vietnam at the expense of maintaining an effective and peaceful international posture, the cost of the war, its impact on the nation's capacity to meet its domestic needs, and the adverse effect the war was having on the domestic economy. It was his feeling that because of these factors and the increasing civilian unrest, political options should be explored which could expose the depth of the unhappiness. The New Hampshire presidential primary is an early and often important political barometer. If something could be done to translate concern into votes using the March 12 election, Officer thought it should be done.

The option that Officer suggested was that I research the possibility of a bipartisan opportunity to express dissent through the presidential ballot. The political vehicle for protest, which Officer initially suggested, was that of placing on both parties' presidential primary ballot a referendum statement that would allow the voters the option of either supporting or rejecting the administration's Vietnam policy.

My research found that only the General Court (New Hampshire's legislature) could approve a referendum item for inclusion with a statewide ballot. The biennial session of the General Court was to be adjourned July 1, 1967, and the likelihood of that body even considering such an article was remote.

The only remaining possibility left to express antiwar protest in the 1968 New Hampshire presidential primary had to be through a candidate or the name of a candidate. Through the spring, summer, and early fall of 1967, only Eugene Daniell's Draft Robert Kennedy effort seemed viable.

The summer doldrums dry up political activity in New Hampshire, and 1967 was no exception. Lyndon Johnson's difficulties in the cities that summer overwhelmed the increasing momentum of the antiwar movement. Riots in Newark, Watts, Detroit, Cincinnati, Tampa, Atlanta, and other cities diverted public attention from the war momentarily, but by early September and with the return of some measure of calm in the cities, concern about the war mounted.

Officer and I discussed the possibility of meeting with Eugene Daniell to attempt to moderate and reorganize his Draft Kennedy activity. Our approach would have been to submerge the public effort to the Kennedy write-in until it was practicable to stimulate the actual write-in vote. An organizational effort would have given visibility to the activity instead of the reverse, which was Daniell's approach. Since Daniell's first concern was with the issue of the war, visibility at an early stage and throughout this activity was important. Creating a viable political alternative to president Johnson was less important to Daniell than registering protest against the war. What Daniell did not understand was that the two activities were inextricably linked and mutually reinforcing. The issue and the protest could not survive politically or be focused without a candidate, and a candidate could not be created without the issue-defining capacity of a well-organized campaign.

The example and organizational model Officer and I considered had been used effectively in the 1964 New Hampshire presidential primary. It was a model that called for sophisticated organization and moderation. It was a model that worked precisely because it filled the same political vacuum that was beginning to appear in the fall of 1967, a vacuum that was not being filled by either the candidates of the Republican Party or the option of writing in a name other than Lyndon B. Johnson on the Democratic ballot.

As was discussed earlier, the 1960 presidential primary of John Kennedy revealed some of the political dynamics of the New Hampshire presidential primary. The 1964 version of that event revealed additional options. Both experiences were to have an important influence on the planning of the 1968 contest and the evolution of Eugene McCarthy as a presidential candidate.

For me, 1964 produced a case study of how the primary could work that was of great influence in my thinking, especially as I discussed with Charles Officer how public concern about the Vietnam war policy might be demonstrated to Lyndon Johnson.

The time lock on the political system was about to open, as it does in New Hampshire every four years. It would be possible to work within the system to demonstrate with votes the desire for policy change. How that might be accomplished was still unknown.

CHAPTER 1

The New Hampshire Presidential Primary

BACKGROUND

The New Hampshire presidential primary is a product of Yankee frugality. The early date was set for 1968 to coincide with the first Tuesday in March, the same day as the annual town meeting. Two elections on the same day saves considerable time and money, and it also results in a larger vote.

The presidential primary was legislated in 1913 as New Hampshire's participation in the "new democracy." Its function was to select the various parties' representatives to the national conventions by popular vote rather than state convention. By act of the 1948 New Hampshire legislature, the presidential preference section of the ballot was added.

The presidential preference section of the ballot made the New Hampshire primary a national attraction. A presidential candidate could benefit from the publicity of New Hampshire's "first in the nation" primary and do so at relatively little cost.

Several factors make New Hampshire a key state. The first is the early date of the presidential primary. The second is the relatively high voter participation. The third is the fact that although a rural New England state by image, New Hampshire has been heavily industrialized in the percent of its population holding manufacturing jobs. The fourth is that New Hampshire has been a "bellwether" state. Within its borders was one of the five counties in the nation that has voted for the winning presidential candidates since William McKinley. According to a study by Professor Robert Dishman of the University of New Hampshire, the barometer counties reflected the thinking of the American public and did so on almost every index that political science can devise. Therefore, it was possible to show by voting patterns that New Hampshire's nine other counties did not deviate greatly from the norm of Strafford County, the bellwether county.

In spite of the national implications of the early primary, it is still a New Hampshire phenomenon. The organization, strategy, issues, and methods need to fit the New Hampshire political mold. The results bear the mark of the state's electorate, and when it comes to the presidential primaries that electorate is at least as sophisticated as any other.

It is, however, impossible to divorce the in-state politics of New Hampshire from the activities of its presidential primary. Thus, it is possible to describe how what happened on the Republican side in the 1964 presidential primary was influenced by the 1961 death of a prominent New Hampshire senator, H. Styles Bridges, and how the events of 1964's presidential primary influenced preparations for the 1968 revival.

The death of Senator Bridges marked the end of New Hampshire's monolithic Republican Party. As will be shown later it was as impossible to detach the 1968 presidential primary from the internal politics of the New Hampshire Democratic Party as it had been to detach the 1964 presidential primary from the internal politics of the New Hampshire Republican Party. The role of the state party is little recognized by those who come to New Hampshire every four years to watch the state's voters consider the new crop of presidential candidates.

The bitter Republican primaries of 1962, which led to the election of the Democrats King and McIntyre, would not have occurred with such intensity had Styles Bridges lived. The power vacuum created by the vacancy in this long held Senate seat caused political chaos in the Republican Party. Almost without exception, those who participated in the devastating Republican state primary of 1962 were products of the various office assignments available in the office of a U.S. senator.

The internal affairs of the Republican Party had always been the private province of Senator Bridges. His power was built upon the personal favors he performed and the funds he controlled. Those who wished the support of the Senator in their activities responded to his direction and leadership. His first concern was to prevent the development of a strong Democratic Party. The second was to eliminate the possibility of factional splits within the Republican organization. Senator Bridges assumed complete internal control of the New Hampshire Republican Party from 1953 until his death in 1961.

By 1964, the free-for-all within the Republican Party had not been resolved. The splits that developed as a result of the 1962 primary contests remained, and the factions gathered around the presidential candidates most closely reflecting their particular views.

THE CANDIDATES IN PROFILE: 1964

Five candidates were listed on the presidential preference section of the March 10 Republican primary ballots. One space was provided for the voter to write in any additional name. Of the five candidates listed on the ballot, three were "also rans." Harold Stassen, Margaret Chase Smith, and a New Hampshire perennial, Norman LePage, qualified in this category and failed to count in the contest. The two remaining candidates, Nelson Rockefeller and Barry Goldwater, entered and waged vigorous primary campaigns.

Fifty-two percent of the New Hampshire Republicans voting wrote in either Richard M. Nixon or Henry Cabot Lodge. In both cases, the result was the outgrowth of two organized efforts and the offshoot of New Hampshire's own internal politics. Both Lodge and Nixon will be considered with Rockefeller and Goldwater as the significant figures in the 1964 primary.

NELSON ROCKEFELLER

As the governor of New York and as a member of a well-regarded and wealthy family, Nelson Rockefeller should have been the man to beat in the New Hampshire primary. He was born in Maine, educated at Dartmouth College in Hanover, and maintained long friendships with his New Hampshire classmates. A frequent visitor to the state, Nelson Rockefeller had both a high recognition factor and a record of long and notable public service. He seemed as much a New Hampshire candidate as one could be who was not actually a native.

Rockefeller lost his acceptability to rank and file Republicans by divorce and then remarriage to a younger woman, who had left her family of four children to marry him. This was an intolerable transgression in the minds of New Hampshire's conservative Republican electorate. It was the one factor in the primary that was clear and irrefutable.

When Governor Rockefeller made his announcement in the middle of November 1963, the polls showed him to be the least acceptable of the four major Republican candidates. The New Hampshire electorate had forgotten the public service record of their friend and could dwell only on the fact of his remarriage. His campaign strategy was clear. He had to place his own good record once more before the people, and in such a way that they would decide that his personal life had not and would not affect his proven capability in public services.

The keys to Rockefeller's campaign were himself and his organization. He had to be in the forefront of this effort since each voter's decision could only be made on the basis of a reaction to the candidate himself.

Although Rockefeller did not fit the conservative philosophic mold most suitable to the organization Republican, he did match the thinking of many nominally committed and registered Republicans. Rockefeller was directing his campaign toward that moderate bloc of voters.

BARRY GOLDWATER

When Senator Goldwater first came on the political scene, he struck a familiar chord in the hearts of many New Hampshire Republicans.

Senator Goldwater's prominence on the national scene attracted many of New Hampshire's more prominent Republican political figures. He was a political leader who more closely espoused their personal brand of conservative Republican politics. They jumped to his support.

Distance from New Hampshire and effective public relations had built an image for the senator that was formidable. The polls showed that Senator Goldwater had a large base of support in New Hampshire and that he would be the person to beat in the March 10, 1964, primary. To win he would need only to continue as he had in the past. Unfortunately for Senator Goldwater, however, the New Hampshire primary demanded more from him than giving hazy red, white, and blue impressions. He was forced to campaign personally, defining himself and his position.

Barry Goldwater was the state organization's candidate. He relied on the Republican leadership to carry his campaign. He took the leadership's advice concerning the issues, how to approach the New Hampshire voter, his schedule of appearances, and the character of the campaign. He was told New Hampshire was a sure thing. All Senator Goldwater had to do was to go to New Hampshire and the adulation would solidify into a vote plurality reflected in the polls.

RICHARD NIXON

As the standard bearer for the Republican Party in the 1960 election, and as an avowed nonparticipant in the 1964 preconvention primaries, Richard Nixon waited in his New York law office while others carried his effort. Nixon had assured his supporters that he would respond to a legitimate draft if this were the result of the July convention.

The New Hampshire Republican Party leadership, which had supported Mr. Nixon in the 1960 election, had allied itself, one person excepted, with Goldwater. Governor Rockefeller had gathered in the remaining actives leaving a single major Republican uncommitted, former Governor Wesley Powell. Always unpredictable, Wesley Powell entered the primary as a "favorite son" candidate. At the last moment, before the nomination period closed, he withdrew his name with a statement in support of Richard Nixon.

In the New Hampshire presidential primary, the potential candidate must agree to have his name placed on the ballot. Mr. Nixon had not and would not agree to do this. Powell called for a write-in vote for the former vice president.

Wesley Powell's core of dedicated followers had been waiting for his advice on the primary contest. With his statement, the remainder of Powell's followers, those not committed to other candidates, rallied in support of Powell's position. The Nixon campaign, headed by Powell, operated for less than one month prior to the March 10, 1964, election date.

HENRY CABOT LODGE

Six thousand miles away from New Hampshire, the U.S. ambassador to South Vietnam, Henry Cabot Lodge, posed the greatest factor of unpredictability in the New Hampshire primary. At sixty-one, the former Massachusetts senator, ambassador to the United Nations and vice presidential candidate, Henry Cabot Lodge had a national reputation that made his name familiar to eight out of ten Americans.

As a neighbor from Massachusetts, it is fair to say that he was even better known to New Hampshirites.

Lodge had long been popular with New Hampshire nominal Republicans. As a liberal Eisenhower Republican, he had not been especially favored by the conservative party organization; however, as the architect of the 1952 Eisenhower primary victory, he was held in a certain awe by all Republicans.

Unable and unwilling to give any direct encouragement to the campaign on his behalf in New Hampshire, Ambassador Lodge went about his duties in Saigon while friends and political amateurs formed a Draft Lodge organization in New Hampshire.

As with Richard Nixon, the consent of the candidate could not be obtained and, therefore, the Lodge name could not appear on the ballot. A slate of delegates was filed as "favorable" to the Ambassador. The national significance of the primary would be the preferential section of the ballot and that depended on the writing ability of the electorate.

The Draft Lodge effort had the advantage of a well-known candidate with whom the public had had long experience. The spectrum of choice was complete for the politically sophisticated New Hampshire electorate.

THE MEDIA

In this election, as in all others in the age of politics by public relations, accessibility to the means of communication was critical. In the 1960s (and still today) New Hampshire had seven daily newspapers, ten weekly newspapers, approximately twenty radio stations, and one commercial and one educational television station. The northern part of the state was covered by television from a channel located in Maine. The Boston television channels were strong and effectively covered two-thirds of the state. The in-state channel located at Manchester carried ABC network programming and competed with the same programming from Channel 7 in Boston and Channel 8 in Maine. Because of the prohibitive cost, television had seen limited use in New Hampshire politics. The in-state channel was not strong enough to attract a wide audience, and the cost of television from Boston was prohibitive for most New Hampshire candidates.

New Hampshire had a large and responsible weekly press. The small circulation papers reflected the political activities of the people in the local communities. Their greatest impact was on the way local affairs were conducted and by conveying certain community social norms and mores. Coverage in a weekly paper, on a regular and favorable basis, could be of great assistance to any political candidate.

Six of New Hampshire's seven daily newspapers were moderate-to-liberal Republican in tone. They were distributed geographically in seven urban centers and, with the exception of one, maintain regional circulation. In no case was there more than one daily newspaper in a given city. Both the Associated Press (AP) and United Press International (UPI) maintained wire service offices in the state.

The exception mentioned previously was the *Manchester Union Leader.* Owned since the mid-1940s by William Loeb, this paper had continually supported a series of right-wing and conservative causes. The paper was consistently partisan and used all the tricks of "yellow journalism" to support its positions. It had long been anathema to sensible political discussion and journalistic responsibility. Skillfully propagandistic, the paper perfected the front page editorial and adjusted its news stories as best serves its interests. President Kennedy said, while speaking in Manchester during the 1960 campaign, that he thought there might be a more irresponsible newspaper in the nation than the *Manchester Union Leader,* but he had never seen it. (Eric P. Veblin, *The* Manchester Union Leader *in New Hampshire Elections,* Hanover, N. H.: University Press of Northern New England, 1975.)

The *Union Leader* had a definite impact on New Hampshire politics. It claimed a state-wide circulation in excess of sixty thousand papers. At least half of this circulation was in the state's largest city, Manchester. Whether Loeb was an arbiter of presidential candidates is questionable. He did, however, frequently determine the issues of a political contest.

STRATEGY

Governor Rockefeller announced his candidacy first and opened his active campaign for the New Hampshire primary early in November 1963. He knew that the polls were running strongly against him and an early start would give him that much more time to convince a skeptical New Hampshire electorate. According to a November Louis Harris poll, Goldwater could expect to gather 62 percent of the prospective vote. Rockefeller was far behind.

As a gregarious and energetic man, Rockefeller knew that his forte was the handshake, a sunny disposition, an easy manner, and the issues. His campaign was pitched on two levels. The first was to ensure maximum exposure to the public. The second was to draw his chief opponent, Barry Goldwater, into a debate on the issues.

Governor Rockefeller began an intensive drive to meet as many New Hampshire voters as possible. He was working to win a bloc of voters described by a Louis Harris poll, as "38 percent disenchanted with the Governor's personal life."

On his frequent campaign visits, Rocky brought with him members of his New York executive staff to apply campaign techniques proven in two successful races for the governorship. A not-too-modern bus was acquired for travel around the state, and Rocky was ever present, waving and flashing a warm smile to those he passed on his journey.

Rocky was often joined by his wife, Happy, in an attempt to dispel the adverse feelings concerning their marriage. She attended all major campaign events and was at his side in most cases when mass media coverage was arranged.

From the very beginning, Governor Rockefeller constantly challenged Senator Goldwater to engage in public debate. With the assistance of a capable staff, Rockefeller researched Goldwater's past statements and proceeded to attack his pronouncements on a broad range of domestic and international issues.

Rockefeller took Goldwater as the single opponent in the campaign. His strategy was to engage Goldwater in every possible way. No strategy had been devised to deal with the two unannounced candidates, Lodge and Nixon, and none was developed.

Before continuing, it is important to mention an additional outside factor. President John F. Kennedy was assassinated in Dallas, Texas, on November 22, 1963.

President Kennedy was a neighbor of the New Hampshire people. He had taken the presidential primary route to his nomination in 1960. His hand had been extended to hundreds of New Hampshire voters, and his presence had graced many homes and places of business in the state. Upon his death, a one-month moratorium on political activity was announced, ending just before Christmas.

The enormity of the tragedy forced the New Hampshire citizens to consider more seriously the vote to be cast on March 10. The voters would now listen more closely and demand solid answers. When the campaign resumed in January, new factors had been added; the complexion changed, and a new balance quickly became apparent.

Senator Goldwater returned to Arizona in January and announced that he would seek the Republican nomination by entering his name in the New Hampshire primary. The *Manchester Union Leader* and the state GOP leadership had been pushing strenuously for this announcement.

Goldwater for President headquarters in Concord had been open before the senator announced his candidacy and was staffed with experienced New Hampshire politicians. The strategy was simply to mold and increase the large Goldwater popularity bulge indicated by the polls. The ethos of New Hampshire politics requires that an announced candidate must meet the voters in their shops, homes, clubs, churches, grange halls, and, especially, on the street. New Hampshire people will not often go out of their way to meet a candidate. To them it is the candidate who comes to the voter to ask for that vote.

Goldwater supporters proceeded to acquaint the public with their candidate and his views. The decisions concerning how the campaign should be presented were left in the hands of the New Hampshire supporters. Goldwater and his office staff followed, without concern, the recommendations of the in-state politicians. Lacking the direction of Rockefeller's professional staff, the all-chiefs-and-no-braves organization of Goldwater's prominent New Hampshire supporters haphazardly went about the task of presenting what they, individually, thought was the Goldwater position. Mass media and public relations were left in the hands of the *Manchester Union Leader.* Use of television and radio was ignored until the very last days of the campaign.

Without effective campaign planning, prominent political leaders are not enough to carry the cause. Goldwater supporters had not analyzed and quantified their candidate. They had not evaluated the basis for his support. They failed to recognize that this man was a Westerner, a political novice outside his own state, and a salable quantity in only those limited areas where he had built an image for himself.

THE WRITE-IN EFFORTS BEGIN

The Lodge and Nixon write-in efforts began early in January. Ambassador Lodge's supporters from Massachusetts came to Concord and opened headquarters on January 10. Governor Powell swung his loyalists away from Goldwater and to former Vice President Nixon. For two campaign efforts seeking the same result, a large write-in vote, the Lodge and Nixon efforts were quite different.

A small core of Lodge supporters came to New Hampshire prepared to conduct a Draft Lodge campaign through the write-in method. As late as January, the candidates' polls and the polls of independent research organizations showed that approximately 60 percent of the voting public was still undecided. This was the workable political capital with which the Lodge people expected to shape a vote for their candidate.

The basic strategy was to develop a "steamroller" of grass root support for the candidate. The most difficult steps of political campaigning had been accomplished. The ambassador was well known by the voting public both in name and political position. The problem was not to woo the voters from another candidate, but rather, to get a voter to commit oneself to Lodge. The Draft Lodge movement's two major tasks were to announce the movement to the voters and then to show the voters how to vote for the ambassador.

A slate of delegates "favorable" to the ambassador was selected. Those chosen were respectable business and professional people, practically unknown outside of their own occupational and social circles, and completely unknown politically. This nucleus of New Hampshire political amateurs went into the field and organized local Draft Lodge committees. Good publicity came from this activity when prominent, nonpolitical people in the communities announced as being "favorable" to the ambassador.

Early in February a mailing went to all registered Republicans. Included was a brochure describing the candidate and the reasons why he should be drafted as the Republican presidential candidate. There was also a pledge card with a message asking that if the voter was inclined to vote for Lodge would the voter please say so and return the card to the Concord headquarters. The response indicated that there was solid support for the ambassador at the local level and that this support, as the election approached, could be expected to increase.

The final step in the strategy was to draw the opposition candidates out with regard to the Draft Lodge movement. During the last weeks of the campaign both Goldwater and Rockefeller stepped into the Lodge set trap by recognizing the movement. Both made statements relative to Lodge's abilities, experience, and present position as the incumbent Democratic administration's representative in Vietnam.

Governor Powell, the perpetual opportunist, recognized the indecision of the voters. His political capital was the residue of his own campaign organization and the public's interest in Nixon left over from 1960. Putting the two together in a respectable write-in effort would revive the former governor's own political chances and incidentally those of the former vice president. Although it was late in the primary campaign, Powell knew his media tactics, his potential support, and his personal audience well.

Powell announced his support for Richard Nixon and solicited the support of his friends. Those who were not committed to other candidates made public statements of agreement and solicited funds for the campaign. The former governor's best medium was television. He purchased several one-half hour programs on New Hampshire's only commercial channel and discussed the reasons why Nixon would be the best Republican presidential nominee. Powell and his supporters placed a series of advertisements in the state's daily and weekly newspapers urging the voters to write in the name of Richard Nixon.

The Nixon effort began too late to enter a slate of delegates favorable to the candidate. In terms of the vote outcome, it is significant to note that the name Richard Nixon did not appear anywhere on the printed ballot. The voter, without assistance from the ballot, had to write in the candidate's name and omit the section of the ballot concerned with candidates for convention delegates.

THE ISSUES

As with Lodge, Nixon was well known to the voters. There was no debate on the issues, and no statements were made on the candidate's behalf that would reveal more than what was already known concerning his position on the current events. The opposite was the case with Rockefeller and Goldwater. Their strategies for the primary campaign required that they make statements concerning specific issues and that they answer the questions of the public and the press.

Governor Rockefeller had one major liability to overcome as a candidate, his divorce and remarriage. It was not an issue that could be debated, reasoned, or canceled; it had to be overshadowed by the other qualities of the candidate. The governor stressed his broad administrative experience in international affairs, in the federal government, and as the two-term governor of New York. He spoke with authority on a broad range of issues on which he knew his opponent, Barry Goldwater, would differ. Three basic issues boiled to the top during the campaign, Social Security, income tax, and the United Nations. The governor supported the existing system of Social Security while his opponent had stated that he favored a voluntary system of old age insurance. The income tax issue, simply stated, was that Goldwater favored a flat-rate tax while Rockefeller favored the existing progressive rate. Both Rockefeller and Goldwater opposed the admission of Red China to the United Nations.

The *Manchester Union Leader* vociferously supported Senator Goldwater and, in many cases, established the issues upon which he had to run. The basic theme of the *Manchester Union Leader*'s attack always raised the same issue: the Rockefeller wealth and re-marriage. Editor William Loeb used the front page editorial almost daily to castigate the governor.

New Hampshire's population is approximately 50 percent Roman Catholic. The *Manchester Union Leader*'s greatest circulation is in the city of Manchester, which is more than of 70 percent Catholic. On March 7, the *Manchester Union Leader* reprinted the following item with a picture of the governor and Happy Rockefeller. Headlined "Rocky Should Withdraw," it read as follows:

> *The Sign,* a national Roman Catholic magazine, makes no secret of its disapproval of Governor Rockefeller's highly publicized divorce and remarriage. The photo and caption below, published by the religious magazine in October, 1962, flayed the New Yorker for his flagrant transgression of our code of life, and called upon Americans of all faiths to repudiate him. Citizens who recognize the need for stern moral standards in high office cannot ignore the fundamental good sense of the magazine's position.

The other six daily newspapers in the state did not participate in this type of journalistic partisanship and character assassination. It was in these papers that the debate on the three basic issues was carried to the public.

Governor Rockefeller cleared each issue hurdle with the aplomb of a candidate who had prepared his campaign strategy carefully. Each issue was raised, developed, exploited, and registered with the voters before the next issue was taken up. Senator Goldwater and his supporters were always on the defensive. Not a single issue was constructed and raised successfully by the Goldwater people. Theirs was a holding action relying completely upon the candidate's personal magnetism.

Reducing the campaign to elements, Rockefeller organized, planned, and timed his campaign expertly. His supporting organization and control of the issues left him free to be an aggressive yet relaxed campaigner. His humor, congeniality, and energy were maintained throughout the campaign. His scheduling took him into the shops, business offices, and gatherings where he could most easily work his personal charm. He was well received by those he met and protected from embarrassment and hostility by good advance preparation.

Senator Goldwater was poorly served by his supporters. Losing the advantage on the issues and meeting increasing public hostility, Goldwater responded emotionally. He lost his dignity by reacting sharply on several occasions. No matter what he said he seemed just a little out of step with the people of New Hampshire. He was not the urbane, solid individual that his image had projected. His tendency to "shoot from the hip" on Social Security, Castro in Cuba, the reliability of U.S. missile defenses, income tax, and the United Nations all disturbed much of the New Hampshire Republican electorate.

The intense conflict between the governor and the Arizona senator did a great service to the write-in campaigns of Henry Cabot Lodge and Richard Nixon. As Rockefeller attacked and broke down the base of Goldwater's support, he created a large bloc of voters who, because of the underlying moral issue, would not vote for the governor but could be attracted to Lodge and Nixon.

Anticipating this trend, the Rockefeller and Goldwater camps began to devote more and more attention to the write-in movements. The basic Rockefeller theme was that he was the only true candidate in the primary and that to vote by write-in would serve no one and might damage the cause of moderate Republicanism. Goldwater relied on his supporter, William Loeb, to define the candidacies of Nixon and Lodge.

With the usual front-page editorial, Loeb wrote under the heading "Nixon Has Failed" an item that reflected upon Nixon's defeat in 1960 and in the California gubernatorial election of 1962:

> No one who remembers the miserable showing Nixon made in the television debates with the then Senator Kennedy would ever want to see him again as the standard bearer and then for the defeat in California by being a poor loser. In a cry-baby statement issued after his defeat, he blamed the press and everyone but himself for his inability to defeat Governor Brown.

He concluded by saying that only Goldwater offered a choice and to select Nixon again would be to repeat the failure and futility of his last attempt.

As for Ambassador Lodge, Loeb unleashed a warning to the voters under the heading "Beware of Lodge." Reviewing the situation in Vietnam, Loeb blamed Lodge for the overthrow of the Nhu family dynasty and for the worsening war effort since the coup.

> It would appear to this newspaper that the present administration was determined to overthrow the strongly anti-communist Diem faction, wanted a Republican fall-guy to give its dirty action a nice, non-partisan look. Ambassador Lodge was apparently stupid enough to fall for this plan and go along with it.

Goldwater deferred any immediate comment on the Lodge write-in; he did not, however, repudiate Loeb's support or any of the individual editorials.

Governor Rockefeller's organization also recognized the potency of the Lodge and Nixon write-in movements. It correctly surmised that the Lodge write-in was the most dangerous threat and turned its attention to that campaign. Late in February, Governor Rockefeller began referring to the "mess" in Vietnam and stating that Lodge would have to share some of the responsibility. This identified Lodge as a candidate and as someone with whom Rockefeller differed politically. Instead of taking the tack of recognizing Lodge as an important Republican leader entrusted with the execution of national policy in a critical and complex situation, Rockefeller split with Lodge.

According to the Lodge organization, the Lodge campaign would have ended if Governor Rockefeller had defended the ambassador at the point when Goldwater and his supporters were initiating their attack. Goldwater said that Lodge had gotten things "all balled up in Vietnam." According to John Grindle of the Lodge organization, as reported in *Newsweek*, "Had Rocky said Cabot and I are together in this—we have to stop Goldwater—it would have pulled the pins out from under us. Instead, Rocky criticized Lodge." The Rockefeller criticism placed Lodge on his own, while it placed Goldwater and Rockefeller in the same camp against the ambassador.

The Vietnam issue was the one issue on which the expert Rockefeller organization had not conducted research. Rockefeller's statement was in haste and lacked the direction and sense with which he approached the other issues in the campaign.

THE RESULTS

The campaign came to a climax during the first week in March. Films of the candidates or discussions by their representatives were featured on the major television channels serving the state. Spot announcements revealing specific stands on issues filled most available radio advertising time.

The Draft Lodge forces scored once more before the election was held. In New Hampshire campaigns it is traditional for the candidates to mail a sample ballot with the candidate or candidates marked as they would wish the people to vote. The Rockefeller ballot was mailed and carefully marked in an indistinguishable black. The Lodge ballot, also printed in black, was marked in red with specific instructions to the voter on how to vote for the Lodge delegates and how to write in the ambassador's name. The instructions and the red ink made writing in the ambassador's name that much easier.

The campaign concluded without a major last-minute issue or strategy shift. Rockefeller was rich and divorced; Nixon had lost elections; Goldwater was a Westerner, a conservative, and untried in national politics; and Lodge would be hurt by previous defeats and the Vietnam issue. The campaign came to a quiet conclusion under the glare of extraordinary national media attention.

Without incident or fraud, the voters went to the polls on a cold, snowy March 10 and some ninety thousand Republicans cast ballots.

The March 10 primary results were scored as follows:

Lodge	33,007	35.7%
Goldwater	20,692	22.4%
Rockefeller	19,504	21.1%
Nixon	15,587	16.9%

Fifty-two percent of the vote cast in the Republican primary was a write-in vote for either Richard Nixon or Henry Cabot Lodge. Neither of these men campaigned personally for the public's vote nor indicated a wish to be considered. Lodge seemed to be the acceptable alternative for a public that was not willing to support either Goldwater's instability or Rockefeller's divorce and remarriage.

There was one obvious loser in the New Hampshire primary, two good showings, and one winner. Senator Goldwater lost on all accounts from what was, in the beginning, his victory. Not a single Goldwater delegate was elected to the convention. The voters turned down, as delegates favorable to Goldwater, the state's most prominent Republican leaders. The Senator's vote total was unimpressive and demonstrated that his stands on the issues would not be popular with the people of the northern industrial states. Governor Rockefeller had struck the Senator hard on the issues and had revealed the weakness of his positions. Goldwater suffered a severe loss of national prestige with his defeat in New Hampshire.

Contrary to what was then stated by the reporters, the vote given to Governor Rockefeller should have classified him as a strong contender. He began the campaign far behind in the early polling, as reflected on the issue of his personal life. Rockefeller had engaged Goldwater and drawn him in with his strategy. Rockefeller gathered a respectable vote which showed him to be a potent campaigner who made one mistake when he attacked Ambassador Lodge. Unfortunately for the governor, the size of his vote was not sufficient to demonstrate that the issue of his personal life had been left behind.

The Nixon vote was the truly unusual vote in the election. Without an organization, without stimulus from outside, and with little time to organize before the election, former Governor Powell convinced a significant number of voters that writing in the Nixon name on the ballot would have meaning. Nixon received almost 17 percent of the vote. This vote was as much to the credit of Powell as it was to the reputation of Richard Nixon.

Without Ambassador Lodge and the Draft Lodge movement, Governor Rockefeller may well have been the top winner in the primary. The Lodge organization's strategy, timing, and use of media were superb. It discovered an undecided electorate, approached it, and captured it convincingly. The vote total was more than significant; it was astounding. No means of explanation from either Rockefeller or Goldwater could possibly diminish the positive nature of this endorsement.

The vote returns revealed the existence of four types of New Hampshire Republicans. The first were the conservative party leaders and those establishment voters who responded to suggestions of those leaders and, in this election, to the voting advice of the *Manchester Union Leader* in its support of Senator Goldwater. These voters were scattered throughout the state but tended to predominate where the conservative establishment of the Republican Party was the strongest.

The second bloc of voters were those of the more liberal Republican establishment. These voters and their leaders tended to support the candidacy of Governor Rockefeller and to receive the endorsement of the liberal Republican press for their activities in the state. Like the conservative Republican establishment vote, this vote was widely dispersed throughout the state but was strongest in those communities where the newspapers and the leadership had been relatively more liberal.

Neither of these two blocs would play a role in the 1968 Democratic Party or have particular influence on what occurred that year. The conservatives would vote for Richard Nixon and the liberals tended to support Governor George Romney and then to write in the name of Nelson Rockefeller. It is the last two voter types that are of interest.

The first of these were the voters that responded to the suggestion of former Governor Powell that they write in the name of Richard Nixon on their ballot. These voters tended to predominate in the high circulation communities of the *Manchester Union Leader,* such as Manchester and its surroundings and the communities between the circulation sheds of the regional daily newspapers. Loeb and Powell had been a political team for more than ten years until their split in 1961. Powell had attracted an antiestablishment Republican vote in his primary contests and had won his two terms as governor with the support of maverick Democrats from these same communities. The strong Powell communities also tended to be of middle or lower middle socioeconomic status.

Loeb could not overcome Powell's residual appeal and failed to hold Powell's loyalists for his candidate Barry Goldwater. Powell's vote bloc tended to be the mavericks of New Hampshire politics and, therefore, not persons closely aligned to either political party.

The final bloc of voters were those independent Republicans that include Democrat-like liberals and nonorganization Republicans, and who tend to be of a higher socioeconomic status. These were the Lodge voters who were able to make a vote decision with a minimum of campaign provided information, and to register that decision in the more demanding manner of the write-in but also through the selection of delegate candidates. These voters, their communities, and their similar Democratic voter counterparts are of particular importance to the explanation of the outcome of the 1968 presidential primary of the Democratic Party.

In summary the 1964 Republican presidential primary gave the observer two basic insights into the dynamics of such elections. The first was the tactic the Lodge organizers had used to attract a vote for their candidate. The pledge card, the use of direct mail, and the careful timing of their strategy were especially attractive to those organizing campaigns for 1968. Secondly, the way the voters broke into blocs and how these blocs responded to changing political conditions attracted considerable interest. The possibility that Democratic voters might respond, like the Republican voters had responded, to the various options, indicated a potential in the Democratic electorate to produce a surprise result similar to that which the Lodge organizers had accomplished.

The 1964 presidential primary was a reference point that helped the campaign planners of 1968 judge the potential of their strategies. It gave them new options that, because they had worked in 1964, might be made to work again in 1968. Without that reference point much of what happened in 1968 might not have happened. To experiment, as the Lodge organizers experimented, would have been much too risky given the issues that were at stake. There had to be some feeling that an effort to test public opinion on the war issues would be politically viable. The Lodge success was a political reality. The conclusion of those considering options for 1968 was that something like it might work again.

CHAPTER 2

Early Chronology

FINDING A VOICE—1967

Accounts of the national search that was going on to find a person willing to be a candidate against Lyndon Johnson have been well documented. It is sufficient to note that a series of separate and unrelated organizational activities and alternative searches were underway not only in Washington, but in many other states as well. The searches, which had succeeded in gaining the attention of those in New Hampshire concerned about the war, were, in order of relevance to the state: the Draft Kennedy movement, the Wisconsin vote "no" option, the California Democratic Council organization, and the New York Coalition for a Democratic Alternative. Little if anything was known of the activities of Allard K. Lowenstein, Russell Hemenway, Maurice Rosenblatt, Curtis Gans, and others as they went from office to senatorial office trying to convince first Robert Kennedy, then George McGovern, then McCarthy to become a candidate in opposition to what was assumed to be the certain renomination of President Lyndon B. Johnson.

All that has been reported subsequently of Lowenstein's search from one possible candidate to the next inside Washington and elsewhere, was unknown to those like Officer and myself who were evaluating our own options in New Hampshire. As September and the political season of 1968 began to close in, the possibility of working with the Draft Kennedy movement in New Hampshire seemed to be the only remaining option. Others in New Hampshire had come to the same conclusion and had already begun to attend the strange meetings that Eugene Daniell would hold in various parts of the state.

Daniell would issue a press release saying a meeting of Draft Kennedy supporters would be held in this town or that, reserve a room, contact a local friend or antiwar activist, and hope for the best. He would arrive at the designated time and place and conduct a rather free-form colloquy concerning the war, its damage to the nation, its cost, and, incidentally, the need to draft Robert Kennedy as an opponent for Lyndon Johnson. Each meeting would begin and end in essentially the same manner—with a press release suitable for use on morning radio and in the morning newspaper. Rather than creating a statewide network of local committees, Daniell left in each of these communities a confused group that had come to his meeting expecting to be involved in establishing a statewide organization. Daniell had neither the staff, the funds, nor the interest to pull the local contacts together into a campaign organization.

One of Daniell's meetings was held in Hanover, fertile ground for antiwar sentiment. Several Dartmouth faculty members attended. It was a relatively small gathering. Roger Davidson, a member of the Dartmouth college government department, relayed an account of the meeting to me. Previously I had expressed skepticism concerning the potential of Daniell's organizational style and had refused an invitation to attend the meeting. The substance of the meeting had been an attempt by the Hanover attendees to extract some organizational concessions from Daniell.

In response Daniell agreed to hold a statewide organizational meeting in Concord. At that meeting it was expected that a statewide Draft Kennedy organization would be formed, officers elected, and an operating committee created. This was, according to Davidson, a difficult series of steps for Daniell to take, but if he did not take those steps, he was told by his potential Hanover supporters that he could not count on their participation.

The search for an alternative candidate was beginning to succeed. Senator Eugene J. McCarthy, Democrat of Minnesota, had indicated that he would consider being a candidate. With the first positive response from a possible candidate, those urging the alternative, primarily Allard Lowenstein, a New York lawyer, former member of Senator Hubert Humphrey's staff, Americans for Democratic Action (ADA), and prominent civil rights activist; Sandford Gottlieb, executive director of national SANE, an antinuclear weapons, antiwar organization; and Curtis Gans, a Lowenstein associate and recent member of the Americans for Democratic Action staff sought to make as many contacts as possible in as many of the primary states as possible. This was to be done to lend credibility to their contention that a sizable organization already existed and could be used by an alternative candidate.

Gans called Davidson saying that he wanted to meet on October 25. Davidson called me and asked if I could spare the time to join him for what sounded to Davidson like a most mysterious meeting. Gans had not been specific as to his mission except to express interest in the New Hampshire political situation and the Draft Kennedy activity.

McCARTHY WILL RUN

A day or so before Gans arrived in Hanover, Officer and I had decided we would begin to discuss with Eugene Daniell how the Kennedy write-in might be organized like the Lodge write-in of 1964. Within a week or so of Gans' surprise visit we expected to have met with Daniell, discussed our ideas, and influenced the direction of subsequent Kennedy write-in activity. Because of these pending decisions and also being skeptical about the need for outside help with Daniell's plan, I was reluctant to join the Gans-Davidson meeting for more than pleasantries and a general status report of the New Hampshire situation.

When he entered the room I immediately recognized Gans as having been an effective proponent of the Democratic Party at a 1959 National Student Association meeting. After introductions, Gans quickly indicated there was a possibility that Senator Eugene McCarthy would run for president against Lyndon B. Johnson, and that there was a possibility that he would enter the New Hampshire primary. Without further warm-up, Gans then asked what I thought of McCarthy's prospects as a presidential candidate.

Stunned, my whole political experience in New Hampshire flashed through my head like a role of microfilm. I remembered that in the spring of 1960, little-known U.S. Senator, Eugene J. McCarthy, was introduced to a student audience at the University of New Hampshire by the Catholic student chaplain, Father Francis O'Conner. He was speaking on behalf of the candidacy of Hubert H. Humphrey, who was then running for the presidency against John F. Kennedy. My impression of that brief exposure was indelible.

McCarthy had politely fended the clumsiness of the conservative priest's introduction and spoke effectively about the state of the nation after eight years of President Eisenhower's passive leadership. The image that remained for me when Gans mentioned the presidential possibility was one of McCarthy's personal confidence and well-stated presentation, but, most importantly, his wry sense of humor. McCarthy had been bright but not insensitive, creative but not arrogant. He welcomed questions, answered them effectively, handled the hostile questions deftly in a manner that left no doubt as to his position but at the same time did not embarrass the questioner. In short, that flashback produced a personality profile that was usable in New Hampshire. Although an obscure U.S. senator, not a recognizable leader against the war, or for any particular cause, McCarthy did possess the visible characteristics that would make it possible to run a campaign for him in New Hampshire.

What caused me to react favorably was that I could place McCarthy in New Hampshire. Eugene McCarthy, I recalled, had addressed an audience of mostly New Hampshire students and had left a strongly favorable impression with that audience.

With the same flashback that contained the clip of McCarthy in 1960, there were also clips of my campaign experiences in New Hampshire and the organization that a full-scale presidential primary effort would require. It might be possible to take a candidate like McCarthy, organize a proper campaign, and generate a sufficient vote to mean something, but that activity would involve considerably more resources and personal commitment than would a write-in effort for Robert Kennedy. Taking on such a task would be close to impossible and at best only slightly possible if many others were willing to help.

Therefore, my answer to Gans' question was yes to the idea that McCarthy might be a candidate, but cautious to the idea that McCarthy might enter the New Hampshire presidential primary. Having just arrived in a new job with Dartmouth College, I was in no position to either explore the possibilities of a New Hampshire candidacy or to commit time to even a high success probability campaign, much less a quixotic antiwar venture.

Gans was the field operative for the Conference of Concerned Democrats (CCD), a hastily organized ad hoc group brought together to support the search for an alternative candidate. What was most reassuring about what Gans said was that the leadership of the CCD had come to the same political conclusions as Officer and I had about New Hampshire. The focal point for registering protest against the war had to be the president of the United States, Lyndon B. Johnson, and his desire for reelection. To be successful the political activity had to depend on those with political experience, whether that be through elective or party office, or extensive experience with the Democratic Party.

In other words, to be successful, a drive to stop Johnson had to come from inside the Democratic Party, using persons familiar with the party processes and with legitimate political reputations. The Gans presentation agreed with my own thinking about what would be successful in New Hampshire. Especially attractive to me was the fact that there would be a live, attractive candidate, not just the Kennedy name, a name that was being unwillingly borrowed as a protest vehicle.

I agreed with Gans on the theoretical points that supported the usefulness of the possible candidacy. I was skeptical, however, about Gans' credentials, especially about the possibility of generating the required local support from politically experienced New Hampshire Democrats. On this latter point I turned the question back to Gans. I had neither the time nor the inclination then, to explore the possibility with other New Hampshire Democrats.

Toward the end of the meeting I gave Gans the names of approximately twenty Democrats scattered through the state. In each case the name represented a person with considerable political experience in New Hampshire politics. They tended to be liberals who might be concerned about the administration's Vietnam policies and people, who, when motivated, would be politically effective. In each case, the person, if favorably impressed, would give Gans other local names for him to contact.

Immediately following the meeting, I went to my office to check on Gans, the possibility of a McCarthy candidacy, and my own mental condition. My first call was to my spouse, Sandy, which established that I was still properly rooted in the same dimension. The second call was to Senator Eugene McCarthy's office to check on Gans and his story. After a bit of confusion I spoke to the senator's administrative assistant, Jerome Eller, who assured me that Gans was on a valid mission. Eller was less candid on the possible candidacy of his senator, however, but this was to be expected. What Eller said was not inconsistent with what Gans said in our meeting.

I learned, subsequently, that Gans had worked for the ADA until the summer of 1966, when he resigned because ADA failed to take a strong stand against the war in Vietnam. Then Gans and Allard Lowenstein formed, with others, the CCD. Lowenstein, then teaching law in New York, was equally fed up with the administration's war policies. The purpose of the organization was to dump Johnson since he appeared to be the main obstacle preventing a war policy change. Lowenstein conducted the search for a candidate. That search, which ultimately produced Senator Eugene McCarthy as a candidate, had stopped at the offices of Robert Kennedy, Frank Church, George McGovern, and Vance Hartke, offering the CCD support if one would become a candidate. With at least a favorable reaction from Senator McCarthy, the CCD mission became to generate the organization it had promised would support an alternative candidate. Without the candidate there was little impetus for the organization, and without the organization it was hard to convince a potential candidate that a candidacy would be more than a crude and politically devastating joke.

Gans was the forerunner sent by the slim CCD organization to scout out the critical primary states for support for the possible McCarthy candidacy. Gans could have easily put together an impressive paper organization in each of the primary states just from the names of those who were most vocal in their opposition to the administration and the war. Instead, however, CCD adopted the more difficult task of finding support for an alternative candidacy from experienced political people in each of the target states. To a large degree the success of the campaign that followed depended on the extent to which Gans and Lowenstein were able to stir up such a cadre of politically experienced individuals for McCarthy.

Without question, the lengthy and fruitless work of those who had first raised their voices in opposition to the war policies of the Johnson administration had stirred the consciences of at least some political activists. To those in New Hampshire, Wisconsin, California, New York, and many other states, who were looking for a way to express opposition to the war, a live candidacy by a respected political leader, within the political system, was by far the preferable protest route. Their experience, their political skills, and their understanding of the political processes could direct the energy of protest within a political system designed to absorb such discontent. They were in contrast to those with political expertise in the national peace movement who had already written off the possibility of creating a force inside the political system that would be powerful enough to evoke a policy change. Later, when the success of the political efforts began to show, some of these groups and individuals joined the effort. Even until the very end in Chicago 1968, some substantial and vocal groups did not join, did not see the efficacy of participating in the political system, and felt vindicated by the result of the Chicago convention.

To support their argument for activity inside the political system, Allard Lowenstein collaborated with a University of Michigan professor, Arnold E. Kaufman, on the following statement. Gans capsulated the argument in each of his subsequent meetings as he pursued the list of twenty names I had given him on October 25.

Why Democrats Should Work to Stop Johnson

Allard Lowenstein and Arnold E. Kaufman

It seems self-evident that Democrats opposed to American policy in Vietnam and distressed by the consequences of that policy at home should oppose the re-nomination of President Johnson who is, after all, the author of that policy. The moral issue could hardly be more clear and the stakes are too high for self-paralysis, however rationalized.

For Democrats who feel their party and nation are headed to disaster, to avoid opposing the President is to abandon a basic principle of electoral democracy. There have rarely been such compelling reasons to work politically for new leadership.

And Democrats who, feeling this way, justify a failure to act politically as an act of political realism make common cause with other Americans who justify their failure to act politically as an act of conscience. Unopposed, these abstainers could fulfill the prophecy they share: the prophecy that the American political system has become too defective to permit effective opposition to a man who is leading the nation to disaster.

We do not believe that. Opposition to the President's renomination is, among other things, an expression of faith in American democracy. But faith in democracy is not enough to persuade tough-minded men to follow a particular political course.

It is our contention that the effort to stop Mr. Johnson's renomination is also the most practical option available to those who would reverse course in Vietnam and reorder the national priorities; that it is in fact, an essential part of any general effort to achieve those goals.

In short, if a President is wrong but popular, political realities may make opposing him difficult, however right; if a President is right but unpopular, supporting him may be a duty, however difficult. But when a President is both wrong and unpopular, to refuse to oppose him is a moral abdication and a political stupidity.

We are convinced that the most effective way to oppose Mr. Johnson is to oppose his candidacy in primaries and at state conventions. Some of our reasons follow.

I. There is no longer serious dispute about the fact that disaffection from Mr. Johnson is extensive and growing rapidly throughout the country. Political sentiment so deeply and widely felt will find some form of expression. If we do not provide constructive alternatives and attractive liberal leadership there will be less competition for other kinds of leadership. Such a development can only encourage increasingly frustrated outbursts on the left, and a Reagan-style reaction among the general public. But this need not occur, if the experiences of the past two months are any guide. In any case, enthusiasm among grass-roots Democrats for a Stop-Johnson campaign is overwhelming, and we ignore the opportunity such enthusiasm provides at our own peril. That so much has been accomplished so quickly without major names, without adequate organization, and virtually without funds, is proof enough of what could be achieved if major figures were to join in creating adequately-financed organizations.One useful by-product of this type of campaign could be the healing of ancient wounds and the development of a new coalition embracing much of the disenchanted left and of the anxious, muddled middle—a coalition that would be based on present realities and needs rather than on fading memories of past political victories.

II. The most foolish course for liberal Democrats is to sit out the Johnson issue, as if by our ignoring it will go away. The fact is that Mr. Johnson will be opposed, whatever liberal Democrats may "decide" to do. In Wisconsin, does one vote "Yes" or "No" when those words appear beside Mr. Johnson's name on the ballot? In California, can one simply avoid the primary contest between the CDC "peace" slate and a coalition of party regulars that may include, and possibly be led by, Mayor Yorty? And if one does these things is the anti-war cause strengthened by the stronger pro-Johnson vote that would presumably result?

Surely it is clear that the one way in which dove sentiment can be made to seem minimal is to leave the organizing of the anti-Johnson effort to groups with little standing as Democrats and with less prospect of reaching effectively the wide spectrum of Democrats who are upset about the President's policies. In short, unless responsible, widely based campaigns are waged in Democratic primaries, the campaigns that will be waged will make peace sentiment seem far weaker than it is.

Such a result, in addition to its impact on the Democratic convention, would almost certainly have sad effects on the situation in the Republican Party. Polls would continue to show that the President is unpopular, and if this unpopularity is not reflected in strong dove showings in Democratic primaries, there would be little incentive for Republicans to seek dove support.

There can be little doubt that the likeliest way to arrive at a Johnson-Nixon or Johnson-Reagan choice in November is for anti-war candidates to run badly in Democratic primaries. On the other hand, well-organized campaigns under responsible leadership can underscore the strength of anti-war sentiment and suggest to the Republicans that their prospects for winning the Presidency may depend on offering dissident Democrats a tolerable alternative. In short, those who would permit the Democratic nomination to go to Mr. Johnson by default or would have the opposition to his renomination in the hands of those least in tune with the general public make it more probable that the Republicans will misread the temper of the American electorate and do the natural rather than the sensible thing.

III. Those who worry about trying to "beat somebody with nobody" need not. There will be an acceptable "somebody" as soon as the depth and extent of Democratic dissatisfaction is clear.

There are admirable alternatives to Mr. Johnson among men not committed to supporting him: Senators McCarthy, McGovern, and Church, for example. But these are men who cannot be expected to rush joyously into so grueling a contest; they cannot be expected to undertake it unless they can be shown that it will not be an act of political hari-kari.

The nature of the situation therefore dictates that a broad-based and growing Stop-Johnson campaign must be underway before decisions about specific candidates can be made. Reiterated predictions that no acceptable candidate will be available are not merely misleading; they can become dangerously self-fulfilling if they confuse people about the importance of indicating opposition to Mr. Johnson's renomination.

IV. The effort to get a "peace plank" in the Democratic platform is a splendid supplement to the basic Stop Johnson strategy. There are some states (and some Congressional districts) in which it may well make better sense to work for such a plank than to mount an effort to win delegates directly opposed to Mr. Johnson's renomination. Furthermore, there are some people deeply opposed to the President's Vietnam policy who for one reason or another are unwilling to oppose the President personally at this time. Such people should be valued allies; for on thing they are a constant reminder of how much further the President's support can erode, should he continue on his present course.

Every activity that can help to keep open debate at the National Convention should be welcomed. The President and his national Chairman, Mr. John Bailey, are already at work to try to head off such a possibility. But many Democratic professionals who may end up supporting the President would rather attend a convention than a coronation. The Michigan State Chairman, Mr. Zolten Ferency, had such people in mind when he blasted Mr. Bailey's odd announcement that the decisions of the Democratic Convention have already been made before any delegates have even been elected.

Much must be done immediately if Mr. Bailey is not to be a more accurate prophet than he is reporter, and there should be no cause for quarrel between those who wish to oppose only the war and those who wish to oppose Mr. Johnson as well.

V. Those who hesitate to oppose Mr. Johnson lest he change his Vietnam policy should rather be among the first to joint in a Stop-Johnson campaign. Nothing is less calculated to persuade Mr. Johnson to change policies than actions that imply that he has, in any case, the support of those who are opposed to those policies. If increasingly effective political opposition induces the president to reverse himself, surely the anti-Johnson effort will not have been wasted.

In that event, no doubt some would continue to oppose Johnson; others would revert to support. But such decisions are not only unnecessary, they are impossible until events raise the questions. To speculate over potential decisions about hypothetical problems not even remotely at hand can be more divisive than enlightening.

* * * * * * * * * * * * * * * * *

The American people are generally appalled by the prospect of a Johnson-Nixon-Wallace choice in 1968. One may hope Republicans will do all they can in their party to avert such a choice.

But it is conceivable that those of us who are Democrats will surrender the party of Franklin and Eleanor Roosevelt and of John F. Kennedy to those whose policies are shattering our hopes for a just society and a peaceful world. To accept the Johnson record as the basis for a national campaign is such a surrender. It may seem difficult at first to fight for the party against the power of the Presidency, but that is how the fight must be made if it is to be relevant.

Fortunately, there is no indication that rank and file Democrats are more than momentarily abashed at the prospect of such a fight. In fact, so many of them care deeply about the stakes that the fight can be won if we have the guts to wage it.

GANS' REPORT

Two days after the October 25 meeting, Gans called to say that he was making progress with the list of names I had given him. The initial list of about twenty names had now doubled. Gans had carried his message to at least one person and usually more in almost all of the critical cities and towns of the state.

Between the first meeting and Gans' progress report, I had discussed the possibilities with Sandy Hoeh. She then held the 2nd Congressional District chair for the New Hampshire Democratic State Committee. Several weeks earlier she had scheduled a 2nd District conference to be held Sunday, October 29 on the campus of Colby Junior College, New London, New Hampshire. Charles Officer was going to deliver a brief talk about the district and the probable issues that the Democratic candidate was likely to face in the fall of 1968. Officer's talk would include his evaluation of the impact on the Democrat Party of the administration's policies in Vietnam. The speech would be critical of those policies and would indicate that in order to have salable political positions by November 1968, New Hampshire Democrats would be wise to moderate their support of the administration. Officer, by opening the door to criticism of the administration from within the party, would be the first step in the strategy to help with Daniell's write-in for Kennedy.

The 2nd District conference would also serve as an important sounding board for assessing the prospects of an anti-Johnson, antiwar drive in the state. Attending would be Democrats from all corners of the district and especially from the major cities and towns that contain most of the district's Democratic voters. These would be the actives, those interested in the day-to-day affairs of politics, skilled in campaigning, and close to the voters.

I had discussed the upcoming conference with Gans at our meeting. We agreed to meet at the conference for a detailed report and to give Gans a further chance to contact more of the state's Democrats. Although Gans' telephone report on October 27 was optimistic, I was not prepared to become involved in an antiadministration activity until many other aspects of the possible campaign were carefully outlined. I wanted to make sure that Gans would not link my name with a campaign at this stage and certainly not until I had had a chance to follow up on the contacts Gans had made and reported back to me.

I called Officer shortly after Gans' Hanover visit to advise him of the possible McCarthy candidacy. The only change this information caused in their plan for the 2nd District conference was that instead of making a specific overture to Daniell, a more general reference would be made to possible outlets for antiwar feelings during the coming year. They agreed that they would not attempt to meet with Daniell but rather would encourage Gans to circulate at the conference and to report his findings. Gans was scheduled to leave New Hampshire October 29.

The conference program went as planned. Officer's message about the challenges ahead for the Democratic Party in 1968 was well received. He said:

> Party unity should be of the highest priority and not be sacrificed for the sake of desires dictated from Washington. Let us keep those who speak dissent within our party in this difficult year, but true to our open democratic traditions, and make our party grow stronger with this year as it has in the past election contests.
> (Press release, 2nd District Conference, October 29, 1967)

I maintained a distance from Gans, letting him talk to those attending by himself alone and without giving the appearance of a cabal in the formative stages. Toward the end of the afternoon I was approached by two friends who were on the staff of Senator Tom McIntyre and Governor John W. King, Charles McMahon and Richard Weston, respectively.

The three of us went into a separate room where I was grilled by McMahon and Weston about the mysterious Gans. Since Daniell was also attending the meeting and promoting the Kennedy write-in, I was as oblique in my answers as I could be without appearing foolish. McMahon and Weston wanted to know who Gans was, what he was doing in New Hampshire, and whether I was involved with him. I was not particularly helpful to either Weston or McMahon because there was not much of substance to report. McMahon was especially interested in Gans since he had been tipped off about McCarthy through Senator McIntyre's Washington office. Since McIntyre was a member of the Armed Services Committee and would be a major supporter of the president in the coming primary, any stir of opposition to a united effort for the president in New Hampshire was viewed as being potentially damaging to McIntyre's stature in the senate and with the administration. It was to be McIntyre's job, in cooperation with Governor King, to deliver the state of New Hampshire via the presidential primary to Lyndon Johnson without Johnson having to be directly involved.

My most direct response to Weston and McMahon was that I had extended to Gans the same courtesy that I would extend to any other Democrat or news reporter who wanted to discuss politics with some New Hampshire Democrats. I said that I had told Gans what the situation was in New Hampshire, given Gans a list of names with whom Gans could check my evaluation, and advised Gans as to the condition of the Democratic Party following the 1966 election. Regarding a possible McCarthy candidacy and whether I thought anything would come of the Gans scouting mission, I was noncommittal. McMahon and Weston seemed satisfied with the conversation but continued to be concerned about Gans.

Before Gans left New Hampshire that afternoon, he discussed his findings with me. The responses Gans found were, in most cases, cautiously favorable. The people he had met were the political people that a successful campaign would depend on for support. Their experience was such that casual enthusiasm or immediate committal to Gans was not their style. They wanted to check with associates in the party, in their communities, and with their families. They were not about to tilt windmills. They knew that a political failure in New Hampshire for the antiwar movement could be a critical blow to the fortunes, not only of the antiwar movement but to many thousands of young Americans they did not want to see go to Vietnam. I assured Gans that if he received anything positive from those he contacted that he should interpret that as a favorable sign.

Gans also had a chance to meet with Eugene Daniell and to gain an impression of him and his activities. Daniell was almost as curious about Gans as were the McIntyre-King staffers. Daniell felt that his drive could bring Robert Kennedy into the campaign and that the candidacy of an unknown, such as Eugene McCarthy, would face great difficulty. To Gans, Daniell's efforts appeared to be a one-person operation. He did not have a organization or even many supporters at the 2nd District meeting. Yet Gans, through his contacts around the state, had found substantial disenchantment with the Johnson administration and saw this as the basis of statewide political opposition to Johnson's renomination.

Gans asked me if I would be willing to call a meeting of those he had contacted to consider further the prospects of the McCarthy candidacy. I remained noncommittal but said that I would be willing to consider doing that if reactions to Gans' visit continued to be favorable in the weeks ahead.

WHERE THERE IS SMOKE THERE IS FIRE

Gans had spread sparks in dry tinder. The smoke was becoming obvious. As early as the Friday before the 2nd District conference, word of Gans' travels was leaking to the New Hampshire press. Stimulated by inquiries from national bureaus, local wire service reporters began to sniff the air for signs of an emerging McCarthy organization in New Hampshire. Although no one was yet committed to such an activity, the string of reporters' telephone calls began to fan the sparks. New Hampshire is a small state where political news travels fast.

A reporter's call to a prominent Democrat, in all likelihood former National Committeeman, William L. Dunfey, produced another call to a Portsmouth Democratic city councilman, Paul McEachern. McEachern had been on my list for Gans, and when McEachern was called he indicated that I had suggested that Gans see him. McEachern was noncommittal in the newspaper account of his story, but the reporter had to attribute the activity to someone in the state other than Gans and referred to me as the "titular leader" of the New Hampshire McCarthy organization. The story led other reporters to the trail. Where there is smoke there shall be fire appeared to be the reporters' slogan as I tried desperately to put the brakes on the publicity that linked me to the yet nonexistent McCarthy candidacy.

McMahon had obviously reported his conversation with me to his boss, Senator McIntyre. Within a day or two of the 2nd District conference, McIntyre called us, talking to Sandy. He asked her what my intentions were with respect to the possible candidacy of Senator McCarthy. She spoke of our concern about the war and the impact the war was having on the possibilities for the party in New Hampshire during the coming year. Sandy said she felt there had to be a political way to express the growing dissent in New Hampshire and the nation without destroying the political system. She said that at that time we had made no commitments to McCarthy, Gans, or anyone regarding an anti-Johnson campaign. In closing, she assured McIntyre that she would let him know if we intended to change that position.

During the week following the 2nd District conference, I made a number of telephone calls to those who had responded favorably to Gans' inquiries and found that what Gans had reported was correct. There was interest in opposing the president on the war. There was a favorable reaction to the possibility that McCarthy might be a candidate. There was also the expected skepticism about running a successful campaign and the size of the possible vote. Too many years in a conservative state with basic patriotic inclinations had made most of those contacted careful about overly enthusiastic political predictions.

Too many good candidates in favorable campaign years had suffered defeats. A difficult media situation, a probable lack of attention for a Democratic challenger in the midst of a vigorous contest for the Republican nomination, weighed heavily against organizing a Democratic protest vote against the president. The peace movement was weak, isolated, poorly organized, without funds, and had not attracted much attention in the state. A New Hampshire campaign for someone like Senator McCarthy would have to start from the very beginning.

Gans called during the last week in October to report that things were moving rapidly in Washington. He asked if I would convene those who had been contacted during the recent visit to meet with Allard Lowenstein. I said that I would commit myself only to the extent of bringing the group together to meet Lowenstein. I felt it was important to share thoughts, reflect on Lowenstein's report, and discuss the reality of such a venture before even suggesting that an organization should be formed. Furthermore, I knew little or nothing about Allard Lowenstein, the CCDs he was representing, or the status of the potential McCarthy candidacy except what Curtis Gans had said during his visit.

My first call was to Sylvia Chaplain, of Bedford, a suburb of Manchester, to ask if we could meet in her home on November 5. The location was convenient for most of those who would attend, and Sylvia had already made known, through Gans, that she was interested in the activity. A long suffering Manchester liberal, member of ADA, and a participant in numerous state, local, and national campaigns,

Sylvia, her spouse Philip, and their living room were important to the early development of the McCarthy activity. The calls to the others on Gans' list went out with most expressing interest and almost all being able to attend.

LOWENSTEIN'S FIRST VISIT

I arranged with Gans to have Lowenstein arrive in Manchester sufficiently ahead of the Bedford meeting so that we could meet, and I could explain the situation and provide some background. Lowenstein appeared younger than his forty years, with rumpled hair dragged forward over his retreating hairline. He arrived with what I subsequently learned was his usual rush, bordering on chaos. I was immediately taken by his enthusiasm but even more by a sense of commitment and purpose that seemed to emanate from him.

With only the barest of introductions, I felt that I could trust Lowenstein, and since Lowenstein had already received a briefing from Gans, I pursued my questions. It was important to know as much as I could about what Lowenstein was up to before I escorted him into the Chaplain living room. I wanted to know whether there would be a McCarthy candidacy, what was the likelihood that McCarthy might enter the New Hampshire primary, what elements of the campaign would be provided from outside New Hampshire, and what the CCD was all about. Lowenstein was as responsive as he could be at that stage in the development of the candidacy. There were many ifs in the answers but few of these were hidden. Where the facts were shaky, his contagious enthusiasm made even the most difficult solutions seem within reach. My appraisal of those expected to attend that evening's meeting was virtually on target with the organizational objectives Lowenstein had in mind.

As a side note Lowenstein was the first migrant to New Hampshire to become "Clean for Gene." He had arrived in a somewhat disheveled state and without a tie. He asked me if he needed a tie for the meeting. I said not particularly, but perhaps in order to accomplish the objective of the meeting it might be a good idea. He went to the John Goffe Mill gift shop, bought a tie that almost matched his shirt and suit, and we went to the Chaplains' home.

THE FIRST MEETING

The living room was filled with at least one or two persons from each of the eight or nine important primary vote-producing communities. As they walked in Sylvia took me aside to say that she had received a call from Eugene Daniell asking if he might come to the meeting. Since the meeting was to be informal and Lowenstein's mission not fully known she felt that there was no reason to exclude him. Toward the end, Daniell and Dr. Martin Shepard, the New York City Draft Kennedy leader, arrived.

I introduced Lowenstein by noting the group's curiosity about his visit and by having those in the group introduce themselves. Lowenstein began by reviewing the administration's unwillingness to respond to the rising volume of dissent of the war, its inability to resolve the problems of the big cities, and its increasingly harsh repression of criticism in the nation. Lowenstein spoke in political terms outlining how the political system could be used to oppose Johnson and the war. The arguments were well received by those in the room. These were political people and they wanted their unhappiness with the Johnson administration expressed in political terms, not in the language of moral and ethical protest.

Lowenstein had two basic points that he wanted the group to consider. The first was the possible candidacy of Senator McCarthy. Lowenstein said the senator had not yet committed himself to be a candidate. Lowenstein felt that in order to stimulate McCarthy's candidacy there had to be in existence in each of the important primary states an organization that would welcome and support his candidacy.

The second point concerned the organization which Lowenstein was developing, the CCD, as a national umbrella organization for antiwar political activity. It was to be the national organization for the Dump Johnson movement and would be a framework for marshaling support and, as importantly, public attention for an alternative candidate. Lowenstein wanted as many of those assembled in the room as possible to plan to attend the CCD national meeting in Chicago, December 2 and 3.

On both points the group was cautious. Each person recounted his or her own feelings about the failures of the Johnson administration and the disaster that was likely for the Democratic Party if Johnson were not challenged and the war policy was not changed. A sense of betrayal by the administration was clear, but caution concerning the difficulty of a drive to replace Johnson on the ticket was also clear. If these people were to trade their personal political capital, they wanted a return that at least left them with some dignity, some sense of the value of the effort, and some recognition as to the level of their political skills. Doubts as to the extent of outside help, especially the financing that they could expect, were uppermost in their minds. This concern was overshadowed only by individual uncertainty as to whether it would be possible to produce a sufficiently large vote in New Hampshire to make the venture respectable.

To a person, the group wanted to think about the Lowenstein arguments before deciding what to do. His enthusiasm had clearly been contagious, but the group felt the need to stand back, examine what it had heard, talk with friends at home, and then consider the possibilities.

The principal purposes of the meeting had been accomplished by the time Eugene Daniell and Dr. Shepard arrived. Shepard and Lowenstein had met earlier, and Shepard, especially, was suspicious of Lowenstein's activities. Lowenstein had access to Senator Kennedy on a personal basis that Shepard neither had nor could establish.

The contrast between Lowenstein's reception from the political people assembled in Bedford and that which Shepard and Daniell had attracted in Concord was upsetting. Shepard maintained that regardless of what McCarthy would do, he and Daniell would continue. He alleged that McCarthy, an unknown, would not be able to bring out the votes necessary to have an impact, much less gain enough recognition to attract an audience. In contrast to Lowenstein's style, Shepard evoked hostility. He appeared as a cynic with a sense of bitterness that did not set well with those attending.

Shepard had an opportunity to capitalize on the gathering, but he had neither the tact nor the sense of timing that Lowenstein's political realism had conveyed. Shepard seemed to be on his own ego trip and Kennedy seemed to be a convenient excuse. Lowenstein, on the other hand, had genuine contact with Kennedy, knew Kennedy's feelings at the time, had begun to generate the McCarthy candidacy, and was obviously interested only in the need to get state organizations going rather than creating food for his own ego. Shepard was unable either to divert Lowenstein or to draw support for his own efforts from those assembled. Those gathered would reassemble with their conclusions in two weeks on November 19.

THE PEOPLE AND POLLS

Politicians feel an almost constant sense of uncertainty. Old-style politicians used to ride by the seat-of-their-pants, never getting too far from the inclinations of their rather homogeneous constituencies. Their opinion polls were taken as they patrolled their districts receiving reports from their workers. They could count on reaping the fruit of the services they directly bestowed. As constituencies became more diverse, the issues more complex, and the capacity to provide direct services more limited, these informal roots to a constituency began to shrivel. Replacing political instinct and seat-of-the-pants politics were the voter survey and the public opinion poll.

Practically everyone in the room with Lowenstein had had some involvement with sample surveying. Sylvia Chaplain had a master's degree in survey research; Peter Freedman used surveys as part of his shoe company's marketing program; and others had used poll results for campaign planning or had helped conduct such surveys. The poll had become important to the campaign planning of the New Hampshire Democratic Party during the preceding decade. In fact, the Democrats had established such a formidable reputation as effective poll users that the Republican Party had begun to commission its own.

Given this experience, the group was not about to trust its own intuition. To be successful with a candidate like McCarthy, the group members felt they should know what portion of the voting public might be responsive to an alternative candidacy, especially one based on issues like support or nonsupport for the Johnson administration policies in Vietnam. During the Lowenstein meeting, the subject of a poll was thoroughly discussed. Everyone felt that such a poll was necessary before they could begin organizing and before a man like McCarthy should risk the peace issues in what might be disastrously hostile territory.

They felt they had a special problem in New Hampshire. The usual barometers of public sentiment in other jurisdictions were badly skewed in New Hampshire by the overriding presence of only one statewide daily newspaper, the *Manchester Union Leader*. The issue transmitting and interpreting process that operated in other states to convey an increasing disenchantment with the Johnson administration, and especially with the war, was not functioning on a statewide basis in New Hampshire.

The group members presumed that they might be representative of a certain like-minded segment of the population, but they did not know how large that population might be or where it was located. Nor did they know how intensely others might share their concerns or even if they would vote in the March 12, 1967, presidential primary. A great deal rested on this point. The Democratic Party had been a minority party for so long that its membership, though growing recently, was still limited. Slightly less than ninety thousand voters were registered in the Democratic Party in 1968 when the first formal report of registrations was made by the secretary of state. Of this number more than 40 percent were located in the state's two largest cities, Manchester and Nashua, and about 50 percent were in Hillsborough County alone. With the *Manchester Union Leader* dominating much of this important Democratic bailiwick, it would be difficult to generate a successful antiadministration, much less an antiwar, campaign.

From all visible signs, the administration's war policies were receiving the support of Democratic Party registrants. If there was an element susceptible to an alternative candidate within the body of New Hampshire's Democrats and especially among the Democrats of populous Hillsborough County, there was little to show for it but those assembled in the Chaplain living room. As mentioned before, because of the Democratic Party's perennial minority status, liberal-minded activists concerned about the future of New Hampshire governmental affairs registered in the Republican Party and voted in its primaries. Occasionally their votes had made the difference between the nomination of a conservative/reactionary candidate and one of more moderate views. Because of this situation, the Democratic Party had been divested of at least some of its natural liberal constituency.

As the political year of 1968 approached, the possibility of influencing Johnson's war policies within the Democratic Party was remote. Republicans and liberals wanting to attack administration war policies were looking at the Republican presidential nominating contest as being the place to have an impact. If the candidate in the Republican primary who was most critical of the administration on the war were to prevail, then a strong political message would be transmitted to President Johnson. Changing parties was then a complicated process in New Hampshire. The possibility that a significant number of these antiwar Republicans would switch to the Democratic Party and thereby be eligible to vote for or against its candidates was negligible.

Faced with this discouraging political situation, the group decided at the November 5 meeting that it would need a poll prior to making a recommendation to Lowenstein or McCarthy about entering the New Hampshire presidential primary. Estimates of the cost of such a poll were in the range of $4,000 to $6,000. That amount was not available to the group. Lowenstein, without a firm candidate, and with only the beginnings of a national organization, was hesitant to commit such an amount. Although he was not critical of the group's concern, he did seem to feel that such a step at this stage would not produce usable results. In retrospect, it is probable that such a poll would have confirmed their worst fears rather than their optimism and could well have derailed their effort.

Since neither Lowenstein nor the CCD had the resources to conduct a national poll, much less a poll in only one of the primary states, it was apparent that the activities, nationally and in New Hampshire, would have to depend on the intuition of the adherents. Not having a poll in the early months and especially not having one in those first few weeks of decision making led to several interesting results. A normal organizing procedure for someone in Lowenstein's position would have been to arrive in New Hampshire with a poll that showed a pool of discontented potential Democratic presidential primary voters could be tapped providing that certain organizational steps were taken. Such a performance would have been the equivalent of premarketing a product in a new sales area. Along with such market delineating data there could have been a campaign strategy that reflected the findings of the poll. The package would be modified to meet the criticisms of those in the Chaplain living room. Any questions about whether the projected results could be met would have been answered by the poll and the presumption of success if the advised strategy were implemented. All that would be asked of those assembled would be their support, willingness to be a "sales force," and advice on how to adjust the campaign concept to operate smoothly.

Lowenstein arrived with none of the tools or preconceptions of the modern market researched campaign. Furthermore, it was clear to most of those who were sitting in that living room that the only way they would get a poll of New Hampshire voter opinion, at that stage, would be to pay for it themselves. The only hard information that Lowenstein possessed was that McCarthy was probably going to be a candidate, the CCD was to meet in national convention December 2 and 3, and that there were hundreds, perhaps even thousands, of persons across the nation who shared a concern about the policies of the Johnson administration. These were the only sure things he offered. The group had to decide individually and collectively whether to support an alternative to President Johnson. Then they would have to act to implement that decision on their own using their own wisdom. Making such a commitment without the trappings of modern precampaign planning and survey research would be difficult. The level of uncertainty was high as the meeting concluded.

CHAPTER 3

The New Hampshire Democrats and President Johnson

JOHNSON RENOMINATION

Just before the session with Lowenstein began, a meeting of the executive committee of the New Hampshire Democratic Party ended. Sandy Hoeh, who as chair of the 2nd Congressional District also served on the executive committee, had left Hanover earlier to attend that meeting. Until that date, the New Hampshire Democratic Party leadership had assumed that it would be united in its drive to deliver the state to Lyndon B. Johnson in his push for renomination. The Daniell-Kennedy write-in activity was viewed by most party leaders as a fringe operation that could be easily isolated. But by the end of that day the start of a substantive split in the New Hampshire Democratic Party had occurred.

Sandy Hoeh arrived at the Chaplain home and reported the results of the executive committee meeting. The principal actors of the Johnson campaign attended and were the Democratic Party leadership of the state, with the single exception of the former gubernatorial candidate, Bernard L. Boutin. A rather elaborate campaign plan had been developed by Boutin and informally agreed to by the major officeholders, principally Governor King and Senator McIntyre. The first public act of the Johnson write-in campaign was to be the discussion of the campaign at the November 5 executive committee meeting. Word of the Gans visit, the possible McCarthy candidacy, and additional stirrings prompted several changes in the original plan.

First, in an attempt to thwart the McCarthy move, Boutin wanted to secure state committee endorsement of the renomination campaign for Johnson sooner than he had originally planned. Second, because of the rumblings from the 2nd District conference regarding the antiadministration feelings of some Democrats, the agenda for the executive committee was modified. A discussion of the soon to be made public write-in drive for Johnson was closely guarded. Governor King made the presentation of the Boutin strategy that would convert the party organization into one large campaign committee for the Johnson renomination drive. An aspect of Sandy Hoeh's report that seemed most alarming to those gathered in the Chaplain living room was that a meeting of the Democratic state committee would be held Sunday, November 19, for the purpose of approving the Johnson campaign plans and endorsing the renomination of Lyndon B. Johnson. As a prelude to that endorsement meeting, a social/fund-raising event was scheduled for November 17, with the featured speaker being Senator Edward M. Kennedy.

As discussed earlier, New Hampshire presidential primaries are frequently politically perilous events for party leaders and officeholders. For a major officeholder, survival is of ultimate importance and to survive being involved in a New Hampshire presidential primary without collecting scars is a miracle. For King, McIntyre, and Boutin, party unity in support of the president was assumed. As leaders of the party, they had every reason to expect that what they said would carry weight with a sizable constituency. On the other side, they were in no position to differ with the president since such a move would be costly in terms of present political security and future rewards. Neutrality under the conditions of late 1967 and early 1968 would not have been an acceptable alternative. In fact, neutrality for a governor about to seek reelection, election to another office, or appointment as a federal judge would be viewed by the president as tantamount to desertion. In 1967 and 1968, one was either for the president or against him. There was no middle ground.

THE BOUTIN STRATEGY

After a string of appointments that had kept Boutin in Washington since the election of John F. Kennedy, he had resigned as the administrator of the Small Business Administration and returned to New Hampshire. Boutin sought to resume his interrupted career by reestablishing himself in New Hampshire and capitalizing on his exemplary record of federal service. When he returned during June 1967 Boutin had every intention of running for governor again, assuming that three-term governor, John W. King would either step aside or run for the U.S. Senate.

Boutin saw the chance to combine the gubernatorial objective with the Johnson renomination mission. His success as the manager of the Johnson campaign would bring him back into the limelight of New Hampshire politics and identify him with the fortunes and successes of his sure-to-be-reelected president, foreshadowing his own gubernatorial candidacy.

At approximately the time of Boutin's return to New Hampshire, the press carried a series of stories about a mysterious individual that President Johnson had sent to New Hampshire to organize his presidential primary. The stories had a particular flavor that would be repeated as the Johnson effort went forward. It appeared from the stories that somehow Johnson did not trust his fortunes to the leadership of the New Hampshire Democratic Party. Eventually both the press and the politicians settled on Boutin as the mysterious individual, although he steadfastly denied having other than friendly connections with the White House or the president's reelection operatives.

Whether Boutin was commissioned to manage the New Hampshire Johnson campaign or not, he arrived in New Hampshire with the plan for Johnson's effort in the primary. Even before he was appointed as the Reelect President Johnson chair for New Hampshire, Boutin outlined the Johnson campaign to party leaders and probably campaign workers.

The Johnson campaign was to be a total party effort. During a conversation with Sandy Hoeh in August 1967, Boutin sketched out the pyramid that would be the organizational shape of the Johnson New Hampshire campaign. At the top of the pyramid were the names of the titular leaders of the Democratic Party—King and McIntyre. Within the same segment with King and McIntyre was the operating head of the organization, Boutin himself. Beneath that point stretched downward an organization that would parallel the organizational structure of the New Hampshire Democratic Party. There would be regional leaders similar to the congressional district chair, county leaders, city leaders, town leaders, committee members, and a campaign connection to each of the ninety thousand-plus members of the registered Democratic Party electorate.

Although at the stage that Boutin described the organizational form the concept appeared to be separate from the Democratic Party structure, it was obvious that the party and the candidate organization would soon become one and the same. Accomplishing the transmutation would be an early objective for Boutin.

Apparently, sometime prior to Boutin's return to New Hampshire, a decision had been made in the White House that Lyndon Johnson would not become an announced candidate for reelection until late in the preconvention season. By this decision, Johnson took the cautious, more traditional route of incumbent presidents. Party surrogates in the respective states managed their affairs, keeping the incumbent presidents out of such politics. The fiction of noncandidacy would be maintained as long as possible for whatever purposes would be served by appearing to be above the political struggle.

The decision left the renomination leadership in New Hampshire with a single alternative. Since Johnson would not be an announced candidate, it would not be possible for his name to be listed on the ballot. The alternative, therefore, would be to ask Democratic voters to write in Johnson's name on the ballot. Consequently the Johnson campaign organization's first priority was to stimulate New Hampshire Democrats to turn out in significant numbers and then to write in the name of Lyndon Johnson. Of secondary importance in the strategy would be the selection of a slate of delegates. Boutin planned to solicit as delegate candidates the state's most prominent political names. These names alone, Boutin felt, would attract the votes needed to fill the delegation with Johnson supporters.

Boutin's planning was conditioned by several important experiences. The party reform effort of the 1950s had dislodged the conservative wing of the party from the leadership. Many of those who had been in the prereform leadership still lurked in the shadows of the party's councils. To Boutin in 1967, these individuals posed the greatest danger to the unity effort he had in mind for the Johnson campaign. In his conversation with Sandy Hoeh that August, Boutin referred to the names of some of the more obstreperous prereformers as representing that minority who would probably not join the write-in effort. When Sandy asked how he viewed the Draft Kennedy effort of Eugene Daniell, Boutin responded by saying that first, Robert Kennedy would come to New Hampshire and support the renomination of Lyndon B. Johnson, and that second, Daniell would not be able to generate much support for his Kennedy write-in effort. Only those ancient malcontents and a few "wild-eyed" radicals would even consider challenging the renomination campaign of the president in New Hampshire, Boutin concluded.

A second experience from Boutin's past that influenced his thinking was the John F. Kennedy primary of 1960. He clearly painfully recalled the effort of the party malcontents to abort the election of the full slate of Kennedy pledged delegates. Those same figures appeared to so occupy Boutin in his planning that he did not recognize the growing opposition to the president's war policies, an opposition composed of some of the same individuals who had helped Boutin reform the Democratic Party in the late 1950s.

A further blinding political event in Boutin's recollection was the 1964 effort to secure a write-in on that year's presidential primary ballot for vice president for Robert F. Kennedy. That movement had been generated in New Hampshire by some of the same persons who had opposed the pledged slate in the 1960 primary. It appeared that this effort was designed to demonstrate a loyalty to the heir Robert Kennedy that was greater than that of John Kennedy's 1960 advocates, like Boutin, who were now Johnson loyalists. An embarrassing situation was developing for Johnson and his supporters early in 1964. Loyalty to the Kennedy family was being placed in conflict with loyalty to the Johnson administration. The conflict left many Kennedy loyalists, now well connected in the Johnson administration, on extremely shaky ground. A significant vote for Robert Kennedy for vice president could be embarrassing to President Johnson. Opposition to the Kennedy candidacy would be interpreted in New Hampshire as ungracious if not actually disloyal. Given the choice, McIntyre, King, Dunfey, and other party leaders met and concluded that the only way to contain the divisive threat of the Kennedy vice presidential write-in was to embrace the effort. In a last-minute announcement, most of the party's leadership, including the senator and governor, enthusiastically endorsed the write-in for Robert Kennedy as vice president on the 1964 presidential primary preference ballot. Only one of the Democratic Party leadership, Democratic National Committee member, Hugh Bownes, stated his preference for Hubert H. Humphrey, the eventual nominee.

Boutin was left to explain the reasons for the Kennedy write-in to an outraged Lyndon Johnson. Fortunately, from his point of view, Johnson secured slightly more write-in votes for president in 1964 than Robert Kennedy garnered for the vice president. That result and machinations of the 1964 primary forced Boutin to ally himself fully with the fortunes of Lyndon Johnson and, in reality, sever his once strong ties with the Kennedy family.

There appeared to be no room in Boutin's thinking for a strategy that would respond to discontent within the party other than to isolate that discontent as had happened in 1960, or to smother opposition in a blanket of loyalties as had happened in 1964. Boutin's plans were based on his own political experiences and confidence that Robert Kennedy would not allow his name to be used in a way that would be construed as disruptive to the Kennedy-oriented New Hampshire party organization.

Unfortunately for Boutin, his most recent active campaign experiences had been at the behest of Lyndon Johnson. As a highly placed political operative in the Johnson administration, Boutin had been used by the administration to carry out some of its political objectives. On several occasions he had been sent into the field, especially in the south and Texas, to assist in organizing election activities for several Johnson supporters. What Boutin gained from that experience was an indoctrination in unit rule, Texas-style politics.

The unit rule, a Texas tradition, worked to systematically remove from consideration minority views, minority representation, and intraparty minority accommodation. Complete and unquestioning loyalty to the party and its leadership was a hallmark of the unit rule process. Minorities were isolated and excluded from the party processes at early stages in either candidate selection or party organization. The result was that the Texas-originated White House political operation had little tolerance for other states' experience with minority inclusion and compromise. Boutin had, apparently, assimilated this ethos without questions.

By the time Boutin arrived in New Hampshire he was fully committed to an unity campaign that was designed to prompt active allegiance to the renomination of the president. The pyramid of interlocking campaign leaders would be vertically pledged to the support of the president in the same way as Boutin himself was pledged to the political operation of the White House. The organization of the New Hampshire Democratic Party and the loyalists of the major elected officials would be unified as on structure. There would be no room in Boutin's campaign concept for anything but total loyalty both to Johnson and to the policies of the administration. A person supported the president or not. No halfway measures were tolerated, especially concerning the Vietnam War.

NEW HAMPSHIRE DEMOCRATS: TRADITIONS AND ETHOS

Boutin had been away from New Hampshire politics for more than seven years when he returned in the spring of 1967. He had lost his sensitivity to the political climate of New Hampshire. It seemed that Boutin thought the politics of the nation had shifted to the model of the Texas-conditioned White House, and that allegiance to the White House and the Johnson-dominated party could overpower New

Hampshire political traditions of individuality and independence. The campaign that Boutin began to implement for President Johnson was not one that was in keeping with New Hampshire's political traditions. It is from this beginning that the critical weakness of the New Hampshire Johnson renomination effort developed.

It might appear obvious that a person with Boutin's New Hampshire experience would outline a campaign responsive to that experience. In fact that may well have been what Boutin did recommend. Boutin's own involvement in the revitalization of the New Hampshire Democratic Party was closely tied to the objective of organizing the nomination of a viable Democratic candidate for governor. Such success meant that aggressive campaigning and thorough organization were necessary to pull the strong candidate through the primary and on to election.

Too often in the past straw candidates and weak candidates closely tied to the Republican opposition had characterized the state's Democratic Party primary. The ethnic blocs of Democratic voters who voted in the state primaries were played against each other. Weak and often unknown candidates with appropriate ethnic surnames were filed to dissipate ethnic voting strength that was needed to nominate strong Democratic Party candidates. Often half a dozen names were listed on the Democratic primary ballot offering an assortment of French-Canadian and Irish surnames. Not infrequently the nominee who was produced from such a crowd of candidates disappeared from political activity after receiving the nomination. The Republican candidate would go on to win in an almost uncontested election.

Boutin, in fact, had been one of the rare Democrats to survive the process with his candidacy in 1958. Careful control of the candidate filings, elimination of straw candidates by demanding adherence to state law regarding the authenticity of candidacies, and thorough organization gave Boutin the 1958 gubernatorial nomination. He went on to run the best race a Democrat had run against the Republican nominee in over twenty years; he lost by a mere 6,835 votes out of 206,745 cast.

To Boutin, therefore, primaries were hazardous affairs. To accomplish the desired results, a tight organization would be necessary.

OPEN PRIMARY TRADITION

There is, however, an important other side to the story. New Hampshire is a state with a long and ingrained primary election tradition. That tradition has produced a widely accepted ethic regarding the open selection of candidates that has endured despite the abuses that the ethic was subjected to by some in the Republican majority. During the era of the leadership of Governor and then U.S. Senator Styles Bridges, the nomination of both Republican candidates and Democratic opponents for major offices was regulated through his office. The Democratic primary was carefully orchestrated to produce only nominal opposition while the Republican primary was structured to prevent divisive internecine warfare.

During the period from the middle 1930s to Bridges' death in 1961, a second variable entered the scene. A progressive Republican newspaper, the

Manchester Union Leader, changed ownership. William Loeb, the son of President Theodore Roosevelt's secretary, acquired the newspaper from the widow of Frank Knox, former secretary of the navy under President Franklin Roosevelt and a former Republican vice-presidential candidate. As a result, the editorial tone of the newspaper changed from that of progressive Republicanism to one of virulent conservatism. The newspaper became an ardent supporter of Styles Bridges and followed Bridges in his anticommunist foray into both domestic and foreign policy. (Kevin Cash, *Who the Hell Is William Loeb?*, Manchester, N. H.: Amoskeag Press, 1975.)

Loeb's power in New Hampshire rested on his ability to use his newspaper to generate controversy that caused a reaction from the politically active public. The tactic remains simply one that takes situations, issues, groups, or individuals and casts their behavior in either a favorable or unfavorable light. Those persons and views Loeb favored are contrasted with those he disliked. Eventually sufficient controversy revolved around the situation to polarize the public's view and to isolate and thereby destroy the effectiveness of the person or the political usefulness of the issue.

Loeb succeeded in this behavior because New Hampshire does not have statewide media alternatives to his newspaper. As he built his case, the other side, the side that might present and legitimize the opposite view, is not presented.

When Loeb found that he could not penetrate the power structure of the state Republican Party with his conservative philosophy, his bully tactics, or his alliance with Senator Bridges, he began to chip away at the Republican organization with his editorials. To overcome the hazards of internecine primary contests, the state Republican leadership had organized to prevent party-destroying primary conflicts. The controllers of this informal mechanism were a group of party leaders almost exclusively located in the capital city of Concord. Loeb labeled them the "Concord Gang."

The key to this control was for the leadership to elect the strongest potential nominee for the office of governor and then to organize the party to support that person with preprimary endorsements and praise. Not falling in step behind the leadership in its effort to maintain control of the statehouse for the Republican Party, and incidentally access to that office for themselves, implied the opposite as retribution, loss of the governorship, and loss of access to its perquisites.

Loeb's attack took the form of redefining the ethics of primary election contests. To him and to the framers of the theory of primary elections, a primary was to be an open process unencumbered by the intrusions of vested party interests. Loeb objected to preprimary endorsements by party committees or major party officials such as county chair, state committee members, or state party officers. He objected to the expenditure of party funds to support the primary election candidacies of those endorsed prior to primary elections. He especially objected to efforts by party leaders to march the rank and file membership of the party to the polls to vote for the endorsed candidate.

Although Loeb's motives may have been questionable, his tactic touched an old and responsive nerve in the New Hampshire body politic. The reforms of the progressives that led to the enactment of the primary legislation were founded on the same principles as those which Loeb had begun to espouse. Politics prior to the adoption of the primary system had been closed and dominated by powerful railroad, banking, timber, and industrial interests. These interests selected the major candidates for public office, bought the legislature, and manipulated the conditions of electoral politics. The early twentieth century reforms the progressives legislated in coalition with populist Democrats had sprung from a perverse, corrupt, and exploitative political environment. (Winston Churchill, *Coniston,* New York: The Macmillan Company, 1906.) Enacting primary election laws and legislating the structure of the party organizations for New Hampshire established, by law, an ethic of open party processes and individual citizen participation in the selection of party candidates.

At the same time Loeb was struggling to open the candidate selection process of the Republican Party, he was also looking askance at the Democratic Party. In its quest to produce a viable nominee, the reformers of the Democratic Party sought to control the primary elections much as had the "Concord Gang" of the Republican Party. Following the minor revolution within the Democratic Party in 1956, the new and liberal leadership began to put the party in order. To do this required an organizational effort from the Democratic leadership to pull a strong candidate through the state primary. In the face of this effort even the slightest aroma of preprimary organization for a specific candidate by the party leaders brought down the wrath of Loeb's editorials on the reformist Democrats.

Since in this case the ends justified the organizational means, in 1958 the reform leadership of the Democratic Party was willing to suffer the bolts from Loeb's pen in order to secure through party leadership the nomination of the strongest candidate, Bernard L. Boutin. Although Boutin was the beneficiary of the preprimary organization and, as such, appreciated the value of a thorough effort, there was a tendency not to appreciate the sanctity of the open primary that Loeb was reestablishing.

What Boutin failed to recognize, when he returned to New Hampshire in the spring of 1967, was that Loeb had been successful. The old ethic had been restored. Primaries were intraparty contests, but officeholders of the party, the party's organization, and the party's treasury were not to be used to support particular candidates in the primaries. The strong sense of fair play fostered by the chipping process of the *Manchester Union Leader* now required that the primaries be open and that individuals should be encouraged to participate not by threats, but through an individual desire to respond to the call of a candidate. Pressure might be applied to party leaders, public officeholders, and those needing access to those in power, but such pressure could not be applied to the mass of a party's membership.

Simply stated, the ethic that the Loeb attacks had revived drew on the positive attributes that had been ingrained in New Hampshire participatory democracy and open political decision making. The premises of this primary election ethic required the neutrality of party officials during the primary contests, the neutrality of the formal committee structure of the party, equal access to the mechanisms of the party for all candidates, no endorsements, and no funds diverted from party accounts for primary election campaigns.

The primary was to be an open intraparty contest fought in a manner that would give no participant a special advantage with an ending that would allow the party to unite behind the victor. As a result of these premises, votes became difficult to deliver. The links that had held the Republican Party together and out of bitter primary fights disintegrated. The old reformers in the Democratic Party like Boutin began to feel the sting of the primary election ethic as they made plans for the renomination campaign of President Johnson.

On his return to New Hampshire, Boutin would find a voting population that now knew something about primary election ethics. Loeb's fair play doctrine, together with several vigorous primary contests, had drawn more voters into primary election activity than ever before. Participation, however, was not on the basis of blocs of votes to be delivered by endorsements from the leadership, but, rather, as the result of much individual decision making and ad hoc organization. The Boutin model for the Johnson New Hampshire primary campaign in 1968 was developed out of his earlier New Hampshire experiences and his activities outside New Hampshire while serving the Johnson administration in Washington. Attempting a campaign based on those experiences would run contrary to the independent mood and the primary election ethic now well established in Boutin's home state.

CHAPTER 4

The Precampaign Campaign

THERE IS AN ALTERNATIVE

Lowenstein left Manchester on the evening of November 5. The group gathered in the Chaplain living room liked what Lowenstein had said. Each person had had significant experience either at the local or state level in New Hampshire's Democratic Party wars. Lowenstein's conversation had been directed at how the political system could be used to oppose the Johnson administration's policies on the war. It was unnecessary to convince any of the listeners that the war was wrong and destructive to the social fabric of the nation. The need for an alternative, at least to dissent through existing political channels, was what each wanted.

Lowenstein had effectively isolated the Draft Kennedy people. They were no longer a factor of much importance in the group's thinking. The alternative candidate was to be Senator Eugene J. McCarthy. Lowenstein wanted to return to Senator McCarthy with a list of primary states where organizations were ready to support his candidacy once the announcement came. His optimism was contagious, but being true to New Hampshire's cautious and conservative traditions, the group members wanted to stand back, test the sentiment on their own communities, rethink what they had heard that evening, and present their considerations at another session. The group would meet again November 19. Lowenstein promised to return to hear the reports and to present his view of the national situation. In the meantime they would also have to react to what Sandra Hoeh had reported concerning the Democratic state committee's plans for the Johnson campaign.

In the days that followed, the pace of the precampaign increased. Lowenstein's travels stimulated activity in a number of states. The national press and electronic media caught the smoke of the many political fires that had begun to smolder.

Pressure mounted in the states where strong antiwar organizations were anxious to support an alternative candidacy. Accelerating national antiwar activity shifted from teach-ins, petition circulating, and informational meetings to political action. The first step was to offer support for a candidate. Lowenstein urged his contacts to organize and then to write, telegraph, and call Senator McCarthy's office urging him to become a candidate. The sheer energy expended by Lowenstein and Gans in their travels generated, within a short month, the critical mass that was to become a national campaign. If they had operated only at the national level or only at the state level they would not have produced the desired result.

Lowenstein had to demonstrate not only to McCarthy but to the national media that an alternative candidacy would be met with enthusiasm not only generally but also by specific political organizing at the state and local levels. He could not stimulate the local organizing unless those he wished to organize heard something about his alternative candidate coming through the national media. When in Washington, Lowenstein would tell of the meetings he had had and the responses he had received. When in the living rooms of the other primary states and before peace activist organizations, he spoke of the disquiet that pervaded Washington and the growing concern about the war in the congress. When Lowenstein was in Washington, leaks to the national reporters prompted calls through the news-gathering services back to the states Lowenstein had visited. State news bureau reporters began checking their sources to find out what had been stirred up by the latest of the Gans-Lowenstein visits. As the momentum increased so did the frequency of the calls. Relatively little activity was already prompting considerable press speculation

TWO WEEKS TO THINK

The New Hampshire group was in a two-week holding pattern. I made several calls to check on local responses. Press stories appeared in the daily New Hampshire newspapers recounting the fact that a group had met to consider a possible alternative candidacy. The stories stimulated interest in the activity at the local level, which gave the contacts of the individual committee members substance. Those who did say they were interested in a possible McCarthy candidacy tended to be persons already opposed to the war rather than those with who might see McCarthy as a real candidate. To most, the possibility of anything more than a token political success in New Hampshire was not seriously considered.

Out of this period came a number of contacts that were important to the development of the New Hampshire campaign, including Gerry Studds. Studds, a Yale graduate of the late 1950s, had taken a job with the State Department shortly after completing a master's degree. He arrived in Washington during the early days of the Kennedy administration. On loan from the State Department, Studds was assigned to help draft Robert Kennedy's Domestic Corps proposals. With John Kennedy's death, Studds left the State Department to become legislative assistant to Senator Harrison Williams of New Jersey.

Disenchanted with many aspects of Washington life and especially with U.S. Vietnam policy, Studds left Washington to accept a teaching position at Concord's St. Paul's School and buried himself in the vigorous life of a prep school teacher. Studds did emerge briefly in 1966 to work with Sandra Hoeh as she developed the Concord organization for the reelection campaign of Senator Tom McIntyre. His only other political activities between his 1965 arrival in New Hampshire and our meeting in November 1967 were participation in the famous 1967 March on the Pentagon and limited contact with Gene Daniell's Draft Kennedy activity.

Having read the press stories about the November 5 meeting, Studds called me to determine the extent of my involvement and the nature of my contact with Senator McCarthy. Shortly after the call, we met for lunch in Concord. Concerned by the antiwar restlessness of his students, Studds' foremost question was about the seriousness of the venture. I recounted for Studds the Gans visit, the Lowenstein meeting, the call to Senator McCarthy's office, and my own evaluations. Studds spoke of his frustration with the direction of U.S. Vietnam policy, his disgust over the Johnson administration's response to criticism, the terror of the March on the Pentagon, and his feelings about the inefficacy of politics. I suggested that they were entering a time when doors of the political system would swing open again and that they had to at least test the system once more. Studds appreciated that with proper organization and resources they might be able to make a dent, and the cost of the try would be far less than a radical action.

The lunch ended with Studds agreeing to come to the next meeting. His closing remark reflected what was to be the sentiment of many young people who ultimately became involved. "I guess we should give the political system one more chance with McCarthy and the New Hampshire presidential primary before we head to the barricades."

Other important recruiting occurred in each home community of those who had attended the November 5 meeting. The possible alternative candidacy was not to be built on a base of preexisting antiwar organizations, but rather created from a new organization developed from the disaffection of those with political experience in the Democratic Party. Once the statewide network of politically experienced leaders was established and local groups were organized by these leaders, then it would be possible to form coalitions with the existing peace-action and antiwar protest groups. This sequence of organizing was important.

If the McCarthy activity had been built on the foundation of existing antiwar organization before attempting to create a politically experienced cadre, it is probable that the radical public image of the antiwar activists would have kept away those politically experienced Democrats who could make the effort succeed.

A consensus among those making the contacts was that a drive, to be successful, had to be mounted within the Democratic Party. It had to be built inside the structure of the New Hampshire primary election process, and it had to be directed specifically toward amassing votes that were clearly Democratic Party votes. Only in this way would it be possible to convince President Johnson that the opposition was not a collection of miscreant radicals outside the processes of partisan politics.

The peace-action and antiwar groups in New Hampshire were composed of a conglomeration of some Democratic Party and some Republican Party activists, resident and nonresident students, radicals, and nonpartisans. To some, there was a feeling of a "curse on both of the political houses," which made it difficult for them to be involved in a political action that would be tied to a specific party. In contrast, the view of the early New Hampshire McCarthy group was that the party to which they had owed allegiance for some years was being taken in a direction that was not true to history. Past involvement in the Democratic Party was as important, in their early organizational planning, as was a like concern about the war. Once a sufficient identity had been established for this group of Democratic Party dissenters, then they felt a coalition could be constructed of others willing to share that common litany of dissent.

Toward the middle of November, a pattern of escalating political events began to emerge. A flurry of reports on the pending McCarthy candidacy dominated the ruminations of the columnists and the dispatches of the wire services. Various state organizations were reporting favorable reactions to a possible McCarthy candidacy. The pro-Johnson organizing effort, active since early in the fall, set the November 19 meeting of the New Hampshire Democratic State Committee as its Johnson renomination endorsement date. In order to orchestrate that meeting properly and to repress any activity on behalf of Robert Kennedy, Boutin scheduled an evening social gathering of New Hampshire's Democrats for Friday, November 17. The star attraction would be Senator Robert Kennedy's younger brother, the senior senator from Massachusetts, Edward M. Kennedy.

THE KENNEDY "ENDORSEMENT"

The invitation to Edward Kennedy had been extended several months earlier and had been accepted by the senator as a personal gesture to those New Hampshire loyalists who had helped with the 1960 presidential primary. The invitation had been extended through Kennedy's senate colleague, Tom McIntyre, on behalf of Governor John W. King and Bernard Boutin. The event was organized as a $5 per person reception. The price and the attraction of the star, Edward M. Kennedy, insured that most of the party's leadership and faithful would be attending, and in fact more than two thousand turned out on that snowy November night.

Because circumstances had begun to change during the last weeks of October and early weeks of November, Boutin saw the social evening as an opportunity to overpower any of those who might be wavering in their support of Johnson. The visual unity of the New Hampshire party's leadership, delivered through Senator Edward Kennedy, he reasoned, should be enough to do that. In fact, in the days prior to the Kennedy visit and in the car from Boston to Manchester, McIntyre and Boutin urged Kennedy to lay to rest any speculation that his brother might be a candidate or that the Kennedy family would lend moral support to any alternative drive for the nomination. Boutin wanted Kennedy to renew the Boutin promise that if a Kennedy came to New Hampshire during the time of the presidential primary campaign it would be for the purpose of endorsing President Johnson or actually campaigning for the Johnson write-in.

Kennedy arrived, spoke, and shattered the Boutin dream. Not only did Kennedy not endorse the president for renomination in unequivocal terms, he only mentioned Lyndon Johnson's name once and then only among the list of the Democratic Party's presidential heroes.

The visible gap between Robert Kennedy and the president had been widening in the weeks prior to the November 17 gathering. Robert Kennedy had broken with Johnson over the war in a speech delivered earlier that fall. Although his public statements continued to support Johnson's renomination and he had privately refused to consider a candidacy for the presidency in 1968, Robert Kennedy was seeking a policy change on Vietnam through his support of those in dissent.

After perfunctory introductory remarks, Edward Kennedy recounted recent conversations he had had with his brother, "When I said I was going to New Hampshire I asked my brother if he wanted me to file a disclaimer removing him as a candidate. He replied, 'Mind your own business.' When I told him about the write-in campaign he said, 'Robert Kennedy spelled R-O-B-E-R-T-K-E-N-N-E-D-Y is not a write-in candidate.'" In his traditional review of the great names in Democratic Party history, the names of Roosevelt, Truman, and John F. Kennedy drew the loudest response. Johnson was extended courteous but not extraordinary recognition.

The thrust of Edward Kennedy's speech emphasized the social and economic responsiveness of the Democratic Party and its leadership during periods of national crisis. He praised the party's tradition of creative internal conflict, its open policies, toleration of dissent, and sensitivity for the excluded and disadvantaged. He said almost nothing about the war except to advise tolerance of dissent.

The climax of his speech began with a warning, "I have heard in recent days that there is a man considering a campaign in New Hampshire for the presidency. This candidacy poses a serious threat to the Democratic Party. This man from Minnesota must become well known to you all so that you will understand the seriousness of his positions. This man, Harold E. Stassen, does not deserve your support." Kennedy's tone, at once playful and yet serious, hushed the audience. The leaders on the platform hung in anticipation of words that would tell the gathered Democratic faithful that Eugene McCarthy was to be feared and could not expect even the slightest encouragement from the Kennedy clan. Those in the room who had begun their early contacts for McCarthy were equally suspended by Kennedy's rhetoric. To the noticeable relief of many gathered in the room and to the visible distress of those on the platform, Kennedy had not singled out McCarthy. He had instead taken all on a rhetorical trip. More questions were raised than answered by Edward Kennedy's performance. He quickly concluded his speech, leaving Boutin, King, McIntyre, and party chair, William Craig, standing on what must have seemed at the moment, a very shaky platform. No ringing endorsement of the president had occurred. No great up welling of emotion had been generated from the crowd to discourage an effort to build an alternative organization from within the party.

During that one evening, I was cornered by fellow veterans of previous campaigns and became the center of one small group of the curious after another. Encouragement for a McCarthy campaign came less from those holding particular titles in the party than it did from those who I knew had the experience to make difficult campaigns succeed. As the evening progressed there were those who were curious, those who wanted to work, those who knew others who would join in local committees, and those who would lend moral support if not open allegiance to our effort. While Boutin and the Johnson write-in leadership were attempting to wrap the gathering in a sense of unity from the platform, an organization of significant proportions was forming in opposition to that effort at their very feet.

Among the more important contacts I made that evening was Jack Dunfey, Bill's brother and president of the Dunfey family's successful corporation. Bill Dunfey had not attended, and I had not been in touch with him since Gans' visit. As a result, it wasn't known whether Bill Dunfey was in support of an alternative candidacy or would be with his old friend Bernard Boutin in support of the renomination of Johnson. Jack Dunfey's comments to me were encouraging. He strongly disagreed with continuing the war and was upset by the impact the war was having domestically. Although Jack Dunfey made clear that because of his family's business ties it would not be possible for him to be involved in any visible way, he surprised me with his vigorous encouragement. I took this to mean that Bill Dunfey was also viewing the effort to find an alternative candidate with the same interest. This meant that when I needed counsel regarding the operation of the possible presidential primary campaign, I could call on Bill Dunfey for that advice.

In retrospect, I thought that Bill Dunfey may well have either contacted or been contacted by Edward Kennedy prior to his visit November 17. Although this speculation is unconfirmed, it was obvious that Kennedy's performance required prompting other than that which the senator received from Boutin and McIntyre on his way to Bedford. Subsequently Dunfey did keep in close touch with both Kennedy brothers on the progress of New Hampshire's McCarthy effort.

THE JOHNSON ENDORSEMENT

The Democratic State Committee assembled for its previously scheduled meeting on November 19 in Concord. The meeting was set to closely follow the "unity" reception held on Friday, November 17. Undaunted by the lack of an endorsement of President Johnson by Senator Edward Kennedy, the Boutin-Craig leadership now sought to convert the Democratic State Committee and its machinery into the Johnson write-in campaign organization. In order to do this Boutin had to secure the endorsement of the State Committee. Such an endorsement would accomplish the conversion, making the machinery of the New Hampshire Democratic Party available exclusively to the Johnson write-in campaign.

The resolution drafted by the National Committee member Joseph Millimet was introduced by Governor King and seconded by Senator McIntyre. Supporting the resolution, King said, "Johnson is in the company of greatness and is not the first president to lose public opinion because of an unpopular war. Of course his popularity is dwindling, but he wasn't elected to please all of the people all of the time." King went on to compare Johnson's war problems with those of George Washington, Abraham Lincoln, and Franklin D. Roosevelt:

> "We elected him because we had faith in his ability to lead this country and to do the right thing, popular or not." He concluded by vowing strong support of the President for re-election, "When the chips are down, the people of this country will realize the fact of life that this man, in four years, has done more in the way of concrete accomplishments for this country than any other President in history. This is the man who has had the tenacity and determination that persevered in the great struggle in Vietnam at the cost of his own personal popularity. And in that situation he is in the company of greatness. For this is not indeed the first time that a President of the United States faced this very same situation.
>
> "I cheer President Johnson for upholding and maintaining that honor in the face of the worst personal abuse any President ever had to endure. In South Vietnam the United States has made a solemn commitment to stop communist aggression, and that commitment is a matter of our national honor."
>
> (*Manchester Union Leader*, November 20, 1967, pp. 1, 14)

The debate continued for almost an hour. Those opposed to the endorsement resolution argued the issue on two grounds. The first was their disagreement with the administration's war policy and the second was the standard argument in favor of an open primary and against endorsements. Chair William Craig said of the debate, "The main difference of opinion seemed to be on Vietnam. No one put it on the basis of a 'Dump Johnson' movement."

Will Brown, Merrimack County State Committee member argued that an endorsement would violate the tradition of avoiding unnecessary conflict within the party that had been established by ending the practice of preprimary state Committee endorsements. An endorsement, he argued, would shut out those in opposition at a time when each and every Democrat was needed to elect the nominated ticket in the fall.

Although not a member of the committee at that time, I requested permission to join the debate. Using a *New York Times* page-one story of that same day headlined, "Kennedy Asserts a Bid by McCarthy Would Aid Party," I read segments of the story datelined Tarrytown, November 18:

> Senator Robert F. Kennedy said today, "It would be a healthy influence to the Democratic Party. It would allow Americans to take out their frustration (over the Vietnam war) in talk instead of violence. It could be a major, important service, for our society."

I then urged that the endorsement resolution be tabled in order to retain an open party until a nominee had been selected by the Democratic National

Convention. Reflecting on Robert Kennedy's comment about "adding excitement," I noted that without a contest in New Hampshire the opportunity to build the state party, through creative conflict, would be lost. Except for the quotation from Senator Robert Kennedy, I had not mentioned Senator McCarthy or the possibility of an alternative candidacy.

The endorsement resolution was approved by a vote of twenty-three to five. In spite of the vote a victory of sorts had been won. Five members of the Democratic State Committee voted in opposition to the leadership's resolution. Already the Boutin strategy of asserting a unified Democratic Party behind the renomination of President Johnson had begun to tremble. The effort to force the endorsement resolution on the party would ultimately work to Boutin's disadvantage. The arguments and the tactics used to line up the votes for the resolution disturbed some committee members. Several would join the McCarthy campaign within the next several weeks stating publicly their opposition to the endorsement and the violation of party organization neutrality that the endorsement represented.

The endorsement gave the *Manchester Union Leader* additional ammunition in its continuing fight against preprimary endorsements. Subsequent editorials would recount the action of the State Committee on November 19 as an example of the strong-arm tactics the party leadership was willing to use to regiment the party. The *Union Leader* now adopted a curious posture that became even more evident as time went on. Although totally in opposition to the antiwar position of those seeking an alternative candidate, the newspaper did editorialize in favor of the minority of the Democratic State Committee and support its position on the basis of political fair play. (*Manchester Union Leader*, February 17, 1968)

What had been a desire to explore alternatives on the part of our group now became a resolve. The language of the Democratic State Committee resolution and the arguments of those who supported its adoption grated our sensitivities. The endorsement meant that for all intents and purposes the state Democratic Party was now the Johnson organization. For those of us who had been considering a McCarthy for President organization this would be the last time for many months that we would share the same room with colleagues of many past campaigns.

THE SECOND CHAPLAIN MEETING

Also on November 19, a meeting took place at the Chaplain's home. Al Lowenstein arrived from Washington and New York with fresh reports of the preparations for the CCD to be held in Chicago on December 2, and the imminent announcement of Senator McCarthy's candidacy. Others arrived from the Concord meeting of the Democratic State Committee with vivid accounts of the endorsement meeting. What seemed to impress those gathered more than the vote was the out-front roles played by Governor King and Senator McIntyre. Most were dismayed at King and McIntyre's willingness to precipitate conflict within the New Hampshire party by seeking the endorsement.

The first order of business for the meeting was to assess the returns of two weeks of local contacts, news reactions, and other in-state indices of the alternative campaign's possibilities. Most attending had discussed the situation with friends and business and political associates. Although far from a scientific survey, the sampling did reveal a substantial disenchantment with President Johnson. Few of those contacted had even recognized Senator McCarthy's name, and except for those who had made up their mind to oppose the war, few seemed willing to accept a single-issue, antiwar candidate.

Lowenstein reacted to the reports with his usual optimism. There was unhappiness with both Johnson and the party leadership for responding to dissent, not by accommodation, but with heavy-handed, shape-up or ship-out tactics. A campaign that harnessed the discontent and turned it into votes, he said, could not be denied by Johnson and his war policy advisors. The time had come for us to make some decisions. Lowenstein asked the group to answer two important questions: would it form a McCarthy for President Committee, and would it send a delegation to the Chicago meeting of the CCD?

The answer to both questions by vote of the group was yes. In order to gain the greatest impact from the formation of the committee, the group agreed that a press conference should be held and the names of the committee released as soon as possible. It would be important to stress that the committee was representative of the major communities where the Democratic primary vote was concentrated. The basic list was developed from those attending, since most of the important sections of the state were represented in the room. The title "steering committee" was selected as representing the intentions of the committee at that stage. I was asked to be the chair of the committee but declined the title. I suggested they avoid permanent titles and formal organization in hopes the activities would attract the prestigious to the effort and that they could draw attention to the fact by announcing recognized titles. During the early stages, I used the title of "temporary chair." Even the title "steering committee" contained an ad hoc tone that was meant to indicate an openness to the venture in contrast to the formalized structure being used by the Johnson people.

Traditionally the presidential primary in New Hampshire has been a way for those interested in politics to become involved in partisan organization. If the key positions in the campaign were filled by those already well known, the newcomer could expect some lesser role. Since political activity, at least in the Democratic Party of New Hampshire, is rewarded in large part by various forms of public recognition, having titles available and room for ad hoc organization multiplied the opportunities for recognition. Since an alternative candidacy depended on widespread participation, the organization that would coordinate that effort had itself to represent informality rather than hierarchy.

When the group completed its discussion about forming a McCarthy for President Steering Committee and agreed to announce the committee, Lowenstein said that he had thought they would come to that conclusion. Always the master of the moment, Lowenstein reached for a brown paper bag at his foot and dumped out on the coffee table in front of him a pile of buttons reading "McCarthy '68." Each person in the room put on a button and stuffed the remainder in their pockets and purses for friends.

Responding to Lowenstein's second point, the group agreed to send a delegation to the December 1 national meeting of the CCD. Philip and Sylvia Chaplain; John Holland, a Manchester attorney; and Gerry Studds said they would attend. Sandy and I were urged to go also. Money for such a trip was short but we promised that one of us would attend.

Before the meeting closed the group returned to their evaluation of the New Hampshire situation. Lowenstein's report from Washington was that McCarthy would have to be encouraged, first, to enter the presidential race, and then to enter the New Hampshire primary. On this latter point we all agreed that if McCarthy ran for the presidency he could not be considered a serious candidate unless he entered the New Hampshire primary. We understood his caution as we understood our own. New Hampshire appeared to be a hostile place for a man labeled an antiwar, "dump Johnson" leader with a strongly liberal record in the U.S. Congress. In order to provide a testing of the water for both the candidate and ourselves, we agreed that McCarthy should come to New Hampshire in some context other than as a presidential candidate.

Practically every candidate who considers entering the New Hampshire presidential primary practices the same ritual. The best format for such visits is usually a speech before a nonpolitical but influential group. The second best is an invitation to be the attraction for a political event, preferably a fund-raiser for the state party. The third and least desirable alternative is to precipitate an event of one's own making such as an invitational dinner, reception, or meet-the-potential-candidate affair. The group wanted an event of the first order for Senator McCarthy.

Two members of the University of New Hampshire's Political Science Department, Robert Craig and Larry O'Connell, were at the Chaplain's that evening. They recalled that a prominent Manchester family, the Sidores, had endowed a lecture series in memory of the late Saul Sidore, founder of Pandora Woolens, Inc. There was to be an evening lecture in Manchester and later a campus appearance at the university in Durham. The coming lecture series topic was to be on the struggle for human and civil rights in the United States. The approximate date of the program, Craig and O'Connell thought, was December 13. The group concluded this would be the perfect format for a McCarthy visit. The group's task was to determine if McCarthy could come and then to have an invitation arranged for him.

THE FIRST PRESS CONFERENCE

On Monday, November 20, Gerry Studds and I checked the list of names that were to be the membership of the New Hampshire McCarthy for President Steering Committee. The membership announcement of that committee would be the first public work of its meetings; we wanted it to express the nature of the concern felt by those considering the McCarthy candidacy and the breadth of that concern within the New Hampshire Democratic Party. In order to avoid any confusion on the part of those listed as the membership on the steering committee, each was called not only to ensure their willingness to be announced as a member, but also to suggest responses that might be given to a reporter.

Each member was advised that the best response would be a personal response. One that recounted why they had decided to object to the party's leadership, what they expected might result from an effort centering on Senator McCarthy in New Hampshire, and how they evaluated the potential for such an effort in their own communities would be in order. They were told by us that it would be of special value to review their own political experience and note their current public and party offices. Our intention at this stage was to project an image of seriousness. We wanted the committee announcement to embody the depth to which the administration's performance, especially its war policies, had caused concern.

New Hampshire press conferences are small affairs by national standards. Our first press conference proceeded with the usual five or six reporters gathered in the small statehouse press room. We had prepared a brief statement announcing the formation of the McCarthy for President Steering Committee which read:

> The McCarthy for President Steering Committee has been formed in response to the interest and urgings of many active party Democrats, Independents, and interested Republicans. It is a committee that has one purpose in mind and that is to urge that Senator Eugene J. McCarthy become an active candidate for the Presidency of the United States.
>
> Our priorities, at this time, are threefold. First, we are prepared to organize a substantial and broad-based effort on behalf of Senator McCarthy in New Hampshire. Secondly, we intend to represent New Hampshire with a delegation from our committee at the December 2–3 meeting of the Conference of Concerned Democrats in Chicago, where Senator McCarthy will make a major address. Thirdly, we intend to organize a campaign to encourage the re-registration of Republicans and Democrats during the re-registration period set by law in early December.
>
> We expect that within a few weeks Senator McCarthy will respond to the numerous speaking invitations that he has received from New Hampshire and that he will visit our state.

The press release contained the announcement of the members of the committee and the appointment of a fiscal agent, attorney John Holland, to handle the financial records of the committee as required by New Hampshire state law.

To make clear the orientation of the committee's activities the release went on to announce the membership:

> We are loyal and dedicated Democrats who find in Senator Eugene J. McCarthy the qualities of leadership which will strengthen our nation and the Democratic Party.

The members of the Steering Committee are:

David C. Hoeh, 29, Temporary Chairman.

Attorney John S. Holland, Treasurer and Fiscal Agent, member of the Bedford School Board and member of the New Hampshire Human Rights Commission.

Attorney Paul McEachern, 29, Portsmouth, former State Representative, member of the Portsmouth City Council and Assistant Mayor.

Representative Jean Wallin, 33, Nashua, State Representative active in local affairs and statewide Democratic campaigns.

Bert Bouchard, 39, Nashua, City Council member, insurance executive.

Sylvia Chaplain, 42, Bedford, member of the New Hampshire Human Rights Commission, active in local Manchester and state party affairs.

Dr. David G. Underwood 3rd, 36, Concord, active in the Concord Democratic Party.

Dr. Roger Davidson, 31, Hanover, assistant Professor of Government, Dartmouth College.

Attorney Bartram C. Branch, Manchester, member of the Manchester School Board.

Robert E. Craig, 34, Assistant Professor, Department of Political Science, University of New Hampshire, active in local and state party affairs.

Gerry E. Studds, 30, Concord, Master, St. Paul's School, previously with the U.S. State Department and Administrative Assistant to Senator Harrison Williams of New Jersey.

Peter Freedman, 47, Bedford, Manchester shoe manufacturing executive, Bedford Town Moderator.

Thomas Breslin, 54, Concord, sub-area director, United Steel Workers Union of America.

Responding to questions from the press concerning the Draft Kennedy activity, I noted that the "committee is not opposed to a movement in the state boosting Senator Robert Kennedy," noting further "that the dilemma being presented to liberal Democrats in the state is only 'within the party' and that by March 12th, the anti-Johnson forces would be supporting either McCarthy or Kennedy." (*Concord Daily Monitor,* November 21, 1967, p. 1) Asked whether McCarthy would enter the New Hampshire presidential primary, I replied, "I'm 50–50 certain McCarthy will enter the New Hampshire Primary," but I was not sure whether the group would run a slate of pro-McCarthy delegates to the National Democratic Convention; a subject that we had not discussed at this early stage.

The press coverage of the conference was good by New Hampshire standards. The morning timing meant that all of the afternoon daily newspapers would receive the wire story for Tuesday's edition and the *Union Leader* would carry it in the city edition which appears as the Manchester edition in the afternoon. The radio stations carried the story at noon and throughout the remainder of the day. Several stations called for actualities which were played that day and with the morning news on Wednesday. A front page with picture story appeared in the *Concord Daily Monitor.*

The first major step toward a campaign had now been taken. By announcing the formation of a political committee, the group was committed to an open candidacy that was now totally dependent upon an announcement from Senator McCarthy. Few of the group entertained the notion that a write-in campaign for the senator was possible, nor were they going to opt for a "wait-and-see" tactic which would have left the field open to the Draft Kennedy people. Their efforts were to be directed toward two basic objectives. The first and public objective was to create the impression that an organization was ready and, most importantly, able to run a campaign, a campaign that would be in opposition to the war and the renomination of Lyndon B. Johnson, as long as he espoused policies continuing the war. The second and private objective was to convince Senator Eugene J. McCarthy that a candidacy in New Hampshire was possible. The group had assumed at the time of the formation of the committee that McCarthy would soon announce his candidacy formally and that the group's efforts, at this time, were less to convince him to be a candidate than to prepare the political base for a campaign.

REGISTRATION OF THE COMMITTEE

On November 27, 1967, I sent a letter to New Hampshire Secretary of State Robert L. Stark stating, "A committee has been formed to promote the candidacy of Senator Eugene J. McCarthy for President. The formal name of the committee is 'The New Hampshire McCarthy for President Steering Committee.'" The letter noted that I was the temporary chair of the committee and that the treasurer and fiscal agent was attorney John S. Holland. The addresses listed were Holland's Manchester law office, 1838 Elm Street, and as campaign headquarters, my home, 2 Ridge Road, Hanover.

Stark's response to my letter dated November 28, 1967, acknowledged receipt but added, "However, in addition, I believe you should comply with the previsions of RSA 70:8."

This response raised an important side issue that introduced a measure of suspense into those early days of the 1968 political season. Apparently my letter was the first to be received by the secretary of state that formally filed a committee in support of a particular candidacy. Although usually a pro forma occurrence in New Hampshire, my letter brought Stark's response and a press statement from him to the effect that by filing, the McCarthy committee was in violation of 70:8 of *New Hampshire's Revised Statues Annotated* which read in part:

> If the political committee is organized to support a candidate in any election, it shall first secure the written consent of the candidate or his fiscal agent, before it receives or spends any money or thing of value, and its officers shall file such written consent with the Secretary of State immediately; but this limitation shall not apply to the political committee of the party to which the candidate belongs in elections other than primaries.

At the time, it appeared that Attorney General George Pappagianis, an appointee of Governor John W. King, had instructed the secretary of state to remind those filing intentions to form political committees of the statutory provision. I immediately contacted Holland to have him look into the matter.

It appeared as though the endorsement strategy the Democratic State Committee had adopted was tied to the Pappagianis interpretation of RSA 70:8. If that interpretation prevailed, then the write-in campaign for President Johnson would be the only legitimate noncandidate-approved write-in effort allowable under New Hampshire law. The effect of the interpretation would be to end any campaign efforts but those that secured either party approval or written approval from the individual on whose behalf the committee was to be organized. In fact, if the interpretation had been applied to earlier situations, the successful write-in efforts of 1964 for Lodge and Nixon would not have been possible.

Although the McCarthy group had not seriously entertained the possibility of running a campaign without Senator McCarthy's active participation, and would, therefore, be able to qualify under the provisions of the law as interpreted, it did raise a question concerning its capacity to organize before Senator McCarthy announced his candidacy. If he did not choose to run in New Hampshire as an announced candidate, the committee's capacity to run a write-in effort would be seriously restricted—they could not ". . . receive(s) or spend(s) any money or thing of value" according to the way the law was now being applied.

THE RSA 70:8 AFFAIR

Holland requested the documentation behind the secretary of state's interpretation and received from the attorney general an opinion that had been directed to the secretary of state, dated October 16, 1967. For reasons not altogether clear at the time, the attorney general had reviewed the statutes pertaining to the presidential primary and had drafted an opinion. It appears that the attorney general's opinion was prepared on inquiry prior to the endorsement action by the Democratic State Committee in which Governor King, the governor's legal counsel, Joseph Millimet (of the same law firm as Holland), and Senator Tom McIntyre played major roles.

Holland wrote the attorney general December 1, 1967, stating:

> Since R.S.A. 70:8 now defines the term 'election' in such a manner as specifically to exclude a presidential preferential primary, it appears that there is no statutory requirements that the consent of the candidate in a presidential preferential primary be filed with the Secretary of State. In fact, it does not appear that a committee established for the purpose of promoting a candidate in the presidential primary is required to file any prior notification with the Secretary of State.

Holland went on to note:

> The news release which I saw in the *Manchester Union Leader* indicated that the Secretary of State had informed the press that our committee was the only committee which had filed. It is a matter of public knowledge that there are committees active in the state promoting the candidacies of Governor Romney, Governor Reagan, Senator Kennedy, Former Vice President Nixon, and perhaps others. Since an inference could be made from the reports in the news that our committee was in some way violating the statute, we would appreciate receiving some clarification. As pointed out above, in my opinion, the provisions of R.S.A. 70:8 relating to the consent of the candidate clearly do not apply to a presidential preferential primary.

Holland's letter prompted the attorney general to review his earlier opinion, which he did and on December 20, 1967, he issued a detailed response. Although the McCarthy leaders felt that the manner in which the secretary of state had handled the release of the McCarthy committee's supposed violation was inappropriate, they were not otherwise inconvenienced by the attorney general's interpretation of RSA 70:8.

The attorney general's opinion applied to the presidential preference part of the ballot and not to the delegate selection portion. In other words, it would be possible for New Hampshire residents to file as candidates for delegate, spend and receive funds for the purpose of supporting their own campaigns for delegate, and while doing so could represent themselves as being "favorable" to the nomination of a particular individual. The limitation applied strictly to the formation of committees for the purpose of promoting write-in candidacies on the preference portion of the ballot.

The attorney general's opinion came in response to a proposition advanced by John Holland that "even if R.S.A. 70 applied to presidential preference primaries, it applies to persons whose names are printed on the preference ballot and not to those whose names are written in because there is a distinction between those who are admittedly candidates for the presidency and give consent to have their names printed on the ballot, and those who neither admit nor deny candidacy and whose names are written in by the voters." (*Concord Daily Monitor*, December 20, 1967)

Pappagianis' answer to this contention follows:

> 1. RSA 58:4 does not require a prospective candidate nominated by petition to inform the Secretary of State that he desires or consents that his name appear on the presidential preference ballot.
>
> It requires that the Secretary of State notify the candidate that unless he withdraws his name for the ballot within 10 days after the receipt of . . . notice . . . his name will appear on the ballot; the Secretary of State shall

> not put the prospective candidate's name on the ballot only if the candidate "signifies" his desire to withdraw his name within the time limit.
>
> Accordingly, one's name may be printed on the presidential preference primary ballot through lack of formal notice to the Secretary of State as to his desires.
>
> Likewise, a write-in candidate may be concerted for a person in the presidential preference primary with the person's silence as to his desires stemming from deliberation, inadvertence, indifference or other cause.
>
> 2. RSA 70:1 defines a candidate as any person for whom votes are sought in an election. Thus, one may be a candidate whether his name is printed on the presidential preference primary ballot as a candidate or whether his name is to be written on the ballot, and, in either case, regardless whether the person seeks votes. The statute is satisfied if votes are sought in an election.
>
> 3. RSA 58:2 states that "every qualified voter " shall "vote" on the ballot of his party for a person to be the "candidate" of his political party for president either by "writing" the names of such persons in blank spaces to be left in said ballot for that purpose, or "by making a cross opposite the printed names" of the persons of his choice, as in the case of "other primaries."
>
> RSA 58:5 authorizes columns headed "candidate" for president and states that "there shall always be one blank space left for writing in the name of a candidate."

Eugene Daniell, not one to shrink from a fight, reviewed the opinion and immediately wrote the following to the attorney general:

> I inform you that I have just organized a committee for the sole purpose of writing in the name of Robert F. Kennedy in the Democratic presidential primary. To make the matter doubly clear I will put an advertisement in the *Manchester Union Leader* on December 26th soliciting funds and supporters for the purpose of this committee. Please understand that this action is taken without the consent or approval express or implied, of Senator Robert F. Kennedy.

In the story recounting Daniell's letter, Pappagianis said that he would "await any action he may take and if I think the action is against the law as this office interprets the law, I shall take the necessary legal steps. . . ." Concluding his comments, Pappagianis said, "I have nothing to say about that portion of his letter that seems to convert a legal issue into an opportunity for partisan activity on his part. As far as this office is concerned the issue is one of law." (*Concord Daily Monitor*, December 22, 1967)

Daniell's response to reporters' questions began to link the rulings to the Johnson effort by saying ". . . in his estimation, the opinion will clearly help Johnson. Johnson is in with the organization Democrats. It's no longer the Democratic Party but the Johnson Party. The opinion will hurt my efforts to draft Kennedy because it is we who have the uphill fight. . . ."

To reinforce his contention that the Draft Kennedy activity was without Kennedy's present or potential support, Daniell said, "We don't want Kennedy's support. We are a movement of people who want to show Kennedy the people are for him because he's the most qualified man to be president." Of the State Democratic Party organization he said, "They wanted to sleep through the primary. The opinion is an excellent excuse to get off the hot seat." (*Valley News,* December 22, 1967, pp. 6, 34)

Daniell had taken the interpretation of the attorney general's opinion out of the hands of the McCarthy committee. He was willing to sustain the controversy and derive whatever benefits might accrue from the issue and the rhetoric amplified many of the McCarthy committee's own sentiments. These were sentiments, however, that the McCarthy committee was not prepared to express nor would these views be especially productive to an effort to restore conscience to the Democratic Party.

Daniell, however, was not one to soft-pedal a hot issue and stated that:

> The A.G.'s ruling has the effect of continuing in office the tragic and unsatisfactory Lyndon Johnson.
>
> He needs no additional organization since his professional backers have already taken over, lock, stock and barrel, the Democratic organization of this state. If you are looking for improper action why not investigate their illegal use of the party's funds and equipment for the principal purpose of re-electing Johnson.
>
> It is well-known that persons unwilling to support their candidate are discouraged from participating in so-called party function. As you know this violates every concept of pre-primary fair play.
>
> Actually, the so-called "Citizens for Johnson" organization is a dummy outfit with only professional politicians for members.
>
> If your (the Attorney General's) opinion is allowed to stand it would be another step to the authoritarian form of government which all loyal Americans despise.

Daniell's press release swirled around the legal issues of the ruling but quickly broadened to encompass the tactics of the Johnson campaign organizers, the endorsement and conversion of the Democratic State Committee into the Johnson campaign vehicle, and linked these tactics with the actions of the state's major Democratic officeholders.

Daniell placed his advertisement in the December 26 edition of the *Manchester Union Leader* as he had promised. Technically the issue was joined but the attorney general still had to declare the violation and to proceed with a prosecution of the case in an expeditious manner.

By December 30, the duplicity of the Democratic committee had been drawn to the surface sufficiently by Daniell's charges for the *Concord Daily Monitor* to editorialize. Under the title "BOSSISM" the main editorial led with "Trying to separate the Democratic State Committee from the Johnson Democratic primary committee is virtually impossible." The editorial went on:

> For this reason the Democrats are thumbing their noses at the Attorney General's ruling about having to get their candidate's consent before soliciting funds. . . .
>
> Such consent, according to the Attorney General, has to be filed with the Secretary of State.
>
> A state committee is supposed to be neutral as to its party's candidates in primaries, but you'd never know that from observation of the Democratic antics this year.
>
> When the committee members are wearing their Johnson for President hats they aren't going to solicit or spend money, they say. All they want is for all Democrats, like them, to vote for Johnson in the primary beauty contest.
>
> When the committee members seek seats as delegates favorable to Johnson, they say, they will spend some money. It will be reported by the Democratic State Committee, they say. Or do they mean the State Committee will spend money in support of the prohibited solicitation of write-in votes for Johnson, without his written consent.
>
> It all gets kind of confusing.
>
> Presumably, if this can be done for Johnson it can also be done by Democratic supporters of Kennedy, McCarthy, or any others who may have supporters in the party.
>
> What is a primary, anyway?
>
> A primary is the device by which the registered members of a political party participate in the popular nomination of the party's candidates.
>
> The Democratic State Committee, or any political party state committee, is committed to the primary principle and is pledged to neutrality as between primary candidates.
>
> This is so because it is supposed to support the winning nominees.
>
> Yet the record shows the Democratic State Committee actually voted, in November, to "Pledge their full support as a committee to take all steps necessary to bring about the renomination and re-election of Lyndon Johnson as President."
>
> Bossism is not restricted to the White House.
>
> (*Concord Daily Monitor*, December 30, 1967)

Through the state committee endorsement, the attorney general's ruling, the Daniell challenge of the ruling, the state committee's reaction to the ruling, and the possible link between the ruling and the Democratic administration in the statehouse, a case was built by Daniell and the press that began to awaken the concern of the voting public.

At this important stage in the Johnson campaign, the press coverage was almost totally devoted to the Daniell sequence of charges, comments on the attorney general's ruling, and the pending development of a court test. Practically every story on the Johnson campaign in New Hampshire carried comments on the Daniell charges and Boutin responses rather than positive accounts of the growing list of Johnson endorsements coming from party leaders. A *Valley News* headline of December 27 summarized the difficulty the Johnson campaign had in separating itself from the attorney general's ruling, "Johnson Forces Set Campaign; Daniell Maps Ruling Challenge," or the December 28 headline in the same paper, "Write-in for LBJ Unaffected by Pappagianis Recent Ruling."

On January 4 the Attorney general and the secretary of state notified Daniell that he was in violation of the statute. Daniell called for an immediate hearing in superior court and filed for a declaratory judgment so that the case could be moved directly to the New Hampshire Supreme Court.

Concerned about delays and about losing the press momentum that he had been able to generate, Daniell wrote to the chair of the New Hampshire Democratic State Committee, William Craig, requesting that the "Robert F. Kennedy Write-in Committee" be placed on an equal footing with the Citizens for Johnson Committee. In his January 13 letter, Daniell wrote:

> So that the Johnson and Kennedy supporters can compete fairly, I ask that the State Democratic Committee give to the "Robert F. Kennedy Write-in Committee" the same privileges they have given to the Citizens for Johnson. Let us operate as one of your sub-committees. We would not expect to have any of your committee's funds appropriated for our use.

In a *Concord Daily Monitor* column dated January 15, Jack Hubbard wrote:

> If you can't lick 'em, join 'em, (and try and lick 'em that way). That's what Franklin Attorney Eugene Daniell tried to do to the Democratic State Committee Saturday, and the immediate results was anger from Johnson Democrats. Boutin's response was, "the committee can't do this. It would violate the intent of the November resolution. The state committee has supported the President, why should it now support Daniell? The proposal would destroy the integrity of our own resolution. How can the state committee have two candidates?"

Daniell's proposal opened a new wound. This time a split appeared within the Johnson camp itself. Attorney Joseph Millimet, legal counsel to the Democratic State Committee, reacted to the Daniell request with the following:

> We have a very difficult situation here. I was the one who authored the resolution to support the President. [Adopted November 19th, 1967] Gene Daniell wants to make the state committee the treasurer for his write-in campaign. As a Democrat not a lawyer, I would like to support him, and even though I think Gene is dead wrong in what he is doing—I would like to see him do it.

Millimet's response was in direct conflict with the opinion of the Johnson leader, Bernard Boutin. Millimet wanted to minimize the damage that might be caused to the New Hampshire Democratic Party by avoiding, if possible, serious infractions of the rules of intraparty primaries. Boutin, on the other hand, had one overriding objective: Build a solid renomination base for the president and cut out of the Democratic Party any who questioned the validity of that drive.

Daniell's suit was transferred from the superior court to the Supreme Court on January 17 without a ruling from the lower court. The Supreme Court called for briefs to be filed by January 31 and indicated that its decision would be forthcoming during the term beginning February 6. On February 9 the court held for the defendant, Daniell stating it was not necessary to have written permission to conduct a write-in campaign for a candidate. (*New York Times,* February 10, 1968)

The finding concluded a protracted legal contest that caused irreparable damage to both the Johnson and Kennedy drives. Daniell spent almost all of his time fighting the legal battle. He did not have a campaign organization operating the Kennedy write-in while he was in court, at the law library, and writing his stinging press releases. The Johnson campaign was likewise employed responding to Daniell's charges and trying to change the image of its activity from its power politics to the image of an efficient campaign organization. At the same time the Johnson leaders were having to contend with cracks in their organization.

THE REREGISTRATION PROBLEM

At the same time as the dispute between Daniell and the attorney general was going on the McCarthy committee was continuing its work. One of its objectives was "to organize a campaign to encourage the re-registration of Republicans as Democrats during the reregistration period set by law." In 1968 New Hampshire maintained a rather tightly regulated party registration system. Membership in a party by fact of registration or previous nonparticipation in a primary and, therefore, status as an independent, were voting requirements. In order for a person registered as a Republican to participate in the Democratic presidential primary that person would have to have reregister as a Democrat ninety days prior to the primary election date.

The reregistration period opened for the 1968 presidential primary early in December and was to end December 12, 1967. This would be the only time that either Democrats or Republicans could switch their registration in order to make them eligible to vote in the opposite party's primary. In their preliminary planning for the McCarthy campaign the committee felt that it would be important to have the campaign sufficiently organized so that it could cause some Republicans to change their registration. The committee hoped that these nominal Republicans might feel that their vote would have greater dissenting impact when cast directly against the administration, in the Democratic primary, rather than for some Republican candidate.

Unfortunately reregistration was a difficult process. The voting lists are maintained by uncompensated supervisors of the checklists who are required to "sit" for the purpose of receiving reregistration requests during periods defined by law. These periods vary in duration and number, and are determined by the population size of the voting precinct. The supervisors may set their own times to meet within the guidelines of the law and are obligated to provide only perfunctory notice of their sitting schedule. As a result it was often almost necessary to hire a private detective to search out the time, date, and place of these reregistration sittings. Also to be considered was the fact that in New Hampshire the voting machinery, with few exceptions, is controlled by locally elected supervisors who are usually Republicans. The closed registration system favored the majority party and changes in that system that would make it more open were resisted.

Organizing a significant reregistration drive would have required a major effort on the part of the McCarthy Steering Committee. To be successful there would have to be an actual candidate ready and willing to challenge Lyndon Johnson in New Hampshire. On the Republican side, Governor George Romney was offering that kind of attraction to both the real and nominal Republicans upset with the Johnson administration. There was, therefore, a certain urgency in the McCarthy committee's effort to encourage Senator McCarthy to announce his candidacy nationally and in the New Hampshire primary prior to the expiration of the reregistration period.

The committee estimated that it might be able to reregister four thousand to five thousand Republicans if it were successful in making known the existence of the reregistration period by publicizing the actual times, dates, and places of reregistration. On this latter point, it was not unusual for the supervisors to select difficult times to comply with the law. Saturday evenings and dates in the middle of long-weekend holidays were often the times selected for reregistration. Only the most dedicated and persistent of those wishing to reregister bothered to take the trouble.

The outcome of the reregistration effort was more successful than the McCarthy committee had expected. While the leadership was occupied with preparations for the CCD meeting in Chicago and with planning the visit of Senator McCarthy to New Hampshire toward the middle of December, others tried to get Republicans to reregister. Although Senator McCarthy did not announce his entry into the New Hampshire primary until long after the end of the reregistration period, his November 30 announcement of candidacy did prompt a significant increase in the number of reregistrations from Republican to Democrat. The committee estimated that upwards of five thousand persons entered the Democratic Party and that a majority of these did so to vote for Senator McCarthy.

While the New Hampshire McCarthy Steering Committee was pursuing its organizational objectives, McCarthy was preparing to announce his presidential candidacy in Washington. E. M. (Ned) Kenworthy, writing in the November 25 edition of the *New Republic,* reviewed what Senator McCarthy had been up to during the period from November 9–13. McCarthy had visited five important states (New York, Minnesota, Michigan, Massachusetts, and Illinois) testing sentiment and gathering pledges of financial support for what McCarthy then described as his "personal confrontation" of Johnson's Vietnam policy. Kenworthy wrote:

By the end of those five days the Minnesota Democrat had reached, if he had not done so earlier, the point of no return.

Sometime prior to November 30, McCarthy concluded his preliminary search for support and committed himself to that "personalized alternative." When he entered the Senate Caucus Room to make his announcement at a press conference, it was a sense of the personification of protest that surrounded him. He was a rallying point, a vehicle for dissent on the war, a senator with standing and credibility. He was not, however, viewed by himself or by many others as being a viable candidate for the presidency.

The press conference was notably low-key. He began his announcement by not saying that he was a candidate for the presidency but saying, "I intend to enter the Democratic primaries in four states, Wisconsin, Oregon, California, and Nebraska. The decision with reference to Massachusetts and also New Hampshire will be made within the next two or three weeks."

In the remainder of his statement, he set forth the tone of his effort, making clear that he was not a candidate in conventional terms:

> Since I first said that I thought the issue of Vietnam and the issues related to it should be raised in the primaries of the country I have talked with Democratic leaders from about 25 to 26 states. I've talked particularly to candidates for re-election to the Senate—Democratic candidates—some House members and also to students on campus and to other people throughout the country.
>
> My decision to challenge the President's position and the Administration position has been strengthened by evident intention to escalate and to intensify the war in Vietnam and on the other hand the absence of any positive indication or suggestion for a compromise or for a negotiated political settlement.
>
> I am concerned that the Administration seems to have set no limit to the price which it's willing to pay for a military victory. Let me summarize the cost of the war up to this point:
>
> The physical destruction of much of a small and weak nation by military operation of the most powerful nation in the world.
>
> One hundred thousand to 150,000 civilian casualties in South Vietnam alone, to say nothing of the destruction of life and property in North Vietnam.
>
> The uprooting and the fracturing of the structure of the society of South Vietnam where one-fourth to one-third of the population are now reported to be refugees.
>
> For the United States as of yesterday over 15,000 combat dead and nearly 95,000 wounded through November.
>
> A monthly expenditure in pursuit of the war amounting somewhere between $2 billion and $3 billion.
>
> I am also concerned about the bearing of the war on other areas of the United States responsibility, both at home and abroad.
>
> The failure to appropriate adequate funds for the poverty program here,

for housing, for education and to meet other national needs and the prospect of additional cuts as a condition to the possible passage of the surtax bill.

The drastic reduction of our foreign aid program in other parts of the world.

A dangerous rise in inflation and one of the indirect and serious consequences of our involvement in Vietnam, the devaluation of the British pound, which in many respects is more important east of Suez today than the British Navy.

In addition, there is growing evidence of a deepening moral crisis in America—discontent and frustration and a disposition to take extra-legal if not illegal action to manifest protest.

I am hopeful that this challenge which I am making, which I hope will be supported by other members of the Senate and other politicians, may alleviate at least in some degree this sense of political helplessness and restore to many people a belief in the processes of American politics and of American Government.

The college campuses especially on those campuses—and also among adult, thoughtful Americans, that it may counter the growing sense of alienation from politics which I think is currently reflected in a tendency to withdraw from the political action, to talk of non participation, to become cynical and to make threats of support for third parties or fourth parties or other irregular political movements.

I do not see in my move any great threat to the unity and strength of the Democratic party, whatever that unity may be today and whatever strength it may be.

The issue of the war in Vietnam is not really a separate issue but one that must be dealt with in the configuration of other problems to which it is related. It is within this broader context that I intend to make the case to the people of the United States.

To say that I'm—as I'm sure I shall be charged—I am not for peace at any price, but for an honorable, rational and political solution to this war, a solution which I believe will enhance our world position, encourage the respect of our allies and our potential adversaries, which will permit us to give the necessary attention to other commitments both at home and abroad, military and non-military and leave us with resources and moral energy to deal effectively with the pressing domestic problems of the United States itself.

In this—this total effort—I believe we can restore to this nation a clearer sense of purpose and of dedication to the achievement of our traditional purpose as a great nation in the 20th century.

(New York Times, December 1, 1967*)*

The statement and McCarthy's response to the questions that followed constitute important political documentation of his attitude toward the venture. As Warren

Weaver reported in his *New York Times* article that day, "During a bantering, low-key news conference, the Minnesota Senator never actually declared himself a candidate for president or contended that he could deprive the president of the nomination."

He viewed his function as being that of the vehicle, the channel, the personification, that would make it possible to manifest the extent of the national concern—a concern he saw as dividing the young from their parents, the campuses from their communities, the present from the future. It was not possible simply to vote "no" on the issue of the renomination of the president. There had to be a focal point, a name but not a great deal more, and certainly not a candidate projecting the impression that he expected to displace the president.

McCarthy did say, ". . . I don't mean to draw off at any point, and I think this challenge would have to go all the way to a challenge for the nomination for the presidency. It may not be me at that point. It may be someone else, but so far as the end result of the effort, I think it has to go to the point of trying to change the policy and direction and also the mood of America." It was a modest beginning marked by realistic language tied to the accepted wisdom that a sitting president was impossible to displace if that president wished to seek renomination. One questioner, in fact, asked if McCarthy's move wasn't actually political suicide, to which McCarthy replied, "Not suicide but it might be execution."

The crucible of the New Hampshire primary would change the tone of the McCarthy effort but the essence remained. McCarthy was responding to a call. There was a spontaneous national movement that needed a point around which to organize. The movement needed someone who sensed the urgency of the time, who could give voice to the sense of urgency, who could respond to the vitality of the concern, and who would remain solid when faced with pressures to adjust from within as well as from without. McCarthy did not describe a traditional political role for himself. He was there because he was willing to respond to the call. That was the only condition. To become a candidate in the traditional sense was not possible in 1967. To have said, "I announce my candidacy for president and I expect to be nominated and elected to that office" would have been a false and misleading statement totally out of step with the needs of the moment. The insincerity of that statement would have driven away the very support that had created the conditions of the draft. There were those who faulted McCarthy in his announcement for his lack of passion, charisma, and firebrand dedication to the cause. They were seeking a leader to speak with their own sense of urgency, an amplification of their concerns, rather than a political educator, one capable of expanding the constituency of dissent with effective argument and carefully put questions.

The reaction to the announcement was extensive though widely varied. The *New York Times* editorialized:

> The decision of Senator Eugene McCarthy of Minnesota to challenge Johnson in the Democratic Presidential primaries now enables those who dissent from the administration's policy in Vietnam to find political expression for their convictions. . . .
>
> It is highly unlikely that President Johnson can be denied renomination if he wants it. Senator McCarthy's more optimistic supporters argue that if he

> should be successful in the primaries, such a show of strength might impel President Johnson to withdraw voluntarily to prevent a hopeless split with the party. We believe this kind of reasoning to be based on a complete misreading of Mr. Johnson's temperament. He is not a man likely to quit under fire.
>
> But it is true that the nation's policy can only be changed by political methods. How the Vietnam issue is fought out within each party and between the two parties in the coming year will go far toward determining the shape of American policy in the next Presidential term. Since Senator McCarthy is a thoughtful, responsible man, he can be expected to clarify the alternatives in Vietnam and usefully contribute to the complex political process by which the American people make up their minds on great issues.
>
> (*New York Times,* December 1, 1967)

Not quite believing what they were seeing, the mystics of the national press began to probe immediately for the hidden McCarthy agenda and the personal motives of his actions. The first theme, that of the "stalking horse" for some other candidate, usually considered to be Senator Robert F. Kennedy, was the most persistent early press question. McCarthy did not fully allay that contention in his press conference when he said that had talked with Senator Kennedy about his decision to oppose the president, and Kennedy "had not tried to dissuade him." He indicated that Kennedy was his second choice as a Johnson challenger. "I would have been glad if he had moved early. I think if he had, there'd have been no need for me to do anything."

The New Hampshire and regional newspapers gave McCarthy's announcement prominent coverage. Major stories appeared in the Boston and New Hampshire newspapers. The *Boston Herald-Traveler* ran a large headline, "McCarthy Tests LBJ in 4 Primaries," with a column head "Seeks Reaction on War Policy." The *Christian Science Monitor* headline read, "McCarthy Rallies War Critics." The New Hampshire newspapers ran page-one stories with headlines like those in the *Valley News,* "McCarthy is Going to Run" or in the *Daily Dartmouth,* "McCarthy Challenges LBJ of Presidency."

The announcement had been received well. Editorial reaction reinforced the seriousness of the announcement. The tone was one of the "test" McCarthy was prepared to make rather than promulgating an aggressive candidacy. Even the "stalking horse" theme took on a jaded aspect when surrogates for the administration (when asked to react to the McCarthy decision) accused him of being a front-runner for Kennedy. The *New York Post* carried a story headlined, "Connally Hits McCarthy as RFK Front." The story read, "Gov. Connally of Texas charged today that Sen. McCarthy is a 'stalking horse' for the Presidential aspirations of Senator Robert F. Kennedy. . . . The Governor, a staunch defender of Johnson's policy in Vietnam, met reporters at Kennedy Airport before boarding a plan for Paris. His charges came after his White House meeting Wednesday with Johnson." The "stalking horse" theme did stimulate interest in the McCarthy activity. It is possible that without the subplot and the reportorial sniffing for intrigue, the McCarthy story might well have died during the next month when there was little for the reporters to cover except the preliminaries of a newly born political venture.

Newsday's Nick Thimmesch in a December 1, 1967, column headlined "McCarthy Aides the Crux," identified an ultimately more important theme:

> The "McCarthy for President" movement has an attractive candidate, a lively issue, the promise of plenty of money and the immediate problem of developing an effective campaign apparatus.
>
> The celebrated Minnesota Senator made his big splash yesterday by announcing that he would enter four primaries. . . . Today, his staffers and supporters are busy arranging schedules and organization in a score of states in addition to those where he will definitely be on the ballot.
>
> Until that organization is formed, McCarthy must rely largely on the Conference of Concerned Democrats and similar groups which have been pushing a "Dump Johnson" movement for two months. . . .
>
> The Senator has not signed on any issues specialists and relies on staffers and friends in universities and in the military for advice on his principal issue, Vietnam. At this point he does not have a staff of the dimension usually required for presidential primary campaign. . . .
>
> At the end of McCarthy's announcement session yesterday, where the Senator showed good wit and poise, a man long associated with liberal causes remarked: "Gene was great today, but he's so casual about organization. Vietnam is the big issue and lots of people are for him. The question is whether he can get well enough organized to make some impact."
>
> (*Newsday,* December 1, 1967)

Thimmesch and others inventoried the support that existed in each of the states where McCarthy would definitely run. What they found was impressive. McCarthy would have to "rely," as Thimmesch put it, on these "groups" until he built his own organization. What he missed was that building McCarthy's own organization had, to a great extent, already been accomplished. This was a legitimate draft. Organizations were really seeking a candidate, whereas usually candidates stimulate organizations to support what they already have firmly in mind.

Thimmesch wrote:

> On the West Coast, McCarthy's initial support is the California Democratic Council, headed by Gerald N. Hill and Edmund Gerald Brown, Jr., son of former Governor "Pat" Brown; California Congressman Don Edwards; and former Oregon Democratic State Chairman Howard Morgan.
>
> In Wisconsin, where McCarthy is popular, Donald O. Peterson, Democratic chairman of the 10th Congressional District Committee, is the organizer. . . . The key men in the New York effort are reformers—Atty. Allard K. Lowenstein, Assemblyman Jerome Kretchmer, City Councilman Ted Weiss and Ronald Eldridge. McCarthy also has the backing of Michigan's most publicized dissenter from Johnson's Vietnam policy, Zolton Ferency, who recently resigned as state chairman.

> A "Citizens for McCarthy" group is active in New Hampshire under the leadership of David Hoen [sic], former assistant to Gov. John W. King and Sen. Thomas J. McIntyre. . . .
>
> He (McCarthy) would also like to get supplemental support in the form of favorite son candidacies from three sympathetic senate colleagues: Indiana's Vance Hartke, Ohio's Stephen Young and South Dakota's George McGovern. Invitations to speak are pouring into McCarthy's office. His first campaign speech will be delivered to the Conference of Concerned Democrats, who are already believers, in Chicago tomorrow.
>
> (*Newsday*, December 1, 1967)

Both Governor John W. King and Senator Thomas J. McIntyre were contacted for their reaction to the McCarthy announcement. King was asked whether he agreed with Senator Robert Kennedy when Kennedy said he thought McCarthy's decision "would be good for the party." King said he disagreed with Kennedy; "My inclination is to support the president. In am not weakening." Later the same day, while speaking in Exeter, New Hampshire, King said, "I have complete confidence that the man who has led this country with vigor and determination and unshakable courage for the past four years will be re-elected for another four year term." He concluded by comparing Johnson with four other presidents who withstood adverse public opinion during the Revolution, the War of 1812, the Civil War, and World War II. (*Valley News*, December 1, 1967)

McIntyre said, "He, Governor King, and the members of the New Hampshire State Democratic Committee will 'do our best' to make sure Senator McCarthy 'gets as few votes as possible if he enters the state presidential primary.'" McIntyre viewed any Kennedy activity as being "much more difficult" than McCarthy's. "The only McCarthy New Hampshire people know about is the late one"—referring to Senator Joseph R. McCarthy of Wisconsin.

"It poses the threat of early injury to the president," McIntyre noted. "It doesn't take too much for the news media to read into the results a possible threat to the president." He added, "His own polls and readings indicated New Hampshire was quite hawkish though he did sense some build-up for a move to get out of Vietnam." He estimated a turnout of forty thousand of the state's eighty-seven thousand registered Democratic voters and thought that would be a good showing.

Earlier, McIntyre had projected that McCarthy would not get more than 10 percent of the primary vote if he became a candidate in New Hampshire. His figures, based on the forty thousand vote total in the Democratic primary, meant four thousand votes. Continuing, McIntyre mentioned that the most McCarthy could expect to receive in the primary was "3,000 to 5,000 votes." (*Newsweek*, November 11, 1967) This statement became an early target for the McCarthy campaigners who could then say that anything above McIntyre's prediction of three thousand to five thousand votes would have to be considered significant.

I had been quoted in an early, unguarded moment as predicting that McCarthy could get "at least one-third" (*Newsweek*, November 27, 1967) of the total vote. As time went on, the numbers game, which McIntyre started and the press would not end, became almost as important as all other aspects of the campaign.

PLANNING A McCARTHY VISIT TO NEW HAMPSHIRE

At the November 19 meeting of the New Hampshire McCarthy Steering Committee, the possibility of a speaking engagement for Senator McCarthy prior to a decision on New Hampshire was discussed. The prospect of the Sidore Lecture Series as the sponsoring forum was mentioned, and in the two weeks that followed I pursued that possibility. The topic was to be "Human Rights, Power and Politics in Contemporary America." The organizer for the Sidore Lectures Committee was Erwin A. Jaffe, associate professor of political science. Already scheduled in his program were Father James Groppi of Milwaukee, Mayor-Elect Richard Hatcher, Gary, Indiana; and William Strickland, former executive director, Northern Student Movement, New York City.

Jaffe had ideas about both the efficacy of establishment politics and the type of individual he wanted to complete his program. Although not radical enough for Jaffe, McCarthy at least was tolerable since he had come out against what Jaffe felt was the "establishment's" war. The especially attractive characteristic of the Sidore Series was that one of the sessions would be presented in Manchester. This meant that the McCarthy committee could have a nonpolitical event for McCarthy outside an academic community. In fact, Manchester offered the best of all possible political worlds for such an event. Jaffe, however, wanted assurances that McCarthy's participation would in no way exploit his series for what was, in his mind, a potentially disreputable political purpose. Jaffe began imposing conditions on McCarthy's possible participation that would have kept McCarthy from any contact with local supporters, the press, and any but those wishing to hear McCarthy's thinking on the topic of the lectures.

Arranging McCarthy's multiobjective New Hampshire visit against the resistance of a politically turned-off host strained all involved. I first had to be sure that an invitation would be issued. To do this I had to reach beyond Jaffe to May Sidore Gruber, the benefactor of the series. She and her late husband, Saul Sidore, had helped to revive the New Hampshire Democratic Party and had assisted John F. Kennedy in the early stages of his campaign for election in 1960. She, I sensed from earlier contacts, would appreciate the objective I had in mind as I attempted to build a base for an antiadministration, antiwar effort in New Hampshire.

Recently remarried, May Sidore Gruber, who commuted between her New York City and New Hampshire Pandora Knitting Company offices, was scheduled to be in New York December 1. I called her to ask if we might to discuss the McCarthy candidacy and McCarthy's possible involvement in the Sidore Lectures. Meeting first in her Fifth Avenue apartment and then for dinner, we (Sandra Hoeh and May Gruber's husband, Sam Gruber, included) discussed the importance of what Senator McCarthy had said in his announcement on the previous day. The possibility of having McCarthy speak in the Sidore Series at beginning of the 1968 political season was not lost on May Sidore Gruber. She saw the opportunity the

Sidore Series had to help make history and to assist in bringing the issues of war and human rights into immediate political focus. Not only did she support the idea of having McCarthy lecture, she said she would convince Jaffe of the value and wanted to host a reception dinner for a select group prior to McCarthy's Manchester portion of the series. She hoped that this latter gesture, the dinner, would lend further impetus to McCarthy's political potential in New Hampshire.

May Sidore Gruber also understood the difficulty I was having with Jaffe. She was sensitive to Jaffe's hopes for the lecture series and asked me to conform as much as I could with Jaffe's wishes. She wanted Jaffe's effort in bringing the two-day program together to be respected; at the same time she assured me that my purposes in having McCarthy come to New Hampshire, in this way, were of equal importance. Concluding the meeting, she asked me to coordinate the arrangements for the Manchester lecture through her son Gene Sidore, now with the family firm in Manchester.

It should be added that rarely in the annals of New Hampshire political events has it been possible to make such uniquely appropriate arrangements for an announced candidate for the presidency. The Manchester lecture would not only provide McCarthy with an excellent forum, but the Sidore Series would also pay his expenses and a one-thousand-dollar honorarium for his visit. Jaffe issued the invitation to Senator McCarthy.

The next step was to convince Senator McCarthy to accept the invitation. The dates were set: December 14 for the evening lecture in Manchester and the morning of December 15 for a colloquium at the University of New Hampshire.

THE CONFERENCE OF CONCERNED DEMOCRATS

Lowenstein and Gans' weeks of activity now culminated in a gathering of representatives from forty-two states in Chicago. It was the first meeting where all the different segments of the McCarthy campaign were gathered in one place. This meeting of celebrities, party officials, students, elected officials, new activists, old activists, minority group members, and labor unionists, both young and old, was a preview of what would emerge as a significant political force. Unquestionably it was an important meeting. Without the reinforcement that the gathering gave to each who attended, the concern the participants felt as individuals in their own states might well have remained isolated.

New Hampshire had special meaning for the CCD organizers. It was to be the first primary, the first test, the first chance to strike a blow; its importance was appreciated by those in other states who would be looking on. Practically from the moment of registration at Chicago's Blackstone Hotel, the New Hampshire delegation was collecting pledges of help from all sections of the country should McCarthy enter the New Hampshire primary. In addition to the delegation from the New Hampshire McCarthy Committee, Eugene Daniell came alone with his Draft Kennedy message. The Blackstone provided an appropriate context for the meetings. In 1920 it had been the scene of the famous smoke-filled caucus meeting that led to the selection, and ultimate nomination, of Warren G. Harding as the

Republican candidate for president. This historic fact, of course, was not lost in the minds of the CCD delegates, although Lowenstein and those assembled did not exactly fit the description of the old-time professional pols who had occupied those rooms in 1920. In fact, Paul Wieck, writing in the December 17 issue of the *New Republic,* said, "They looked respectable, mostly middle class, and middle aged."

Lowenstein had several reasons for urging the New Hampshire delegates to attend. Among these he hoped that from New Hampshire he might secure legitimacy for the intraparty activity of the CCD. As the time for the CCD meeting neared and McCarthy announced his candidacy, the most important reason for the New Hampshire group to come to Chicago was the chance to present its case for McCarthy's entry in the New Hampshire primary directly to the senator himself.

Lowenstein had asked Sandra Hoeh, at that moment one of the highest officials of the Democratic Party in the nation willing to be identified with the McCarthy candidacy, to join the National Steering Committee of the CCD. As the chair of the 2nd Congressional District of New Hampshire for the State Democratic Committee, her position was approximately number three in the hierarchy of the New Hampshire party. Few others at that level had been willing to join Lowenstein's efforts at this stage. At twenty-six, she represented both the concerns of younger Democratic party members and a desire to see her party maintain its pledges of peace made during the 1964 campaign. Summarizing this view, Wieck wrote, "The Hoehs expressed the prevalent opinion that this was to be a 'within-the-party' campaign. They do not want to split and form a third party." (*New Republic,* December 17, 1967)

The conference followed the pattern set in the twenty-eight states where Lowenstein and Gans had either established organizations, as in New Hampshire, or had drawn existing organizations into their fold, such as the California Democratic Council. They always stressed respectability, moderation in other words, the very image of a good citizen concerned about the future of his or her nation. Lowenstein and Gans did not want the radical left, and, in reality, the radical left had already withdrawn from the political system.

The students attending had been carefully limited by Lowenstein to prevent hordes of college-types from diluting the establishment patina of the gathering. Those who did attend, and there were a considerable number, were properly attired and, except for age, comparable with their seniors. Both Lowenstein and the students realized that an adult identity for the meeting was necessary. Lowenstein had been a past president of the National Student Association and through the years had kept in contact with the subsequent leadership of NSA including its recent past president, Sam Brown. Lowenstein had asked Brown to chair the student meetings of the Chicago conference.

An important part of the conference turned out to be the caucus sessions that were held by the students. A network of contacts was woven in these sessions that became important later. Barbara Underwood, who, with her spouse David, became one of the leaders of the McCarthy campaign in Concord, New Hampshire, wrote in an unpublished manuscript:

> During one of the meetings, where about 45 students attended, the debate went on for over an hour around a name that they would call themselves. They wanted to merge several fragmentary groups into one national McCarthy organization and under one title. They eventually settled on "Young Citizens for McCarthy."
>
> The name "Students for McCarthy," they thought, would damage the Senator's cause. Today's connotation of student, they argued entails subversive, anarchistic, or juvenile behavior. Sam Brown argued for the more inclusive name because he thought the organization should appeal to a more inclusive body of people. He said, "The name is a symbol and it would be ridiculous for us to cut ourselves off from two-thirds of the youth in the country by choosing such a restricted name as "Students for McCarthy."
>
> The "Young Citizens" planned to set up chapters in the areas or states where McCarthy planned to enter primaries: Wisconsin, Massachusetts, Nebraska, Oregon, and California. Most of the money for these operations, said Brown, would come from the national McCarthy for President organization. Lowenstein said during the course of the conference that more than one million dollars had been received in pledges. Brown added, "You know Allard, he's the perpetual optimist."
>
> (Barbara Underwood, *St. Crispin's Day, Gene McCarthy in the New Hampshire Primary*, Concord, N.H.: unpublished manuscript, 1970)

Through the Chicago meetings a theme for student involvement emerged. The ability of people like Sam Brown to articulate the feelings of the students and yet understand the realities of the political climate toward students and the negative reaction young people had caused was important to the eventual organization of productive Young Citizens participation in the campaign. The distinction between the regular Young Republicans or Young Democrats organizations and such groups as the Young Citizens for McCarthy was the difference between auxiliary functions and full partnership. The partnership was Lowenstein's objective.

There was, however, a subtle clash of wills in Chicago that also set an important tone that underlay the theme of 1968. Lowenstein had created the Dump Johnson movement, stimulated the search for an alternative candidate, and begun the effort to bring together a coalition of new and existing groups able to organize a campaign. The culmination of that effort was the nationally organized CCD, meeting in Chicago, and the "yes" answer from McCarthy to be a candidate. With that "yes" McCarthy replaced Lowenstein as the leader; whether he or Lowenstein actually perceived the transfer of leadership, it had occurred. McCarthy began to take charge and to show his independence by resisting Lowenstein's plan to have McCarthy make his candidacy announcement before Lowenstein's assemblage Saturday evening, December 2.

Further evidence of McCarthy's desire to assert his own style came early in the first plenary session of the conference. Lowenstein had gathered his stars on the platform, and they exhorted the audience with the importance of the meetings that were about to begin. McCarthy appeared, having just arrived from the airport. Lowenstein, hoping for the dramatic entrance to be staged that evening, was clearly surprised by McCarthy's sudden and informal appearance. Following the ovation and a brief response by the senator, Lowenstein was surprised when McCarthy did not leave the stage but wished to linger and respond to questions.

The carefully stage-managed presidential candidates of recent memory were willing to answer questions on occasion, but the setting was usually arranged to control the hazards of misstatements. Unfriendly questions could be deflected, weak answers could be smothered, and the right questions would be expected from the friendly. Rather than exposing McCarthy directly to his questioners, Lowenstein stood as the translator of the questions to Senator McCarthy. It quickly became clear to most in the hall that McCarthy was not only willing to handle his questioners but was eager to do so. The obvious questions regarding the war and administration policy in Vietnam slipped easily through the Lowenstein screen to McCarthy. Eventually, Lowenstein could not resist embellishing a question or two or adding his own response. Two stars were on the stage. Lowenstein was fading; he was not the candidate; the candidate was there, and the candidate was beginning to assert his own personality. When the questions on the war beginning to diminish, questions on the problems of the cities followed, and then a question on McCarthy's feeling toward birth control. Lowenstein would not pass that particular subject through his screen. McCarthy, capable of hearing the questioner, responded under his breath, "Yes, I am in favor of intrauterine devices for sacred cows." The session adjourned.

That evening the conference reconvened in plenary session. Lowenstein's sense of staging meant that the image to be projected through the reporters and the electronic media would be as close to that of a national convention as was possible. A band was even playing the usual convention fare.

The parade of speakers to the podium began with a series of brief exhortations from the emerging leadership of the CCD. Then Allard Lowenstein was introduced. The overflow gathering of more than four thousand people exploded as Lowenstein's eloquence and charged rhetoric jumped from exhortation to challenge to predictions of accomplishments for the future. Repeatedly interrupted by cheers, Lowenstein mapped a direction that was enthusiastically endorsed by the gathering. Concluding his lengthy and emotional speech, Lowenstein introduced his now highly charged audience to its new hero, Senator Eugene J. McCarthy. The man who had brought the conference into being had, whether he realized it or not, just given his last speech as its leader. Lowenstein was memorable, but the power of his language and the dominance of this energy violated the "one star rule" of American politics —a rule that even many experienced political activists did not fully appreciate, a rule that Senator McCarthy would quickly make known to the gathering and to Lowenstein.

As McCarthy began to speak a confused quiet came over the audience. They had been taken to the heights of emotion by Lowenstein, and now before them was a gray, distinguished presence with a compelling message but a quiet presentation. McCarthy, it became readily apparent, did not intend to run a fire-charged campaign. He apparently felt that the issues were already too explosive and that if a larger public was to understand the urgency of the time, the issues would have to be discussed calmly and rationally. He was not going to make promises that could not be kept, and, more importantly, he would not allow expectations to run higher than they should. His ascendancy to the leadership of the antiwar movement that night was not brought about by further charging the emotions of his audience but by quieting them. Not a few considered his speech dull and uninspired. McCarthy has commented that he felt it was one of his best. (Eugene J. McCarthy, *The Year of the People*, Garden City, N. Y.: Doubleday and Company, 1969, p. 29)

He called on the Democratic Party to recapture the spirit of Adlai Stevenson and John F. Kennedy. Concluding his remarks, McCarthy set forth his credo for the coming contest:

> The message from the Administration today is a message of apprehension, a message of fear, yes—even a message of fear of fear.
>
> That is not the real spirit of America. I do not believe that it is. This is a time to test the mood and spirit:
>
> To offer in place of doubt—trust.
>
> In place of expediency—right judgment.
>
> In place of ghettos, let us have neighborhoods and communities.
>
> In place of incredibility—integrity.
>
> In place of murmuring, let us have clear speech;
>
> let us again here America singing.
>
> In place of disunity, let us have dedication of purpose.
>
> In place of despair, let us have hope.
>
> This is the promise of greatness which was stated for us by Adlai Stevenson and which brought to form and positive action in the words and actions of John Kennedy.
>
> Let us pick up again those lost strands and weave them again into the fabric of America.
>
> Let us sort out the music from the sounds and again respond to the trumpet and the steady drum.

A quiet, almost contemplative audience rose in a standing ovation as McCarthy's concluding phrase drifted in the haze of the room. He had been interrupted by applause only occasionally in his address and then less because of the emotion of his delivery than by the power of his words. The contrast between Lowenstein's emotional vigor and McCarthy's quiet arguments and concluding poetry was read by the reporters as having produced disappointment in the minds of his audience.

I recall being asked by several wire service reporters, a columnist or two, and even some network personnel, "Weren't you disappointed in McCarthy's speech?"

My response was that this was a difficult time and that shouting and emotion were not what would make a political movement. People, I felt, needed a chance to consider the whole situation, to interact with the speaker, probe their own minds not as a reflex to an emotional address but in response to a thoughtful one. McCarthy's style, his power to quiet an audience and to get his listeners to think and then to respond was a power that would be greater in 1968 than that of emotion.

Yes, I said, it was fun to listen to Al Lowenstein and to shout and applaud his rhetoric and his vigor, but I agreed with Lowenstein. One would either have to agree totally with Lowenstein or disagree totally. There were no other choices. McCarthy gave the listener a chance to consider the message, to agree or not, or to change perspectives. It was this tone that many who would be returning to their various states to organize McCarthy's campaign felt was the new spirit—the McCarthy spirit.

The next day, Sunday, December 3, the CCD concluded its business and for all intents and purposes began the metamorphosis that would emerge as the national McCarthy campaign. Writing of the CCD meetings, Paul Wieck said:

> Perhaps the most impressive thing about Chicago in early December was the ease with which the Conference of Concerned Democrats lined up officially behind the McCarthy candidacy. As a group, reform liberals are notoriously garrulous, often purists. Zolton Ferency of Michigan pinpointed this tendency in his speech before the conference when he said he's seen a "whole convention hung up over whether it should be a comma or a semi colon." The ingredients for a hang-up were there when the delegates arrived. Large numbers of them privately yearn for Bobby Kennedy, the heir apparent of their political dreams and the one man they're convinced could really up-end LBJ in 1968. No doubt, many left Chicago hoping Senator McCarthy will only serve to break open the convention through a series of primary wins, and in the process, open the way for RFK. Yet, they readily agreed to a unanimous endorsement of Senator McCarthy.
>
> (*New Republic,* December 10, 1967, p. 10)

A resolution was introduced in the concluding plenary session of the conference and passed without dissent, reading:

> Whereas this nation is in desperate need of the kind of courageous and dynamic leadership which alone can bring peace and unity to our tragically divided country, and whereas the Democratic Party should be the instrument for providing that leadership;
>
> And whereas Senator Eugene J. McCarthy is a statesman who possesses the qualities of courage, leadership, humility and vision needed to instill faith in our government,
>
> Therefore, be it resolved: that this conference of Concerned Democrats representing all sections of this great nation, meeting at Chicago, Illinois, this 3rd day of December, 1967, does hereby enthusiastically endorse the candidacy of Eugene J. McCarthy for the 1968 Democratic nomination for president.

The national press, always waiting in the wings of such meetings for signs of dissolution and conflict came away, as did Paul Wieck, with a sense of amazement, even awe, that the conference had been able to pursue its tasks without major disruption.

The major reason why six persons had traveled the eleven hundred miles from New Hampshire to Chicago was to meet with McCarthy. The CCD schedule provided for state or regional meetings to discuss political action and to have the chance to talk directly with the candidate. The primary states that McCarthy had already said he would enter tended to control the action in each of the regional sessions. For New England, the options were New Hampshire and Massachusetts. Both were waiting for a decision from McCarthy. Lowenstein had told the New Hampshire delegation before it left New Hampshire that it would have to present a strong case to McCarthy in order to get him to seriously consider entering the New Hampshire primary. Lowenstein felt that McCarthy was not sure that an antiwar, liberal candidate could make a reasonable test in New Hampshire—a state known for its conservatism and unsympathetic press. The group's second mission was somewhat shorter in its range. I needed a decision from McCarthy regarding whether he would accept an invitation from the Sidore Lecture Series to participate in the December 14–15 programs.

Gerry Studds and I had discussed what our arguments should be when we introduced ourselves to McCarthy and then described why he should consider the New Hampshire race. The essence of the argument was that New Hampshire was first and tough, or at least so it seemed to the world. If McCarthy ducked New Hampshire he might have difficulty proving that his effort was serious even if he did go on to successes in friendly Wisconsin, Oregon, California, and Massachusetts. New Hampshire produces a large media effect for relatively few dollars spent. Campaigning in New Hampshire is manageable. The Democratic primary vote is concentrated. If McCarthy intended to campaign in Massachusetts then time, money, and energy spent in New Hampshire would condition the neighbor state for its later primary.

During the Thanksgiving period, Gerry Studds had spent some time analyzing the results from previous New Hampshire presidential primaries. As a result of this work Studds and I would be able to give McCarthy a precise breakdown of the time he would have to spend in New Hampshire. The proposal we prepared outlined a twelve-day campaign schedule showed that it was possible, in that time, to cover as much as 75 percent of the potential Democratic primary vote. In addition to the actual schedule, we had a rank order list of each New Hampshire city and town that produced a meaningful Democratic primary vote. This was a list that would be the basis for expanding the campaign schedule as needed.

Perhaps the most effective argument we thought could be made involved the type of organization that was already assembled in New Hampshire. We felt that the membership of the steering committee and the list of contacts throughout the state argued in favor of the New Hampshire contest.

At the New Hampshire delegation meeting with McCarthy, the six McCarthy delegates from New Hampshire were expanded by Eugene Daniell and several delegates from the nonprimary states of Maine and Vermont. When McCarthy arrived there were perhaps as many as twelve people assembled.

Following introductions and questions concerning when he might make a decision about New Hampshire, each of the McCarthy people, as if by prearrangement, presented an argument in support of his entry. Studds reviewed his research and the possible campaign schedule. I noted that this was not a group of amateurs and that we were ready to run an effective campaign.

Jack Holland reviewed the importance of New Hampshire as the first primary and its value as being a tough state for his candidacy. Sylvia Chaplain recalled other primary campaigns that she had been involved in, the importance of organization, and an early start. Philip Chaplain first discussed the moderate cost of a campaign, but then with conviction said that for McCarthy to campaign creditably and to really test opinion on the war, New Hampshire was essential. The newly found friends from the neighboring states pledged their support if McCarthy entered the New Hampshire primary. They would come to work, send money, and do anything that would help the cause.

Senator McCarthy told the group that he was impressed with the work they had done and with the organization they had. He was given copies of the statistical analysis, the schedule, and the membership of the steering committee. Unlike some of the caucus sessions that McCarthy would visit that afternoon, the New Hampshire meeting had no questions challenging McCarthy's intentions or revealing uncertainty as to the organizational leadership of his campaign in a particular state. The New Hampshire delegation obviously was looking for a "yes" decision—one that would serve as marching orders.

In response Senator McCarthy was encouraging. He said he was impressed by the preparations and that he was "inclined to enter the primary but that he had not yet made up his mind." Later, when asked by a reporter how the New Hampshire meeting with the senator had gone, I said, "I bet he enters." Since the meetings were closed caucuses with the press outside, there was a scramble for news. Before the Massachusetts caucus, McCarthy announced that he would enter their primary. His decision on Massachusetts came when Senator Edward M. Kennedy stated that he "had no intention of running as a favorite son candidate" in the state's April 30 contest. That meant that of the original list of six primaries, only New Hampshire was left without a decision.

Even though the caucus sessions were closed to the press, I had a problem. I wanted to discuss the plans for the senator's visit to New Hampshire, but with Gene Daniell in the room it was not possible. I followed the senator into the hall, mentioned that an invitation to speak at the Sidore Series would be coming, and asked him to accept. McCarthy said simply, "Yes," and asked me to work out the details with his administrative assistant, Jerry Eller.

I had talked with Jerry Eller on the telephone several times earlier but this was our first meeting. We huddled for a moment discussing the outline of the Sidore Series arrangements, and then I asked how the reporters should be handled. His response was "keep them guessing." This was not exactly the response I needed in order to keep my then productive relations with the New Hampshire press alive. In other words, I guessed that I could not expect detailed help from the senator's office; I would be on my own. This also appeared to be a part of the challenge. Could the locals be professional and keep the momentum up on their own without frustration or demagoguery?

My brief exchange with Eller, the indecisive meeting with McCarthy, and the tone of the senator's speech highlighted a series of problems that Paul Wieck summarized:

> This brings me to another of those inevitable "ifs" that kept surfacing in Chicago—Senator McCarthy himself. Although he has been steadily escalating his campaign since the idea of actually running against President Johnson began to take room in his mind, a good many of his troops are, as I say, further down the road than he is. In fact, he still gives the impression from the podium that he is challenging President Johnson to a polite debate, or perhaps, a seminar instead of a no-holds-barred fight for the most powerful office in the world. Despite this, support escalates.
>
> The problem is, Senator McCarthy doesn't seem quite prepared for it. His troops, already deeply committed, came to Chicago to get two things—marching orders and an idea of the funding they will have to carry them out. A couple of delegations went home disappointed because neither were provided. As of this writing, Senator McCarthy still hasn't selected a campaign manager (he's looking over a list of top echelon men, a fund chairman or a press secretary. This, of course, can be remedied easily. However, there is a danger that the nationwide organization put together by Lowenstein and his aides will be allowed to dissipate itself without proper leadership. . . .
>
> (*New Republic*, December 16, 1967, p. 11)

The New Hampshire delegation to the CCD meeting in Chicago was now complete. In the language of 1968, McCarthy's New Hampshire supporters had made their case. We were encouraged by McCarthy's reaction and felt comfortable with him as a candidate. Our uncertainty was that of not being able to proceed when we felt that so much had to be done. We had not been successful in getting McCarthy to say "yes" to New Hampshire. Since McCarthy was delaying the decision, New Hampshire supporters would not be able to issue a definite call to work on their first goal—the reregistration of Republicans prior to the December 12 deadline. All that we could offer was a positive impression that McCarthy might enter. In response to a UPI question, I said, "I think his decision will be made during the trip to New Hampshire this month but his decision will probably not be announced until shortly after his trip is ended." (*Valley News*, December 4, 1967)

Shortly after returning to New Hampshire I wrote the following letter to Senator McCarthy:

> Enclosed are clippings taken from several local New Hampshire newspapers. This is not a complete set but does represent the interest that the prospect of your candidacy in New Hampshire has stimulated. Other New Hampshire

> newspapers have given equal or better coverage to the subject and additional editorials have been written favoring your candidacy.
>
> We sincerely hope that this interest plus, the New Hampshire McCarthy for President Steering Committee's expressed interest in your entering the New Hampshire primary will encourage you to do so. Our visible committee is like an iceberg. In the week since you made public your candidacy we have received numerous direct and indirect indications of broad organizational support. The frequent comment is "When he announces his New Hampshire intentions we will be with him and you can use my name." This includes party leaders, public officials, prospective candidates for 1968 offices extending to Congress, students, and more.
>
> We wait encouragement from you, and a decision shortly after your December 14 and 15 visit to New Hampshire indicating that you will enter this primary. When that happens local committees will be formed in all of the major cities, in each academic community, and an expanded organization will be staffed at the state level. We are a machine ready to run as soon as you flick the switch.
>
> I have been involved in ten years of Democratic campaigns in New Hampshire and have never before seen such dedication, willingness to commit time, energy, and funds, from people who are hardened realists about the political process. We do not intend to lead you astray.
>
> We think we can campaign effectively for you and with you in our state. We feel that the quality of the dissatisfaction with President Johnson is such that a well managed and structured campaign on the issues will meet with qualitative and quantitative success. . . .

Up to this point it had been possible to develop the McCarthy New Hampshire activities through stimulation from Al Lowenstein and Curtis Gans. At the end of the CCD meeting, it was clear that direct operational contact with McCarthy was now essential. Without a national presidential campaign organization or even a campaign manager, communication would have to be established through the Senate staff.

After the regional caucus meeting with McCarthy and the brief conversation with Jerry Eller, I met with Al Lowenstein. I described the meeting we had just had with McCarthy, noting that even in private McCarthy had not given an indication as to how he would decide on New Hampshire. I admitted that my delegation felt a bit discouraged. We were convinced that we had made an irrefutable argument and that McCarthy could not properly make the test of the war policy or develop a solid national candidacy without entering the New Hampshire primary. I asked Lowenstein what the New Hampshire committee's next steps should be. Lowenstein suggested pursuit. Pursuit had apparently won the day with McCarthy, in Lowenstein's mind, when he successfully convinced McCarthy to become a candidate.

Lowenstein suggested that I should follow McCarthy to his next stop, a large gathering on Monday, December 4 at a Great Neck, Long Island, temple where he would be speaking and raising funds. Since I would be returning from Chicago through New York, pursuit might be possible except that I had to return to New

Hampshire to work and to begin the arrangements for the December 14–15 lecture visit. Sandy made the trip to the Great Neck meeting. Again McCarthy was receptive to her review of the New Hampshire delegation's arguments for his entry in New Hampshire, but he remained noncommittal. It was now clear McCarthy's New Hampshire supporters would have to wait until he visited the state later that month.

STATUS OF THE CAMPAIGN: EARLY DECEMBER

The combination of the announcement of McCarthy's national candidacy, the surge of various state activities for McCarthy, and the publicity given to the CCD began to stir the smoldering dissident Democrats fire. The CCD had brought the activities and individuals of the state organizations in contact with the national press. Reports and columns were written about the conference. As an example, Paul Wieck (one of the more perceptive of those writing during the early months of the campaign), writing in the *New Republic*, said:

> In many respects, the Chicago weekend offered a study of the strengths and weaknesses of the McCarthy movement punctuated by a series of "ifs."
>
> "If" the mood of the electorate is really such that a major effort can be made to deny renomination to President Johnson, a good start has been made.
>
> This will be answered early—by the working class Catholics in Massachusetts and, possibly, New Hampshire; by the farmers in Wisconsin and Nebraska; by the Negroes in the ghettos of Milwaukee and Boston; by the white collar workers in the Boston suburbs.
>
> If the answer is "yes, the mood is there," Senator McCarthy will assuredly return to Chicago next summer with a sizable block of delegates in as much as the Democratic Party's structure, outside Chicago and a few machine-oriented states in the Northeast, is, at best, a shell. It wouldn't resist a massive, well-funded effort riding the crest of a voter mood. Thanks, in part, to the way President Johnson has run, or failed to run, the Democratic National Committee.
>
> If that answer is "yes" one can expect top officials in the party to come forth as the months roll by.
>
> Its long-range significance could be to recharge the batteries of a tired party structure and convert it in many areas into a vehicle responsive to the will of the electorate.
>
> If Senator McCarthy accomplishes nothing more than this, he will have made a valuable contribution. Much now rests with him.
>
> Even if all the "ifs" turn out right, he must still throw himself into a hard-hitting, personalized campaign that will arouse the interest of the voters if all this is to be translated into convention delegates.
>
> The beginnings—but just beginnings—were to be found in Chicago the first weekend in December.
>
> (*New Republic*, December 16, 1967)

When uncertain campaign workers read encouraging stories, such as the above, in influential national magazines, and read similar analysis in the columns of their daily newspapers, and also began to see the networks extensively cover early national meetings, confidence was created. When the travelers returned home from Chicago to find editorial support in their local newspapers the recharge was immediate. Under the headline "An Overnight Phenomenon," the *Concord Daily Monitor* wrote the following in its lead editorial on December 5, 1967:

> A person can rise to national prominence in this country in a surprisingly short time.
>
> The latest example is Senator Eugene McCarthy, endorsed as a Democratic candidate for the party's nomination for President by dissenters to the policies of President Johnson. . . .
>
> Accentuating the rapidly spreading awareness of his presence as a national figure is the degree to which it has evoked concern by the Democratic regulars who support the President's presumed ambition to succeed himself.
>
> The loud cries of pain, especially from Senator McIntyre of New Hampshire, and Governor King's studied efforts to dismiss Senator McCarthy as a nonentity, belie their expressed confidence in the President's cause.
>
> Related is the release of Secretary of Defense McNamara at this particular moment and the subtle drawing back of Senator Robert Kennedy from his unconditional endorsement of President Johnson's candidacy.
>
> McCarthy has been boosted by those with whom he dissents to the position of stalking the nomination for Senator Kennedy, whether he planned it that way or not. . . .
>
> Whatever McCarthy does, he is encouraging Democrats to change horses, something a lot of them have been thinking about, as the popularity polls reveal.
>
> He favors free choice by Democrats of their party leadership and he is capable of using inspirational language in support of such freedom.
>
> His personal political future seems to be of no concern to him, which is one reason he has already attracted a respectable following.

On the same day Louis Harris released his latest poll which showed that "Senator Eugene McCarthy would lose a nationwide primary battle against President Johnson for the Democratic nomination for President by almost 4 to 1 if it were held today." (*New York Post,* December 5, 1967)

The survey showed that a national cross section of Democrats preferred Johnson by 63 percent to McCarthy with 17 percent and 20 percent were undecided. The story went on to say:

> McCarthy runs weakest in precisely those regions where his backers have been urging him to confront Mr. Johnson. In the East, including New Hampshire

> and Massachusetts, McCarthy trails by 72 to 11 percent. In the Midwest, including Wisconsin, the Senator has a 67 to 19 percent disadvantage. . . .
>
> Mr. Johnson makes his poorest showing against McCarthy in the South, where LBJ leads by 54 to 20 percent with 26 percent undecided. . . .
>
> It should be pointed out that the results represent the situation at a time of weakness for any challenger—before he has had an opportunity to develop as a serious alternative in the public mind. How much the Senator could gain on the President would depend partly on the kind of campaign he waged, the support he could organize and what happened to the prevailing mood about the Vietnam war, likely to be the principal issue of any such confrontation.
>
> The potential for which McCarthy might aspire was recorded by Senator Robert Kennedy of New York in the Harris survey where he led President Johnson in preference for the Democratic nomination by 52 to 32 percent. The gaps between McCarthy's initial support and Kennedy's demonstrated support are greatest among young people, Negroes, women and Catholics.
>
> If McCarthy could rally support among such voters in New Hampshire, Massachusetts, Wisconsin, Oregon, or California primaries, he might make a contest of a campaign against President Johnson.

From these accounts could be read important implications. The first was that a 17 percent level of favorable recognition was reported five days after an announcement of candidacy which had not been preceded by the usual preannouncement buildup. This indicated an important foundation of support. The sizable undecided percentage was also encouraging, considering a campaign had not begun. Thirdly, the early comparison between Johnson and Kennedy indicated that Johnson's 63 percent against McCarthy was anything but rock hard. In fact the hard commitment to Johnson was only at the 37 percent level. The fourth, and most important implication, was that to strike an early blow McCarthy would have to enter and do well in one of the states where he was perceived by the poll to have a difficult contest. Given the size of the swing vote to Kennedy and percent undecided, such a contest, even in conservative New Hampshire, might be possible for McCarthy. Certainly a campaign could succeed beyond the 10 percent or three thousand to five thousand vote level that Senator McIntyre predicted would be necessary to be considered significant. The problem remained one of convincing McCarthy to run in New Hampshire.

THE DECEMBER 14 AND 15 NEW HAMPSHIRE VISIT

Orchestrating the plans for Senator McCarthy's participation in the Sidore Lecture Series called for major diplomatic experience. Professor Jaffe had his particular ideas as to how the visit should occur. He was completely opposed to any hint of

McCarthy's political potential either in New Hampshire or, for that matter, nationally. Anything that hinted of the trappings of politics, especially meetings with potential New Hampshire supporters and conveniences for the media, was not to be allowed. McCarthy was to perform only within the context of Jaffe's lecture series format. Concerns beyond that format would be restricted.

On the other side, in Manchester, Gene Sidore represented the Sidore family interests in the lecture series. With some perception of the role the family might play in launching a New Hampshire McCarthy effort, he posed a different problem. Sidore would be making the arrangements for the speech, organizing the preceding dinner, distributing the tickets, and considering accommodations for the media.

Conflicting with the visible and hidden agendas of Jaffe and Sidore was the agenda of the McCarthy Steering Committee. We had sought the Sidore invitation to allow McCarthy the chance to speak before a New Hampshire audience, meet with New Hampshire and national reporters in the state, and meet with the New Hampshire McCarthy committee, and give us a chance to pursue arguments supporting his entry in the primary. Such a generally acceptable agenda quickly became most difficult to pursue in the face of Jaffe's obstinacy and the prerogatives being defended by Gene Sidore. In fact it appeared that once McCarthy was delivered to the site of the pre-speech dinner he would slip from the hands of the steering committee for good—fully protected from any hint of any political motive behind his visit.

I was willing to grant all concessions but one to ensure that the visit actually occurred: There had to be a private session in which McCarthy could meet with the members of the steering committee. Sidore supported the idea as long as he could be the host, have it at his home or a site of his choice, control the presence of McCarthy, and even the order of the meeting. Jaffe would not tolerate the intrusion of a political meeting on his plans for the lectures. Neither was sympathetic with the idea that reporters should be allowed special access to either the Manchester lecture or the University of New Hampshire appearance in Durham. Certainly the press was not to be allowed to meet separately with McCarthy. The idea of a press conference was repugnant to both Jaffe and Sidore.

Obviously the private meeting and some opportunity for media contact were essential to the steering committee's efforts to introduce McCarthy to New Hampshire. The privileged few who would join him for dinner and the somewhat larger group that would gather for his speech would not provide the exposure that would stimulate interest in his candidacy. McCarthy had to receive amplification that only the media can provide. Making arrangements in the face of Sidore's and Jaffe's resistance occupied my full attention for most of the ten days prior to McCarthy's scheduled arrival.

Gradually it became possible to separate the two events. Jaffe would control the schedule in Durham, and Sidore, becoming more cooperative, and I would schedule the Manchester/Bedford portion. I was happy to see the two events separate and the emphasis, for political purposes, shift fully to Manchester.

Following a series of telephone calls from New Hampshire reporters recounting their difficulties with Sidore, I discussed with him the media needs and the objectives of the McCarthy visit. He agreed that a press conference should be held prior to any of the scheduled events. At that conference, the full range of media tools and technology would be acceptable. During the dinner, however, the reporters would be excluded, and during the lecture the photographers would not be permitted to circulate in front of the lectern either before or during the McCarthy speech.

Negotiating the meeting of the steering committee with McCarthy following the lecture proved to be more difficult. Sidore felt that as the Manchester host of the lecture he should control all Manchester activities. Jaffe returned to the scene expressing his desire to pick up McCarthy immediately following the lecture and hustle him quickly out of town for the one-hour ride to Durham. I was urging that the meeting be held at Sylvia Chaplain's nearby Bedford home and that the McCarthy Steering Committee should control the invitation list.

Having reached a point of impasse on some issues, it was necessary to involve the senator's office. I assumed that as the preparations for the visit progressed the office would be in rather frequent contact with me and would, shortly before the actual date, send an advance person to review the arrangements. The possibility that an advance person would come was always a key card in my hand as I negotiated with Jaffe and Sidore. What I could not extract that was politically important could be affirmed by the advance person's direct communication. Telephone talks with Jerry Eller and McCarthy's secretary, Jean Stack, assured me that I was to control the visit. The schedule would be cleared with me, and my concerns regarding the in-state press conference and the meeting with the steering committee would be accommodated.

Final arrangements were made and the schedule drafted. A meeting of the steering committee had been held December 6 at the Chaplain home to report on the Chicago CCD meeting and to plan the committee's involvement in the McCarthy visit. Gerry Studds and I arranged to meet the senator in Boston at Logan International Airport and drive him to Bedford for the press conference at the Sheraton-Wayfarer Inn. At no time prior to the senator's arrival did an advance person appear in New Hampshire. Accounts of the McCarthy style and organization began to outline his approach to the campaign. Writing in the *Washington Post,* Walter Pincus said under a headline reading "McCarthy a 1-Man Show":

> A normal candidate making a serious run for the presidential nomination would gather around him a staff of political professionals. McCarthy, however, is far from the normal candidate. With his administrative assistant, Jerome Eller, he has kept personal control over each move. Even now he plans only a skeleton national organization with nearly autonomous state committees operating where he will enter primaries.
>
> The extent of McCarthy's effort, therefore, rests almost entirely on his own shoulders. He talks of the campaigning ahead with an ease and detachment that on the surface, at least, belay the charges that pique, bitterness and ambition led him into the fight. . . .
>
> (*Washington Post,* December 3, 1967)

It was evident to Studds and me that McCarthy had some measure of confidence in our perception of the New Hampshire scene and capability to understand the political role he was playing. At each step in the preplanning from Chicago onward, we were reassured that we were being perceived as experienced and creditable—advantages that were valuable to the process of creating the proper political climate for McCarthy in New Hampshire. McCarthy, however, was not to be the usual candidate, as the *Washington Post* and several other accounts of his early activities indicated.

The Lowenstein-Gans contacts, which had helped us prior to the Chicago gathering, had faded. No campaign organization existed except in the senator's office. All our plans and detailed scheduling for the visit were cleared by telephone and not checked by an on-the-scene advance person. What was obvious to us was the fact McCarthy was reviewing the schedule. He would not be put into situations where he might be politically uncomfortable, but he was not concerned about having a detailed schedule. From this we learned that McCarthy was truly placing his trust in those active at the state level and that he would allow room for events of opportunity in the schedule. At the same time Studds and I sought to perform the scheduling tasks as professionally as possible given the lack of time and the unavailability of a person experienced in advancing Senator McCarthy's political visits.

December 12 newspapers carried the report that McCarthy at last had appointed a campaign manager. The *Valley News* (December 14, 1967) reported:

> Blair Clark, who helped launch the *New Hampshire Sunday News*, in Manchester, N.H., will manage Sen. Eugene McCarthy's campaign for the Democratic presidential nomination.
>
> Clark, 50, of New York City, worked for the *St. Louis Post Dispatch* from 1940 to 1946 before going to Manchester. Afterward, he worked briefly for the *Boston Herald-Traveler*.
>
> Clark joined CBS news in 1953 and became general manager and vice president in 1961.
>
> In 1952 he was public relations director of the national Harriman for President Committee.

Studds and I learned later that Blair Clark, an heir to the Clark Thread fortune, had come to New Hampshire in the middle 1940s to organize a Sunday newspaper. He and Bernard McQuaid ran the *New Hampshire Sunday News* until William Loeb acquired the *Manchester Union Leader*. Loeb offered to buy the *Sunday News* from Clark and McQuaid. If they did not sell, Loeb indicated that he would publish his own Sunday edition of the *Manchester Union Leader*. Given that choice, Clark and McQuaid transferred ownership to the Manchester Leader Corporation. (Cash, op. cit.) McQuaid remained as publisher and Clark left New Hampshire for CBS. He was, therefore, familiar with the political environment of New Hampshire and intimate with the recent publishing history of the *Manchester Union Leader*. We were told that Clark would be joining the senator on his visit and that we would have a chance to meet with him concerning the New Hampshire primary.

To bring McCarthy to New Hampshire Studds and I drove his station wagon to Boston, parked as close to the terminal as we could without risking a parking ticket, and went to the gate where the senator was expected. To our surprise several reporters, a television station's film crew, and several of the curious were assembled. I had released the time of McCarthy's arrival but did not realize that it would provoke any serious attention.

The airplane arrived and approximately a dozen passengers hurriedly got off the plane. Several were recognizable as members of the national press; they were people we had met in Chicago. McCarthy and Eller followed. A walking press conference of sorts was held as McCarthy followed us to the baggage claim area. The camera crew filmed while the television reporter attempted both to interview McCarthy and urge him to permit a longer interview in a room set aside for VIP events at the airport.

While not being discourteous, McCarthy did say that little time was available for an interview. Eller said to us, "Let's keep moving and shake the press." Eller and I moved to the baggage claim area. There before us were Ned Kenworthy of the *New York Times*, Ward Just of the *Washington Post*, Harry Kelley of the AP, and several others. All were looking for bags and rides to New Hampshire. They apparently thought this would be the conventional presidential candidate's visit to the first primary state, and, although it was billed as a nonpolitical lecture, they did not believe that such a thing could exist. If not a press bus to take them to New Hampshire, they at least expected an entourage of automobiles. Not anticipating such press attention from outside New Hampshire and not having been advised to expect a crew of reporters to care for, we had only one car, Studds' Chevelle.

McCarthy said that he had announced that his visit would be nonpolitical in nature, that he would be giving a lecture, and that no decision concerning his involvement in the New Hampshire primary would be announced during this visit. By word and by action McCarthy was making clear what he had said. A nonpolitical lecture visit was to be just that, and the political overtones of service to the national press, which usually accompany preliminary testing in New Hampshire, would not be a part of this visit. The reporters were taking no chances. Many other overt tests of the New Hampshire political waters would have offered chauffeured limousines, free meals, and drink to attract a press entourage of the sort that straggled out of Boston's Logan Airport that December afternoon. With Eller continuing to urge no accommodation to the reporters, we almost ran to Studds' car and headed off to New Hampshire with a reporter's car or two trying to follow.

En route to New Hampshire, Studds and I briefed the senator on the New Hampshire situation, the schedule, persons he would be meeting, and our objectives for the evening. Part one of the schedule, the press conference, went routinely. McCarthy refused to reveal his intentions concerning New Hampshire, responded to a series of questions about Vietnam policy, and concluded with some comments on the national political situation.

The Sidore reception and dinner followed. A number of the prestigious of the New Hampshire liberal political community were present. Following introductions McCarthy responded with understated remarks concerning the national scene and his visit to New Hampshire. He was cordially received and left the group comfortable and assured. This was a feeling that would be sensed widely as the weeks went on.

As the appointed hour for the speech neared the McCarthy committee's preparation began to show. Our desire to have McCarthy exposed to New Hampshire through a Manchester meeting was a risky venture. It is usually hard to attract an audience of any size in New Hampshire, except on a campus, and especially hard on a Thursday evening. To attend, many would have to drive an hour or more each way, and to have an audience of a reasonable size at least half of it would have to be composed of persons willing to spend that amount of travel time.

By eight o'clock, a crowd estimated at fourteen hundred had assembled, an unheard of audience for a New Hampshire political event. A sense of eager anticipation seemed to rise in the convention hall. In the two short weeks since his announcement and the Chicago meetings, McCarthy had sparked sufficient interest to draw a full house in a state known for its casual regard for the politically ambitious, famous, or about to be famous.

Following a brief introduction McCarthy stood before an audience that erupted with applause and rose as a body in a standing reception. As the audience quieted he began his speech. Recalling the event, Gerry Studds reported:

> It was a forum, I believe, on civil rights and Senator McCarthy was to speak on housing as one of the new civil rights. The people who came clearly had come not to hear about housing, nor to hear about civil rights but to see the man who had just declared that he was going to oppose Lyndon Johnson.
>
> It was a golden opportunity and it was a disaster. McCarthy gave a speech which, while substantively fine, was totally non-political and he gave it in his flattest conceivable style.
>
> (Gerry Studds, McCarthy Historical Project Transcript, p. 8)

My reaction to the speech was more positive than Gerry Studds', but I was disappointed to a certain extent as well. While it was an excellent statement of new civil rights activity, McCarthy mentioned the war as such only once during the almost one hour of his address. The people in the audience, on the edge of their seats waiting for him to depart from his announced topic to discuss the Vietnam war, were still left waiting on the edge of their seats when he closed his lecture. For those who listened to the content and reflected at all on its strength, the charge that would later be leveled against McCarthy as being a one-issue candidate would sound ridiculous. But that evening, McCarthy did as he had been invited to do. He delivered a thoughtful lecture, academic in content and tone, without inflammatory rhetoric or intonation. He was interrupted several times by courteous applause when he outlined the essence of his new civil rights:

> In addition to those traditional and constitutionally guaranteed legal civil rights, we must move on to establish a whole new set of civil rights which we consider to be the rights of every American citizen. First among these

> must be the right to a decent job which returns him satisfaction as an intelligent and creative person, and also an income with which he can support his family in dignity and in decency. This is not a simple declaration of a desirable objective, such as it was in 1946 when we passed the full-employment act, but rather an objective statement which must be realized within a period of two or three years. In order to secure it in the first instance, we must move on the question of income. The federal government must proceed to determine what a minimum income is and attempt to insure it for all Americans.
>
> The second new citizen's right which we must pursue is the right to adequate health care without regard to income or without regard to race or without regard to habitation. This is a right which is not specifically guaranteed under the Constitution, but is very clearly implied in the concept of equality and in the search for happiness which is basic to the whole American way of life. To secure this right, we must have a federally subsidized insurance program so that no citizen will be deprived of health care because of a lack of funds, because of income, or because of a lack of facilities. . . .
>
> Third, every American must now be accorded the right not simply to equal education or a kind of average education, but to that kind of education and that amount of education which is necessary to develop his full potential. This for the most talented among us, whose gifts, of course, must be brought to serve the whole society, but also for those of average gift, and those who are most handicapped and least gifted, but who have the potential to come to some knowledge of the truth no matter how limited that knowledge may be. In order to secure this right, we must have a massive program to upgrade the education of our adults who have been trapped in the poverty syndrome. . . .
>
> The final new citizen's right which I will speak of to you tonight, is the right to a decent house—not a house in isolation, not a house in a ghetto, but a house in a neighborhood which is part of a community which must be a part of the United States of America.
>
> (McCarthy, op. cit., pp. 303–305)

It was good, it was strong, it was needed, but it was not what most troubled those assembled. McCarthy closed without stirring his audience. Many were surprised that the speech had ended; there was a moment of silence then applause, some standing, and McCarthy left the podium and the hall. Studds and I joined him as he returned to his room. Although surprised that he had not attempted to move his audience with some words on the Vietnam War, I was impressed with the content of his lecture. I also had been closer to the conditions set for the event by the Sidore Series invitation than had been Studds or others on the steering committee.

It was a time for a candidate who could get people to listen. Each candidate has a style and is unique. McCarthy was not John Kennedy nor Hubert Humphrey nor Lyndon Johnson. He was a man with his view of the way he would create his campaign and project his own personality. In each candidate there are assets and liabilities. McCarthy's New Hampshire supporters would all have to learn what these were and how to use McCarthy's personal qualities as they emerged.

As I met McCarthy as he was leaving the podium, I congratulated him on the speech, indicating that I felt McCarthy had stated important issues that could well be lost in a candidacy that was being labeled as devoted to just one issue. My comments were restrained since I too felt a measure of disappointment in that McCarthy had not taken advantage of the gathering to build enthusiasm for his candidacy in New Hampshire. If a conclusion were possible from McCarthy's delivery, it was that McCarthy still was not committed to being a candidate in a New Hampshire run. In fact some reacted by saying that his approach to the audience was one designed to "turn off" interest so that an announcement made later that he would not enter would not be greeted with great disappointment.

Gerry Studds recalled:

> I remember I took the senator immediately from the podium after he finished, back to his room in the motel. And I was trying to think of something appropriate to say under the circumstances. And he put his arm around me and said, "I think we really got them that time. I could feel it." I said to myself, Oh, my God. He thought that he really had them in the palm of his hands.
>
> We may have overdone or the University of New Hampshire officials may have overdone their emphasis to him initially that it was to be a non-political speech. It certainly was.

The irony of the speech was that on April 11, 1968, in response to charges that McCarthy was a one-issue candidate and not concerned about urban and racial issues, he gave almost exactly the same speech before a Boston University audience. With major advanced billing as an important statement of McCarthy's civil rights position, McCarthy delivered the Manchester speech to an enthusiastic audience and received wide national coverage for both its content and delivery.

When final arrangements had been made for McCarthy's visit, the members of the steering committee were notified that there would be a meeting following the speech at the Chaplain's home. Although this was to be a no-press, steering committee-only private meeting with McCarthy, I did suggest to members of the steering committee that they invite persons from their communities who would be likely to support McCarthy. To the last moment, Jaffe resisted the plans for the meeting. He conceded grudgingly only because McCarthy agreed to meet with the steering committee. Jaffe's conditions were that the meeting be short, composed of the steering committee members alone, and with no reporters in attendance. Only on the size of the meeting did I deliberately violate the agreement. The time would be short, and no reporters would be permitted since a frank and open exchange was the objective. The gathering, however, would be considerably larger than Jaffe would have liked.

THE MEETING

One of the first persons McCarthy met as he came through the door was Mrs. Macy Morse, a campaign experienced Nashua Democrat—a mother of thirteen children—several of whom were in the military service at the time. Petite, attractive, and always sparkling, Macy startled McCarthy by asking, "How's your health? Well you know if you enter the New Hampshire primary you will have to work very hard." In a direct way Macy summed up the sentiment of the assembled. His audience was disappointed, even bored, by his speech. As Barbara Underwood recounted, "McCarthy looked to them [his audience] like a gray, tired, old college professor." But when he entered the Chaplain home she wrote, "He seemed taller and more attractive in the smaller gathering. He had dignity and a certain amount of charm. He really did look and act like someone who could be president."

I took several minutes to make sure that McCarthy was introduced to everyone. Some of the disappointment began to fade. As political people, coming to what they perceived as a political event and expecting a statement of the McCarthy campaign credo, they could not quite believe what had happened. He had given them food for thought when they expected a battle plan or at least a sketch of why they should join the march. Those few who had caught the meaning of his words were taken by them, but the delivery and the lack of fire left all with a sense of a nonhappening.

As he entered the Chaplain living room, McCarthy said, "What is this? It looks like a government in exile." His remark both reassured and solidified with a note of serious humor that set the tone for the next hour. I guided McCarthy to a comfortable chair at the end of the room. In front of him the fifty to sixty persons found chairs, sat on the rug, or leaned on a piano. It was crowded, but comfortable enough. Most members of the steering committee and those who wanted to say something stood back or peered over shoulders near the entrance.

I introduced McCarthy by saying, "Tonight we have had a chance to hear you speak, now we would like to tell you what we see are your chances in New Hampshire and what we would like to do for you in this primary."

One of the first persons I asked to speak was Dennis Sullivan, recently elected as mayor of the city of Nashua. A maverick Democrat who had taken a leave from his job as a postal clerk to run for mayor, Sullivan professed to reflect the view of the New Hampshire workers. Sullivan was also the senior elected official in the room.

Although he had not been involved in the McCarthy activity, he was attracted to the meeting by his opposition to the Johnson administration and the renomination endorsement of the Democratic State Committee. His comments about the impact of a possible New Hampshire McCarthy effort were disjointed and confusing. He was clear, however, in his view that it was desirable to confront the Democratic Party organization of the state. He concluded by saying that he did not want to give McCarthy a bum steer. He did not think McCarthy's antiwar position would be well received in New Hampshire and advised him not to stake too much on a New Hampshire race. Issues of intraparty fair play, and adverse reactions to the

Johnson administration and New Hampshire Democratic Party heavy-handedness, he felt, were more likely to produce results.

Others, like David Underwood of Concord; John Holland of Bedford/ Manchester; Paul McEachern, deputy mayor of Portsmouth; Jean Wallin, Nashua state representative; Joseph Welton, Nashua Democratic Party chair; and Ron O'Callaghan, Democratic Party activist of Laconia, were basically positive toward the prospects of a live candidacy and about the organizations they could generate for such a candidacy in their communities. John Wiseman, a Keene State College history professor, recounted the independent organizing efforts that were already well under way in his city.

The most startling comments of the evening came from John Teague, a member of a prominent New Hampshire Republican family. As Barbara Underwood recalled in her account, there were few students at the meeting and only one spoke. Teague, an Amherst College senior, head of the Amherst College McCarthy for President group, had become a Democrat much to the surprise of his conservative Republican father. "Students," he said, "are tired of protests. They are tired of sit-ins and women pushing baby carriages in protest marches . . . they are tired of burning their draft cards, and all of the usual kinds of war protests. We want to push the political system just as hard as it can be pushed to see if we can accomplish anything."

He concluded by urging Senator McCarthy to be a serious candidate for the presidency and to say that he is running for president. "If this happens and young people get the message clearly, then thousands will join the campaign." With these words, Teague had captured the mood of the evening. Perhaps making McCarthy, as the personification of the war issue, the focal point of protest would not be enough. McCarthy had to become a serious candidate for the presidency. If he entered the New Hampshire primary he would have to understand that such a condition would be the consequence.

Macy Morse, who had asked McCarthy about his health when he arrived, now spoke more personally. As the mother of eleven sons, two of whom had served in Vietnam, she recounted how disturbed her boys were with what was going on over there and how concerned she was about the fate ahead for others of her family if the war continued. She then renewed her description of New Hampshire campaigning and urged McCarthy to run in New Hampshire, and, more importantly, to run hard.

A comment from a Republican who was interested in McCarthy was that he would support McCarthy if McCarthy ran in New Hampshire, and he expected that many other Republicans would do the same. In reply the senator said, "Yes, at this point there is no indication that the Republican Party will come up with anyone better than the present administration.

"My purpose in announcing my candidacy in November was threefold. First, I want to challenge the administration's course in Vietnam and to bring about a public debate or discourse on the issue. Secondly, I want to bring about a change in the present administration. And third, I want to be elected president of the United States."

With the exception of Mayor Sullivan's early comments, the tone of the remarks had been serious, positive, and encouraging. Little had been glossed over.

McCarthy had to know from the comments that New Hampshire would be tough but that he could count on the support of a considerable group of experienced workers. With this as background, I felt safe in turning to our steering committee's skeptic, Peter Freedman.

Freedman began by telling McCarthy that he didn't think McCarthy would do well among the blue-collar New Hampshire workers. He recounted conversations he had had during the past weeks with Manchester Democratic mill workers who thought that McCarthy meant Joe McCarthy and that the best solution to the Vietnam situation would be to "bomb it off the face of the earth."

McCarthy responded by saying, "No, I don't imagine I will do well with the labor vote. I don't think I will do well with them in Minnesota either, but I don't think it will be much of a problem." But in the final analysis, if he did get the Democratic nomination, the labor vote would go either to him or George Wallace, rather than to the Republican candidate. McCarthy said he would not consider running as a third-party candidate.

Freedman went on with his account of the informal polls he had taken among his workers in the Democratic cities of Manchester and Claremont. Both samplings showed that his workers held "hawk" positions on the war. He concluded with the question, "Senator, don't you think you should have a poll before deciding whether to enter the New Hampshire Primary?" McCarthy reflected a moment, then said, "No, I don't think so; I think a poll would be very discouraging." This comment seemed to encapsulate the nature of his effort and unified the gathering's commitment to him in one quite prophetic response.

The senator then asked several questions about when a decision on entering New Hampshire would have to be made. David Roberts, Dartmouth College professor and member of the Draft Robert Kennedy Committee, said that an organizational meeting would be held on December 28 and that that would be the final date before the organization would be fully committed. Roberts added he felt that organizing two conflicting efforts to provide an alternative to President Johnson could not work. In his mind it was clear that if McCarthy entered the New Hampshire primary the Draft RFK movement would shift to the McCarthy candidacy.

In response to a question concerning New Hampshire specifically, McCarthy said, "You know the New Hampshire electorate is known to be somewhat mischievous in nature. I don't really know how we would do here. My time is very much committed to the Wisconsin campaign, and I planned to make a trip to the Far East stopping over in Saigon and Japan. I will have to let you know later."

I was about to bring the session to a close when McCarthy said that he greatly appreciated the meeting and that it had given him a great deal to consider. He then said, "I had better leave before I do something rash." The meeting ended. McCarthy talked casually while the car was summoned.

Commenting on the meeting in her account, Barbara Underwood wrote, "It is one thing to be a critic of the president from the Senate Foreign Relations Committee; it is another to suggest that you might be a better substitute. And yet,

McCarthy seemed of presidential stature there in the living room at Bedford, that is if his 'mission impossible' could ever be completed."

Studds and I thought that the meeting had gone exceptionally well. The right tone had been maintained. A frank discussion of New Hampshire, its political problems and potential, had been accomplished in a way that showed McCarthy the sincerity of those who would be the activists. All of the hard questions concerning McCarthy himself as a candidate, and New Hampshire as a test of his candidacy, had been raised. McCarthy's responses were thoughtful, perceptive, and reassuring, not concerning his decision as to whether he would enter New Hampshire, but his competence as a candidate. The negative feelings left by the earlier lecture had been turned around by his responses and his presence. Studds and I were genuinely proud of our efforts and those of our steering committee associates, but were we closer to a positive decision from McCarthy about New Hampshire?

Although we felt that our portion of the December 14–15 visit was now over, it suddenly occurred to us to follow McCarthy to Durham that next day. We felt we should at least maintain contact with McCarthy, if not some measure of responsibility for him, until he was safely out of Erwin Jaffe's hands and away from New Hampshire.

Our intuition was correct. Leaving Concord early the next morning, we arrived in Durham in time to hear most of the panel presentations organized by Jaffe. It was an uncomfortable forum for a person like McCarthy, who sought to defuse emotional intensity and redirect energy toward available political channels. McCarthy managed to survive assaults from the more radical members of the panel on both the political process and on McCarthy himself for indulging in such two-faced hypocrisy as actually running for political office. Shortly after we arrived, Jerry Eller found us, much to his relief. Eller wanted to extract McCarthy from the panel and from Durham as quickly as possible before McCarthy suffered serious political damage.

David Wilson, a columnist for the *Boston Globe* and producer of a Massachusetts issues program for the *Globe*'s television station, had arranged with Eller for McCarthy to appear on the program prior to his early afternoon departure. With that commitment in hand, it was possible to organize McCarthy's exit.

To our surprise, Studds and I found that Jaffe had made no plans to provide transportation for McCarthy to Boston. Seeing our chance, we offered our service—an offer that Eller quickly accepted.

The press that had been following McCarthy the previous day had continued to pursue him in Durham. The critical question about McCarthy and New Hampshire was asked repeatedly but the answer remained noncommittal. Studds and I were optimistic that the answer would be "yes," especially after the meeting of the previous evening. But McCarthy had not given a hint to anyone. Jerry Eller had a list of reporters' names who wanted exclusive interviews with McCarthy. Time for such interviews was always scarce but especially so since McCarthy's announcement. Eller picked David Halberstam, then writing for *Harper's* magazine, to ride with them to Boston.

With McCarthy now on the road to Boston, away from Jaffe and moderately unscarred, Halberstam began questioning him about the reasons for his candidacy, his perspective on Vietnam, and related foreign policy and political issues. Jerry Eller wedged between Studds and me in the front seat. McCarthy and Halberstam were in the back seat and a St. Paul's School student of Studd's, Dan Barney, was stashed in the cargo space of Studds' station wagon.

Near the end of the one-hour drive to Boston, Halberstam began a series of questions on the primary states that ended with one on whether McCarthy would enter the New Hampshire primary. To this point the interview had been interesting but not particularly revealing. Road noise made hearing all of the exchanges difficult but with this question both Studds and I perked up. McCarthy's response was, "I'm not inclined to enter at this point." I was disappointed but not surprised. I did not expect that McCarthy would tell a reporter something he had not confided to those who would shepherd his fortunes in New Hampshire. It also occurred to me that this was the candidate speaking. What would the absent manager, Blair Clark, have to say? With this in mind, I leaned over to Jerry Eller and asked what I should do to make the case for McCarthy's entry into the New Hampshire primary to Blair Clark. Eller said I should get in touch with Clark and outline the rationale for a McCarthy New Hampshire candidacy to Clark as soon as possible. (Blair Clark did not come to New Hampshire with McCarthy as planned. He had made a quick trip to California to quiet a feud that was developing there between several organizations committed to McCarthy's candidacy.)

The WGBH-TV interview was excellent, and McCarthy did not repeat his comment to Halberstam about New Hampshire. For the purpose of the taping, at least, McCarthy remained uncommitted with respect to New Hampshire. A police escort was waiting for the trip from the television station to the airport. After three blocks, the police car stopped, a *Globe* reporter hopped out saying that he had forgotten his bag at WGBH and the police car was taking him back. Studds would have to get McCarthy to the airport on his own. Studds made some comment about the power of the press while I was trying to figure out the quickest route to the airport. In the rush, courtesies were exchanged and McCarthy thanked us for our efforts and said that he would be in touch with us soon.

As we left Logan International Airport we realized that the visit was over and we had not received the answer or even a hint of a positive answer, to the question they had been pressing since Chicago. We were tired, depressed, and confused. Had we made a mistake somewhere that put McCarthy off? Had the Chaplain meeting been too open and direct? Was there some other argument that we had missed or were not aware of that was influencing McCarthy's thinking about New Hampshire? We reviewed each question and found that those parts of the visit we had controlled had gone well.

In our review of the previous two days, there was one point that seemed to have troubled McCarthy. He seemed concerned about the amount of time he would have to spend in New Hampshire to have an impact. The theme of the Chaplain meeting had been that candidates have to work hard to succeed in New Hampshire. Originally Studds and I had advised that twenty-five days be set aside for New Hampshire campaigning.

We concluded that perhaps this was the issue that might be putting McCarthy off. Twenty-five days was a lot of time to invest in a long-shot primary when better options appeared in Wisconsin and even in the Massachusetts primary in late April. Could we shorten the amount of campaign time that would be necessary, especially in view of the attention McCarthy was gaining via the media in the weeks since his announcement? We agreed that this had to be the approach. New Hampshire had to be shoehorned into the McCarthy campaign schedule. We thought that effective scheduling that reduced the time required to campaign and increased the effectiveness of that time might reopen serious consideration of New Hampshire for McCarthy.

NEW HAMPSHIRE REACTIONS TO THE VISIT

Studds and I realized that McCarthy had been less than a stunning success in the public sessions of his visit. The Chaplain meeting had offset that feeling to a considerable degree for those who had attended, but that was only a small percentage of those who had come to the Bedford lecture or to the Durham colloquium. The feedback from the Bedford lecture was especially discouraging. Ward Just wrote of the McCarthy visit in the *Washington Post* (December 17, 1967) under the headline "McCarthy's Non-Campaign in N.H.":

> Only once did he come alive, and that was bantering with reporters after the exchange with Strickland. Somebody mentioned an article in the *New York Times* that obliquely compared him to Sir Thomas More, the great anti-establishment Englishman who is one of McCarthy's personal heroes. "That's you all right," said one of the reporters. "Yeah," said McCarthy, "I'm a stalking horse for Sir Thomas More."
>
> "They never heard of More in Manchester," said one of the reporters laughing.
>
> "I'll split the vote," said McCarthy.

Ned Kenworthy's *New York Times*' (December 18, 1967) story was headlined, "Even Backers Found His Performance on New Hampshire Trip 'Half-Hearted'." He wrote:

> "The group backing McCarthy is a pretty responsible group, and they feel they have a chance in New Hampshire," a prominent Democrat here (Keene), who is an ardent supporter of President Johnson, said today.
>
> "However," he added, "if McCarthy comes into the New Hampshire primary on a half-hearted basis, he better stay home. . . ."
>
> When he departed, everyone, including his backers seemed a little puzzled and disappointed, precisely because his whole performance struck them as "half-hearted."

The most stinging blow came in an editorial written in the friendly *Portsmouth Herald*.

> Spoken reaction to the New Hampshire appearance of Senator Eugene McCarthy last week indicated that the Minnesota Democrat came closer to laying an egg than lighting a fire as far as his quest for presidential support is concerned.
>
> "Strictly lackluster" is the prevailing opinion of McCarthy's efforts during two speaking engagements in the Granite State.
>
> While it is true that certain contextual limits on McCarthy's speeches kept him away from politics and within the realm of 'academic interest', this didn't mean that he had to be so inexpressive in his delivery.
>
> The impression he left behind him was overwhelmingly negative, causing many of his embarrassed partisans to wonder if they hadn't been premature in placing their faith in them.
>
> It's not that they feel McCarthy is leading a wrong cause but that he may prove the wrong leader of a right cause, for where causes are concerned, effective leadership must be at least zestful.
>
> The McCarthy mien in New Hampshire seemed almost a repudiation of that idea. The Senator was not only dull and uninteresting, his attitude of imperturbability showed through as pure want of enthusiasm for his own purpose. . . .
>
> The amount of excitement a politician generates is no way to measure his worth, yet practicality commands that he try to arouse the voters to his own sense of earnestness in appealing for their support. McCarthy failed to achieve even that modest level of expectation.

Fortunately December 15 was followed by the Christmas holidays. At another time during the year, the disappointments of the McCarthy visit might have been the subject of considerable public and press chewing, but in the holiday season, politics, no matter how urgent, receded behind a nostalgic veil of evergreen, holly, mistletoe, and festivity.

Ironically one who did get caught up in the spirit of critique was Professor Erwin Jaffe. As a courtesy gesture I wrote to him December 19:

> We want to thank you for your cooperation and forbearance during Senator McCarthy's participation in the Sidore Lecture Series. We recognize that his participation was quite different, in fact, from that of the others simply in terms of the attention which he commands just by stepping across the New Hampshire border.
>
> From talking with persons who attended the series, the highlight was the Wednesday night session with Reverend Groppi, Mayor Hatcher and William Strickland. . . .
>
> Considering the nature and complexities of a visit by a unique national political figure, we were pleased that the program proceeded without conflict

or major incident. The only unhappiness that we all felt was the Friday morning coffee reception which was swamped by the press before the students had a chance to walk from the Field House. [An incident that especially bothered Jaffe but was the result of his not preparing opportunities for the press to question the panelists including those other than McCarthy.]

Once again we wish to thank you and the Sidore Committee for the evening time and the congeniality with which Senator McCarthy and the press corps were accommodated. I hope the next visit by Senator will be political and less laconic.

On December 30, Jaffe replied:

Thank you for your letter of December 19.

I am, of course, pleased with the results of the three days of discussion. Three of our speakers gave themselves fully to the program, and the effects were startling, and hopefully, permanent. The fourth visitor, Senator McCarthy, was indeed "different." His performance was dismal, uninspired, lackluster and unimaginative. And his office was responsible for every kind of foul-up, including: (1) inviting the cameramen to film the Senator in an alleged "dialogue with students" during the coffee "hour," in spite of my repeated efforts to reserve the few moments for private meetings with students, and (2) walking out on the TV interview because of a nine-minute delay (in fact, in my presence earlier that morning the decision had already been made to escape as quickly as possible so that the short delay was a mere pretext). No, the Senator neither performed as a candidate nor a president. Indeed, what his purposes were in coming here is beyond my poor capacity to guess.

I'm sorry for the heated words. I still think your interventions were unfortunate and destructive of the purposes of what is a very precious UNH asset, the Sidore series. Never again will I permit any candidate and his associates to use our good offices for their purposes.

However, all of that is unimportant. What is important is that people like you and Sandy and your associates—people like myself looking for some virtue in a sadly degenerated political system—waste their time and talents on the likes of Eugene McCarthy. We are desperately in need of leadership and integrity; in good faith, you have worked hard for someone who turns out to be another misguided and unknowing hypocrite who cannot possibly transcend the system that produced him. And the question for all of us is "what are we going to do now?"

Fortunately the introductory phase of the steering committee on behalf of Senator McCarthy was finished. Studds and I felt that in spite of Jaffe's comments we had accomplished the major objectives of the visit. McCarthy had been favorably impressed by the effort and the sincerity of those who had come to meet him. Some would be momentarily put off by McCarthy's style, but upon reflection we found that all wished to renew the pressure to make sure that McCarthy did enter the New Hampshire primary. We now wanted the chance to test our own political acumen.

As a footnote, Jaffe did eventually shed his disillusionment and radical critique enough to become involved in the McCarthy campaign. He would be followed by others of a like mind back into the political process that they had viewed with such skepticism a short while earlier.

Hearing the rumblings of disappointment coming from those who attended McCarthy's Wayfarer lecture along with the reports of the press, the Citizens for Johnson leader saw the chance to attack. Until then they had been on the defensive trying to explain their policy of preprimary endorsement and fending off Eugene Daniell's charges of conspiracy. They had failed to attract much press attention for the growing list of prominent Democratic leaders who were endorsing Johnson's renomination. To improve their public relations they began to comment on the lack of success, in their view, of McCarthy's visit to New Hampshire.

Of the Johnson Committee's tactic, Kenworthy wrote in the *New York Times* (December 17, 1967):

> Democratic leaders here are not afraid that Senator Eugene J. McCarthy will decide to enter the New Hampshire Presidential Primary on March 12. They are daring him to enter.
>
> In the hope that the Minnesota Democrat will take their dare, the party leaders, with President Johnson's blessing, are hard at work on a write-in campaign for the President.
>
> In issuing their challenge, the leaders take the same high ground staked out by Senator McCarthy in justification of his own challenge to the President—that the issue of the Administration's Vietnam Policy should be "personalized" and fought out within the party in the Presidential primaries.
>
> "I believe McCarthy is coming in," Bernard Boutin, State committeeman and campaign director of the New Hampshire Citizens for Johnson, today. "It is logical for him to come in. He knows that if he has a chance to make a dent on the President's policies, he must make it here."
>
> Mr. Boutin makes plain that there are very good practical reasons behind the desire of Democratic leaders to have Mr. McCarthy add New Hampshire to the five other primaries he plans to enter.
>
> "My opinion is that the President has a hell of a lot of support in this state," Mr. Boutin said. "The average age is high. They (the older citizens) need help for medicine. And New Hampshire is hawkish state. It has always been conservative. Any time there's been a national crisis, they (New Hampshire men) beat their breasts and say, 'We're with it'."
>
> Furthermore, Mr. Boutin says, whatever divisions there may be within the party organization do not center on Vietnam.
>
> "The leaders of the party are completely in back of the President," he said. "Twenty-five city and town (Democratic) committees have endorsed the President's policy."

> And Mr. Boutin finds "symbolic" of the President's strength a recent resolution passed unanimously by the 11 Democratic and 3 Republican alderman of Manchester endorsing the Administration's Vietnam policy.

The holiday period didn't help Boutin in his efforts to marshal the already committed leadership of the Democratic Party. The "dare" was noted by Studds and me as an interesting tactic, but of greater consequence was the fact the Johnson campaign leadership recognized Senator McCarthy's presence and offered to engage with him in political combat in New Hampshire. Boutin, and in all probability the White House, felt sufficiently confident of the New Hampshire outcome to challenge McCarthy to his certain political death in safe pro-Johnson New Hampshire turf. If McCarthy were foolish enough to enter under those circumstances, then they would eliminate him before Wisconsin. If he did not enter, they could charge him with avoiding the first and toughest test of his candidacy and the issues it represented.

Studds and I found a strategy evolving that could be used in two ways. The fact that the Johnson committee chair had "dared" McCarthy to enter further indicated the extent of their overconfidence with respect to both their candidate and the political ethos of New Hampshire.

The second aspect of the strategy meant that the "dare" required the Johnson committee to recognize the results of the primary. They could not escape the result by depreciating a possible McCarthy success because they had to get voters to write in Johnson's name. Tied to this was the fact that there was now a direct confrontation in the making, and we knew this would appeal to Senator McCarthy's competitive spirit.

In retrospect, it is conceivable that if McCarthy had stormed New Hampshire on December 14 and 15, and had ignited a political fire through rhetoric and/or charisma, the Johnson managers might have retreated to a more cautious position, refused the challenge to engage with McCarthy, and scaled down their campaign on behalf of Lyndon Johnson. Such a shift in the Johnson campaign strategy could have had at least one effect on the McCarthy campaign. McCarthy might well have not entered the New Hampshire primary at all but concentrated his effort in those states where the confrontation with Johnson was more direct.

THE STRATEGY AND SCHEDULE PROPOSED TO MCCARTHY

As agreed, Studds and I pulled together a concise statement of the reasons for entering the New Hampshire primary together with a detailed schedule of the time that Senator McCarthy would need to campaign. Studds left Concord for his parents' Cohasset, Massachusetts, home shortly after McCarthy's departure from New Hampshire. Though not optimistic, Studds promised me to give our effort to convince McCarthy one more try. Studds would pull together in a concise memorandum the arguments we had made to McCarthy and attach the detailed schedule. I, in the meantime, attempted to make telephone contact with Blair Clark to discuss our concerns and gain some sense of whether McCarthy was still considering a New Hampshire campaign.

To make contact with Clark was difficult. No campaign headquarters had been established nor were there campaign telephones. Clark was traveling extensively to meet with campaign committees in the states where McCarthy had said he would campaign and spending the remainder of his time between his New York City apartment and the senator's Washington office. I left messages in all conceivable places hoping Clark would return a call or that with luck I might catch him at one spot or the other. Failing in these attempts, I then placed all of our hope in the arguments of the memorandum that Studds was drafting.

The memo and the schedule titled, "Senator McCarthy and The New Hampshire Primary" were mailed to Senator McCarthy December 22 with the following cover letter. A copy of the memo and the letter were also addressed to Blair Clark in care of the senator's office. The letter read:

> Dear Senator McCarthy:
>
> Since your recent visit to New Hampshire Gerry Studds and I have discussed the possibility of your campaign in New Hampshire and have attempted to summarize the time requirement and the mechanism of such a campaign.
>
> Gerry is responsible for the statistical work enclosed and for drafting the analyzed schedule. We think that this schedule coupled with strong internal and external media support, direct mail, and telephone canvass will produce the desired result. The organization is ready to go and prepared to program each of the campaign elements.
>
> Since the enclosed was prepared, the New Hampshire Attorney General ruled that permission must be secured from a candidate before funds may be solicited or expended in a Presidential Primary in his behalf. This ruling effectively eliminated the write-in campaign planned by the LBJ committee. They will not be able to expend funds to stimulate the write-in and will either have to shift to a "stand-up" candidate or concentrate on the delegate section of the Primary ballot.
>
> We hope the enclosed reaches you in time to assist you in forming your campaign strategy and that you will enter the New Hampshire primary with the intention of winning. Please be in touch with us if there are questions on the enclosed. We are willing to meet with you and your staff at any time to discuss your potential effort in New Hampshire.
>
> Sincerely,
> David C. Hoeh, Temporary Chairman,
> McCarthy for President Steering Committee

(At this stage Studds and I were operating on the assumption that the attorney general's opinion would apply to the Johnson committee. The full meaning of the Johnson renomination endorsement by the Democratic State Committee was not clear at the time of the letter to McCarthy but was just beginning to emerge through the probing of Eugene Daniell on behalf of his Draft RFK Committee. Our position at that point was to keep the Johnson forces on the defensive while not being particularly concerned about the nature of the actual confrontation. The letter reflects this early naiveté on our part.)

Our memorandum read:

Senator McCarthy and the New Hampshire Primary

The following factors (listed in no particular order of priority) ought to be given consideration:

• We already have the nucleus of an experienced, broadly representative, and committed organization—several of whom are prepared to take partial leaves of absence in order to give the N.H. campaign professional guidance. [If McCarthy entered, Gerry Studds hoped to receive a partial leave from St. Paul's School to manage the effort. Senator McCarthy wrote making such a request of the Headmaster but it was denied.]

• We already have done statistical research to a degree without precedent in this state. We have pinpointed the Democratic primary vote with considerable precision, both statewide and by congressional district.

•We have already acquired the voting lists for the entire state (all registrants: Democratic, Unaffiliated and Republican). (Prof. Robert Craig had secured most of these lists for public opinion surveying proposes. He was willing to make lists available to anyone who asked for them. The McCarthy campaign was the only organization to make such a request.)

• We are encouraged about the possibility of a write-in effort for Senator McCarthy on the Republican ballot (particularly given the number of Republicans who were willing to change their registration this month even though Senator McCarthy was not yet a candidate in New Hampshire).

• We envision a massive mailing effort—of the quality and extent of the Lodge effort in 1964—to all registered Democrats and Independents.

• We have access to almost unlimited volunteer help which we foresee utilizing for a) addressing and stuffing envelopes b) door-to-door canvassing, and c) telephone canvassing.

• Campaigning in Massachusetts and New Hampshire is, in many ways, a single "package"—there is a great overlap of radio, TV and newspaper coverage. Activity in one state is covered in great detail in the other.

• Sen. McCarthy's candidacy in New Hampshire would lead to the almost total dissolution of the RFK "movement" here, most of whose Executive Committee have already indicated a desire to work for McCarthy.

• Every minute spent in New Hampshire in January, February and March will bring massive, national exposure for Sen. McCarthy; New

Hampshire is the principal focus of the national media during this period; the troops in Wisconsin, Massachusetts, California, Oregon, etc. will read of, see, and hear the Senator every day he spends in New Hampshire.

• The stated aims of the Senator's national candidacy lead him logically to New Hampshire—There are many people here, as in every other state, who want, and need, someone for whom they can work and vote.

• Many officials of the New Hampshire Democratic Party have already publicly endorsed Senator McCarthy and hailed his courage. What happens to them if he bypasses New Hampshire.

• An effective campaign here is relatively inexpensive—$50,000 would sustain a major statewide effort of the magnitude and quality we envision.

• There is nothing to be lost—and a great deal to be gained—by coming into New Hampshire:

a) Given the general impression that this is a "hawkish" state and a "conservative" state—plus Senator McIntyre's extraordinary prediction that McCarthy would get 3,000-5,000 votes, anything better than that can be hailed as a stunning performance (and we can do considerably better than that).

b) The Senator would reaffirm the seriousness of his national candidacy by his willingness to enter against odds (e.g., JFK in W. Va.).

c) A victory here—which we think we ought to shoot for—and which seems to us far more within the realm of possibility than it did a month ago—would have major national repercussions.

• There has been a clear, panic reaction to the threat of McCarthy's candidacy among the Party hierarchy in this state—and with real reason. Many prominent Democrats have quietly refused to serve on the LBJ Committee.

• If we are to move on the Senator's behalf, we must get going yesterday, e.g., in the city of Keene, a McCarthy committee, with 90 adult volunteers, has already located office space for headquarters and is awaiting word from us to install phones and begin operations. Similar efforts throughout the state need rapid encouragement.

Finally, New Hampshire Democrats—just as Democrats everywhere else—are deeply concerned about the present leadership of their party and their country—and they want an opportunity to express that concern.
(Signed)
David Hoeh
Gerry Studds
for the N.H. McCarthy for President Steering Committee

The memorandum of arguments was followed by a document entitled, "12 Day Schedule—Explanation" which read:

> The percentage figures for each town represent the average percentage of that town's vote in the last three Democratic primaries (1960, 1964, 1966)—computed both as a percentage of the total, statewide vote and as a percentage of the vote in its congressional district.
>
> These towns, then represent over three quarters of the total Democratic primary turnout (N.B.: It is far less dispersed than is the Republican vote.)—and they include every single daily paper (9) and three major weeklies in the state.

The full schedule considered the time needed (twelve days), the places to be visited either by name or by cluster of names, the importance of each place or cluster by the percentage that cluster represented of the statewide primary vote, and percentage of the respective congressional district within which the cluster was located. The schedule, as developed, would cover areas of the state that contained 76.8 percent of the statewide Democratic primary vote, 79.7 percent of the vote in the more compact lst Congressional District, and 72.4 percent of the vote in the geographically larger 2nd Congressional District. With proper scheduling, advance work, and good local organization supported by well-managed statewide activities, Studds and I thought the schedule would provide Senator McCarthy with enough exposure to draw a meaningful vote. With the exception of the Berlin cluster, all of the others either contained a daily newspaper or were served by one nearby. The 20 percent of the statewide vote not contained in the cities and towns included in their list were scattered widely in the smaller towns of the state.

Reflecting later on the schedule and memorandum, Studds recorded, "That document is actually one of the few pieces of paper that has emerged from the campaign of which we are very proud. . . ." We told him (McCarthy) that we felt rather presumptuous giving national arguments, as we sat up there in the "woods," but that were McCarthy to wait, if Wisconsin were going to be his first primary, that the months of January, February, and March would be rather bleak ones in terms of national publicity for him, the national media would be in New Hampshire in any event for the primary in March, and this is where the spotlight would be for these three months.

It would be crucial for the troops in California, Oregon, Wisconsin, and everywhere else to be reading and hearing about him at that time and not to have him in Vietnam or God knows where else he was going. We told him that if he meant what he said, he damn well ought to be in New Hampshire anyway because there are people here who feel very strongly and want someone to work for.

WAITING

Since McCarthy left New Hampshire December 15, Studds and I had had no communication with him and had been unable to make contact with his manager, Blair Clark. The memorandum was mailed; it was our last effort to convince McCarthy and his Washington advisors of the merits of a New Hampshire contest.

In the meantime, press accounts gave us little to hope for. New Hampshire reporters continued to call me in Hanover for reactions to the story coming from Washington that a "no" decision had been made on New Hampshire. Since I had had no contact with McCarthy since his departure, I repeated the same evaluation that I had when McCarthy left. I expected a decision would be made shortly after Christmas. Though not stated, I also expected to be told of the decision before it was announced to the press either by McCarthy or his campaign staff. Until then, I would assume that all else was the product of the Washington rumor mill.

On December 23, Studds called me to read a page-one story in the *Boston Globe*. The reporter was James Doyle, a person known to us to have close ties to McCarthy. The headline read, "Senator McCarthy to Avoid New Hampshire Primary." The continuation headline read, "McCarthy Plans Turn to Bay State Primary." Gerry Studds was shocked. "We were pretty deflated. Nobody had told us that, and we had spent a good deal of time talking to the Senator, while he was here and in Chicago, and we rather regretted having to read about in the paper." (Studds Transcript, p. 12) The story's lead read:

> Sen. Eugene McCarthy has made a firm decision to avoid the March 12 New Hampshire primary. The only decision pending is how and when to announce the fact.

And went on:

> One possibility is that a peace candidate not identified with the McCarthy forces will run as a stand-in. This plan, which would minimize the risks of a big loss and still benefit the McCarthy candidacy if the votes happen to be there, is under serious consideration at the moment. . . .
>
> McCarthy's decision to stay out of New Hampshire was a concession to the political realities. Some of his supporters had urged that he enter the primary, saying that if he was going to make an issue against President Johnson's conduct of the Vietnam war, he could hardly begin by skipping the first in the nation primary.
>
> But the more cool-headed among his brain trusters suggested that running in New Hampshire could deal a crushing blow to the entire McCarthy campaign.
>
> The Democrats there are showing a unique unity over the primary, and the Democratic vote is so small and concentrated within the few industrial centers that an attempt to overcome the organization would be difficult.
>
> Besides that, the national spotlight will be on the Republicans in New Hampshire, with Nixon and Romney fighting what might be a death struggle for their party's nomination. McCarthy would risk being depicted as an eccentric loner, a sort of Democratic Harold Stassen with practically no impact on the public or press.

Table 4-1: New Hampshire Democratic Primary Twelve-Day Schedule Senator Eugene J. McCarthy

Time	City	% Vote Statewide	% Vote Ist C.D.	% Vote 2nd C.D.
½ Day	Portsmouth	1.5	2.4	
	Newmarket	1.0	1.7	
		2.5	4.1	
½ Day	Hooksett	0.6	1.0	
	Allenstown	0.9	1.4	
	Pembroke	1.2	2.1	
		2.7	4.5	
1 Day	Berlin	6.3		15.7
	Gorham	0.6		1.5
	Northumberland	0.6		1.5
		7.5		18.7
1 Day	Pelham	0.8	1.2	
	Salem	2.2	3.6	
	Derry	0.8	1.4	
	Hudson	1.6	2.7	
		5.4	8.9	
1 Day	Laconia	2.0	3.3	
	Franklin	1.2		3.0
	Concord	1.7	—	4.4
		4.9	3.3	7.4
1 Day	Rochester	2.0	3.3	
	Somersworth	3.0	4.9	
	Dover	2.2	3.6	
		7.2	11.8	
1 Day	Hanover	0.7		1.7
	Lebanon	0.8		2.1
	Claremont	2.0		5.0
	Newport	0.8		2.1
		4.3		10.9
1 Day	Keene	1.5		3.9
	Jaffrey	0.4		1.0
	Greenville	0.6		1.6
	Milford	0.8		2.1
	Wilton	0.4		1.1
		3.7		9.7
3 ½ Days	Manchester	27.3	44.8	
	Goffstown	1.4	2.3	
		28.7	47.1	
1½ Days	Nashua	9.9		25.7
		76.8	79.7	72.4

> The further danger is that a big flop in New Hampshire would spill over into Massachusetts, demoralizing the campaign workers and conditioning the Bay state voters to view McCarthy as a loser.
>
> Both the McCarthy forces and the White House view Massachusetts as one of the crucial battles in the campaign, as evidenced by the fact that the President might allow State Chairman Lester Hyman to enter his name in the primary if he feels the McCarthy threat needs a decisive defeat.
>
> That is why the McCarthy advisers sitting around the coffee table in the Capitol Hill Hotel decided to forego the New Hampshire effort, and conserve their strength for the April 30th primary in Massachusetts.

December 23 was a Saturday and the beginning of the Christmas holiday. There was little I could do to check whether the story was correct or not. December 28 was the date the steering committee had given McCarthy as the last day to decide. Because of the plans to organize that the Draft Kennedy people were making, a decision to enter the primary much after the first of the year would not provide enough time to organize an effective campaign for McCarthy. I knew the steering committee would become anxious and might even dissolve since no word from McCarthy had been received since his December 15 visit.

Early Tuesday morning, December 26, I placed the usual series of calls to Blair Clark with messages for a return call. Late in the afternoon of the next day Clark finally called. The reason for the call was to assure me that, contrary to what would be heard on Walter Cronkite's CBS-TV "Evening News," a decision regarding New Hampshire had not yet been made. I asked Clark to confirm his call with a telegram, which arrived the morning of December 28 and read:

> It was good to talk to you yesterday and I send you this wire simply to confirm what I said on the phone, that the McCarthy decision on the New Hampshire Primary is still not made, despite press reports, that it is being actively considered from the point of view of scheduling and where the best effort can be made nationally, and that you and your group will be the first to know when the decision has been made within the next several days. Many thanks to you and your colleagues.
>
> Sincerely,
> Blair Clark

I immediately sent a memo to the members of the steering committee and a larger list of those titled "friends." Since the key December 28 date was the Thursday before the New Year's holiday weekend, little would happen between then and January 2. In my conversation with Clark, I did discuss the significance of the December 28 date in terms of Clark's planning for the New Hampshire decision. I indicated that I did not expect anything irrevocable would happen on December 28, and that most of those who would form the leadership of the Draft Kennedy organization had already agreed to shift to McCarthy if he were to enter the New Hampshire primary.

My memo to the committee opened as follows:

> The question is, where do we stand? The answer is that we now serve by standing and waiting. This has been our posture since Senator McCarthy's visit to New Hampshire December 14 and 15. . . .
>
> Since his New Hampshire visit, he has taken the important steps to equip his campaign with the necessary national staff to begin the important scheduling work and strategy planning that had not been accomplished at the time of his New Hampshire visit. Numerous meetings have taken place in Washington and the results have been reported in various and sometimes, inaccurate ways. It has been my position to await the outcome of these meetings knowing that the N.H. McCarthy for President Steering Committee had made strong and compelling cases for entering the N.H. primary. . . .

I then recounted the conversation with Clark and the contents of the telegram. Since the memo had a rather neutral tone and since I wanted to indicate that I expected a positive decision from McCarthy, I ended by setting a probable meeting time for the end of the first week in January. I also enclosed petition forms that had to be circulated in each congressional district in order to place the senator's name on the ballot. My final note was:

> Our organization has grown considerably. It is now expensive to mail and the phone bills are piling up. Any financial help, at this stage, would be greatly appreciated.
> A HAPPY NEW YEAR????

That evening Walter Cronkite reported that McCarthy definitely would not enter the New Hampshire presidential primary. My memo would arrive the next morning. In addition I had called a number of the steering committee members so that Clark's information could be spread among the local supporters.

STRATEGIES AND COUNTERSTRATEGIES: SUBJECT, NEW HAMPSHIRE

James Doyle's account of a decision against New Hampshire was not incorrect. A strong argument for not entering New Hampshire had been made. Parts of that argument filtered into Doyle's story but other parts did not. The additions to the Doyle account were told to me after the elections of 1968 by Russell Hemenway, executive director of the Committee for a More Effective Congress. Hemenway, as executive director of a prominent fund-raising organization for liberal candidates of both parties, assumed a covert role in the early machinations of the search for a Democratic alternative. Although he did not surface often during the year, his contacts, advice and persistent willingness to offer constructive help contributed greatly to the results of 1968.

According to Hemenway's account, there was consideration given to the fact that McCarthy's success in states like Wisconsin might prompt Robert Kennedy to reconsider his decision not to be a candidate in 1968. They felt that if such a reconsideration did occur then a serious blow might not only be dealt the McCarthy effort but also the protest mission against the Vietnam war. To counter this possibility, Hemenway had argued that by skipping the New Hampshire primary neither a positive nor negative impact would result. As Doyle had reported, a negative result in New Hampshire could have meant an end to the antiwar effort for McCarthy or anyone else in 1968. A positive result, Henemway argued, might prompt Kennedy to reconsider, thus probably derailing McCarthy and opening Kennedy up to charges of political opportunism. To avoid New Hampshire would prevent both from happening.

Hemenway went on to argue that waiting until the April Wisconsin primary for the first major push would foreclose Kennedy from entering any of the subsequent and especially important California primary. The closing date for filing petitions of candidacy in California was just before the Wisconsin primary. Kennedy would either have to take a long-shot risk and change his public stance before the Wisconsin test or be eliminated from the all-important California test altogether.

Hemenway was sufficiently close to the McCarthy candidacy to know how poorly prepared and understaffed the effort was even as late as the end of 1967. Few political professionals were willing to take the political, social, and economic risks of joining such a quixotic effort even if they were inclined to support McCarthy's views on the war and the national condition.

It was Hemenway's advice to McCarthy to delay his announcement. During the delay, Hemenway argued, campaign preparations could be made, and McCarthy might travel extensively gaining national attention both through speculation as to a candidacy and from actual reflections on the U.S. foreign policy situation. The actual announcement of candidacy could come in time for the critical primaries but not, in all probability, until after the first of the year. In this way the time would be occupied, New Hampshire avoided, and the principal test, Wisconsin, developed into an important political climax. (David C. Hoeh conversation with Russell Hemenway, winter 1969)

A major piece of this scenario fell out when McCarthy announced his candidacy November 30. If McCarthy did not enter the New Hampshire primary, then the hiatus between his announcement and the Wisconsin primary would be difficult to fill. As an announced candidate he would also have difficulty traveling as a fact-finder for the Senate Committee on Foreign Relations.

The confusion in the press resulted from the fact that Hemenway's argument actually did prevail for a considerable period of time. Probably the Hemenway opinion was dominant in McCarthy's mind when he visited New Hampshire December 14 and 15.

The countervailing force in the McCarthy decision-making process was Blair Clark. Clark arrived in the McCarthy camp at the point when the decision against entering the New Hampshire primary had almost been made. In the first days of his time as manager, Clark had had to rush to California. Other pressing political tasks in the states where McCarthy was already committed to campaign kept Clark away from a review of the New Hampshire situation until after the Christmas holiday.

Clark's meeting with McCarthy to review the New Hampshire decision was more accidental than deliberate. According to Clark, late December weather forced McCarthy and Clark to take a train to New York from Washington rather than the brief shuttle flight. During the trip, Clark brought up the subject of New Hampshire, recounted his experiences in the publishing business there, and urged McCarthy to reconsider the possibility of entering the primary. Of major concern to Clark was the appearance that McCarthy was ducking a difficult primary, New Hampshire, for an easy one, Wisconsin, and that the time between his announcement and the Wisconsin primary would keep the political momentum irretrievably in the direction of Johnson. Clark reported later that McCarthy liked what he had seen in New Hampshire and his contact with the organization developing there for him. By the time the train arrived in New York, Clark had convinced McCarthy to reopen the consideration of New Hampshire. (David C. Hoeh conversation with Blair Clark, spring 1969)

THE ANNOUNCEMENT

I had made plans to visit relatives in Vermont and ski during the New Year's holiday weekend, but planned to return to New Hampshire for a local New Year's Eve party. Sandy and I had spent the last two months in a variety of activities for the McCarthy effort and badly needed to be away from the telephone and the waiting for a decision. Almost as we walked in the door on our return from Vermont on December 31, the telephone rang. Blair Clark was calling. He wanted to come to New Hampshire the next day to meet with me and members of the McCarthy for President Steering Committee. I said that it would be impossible to make the calls to set up the meeting for January 1 but that I could do it for January 2. I tried to push Clark for details on the possible agenda for the meeting, indicating that the steering committee would not be in the mood for another indecisive review. Clark said he wanted to meet with the committee before committing himself or McCarthy to a final decision. I then agreed to gather as many of the committee members as possible at the Chaplain's home in Bedford for the evening of January 2, 1968. I made calls to the committee members during the afternoon and evening of New Year's Day and was able to contact most of them. My memo of December 28 had arrived and was viewed as optimistic news. The members were now ready for the challenges of a new year.

Contacting Gerry Studds presented a particular problem. Studds had made plans to visit friends in Washington and New Jersey. After several telephone calls I finally contacted Studds in New Jersey and asked him to meet me at the Sheraton-Wayfarer for dinner with Clark prior to the 7:30 P.M. meeting. Having come this far in our efforts, Studds was not about to miss this episode.

Sandy, Gerry, and I met Blair Clark for the first time in his Sheraton-Wayfarer room. Tall, lanky, and casual appearing Clark immediately made us feel comfortable by complimenting us on our persistence. He said that he had come to New Hampshire to make a final assessment and that a decision on whether or not McCarthy would enter the primary would be made within twenty-four hours. During the discussion Clark was interrupted by a telephone call from Senator McCarthy. Quietly discussing situations in other states and parts of the campaign, Clark suddenly motioned that McCarthy would like to talk with me.

McCarthy's question concerned the status of the LBJ write-in effort. He wanted to be sure that a direct confrontation with Johnson would be possible. I explained that since the last time I had written, a clarification of the attorney general's position had been received. The Democratic Party endorsement of the Johnson renomination effort constituted a legal action that allowed them to run the write-in effort without specific approval from Johnson. Daniell was challenging the interpretation for the Draft RFK Committee but if he (McCarthy) entered the primary, a clear contest between Johnson and himself would be possible. McCarthy seemed pleased with this information and ended by saying that he did not want to waste time in efforts that did not present a clear test of the issues.

During dinner we reviewed the New Hampshire situation for Clark, the status of our organization, the problems we anticipated, and the opportunities the New Hampshire primary offered the campaign. Clark listened attentively and then remarked that he did not wish to make a decision on the specifics of a New Hampshire organization until he had had a chance to review the situation. He then commented on the miseries of his recent trip to California. It was clear that Clark had been burned by the squabbling in that state, and he was not going to get caught between competing campaign organizations again. We immediately assured him that the New Hampshire McCarthy for President Steering Committee was the *only* committee of the sort, that we were unified in our efforts, politically oriented, and not particularly concerned about doctrinal purity. In other words we just wanted to get going with the primary election tasks at hand. Clark seemed visibly relieved.

At this point I was called to the dining room telephone. Senator McCarthy was on the line. In barely audible tones he said, "Dave, I have decided that I will enter the New Hampshire primary." I responded by saying we had been waiting for that word for a long time and were ready to go to work. Not wanting to let the conversation or the decision drop at that point, I said that I would like to announce the decision in New Hampshire at the same time or before McCarthy made the announcement in Washington. I explained that the New Hampshire reporters and wire service personnel had been extremely cooperative in the past weeks and that I wanted to give them the head start on the story. McCarthy said that this would be okay and that I could hold a press conference the next day before noon and that McCarthy would hold one in the early afternoon.

I reviewed the conversation we were having with Blair Clark and asked McCarthy how I should relay the contents of the telephone call to Clark and to the meeting we were about to have. McCarthy said that I should use my judgment and handle these things as I wished.

I returned to the table, looking, according to Gerry, like I had just swallowed a canary. I told Clark that the telephone call was from "your boss," Senator McCarthy. "He has just told me that he is going to enter the New Hampshire primary." Blair Clark's chin, according to Studds, "sort of fell into his soup, I dropped everything, and I thought Sandy was going to faint. We were not prepared for it at that time." (Studds transcript, p. 13)

I knew that it was essential to maintain the trust of campaign managers. Having dropped the bomb that, in reality, undercut Clark's mission, I had to indicate to Clark that my relationship with him was essential to the success of the venture we now were about to undertake. I said something to the effect that I greatly appreciated hearing the word directly from Senator McCarthy and that his call affirmed our sense of confidence in him and the feeling that he had confidence in us. But what was important was to establish an effective working relationship between those in New Hampshire and the head of the national campaign. Without that, there would be little chance of success in New Hampshire.

Clark recovered from his surprise, muttered that of course he could call McCarthy back and further delay or change his mind, but that since we had a decision and the details of an announcement had been outlined, we should now plan the announcement, give the news to the committee, and get on with the campaign. That was Blair Clark's style. No point rehashing the events of the past two hours. There was too much to be done and there was little time available.

We agreed that a press conference could not be held on the basis of a personal telephone call. There would have to be a document of some sort from McCarthy that could be released since we were going to make the announcement in New Hampshire. We concluded that a telegram would suffice and that we had better draft the telegram, check the contents with Senator McCarthy by telephone, and ask that he send it to us for the record.

Every action of the New Hampshire McCarthy Steering Committee up to the moment of the telephone call from McCarthy had been carried out on the basis of speculation. We now had the decision, and our minds had to shift from speculation to operation. The announcement would be relatively easy to accomplish; fulfilling our promise and expectations would take considerably more energy and help. We began to explore these issues with Blair as we finished dinner, drove to the meeting, and then conveyed to the steering committee what now seemed old news: McCarthy's decision. In response the same stunned look also crossed the faces of the fifteen or twenty members of the steering sommittee who had been able to attend the hastily called meeting.

I reviewed how the announcement would be made, Studds reviewed some of the immediate organizational priorities that would have to occupy the committee during the next week, and Clark outlined the status of the national campaign and what help the committee could expect. He also roughly outlined McCarthy's schedule for the next several months and set January 26 as the probable date of McCarthy's first campaign visit to New Hampshire. Clark said we should not expect many more than the twelve days of McCarthy's time in New Hampshire.

Before the meeting adjourned we agreed that several tasks had to be accomplished simultaneously. With the "go" decision, local and statewide organizing could begin. A state headquarters would have to be located, and a schedule for McCarthy's first campaign trip would have to be prepared by Nashua, Manchester, and Concord members. Money to support all that had to be accomplished in ten short weeks suddenly became a burning issue. Clark assured the committee that funds would be available. The committee advised Clark that it did not have money, would only be able to raise a small amount in New Hampshire, and would not spend or obligate money in the campaign that the committee did not have in its account. Studds and I drafted a telegram for Clark to review before the meeting ended. We then called McCarthy to check the text of the telegram and the timing of the release.

By 9:30 A.M. the following morning, I had called the "dean" of the New Hampshire press corps, D. Frank O'Neil of the *Manchester Union Leader* to announce that I would be holding a press conference at the statehouse press room, in Concord, at 11:00 A.M. O'Neil would notify the other reporters and make the arrangements for the conference. I made a sufficient number of copies of the "telegram" for the press.

It took a moment for the mind-set of the reporters to change from that of knowing that McCarthy would not enter to actually understanding what I had just read. There were one or two questions about whether McCarthy was holding a similar conference in Washington or how the message would be confirmed by him. They sensed that an important national scoop was in their hands, and they rushed to the nearest telephones to call in a story lead and the text of the telegram.

As we left the press room, Studds and I looked at each other and almost simultaneously said, "What have we gotten ourselves into now?" The full weight of not only the McCarthy candidacy but of the impact a failure in New Hampshire would have on the issues of Vietnam policy suddenly became incredibly real. It was a lonely moment, and we mentally inventoried the resources we had at hand to assume the responsibility.

Given even an optimistic view we had a total of $500 in the campaign bank account, no headquarters, no telephones, no mailing address, no manager, no materials, and only a tenuous tie to Blair Clark. Both of us were holding full-time jobs that required constant attention.

Recalling the event Studds said, "We enjoyed this one because it was not particularly well attended. There were the local reporters of the UPI and the AP and a few others who had obviously come to hear us say, 'Well, we're terribly sorry, but Senator McCarthy is not entering New Hampshire'. Their expressions were rather fun to watch as we read the telegram."

Studds recalled our work on the announcement telegram, especially one important sentence: "So far as I know, this was the only time that Senator McCarthy, at least in the first two or three months, and certainly in the New Hampshire primary, said, 'I am running for the presidency of the United States.' I wrote that sentence the night before, and I was damn sure he was going to say that when he declared his entry in New Hampshire. So the telegram began by referring to his running for the presidency of the United States. I had been sick and tired of people telling me that's not what he is running for. So he said it that time."

The telegram read:

> I have decided to carry my campaign for the presidency of the United States into New Hampshire. I will enter the New Hampshire primary. My name will be entered in the presidential preference section and, with your committee's valuable help, we will run a full slate of pledged delegates.
>
> I plan, as you know, to campaign in five other state primaries, but am now satisfied that I will be able to devote to the New Hampshire primary the time that is required. It is important to give the Democrats of New Hampshire the opportunity to express freely their choice on the grave issues facing our country. I will press my campaign vigorously.
>
> I thank you for what your committee has already done and look forward to working closely with you in the weeks to come.
>
> Addressed to: David C. Hoeh
> Signed: Senator Eugene J. McCarthy
> Dated: January 2nd, 1968

I left Studds in Concord with his first task to find a suitable storefront for a headquarters and returned to Hanover to discover that the national press had been burning our home telephone line. Sandy greeted me with a long list of numbers, names, and news organizations that had called me for additional information or to record an interview. McCarthy's confirming press conference was held in Washington later that same day, as scheduled.

The story drew front-page attention across the nation and held the lead position in many radio and television broadcasts throughout that day. The New Hampshire AP version of the story, datelined Concord, under the byline of Adolphe V. Bernotas, read:

> Senator Eugene McCarthy, D-Minn. an opponent of President Johnson's Vietnam policy, will enter New Hampshire's March 12 Democratic presidential primary, David Hoeh of Hanover, the senator's chief Granite State backer, told newsmen today. . . .
>
> Until very recently, McCarthy had indicated he would use the Massachusetts primary as his test of New England sentiment. However, Hoeh said today, there was no clear reason why McCarthy changed signals.
>
> "He isn't running just to make tests—he's seeking the presidency,"Hoeh added.
>
> McCarthy had called off plans to tour Europe and Southeast Asia, Hoeh said, and would be in New Hampshire within the next two weeks to campaign "in excess of 12 to 15 days."
>
> Hoeh said his group plans to spend $50,000 "to do a good job in the campaign."

> He added that the organization expects McCarthy to pull 'about a third' of the state's 80,000 Democratic votes. . . .
>
> Hoeh said the group is already circulating petitions to get on the ballot. Fifty signatures from each of the two congressional districts in the state are required.
>
> Some of the strength shown for Senator Robert F. Kennedy, D-N.Y., will be drawn away by McCarthy's announcement, Hoeh maintained.
>
> He added: "A number of their members said they would join McCarthy."
>
> "A drive to pick up independent votes will be undertaken," Hoeh said.
>
> McCarthy's campaign, Hoeh added, would require "close campaigning. You can't substitute media for effectiveness of meeting the people."
>
> Hoeh said the group has not yet decided on potential delegates.
>
> He added the organization went with pledged rather the favorable delegates because "it gives us control over the structure of the delegation. We can distribute the delegates where the votes are."
>
> In answer to a question on how McCarthy would do in the state's two biggest cities—Manchester and Nashua—Hoeh said: "there is considerable support, especially in Nashua."
>
> He said that in Manchester 'there is no special love for Johnson.'
>
> "Manchester is the kind of city where McCarthy would have appeal." Hoeh said.

While covering essentially the same New Hampshire news, Ward Just, writing in the *Washington Post,* reported a capital view of the story:

> McCarthy's aides insisted that the decision to go into New Hampshire did not represent a change in plans. Last week in a radio interview the Minnesota Democrat said the primary was "not a significant test," and indicated privately that he would avoid it.
>
> Organization Democrats in New Hampshire led by Bernard Boutin, have virtually dared McCarthy to oppose the President.
>
> In an interview last month, Boutin predicted that the President would swamp McCarthy in the March 12 primary, even though McCarthy's name would be on the ballot and voters would be obliged to write in the President's. Yesterday, Boutin was unavailable for comment.
>
> "We don't expect a landslide or anything like that," said one of McCarthy's campaign aides yesterday, "but we expect to do well." The New Hampshire test will be the first direct confrontation between the President and his critics since the 1964 presidential election.
>
> McCarthy aides in Washington said that one of the principal factors in the Senator's decision to vie with the President in New Hampshire was an optimistic report from Hoeh, and from McCarthy's national campaign manager, Blair Clark, who canvassed the state over the New Year's weekend.

Hoeh reported that the President was not popular in New Hampshire, and that support for the McCarthy candidacy was growing. Hoeh reported some defections from the regular Democratic organization, but that group will still regarded as solidly pro-Johnson.

One analysis of McCarthy's decision to enter the primary turns on the criticism of his candidacy as "non-serious." Last week McCarthy confessed himself to be "a little disappointed" with antiwar Democrats who have refused to support him with "the excuse that I am not a serious candidate. . . ."

Political observers here reasoned that if McCarthy did not enter New Hampshire, with its wide newspaper and television coverage and opportunity to challenge Lyndon Johnson, the charge of "non-seriousness" would grow in currency and plausibility.

A McCarthy aide said yesterday that the fact that a campaign for Mr. Johnson was being organized was a "major factor" in McCarthy's decision to add New Hampshire. . . .

Although Bernard Boutin was unavailable for comment, Governor John W. King, did issue a brief statement concerning the McCarthy announcement, which was distributed in the State House press room before the McCarthy press conference concluded. It read:

> Senator McCarthy is welcome to bring his campaign into the New Hampshire primary. While I do not agree with his political view points, a full discussion of the issues in the great tradition of American politics can only be beneficial.
>
> I am confident that the vast majority of New Hampshire Democrats support President Johnson, and his domestic and international policies justify that support.
>
> On March 12, the New Hampshire Democrats will have the opportunity to conclusively show their support for one of our country's greatest and most successful Presidents, President Lyndon Baines Johnson.

With King's statement, timed to ride, if possible, with the McCarthy announcement story, the battle was joined. The confident Johnson renomination leadership were sure they could demolish McCarthy in New Hampshire. There would be no question but that there would be a direct confrontation between the two in New Hampshire.

NEW HAMPSHIRE PROVIDES THE STAGE

Now that McCarthy had agreed to enter, Studds and I could seriously consider organizing the actual campaign. Our preliminary analysis as reflected in the memorandum of December 22 would be the background plan, but a further evaluation would be necessary to cast the campaign properly.

As with the ethos of primary elections which dictated party organization neutrality, there was a second ethos concerning presidential primaries. New Hampshire provides the stage, the audience, and, frequently, the principal directors of a campaign, but the production is paid for with money from outside the state. To some, principally the communications industry and hotel, motel, and restaurant operators, the New Hampshire presidential primary is an economic boon during the winter period of slack business. To others it is quadrennial entertainment relieving the "cabin fever" of the long winter.

In our meetings with Lowenstein, Gans, and later McCarthy and Clark, I had made it clear that only a small amount of money could be expected from the New Hampshire populace itself for use in the primary campaign. New Hampshire's small population, approximately seven hundred thousand persons in 1968 and low per capita income, $3,023 in 1969, meant that the resources to support a campaign of national impact on a New Hampshire presidential primary had to come from outside the state. In this ethos there lay a part of the our strategy.

From the earliest stage of the Johnson effort in New Hampshire there were rumblings. First, who was the mysterious "man from Washington?" Second, how much money would the Johnson leaders bring in to spend for their campaign? Third, when would the "heavies" arrive from Texas and Washington to take over Boutin's operation?

In reaction, Boutin stated a policy that the effort on behalf of the president would be "homegrown" and "home financed" and that its organization, leadership, strategy, and funding would be the responsibility of New Hampshire people. The vote in the New Hampshire presidential primary would be an expression of New Hampshire gratitude for the accomplishments of President Johnson, a gift to the president.

By reacting this way, Boutin had again violated an essential political ethos. It was obvious that if he and his committee were that concerned about the impact of outside money, personnel, and ideas there had to be something to fear. The reporters and numerous political observers could not all be wrong about the heavy-handedness of Lyndon Johnson's domestic politics. Boutin, again, was on the defensive, a position the McCarthy leadership hoped to nurture.

Boutin's only source of staff, therefore, was that available from inside New Hampshire or through the loaning of office staff by Governor King and Senator McIntyre. The only source of money for Boutin's effort was to be the New Hampshire Democratic Party's minuscule coffers, the pockets of its sustaining contributors, and those who could be convinced that they had better contribute if they wished to maintain favorable relations with the sure-to-be reelected president.

On the other hand, the McCarthy campaign could play by the usual New Hampshire rules. The money would be imported. The national campaign office was expected to provide most of the campaign materials and media resources for the effort. Stretching the ethos slightly, we expected to attract a number of outside workers to assist in the actual operation of the campaign. There was, of course, a risk in this strategy, especially when it came to importing volunteers and campaign operatives, but there was no real choice.

Johnson would not enter the primary but he would not duck either. His fate was placed in the hands of his political surrogates in Washington and New Hampshire. There would be no time for politics in the public stance of his administration during the primary contests ahead—at least as far as his personal involvement was concerned. The polls assured him that his direct participation would not be necessary. Bernard Boutin, however, held an important card that Studds and I discovered early in our preliminary planning. In the name of the Democratic State Committee Boutin had blocked by reservation the largest hall in the state, the Manchester Armory, for Thursday, Friday, and Saturday evenings, March 6, 7, and 8. He would be able to hold this space until a specified period, approximately 10 days prior to the actual reserved date. Our question was, how would this space be used? Would the president be brought out of his nonparticipation stance, fly in to Manchester, and attempt a dramatic recreation of his successful 1964 visit? Or was the reservation just good strategy on Boutin's part to prevent the Republicans from staging their own political spectacular, thus completely shutting out the Democrats in the last moments of the New Hampshire primary?

This would be just the beginning of our tactical joust with the Johnson people, but it revealed two aspects of the contest. The first was that there would be direct confrontation between the campaigns supporting the opposing candidates. The second was a mutual awareness that this was not the ultimate fight but only a preliminary. The ultimate fight was still the one that would pit the nominees of the two parties against each other in the November election. As both were Democrats, they were constantly looking over their collective shoulders to see what was happening among the Republicans.

On both sides of the Democratic campaigns optimism was necessary to reinforce efforts at that early stage of the campaign. Boutin was leading from strength. He had determined that a posture of invincibility was necessary to create the impression of a self-fulfilling prophecy of victory while at the same time making those who questioned the prophecy seem foolish. On the other hand, if the McCarthy strategy had been to talk only in terms of minuscule percentages, we would have had considerable difficulty recruiting workers and raising funds.

Boutin's error, initially, was that he sought to overpower with rhetoric. He fell into his own confidence gap. Instead of being more modest in his predictions, he tended to project absolute certitude in his high projections. Starting with a "win" projection of 60 to 70 percent meant that Boutin had almost nowhere to go but down.

The use of Democratic State Committee funds to support the Johnson campaign added more energy to the contest between the Johnson and McCarthy campaigns. Having secured the party's endorsement and then having converted the party organization into the campaign committee for Johnson, the New Hampshire, primary ethos issue of party neutrality had been fully raised. At the McCarthy announcement press conference, O'Neil of the *Manchester Union Leader* asked me a question concerning the use of the Democratic Party's funds to run the Johnson campaign. His newspaper had seen the intraparty contest between Johnson and

McCarthy as an excellent chance to renew their assault on the practice of preprimary endorsements. The article recounting my reply read:

> The decision of the Democratic State Committee to use party funds to support the "Citizens-for-Johnson" effort in the New Hampshire presidential primary was under fire from a second wing of the party yesterday [the first "wing" being Eugene Daniell].
>
> David C. Hoeh of Hanover, state chairman of the McCarthy for President steering committee, told his press conference at the State House that "a lot of Democrats are distressed" by this move on the part of the official party organization.
>
> "Personally, I had my name on a $1,000 note for the State Committee not too many months ago. It's probably spent by now. But I certainly wouldn't like to think this was being used for the Johnson primary campaign. Neither would some other Democrats who are members of the $100 Club."
>
> Asked if this could have a serious effect on party efforts in this state after the primary, Hoeh expressed the opinion that it would "have a bad effect" on fund-raising "later on."

By opening the issue of the use of party funds, I was further placing the Johnson effort on the defensive. The press would be watching for reports of heavy media purchase, billboard reservations, or other evidence of large amounts of money being available to Johnson's campaign. Boutin was already sensitive to this concern and was, publicly and to a very large extent privately, operating on funds generated internally in New Hampshire. My charge now made the use of Democratic State Committee funds equally controversial. Boutin would have to run a conservative campaign, even if extensive funding were available. He certainly could not obligate the Democratic Party of New Hampshire to additional borrowing while a considerable debt still remained to be repaid as a result of the 1966 campaigns.

DRAFT RFK REACTIONS

McCarthy's announcement took Eugene Daniell by surprise as well. Like the rest of the nation, Daniell thought that McCarthy would bypass New Hampshire when the RFK organizing deadline of December 28 came and passed. Again, Daniell, not one to keep in close touch with his associates, did not realize that many of his best potential workers were holding back in hopes that McCarthy would enter New Hampshire. Press reaction was that the future moves of Daniell's organization are uncertain but "most observers believe Daniell will continue undaunted." (*Boston Globe,* January 4, 1968)

Daniell was in the midst of his court contest with the New Hampshire attorney general concerning the legality of a write-in campaign and had not really considered his options if McCarthy actually entered. Revealing this condition he said, "Whatever we do is up to our executive committee. But I know that we will continue with a slate of delegates. The second committee—the RFK write-in committee—will probably run a write-in effort." (*Boston Globe,* January 4, 1968)

Daniell reported that he admired McCarthy but that he still believed that Robert Kennedy was "the best man for the job of president." Daniell appeared to be weakening under the pressure of his legal battle, a dissolving campaign organization, the limitation that his committee was placing on his political style, and the organizational success of the McCarthy Steering Committee. His reference to a "slate of RFK delegates" did, however, give Studds and me pause.

We had not considered seriously the issue of delegates before the announcement press conference. Daniell's emphasis on the delegate selection issue made us begin to consider what our interest might be in the selection of the delegates and, more importantly, what Daniell's interest was.

Was it possible that Daniell, a previous delegate to several Democratic Conventions, was at least as interested in being a delegate again as he was in the RFK draft? This would be a question that would reemerge in the weeks ahead. At this time, however, it seemed desirable for us to make only oblique, usually complimentary, references to Daniell in order to avoid any confrontation with him. As long as Daniell was attacking the Johnson organization and raising the more radical of the antiwar charges, the McCarthy organization benefited by appearing to be the more reasonable, especially the more moderate, of the two antiadministration movements in New Hampshire.

CHAPTER 5

Early Campaign Operations

FIRST DAYS

In a speech before graduates of the Amos Tuck School of Business Administration of Dartmouth College in the spring of 1968, I said:

> Since the art of politics has not become a structured form, despite the attempts of numerous political scientists and the Kennedys, it is possible to continue the process as a "free-form" almost as varied as the totality of human response. In other words, each campaign has its own conception, birth, life, and death—a data producing incident, unique in the history of man. That, for the unrestrained mind, is what makes politics fascinating and alluring.
>
> . . . You will find the special art of campaign management more like an infectious disease than an occupational attraction. If you once become involved and the spirit of competition, desire to influence history, or simply a fascination with the political game gets under your skin from that time on your life may well be colored by the disease.

Politics may be "free-form," but political events, especially campaigns, also have a "stream of consciousness" aspect that requires special understanding. Studds and I felt that we had identified the limits of the political consciousness for the McCarthy effort and had described these in the December 22 memorandum to McCarthy. Bringing a campaign into operation would require less lofty concepts or actions. The campaign was born with the January 3 press conference announcing McCarthy's entry into the New Hampshire primary. Now the campaign had to crawl before it could walk and walk before it could run.

The first major decision we faced was the location of a headquarters. In what city should it be located? Traditionally Democratic presidential primary candidates have centered their campaigns in Manchester, the city containing the largest number of Democratic Party registrants. The Republicans usually selected Concord, which was closer to the center of their constituency.

Both Studds and I were concerned about the outward appearances of the campaign. Even at this early stage we anticipated that a number of young persons would be involved and that their appearance would not always be helpful to the McCarthy image. Long hair, beards, short skirts, and other recently evolved symbols of the "youth culture" might provide the *Manchester Union Leader* and Manchester's less tolerant public officials with a way to embarrass the McCarthy campaign without confronting the real campaign issues.

Late in the Spring of 1967, an antiwar demonstration at the U.S. Army induction center in Manchester, had been broken-up by the use of questionable police tactics. The *Manchester Union Leader* praised the police for their sternness and the Democratic Mayor, Roland Vallee and the Democratically controlled Board of Aldermen passed a resolution condemning the demonstrators and praising the police action. With this in the background, we did not want to enter Manchester with the campaign until it was adequately organized.

In contrast to Manchester's more conservative partisan Democrats, Concord's role as the state capitol and local progressive Republican climate made it appear as a more favorable location for the McCarthy headquarters. These social/political realities were tied to the fact that the wire services were located in Concord, and Concord was convenient for Studds, a resident, and me, commuting from Hanover.

It took Studds more than a week to actually find a headquarters site and then what he found appeared to be far from ideal. I hoped that we could locate an empty storefront on Concord's Main Street, a location that would offer visability for the campaign. What Studds found was the recently vacated Ralph Pill Electrical Supply Store on Pleasant Street Extension. In the heyday of the railroad, Pleasant Street Extension had been a busy thoroughfare. Now it served only as an automobile route to a new shopping center located on the site of the old railroad station and rail yards. The store was away from Main Street, and therefore few pedestrians would be passing by. There would be some parking for campaign workers, but otherwise there was little to make its location attractive.

Inside, to quote Gerry Studds, "It was in absolutely wretched condition. . . . There are two to three inches of electrical commotion all over the place. There were wires hanging out of the wall. It looked like a medieval torture chamber, and it was too big. We didn't know what the hell to do with it. There was a full-length basement and an enormous room behind the showroom in the front." (Studds transcript, p. 14) With our first college volunteer, Dennis Donahue, a Dartmouth senior, we began the campaign by sweeping out the mess. There was a small office to the right of the front door with a "fishbowl" window facing toward the show space of the store. This would be the office we needed, but it was only about eight feet by ten feet in size. It would be a crowded work space, but it did provide separation from the barnlike space of the store. There was no furniture, plenty of wires, and parts of electrical fixtures but few lights. It was dark, dingy, dusty, and dirty. The rent would be more than $100 per month, not including electricity or heat. This was a high price to pay for a headquarters when it was the usual New Hampshire experience to receive the use of storefront space as a campaign gift. The campaign's bank balance was still only $500. The deposit and first month's rent would draw most of this current cash.

Commenting on the early campaign Studds said later, "Those first days were rough. . . . We had no money. I had five personal checks spread around the city of Concord including the check for the rent for the headquarters, and the pledge that they would be held as security and not cashed because they couldn't possibly have been cashed. I would have been overdrawn." (Studds transcript, p. 15)

Holland called me to see what he could do about getting money from the national campaign to cover Studds' checks and the early obligations. He said with the checks already written and costs projected for the next several weeks, the campaign would need about $5,000. Al Lowenstein, during the early meetings and at the Chicago CCD meeting, had made much of the fact that more than $1 million had already been pledged for the McCarthy campaign. With this in the back of our minds, Studds and I had little concern about funding the modest costs of the New Hampshire effort. I called Blair Clark, stated our financial needs, indicated the urgency of the situation, and reminded him that we would not go into debt to run the campaign. Of course we had already violated that rule to the extent of Studds' drafts on his own meager accounts. Clark hesitated, but said that something would be coming soon.

With McCarthy's January 3 announcement, the New Hampshire campaign began receiving a number of small checks and offers of help from across the country. The offers and contributions were reassuring, but the money did not constitute an amount sufficient to meet even early bills. Within a little more than a week, I received two checks each for $2,500 made out to the N.H. McCarthy for President Campaign. The first was signed by Blair Clark and the second was signed by Martin Peretz. Martin Peretz, a professor of social science at Harvard, peace activist, and independently wealthy, was an early and continuing source of funds for the 1968 antiwar and McCarthy political efforts. Both checks were drawn on their respective personal checking accounts. What had happened to the "$1 million" in pledged money was unknown.

DEVELOPING STRATEGY

Wanting desperately to get the campaign into as many hands as possible, Studds and I called a meeting of the steering committee for Sunday evening, January 7. In the notice I sent announcing the meeting, I wrote:

We now have the chance to pave the way for Senator McCarthy in his campaign for the Presidency. This effort, and our work in the next few weeks, may change the course of history. We, individually, and as a committee, have accepted a considerable responsibility. We must now organize to pursue our goals effectively and efficiently.

Our first step is to put our state organization in order so that we can begin to fully structure the campaign. To do this, the Steering Committee asks that those receiving this notice attend a meeting . . . at the home of Dr. and Mrs. Warren Eberhart, 110 School Street, Concord, N.H.

The purpose of the meeting is to discuss in detail the steps that must be taken between now and March 12th. An agenda for the meeting will be prepared so that all of the important items are covered and so that a full perspective on the campaign is made clear to all.

Items needing attention now and/or in the future should be considered by you before attending the meeting.

1. Circulate the nominating petitions as soon as possible. Completed petitions should be forwarded to me.

2. Compile lists of those interested in forming a local McCarthy for President Committee or county committee

3. We need money—further instructions on the specifics of fund-raising will follow but preliminary contact now will bring better results later.

4. Take a look at a calendar of events for the next ten weeks noting those days when Senator McCarthy could fill a good campaign day in your area. This early work will background the kind of scheduling that will make the best use of the Senator's limited campaign time.

5. Compile lists of volunteers willing to participate in the campaign. Be sure the list is complete with addresses and telephone numbers. They will make it possible for us to move the campaign quickly when the telephoning and mailings must be handled.

6. Look for good locations for headquarters in the larger towns and cities. Be prepared to staff and support headquarters operations with volunteers.

A REMINDER—We are engaged in a rough fight, with people who are skilled in the profession. We must be careful in our activities in order to be able to wage an effective campaign. We must, however, keep our eyes open and be willing to speak out when the wrong strings are pulled.

In addition to the original steering committee membership, copies were sent to persons in each of the major primary vote-producing cities and towns who had expressed an interest in McCarthy. With the announcement Studds and I had reason to expect that individual and group antiwar activities could be brought under the leadership of the steering committee to support the New Hampshire McCarthy campaign.

The greatest uncertainty of a New Hampshire campaign is the weather. For outsiders the weather often makes New Hampshire impossible—impossible to get to and impossible to leave—but for residents the weather is a fact of life to be enjoyed or overcome. The first organizational meeting of the New Hampshire McCarthy campaign, Sunday evening, January 7, found people "overcoming."

Late that afternoon it began to snow lightly north of a line that crossed the state at Concord. South of that line the snow was wet and freezing. Travel was difficult. The group coming from the Seacoast and the University of New Hampshire at Durham stopped to move furniture out of a burning house by the side of a slippery road. The librarian from Franklin Pierce College in Rindge rang the Eberhart's door cold and wet after hitchhiking from that southwestern town. Groups of three or four had arrived from Nashua, Manchester, Keene, Portsmouth, Durham, Laconia, Hanover, and several other towns until almost thirty persons were gathered in the Eberhart living room.

I called the meeting to order and began to go through the agenda that had been circulated prior to the meeting (see page 146). The first step was to create an organization that would assume the statewide responsibilities of the campaign, the candidate schedule, and organization of the localities. Studds and I had come to the meeting with a series of specific proposals.

Studds said that headquarters of one sort or another should be established in the twelve cities and then, in descending order of population and voter turnout, the larger towns. In some cases we advised forming area headquarters to support activities in several cities and the surrounding towns. In the case of the smaller towns, but those with a high proportion of voter participation as recorded in the 1964 presidential primary, we advised establishing a "home" headquarters, borrowing a page from Romney's campaign manual. Coupled with the organizational objective for these headquarters was also a campaign scheduling priority. We expected that Senator McCarthy would be visiting New Hampshire within two or three weeks. The campaign's top organizational priority then had to be the cities where McCarthy could campaign without time lost to travel and where the broadest media coverage would be possible. Studds and I used the following analysis of the most recent presidential preference primary, 1964, to determine the cities and towns that would receive our highest priority attention. The first priority would be the opening and staffing of a state campaign headquarters. The committee agreed with the decision to locate the headquarters in Concord. Our next priorities were the cities which, in all but the case of Franklin, had populations in excess of the towns. Then considering the scattered noncity population, we selected those towns having a population of two thousand or more and ranked them according to their respective size and ratio of Democratic voter participation. The organizational task then presented to those gathered in the Eberhart living room was to begin moving down the cities list from Manchester to Franklin and then down the towns list from Salem to the smallest incorporated community in New Hampshire, Waterville Valley. (Tables 5.1 and 5.2 contain the data used to rank our organizational priorities.)

N.H. McCarthy for President Committee, January 7, 1968

AGENDA

Establishment of Storefront HQ in Top 12 Cities

Nashua	Manchester	Keene
Berlin	Concord (state HQ)	Somersworth
Portsmouth	Claremont	Laconia
Rochester	Dover	Salem

Assignment of Responsibility

A) Opening of HQ
B) Formation of local committee
C) Responsibilities of local committee

Establishment of Home HQ in Other Important Towns

1st C.D.		2nd C.D.	
Hudson	Pembroke	Franklin	Newport
Goffstown	New Market	Milford	Lebanon
Allenstown	Derry	Gorham	Greenville
Pelham	Hooksett	Hanover	Northumberland
Hampton	Plaistow	Lincoln	Jaffrey
Exeter	Merrimack	Wilton	Littleton
Rollinsford	Bedford	Winchester	Peterborough
Epping	Seabrook	New Ipswich	Lancaster
Tilton	Farmington	Swanzey	Ashland
Londonderry	Meredith	Troy	Hinsdale
Pittsfield	Durham	Andover	Hillsborough
Milton			

Assignment of Responsibility

A) Designation of home
B) Formation of local committee
C) Responsibilities of local committee (see separate sheet)

By simply reading the name of the key city or town we were able to list as initial organizers those in the room who were willing to begin the organizing. There were strong leads in many communities, organizations in a few, the nucleus of organizations in others, but almost nothing in the largest city, Manchester, and in three strongly Democratic cities, Rochester, Somersworth, and Dover. The total blank was Berlin. Berlin, the northern most city in New Hampshire, would present the campaign with a special challenge. Isolated by the barrier of the White Mountains from the populous southern part of the state, Berlin had grown up as a paper-making wood-processing city. A tradition of strong union organization, bread-and-butter Democratic Party allegiance, and a population composed mostly of French-speaking Canadians made Berlin unique among New Hampshire's cities.

Realizing that the campaign had to be developed rapidly in order to work, Studds and I outlined what was ahead. Ten weeks remained before primary day March 12. During that time many tasks would have to be accomplished. The first would be to identify local supporters in each of the priority/important Democratic-vote-producing communities. The second would be to identify or organize events that would be appropriate for Senator McCarthy to attend. A "shelf" of possible campaign activities had to be inventoried for each of the key cities and towns. The local organizations would be responsible for maintaining this "shelf." They, I advised, should be able to suggest on short notice activities that could be arranged as an effective schedule for the candidate.

The third important local responsibility was to fund the activities that would be assigned. Each of these local efforts would require a local organization that would be a miniature campaign. Too much had to be accomplished in too short a time to permit centralized management and control of all of the campaign's essential activities. Furthermore Studds and I felt that without a large central campaign staff capable of organizing and advancing each activity of the campaign, it was necessary to rely heavily on the ingenuity of the local activists. Both of us had developed an appreciation for the effectiveness of the local groups in the early stages and were impressed by the sensitivity of the local groups to both the needs of a national candidacy and the political traditions of their own communities.

At this stage the local organizations in many states and in a number of New Hampshire communities were further developed than were either the state or the national McCarthy organization. As an example the Keene area committee was ready to proceed. All the committee wanted to know was whether it should go ahead, whether its plans were constructive, how it should relate to the statewide effort, and whether there would be financial assistance for its headquarters. The Keene committee set a pattern that would be followed in almost all of the local efforts of the campaign. The local committees were encouraged to do what they thought they could do effectively and what they could sustain with locally raised money and locally recruited volunteers.

With Concord, the state headquarters site, the local committee would be expected to staff both the local effort and help with state activities. Funding for the

Table 5-1: New Hampshire Democratic Vote by Cities—1964

City	County	Population 1960	Democratic Pres. Primary Vote 1964	Democratic Vote as % of Checklist	Number of Names on Checklist 1964
Manchester	(Hillsborough)	88,282	8,900	18.8%	47,298
Nashua	(Hillsborough)	39,096	3,486	14.8	23,517
Concord	(Merrimack)	28,991	760	4.7	16,148
Portsmouth	(Rockingham)	25,833	442	3.7	11,800
Dover	(Strafford)	19,131	1,760	16.7	10,506
Berlin	(Coos)	17,821	3,306	30.0	10,985
Keene	(Cheshire)	17,562	777	8.5	9,118
Rochester	(Strafford)	15,927	681	7.8	8,722
Laconia	(Belknap)	15,288	769	9.2	8,328
Claremont	(Sullivan)	13,363	757	10.0	7,498
Lebanon	(Grafton)	9,299	251	5.6	4,457
Somersworth	(Strafford)	8,529	861	15.2	5,645
Franklin	(Merrimack)	6,742	398	9.7	4,077
CITY TOTAL:	***54.9%**	**305,864**	**23,148**	**13.7%**	**168,099**
STATE TOTAL:	***57.6%**	**606,921**	**41,436**	**11.8%**	**349,667**

* Percent of city population registered to vote.

Table 5-2: New Hampshire Democratic Vote by Counties and Towns of over 2,000 population—1964

Towns (Pop. 2,000+)	Pop. 1960	Democratic Pres. Primary Vote 1964	Democratic Vote as % of Checklist	Number of Names on Checklist 1964
Belknap Co. *(60.4%)	**28,912**	**1,509**	**8.6**	**17,483**
Belmont	1,953	86	7.6	1,119
Gilford	2,043	67	4.8	1,385
Meredith	2,434	138	8.5	1,619
Tilton	2,137	109	7.6	1,420
Carroll Co. *(72.1%)	**15,829**	**469**	**4.1**	**11,416**
*Conway	4,298	89	3.2	2,782
Wolfeboro	2,689	74	3.8	1,918
Cheshire Co. *(54.4%)	**43,342**	**2,290**	**9.6**	**23,621**
Hinsdale	2,187	116	10.0	1,159
*Jaffrey	3,154	256	13.4	1,900
*Swanzey	3,626	113	6.5	1,737
Walpole	2,825	77	4.6	1,663
Winchester	2,411	206	16.6	1,239
Coos Co. *(57.4%)	**37,140**	**4,883**	**22.9**	**21,321**
Colebrook	2,389	114	10.8	1,046
Gorham	3,039	318	18.5	1,710
Lancaster	3,138	163	9.0	1,794
Northumberland	2,586	376	26.8	1,400
Grafton Co. *(55.3%)	**48,857**	**2,125**	**7.8**	**27,021**
Enfield	1,867	90	8.3	1,072
*Hanover	7,329	289	10.4	2,762
Haverhill	3,127	63	3.7	1,670
*Littleton	5,003	228	6.6	3,450
*Plymouth	3,210	109	6.0	1,787
Hillsborough Co. *(57.1%)	**178,161**	**16,789**	**16.4**	**101,895**
Amherst	2,051	67	5.2	1,288
*Bedford	3,636	229	10.4	2,199
*Goffstown	7,230	664	16.0	4,148
Hillsborough	2,310	95	6.9	1,367
*Hudson	5,876	761	23.1	3,285
+Merrimack	2,989	291	15.9	1,826
*Milford	4,863	413	11.8	3,497
Pelham	2,605	400	24.7	1,614
+Peterborough	2,963	180	9.3	1,924
Wilton	2,025	175	14.4	1,215
+Greenville	1,385	338	44.4	760

* Percent of county population registered to vote.

(continued)

Table 5-2 (continued)

Towns (Pop. 2,000+)	Pop. 1960	Democratic Pres. Primary Vote 1964	Vote as % of Checklist	Number of Names on Checklist 1964
Merrimack Co. *(59.9%)	**67,785**	**3,339**	**8.2**	**40,665**
+Boscawen	2,181	104	9.2	1,126
*Hooksett	3,713	264	10.3	2,547
Hopkinton	2,225	107	6.7	1,594
*Pembroke	3,514	625	22.9	2,720
Pittsfield	2,419	129	10.1	1,271
+Allenstown	1,789	240	20.4	1,174
Rockingham Co. *(58.1%)	**99,029**	**5,422**	**9.4**	**57,613**
*Derry	6,987	390	9.2	4,224
*Epping	2,006	211	16.6	1,266
*Exeter	7,243	284	6.6	4,267
*Hampton	S,379	288	7.7	3,712
Londonderry	2,457	180	11.6	1,544
Newmarket	3,153	424	23.8	1,779
Plaistow	2,915	307	15.6	1,963
Rye	3,224	76	4.1	1,833
*Salem	9,210	1,104	15.5	7,082
Seabrook	2,209	197	13.8	1,422
Strafford Co. *(55.2%)	**59,799**	**3,097**	**9.3**	**33,040**
*Durham	5,504	124	7.2	1,710
Farmington	3,287	195	9.3	2,070
Rollinsford	1,935	257	20.3	1,162
Sullivan Co. *(55.2%)	**28,067**	**1,513**	**9.7**	**15,592**
Charlestown	2,576	52	3.9	1,325
*Newport	5,458	411	13.8	3,044

* Percent of county population registered to vote.

state headquarters would come from the national campaign treasury, but much of the local effort would have to be financed from local funds.

Studds and I advised those attending not to commit themselves, either in terms of activity or expenses, to more than they thought they could sustain. Second, we warned against careless press statements, speaking for Senator McCarthy, or representing him or the campaign with respect to issue positions or activities other than their own. Any state or national campaign policy questions or issue positions would be directed to the state headquarters and to me or Studds.

One question remained. How would the McCarthy effort relate to Republicans? Since the reregistration period was long since past, and since Governor George Romney had taken positions opposing the Vietnam War, it seemed advisable not to adopt a Republicans for McCarthy strategy.

In the discussion Professor Robert Dishman argued that he didn't think that many Republican liberals could be induced to vote for McCarthy as long as they had two of their own kind to vote for. (Nelson Rockefeller was still on the minds of many liberal New Hampshire Republicans.) Second, Dishman thought that an attempt to do any active campaigning for Republican votes would help Nixon more than it would help McCarthy. (Underwood, op. cit., p. 33). To actively seek Republican write-ins for McCarthy at this stage would appear presumptuous and could in the end keep away votes that might otherwise come to McCarthy.

The meeting ended with a mild sense of confidence but with an even stronger feeling of the importance of the tasks ahead. A monstrous task remained that each person who sat in the Eberharts living room that evening intensively felt. Both Studds and I were somewhat less lonely than we had been on January 3, but four days had passed and little had been accomplished. Studds would have to return to his teaching position at St. Paul's School and I would again be isolated by the fifty miles separating Concord from Hanover.

At best campaigns have difficult early periods. Often the start-up problems are reduced through lengthy preliminary meetings that usually precede major political ventures. During the usual precampaign preparation scores of tasks have to be accomplished which prepare the participants for the campaign while at the same time providing a testing period. Virtually everything that can be anticipated in a campaign has its own lead time. Most campaigns have the luxury of some relatively quiet stumbling time in which to plan for a campaign.

For the national McCarthy campaign or the New Hampshire effort no such preparation time was available. The campaign had to develop rapidly on a number of fronts without the planning, the testing, or the caution that precedes similar events. Ten weeks was an incredibly short period in which to organize an effective campaign for Senator McCarthy against even a limited effort for the incumbent president.

With a little advice and some cautions, Studds and I released the local campaigners. Although our experience warned against such loose management, we felt that the bond between the selfless objectives of McCarthy's effort, concern about the war, and a certain desire to be professional would somehow keep the locally based campaigns under control. If the local leadership had trouble, or needed to check an activity or wanted to report something, they were advised to call me or Studds. They were advised especially to call before acting if there was a question. Because of the quixotic nature of the effort, few if any of the New Hampshire committee members, state or local, viewed the campaign as in any way enhancing their own personal or political futures. As a result of this basic difference, cooperation, coordination, and communication were the watchwords. It was a campaign of equals, equally stressed, equally responsible, and equally entitled to taste the success. The tone of the campaign was set.

By Monday morning, January 8, several harsh realities again hit Studds and me. We knew that to operate a statewide campaign someone would have to be in continuous charge of the effort. Studds had requested a leave of absence but in spite of a supporting letter from Senator McCarthy endorsing the request, it was denied.

Studds would have to fulfill the duties of a preparatory school master and snitch what time he could to oversee the campaign. At least he was based in Concord. I was also unable to leave my position at Dartmouth. For more than half of the remaining weeks we engaged in a spatial juggling act. I was almost always accessible by telephone at my office or home. Studds would slip away from St. Paul's between events to check into headquarters, to telephone, or to supervise a growing group of his students who were becoming interested in the campaign.

Almost every evening at about 5:00 P.M., I would drive the fifty miles to Concord, meet Studds at St. Paul's School for dinner, then spend the evening at the headquarters. I would leave Concord at 11:00 P.M. for the return drive to Hanover.

Fortunately, the "let the local organizations loose" to develop strategy worked at least as well in Concord as it did in other parts of the state. By Friday, January 12, Sandra Hoeh had the first organizing meeting of the Concord committee. Approximately a dozen people attended, an organization was formed, Dr. David G. Underwood was elected the local chair, and a schedule for keeping the Concord state headquarters open was drafted. Between Barbara Underwood and Marsha Macey, the co-chair, their friends, and their children (elementary school-aged), the headquarters was kept open, the telephone answered, furniture provided, a sign painted, and the early semblance of campaign activity began to take shape. (Underwood, op. cit., p. 34)

As Studds and I were struggling to organize a campaign in New Hampshire, a similar effort was underway in Washington. Unknown to us at the time, obstacles were facing Blair Clark and Senator McCarthy's senatorial staff, his family, and his Washington friends. We were assuming that things were moving rapidly in Washington, and when we were ready for Washington help it would be there. Fortunately, perhaps, we did not visit Washington until after the New Hampshire primary nor did we wait for Washington directions. We knew enough about the New Hampshire situation and about Senator McCarthy to organize with a minimum of contact with Washington.

With local organization beginning, we now turned to finding personnel for the statewide campaign. Since neither of us could work full-time, this meant that several important functions such as press/media activity, scheduling, and schedule advance work would have to be carried out by others. We assumed again, as we had during the McCarthy's December visit, that some of the advance work would be the responsibility of the New Hampshire campaign but that the major responsibility for advancing local schedules for Senator McCarthy would be covered by persons assigned from Washington. We also assumed that scheduling would be coordinated through a New Hampshire contact with Washington. We felt that press activity would have to be covered in New Hampshire either by someone available for the job in the state or brought in from Washington and assigned to New Hampshire. The former situation was preferable since experience with New Hampshire reporters and media was important to establish credibility while avoiding mistakes.

The first to join the campaign in a full-time paid capacity was a New Hampshire ex-newspaper reporter, Bill Gallagher, who was then self-employed as a photographer.

Bill lived in Lebanon, had written for the *Valley News,* and was familiar with the New Hampshire press situation. In addition, his photographic abilities would help support both the public image of the campaign and provide file photos to be used in preparing campaign materials. To get a photograph in a New Hampshire newspaper other than the *Concord Daily Monitor* or the *Manchester Union Leader,* the photograph had to be supplied complete with story and caption.

After some struggling with the scheduling problems, Studds and I concluded that there was only one person in New Hampshire with the experience to coordinate Senator McCarthy's in-state schedule and that was Sandra Hoeh. Sandra operated statewide via her telephone to check, arrange, adjust, and then to evaluate each of the senator's visits to the state. This also meant close coordination with the local committees, the state headquarters, the senatorial office, local committees, the national campaign headquarters, and the press.

With scheduling chores came the need to have the proposed campaign schedules effectively advanced to check times and to review the detail of each event that was advised in the schedule draft. The first person who accepted the task disappeared in the midst of the preparations for the McCarthy's first visit. The help Studds and I presumed would come from Washington did not materialize satisfactorily. By trial and error and by field-training our own volunteers, the ability to advance schedules developed in the campaign. During the early stages that advancing was more fiction than reality and gave us tremendous concern.

The major hole in the campaign continued to be management. Since the McCarthy effort appeared from the outside to be on such shaky political ground, few professionals with campaign experience were willing to accept the economic uncertainty of working for Senator McCarthy. There was no one in New Hampshire beyond Studds and myself with the experience who was also willing to assume the managerial job. The same was true nationally. The job would remain unfilled until Curtis Gans was assigned to New Hampshire.

What we learned later was that any warm body with even a smidgen of experience who walked into the Washington headquarters was assigned to work there. Only those who had recently changed jobs, lost jobs, had independent incomes, or had recently graduated from college appeared to be willing to sign on with the campaign in anything but a part-time or voluntary capacity. The political pros were not available to McCarthy and as a consequence New Hampshire went without a full-time manager for at least half of the ten-week campaign.

The task second only to organization was to create a mailing list to use in contacting New Hampshire's registered Democratic and independent voters. New Hampshire's elections were then conducted by use of paper ballots in all but Portsmouth and one ward in the Manchester. The voting lists were compiled and published by the supervisors of the checklist in each of the voting districts. Since the supervisors met only occasionally to perform their duties and were compensated little if at all, the objective of their work, the checklist, became their pride and joy and often almost a secret document. Of course the required number were printed and properly posted for each election, but few if any extra copies were available.

The McCarthy campaigners needed only a particular list, the one used to record the votes cast in a primary election. That list and only that list would have the names of the voters with a party identification. The most recent primary election had occurred in the fall of 1966. Getting the local checklist of the high-priority cities and towns for the 1966 fall primary election proved to be a difficult early task for each of the local McCarthy committees. Although by law these lists are open for public inspection, that did not mean that a copy of the list had to be provided for inspection or that an up-to-date list had to be maintained and made available upon request. In fact, more than a few of the checklist supervisors kept their up-to-date record in a card file which was legally something between a public record and a private collection in their mind. A McCarthy worker might be given an old copy of the list, or directed to the most recent list posted in a dark corner of the town hall or ward house, or not find anything but a carefully protected card file.

It should be noted that there is a pretense of bipartisanship attached to maintaining the local checklist of voters. Of the three supervisors, one has to be a member of the opposition party. Since the party that controls the voting machinery, of which the checklist is the most important part, frequently controls the results of elections, the minority Democratic Party in New Hampshire often had a difficult time gaining access to the lists. As a result, in the early days of the McCarthy effort collecting voting lists called for ingenuity and persistence. Much local volunteer energy was devoted to searching for the lists or copying them from the faded sheets posted in ward houses, polling places, or from a card file. The Republican-dominated towns had always been suspicious of Democrats asking for the lists and now, with the upstart Democrat McCarthy challenging LBJ, even the minority of Democratic supervisors were uncooperative. As the quest for the lists failed more than once, Studds and I considered a formal protest to the attorney general, but even that offered little promise since the attorney general was an appointee of the incumbent governor, Democrat and LBJ backer, John W. King.

The lists were of vital importance to the campaign. Names from the lists would be transferred to mailing labels which would give the campaign a way to reach all registered Democratic and Independent voters. The only other way to accomplish this objective would be to blanket mail to the targeted cities and towns. Such a blanket mailing would have been expensive and not sufficiently focused to accomplish the objective of reaching targeted registered Democratic and Independent voters.

Following the difficult job of collecting the local checklists was the even more formidable task of using the lists to prepare mailing labels—especially in the era before word processors and personal computers. Typing these labels was the first important but obviously uninspiring volunteer task of the campaign. Approximately one hundred thousand names and addresses had to be taken from the voting lists, typed on four-carbon label sheets, and then carefully stored by zip code until the time when they would be used for the first mailing. Since the effort to gather the lists was difficult and the lists were hard to photocopy, most were kept safely in the headquarters. This meant that volunteers had to be recruited to do the typing and someone else would have to supervise the list library. The Concord headquarters was the list repository and became the place where most of the label preparation and mailing was accomplished. This meant more work for the Concord McCarthy committee.

Studds and I assumed responsibility for specific New Hampshire-based tasks such as scheduling, organization, and overall campaign planning. We would facilitate an eventual mailing by seeing that mailing labels were prepared, strengthen the effectiveness of the campaign through state and local organizing, and promote these efforts through state generated publicity. We assumed that almost everything else needed to make the campaign successful would be provided from Washington. This meant that the items that were to be included in the mailing, the campaign materials such as brochures, posters, bumper stickers, etc., would be delivered from the national headquarters. In addition all but that publicity that was specific to New Hampshire activities would also come from Washington.

Bill Gallagher would publicize the organization of the local committees, campaign schedules, and replies to charges developed at the New Hampshire level. Advertising media and materials would be a Washington problem, and one that Studds and I thought we could safely ignore while concentrating on the numerous tasks requiring immediate attention.

Exceptions to this began to occur immediately, much to our distress. Some basic materials were needed immediately in order to give the campaign identity, such as stationery, envelopes, press release paper, and a headquarters sign. Along with these items, it was important to reserve billboard space to increase McCarthy's recognition in New Hampshire. Mervin Weston, a member of the earliest New Hampshire McCarthy committee, owned an advertising agency and agreed to help us with the graphics space reservations and ordering of the essential materials. The only material for McCarthy that anyone had seen were the buttons Lowenstein had brought with him in November and a few others leftover from McCarthy's recent Minnesota senatorial contest. The senatorial button was a simple, distinctly lettered item using two shades of blue, one navy, the other aqua. Weston felt the type style would perform well but asked what the campaign slogan would be. After a series of telephone calls to Washington, I discovered that no slogan had been selected. Several more calls were made to discuss some New Hampshire suggestions. For lack of a better phrase and for expediency, the slogan THERE IS AN ALTERNATIVE—McCARTHY FOR PRESIDENT was accepted.

Even such a simple item as an official campaign photograph did not appear to exist at that early stage. Photographers who had accompanied McCarthy on his first New Hampshire visit were contacted for proof copies of any photos they might have. The photo files and graphic art resources that are usually well set before most major campaigns begin were simply not available. This meant improvisation was the rule.

CHARGES AND COUNTERCHARGES

To establish credibility for the New Hampshire organization and to counter what appeared to be the total takeover of the Democratic Party by the LBJ leadership, I challenged the use of Democratic Party funds to support the Johnson campaign. As part of our strategy, Studds and I wanted to keep the LBJ organization on the defensive as much as possible. In a David and Goliath contest such a strategy would be difficult, but there appeared to be some points of vulnerability.

The issue raised by the Robert Kennedy write-in leader Eugene Daniell tipped me off to the fact that the LBJ leaders intended to not only convert the Democratic State Committee organization into an LBJ campaign committee but that they intended to finance the LBJ effort with funds raised to support the New Hampshire Democratic Party itself. Frank Merrick, writing in the January 6, 1968, edition of the *Concord Daily Monitor*, said:

> Sen. Eugene McCarthy's entry into the New Hampshire presidential primary could possibly pose problems for Democrats in the state general election next November.
>
> The stickler is that the Democratic State Committee is spending funds on President Johnson's candidacy, despite the fact that two dissident Democratic groups exist.
>
> David C. Hoeh, McCarthy's state chairman, put his finger on the problem when he noted that some of the members of his group contributed some of the money being spent on Johnson. Hoeh said the money was intended to help finance the operations of the state committee and its full-time staff, not to help get Johnson elected.
>
> This might well hurt the state committee's ability to raise money from within the state for the regular election, he said.
>
> Traditionally, at least in state elections, political committees such as the Democratic State Committee, stay neutral until after the September primaries. But the state committee voted to endorse Johnson and campaign on his behalf.
>
> Because of Atty. Gen. George Pappagianis' ruling on campaign committees, the Citizens for Johnson Committee set up by the state committee technically will be spending money contributed to the party, not to a campaign for Johnson.
>
> Thus, Hoeh could be right, the situation could produce rancor that carries over into the state elections. Just how serious the situation becomes depends, of course, on how much support McCarthy and the unauthorized Robert F. Kennedy movement get.
>
> Bernard L. Boutin, Citizen for Johnson co-chair, concedes that having McCarthy's name on the ballot will make it harder to give him a drubbing in March but says his committee will not change its plans for a Johnson write-in.
>
> There was theorizing after McCarthy's announcement that pro-Johnson Democrats might switch to a favorite son campaign or, even more a remote possibility, Johnson might permit his name to be on the ballot.
>
> The theorizing was based on the fact that what matters to Johnson is how the primary results look to the rest of the nation. He needs a wide victory margin. A close margin could hurt, even if caused purely by not having his or a favorite son's name on the ballot.
>
> (*Concord Daily Monitor*, January 6, 1968)

By alleging a misappropriation of Democratic Party funds, I built on the sensitive "fair play" in primaries ethos that had been nurtured by the *Manchester Union Leader.* Boutin was obviously uncomfortable with having to answer reporters' questions concerning the organization of the LBJ campaign and how that campaign was to be funded.

Instead of being able to discuss the positive record of LBJ and the numerous endorsements LBJ was receiving from the state, county, and local leadership of the New Hampshire Democratic Party, Boutin was constantly defending his actions. To Boutin it seemed that the only items of interest to the reporters were the campaign's funding and what Boutin thought McCarthy's impact would be. The LBJ committee's press releases received little or no newspaper attention.

From the earliest point in the campaign, I realized that a campaign against an incumbent president from within the Democratic Party would stimulate press attention. Such a conflict would make news which would amplify the effort beyond any capacity to buy advertising media. Beyond being an attraction as a media event, the sympathies of many of New Hampshire's reporters were with the antiwar challenge and the underdog McCarthy. New Hampshire's wire service reporters, newspaper writers, and radio reporters were almost all in their twenties. They were our contemporaries and found us to be helpful and open to their questions and willing to provide newsworthy tips. Most importantly these reporters were also willing to call for a response from the McCarthy campaign before sending a LBJ campaign charge out over the wires.

The decision to have McCarthy's announcement to enter the New Hampshire primary take place in New Hampshire had given most of the reporters their first national and international byline. This important foundation of shared interests gave the McCarthy effort an essential boost during the January weeks when the campaign was stumbling to organize. Simply stated, the New Hampshire McCarthy campaign was good news. It was spontaneous, had human interest, and had the appealing vitality of a grass root political movement.

Within the first two struggling weeks of the campaign Studds and I had been successful in giving the effort vitality. Part of this success came from McCarthy's own unique political posture and part from the growing frustration of the voting public with things as they were early in 1968. But, undeniably, the growing McCarthy campaign in New Hampshire and nationally was lively news, even optimistic news. It was appealing in contrast to the ponderous news of the LBJ administration and the depressing news from Vietnam and the American cities.

The McCarthy effort was coming to life in New Hampshire. It was beginning to find its place in the public's stream of consciousness. The art form of campaign politics requires that a campaign organization project consistency with the public image of the candidate, respond to the ability of the voter to tolerate issue contents, and adapt to the particular political climate of a jurisdiction. To be successful, each of these constraints had to be carefully observed. Since this campaign began differently, had different objectives, and sought different methods, it started by bending if not actually breaking many of the conventions of political activity. Its success could be ensured by continuing to be distinct and continuing to find different ways to organize and gain the allegiance of the New Hampshire voters. The importance of the biography of the New Hampshire campaign is that the leaders were able to calculate the risks and then reach out to the voters in a manner that produced the desired results.

Electoral politics is at best a chance. When there is a competitive situation the odds are even. As a result most campaigns are conservative, seek to avoid risks, minimize exposure, and attempt to control events. To outward appearances, campaigns are often boring, narrow, lack imagination, concentrate on accepted or acceptable societal standards, and fail to strain either the mental or institutional capacities of the population. Under the best of circumstances campaigns create excitement through images, hoopla, style, rhetoric, and method but rarely through serious debate or constructive dialogue. To accomplish anything with the McCarthy candidacy in New Hampshire, Studds and I realized that many of the rules of campaigns and the lessons of our own campaign experiences would have to be quickly and carefully examined and new rules created in order to make the McCarthy candidacy work.

CHAPTER 6

Early State Campaign Operations

MAILING AND VOLUNTEERS

In the December 1967 memorandum to Senator McCarthy, Studds and I wrote:

> We envision a massive mailing effort—of the quality and extent of the Lodge effort in 1966—to all registered Democrats and Independents.

Coupled with this promise was an assumption also stated in the December memorandum:

> We have already acquired the voting lists for the entire state (All registrants: Democratic, Unaffiliated, and Republican).

Acquiring the lists and making such lists into something usable for mailings were two quite distinct tasks, as we found out shortly after the state headquarters opened in Concord. We had assumed that the lists would be readily transferable to mailing labels and that these labels could be used to direct the basic messages of the McCarthy candidacy. What we found was that the lists were anything but orderly, most omitted proper addresses, and some important communities were missing altogether.

The plan called for two distinct mailings. One would be to the registered Democrats and the other to the unaffiliated or independent voters. Therefore, each checklist had to be reviewed twice to produce labels for each class of voters. The major problem, however, was that many New Hampshire communities do not record the address of the voter on the checklist. This meant that reverse telephone directories, regular telephone directories, or city directories had to be used to find the correct address for each voter.

When the first of the Concord volunteers arrived at the headquarters and began struggling with the lists, a deep shudder was felt in the young campaign. Approximately 110,000 names had to be taken from the voting lists to construct the basic mailing file of the campaign. As soon as the first checklists were examined and the first label sheets put into a volunteer's portable typewriter a telephone call was made to Studds and me. What we thought would be a simple task vanished in chaos.

Much of the campaign had been predicated on the Lodge write-in model. The variation of the model that we felt would succeed for McCarthy was that, in addition to the registered Democrats, we expected to attract a significant number of independents into the Democratic column to vote for Senator McCarthy. To have this happen a direct personalized appeal had to be made. The independent voters had to receive a letter from Senator McCarthy urging them to vote for him. The appeal to the Democrats was almost the same as that which had been directed to the registered Republicans by the organizers of the Lodge effort in 1964. There was an alternative to Lyndon B. Johnson, and there were substantial reasons for considering a vote for McCarthy.

It was unthinkable to abandon this keystone of the McCarthy campaign effort in New Hampshire. The mailing was essential and it had to be personally addressed. Weighing alternatives Studds and I considered scrapping the mailing as a direct appeal and blanket mailing to the critical cities and towns instead. Such a blanket mailing could be accomplished by using a commercial direct mailing house, but the message would be indiscreet and impersonal because it could not be targeted at specific voting groups. Any appearance of professionalism on behalf of Senator McCarthy would be lost by such a broadcast approach. At this point we made our first appeal for help to the McCarthy national headquarters. Previously an appeal for a manager and an advance person had been made, but not a request for volunteers. By late January the first trickle of volunteers had begun. The mailing label job was still proceeding at a ponderously slow pace, but between the dedication of local volunteers and the vitality of those willing to come all the way to New Hampshire to help, the right mood for the miserable job was set.

DELEGATE SELECTION STRATEGY

Almost the furthest thing from either our minds was the possibility that delegates would be elected representing McCarthy. The campaign concept was to dent the political armor of Lyndon Johnson by showing that a significant segment of his party was willing to vote against him when given the opportunity. There was no question in the minds of any of those involved in the campaign that if Lyndon

Johnson wanted the nomination he had it. From all of the evidence in New Hampshire, Johnson not only wanted to be renominated, but he also wanted a vote of approval for his policy in Vietnam. Johnson, it appeared, would only be vulnerable on the presidential preference side of the two-part New Hampshire ballot, and this is where the McCarthy leadership would focus the campaign.

On January 7, 1968, the *New York Times* published the following editorial which reminded Studds and me of the importance of the delegate portion of the ballot:

McCarthy in New Hampshire

> Early in 1952 President Truman had privately made up his mind to retire, but organization Democrats in New Hampshire persuaded him to enter his name in the state's primary. Otherwise, they argued, a slate of political unknowns pledged to Senator Estes Kefauver of Tennessee would win by default. "If the boss doesn't win that primary," one Truman aid remarked at the time, "those New Hampshire fellows better not show their faces around the White House."
>
> The unexpected happened. Senator Kefauver, with his coonskin cap and tireless handshake, routed the better known Truman delegation.
>
> Senator Eugene McCarthy can take some comfort from this history. President Johnson today has the backing of the Democratic party organization and of most of the leaders. But party organizations do not count for much in New Hampshire, and leaders can often deliver nobody's vote but their own. Under these circumstances, Senator McCarthy was well advised to change his mind and enter the New Hampshire primary.
>
> President Johnson, taking care to avoid the fiasco that befell President Truman, has refused to authorize the use of his name in New Hampshire. As a result, his supporters are running as delegates "favorable" rather than "pledged" to him and are seeking write-in votes for him on the preferential side of the ballot since his name will not be listed. This cautious approach will enable Mr. Johnson to claim all the credit for a victory and to blur the significance of a defeat.
>
> The history of Republican primary voting in New Hampshire is likewise encouraging to Gov. George Romney the G.O.P. underdog. In 1952 in the Republican primary General Eisenhower, absent in Paris, defeated Senator Robert A. Taft, who campaigned vigorously. Four years ago a write-in campaign for Henry Cabot Lodge swamped the two Republican front-runners.
>
> Against this background of insurgency and independent thinking there is no reason to suppose that New Hampshire voters are particularly conservative or hawkish. Governor Romney can thus afford to discount the polls that show him running far behind former Vice President Nixon and to rely upon his own formidable talent for man-to-man persuasion. New Hampshire is not going to decide the nomination in either party, but no one should underestimate its capacity to manufacture political surprises.
>
> (*New York Times*, January 7, 1968)

Given this reminder, Studds and I concluded that a slate of delegates had to be filed in order to show the seriousness of the New Hampshire McCarthy campaign. Without delegates the campaign would be criticized as being just an effort to embarrass the president and to assist the Republican Party in winning the election in November.

I was unfamiliar with the political importance of the delegate filing process and called former Democratic National Committeeman William L. Dunfey to ask his advice. My question concerned how Dunfey perceived the difference between the two classes of delegates—those "pledged" and those "favorable." Studds and I knew the legal difference, but were not fully aware of the political advantages. Dunfey explained that filing a delegation "pledged" to the McCarthy nomination would give those making the slate complete control over the number of delegate candidates that would be filed under the label. Each "pledged" delegate had to have written authorization from the candidate before being permitted to file with the label "pledged." He pointed out that anyone could file as a "favorable" delegate candidate by simply paying the $10 filing fee. He also noted that the Johnson write-in leaders were so sure of their candidate's vote-getting power that they did not plan to control the number of individuals filing for the delegate and alternate delegate slots.

With this advice Studds and I adopted the "pledged" delegate strategy and agreed to control the number of candidates. To make this strategy work, however, we had to discourage individuals from filing as delegate candidates "favorable" to the nomination of Senator McCarthy. Unfortunately, even before this decision had been made, two McCarthy supporters from Cheshire County (Keene area) had already filed as "favorable" to McCarthy.

After the conversation with William Dunfey, Studds and I concluded that we had to develop a full slate of candidates. The delegates and alternates were assigned to New Hampshire in accordance with the rules of the Democratic National Committee which meant first, delegates were to be elected by congressional districts, and second, since New Hampshire had supported the election of the Democratic candidate in the previous election (1964), it was entitled to a reward—an increase in the total size of the delegation. The number of slots in each of the state's two congressional districts were twelve delegates and twelve alternates, a total of forty-eight candidate openings.

Gerry Studds agreed to make it his job to fill the forty-eight spots. The strategy we adopted was to attract attention to the McCarthy New Hampshire effort by awarding places on the ballot on the basis of geographical distribution. The usual strategy, the one used in the John Kennedy delegate selection fight of 1960, was to select delegate candidates on the basis of prominence and location. The latter criteria meant that most of the 1st Congressional District candidates came from Manchester, the largest Democratic Party city, and from Nashua and Berlin, the 2nd Congressional District's largest Democratic vote-producing centers.

We concluded that the likelihood of electing delegates was remote, so instead of geographically concentrating delegate candidates from a few of the most populous cities of a district, we decided to seek candidates in a manner that would geographically disperse the campaign. We also sought to reward with delegate positions those prominent figures who had come out in support of Senator McCarthy.

With forty-eight places to fill, Studds had assumed a considerable task. His first telephone calls brought somewhat strange responses. Instead of immediately saying yes or no to his request, many responded by saying they would have to check their plans for the coming summer. They said they would not become candidates unless they were free to attend the convention scheduled for August. It had not occurred to us that more than a delegate or two would be elected, and even in our most optimistic projection we had not expected that these people would actually go to Chicago in August. The failure of these people to help the campaign by lending their names to the effort for purposes of filling the slate caused some serious problems. As a result, the job of filling the slate became one of convincing supporters of potential value to the slate to allow Studds to add their names to his list. At the same time, he now found that several of those who he had thought would become candidates were now reluctant to do so because they had conflicts with their summer schedules and the dates of the Democratic National Convention. This reaction startled both Studds and me because the real purpose of their delegate strategy was to show the seriousness of the campaign by filing locally prominent names as delegate candidates.

According to New Hampshire Revised Statutes Annotated Chapter 57, Section 53:5, "The name of a candidate shall not be printed upon any such ballot unless not more than sixty nor less than thirty days before the primary he files with the secretary of state a declaration of candidacy. . . ." The thirty-day filing period began January 13th and would close Saturday, February 10 at 5:00 P.M. Studds kept the names of the campaign leaders in reserve and contacted geographically dispersed campaign workers. Again he faced the problem of having serious voids in the list. Principally these voids appeared in the southeastern area of the state, Rochester, Somersworth, and Dover, and in the north, Berlin and Gorham.

Studds roughed out a slate from those who were willing to run. It became obvious that building the ideal slate would take more time than was justified. Consequently Studds began assigning places in the slate to the leadership, including his own name, my name, and Sandra's as alternates. Even with such action taken, however, there still remained a number of slots unfilled.

A second problem occurred during the same period. The "pledged" delegate candidacy required the written consent of the candidate for president and that consent had to be filed prior to the expiration date of the filing period on February 10. McCarthy was scheduled to visit New Hampshire late in January and probably would not return to the state again until after the expiration of the filing date.

We concluded that it would not be possible to complete the slate before McCarthy's late January visit. Getting the final slate to McCarthy for signing prior to the February 10 deadline would be chancy, given the senator's possible international travel plans and the vagaries of New Hampshire weather. I proposed that a blank statement be prepared with space for forty-eight names. An appropriate consent statement and a space for Senator McCarthy's signature were added. This solution received Blair Clark's approval. When Senator McCarthy arrived in New Hampshire on January 26, he signed the blank slate, and Studds continued the job of finding candidates to lend their names to the list.

At the same time the Johnson committee was announcing the names of the prominent New Hampshire Democratic Party leadership who were filing as delegate candidates "favorable" to the renomination of President Johnson. In addition to the approved candidates a large number of spontaneous filings occurred. By the end of the filing period there would be twenty-six Johnson delegate candidates in the 1st Congressional District and nineteen in the 2nd Congressional District for the twelve allocated spots for each district.

DISSOLUTION OF THE RFK WRITE-IN CAMPAIGN

By letter dated January 2, 1968, addressed to Eugene Daniell, the leader of the New Hampshire Kennedy write-in effort, Robert F. Kennedy asked Daniell to "cease your efforts in my behalf." (*Boston Herald-Traveler*, January 7, 1968) Daniell's reaction to what he said was the first communication he had received from Kennedy, was that the request "had not changed anything." (*Boston Herald-Traveler*, January 7, 1968) Daniell continued his effort to file delegates "favorable" to the nomination of the New York Senator and to solicit a write-in vote for the Senator on the March 12 presidential primary ballot.

At the same time Robert Kennedy wrote Daniell asking him to "cease" activities in his behalf in New Hampshire; he stated that he would "remain neutral in the Democratic Presidential Primaries." Kennedy stated that he did not think he would "further the cause of peace in Vietnam by throwing his support to Senator Eugene J. McCarthy." (*New York Times*, January 9, 1968) In the same statement Kennedy reaffirmed his contention that "Mr. McCarthy's entry into the Presidential race was a healthy influence, because it helped channel protest within the limits of the democratic process."

This equivocation on the part of Kennedy presented serious problems for the New Hampshire and national McCarthy campaigns. McCarthy himself had expected that when he took the first step to focus protest toward the political system he would receive the support of his congressional colleagues who had been outspoken in their opposition to the war in Vietnam. However, as late as his entry in the New Hampshire primary, not one member of the senate had come forward to support his position. Especially distressing to him and to the evolving campaign organization was the fact that Robert Kennedy continued to play a coy game in the political wings of both those opposing the war and those supporting the renomination of Lyndon Johnson.

In a column published January 8, 1968, Mary McGrory alluded to the dilemma of this frustration when she wrote:

> Since Nov. 30, when he (McCarthy) announced his intention to challenge the President, McCarthy has been accused by the Johnson forces of being a stalking horse for Senator Robert F. Kennedy. The RFK followers, complaining of McCarthy's inertia, have begun to call McCarthy "a stalking horse for Lyndon Johnson."
>
> (*Boston Globe*, January 8, 1968)

While Studds and I tried to ignore Daniell's efforts and avoided any direct conflict with him, his activity remained a problem in our effort to develop a unified opposition to Johnson. The same situation occurred nationally and slowed what Blair Clark and McCarthy thought would be a significant movement of money and endorsements to McCarthy during those important early weeks following his announcement. In the four primaries McCarthy had said he would enter, all were almost totally dependent on funds raised in their states to support the McCarthy effort.

Kennedy's impact diverted attention from McCarthy as a serious candidate toward his possible role as an RFK stalking horse. For the early weeks of 1968, the influential *New York Times* focused much of its attention to the prospect of a Kennedy candidacy, to the point of all but excluding coverage of McCarthy's budding campaign. The secondary impact of *Times* coverage was to distort other media interest in McCarthy and especially the McCarthy effort in New Hampshire. Since staff to cover anything but local events and an occasional state event are severely limited in most instances, the regional press takes its cues from as reliable a source as it can find. Beyond that conditioning was the fact that Robert Kennedy was of special regional news interest. His family was overwhelmingly prominent in Massachusetts, and he was currently serving as the junior U.S. Senator from nearby New York State.

While perhaps not significant to the casual observer of New Hampshire politics, the *Daily Dartmouth*, the student-run newspaper of Dartmouth College, played a particularly interesting role in the New Hampshire McCarthy campaign. The *Daily Dartmouth* picked up the editorial inclination of the *New York Times* from the beginning and as a result the *Daily Dartmouth* speculated as to the impact of McCarthy's New Hampshire announcement on the possible candidacy of Robert F. Kennedy. In its first interview with me immediately following McCarthy's New Hampshire announcement, the *Daily Dartmouth* headlined the story, "Can McCarthy Lure RFK Backers?" (*Daily Dartmouth*, January 5, 1968) The lead read:

> David C. Hoeh, Associate Director of the College's Public Affairs Center and head of the McCarthy for President movement in New Hampshire, predicted yesterday that support for Robert Kennedy will "dry up" in the wake of Minnesota Senator Eugene McCarthy's announcement. . . .

The consequence of the *Daily Dartmouth*'s emphasis as well as that of the *Times* was to reflect on the emerging national political scene from the perspective of its potential impact on RFK. Subsequent interviews, both in the *Daily Dartmouth* and on the popular student-operated radio station WDCR, took this theme. This effectively diverted student and faculty attention from the significance of the developing McCarthy effort in New Hampshire. The impact was seen especially among those individuals who carefully calculated the investment of their political and intellectual capital. These people, anticipating a possible Kennedy announcement, tended to be cautious and avoided becoming involved in the campaign. Only those few faculty, residents, and students who strayed from Hanover to become involved in various protest or political events were attracted to the McCarthy activity.

Daniell's activity on behalf of Kennedy was noisy enough and significantly reinforced by media sources to perpetuate the prospect of a roughly equal contest between McCarthy and Kennedy. Given that prospect, many chose not to become involved. This was a situation that for many did not change until after the final returns had been recorded on March 12.

On January 16, Daniell filed himself and five others as delegate candidates favorable to RFK. In the following weeks additional delegate and alternate candidates filed as Daniell tried to keep the write-in effort alive by emphasizing the importance of the delegate filings. There was, however, no substantive organizing on the part of the RFK committee during January.

Early in February, Theodore C. Sorensen, a former top policy aide of President John F. Kennedy, asked to meet with the members of Daniell's RFK committee. The session was scheduled for February 7. At that time Daniell had been successful in filing fifteen candidates for the delegate slots favorable to the nomination of Robert Kennedy. Sorensen came accompanied by William L. Dunfey.

Dunfey had arranged the meeting in hopes of discouraging the Daniell group from continuing their unauthorized efforts on behalf of Robert Kennedy. He felt that bringing someone like Sorensen to New Hampshire would convey the message in irrefutable terms. Sorensen met with the group and urged them to "cease and desist" in their efforts to secure a write-in vote for RFK. Sorensen followed the meeting with a press conference in which he described the message he delivered to Daniell's committee.

Sorensen described himself as a "friend, lawyer, and unofficial advisor" to Senator Kennedy. In his press conference he explained, "New Hampshire Democrats will have a choice in next month's primary between two real candidates, U.S. Senator Eugene J. McCarthy and President Johnson." He noted that "to cast a ballot for a non-candidate is a wasted vote. Therefore, if even one vote is cast for him (RFK) in the New Hampshire primary the senator will regard it as one vote too many." He concluded by saying, "Senator Kennedy wanted me to persuade everyone supporting him in this drive that they are performing a grave disservice to the senator, his beliefs, and the Democratic Party." With this Sorensen reaffirmed Kennedy's noncandidacy by repeating Kennedy's statement, "I will not be a candidate against President Johnson this year under any foreseeable circumstances." (*Manchester Union Leader*, February 8, 1968)

Sorensen's visit had its intended impact. Major media attention gave the visit front-page coverage and illustrated Kennedy's reluctance to be identified with the New Hampshire write-in effort. Dunfey had carefully assessed the situation and determined that Kennedy's political future could be seriously harmed by Daniell's poorly organized effort in New Hampshire. Sorensen was the chosen messenger with authority to speak for the senator. Kennedy was not running in New Hampshire and no authorization, direct or indirect by omission or commission, could legitimize the use of his name by Daniell and his group. Daniell held his "press on" position but his group began to have serious doubts. Never a large organization, Daniell began to receive calls from his supporters and even from several of those who had filed as delegate candidates favorable to RFK. With this pressure, Sorensen's visit, and the successful conclusion of his legal action, Daniell issued the following statement on February 9, one day before the close of the delegate filing period:

Statement of the Members of the New Hampshire RFK in '68 Committee Made at a Meeting Held at Their Manchester Headquarters 51 Newberry St. on February 9, 1968

> The New Hampshire R.F.K. in '68 Committee will continue to do all in its power to support Robert F. Kennedy and the principles he has so courageously expressed.
>
> In deference to his request we encourage all his many loyal friends and sympathizers not to write in his name in the coming presidential primary, but as the best means of giving support to his views and in particular those concerning Vietnam, we unanimously endorse and will actively work for the presidential campaign in this state of Senator Eugene McCarthy.
>
> We feel that all those who seek to perpetuate the glorious traditions and democratic principles for which the late John F. Kennedy gave his life, must condemn the present tendency of the New Hampshire Democratic Party, under the domination of "Citizens for Johnson," to adopt the tactics so common to authoritarian and communist countries. In particular, we oppose the undercover intimidation, numbered identification cards, and many less subtle means of interfering with the free choice of New Hampshire voters. We further deplore the absolute refusal of the Johnson supporters to publicly debate the issues now facing this great state.
>
> Fully understanding that Robert F. Kennedy is not, and will not, except in case of unforeseeable developments, going to become a candidate for president, and further giving due consideration to his expressed disapproval of any delegate to the Democratic National Convention running favorable to him, we nevertheless feel that this is a decision peculiar to each individual in which the Senator would not presume to dictate. Some of our Kennedy delegates wish to continue and we pledge our support to them. A majority of our delegates, in view of the plea of Senator Kennedy, have decided to withdraw as delegates.
>
> As a Kennedy organization we pledge ourselves to one hundred percent support of Senator Eugene McCarthy and his New Hampshire campaign. We offer our services in any capacity and are united in our complete opposition to Lyndon B. Johnson.
>
> Approved by a unanimous vote,
> (Signed)
> Eugene S. Daniell, Jr., Chairman

An event of significant political proportions to the fledging McCarthy effort had been accomplished. A potentially divisive companion effort had been eliminated without acrimony. The pressure to end the RFK write-in had come from Robert

Kennedy himself, which could be interpreted in two ways. The first, and least apparent, was that he wished to protect himself from a weak and potentially surrogate managed political event. But second, and of greater importance, was the appearance of support for the New Hampshire McCarthy effort that could be read from Kennedy's request.

Kennedy was a prominent critic of the Johnson administration's Vietnam policy whose early statements had encouraged those organizing the McCarthy effort. Sorensen's only reference to the McCarthy campaign during his New Hampshire visit was that "it speaks for itself." (*Manchester Union Leader*, February 8, 1968) Reacting to Daniell's announcement, I issued a brief statement dated February 11, which read:

> We are delighted with this development. It unites all those in New Hampshire who with both Senator Kennedy and Senator McCarthy take strong issue with the manner in which Lyndon Johnson has broken the pledges he made to the Democratic Party and to the American people in 1964.

With my statement was also a statement from Sandra Hoeh, Democratic State Committee 2nd District chair, concerning Eugene Daniell's success before the New Hampshire Supreme Court and that court's reversal of the attorney general's ruling on the issue of political contributions. The statement further demonstrated the positive aspects of Daniell's effort and linked the McCarthy campaign with the legitimizing value of the New Hampshire Supreme Court's finding on behalf of Daniell. The statement read:

> The decision announced by the N.H. Supreme Court—to the effect that a candidate's consent is not required before money may be raised and spent in his behalf—compounds the tragedy of the New Hampshire Democratic State Committee. Making the New Hampshire "Citizens for Johnson" effort a subcommittee of the Democratic State Committee was disgraceful from the beginning. Ironically, it has now also become unnecessary. To convert the State Committee into an active campaign organization for a candidate (not to mention a non-candidate) in a primary election is a perversion of the legitimate role of the Committee and a flagrant distortion of the primary process.
>
> As a member of the Executive Committee of the Democratic State Committee, I call on the members of the Committee supporting Lyndon Johnson to think for a moment about what a primary is for. I call on them to apologize for their misuse of our Committee, to recall all Johnson literature and materials bearing the imprint of the Democratic State Committee, and to organize themselves as one group of Democrats supporting one of the two Democratic candidates in the coming primary. The people will decide on March 12th who our Party's candidate will be.

The two events gave the McCarthy campaign an important strategic as well as an important media success. The campaign had developed sufficient strength not only to draw attention to but to capitalize on events that were external to the campaign. The combination of events into an important political statement demonstrated to observers that the campaign was in capable hands and that it could be responsive to the political events that were not necessarily developed by the campaign or generated outside of the state.

On the other hand the Johnson campaign suffered at least two critical blows during the period. The first was that Robert Kennedy was clearly assuming a hands-off position. He would not come to New Hampshire to campaign for the renomination of Lyndon Johnson as Bernard Boutin had contended he would eight months earlier. At the same time he also lost the potentially divisive activity of Daniell and his write-in effort. The dissenting forces in New Hampshire were now joined behind Senator McCarthy and under the leadership not of the maverick Daniell but of respected Democratic Party workers and established local, county, and state leaders.

McCARTHY DELEGATE SLATE FILED

Daniell announced that he was ending the RFK write-in effort by press release dated February 9. The filing period for delegate candidates closed Saturday, February 10 at 5:00 P.M. Studds had been feverishly trying to complete the McCarthy slate of twenty-four delegate and twenty-four alternate delegate candidates as the deadline approached. Two serious problems remained as the last week of the filing period began to close. The first was that, in spite of his best efforts, the slate did not contain names from either Manchester or Berlin. Second, in order to file for delegate each candidate had to present himself or herself personally at the office of the secretary of state in the state capitol, Concord. Individual schedules and possible bad weather made this requirement a serious hurdle.

Studds and I had been successful in getting two persons who had filed on their own as favorable McCarthy delegates to withdraw with one subsequently being included in the pledged slate. Otherwise the record of McCarthy delegate candidate filings was clear of all names except those approved by Studds and included in the pledged slate. Unfortunately as the week came near an end, Studds still lacked a sufficient list of persons willing to file as candidates.

In the last seventy-two hours before the filing period closing, Sorensen came to New Hampshire, Daniell hedged on whether to end the RFK write-in, Studds needed delegate candidates, and I wanted to seal the end of the RFK effort as amicably as possible. I suggested to Studds that perhaps Daniell could be encouraged to fold the RFK tent if he and some of those who had already filed as RFK delegate candidates were offered places within the slate of "pledged" McCarthy delegates. He might react against the suggestion with a charge that we were trying to "buy him off," but since the interests of Daniell and the McCarthy organization were shared, the contact was certainly worth a try. In addition Daniell had filed delegate candidates who resided in both Manchester and Berlin. If these filings could be switched to McCarthy, the geographical distribution objective of the McCarthy slate would also be accomplished. When contacted by Studds, Daniell was favorable. He agreed to issue his February 9 statement ending the RFK write-in, withdraw as a favorable delegate candidate for RFK, and refile as pledged delegate for McCarthy. He said he would also call each of those who were filed as RFK delegate candidates asking them to withdraw and offer to those residing in areas where the McCarthy slate was deficient the chance to refile either as delegate or alternate candidates pledged to McCarthy.

In his conversation with Studds, Daniell indicated that a number of those who had filed for RFK did so at his request and were not particularly tied to the idea of being candidates. Others Daniell had convinced of the importance of being delegate candidates, and these he expected would want to join the pledged McCarthy slate. With Daniell's blessing and full cooperation, Studds now contacted those Daniell suggested would want to refile to schedule their trip to Concord and to help them through the procedures at the secretary of state's office. Several were able to make the change during Friday, February 9 but the last five or so slots could not be filed until Saturday. All was moving smoothly until Studds awoke Saturday morning to find that it was beginning to snow. By noon New Hampshire was in the midst of a serious storm. Roads were hazardous and the predictions were for increasing snow and freezing conditions. As late as noon several of those who had promised to make the trip to Concord had not arrived. Studds called and found all the late filers were on the road. I called Studds to check on the progress of the filings at about noon and found Studds deeply worried that the late filers might not make it through the storm in time for the 5:00 P.M. closing. I said I would leave immediately for Concord to help, but I was also faced with the worsening weather. By approximately 4:00 P.M., when I arrived in Concord, the last of the delegate slate had filed.

Forty-eight names, no more and no less, were filed for the forty-eight slots on the McCarthy slate. The RFK effort had been successfully folded into the McCarthy organization and symbolically sealed with the additional gesture of filing their geographically prominent candidates for McCarthy. On the other hand the Johnson organization, unwilling to control delegate candidate filings, was now stuck with lists of favorable candidates far in excess of the slots available. The strategy had worked better than we had expected. And the challenge of New Hampshire weather had not been an insurmountable barrier.

EARLY SCHEDULING AND FIELD OPERATIONS

Senator McCarthy's first campaign visit to New Hampshire was scheduled for Friday, January 26 and Saturday, January 27. Scheduling, the related support and logistical problems are always a major challenge in a campaign but especially in a New Hampshire presidential primary. This situation results from the fact that both the national campaign and the state organization are usually either inexperienced or rusty.

Beyond the inexperience and nervousness of a campaign venturing into New Hampshire is the fact that the serious efforts attract great press and electronic media attention. New Hampshire is the first. Consequently there is little else for the reporters and columnists to talk about except New Hampshire, the candidate, the campaign, the human interest stories, and the trivia that in later primaries will fill space occupied by analyses of past primaries, delegate selection, conventions and caucuses, issue debates, and related nomination-seeking events. As Studds and I learned when McCarthy arrived in Boston for the Sidore Lecture early in December, the reporters were attracted to New Hampshire and could not be discouraged from visiting even with an unannounced candidate. Once a candidate had announced and was scheduled to visit New Hampshire, the campaign considered that factor in its plans and made every attempt to maximize the potential for positive news. The campaign also understood that almost every step, statement, and activity would be under the probing scrutiny of the media. The campaign needed a full-scale press operation to provide copies of campaign schedules, press statements, advanced copy of speeches, and photographs to be sure that the media coverage would be adequate and positive.

The media seemed to respond to what had become known as media events. These were either regular campaign activities that attracted attention or staged episodes of human interest value that could be easily encapsulated for television viewing. There has become what amounts to a gray area in presidential campaigns between what is a legitimate means of identifying with the public and producing a circus act. The temptation is strong to perform in the center ring of the traveling show of a presidential campaign. Some candidates resist, others succumb. All have to reveal their humanity in these media rites or risk being labeled "aloof" or "detached" or "not down-to-earth." The pull to contrive and perform is tremendous upon all involved—candidates, campaign leaders, workers, and even the media. As campaign managers we were in turn faced with the difficult task of determining what would be viewed as a legitimate event that could be contrived and what might not be. Furthermore, we had to develop ways to respond to spontaneous situations to capture media impact and concentrate on how they could be properly managed to cast the most favorable light upon the candidate at any given time. For the McCarthy leadership there was always the utmost seriousness of the underlying issues of the McCarthy candidacy. It may have been, or even be now, appropriate for some candidates to run for the highest office of the land in the middle of a traveling circus, but from what Studds and I had seen of McCarthy this was not his style.

I wanted to present McCarthy in the Kennedy tradition of well-organized, fast moving, diverse, and street-level campaign activity. That model meant beginning the campaign day early, working constantly through the day, and ending late in the evening. It meant finding a series of activities that would make news, be symbolic, show the candidate's humanity, and reveal his intellectual capacities. The spectrum had to be cast within a schedule that would both reflect the qualities of the candidate while responding to the political ethos of New Hampshire.

I recalled that John F. Kennedy began his 1960 presidential drive with a press conference at the city hall in Nashua on January 25, just eight years earlier. For a campaign that felt its antecedents to be the lost spirit of JFK, no better symbolic place to begin the McCarthy drive could be found. The Nashua committee could schedule the appropriate greeting before the statue of the late president near the city hall steps, a press conference opening the campaign could follow, and then perhaps a main street handshaking tour followed by a neighborhood coffee reception. Studds and I discussed the rough outline of the morning with Jean Wallin, a Nashua state representative and McCarthy supporter. She agreed to make arrangements for the scheduled activities and scout places that would be appropriate and hospitable stopping points during McCarthy's street tour. The populous spine of New Hampshire runs from Nashua on the border with Massachusetts to Manchester, approximately twenty miles north of Nashua, to Concord approximately twenty miles north of Manchester. A convincing first day of campaigning had to cover each of the three principal New Hampshire cities. By doing this the maximum in-state media impact would be available and perhaps, with the Nashua stop, some Boston television and press coverage would also be attracted.

While Studds and I were confident of the scheduling abilities of those in Nashua, Manchester had not developed its own McCarthy committee. There are, however, two things that any candidate can and must do in Manchester. The first is to have a visible luncheon at one of the busy downtown restaurants and, if possible, be joined in that luncheon with prominent community leaders. The second is to shake hands with workers during a shift change at one of the plant gates in the historic Amoskeag Millyard.

Without an organization to build a full schedule and with the need to get to Concord before the end of the workday, we decided to shorten the Manchester visit to the "visible" luncheon, a brief block or two handshaking tour on Elm Street, and then a shift change at one of the plants in the Millyard. In the back of our minds was the reaction that McCarthy had received to his December speech in Bedford. Somehow during that first campaign visit, the less than exciting taste of McCarthy's lecture had to be erased. The best place to do that would be Manchester. Finding a place and guaranteeing an audience would be difficult. The local supporters, especially John Holland, the campaign treasurer, told us that St. Anselm College would be willing to host a speech. We were pleased that a college site was available because there would be less audience problems. Also, the conservative Catholic school would be the backdrop for McCarthy's issue critique. The speech would end the campaign day. A Friday evening was not the best time to schedule a political speech, but again the risk had to be taken in order to strengthen McCarthy's image.

Concord was also a required stop during the first visit since McCarthy might not return to New Hampshire before the closing of the candidate filing period on February 10. McCarthy would have to arrive in Concord before the secretary of state's office closed. This meant we had to get the required number of signatures—fifty names from each of the state's two congressional districts—and prepare the other details of an accurate filing.

Although Studds and I had given the signature petitions to the original steering committee members much earlier, little had been done in the rush of the early campaign to stimulate circulation. Often candidates like to file signatures far in excess of the small number required in order to show their statewide strength and appeal. Because the time was so short and many other scheduling and organizational tasks needed attention, we decided to collect just the required number of signatures. This meant that valid signatures had to be secured from each of the congressional districts and that these had to be available and in proper order for McCarthy's filing on January 26. Studds began this task along with his effort to complete the delegate candidate slate.

A McCarthy visit to Concord late on a Friday afternoon would not offer much opportunity for effective campaigning. About all that could be scheduled was a brief handshaking tour along Main Street and an official headquarters opening. The Concord committee felt it could bring out a crowd to headquarters if a reception and meet-the-candidate session were added to the ribbon cutting. Following the headquarters opening, McCarthy was scheduled to return to Manchester to relax and prepare for his speech at St. Anselm College in the evening.

Studds and I felt a reasonably good schedule had been created for McCarthy on his first campaign day. There was an open question concerning possible campaigning on the next day, Saturday, January 27, but this remained uncertain in Washington. A Saturday schedule would be difficult this early in the campaign, and winter Saturdays are difficult days. Most campaigning happens during the week when factories are in operation, children are in school, and coffee klatches can be arranged. Visits to shopping centers, a winter carnival, ski area, hockey rink, or outdoor recreation activity are possibilities, but schedules are heavily dependent on favorable weather, careful advance work, and considerable dead time spent traveling. The major outdoor winter attractions draw more out-of-staters than New Hampshirites, and while this would help McCarthy with the upcoming Massachusetts primary, it was not particularly valuable for the New Hampshire effort. There appeared to be few scheduling options for Saturday, January 27, so Studds and I left the day to McCarthy's inclination and chance.

EARLY VOLUNTEERS

A desperate feeling of loneliness began to creep back into the minds of Studds and me as the activity of the first two weeks of the campaign increased. The loneliness came as a result of knowing how much had to be done, and not having others either to call upon or to hire to do the jobs. Local volunteers could not accept assignments that conflicted with home or work schedules, there were no colleges or universities to tap for volunteers, and, furthermore, only Studds and I had had sufficient previous campaign experience to know what had to be done and how to organize the tasks. We were confronted with a serious dilemma. There was not enough money in New Hampshire, nor did there appear to be enough money in the campaign to hire people to fill the jobs.

We both concluded that the solution to our problem was to get help. Since the December 2 Chicago meeting of the CCD, I had been receiving letters from those in other states offering to come to New Hampshire to help in a campaign if McCarthy entered the New Hampshire presidential primary. After the January 4 announcement this trickle of volunteer offers increased and included telephone calls, more letters, and even volunteer offers with contribution checks included. I contacted those who had written to see whether they could come to New Hampshire to help. I also called the Washington McCarthy headquarters to see what it could do to turn up volunteers.

Operating with extreme caution, Studds and I agreed that no blanket invitation to come to New Hampshire would be issued. We were both concerned about the impact on the voter of out-of-state volunteers, but there was no choice. We concluded, first, that out-of-state volunteers would be assigned to less visible jobs. Second, they would be placed in close contact with or under the supervision of local volunteers in order to acclimate them to New Hampshire politics. Third, no one would be allowed to come and work without having first talked to either Studds or me before coming, and having met with one of us before being assigned. In this way we could control who came, how they looked, what they would do, how visible the assignment would be, and whether a positive experience would result. Neither liked the conservative stance they felt they had to take, but because of the political climate, and the negative social reaction to long-haired, bearded, unkempt, protesting, hippie-like youth, we felt we had no choice in this posture either. By prescreening we could discourage those who might not be serious, those who might be destructive to the campaign, and those who were not prepared to work hard and constructively. The campaign could only succeed, we felt, if those who came to help out were willing to work and even sacrifice appearance for the sake of the antiadministration, antiwar objective.

In spite of these constraints, the trickle of volunteers began. I had several Dartmouth students working both in the Hanover area and Concord. Studds involved several of his St. Paul's School students in Concord area activities, and slowly the calls began to pay off. Sam Brown, former National Student Association activist and a friend of Al Lowenstein, then working out of New York with the Coalition for a Democratic Alternative, sent a graduate student, Dan Dodds, to Concord. Dodds was in a graduate program in urban affairs that called for a field practicum. He hoped the campaign would apply. The practicum, if acceptable, would keep him out of the draft. On almost the same day, Eric Schnapper, a Yale law student, arrived. Dodds was over six feet tall, blond, quiet spoken, and somewhat slow in what he did. Schnapper, about five feet ten inches tall, thin, and dark haired, was intense and quick. The contrast was remarkable.

Within a day or two of the first volunteer arrivals came John Barbieri of Connecticut, who had just returned from a two-year hitch with the Peace Corps in India. He had been back long enough to visit his Hartford home, check in with the McCarthy campaign through Sam Brown, and had come directly to New Hampshire. John was ready to work on the campaign as long as he could. He had had to return to

Hartford immediately upon his arrival from India because his Selective Service Board wanted him to report for possible induction. To his Selective Service Board, the Peace Corps would not be acceptable as an alternative to induction in the armed forces.

Within a day or so after John Barbieri arrived, a Yale English graduate student named Dianne Dumanoski came to the Concord headquarters. Her concentration on early English literature faded as the McCarthy candidacy began, and she took a leave from school to join the campaign. The four constituted the first volunteers to join the New Hampshire effort from outside of the state. None had had any significant experience in a campaign. They were bright, energetic, and totally committed to the campaign.

As the first two to three weeks of the campaign went by, other volunteers joined the campaign. Some came for a vacation week while others prepared to stay for longer periods. Some came intending to spend only a week and then remained for a second and third and then were totally caught up in the effort.

Studds and I either together or individually spent time with the volunteers providing them with a background on the campaign, New Hampshire, and the political expectations of the effort. During the first several weeks an oral history and indoctrination course developed that was passed from volunteer to volunteer as a rite of passage into the campaign. Eventually a sketch of New Hampshire political history, legend, dos and don'ts was compiled and mimeographed. Each volunteer received a copy, was required to read it, and informally quizzed on the contents. The earliest arrivals became the pros to be succeeded by later arrivals who quickly became equally professional.

ADVANCING THE FIRST CAMPAIGN DAY

The hallmark of the modern campaign is advance work. The advance person is the scout who is supposed to check all of a campaign day's details, adjusting the schedule to meet the personal needs of the candidate, providing opportunities for the media, and maintaining both the ethos of the campaign and the locality of the campaign. It is a difficult, demanding, and often thankless job. A good campaign day is a work of art that occurs as much by chance as by design but is always subject to critical review. The critics are the candidate, the media, the local committee, and virtually all others who have a hand in making the events that occupy the candidate's time and project the campaign's message. The best laid plans of the schedulers do not always guarantee results. Too often it is the unexpected that will make or break a campaign day, and it is quite often the unexpected that receives the attention of the media to the exclusion of the preplanned message.

Studds and I knew the importance of both good schedules and good advance work. The rough outline developed for McCarthy's first day in New Hampshire would have to be timed, prerun, checked, and adjusted. We were hampered in this task from having only brief exposure to McCarthy as a person and even less to him as a candidate. We had no idea how fast or slow McCarthy would work, what kind of reaction he would receive, or what activities were his favorites. We knew he had worked hard in his Minnesota election contests and that Minnesota contained much the same mix of rural small town and urban industrial areas as did New Hampshire. Since in-state media, especially television, was insignificant, McCarthy would have to meet the voters on the street, in their places of work, in their homes, and where they gathered. He would have to handshake his way through a schedule and find a way to communicate his issues and his qualifications through these informal contacts.

On Sunday, January 14, we began the precheck of the first day's schedule by visiting Jean Wallin in Nashua and then meeting with contacts in Manchester. The Nashua schedule seemed well set. The mayor would welcome McCarthy, a press conference was scheduled, and the right stops on a handshaking tour on the street would be identified. Manchester was less secure. The visible luncheon spot was okay, but shift changes at the local factories were not known. A shift change takes about fifteen minutes and must be timed accurately. The Concord end of the visit was also well in hand, but was much less critical as to the timing than was the Manchester stop.

We were reasonably satisfied with the preliminary check of the schedule and went on to other campaign tasks. We expected that the advance crew would make the final check and adjust the day to conform with earlier experiences with McCarthy's campaign pace and style.

Studds and I still wanted to couple future scheduling with an in-state advance person who would ultimately work with the national crew. Blair Clark had authorized us to hire an in-state advance person and to do this prior to the first McCarthy visit. I met with Bob Call from Portsmouth, outlined the responsibilities of the job, and then said I expected that an advance person would be coming into New Hampshire well before McCarthy's first visit to check the arrangements. In the meantime Bob Call was to check the schedule in detail, especially the shift change times in Manchester and the arrangements for the Senator's evening address at St. Anselm College.

Several days before McCarthy was to arrive Studds received a call from New York to say that Sandy Fraucher would be arriving to advance the senator's visit. A check with Blair Clark assured Studds that Sandy Fraucher was an experienced advance person and, while young, had developed a considerable reputation advancing John Lindsey's campaign in New York City. We were a bit concerned that such experience might not be entirely relevant to New Hampshire, but since we had Bob Call as our own advance person, we felt things would probably go relatively smoothly, at least for the first campaign trip.

Sandy Fraucher arrived in Concord late in the afternoon of the Wednesday before McCarthy's scheduled Friday arrival. He left his shirts for Studds to have cleaned, phoned Bob Call, and set up a meeting to go through the schedule the next morning. They missed connections in Nashua but got together in Manchester. Neither seemed to know their way around, missed meetings with the campaign's Manchester contacts, and didn't final check shift change schedules. They finally made local connections, but the day had gone before they could confirm all of the details. The Concord arrangements were left to the Concord committee without any review except that given earlier by Studds and me. Fraucher picked up his shirts and departed from New Hampshire. Bob Call returned to his Portsmouth home. Both assured us that the schedule was set and would be okay.

FIRST DAY LOGISTICS

Assuming that everything would go according to schedule during that first day, Studds and I were concentrating on how to transport the senator and those traveling with him through three New Hampshire cities. Dodds and Schnapper were assigned the task of getting cars and assembling a small motorcade. I insisted that there be at least one extra car in the motorcade and preferably two. From past experience I knew that, given New Hampshire weather and its effects on automobiles, something might happen. Either a car would not start or under the pressure of the day someone might misplace some keys. Schnapper, who seemed the most confident, was assigned to drive the senator. To do this and not get lost in this unfamiliar state Studds had sent him out to prerun the route.

We tried to duplicate each system in this campaign day so that, if and when something went wrong, there would be a backup. Extra cars, extra people, extra checks, and extra rechecks were set up to ensure that nothing would be completely missed. McCarthy would arrive in Nashua from Boston by car, being driven by several members of the Massachusetts McCarthy organization. A bus would bring the media following McCarthy and this bus would carry the reporters through the day.

Earlier, Russell Hemenway, executive director of the National Committee for an Effective Congress, had called to say that several potential financial supporters of McCarthy would be observing the day's activities. They would be traveling in their own car but would be watching closely to see whether they thought the campaign had a chance. He hoped that we would keep this in mind since, if the schedule "bombed" or McCarthy appeared ineffective, substantial financial support would disappear. In addition to the microscope of the national media, we now had to be conscious that our efforts would be viewed by potential financial backers who had had no previous political campaign experience.

Thursday, the night before McCarthy's arrival, it began to snow heavily in New Hampshire. Fortunately McCarthy had been scheduled to be in Boston that day and had arrived there before the snow slowed air travel into the city.

THE FIRST CAMPAIGN DAY

During the night the snowstorm ended. New Hampshire road crews are famous for being able to clear the state's main highways to almost bare pavement within a few hours after the end of a storm. About six inches of white, fluffy snow lay on the ground and hung from the branches of the hardwoods and the evergreens. The sky was that deep, cloudless blue that follows only after a storm. The temperature was in the low thirties but with intense sun the air felt warm, almost with a touch of spring.

Studds and I were elated with the changed weather when we met early that morning at the Concord headquarters. Schnapper and Dodds were waiting with the cars for the motorcade. With them were two new faces who had come into town the night before to help with the campaign. We were now faced with a wrenching problem. Both of the new young men were neatly dressed, sport coat and tie according to some perceived dress code, but one had a lengthy beard and the other long hair. Both were about to jump into a car to follow along during the day's activity helping to drive, hand out materials, or do whatever was needed. Both Studds and I knew appearances were only a small part of what the generation of the late 1960s was experiencing. Appearances did not bother either of us as long as individuals worked hard and behaved in a way that lent credit to the effort.

But this was McCarthy's first day in New Hampshire. Studds and I were particularly sensitive to that fact that the only television image that might be projected from New Hampshire would be of bearded, long haired, miniskirted, antiestablishment appearing young people. This could not be allowed. Studds took both aside and explained the situation. As much as he hated the task it had to be done and, to their credit, they understood. Their response to Studds' request not to come was that they had come to New Hampshire to help McCarthy and not hurt him. If Studds felt that their appearance would hurt McCarthy during this campaign day they would not travel. In fact Studds asked that they not even come close to the campaign that day. He suggested that they remain in Concord, help with preparations for McCarthy's visit later in the day, and when he arrived get out of sight. This was probably the toughest job Studds had to do during the whole campaign. It was not necessary to mention appearance again. Like the political history lesson that became required reading during the campaign, volunteers were either "clean cut" and out front or they accepted back-room, invisible assignments.

McCarthy had been fund-raising in Boston the previous day and had been unusually successful. Robert Healy of the *Boston Globe* wrote in his column dated January 26:

> McCarthy raised $50,000 in two appearances in Boston on Thursday. At the luncheon at the Somerset Club, one woman gave him a check for $1000. When he finished his talk she wrote out another check for $4000. At that luncheon there were about 30 persons. They were substantial people—bankers, businessmen, educators. Some were Republicans. Some had never been involved in politics. Each gave at least $1000. At the cocktail party later in the afternoon there were between 150 and 200 persons. They contributed $100 each. McCarthy then is not just attracting the hippies and the peace groups. His appeal is broader. It is beginning to capture people who are genuinely frustrated by United States involvement in Vietnam. Both affairs Thursday proved this. . . .

McCarthy's car arrived in Nashua on time followed closely by the press bus. A group of perhaps fifty had gathered anticipating his arrival on the plaza in front of Nashua's City Hall. It was a bit after 9:00 A.M., a little early for the shoppers. But the activity and especially the sight of news cameras, and reporters began to swell the crowd. CBS had sent Roger Mudd, the Boston stations had sent reporters well known to Nashua residents, and the wire services had sent in their top reporters.

We greeted Senator McCarthy and directed him to the place where the bust of President Kennedy stood on a pedestal just in front of the city hall steps. McCarthy gazed rather solemnly, reading the inscription engraved in gold on the face of the black granite pedestal to himself.

In Memorium
President John Fitzgerald Kennedy on January 25, 1960
This City Hall Plaza was John F. Kennedy's First Campaign Stop in the Nation
for the Presidency of the United States of America

Still and news reel photographers clicked and ground away as the challenge of that precedent became obvious. Then McCarthy shook hands with those who had gathered, and exchanged friendly greetings and informal words of welcome.

The press conference had been scheduled for 9:30 A.M. When McCarthy entered the city hall auditorium at 9:15 A.M. the camera crews were still struggling to assemble their microphones, lights, and cameras and the audience was almost entirely composed of empty chairs. Almost no one had experienced a candidate who arrived on time much less one that was early. There were some awkward moments as the chairs began to fill. Studds and I went to find the mayor who was scheduled to greet the senator.

The New Hampshire press office had released a schedule for the day and copies were available for the press, but we expected that an advance release of the senator's remarks would be available for distribution. Sandy Fraucher appeared but he had no advance text nor did he have a copy of the schedule for the day. Studds and I were also looking for Bob Call who was expected to guide us through the day.

The mayor, Dennis Sullivan, finally arrived saying that he had been ill and had just come from his bed for the occasion. In a few words Sullivan extended the welcome of the city but did not offer further encouragement. McCarthy responded briefly and without text. He called the Granite State primary a special challenge, as he put it, "The primary has the reputation of being the harshest political judgment in the country." (*Rutland Herald,* January 27, 1968)

McCarthy set the theme of his campaign through his response to reporters' questions. One asked, "Why aren't you conducting a more forceful campaign?" "I don't intend to shout at people around the country. I don't think the people in New Hampshire want to be shouted at. The issues I want to get out are not best served by table thumping," he responded. (Underwood, op. cit., p. 5)

The press asked how his campaign was going so far to which McCarthy replied, "All right." Someone asked him to be more enthusiastic, but he repeated, "I think all right is an honest statement. We haven't despaired yet. We haven't folded up our equipment and left the room." He concluded the press conference by noting that the prediction was that he would be lucky to get 10 or 12 percent of the vote on March

12. He said that he expected the figure to be far higher. "We're going to run to win, that's all." (Underwood, op. cit., p. 5)

McCarthy, now well ahead of the scheduled time for the end of the press conference, visited several city hall offices to shake hands and chat with city employees, then went out to the street, greeting a few more of the early shoppers. A nearby coffee shop had been scouted by the Nashua committee as being the place where McCarthy might meet voters on their midmorning coffee break. The entourage jammed in around the surprised customers perched on their stools. In the coffee shop McCarthy quietly introduced himself, excused the interruption, and moved easily from patron to patron.

In spite of the unscheduled tour of city hall offices and the visits on Main Street, McCarthy was still running ahead of schedule, and few people remained on the sidewalks that McCarthy had not already met. It was time to move to the next stop, another example of the New Hampshire tradition of campaigning, a coffee party at the home of attorney Joseph Welton, then the Democratic Party chair in Nashua and an early McCarthy supporter. The entourage now numbered ten to fifteen cars and the press bus wound through Nashua's residential area. The reporters were anxious to see how McCarthy performed in this domestic setting and proceeded to crowd out those Welton neighbors who had come to hear and question Senator McCarthy. Studds and I did not want the coffee to be an extension of the press conference, nor did we want the presence of the reporters to repress the Welton neighbors. We had to make a decision between media access to McCarthy or voter access. We decided on the side of the voter and quietly asked the press to adjourn to the kitchen and hold their questions until McCarthy had had his chance to meet voters and respond to their questions.

During the session Studds and I became a bit concerned with the pace that had been set during the day. McCarthy was running as much as one-half hour ahead of the schedule. Neither Fraucher nor Call had shown up in Nashua. I made a quick telephone call ahead to John Holland in Manchester to see if he had seen either of them and to warn him that Senator McCarthy would be arriving in Manchester approximately fifteen minutes earlier than planned.

McCarthy recorded and filmed several interviews for the Boston television stations that were following him that morning. The Boston reporters and crews then left the campaign just before noon in order to process their film and prepare for late afternoon deadlines. I then asked Dodds to bring the senator's car to the house in preparation for the trip to Manchester. A few moments later Dodds returned saying that he could not find the keys. Schnapper brought up a reserve car and led the entourage safely out of Nashua. Dodds remained behind to search for the keys and catch up later.

In spite of the delay and slow driving, the campaign arrived at the Puritan Restaurant in Manchester fifteen minutes early as I had predicted. Holland was there to greet McCarthy but he whispered to me that others he had invited to join in the luncheon had not yet arrived. Again people assumed that campaigns always run late and for them to be on time, certainly not early, would be enough. Studds grabbed Senator McCarthy's arm and began an impromptu handshaking tour of the

Elm Street sidewalk. The press tagged along to check on the local residents' reactions to McCarthy in this, the most hostile of New Hampshire territory. Most people were startled, did not recognize McCarthy, but when introduced were friendly, usually wishing him good luck.

Using approximately ten of the extra fifteen minutes in the street tour, McCarthy returned to the restaurant and, followed by the somewhat smaller press corps, was ushered to his table through the main floor to the rear of the crowded second level of the restaurant. Studds and I had expected that he would move slowly through the restaurant shaking hands and introducing himself or being introduced by John Holland. It quickly became obvious that McCarthy, unlike many other politicians, did not enjoy interrupting people as they were eating. I tried to get McCarthy to appreciate that in this restaurant and at noontime people were there to be interrupted and that in a certain way they expected that McCarthy would pass among the tables and booths greeting each of them. Apparently this was not McCarthy's style. The luncheon went well but faster than scheduled since McCarthy had not tarried on entering the restaurant nor did he change his ways when leaving. He greeted a few of the other patrons but mostly those introduced to him by those who had joined him for lunch.

The major disaster of the day was about to occur. In his account of the day Studds recorded the following:

> McCarthy's first campaign visit to the state . . . was a nightmare. David (Hoeh) and I . . . had hired a local advance man who turned out to be some kind of a character who never showed up and that trip was advanced 20 minutes ahead of the Senator's arrival (at each stop) by David and myself. I never want to live through anything like that again!

The telephone calling we began in Nashua increased when we arrived in Manchester. Neither advance person had appeared and the next stops on the schedule called for McCarthy to be in the Amoskeag Millyard to shake hands with workers changing shifts. A time for this was listed, but it had not been confirmed. Holland and the other Manchester local supporters had thought these details had been checked. I now wanted to add something to the schedule to pick up the pace and fill in the extra time that was available.

Studds and I bounced in and out of the dining room making desperate telephone calls first to confirm the shift change mentioned in the schedule, and second, to try to add another event, possibly a plant tour or another shift change. The situation was desperate. McCarthy was about to leave the restaurant for his next stop. Originally we had wanted to have McCarthy walk along to the newly acquired storefront that was to be the McCarthy Manchester campaign headquarters. But shortly after the lease was signed and a day or so before McCarthy was to arrive, the ceiling of the main room fell in, leaving the place a mess and a hazard.

McCarthy was now out on the street, still not quite sure what would happen next. I began a handshaking walking tour with McCarthy north along the east side of Elm Street while Studds and Holland went to telephone booths to call in search of more definite shift change times. Although it was reasonably warm and sunny there were not many people on the streets during an early Friday afternoon, so I began taking McCarthy into several of the larger stores to circulate among the customers. To make sure that no incidents occurred, I sent Eric Schnapper ahead to check with the store manager to be sure that he would welcome McCarthy's campaigning. McCarthy also made known his preference. No campaigning in beauty parlors. "Women," he said, "did not like being seen by strangers when under a dryer or wrapped up in towels." (DCH recollection) He also cautioned about barbershops as being places of strong opinion with little likelihood of being able to counter the barber's view. "It's as hard to argue with a man holding scissors or a razor as it is to talk while in a dentist's chair," he quipped.

The west side of Elm Street was in the shade, with even fewer people on the street and smaller shops. McCarthy moved quickly making his way back to the place where the cars were waiting to take him to the next campaign stop in the Millyard.

Studds was almost sure of the shift change but still had not been able to confirm it or another change to his satisfaction. The place, the Brookshire Knitting Mills, was in the middle of the Millyard along a narrow street that had been designed for rail and horse-drawn wagon service. The cars could enter but not the bus. McCarthy arrived, the press ran to catch up with him from the bus that was parked outside, and all stood in eager expectation for the flood of workers to stream down steps, past the senator's outstretched hand. They waited for ten, then fifteen, then twenty minutes, while Studds and I nervously tried to find out what had gone wrong in their scheduling. The Brookshire Mills were owned by the Sidore family and under this management were assumed to be friendly. We had also assumed that our advance people had been in touch with a member of the family to prearrange the visit. As they soon found out, no one had checked with the Brookshire management. We asked if the shift were about to change soon but were told that the largest number of workers had left approximately five minutes before McCarthy had arrived. I tried to arrange an in-plant tour but found that permission to do this had to be secured well in advance.

At this inopportune time Sandy Fraucher arrived, complaining loudly that McCarthy was standing outside of a nonunion factory about to greet nonunion workers. The reporters finally had something to write about and began taking notes. I grabbed Fraucher by the sleeve and took him aside, explaining in a stage whisper, that John F. Kennedy had toured this factory in 1960 and that the Sidore family offered their workers benefits that most textile contracts had not even begun to include. Through it all McCarthy chatted with reporters, remained calm, and greeted the few workers who straggled out the door.

In the group observing the confusion was Russell Hemenway and the small group of New Yorkers he hoped would financially back the campaign. Up until this point the day had gone well to the outsiders. The schedule and the logistics seemed professionally handled and what few problems had developed were known only to Studds and me. Now the campaign was aground in the Millyard with little or nothing to do but wait.

As Studds recalled:

> We made the famous mistake there. We got him five minutes late to the factory gate and he had just missed the bulk of people which all the national press picked up to show how bad the organization in New Hampshire was. The organization in New Hampshire had been naively assuming that a candidate for the Presidency of the United States would be preceded by some advance men. Some of us had worked on Kennedy campaigns before and we had some disillusioning still to go. But we learned after that point that if there was going to be advance work we were going to do it. . . .
>
> (Studds transcript, p. 21)

The doorstep of the Brookshire Knitting Mills became a symbol of a low point of the campaign. Every story about McCarthy's first visit to New Hampshire carried at least a paragraph about the doorstep, and the key theme of the next two days' coverage of the campaign focused on the doorstep either in words or in film. As an example one reporter wrote:

> It also became clear early in the day that McCarthy's New Hampshire organization has a long way to go to take on a patina of professionalism.
>
> Item: McCarthy is scheduled to have dinner in a busy downtown Manchester restaurant, where well-heeled business types eat, with a small group of supporters. The dining rooms, upper and lower, are filled with people. McCarthy has lunch, shakes hand with one or two people who come to his table, then walks out without visiting one single table or shaking another hand.
>
> Explains his aide when asked by a reporter what the man is doing: "We're behind schedule."
>
> Item: McCarthy is scheduled to visit a textile plant at 3 P.M. to shake hands as the workers get off their shift. He arrives at the plant slightly before 3 P.M.
>
> But the shift got out at 2:45 P.M. So he stands in the cold and slush, or in the plant entry waiting for another shift to get out half an hour later.
>
> The result—about 30 minutes spent waiting to shake the hands of less than 20 women who were obviously in a big hurry to go home.
>
> (*Rutland Herald*, January 27, 1968)

Another caught the same scene but found something in the event that revealed McCarthy's character.

> At Manchester's Brookshire Knitting Mills, a schedule mix-up found the campaigners arriving 10 minutes after a large 2:45 P.M. shift let out.
>
> The next flow of workers was to occur at 3:15 P.M. McCarthy and his staff spent the time between the millyard, where heavy slush from the day's traffic mingled with ruts carved from ice, and the front lobby, where the weather was more clement. Then only about 15 women came out. "I'm

> sorry, Senator," an aide confided. "Our man fed the wrong information about this." "That's all right."
>
> Later, traveling between Manchester and Concord . . . McCarthy noted, "Yes it has been a good day. Well planned."
>
> (*Boston Globe,* January 27, 1968, p. 8)

McCarthy was not easily ruffled by miscues or schedule mix-ups. Studds and I were personally demolished by the disaster in Manchester, but since McCarthy had been so understanding and forgiving we promised each other that nothing like that would happen again if we could control it in any way.

Quietly, McCarthy said, "Let's go," to Studds and me. Sensing that the press was let down by the stand in the cold, McCarthy climbed aboard the press bus to ride with the reporters to Concord. The lead car again slowed the pace as the campaign was still ahead of its scheduled arrival in Concord. While fumbling in the front of the office of the Brookshire Knitting Mills, I had called ahead to Concord to warn them of an early arrival at the statehouse. The well-organized Concord Committee quickly made the appropriate calls to the local reporters and photographers so that they would be on hand for McCarthy's filing and to local supporters who could be expected to attend the headquarters opening.

Both McCarthy and the reporters who had ridden with him on the bus came off in a jovial mood as if nothing unfortunate had happened during the previous stop.

McCarthy entered the statehouse, and went directly to the secretary of state's office where we produced the appropriately signed petitions and forms necessary to make the filing official. The reporters asked the number of signatures and the reply was, "Just the number required. We did not attempt to produce more than this number." The filing was official no questions were asked concerning the names nor problems encountered in the exercise.

McCarthy then went to Governor John W. King's office to pay a courtesy call. The *Boston Globe* account of the meeting read:

> It was a courtesy call on the governor, the kind visiting high-level politicians make when on someone else's home ground. The chat between Sen. Eugene McCarthy and Gov. John W. King was brief.
>
> "Is this your official start?" King small-talked as they sat on a black leather couch in his office. "Yes," said McCarthy.
>
> "You will find that people here will treat you courteously. You will like campaigning here. I did. I wouldn't have done it three times otherwise. I hope you will say what a beautiful state we have here," said King.
>
> "Yes, it is. I have already said how it reminds me of Minnesota," said McCarthy.
>
> Then, Friday afternoon, the two men shook hands, probably the last time until March 12. . . .
>
> (*Boston Globe,* January 28, 1968, p. 1)

Following the official filing and the meeting with the governor, McCarthy seemed to catch the spirit of the campaign. His ride from Manchester to Concord in the press bus had been stimulating and his reception in Concord reassuring. Now he left the statehouse to walk the three blocks to the state headquarters. On his way he greeted people on the sidewalk. Here the reception was more cordial than it had been since Nashua. As he rounded the corner from the statehouse to Main Street he was met by Vincent Dunn, Jr., the eight-year-old son of New Hampshire's banking commissioner, who was holding a copy of McCarthy's book *The Limits of Power.* The boy asked the senator to autograph the book. I then took the opportunity to usher McCarthy into the offices of the Banking Commission and to introduce him to Vincent Dunn, Sr. Dunn and his wife Miriam were becoming increasingly helpful to the McCarthy effort and would become heavily involved before the end.

As was usual for the day, McCarthy arrived at the headquarters a bit ahead of schedule which meant that things were not completely ready for the reception nor had all the people gathered. Before he left about fifty persons filled the room. Speaking briefly, McCarthy thanked them for their interest and commented on his first day:

> If what I have seen in the three towns I have been in is indicative of a general response, we'll settle for 55 per cent of the vote. I have never had as encouraging a response, even in my own state. And in spite of the "mischievous" New Hampshire voter, I might have a chance to win. I want you to know the burden you bear, and thank you for working in this common cause.
>
> (*Concord Daily Montitor,* January 27, 1968, p. 12)

He made a point of greeting and talking with each person in the headquarters and promised to return again before the end of the campaign in order to meet those who had not arrived before he had to leave for his next stop, a 5:45 P.M. reception, part of the annual meeting of the New Hampshire Bar Association.

McCARTHY'S SECOND MANCHESTER SPEECH

On January 12, 1968, William Loeb, the controversial editor and publisher of the *Manchester Union Leader,* printed one of his famous front page editorials titled, "Addressed to Democrats Only." It read:

> It is good news to all patriotic Democrats that Senator Eugene McCarthy has announced that he will authorize a write-in candidacy for himself in New Hampshire.
>
> Here is the opportunity for every patriotic, sensible Democrat in the state of General Stark to indicate just how little he thinks of anyone who goes around giving speeches which serve to prolong the war, as Sen. McCarthy is doing by attacking President Johnson's and this nation's commitment to the defense of freedom in Vietnam.

Dissent, of course, is the right of every American. But carping dissent in war time, with the enemy at our throats and killing our boys in Vietnam, is NOT a right.

IT IS A DISGRACE!

It is difficult for this newspaper to believe that Sen. McCarthy doesn't understand that every speech he makes in favor of our withdrawal from Vietnam, in favor of what amounts—no matter how carefully disguised—to surrender to Communist aggression, costs the lives of many American boys.

Whether Sen. McCarthy knows it or not, those speeches of his are written in blood—not his blood, but the blood of American boys who are killed because this war is prolonged by those speeches.

When rulers in Hanoi hear a speech by McCarthy, or Bobby Kennedy, or all the other chickens who want to pull out of Vietnam, who want to run home with their tails between their legs like so many licked yellow curs, they say: "All we will have to do is to wait long enough and those crazy Americans will be fighting among themselves so hard they won't be able to beat us."

Editorials won't beat Sen. McCarthy or the whole barnyard of crazy chickens, but the patriotic, sound Democrats of New Hampshire have a golden opportunity in this election to support overwhelmingly—those delegates pledged to President Johnson and give Sen. McCarthy as few write-ins as is humanly possible.

Let NewHampshire, the State whose motto is "Live Free or Die," once again show the nation that, Democrats or Republicans, we are eagles and not plucked chickens.

(Signed)
William Loeb, Publisher

The questions the McCarthy organizers faced was what impact would such statements have on the turnout of the St. Anselm speech, and what impact would this rhetoric have on the Manchester voter? Would there be a crowd for the St. Anselm speech? Would the crowd be friendly or hostile? These were the concerns we had as we arrived at St. Anselm to check the arrangements for the speech.

Studds had gambled in favor of holding the speech in the large gymnasium of the college rather than in some smaller but easier to fill space. After making the decision to use the larger space, Studds sent out the word to the nearby cities of Nashua and Concord and even to the well-organized Keene committee some distance away. These committees were urged to contact as many of their allies as possible and encourage them to help fill the St. Anselm hall.

To our relief, some time before the 8:00 P.M. speech schedule, the hall began to fill. By the time McCarthy arrived most of the seats were taken and some people were standing to the sides and sitting on the floor. This was not to be a lecture but rather it was billed as a major foreign policy address. Studds and I also wanted it to be a campaign speech, if not in fact than at least in that the candidate would be received and treated as if he were campaigning. We asked the known McCarthy supporters to disperse throughout the crowd and to be responsive. “McCarthy,” we said, “will not shout nor become animated in his presentation. He will make subtle references that should draw a response and he will draw important illustrations that will be understated. When these occur the audience should respond. It will be up to McCarthy’s supporters to lead that response. And when McCarthy enters stand and clap and whistle to provide him with as warm a reception as possible.”

McCarthy entered as scheduled, the audience rose, clapped, and some cheered. He was introduced by the head of the monastic order that operates St. Anselm College, with references to McCarthy’s own strong Catholic background. There had been little need to prepare the audience for McCarthy on this evening. He quickly brought them close to him and carried them through a speech that was deeply serious but laced with humor and referenced with illustrations drawn from his own understanding of monastic orders and the rites and traditions of the Roman Catholic Church.

The speech ended with a standing ovation that sent supporters and the curious away with a renewed interest in his campaign and dedication to the effort. The only two notes of dissent were a banner over the podium that read “Go Hawk Go” but this referred to the St. Anselm basketball team and one older priest who left the room. We had planned the event to happen without a question period following the address. We did not want to open the senator to potential harassment which would be the news of the evening rather than the content of the speech.

There had been no advance text of the speech released, something that is usual in a presidential campaign and something that the media had come to expect. Studds and I had expected that copies of the speech would be available from the McCarthy national office either to be distributed by us for release prior to the speech or to be given to the New Hampshire campaign’s press officer, Bill Gallagher, for distribution by him. Neither occurred and the reporters, long used to following a speech line by line in a text, noting departures from the text and marking the text for use in their stories, had to cover the speech as a news event.

Bill Cardoso, the New Hampshire reporter for the *Boston Globe,* complained to David Underwood, the Concord McCarthy chair, that McCarthy hadn’t said anything new that evening. “I couldn’t stop the presses on this speech and make them break into the type with a new story. I’ve already missed my deadline. There were no early press releases available.” (Underwood, op. cit., p. 12)

Russell Hemenway had also been talking to Cardoso who had raised an additional sore spot from his view in that McCarthy had not held a question and answer session following the speech. Hemenway responded, “Gene McCarthy is terrific on questions and answers. There is no need to shield him from a hostile audience. He handles them perfectly. There isn’t another candidate I know who can get up and make a speech like Gene McCarthy did tonight without a prepared text.” (Underwood, op. cit., p. 12)

The comment frequently heard among the reporters around presidential campaigns is that the candidate “didn’t say anything” or (if they are charitable) “didn’t say much that was new in his speech.” The comment reflects the fact that the reporters hear most of a candidate’s speeches, read a great deal about the candidate, and are in many ways better informed as to the manner and style of the candidate than is almost anyone else in the public. This creates a cynicism that comes from familiarity, a cynicism that tends to be reflected in what they feel is important to report or how they perform their job when there is little to report.

On the other side of this coin is the candidate and an unwritten rule that repetition creates positions, issues, and ultimately an image which provides the candidate with recognition and identity. Candidates are constantly searching for themes, ways of using the language to create a response, to convey their thoughts, to reveal their personal qualities. Once those vignettes of an issue, a position on the issue, and the style of the candidate have been found to solicit audience response they are repeated. Unlike the reporters each audience is new, and each audience wants to be given the opportunity to take full measure of the candidate.

If the listener has heard and seen the candidate make a particularly valid point in a television interview or speech excerpt, that viewer, when part of the candidate's speech audience, wants to hear that statement again and preferably with the same phrasing, intonation, and emphasis that stimulated his or her interest in the other medium. What is refreshing about covering the New Hampshire primary is that the candidates are groping to find those themes, phrases, and the pace of delivery that will distinguish them from the others. McCarthy was in the process of establishing his style while the reporters were trying to fit him into some familiar mold of what a candidate should be, say, and do.

Following the speech McCarthy returned to his downtown Manchester hotel room where, Studds and I, and the recently arrived Blair Clark, conducted a review of the day with the senator. McCarthy was genuinely pleased with his reception. Studds and I were happy that the day had had only one serious problem and that the speech had not only drawn a respectable audience but that the senator had been exceptionally well received. We were also delighted with the relationship that was beginning to develop between us and the candidate.

We learned that McCarthy could work hard; could sustain enthusiasm through a long day of campaigning; was effective in press conferences and shaking hands on streets, in stores, and at factories; had a commanding presence; suffered mistakes without visible irritation; could make something out of the unplanned and unexpected; was flexible; and could stimulate an audience. In short, we had been right. McCarthy would be an exceptional candidate in New Hampshire. He did not create or attract hostility, and when he encountered opposition he turned it comfortably to his own advantage.

In response to Blair Clark's questions concerning our view of the day, we reviewed our reactions to each event, and apologized for the error at the factory, but felt the day had gone better than we had hoped or expected. McCarthy felt the same way and at that point showed how he had prepared for New Hampshire. He rolled up his pant leg to show the bottom of a pair of long underwear that had kept him warm while moving through the minefield of a schedule. We reminded Clark of our advancing problems and hoped that in the future there would be better help with advance work from the national campaign. We also noted that we still did not have anyone to work full-time as a manager, and our own time was just not enough to ensure that every aspect that had to be done would be done.

EVALUATING THE FIRST DAY AND FIELD OPERATIONS

Studds and I began checking to see how the press had reacted to McCarthy's first New Hampshire visit. The word from Washington was that as far as the national television was concerned the big story had been the mistake at the factory gate. This, according to those who were observing, had been the major image that the nation had seen as a result of McCarthy's first New Hampshire campaign visit. The timing of the mistake had made it even worse because it happened just prior to the evening and weekend deadlines for the networks, a number of the major newspapers, and news services. This was the story they could use; everything else that happened that day happened too late for their use.

A sample of newspaper headlines read:

"McCarthy Roams In Granite State" sub-head: "Low-keyed Approach as Senator Kicks Off Anti-LBJ Drive." (*Rutland Herald,* January 27, 1968)

"McCarthy Leaves N.H.; Romney Still Plugging" Sub-head: "McCarthy Bases Hope on Voter Independence" (*Boston Herald,* January 27, 1968)

"N.H. 'Courteous,' McCarthy Told" Sub-head: "3-1 Defeat Seen for McCarthy" (*Boston Globe,* January 27, 1968)

"N.H. Race Warms Up, McCarthy Meets The Governor" (*Boston Globe,* January 28, 1968)

"McCarthy Moves Through N.H. with the Slow Step of a Priest" (*Washington Post,* January 28, 1968)

"McCarthy Runs Genteel Campaign" (*Washington Post,* January 28, 1968)

"McCarthy Launches 'Challenge' to LBJ" (*Manchester Union Leader,* January 27, 1968)

"McCarthy Keeps at N.H. Voters" (*Christian Science Monitor,* January 27, 1968)

"Dove Candidate Warns of Growing Militarism" (*Rutland Herald,* January 27, 1968)

"McCarthy Stumps in New Hampshire" (*New York Times,* January 27, 1968)

Below the headlines an interesting story began to emerge. The reporters were trying to figure out who this man was and how he would fare in New Hampshire. At first they were looking for signs of hostility toward the "dove" candidate from those he met on the streets. Even under some rather intense grilling in front of network sound cameras, Roger Mudd was unable to get a negative response from those who had just met McCarthy. Not many knew him or had heard of him but what they experienced as McCarthy met them on the street was positive. The reporters could not find hostility toward this man who had come to challenge an incumbent Democratic administration and a war.

A point that did give us some concern was that several reporters attempted to lump the Romney campaign together with McCarthy and to contrast their campaign styles. Romney had just ended a six-day tour of the state a week earlier and was scheduled to return for a two-day swing on January 27–28. Romney was attempting to take New Hampshire by storm. A high-pressure, professional campaign had been organized for him that had him working long days, traveling extensively, and always acting the booster. His street manner was forceful, quick, and aggressive. He thrust himself into virtually every situation to the delight of the reporters and photographers who followed. He was viewed as the candidate most likely to succeed with the issue of an alternative to the Johnson administration's policies in Vietnam. He attracted attention wherever he went in the state and was seen as the man to watch during the 1968 New Hampshire campaign season. Consequently everything that McCarthy did or failed to do in New Hampshire was contrasted with Governor Romney and what the press felt were Romney's strengths as a campaigner.

Under the heading "McCarthy in New Hampshire," the *Rutland Herald* editorialized:

> Judging from reports coming over the frozen Connecticut River, Sen. Eugene McCarthy is running a real risk of being mistaken, for perhaps just a Minnesota Farm-Labor candidate. This unkind assessment of a loyal Democrat's young presidential primary campaign is based on the facts he is following the Romney trail around New Hampshire (without the folksy Romney touch) and is "opposing" a rival who isn't even entered in the race but whose supporters include the cream of the state's Democratic organization.
>
> McCarthy isn't running against Romney, but it is evident from newspaper and television reports that if the two men were selling vacuum cleaners Romney would probably sell out before McCarthy made his first sale.
>
> While Romney has glad-handed factory workers and farmers and regaled affluent middle-class New Hampshire with his manly charm over tea cups, McCarthy has opened his campaign with nothing more than polite, professional phrases and a somewhat wan smile. Since both men have hopes of winning some of the state's registered Independent voters, they are in fact rivals.
>
> It seems doubtful McCarthy can rally enough support from the Hanover intellectuals and other groups opposing the Johnson war policy to

> make even a dent in the state's Democratic cheering section led by the Johnson trio of Gov. John W. King, Sen. Thomas Sen. Thomas J. McIntyre, and former General Services Administration, Bernard Boutin.

The editorial went on to conceed that McCarthy had made an "interesting point" in his St. Anselm speech "when he warned his audience of a growing militarism in American foreign policy. . . . He even cited former Republican President Eisenhower's recent warning that the military establishment was growing too powerful. . . ." But the editorial concluded:

> It wasn't McCarthy's fault that he stepped into New Hampshire in the shadow of the Pueblo incident. But one wonders if that shadow makes much difference. His campaign seems to be a little shadowy anyway, and "opponent" is only a write-in shadow.
>
> (*Rutland Herald,* January 29, 1968)

The story that led to the editorial had picked up the contrast in styles between McCarthy and Romney but had misread the reaction:

> It became clear early in the day that the Senator is going to run a down-style campaign, free of the usual flowery oratory and American-way-of-life speeches.
>
> The McCarthy approach is low-keyed, intellectual, reasoned,—in a word, amateurish when compared to (the) style of campaigning the public is accustomed to.
>
> He's not forceful when handshaking on the street, if he is compared to Michigan Governor George Romney, who excels in the thrust-pump-and-smile technique.
>
> (*Rutland Herald,* January 27, 1968)

The contrasting styles presented a problem in the early campaign management, but Studds and I had been pleased with what we had seen in McCarthy as a campaigner and were skeptical of the reporter's reaction to Romney. To us McCarthy showed quiet confidence, strength, and resolve—something that would make it possible to build an effective campaign organization around.

Ward Just, writing in the *Washington Post,* had caught a bit of what the campaign would be.

> There will be five more trips like this one before the presidential primary March 12, trips with journalists laughing and asking repetitive questions to which they will receive repetitive answers at the state press conferences, awkward dialogues in living rooms, and meetings with money men who will insist on computers to "profile" the vote by ethnic group and religion

> in New Hampshire. McCarthy will say yes, no, temporize a little, back, fill, and finally decide: No. He will surely say no to the professionals. "You can't package religion and politics" he says.
>
> Of course, he is wrong. You can. Kennedy did. McCarthy has the wrong kind of cool for 1968 (sic).
>
> (*Washington Post,* January 28, 1968, p. A4)

But Just's conclusion showed that he was trying to fit McCarthy into a convenient mold as well. After the one day, we knew that McCarthy would not tolerate packaging. His theme, which slowly began to emerge during that day, was the word "reconciliation."

Studds and I now had an experiential basis to make changes in our view of the campaign. McCarthy was not a Kennedy, and he was not dependent upon a staff of writers, researchers, press officers, advance people, and managers. He was independent and remarkably self-reliant. The national campaign had not only failed to provide personnel to support his visit, but it seemed to us that we now knew McCarthy's campaign style as well as anyone else—at least as he had shown it in New Hampshire. On this basis adjustments would be made.

Since there would probably not be advanced texts of McCarthy's speeches, each speech would have to be recorded and transcribed for the press. Since the advance operation had failed both in New Hampshire and from the national campaign, I assigned that job to the one person who had advanced effectively, Eric Schnapper. Schnapper would also be the chief driver for McCarthy since he would be the one most familiar with the routing between campaign stops. All subsequent advance work would be based and directed from New Hampshire.

The first day schedule had depended on the work of the two best organized local committees in the state at that time—the Nashua and Concord McCarthy people. The mistake had been in Manchester where the committee was new, inexperienced, and thin on members. All subsequent scheduling would be handled through Sandra Hoeh from our home in Hanover. She would coordinate the interests of the national campaign, McCarthy's senatorial office, local committees, and the state campaign in building the remaining campaign days for the senator.

Blair Clark had still not been able to assign someone to fill the full-time manager position for the New Hampshire campaign. We were desperate for this assistance as items requiring attention began to pile up. Organization, other scheduling, media, canvassing, and support activities were all beginning to reach the point in the campaign where attention was needed.

HELP ARRIVES

Shortly after the McCarthy New Hampshire announcement, Russell Hemenway called me to offer his help and advice. As executive director of the National Committee for an

Effective Congress, he had had considerable experience assisting in the financing and management of political campaigns. He did not know either Studds or me and was quite sure that neither of us had the experience or background to successfully manage McCarthy's New Hampshire effort. In fact, as mentioned earlier, Hemenway had been opposed to McCarthy's New Hampshire venture but now was determined to help in any way possible. In his call, he inventoried the essentials required to support a successful campaign. I recall being asked whether there was adequate headquarters space, whether the space was large enough to absorb the expansion of the campaign, whether enough telephone lines had been installed, and a series of other questions concerning the logistical support of a major campaign. I assured Hemenway we had had extensive campaign experience and that either we had taken care of the item on Hemenway's list or were cognizant of the need. I recited my own list of needs which had money and a full-time, experienced manager at the top.

Prior to his call, Hemenway had contracted with a data processing firm in New York headed by Harry Harris. Hemenway had raised enough money on his own to acquire approximately $25,000 worth of services from Harris which he now wanted to use in the New Hampshire campaign. Hemenway was anxious to have Harris explain his potential service, and not having poll data to confirm or deny my personal assessment of the mood of New Hampshire, I was interested in seeing what Harris had developed.

Harris came to New Hampshire with Hemenway on January 15 to explain the content of his work and show examples of the analysis he had made. Hemenway felt the analysis would be especially useful to Sandra Hoeh as she began building McCarthy's future campaign schedule. He expected that the analysis would target the key areas and voting population characteristics. A meeting of the McCarthy statewide committee was called to hear Harris' presentation in hopes that the analysis would be of benefit in the activities of the local organizations.

The analysis was heavily based on U.S. census data, employment statistics, and voter registration patterns. Harris' presentation confirmed what the local organizers knew about their own areas and what Studds and I knew about the state. Perhaps in a larger state or for organizers who were not locally based such a profile might have been useful, but for the emerging McCarthy organization in New Hampshire it did not provide anything in the way of new data, perceptions, or analyses than was already a part of the operating experience of the campaign. The listing of key communities that Studds had prepared as part of the December 23 memorandum to Senator McCarthy conveyed the same understanding of the political dynamics.

Following the meeting, Studds and I met privately with Hemenway and Harris to discuss the assistance that the campaign did need. I asked if Harris had any way of generating the mailing lists from the checklists that were then being hand typed. The answer was no. Hemenway saw quickly that his investment had been misplaced. The New Hampshire leadership had developed and internalized in its strategy all of the essential data from which to schedule and orient the campaign.

Later Hemenway asked me to come to New York to go through the profiling process further. Since I was not involved in the detail scheduling and Sandra Hoeh was, she went to New York City to meet with Harris and Hemenway. On the same trip she appeared on David Susskind's program to discuss the New Hampshire campaign with other guests Allard Lowenstein; Zolton Ferency, former Michigan state Democratic chair; and Donald Peterson, Wisconsin McCarthy chair.

On her return she rented an automobile to bring a load of campaign materials freshly printed by the New York based Coalition for a Democratic Alternative. On her return her car slid into a guardrail along Interstate 91 near Brattleboro, Vermont. Uninjured but also unwilling to drive in the snow without snow tires, she waited for me to drive south from Hanover. On our way home, we detoured through Keene and Concord to deliver the materials to a local committee and the state headquarters. The date was January 23, a day when the campaign still seemed very small and in the hands of few people with a great deal to be accomplished.

The complete Harris analysis was of only slightly more value to the campaign than the summary had been. With the analysis, however, came a wall-sized map that was prominently displayed at headquarters. On the map was plotted Harris' targeted voting areas. Since this analysis and display confirmed the strategy we had developed, the map remained useful as a reminder and as a means of orienting newly arrived volunteers.

No other data analysis or polling process was available to the campaign. Hemenway shifted his attention to helping where I suggested, principally with funding and subsequently with media development.

CHAPTER 7

External Events

"FEEDING OFF THE LAND"

At some point early in the campaign, Senator McCarthy was asked how he expected to run a successful campaign against an incumbent administration of his own party. Was there a secret he possessed or did he have some basic strategy that would prove invincible as the campaign year began to unfold? To this McCarthy responded that no, he did not possess a secret formula for success but that he did have a basic faith in the goodness of the American voting public and that he intended to survive by "feeding off the land." The image of a foraging army or swarm of locusts came to mind immediately, which was not exactly an improper image as things turned out. But what McCarthy had in mind was his own capacity to make political hay out of events, situations, and times that could not be foreseen.

To a considerable extent, McCarthy felt that history did not just occur. His political career had been a demonstration of his ability to reap benefits from events that were not entirely of his making, to create advantages for himself, and to grasp a moment and turn it into a positive political event. McCarthy had established himself as a formidable national political force when he directly confronted and challenged the junior senator from Wisconsin, Joseph McCarthy. On June 22, 1952, when Joseph McCarthy was at the peak of his national power, the little known member of congress from Minnesota, Eugene McCarthy, agreed to meet the senator from Wisconsin in a televised debate on the prominent "American Forum of the Air" program. In so doing, Eugene McCarthy became the first member of congress to oppose Senator McCarthy in a public debate.

In his account of the debate, Albert Eisele wrote: "Some of the things he [Congressman McCarthy] said were strikingly similar to the language he would use fifteen years later in criticizing U.S. policies in Asia." (Albert Eisele, *Almost to the Presidency, A Biography of Two American Politicians,* Blue Earth, Minn.: The Piper Company, 1972, p. 113)

> *Senator McCarthy:* We know we have lost an average of 100 million people a year to Communism since the shooting part of World War Two ended. Not 100 thousand, 100 million. Since the shooting part of World War Two ended, the total lost has been about 700 million people. Right, Gene?
>
> *Congressman McCarthy:* Senator, I don't think you can say that we have lost them. We never had them. Of course, it is not our policy to have people. I think that we can say that we have saved much from communism through the sound foreign policy which the Democratic administration did initiate, and which was given bipartisan support by the Republicans as long as it seemed to be going along very well.
>
> *Senator McCarthy:* You said we never had these people. We had the Chinese people, 450 million of them, as our friends for over a hundred years. This present administration has betrayed China.
>
> *Congressman McCarthy:* I don't think we have betrayed anyone. If we look back at American foreign policy it becomes clear that we have not had a consistent foreign policy since 1920.
>
> *Senator McCarthy:* Since 1930.
>
> *Congressman McCarthy:* Since 1920. . . . Let us go back and re-examine our Far Eastern policy for a minute. The U.S. did support the "Most Favored Nation" treatment in the Orient, and that was the basis of our policy until about the year 1900. Actually all this meant was that if anybody was exploiting the Chinese and the Orientals, we insisted that we have the same right to exploit them. After 1900 we began to talk about the "Open Door" policy. This meant we were willing to exploit them in greater degree than anyone else if we could get the advantage.
>
> *Senator McCarthy:* Let us bring it down to date, if we may. As of tonight there exists one of the most treasonable, traitorous orders that has ever been issued by any nation in war or peacetime. I am sure you will agree, Gene.
>
> *Congressman McCarthy:* I am not sure.
>
> *Senator McCarthy:* There exists as of tonight an order to our Seventh Fleet, which says that if our friends on Formosa, if they try to stop the Communist shipping, our Seventh Fleet will sink our friends, and shoot their planes . . . If that is not treason, I ask you what is treason?
>
> *Congressman McCarthy:* I would deny it is treason unless the words "conspiracy" and "conspirator" and "treason" have been redefined. You have to look at it in relation to the whole problem of the Far East. The question is one of whether we are in an all-out war in that area or not. . . .

Eisele concluded by writing, "While there is no evidence to suggest that the debate marked the beginning of Joseph McCarthy's eventual decline, at least one observer felt it was the first time anyone had shown that the Wisconsin senator could be successfully debated. 'The fallacy of Senator McCarthy's invincibility in debate was exploded on Ted Granik's 'American Forum of the Air,'' Harry MacArthur, television critic for the Washington *Evening Star*, wrote afterwards." (Eisele, op. cit., p. 114)

For those who had just come to know Senator McCarthy in the short time prior to his announced presidential candidacy and since that announcement, it quickly became clear that he would build his campaign from the opportunities that occurred as the campaign developed. McCarthy liked to see what individuals would do on their own. He had become a candidate to "test" the administration concerning the Vietnam war policy. McCarthy would be the focus, the personification of the test, but the effort would have to be made by others in the ways they perceived the test could be made in their own jurisdictions.

Among those who did not understand this brand of political behavior were many of the columnists exemplified by a January 20, 1968, article written by Robert Kennedy's friend Jack Newfield of the *Village Voice:*

> Let the unhappy, brutal truth come out. Eugene McCarthy's campaign is a disaster. It has been run as if King Constantine was the manager.
>
> McCarthy's speeches are dull, vague, and without either guts or poetry. He is lazy and vain. His failure to jump on issues like Robert McNamara's firing or Gen. Hershey's recent manifestos reveals a serious deficiency of political instinct.
>
> He has put together a campaign staff of amateurs and burnt-out Stevensonians. He has said nothing of consequence about the cities, the poor, the draft, or the Third World. . . .
>
> Every professional politician who has had any direct experience with McCarthy's campaign has come away in despair. It is so inept it almost seems that only a paranoid view of his intentions can explain its failure. . . .

In this context the earliest McCarthy successes came as tests conceived and managed by those who welcomed the opportunity to focus their opposition to the war policy through the political system. Delegate selection was the first stage in the effort. It was these early victories that lent legitimacy to the McCarthy challenge. If dissent actually could be translated into delegate votes, then something more than fringe politics and irresponsible protest was behind the antipathy to the Johnson administration.

MASSACHUSETTS

During his visit to New Hampshire in the fall, Massachusetts Democratic State Chair Lester Hyman mentioned the problem he was facing in his attempt to either get President Johnson to run in the April 30 Massachusetts primary or to convince some other prominent officeholder to run as a stand-in. The Kennedy family, principally Senator Edward Kennedy, had continually refused to become involved in the problem.

Under Massachusetts law a candidate's name could be entered in the primary in two ways. The first was that the state party chair could submit names to the Massachusetts secretary of state. These names will appear on the ballot unless the person named requests the withdrawal of their name. A name can also be placed on the ballot through a petition signed by twenty-five hundred voters, with no more than five hundred signatures from any one county. The filing deadline for either method was March 5. (*New York Times,* January 10, 1968)

Paul Counihan, McCarthy's Massachusetts campaign manager, picked up the petition forms early in January because Hyman had stated that unless he heard otherwise from the White House he would "put up only one name—that of the president."

Hyman was on the spot. Johnson would only allow his name to be entered if Hyman would assure him that he would overwhelmingly beat Senator McCarthy. Johnson was also concerned by what might result from such a direct confrontation if that confrontation revealed a weakness in his renomination effort. He was always looking over his shoulder to see what Robert Kennedy might be considering, and the Massachusetts primary without Kennedy support could be exceedingly hazardous ground.

Counihan gathered his petitions quickly, developed full slates of McCarthy delegates running in each of the congressional districts, and prepared for a full-scale confrontation. One after another, however, prominent Massachusetts politicians graciously declined the offer to stand in for President Johnson. Several, including then Postmaster General Lawrence O'Brien, offered to stand in if asked to do so by the president. (*New York Times,* January 10, 1968) No such call came. Edward Kennedy refused to run as a "favorite son," again saying he would only do so if asked by the president.

The process had left the organization of a campaign on behalf of the president's renomination in great disarray. This advantage left the McCarthy organizers in full possession of the field. By the early weeks of February, it was clear that McCarthy would be unopposed in the Massachusetts primary. Hyman failed in his attempt to convince the president to enter his own name and Johnson would not put himself in the position of asking a stand-in to carry his campaign in the state. Although a slate of prominent political figures was assembled as delegate candidates, the likelihood of their election was also in doubt without the leadership of a campaign. Given the McCarthy organization's strength in many of the congressional districts, it was possible to project McCarthy delegate victories long before the April 20th primary and to forecast McCarthy delegate domination of the Massachusetts delegation to the Democratic National Convention.

This early success and the confusion it created in the Johnson effort greatly strengthened the New Hampshire McCarthy campaign. The actual events were well covered and analyzed in the Massachusetts media that also dominate the New Hampshire markets. Workers and funds that would have been required to support the Massachusetts campaign now were available for New Hampshire.

MINNESOTA

When Senator McCarthy arrived in New Hampshire for his first visit, his usual traveling staff member, Jerry Eller, was not with him. Eller was in Minnesota where he was helping the McCarthy organization there to participate in the early stages of the delegate selection process in McCarthy's home state.

Minnesota based its 1968 state convention delegate selection system on open precinct caucuses. The caucuses could be attended by anyone eligible to vote in the next general election who was not registered as a member of another political party. The precinct caucuses selected delegates to participate in the county conventions which, in turn, elected delegates who would participate in both the state convention, where the delegates-at-large were chosen, and the congressional district conventions, where the other delegates were chosen.

A quiet organizing effort had been underway in Minnesota to get McCarthy supporters to attend the open precinct caucuses and attempt control of the delegates selected at this first stage. Eller reported that the "nuns were filing by on their way to the caucuses, two by two." McCarthy had extensive support in the Minnesota religious community of the Catholic Church, and this support was once again coming out to help him in 1968. Eller recognized the nuns from their previous work, but few others did because in the time between the 1964 caucuses and the 1968 meetings the clerical habit had been set aside for "civilian clothes."

Even in Hubert Humphrey's home precinct, Humphrey's son and son-in-law had been granted places on the delegations only out of the courtesy of the McCarthy dominated caucus. An Eller projection had McCarthy controlling enough of the eventual delegates to either have control of the delegation or be near the break-even point. Humphrey was not able to control the delegation selection in his own state. McCarthy had his first major victory. Protest had now been turned into actual delegate votes for the Chicago nominating convention. Word of this result came in to New Hampshire during the next several days, further strengthening the resolve of the campaign and measurably raising the spirit of the candidate.

AMERICANS FOR A DEMOCRATIC ACTION ENDORSEMENT

A bitter struggle took place between members of the old Democratic coalition of unionists, civil rights leaders, intellectuals, and liberal politicians which had held together since the defeat of a Dump Johnson resolution at a 1967 meeting of the executive board. Al Lowenstein, a long-time ADA activist, had introduced the resolution early in his Dump Johnson effort to stimulate McCarthy's candidacy announcement. Now that McCarthy was actively campaigning, the issues of endorsement bubbled to the surface again, but this time with the support of many more board members than had been attracted to the earlier negative motion.

The board was scheduled to meet February 10 and 11 to consider the endorsement. Prior to the meeting the issue involved was less whether a resolution of endorsement would succeed but more whether those supporting President Johnson would walk out of the organization. The question on the minds of each of the board members was whether the organization, which had been the liberal conscience of the Democratic Party for more than twenty years, could survive the issue.

Supporting the resolution were the then president of the ADA, John Kenneth Galbraith; influential liberal Washington lawyer, Joseph A. Rauh, Jr.; and former presidential staff member, Arthur Schlesinger. In an attempt to placate the minority of the ADA board opposing the McCarthy endorsement, a substitute resolution drafted by Galbraith was substituted for the stronger draft originally proposed by Rauh. The substitute conceded that "a part of our membership does not agree" with the position, but this was not sufficient to prevent the threatened result. (*Boston Globe,* February 11, 1968) By a vote of sixty-five to forty-seven the ADA Board endorsed Senator McCarthy's candidacy. Those close to the Johnson administration and most of the union leadership that had been part of the organization since its founding, walked out. With his resignation, former ADA president and then special counsel to President Johnson, John Roche said, "I don't go on trips into a political disneyland." (*Keene Evening Sentinel,* February 12, 1968) Labor leaders, I. W. Abel, president of the Steel Workers, and Louis Stulberg, president of the International Lady's Garment Workers, resigned, along with Representative Henry Gonzalez, Democrat of Texas, and Leon Keyserling, former chair of the president's Council of Economic Advisors. Despite the loss of these prominent members, the leadership of the ADA believed the group had "gained prestige by endorsing peace candidate Eugene J. McCarthy's presidential bid." (*Valley News,* February 14, 1968)

In addition to demonstrating the willingness of a number of prominent national liberal leaders to go out on a limb for Senator McCarthy, the endorsement produced important press recognition of McCarthy's growing national campaign. The *Boston Globe* ran a front-page, four-column story in its Sunday, February 11 edition headlined: "The Democratic Campaign: 2 VICTORIES FOR McCARTHY, Gets ADA backing . . . and Bobby's N.H. Team." (*Boston Globe,* February 11, 1968, p. 1)

Each of these events added to the credibility of McCarthy's challenge within the Democratic Party. To have this support in the form of delegates, nonchallenges by Johnson, and endorsements from recognized individuals and organizations gave the McCarthy campaign legitimacy. The effort could not be disregarded as a fringe movement of malcontents but had to be recognized as a substantial welling of national concern. The press also began to appreciate what was happening and covered the McCarthy story more sensitively. The campaign was making legitimate news that had to be taken into account on a regular basis.

THE REPUBLICANS

In our December 23 memorandum to McCarthy, Studds and I had suggested:

> We are encouraged about the possibility of a write-in effort for Senator McCarthy on the Republican ballot (particularly given the number of Republicans who were willing to change their registration this month even though Senator McCarthy was not yet a candidate in New Hampshire).

At its first organization meeting after McCarthy's announced entry into the New Hampshire primary, the steering committee decided not to campaign overtly for either Republican write-in votes or to attract Republican workers away from those campaigning in New Hampshire for the Republican nomination. This decision was based on the New Hampshire political ethic that one should not muddy another party's pond—an ethic that was especially revered by those who led the McCarthy campaign. Initially there were two major Republican campaigns. Former Vice President Richard M. Nixon and then governor of Michigan, George Romney. Both saw New Hampshire as the first important test and had spent great time, money, and effort preparing for the contest. In the wings were two other prominent political figures: the governor of New York, Nelson Rockefeller, and retired General James Gavin. Harold Stassen and a clutch of lesser known individuals ultimately filed on the Republican ballot—even one man named Herbert Hoover.

PRELUDE

From the beginning, New Hampshire looked like an important battleground for the Republican Party. Observers assumed that President Johnson would stroll to renomination. But increasing antiadministration feeling, whether focused on the war policy or on other aspects of the administration's record, meant that the nominee of the Republican Party had a chance to defeat the incumbent president.

Each candidate approached New Hampshire as if engaged in an artful form of courtship. First there was a scurrying among those who wanted leadership positions in the respective campaigns for their own purposes and to be with a "winner" early in the presidential season. Then there was the courting of those who were seen by the candidates as having valuable political skills and/or followings that would assist the candidate. Finally there was the sorting and signing up of campaign leaders and committees. Each step revealed something of the image the candidates wished to project and the style of their subsequent campaign.

Nixon, wanting to avoid the trap that had befallen Goldwater in 1964, carefully avoided reestablishing his ties with many of New Hampshire's prominent conservatives and previous supporters of his campaigns. He selected as his state chair a young, recently elected state representative from Hillsborough named David

Sterling. The appointment lent freshness and energy to the Nixon effort, which was a direct attempt to bury Nixon's image as a retreaded loser. Behind David Sterling, Nixon assembled the usual assortment of prominent people who had supported Nixon in the past and who found his conservative posture more to their liking. But Sterling was in front and he served as the visible New Hampshire leader of Nixon's campaign. The image was decidedly more to the center of the political spectrum than had been the case in Nixon efforts in the past. Behind the facade were the same gray politicos who were attracted to Nixon in New Hampshire, but to the public the image was comfortably contemporary.

Romney relied heavily on his close ties with Governor Rockefeller in his search for a New Hampshire campaign group. To many Romney appeared as the fresh face in the crowd and the one who could most effectively take on President Johnson in November. He had taken positions in opposition to the administration's war policy and had attracted considerable support from the establishment dissenters in the Republican Party. Romney was viewed as a Republican liberal and attracted as New Hampshire supporters many of those descended from the New Hampshire progressives. Romney selected as his chair William R. Johnson, an attorney, member of the state senate, resident of Hanover, and recognized leader of the Republican liberals. He inherited as his organization those local supporters and friends of Nelson Rockefeller who had campaigned extensively for the 1964 nomination and a sizable group of individuals, Republicans and Independents, who saw Romney as the only viable alternative to the war policies of Lyndon Johnson's administration.

The *New York Times* reported under the headline "Presidential Warm-Up" on November 5, 1967, that "the political lines in Manchester and Hanover, in Keene and Coos Country [sic] are being drawn unusually early this year":

> David Sterling . . . quotes a straw poll that gives the former Vice-President 59 per cent, Governor Reagan 16, Governor Rockefeller of New York 12 and Governor Romney 6.
>
> Hard by the gilt domed colonial Capitol downtown there was an operating Romney headquarters and a dark untenanted second-floor room that purported to be the action center of a write-in campaign for Gov. Ronald Reagan of California.
>
> Romney spent three days in and out of New Hampshire a week ago, his first real politicking there. . . ."
>
> (*New York Times,* November 5, 1967)

The press followed each campaign closely as the respective strategies were revealed.

NIXON: NEW HAMPSHIRE 1968

Nixon had always done well in New Hampshire, and his nomination organization fell quickly in step behind the New Hampshire and national leadership he had selected. The New Hampshire local supporters knew exactly where the votes were that had gone to Nixon in the past and were ready to dust off these votes for him again in 1968.

The media effort became the most prominent part of the Nixon campaign. Billboards stating "Nixon's the One" with the candidate peering into an open attaché case sprang up all over New Hampshire. Nixon surrogates campaigned extensively for him in the small towns and ex-urban neighborhoods where the Republican vote was scattered. Nixon's few visits were carefully orchestrated appearances where the semblance of access and informality was conveyed to the public, but actual contact with him was almost totally limited. On February 1, a page-one advertisement in the *Union Leader* announced Nixon's campaign beginning with an open house.

On the next day William Loeb published one of his famous page-one signed editorials endorsing Richard Nixon's candidacy. The story that appeared on page one under a picture of Nixon and his family contained the following as indications of how the *Manchester Union Leader* would handle Nixon's candidacy and how Nixon would campaign in New Hampshire.

> Nixon, no stranger to the New Hampshire hustings, will fire his opening guns at a noon press conference today at the Holiday Inn at Manchester, and will remain in the state for the remainder of the weekend.
>
> The highlight of his first campaign swing will be Saturday night's testimonial dinner . . . in Concord where a capacity crowd is assured for the convention hall. The hall has a capacity of close to 1,200.
>
> The former presidential standard bearer of the Republican Party—he lost out in a "squeaker" to President John F. Kennedy in 1960—will be accompanied to New Hampshire by his wife, "Pat" and his two daughters, Tricia and Julie. . . .
>
> This afternoon from 5 to 7 P.M. the Nixons will be hosts at a reception for the New Hampshire press and their families at the N.H. Highway Hotel. This is billed by the Nixon committee as a "non news-making" event. There will be no speeches or press conference at this time.
>
> On Saturday the Nixon family will return to Manchester for a two-hour public reception at St. Anselm's College, Goffstown, just outside Manchester. This will take place from 1:30 to 3:30 P.M.
>
> They will go back to the N.H. Highway Hotel in Concord late Saturday afternoon to prepare for the 7 P.M. Nixon for President dinner at the hotel's convention hall.
>
> The former Vice President will stay overnight at the hotel and is expected to remain there most of Sunday working on future plans for his campaigning in the Granite State. There are no public events on Sunday.
>
> Monday morning the party will leave for Manchester, where Nixon is slated to take-off for Green Bay, Wisconsin and more campaigning, at 11:50 A.M.
>
> (*Manchester Union Leader*, February 2, 1968, p. 1)

Large crowds greeted Nixon during his one-weekend tour, and he was well received by the press. Relman Morin, an AP special correspondent, wrote in a story carried by the *Manchester Union Leader:*

> As a campaigner in his second bid for the presidency, Richard M. Nixon is giving a virtuoso performance in New Hampshire.
>
> He ranges from the big speech at the overflow dinner to quiet question and answer sessions with small groups in small rooms; from massive receptions to leisurely strolls through the snow and slush, shaking hands with villagers.
>
> At one moment his facial expressions mirror the image of the thoughtful statesman, in the next, he is a quipping politician, having a good time and enjoying the laughs.
>
> Nixon has been very versatile in his three days in New Hampshire, scene of the nation's first presidential primary.
>
> He has added a new weapon to his armory—wit. . . .
>
> (*Manchester Union Leader,* February 4, 1968, p. 1)

In his short three-day campaign swing in New Hampshire, Nixon conveyed the image of an accessible, human, thoughtful, yet hard-working candidate. His schedule had been carefully developed to present each of these facets and to counter lingering doubts as to his capacity to engage in and win a rough campaign fight. When Nixon left New Hampshire that Monday morning, he left behind a clear image of a mature and effective campaigner. Although time for a possible return visit to New Hampshire was reserved in his schedule, Nixon did not campaign again—it was not necessary.

Mailings, radio and television commercials, surrogate campaigners, newspaper advertising, Loeb's aggressive support, and a carefully organized mailing effort carried the campaign for him. He was off to more difficult states with the assurance of a percentage player.

ROMNEY: NEW HAMPSHIRE 1968

Governor George Romney of Michigan opened his New Hampshire campaign drive first. He hired as his campaign planners the two persons who had organized the Henry Cabot Lodge write-in during the 1964 New Hampshire primary, John D. Deardourff and David B. Goldberg. Following their surprise success in 1964, Deardourff and Goldberg had formed a consulting firm named Campaign Consultants Inc. (CCI). Tom Henshaw, writing for the *Sunday Herald-Traveler,* said:

> The hottest new item on the political shelf in this presidential year of 1968 is the professional consulting firm which, for a flat fee, will show an aspiring mayor, governor, or even president how to best run his campaign.
>
> (*Sunday Herald-Traveler,* January 7, 1968, p. 53)

CCI had turned down an offer from Richard Nixon earlier and began working on the Romney campaign in February 1967. They assembled a campaign organization for New Hampshire which tied back to Romney's national campaign. In the organization were a number of campaigners who had had close ties either to Nelson Rockefeller directly, to roles in his administration in New York state, or to liberal Republican candidates such as John Lindsay, then a Republican and mayor of New York City.

To give Romney a boost early in his New Hampshire campaign, Governor Rockefeller and Governor Chaffee of Rhode Island came to New Hampshire on January 2 to meet with New Hampshire Romney supporters and to give the effort their full support. The visit was also designed to end speculation that Rockefeller would become a candidate. With Rockefeller fully in support of Romney and Romney identified as the ultimate hope of the moderates of the Republican party, the campaign's managers felt that the Romney energy and personality would attract the needed support. The next step in the plan called for Romney to blitz New Hampshire in a six-day campaign visit.

The *Manchester Union Leader* paid special attention to Romney in these early weeks. Columnist D. Frank O'Neil wrote:

> In this case (referring to the Lodge write-in of 1964) they (N.H. Republican voters for Lodge) were "snowed-under" by a cleverly managed public relations campaign, one that was master-minded by a couple of people who are now trying to sell the same "soap-suds" type of campaign on behalf of Governor Romney of Michigan.
>
> (*Manchester Union Leader,* January 10, 1968, p. 1)

Romney's antiadministration position on the war in Vietnam gave the *Manchester Union Leader* a special opportunity to criticize Romney while he was engaged in his dawn-to-dusk effort to woo Republican voters. In a famous visit to Vietnam to view the war theater, Romney had returned as a supporter of the war effort. Later he changed his position stating that he felt he had been "brainwashed" by the Pentagon and the Vietnam-based military. Romney was never quite able to shake the implications of that phrase. Many became skeptical of Romney's ability to make sound policy judgments and to keep from being swayed by advisors and briefings. Senator Eugene McCarthy, when asked about Romney's brainwashed statement, said that he felt brainwashed was an overstatement. "All that was needed in the case of George Romney was a light rinse."

The *ManchesterUnion Leader* felt that Romney was vulnerable among the conservative Republicans of New Hampshire on both his policy position on the war and the implications of the brainwashed statement. It also sensed that the Romney leadership was having difficulty exciting interest in Romney. The editors began to chip away at Romney. The UPI article datelined Concord was headlined, "Romney Deals Verbal Cut to Military Effort in Vietnam."

> Michigan Gov. George Romney yesterday dealt a verbal blow to the military in Vietnam while urging the U.S. and other major powers to increase efforts

to achieve talks between the Saigon government and the National Liberation Front of North Vietnam.

The Republican presidential hopeful told a news conference, "my general feeling is we have relied too heavily on search and destroy rather than clear and hold."

(*Manchester Union Leader*, January 12, 1968, p. 1)

From the beginning, the Romney campaign developed substantial problems. First, it was unable to stimulate much interest. Second, the organization that did evolve was carelessly managed. Third, the press attention for Romney was confusing and those items the campaign thought would help often backfired. Fourth, Romney himself was badly scheduled. Instead of winning voters by his extensive campaign, familiarity seemed to breed contempt. Because of Romney's campaign impact on the McCarthy effort, it is important to recount some of the details of Romney's New Hampshire failure.

THE ROMNEY ORGANIZATION

Each campaign tries to create an image for itself that is distinct. The Romney managers created the idea of a series of "home headquarters" that would serve as local organizing centers and provide identity for the candidate at the neighborhood, small town level. Opening these "headquarters" would give something for the candidate to do in places where there was little opportunity for conventional campaigning—especially in the small towns where the Republican vote resided and during the winter campaign season. An excellent concept, it had to be done carefully to be successful.

On his campaign travels Romney rode in a Winnebago vehicle that was equipped as a headquarters and a place to relax between stops. When scheduled to come into a town, an advance group of "Romney Girls, five Colby Junior College students, all various shades of blonde, who wore red, white, and blue Romney mini dresses would arrive ahead of Romney and warm the audience [usually in a home headquarters] with several Romney campaign songs." (*Concord Daily Monitor*, January 17, 1968) On one of these campaign swings Romney logged more than two thousand miles of small town stops, plant gate and main street handshaking, and home headquarters openings.

The fault with the home headquarters came when a list of these locations was announced. On the list were a number of individuals who were not active in his campaign. In fact, Studds and I screened the list carefully and found several persons who were active McCarthy supporters who did not have a Romney home headquarters or any intention of opening one. Their names had apparently been added to the list from early campaign activities that had been attended by persons opposed to the war before McCarthy's candidacy in New Hampshire. On January 18 Romney announced that twenty-five headquarters had been established in the Concord area, and that these were the "first of 10,000 that will hopefully be in existence before the Republican National Convention next August," and as the *Concord Daily Monitor* reported January 18, 1968:

> In New Hampshire Romney forces are nearing the end of an effort to establish 500 home headquarters before the March 12th primary. At last count, they had secured more than 400, Romney officials said.

On January 20, William Johnson began correcting, publicly, the list of home headquarters he had issued two days earlier. The public relations impact of the original announcement dimmed as the inaccuracies of the list were revealed.

As Studds and I had noted, the idea of the home headquarters was good, and we suggested that the McCarthy Steering Committee borrow the concept. Those communities that would not be able to find or support a storefront headquarters should be organized around a home headquarters. Volunteers would have a place to go, literature could be distributed from the designated homes, and telephoning for election day activity could be organized around these headquarters. They would not, however, act as the focus of McCarthy's local campaign stops. For a Democratic candidate other activities took precedence.

The Romney campaign schedule was a masterpiece, representing how the campaign thought Romney could storm New Hampshire. He was known to be energetic and personally engaging. A typical schedule had Romney outside of a factory greeting workers at 6:30 A.M., an 8:00 A.M. breakfast meeting/speech, mid-morning opening or visiting home headquarters, a high school or college speech, a noon luncheon with a service club, more home headquarters meetings in the afternoon accompanied by street campaigning, a radio interview, a meeting with a local newspaper editor, perhaps a break from campaigning for dinner or a dinner speaking engagement, and often a speech or a meeting with workers in the evening with the campaign day ending for him after 11:00 P.M. The next morning began again with the 6:30 A.M. plant gate handshaking.

The Romney managers wasted their candidate. On his first campaign day he stood outside of a Nashua factory in twenty-degrees-below-zero weather reaching for the hands of workers who were a bit puzzled to see a grown man standing outside in the biting cold and darkness of the early New Hampshire dawn. The hands he was reaching for were mostly those of Democrats.

Mixed in the schedule were what the managers felt were required media events. They thought Romney should be photographed on skis. He did not ski and appeared in a well-circulated photograph awkwardly trying to stand up on skis. What his managers did not realize was that people come to New Hampshire to ski, but most of Romney's potential New Hampshire voters didn't. His schedule provided a photo opportunity near a quaint, snow-covered bridge. Romney, well known for his jogging, appeared one afternoon in jogging shorts, sneakers, and a light shirt ready to demonstrate, for the curious along Concord's Victorian Main Street as well as the photographers, the jogging style that had made him so well known. For some reason he had to wait in the cold for the event to be orchestrated and lost his temper. He did jog, but the whole exercise lost its meaning—if there ever had been one. Romney succeeded in reinforcing only one image and that was not one that lent any particular value to his campaign. He was energetic but perhaps it was true that he could be easily led by his managers and brainwashed. He certainly did not cast an image either of identity with the New Hampshire Republican voter or competence to be the next president of the United States.

With Nixon's carefully staged visit early in February, whatever momentum Romney had succeeded in building with his attempted blitz faded by contrast. Nixon appeared like a person these voters—voters who had supported him in large numbers before—would like as their president. Romney's campaign was entertainment, almost a circus, except that he was trying valiantly through it all to say something serious and important about the impact of the war policy in Vietnam and the impact of the Johnson administration on the national morality.

ROMNEY'S "SECRET WEAPON"

Early in January 1968 the Romney leadership revealed that it had the capacity to prepare forty personalized letters per minute and had mailed more than eighty thousand letters during the same week. Their "secret weapon" was a computer-driven printer capable of producing twelve hundred lines of typing per minute. William Johnson reported that the "names, addresses, telephone numbers and occupations of 130,000 Republicans have been put on computer tape, leaving about 15,000 yet to do." The names had come from precinct checklists with city and town directories used to match husbands and wives and to get occupations. (*Valley News,* January 13, 1968)

The Nixon campaign was using a mechanical letter-writer that produced three hundred letters a day with twenty-seven thousand their total to that point in the campaign. The battle of the letters was on, and from the early report Romney's computer-based operation was in the lead. The Nixon campaign's reaction was that it "did not consider using a computer in their mailings." It was using a hand personalizing method for its letters that took longer and did not involve a computer. (*Valley News,* January 13, 1968) With Nixon running three to one ahead of Romney at that point in the polls, the campaign was sticking to tried and true methods.

William Johnson had borrowed student and graduate assistant help and purchased computer time on the sophisticated computer equipment based at Dartmouth College. His delight at the ability of this system to produce letters, maintain lists, and sort for special interest constituencies was too much for him to contain. The computer was the campaign gimmick of 1968, and William Johnson was the proud father or, more appropriately, midwife. Unfortunately the revelation of the "secret weapon" fell into the *Manchester Union Leader*'s view of the Romney campaign as a bit of soap-selling hucksterism. A bit too slick, sophisticated, and unsettling for many New Hampshire voters who saw the "secret weapon" as a device to manipulate voters. It violated the ethic of making an independent choice and raised suspicion. In reality there was no need for Johnson to crow about his voter contacting operation. If the letters had been quietly produced, mailed, and read, the impact would have been considerably greater than was the fear he, perhaps, thought he could evoke in the Nixon camp.

Efficiently operating the sophisticated direct and personalized mail has power through the creditability of the "direct line" and the believability of the personalization.

Johnson deflated that credibility when he allowed his secret weapon to become public, and when he went into great detail concerning its operation and potential. This was also the beginning of the era of the public's concern with who was keeping personal records and why, and when Johnson also indicated that he had hoped to include data on how frequently each Republican goes to the polls the specter of some form of an invasion of privacy became evident. Johnson's use of the phrase "data bank" coupled with a *Concord Daily Monitor* headline which read, "Romney's Race Aided by Secret Computer," was enough to raise great concern and suspicion. (*Concord Daily Monitor*, January 11, 1968) An organization aide and an operational advantage which, if it had been quietly used might have helped Romney's campaign, became of negative value. Suspicion increased, the letters that were mailed arrived with considerably less credibility, and Romney was given a controversy to deal with when he was trying to establish rapport with New Hampshire voters.

(William Loeb adopted a unique front page editorial style. He used type face and style changes to emphasize his point of view and make comments within the editorial.) Loeb focused the suspicion with one of his first-page signed editorials that read:

Us Guinea Pigs in New Hampshire

For the last two weeks the campaign managers of Gov. Romney have told half a dozen national publications—with remarkable candor—precisely what they are relying on to win the New Hampshire primary.

The mainstay of their campaign is not the qualifications or ability of Gov. Romney to dig himself out of the quicksand of contradictions where he has been floundering for months. Their "secret weapon" as Warren Weaver of the New York Times wrote a week ago, "is not even in New Hampshire."

It is a giant computer, an electronic data bank, based in New York City, that will be working overtime to rescue Gov. Romney's flagging political fortunes.

Into that computer the Romney organizers have fed not only the voter lists of all New Hampshire Republicans and Independents, but also as much personal background as they could dig up in four months of scouring the state.

Inside this "People Bank" in New York City, the voters can be segmented in seconds into Catholics, Protestants, Jews, married, divorced, single, rich, poor, old, young, union man and businessman, black and white, male and female, government worker, home owner, renter—and we don't know what else.

When all this personal data is coupled with analyses of opinion surveys and behavioral studies, the potential for manipulating the electorate of New Hampshire is enormous.

The Romney managers are aware of this potential—and frank about it.

They have bragged that within a matter of a few hours they can have "tailored" pieces of literature in the hands of any special interest voting bloc in the state.

The letter that goes to the young, Roman Catholic, union worker in Manchester can be wholly different than that sent up to the Protestant, small town, upstate, middle-aged businessman.

Each of these letters would be prepared by social scientists in New York, then mass-produced, inserted, stamped by computer, trucked to New Hampshire and mailed.

Yet, each of these computer-produced letters would appear to all the world to be a personalized note written and signed by either Mr. Johnson, or Gov. Romney or Gov. Rockefeller himself!

A few years back a rather frightening book was written entitled *The 480.*

Its theme was that a small group of behavioral scientists, using a computer and massive personal data on each American voter, could subdivide the country into 480 "voting segments," make "tailored appeals" to each of these segments—and elect any man they chose to be President of the United States.

NEW HAMPSHIRE IS TO BE THE TESTING GROUND OF THIS KIND OF "PROGRAMMED POLITICS" AND YOU THE VOTERS OF THIS STATE ARE TO BE THE GUINEA PIGS.

If Gov. George Romney—a man almost without comprehension of the magnitude of the crises this country faces abroad—can be put across to the New Hampshire voter by a complex of data banks in New York City, the lesson will not be lost on other men with similar ideas.

Despite the confidence of the Romney camp in their computer, we don't think it will work. We hope that you cannot sell a presidential candidate the way you sell cigarettes.

The best defense against this sort of effort to manipulate the electorate and exploit the racial, religious, income and regional differences among us—is the basic good sense of New Hampshire.

From the Romney camp comes word that the first to be hit with the special interest mailings will be the voters over 60.

Maybe this editorial will help them to know beforehand just what they are getting.

(Signed)
William Loeb, publisher

(*Manchester Union Leader,* January 27, 1968, p. 1)

Romney's Rockefeller Problem

In spite of Governor Nelson Rockefeller's early, continuing, and vigorous support for Romney, there remained a sizable group of skeptics in New Hampshire. When the February 10 closing date had passed, sixteen delegate candidates had filed as being "favorable" to the nomination of Governor Rockefeller. By February 18 the *New York Times* reported that Proffessor John A. Beckett of Durham had been selected chair of a delegate candidate committee which was organized for a write-in campaign on behalf of the New York governor.

Announcing the effort one of the members of the committee said, "They expected that the write-in would pick up a large portion of the Henry Cabot Lodge write-in vote cast in 1964." The basis for the organizing was the fact that many continued to view Romney as a stand-in or stalking horse for Rockefeller. If Romney failed, then these analysts were sure that their preferred candidate, Rockefeller, would announce his candidacy. If they could generate a sufficient write-in vote for Rockefeller in the New Hampshire primary, they felt that the demise of the Romney campaign would result and at the same time Rockefeller would consider challenging Nixon for the nomination.

Until the January 28 release of a Gallup poll, Rockefeller had been as much as fourteen points ahead of President Johnson in these surveys. The January 28 release had Lyndon Johnson running ahead of each of the four most popular Republicans with the highest approval, 48 percent, in some time. Rockefeller remained the candidate supported most frequently by voters to defeat or run against Johnson. (*Boston Globe,* January 28, 1968, p. 1)

Romney, in spite of extensive New Hampshire campaigning and an impression of gaining strength, did not appear to move either in the public straw polls in New Hampshire or in his standing among other Republicans mentioned as possible candidates nationally. The Rockefeller write-in organizers perceived this weakness and began actively to hold out hope for a Rockefeller nomination.

In the early stages of the Romney campaign a number of young volunteers had been attracted by his antiwar stand. One of these was Allison Teal who had become a key staff worker in the Romney Concord headquarters. Shortly after Eric Schnapper arrived to work on the McCarthy campaign he met Allison. Their mutual political interests led to frequent discussions of their respective campaign experiences. Schnapper began reporting to Studds and me that not all was going as well as the press releases and progress reports from the Romney headquarters told.

In addition to this cross-referencing of antiwar candidacy was the activity of the press. Lewis Chester and Bruce Page of the *London Times* had regularly followed the activities of the election, especially the antiwar candidacies of Romney and McCarthy. Late in February they stopped by the McCarthy headquarters to chat with Studds and me. They had just come from the Romney headquarters about four city blocks away and reported that the place was like a morgue. "People were standing around as if someone had died and no one knew exactly how to respectfully dispose of the body."

Studds and I had begun to revive our early feeling that a number of nominal Republicans would be attracted to write in Senator McCarthy's name on their ballot. We also felt that Republicans for McCarthy organizing would lend credibility to McCarthy as a candidate who could appeal to voters across the political spectrum. Such a view, if supported by votes, would strengthen McCarthy as a candidate who, if nominated, could win the November election against the Republican nominee. We urged our local organizations to actively organize among Republicans who without Romney had no other antiwar candidate to support.

On February 28, Governor Romney declared that he was withdrawing from the New Hampshire Presidential primary. His campaign had failed to generate any momentum. A possible write-in for Governor Rockefeller was gaining and threatened to push Romney into a third place New Hampshire finish. If this happened Romney's advisors felt it would end prospects for any candidate being successful against Nixon. By withdrawing, Nixon would be denied a decisive win against a serious opponent, then, perhaps, some other Republican could pick up from there and challenge Nixon for the nomination.

The demise of the Romney campaign released volunteers and local moderate/liberal Republican energy to work on the McCarthy effort. Republicans for McCarthy committees organized, letters supporting McCarthy were circulated to former Romney activists, advertisements urging Republicans concerned about the policies of the Johnson administration were placed by these committees, and fund-raising began. Isolated and frustrated Republican liberals began to appear at McCarthy campaign stops and express their support for him. Studds and I were willing to help individuals become organized but felt that if ads were placed, letters mailed, etc., these should be circulated by the McCarthy Republicans themselves, not simply as an adjunct to the McCarthy campaign. The Republicans for McCarthy appeal would then be distinct and could be stated in terms of why these individuals were supporting McCarthy. This could be done exclusive of the appeal that the McCarthy campaign was itself making to Democrats and Independents.

When Romney ended his campaign, segments of the media thought the interesting part of the New Hampshire primary was over for 1968. CBS and ABC canceled their hotel and motel spaces, stopped preparing for extensive election eve coverage, and left New Hampshire. Other news-gathering organizations and several of the major newspapers greatly reduced their coverage of the remaining campaigns. The indications were that Nixon would win easily over the write-in effort for Rockefeller and that President Johnson was at least a three-to-one leader in the campaign with McCarthy. Given that prospect, a fait accompli could easily be reported by a few local stringers and the budget-rich NBC, which continued its election eve preparations.

THE LBJ NEW HAMPSHIRE CAMPAIGN

The Johnson campaign developed according to the plan that Bernard L. Boutin had outlined to Sandra Hoeh during their August 1967 meeting. Following the Democratic State Committee's endorsement of the Johnson renomination bid November 19, other local and county committees and prominent Democratic Party leaders and officials began endorsing the renomination of the president as well. Each of the significant endorsements received the attention of a press release from the Democratic State Committee headquarters and local or statewide media distribution. In carefully orchestrated succession the Johnson campaign leadership began filing for the delegate places. Again, each of the principal and approved filings was accompanied by a press release that kept the efforts of the committee before the public on almost a daily basis.

Shortly before Senator McCarthy was to make his first campaign visit to New Hampshire, Robert Novak, a nationally syndicated columnist, called the McCarthy state headquarters inviting Studds and me to join him for dinner. Evans had been spending the day with Bernard Boutin and other members of the LBJ committee and now wanted to contrast his experience with our view of the contest.

The urbane Evans graciously hosted a quiet dinner in the dining room of the New Hampshire Highway Hotel just outside Concord. He put us both at ease, and we discussed what was happening and what we perceived our efforts would accomplish.

Evans was impressed by what Boutin had told him of his campaign plan and the extensive list of endorsements Boutin had gathered around the state. I responded that I felt if someone was asked for an endorsement that is what they would give. If someone was asked to work then that is what they would do. In the case of the Johnson campaign, I felt endorsements were contrary to the nonendorsement ethic in New Hampshire and might hurt the Johnson effort rather than help. As for the campaign plan, I responded that I did not see it as being particularly unique. It still rested on the hard work of volunteers who did not seem to be volunteering and on the backs of those who had endorsed the renomination effort but were doing little else. To Studds and me it appeared as if the endorsers were busier congratulating each other over the endorsements and predicting how badly McCarthy would be beaten than actually stirring up a Johnson vote. An air of self-assurance about the three-to-one defeat of McCarthy and the ultimate success of Johnson, not only in New Hampshire but in November as well, kept the energy and volunteer levels relatively low in the Johnson camp. To us, the Johnson campaign seemed narrowly based with few persons actually involved in the work, arrogant, and overconfident. We explained the reasons for each of these conclusions to Evans.

We began by reviewing how rapidly our organization had developed before McCarthy announced, how it sustained itself before McCarthy entered the New Hampshire primary, how it had grown since the January 3 beginning, how dedicated and effective the volunteers at the local level had become, the useful press attention the campaign had already received, and how a substantial flow of outside volunteer assistance to operate the state headquarters and staff the priority local headquarters had begun. Both of us described our own experience with campaigns and politics in an effort to counter Evans' impression of the professionalism of Bernard Boutin, his committee, and the support he was receiving.

The evening ended with Studds and me thinking we had convinced Evans of our effectiveness, ability, and the reality of the McCarthy challenge in New Hampshire. Evans' column was printed January 25, the day before McCarthy arrived for his first New Hampshire visit. Studds read it first and called me in outrage. The heading read "LBJ Turns on Heat to Roast McCarthy," and went on:

> Concord, N.H.—The real surprise in the campaign for the March 12 Democratic presidential primary is not the disorganized nature of Sen. Eugene McCarthy's campaign but how the much-maligned regular party organization here is building a well-oiled machine to support President Johnson.
>
> On the eve of McCarthy's first campaign visit here Friday for his battle against Mr. Johnson, the state of the senator's campaign is easily depicted:

> not until this week did his campaign headquarters in Washington send a single advance man to survey New Hampshire and confer with McCarthy's original supporter and now the manager on the scene, Dartmouth College public affairs man David Hoen [sic].
>
> In contrast, McCarthy, the only name on the ballot, faces what looks to be the most formidable and highly organized campaign ever fielded in this state, promoting the write-in of Mr. Johnson's name against McCarthy. Headed by Nashua businessman and former Washington bureaucrat Bernard Boutin (who handled Sen. Estes Kefauver's winning primary campaign in 1956 and John F. Kennedy's in 1960) the Johnson organization is developing a campaign concept based on careful organization wholly new to New Hampshire.
>
> If successful, it will undermine the habitual primary campaign approach of non-organization Democrats like Kefauver, who conducted hamlet-to-hamlet, handshaking tours that overwhelmed the voters.
>
> But Kefauver's stunning upset of Harry Truman in 1952 came against the back drop of a weak, almost non-existent Democratic Party organization. Kefauver filled a power vacuum by going directly to the voters, with little if any resistance from the regulars.
>
> Now, however, the Democrats not only have the governorship and one U.S. Senator but are also organized. They are breaking down the state's 87,500 registered Democrats into 2000 neighborhoods, with one coordinator for each. Every Democratic voter will be handed a pledge card, with a detachable blank addressed to the White House telling President Johnson why the voter will write in his name on Mar. 12.
>
> Campaign plans seldom live up to advance billing. But if Boutin, backed by Gov. John King, does half as well as his blueprint, McCarthy will be facing a defeat close to annihilation.
>
> Moreover, McCarthy's problems only start here. A confidential poll taken for the state organization by Oliver Quayle shows that, although 60 percent of the state's Democrats say they know who Sen. McCarthy is, some of them are confusing him with the late Sen. Joseph McCarthy of Wisconsin. These Democrats identify Gene McCarthy as a hawk on the war in Vietnam when, in fact, the main reason for his campaign against Mr. Johnson is his opposition to the President's firm stand in Vietnam.

Evans went on to recount Studds' reaction to the first McCarthy visit to New Hampshire in December, the impact of his lecture, and John Teague's charge to McCarthy to "run hard for the presidency" made at the Bedford meeting following the Senator's lecture. He concluded his column:

> Thus, the prospect is bleak for McCarthy. He did not really want to come into New Hampshire in the first place but bowed to advice that if he passed up the first primary in the nation his candidacy would suffer still more from a lack of credibility.

> The one bright spot since his entry is that the chance for a large write-in for non-candidate Sen. Robert F. Kennedy, has sharply declined . . . Eugene Daniell . . . is still running several candidates for convention delegates pledged to Kennedy. But Daniell is now planning to vote for McCarthy in the preferential primary.
>
> That will help McCarthy, but not enough. A McCarthy vote of more than 20 percent would be a surprise, and a total of less would be an undisguised disaster.
>
> (*Boston Globe*, January 25, 1968)

In our view, Evans had bought the Johnson campaign story entirely. He had selected from our lengthy dinner conversation only those few comments that revealed uncertainty with McCarthy, problems with the national campaign headquarters, or reactions to McCarthy's precampaign visit. Studds and I felt we had been taken by the slick and engaging writer. We feared that on the day before McCarthy's first visit the conclusions of a major national columnist would seriously undercut our fledgling campaign. Above all we felt we had been and were operating in a professional manner, using limited resources effectively, analyzing the situation carefully, and responding to an offensive posture toward the defensive Johnson campaign. To have a seasoned observer of the national political scene describe our efforts as he did in his column was a severe blow to a campaign ego that was just beginning to feel the first flush of confidence.

Fortunately Evans and Novak's column does not circulate widely in New Hampshire. The reporters who arrived with McCarthy the next day had read it and with the problems at the Pandora Sweater factory gate during McCarthy's first campaign day, they and many political observers outside New Hampshire seemed to find Evans' assessment to be accurate. The view that seemed to be circulating outside New Hampshire, that the McCarthy campaign didn't have a chance and was "disorganized," gave Studds and me problems. Money to run the campaign was not arriving rapidly enough to support even our modest early efforts and certainly not in amounts large enough to sustain a nationally oriented, Washington-based campaign organization. Without the ability to hire staff, develop campaign materials, support field operations, and keep in touch with state and local McCarthy committees, the campaign stumbled badly in the early weeks of January.

Studds and I had tried to point out to Evans that while his image of the national headquarters and a centrally directed campaign might be correct, his image of what was developing for McCarthy at the state level was not. What had impressed Evans about the Johnson New Hampshire campaign were the very attributes of that campaign that held the greatest opportunity for McCarthy's success. A tightly controlled, centrally managed campaign organization highlighted the same negative attributes of the Johnson administration that people at the "grass roots" had begun to fear. Studds and I sensed a basic alienation from and distrust of the Johnson dominated national government. The giant personality of Johnson himself seemed to frighten people. His style and his real or imagined ability to overpower the institutions of the federal government and to stifle opposition had begun to create a considerable reaction.

Evans had mentioned several details of the Johnson campaign that intrigued Studds and me. The first was the organizational concept of Boutin's effort which was to depend on "2000 neighborhoods, with one coordinator for each." (*Boston Globe,* January 25, 1968) Boutin, I recalled, was dusting off a page from the 1960 Kennedy campaign when, to avoid useless local struggles over titles in the campaign, the John Kennedy organizers used the title "Kennedy Secretary" as the means of identifying the local organizer. Boutin revealed by this that he expected difficulty in getting his campaign job done by using only the local Democratic Party organizations—something that Evans did not appreciate when he wrote his column.

Second, Boutin had taken the idea generated by the Lodge write-in campaign of 1964 of a "pledge" card. The impact of Lodge's surprise victory in the 1964 Republican presidential primary had conditioned the organizations of each of the principal campaigns, Republican and Democratic. Although Studds and I were not surprised by Boutin's use of a pledge card, we were interested in what form this effort would take.

A basic element of any political campaign is to know what the opposition is doing. In the case of the Johnson campaign, this became a relatively easy task. First, in their self-confidence the leadership was not reluctant to discus the organizational concept of the campaign with the press. Boutin had done this with Evans. Second, close ties and friendships had been built up over the years between us and many of those working on the Johnson campaign. This friendship had long preceded 1968s politics and would continue after March 12. We were aware, however, that there was dissension within the Johnson camp. Bernard Boutin had returned to New Hampshire to manage President Johnson's first renomination test. The concept and organization manual on the campaign had been developed through his advice while still in Washington. When he returned to New Hampshire he adopted a rather inflexible leadership role that allowed for little, if any, dissension from his concept of the campaign.

Late in January, the first rumblings of this dissension became apparent. Boutin expected all of those who had endorsed Johnson and those who had at one time expressed a willingness to help to fall into line behind him and the top leadership of the Johnson effort. Any criticism was viewed by Boutin as a form of disloyalty. To him there were ninety thousand Democrats in the state who had to be reached and told how to support their president by writing in his name. A New Hampshire success for Boutin's campaign concept would propel Boutin to the national leadership of Johnson's campaign. The personal investment for Boutin was enormous. Winning was the only acceptable result. To others winning was important, but keeping the New Hampshire Democratic Party alive and friendships viable after the primary was at least as important.

Shortly after Evans' column appeared, Studds and I were given a package of the Johnson campaign's organizational materials. One of our volunteers had been given the kit by a disgruntled Johnson supporter. The kit contained a sixteen-page mimeographed document titled, "New Hampshire Citizens for Johnson Campaign Checklist for the President Johnson 'Write-In' Campaign, New Hampshire—March 12, 1967 [sic]." With the document were ten attractively presented pictorial brochures titled, "A Strong Man in a Tough Job," five green and white vinyl bumper stickers that read, "I Support President Johnson," along with a mimeographed slip that said "Bumper *must* be wiped clean before attaching"; four preaddressed and stamped envelopes; a one-page item titled, "Notable Accomplishments of the Vice President, Hubert H. Humphrey"; and twenty serially numbered three-part wallet-sized cards. The first card read, "N.H. Democrats are 90,000 Strong, I have pledged my support to President Johnson, and though he is not an announced candidate, I am writing his name in on my ballot in the March 12th New Hampshire Presidential Preference Primary," with space under the pledge for the voter's signature. Part two of the card was titled "White House Copy" and read "President Johnson, I pledge my support to you and will WRITE-IN your name on my ballot in the March 12th New Hampshire Presidential Preference Primary, Name __________ (print clearly) Address __________ Tel. No. __________ and two boxes: Democrat or Independent, (As an expression of your support this card will be forwarded to President Johnson at the White House in Washington, D.C.)."

Part three, titled, "Headquarters Copy," repeated the name, address, telephone number, voter status, note space for services needed such as "transportation, baby-sitter, and remarks," and as with the other two the serial number was repeated. The preaddressed and stamped envelopes were for the return of these last two coupons to the Johnson headquarters in Manchester.

The whole package was carefully developed and well presented. A brochure folded out to a sheet of high-grade paper with a sample ballot on one side with graphic instructions for writing in the president's name, and on the other a selection of pictures showing President Johnson in his "Tough Job." Johnson was shown quietly in his office, meeting with senate leaders Mansfield and Dirksen, with Dean Rusk in a cabinet meeting, a face-to-face conversation with Premier Kosigin of the Soviet Union and listening to a General in some military field station. The photographs conveyed the burdens of the Presidency and Johnson's thoughtful leadership in that job. The brief text read:

> There is no tougher job in the world than being President of the United States—and never has it been tougher than it is now.
>
> You, along with 200 million other Americans, look to him for decisive action as we face the most serious challenges ever to confront our nation and the world.
>
> An effective President must avoid weakness . . . avoid backing down when the going gets tough . . . and he must forego the impulse to let loose . . . because as the leader of the most powerful nation on earth, he can trigger the destruction of civilization with a single word. He must follow the responsible course . . . enduring the wailing of the peaceniks and those who would surrender.
>
> He must be a man of dedicated strength and President Johnson is . . .
>
> A STRONG MAN IN A TOUGH JOB
>
> The job is made tougher because the courageous course is never easy. He assumed office under the most trying circumstances . . . and besides carrying out, to the letter, every one of President Kennedy's programs, he has

> gone beyond as he strives for an ever better America. It is not easy for a President to crusade for expanded opportunities for all Americans . . .when most Americans are already living better than any people in history.
>
> President Johnson is a tireless worker.
>
> He has done a remarkable job . . . and with our support he will continue as one of our greatest Presidents. Your endorsement will bolster President Johnson's determination.
>
> Both he and the country look to New Hampshire as the first state in the nation to reaffirm its unflinching devotion to convictions of honor.
>
> Your write-in vote can set the pace for the entire nation as an overwhelming endorsement of this strong man in a tough job. Your vote is both the source and measure of his strength.

The theme had been carefully chosen to attract feelings sympathetic to a president in a difficult position. The writers of Johnson campaign material emphasized the positive quality of strong leadership in difficult times. Advice concerning the strategy reflected an underlying strain in the Democratic Party electorate that "strength" was preferable to "weakness" and that strong leadership was preferable to uncertain challenges or disorder. The campaign concept from brochure to instructions to pledge cards was one of unifying behind the President to provide security and national solidarity.

To defeat such a strategy would mean that Studds and I would have to pick it apart or it might, conceivably, fail of its own overconfident volition. The instructions circulated with the campaign materials began to give us some help in countering the Johnson strategy.

The introduction to the instructions read:

> On March 12th New Hampshire will vote 50,000 strong for President Lyndon B. Johnson.
>
> There are over 87,000 registered Democrats and over 127,000 "Independents." The goal is attainable—with hard work.
>
> But—the job is difficult since the President's name will not be on the ballot and it will be necessary to write-it-in.
>
> That then, is the goal for our campaign—by March 12th N.H. will have 50,000 write-in votes pledged to the President. . . .

In a section titled "Tips for Organization," the instructions outlined the campaign structure.

> 1. The Neighborhood Coordinator: The backbone of the entire campaign is the Neighborhood Coordinator. In most cases these coordinators will be women although there is no real preference. . . . Each "N.C." will have responsibility only for his or her neighborhood, consisting of a street or streets assigned by the Town or Ward coordinator.

The "N.C." was expected to contact all Democrats and Independents living within the assigned area. Each was responsible for from thirty-five to fifty voters. The "single most important activity of the entire campaign will be the Pledge-Card Drive. This will be handled by the Neighborhood Coordinator . . . and . . . will be his *top priority* project prior to Primary Day." The instructions went on to discuss the other roles in the campaign including: 2. The Town or Ward Coordinator, 3. The City Coordinator, 4. The County Coordinator, 5. The Check List Committee, 6. The Transportation Committee, 7. The Finance Committee, 8. The Baby Sitter Committee, and 9. The Publicity Committee. Item 10 called for "Weekly Progress Reports to be filed from the County, City, & Town" on an attached report form.

The most intriguing portion of the instructions was that page devoted to "The Pledge-Card Drive." The pledge-card drive gave the organizational pyramid an activity that would substitute for the fact that there would not be a live candidate traveling in New Hampshire and none of the activities to supporting a candidate in the field would take place. Circulating pledge cards and getting signatures would be the important activity and the cards themselves would be the basis on which the get-out-the-vote effort would be focused on election day. The instructions were explicit:

> As stated earlies [sic], this activity is perhaps the most important single activity in the campaign. Thereare [sic], as you know, approximately 90,000 registered Democrats in New Hampshire. We want to show the President that New Hampshire Democrats are practically "90,000 strong for President Johnson." At the same time we want [sic] to be sure that all New Hampshire Democrats (and Independents) are fully aware that they should go to the polls on March 12th and write the President's name on the ballot.
>
> To accomplish these objectives, pledge cards will be distributed to each neighborhood coordinator for use in his neighborhood. Each N.C. will, during this personal call on the voters in his neighborhood, ask the voter to sign the card indicating that he (the voter) intends to write in the President's name on the ballot on March 12th.
>
> The card is divided into three sections. The voter who signs the card will keep one section, the second section will be mailed or delivered to state headquarters by the N.S. and the third section will be retained by the N.C. for reference on Primary Day. (Space is provided in this section for notes as to transportation required, baby sitters, etc.)
>
> The sections of the cards that are to be sent to state headquarters should be collected and mailed in quantities as they are accumulated. Envelopes for mailing are provided in the campaign kit. This section of the cards will be forwarded by state headquarters directly to the President to indicate to him the support of New Hampshire voters.
>
> This activity is vital. It is one which should receive the utmost attention and effort of each neighborhood, ward, town and city coordinator. Almost every voter who signs a card will go to the polls on Primary day and will write in President Johnson's name. From the moment he signs the card,

> that voter has a new and real interest in the campaign—he has taken a first step, and he will follow it up on March 12.

The pledge-card tactic seemed to cross the grain of independent-minded New Hampshire voters. If it could be made to be seen as an embodiment of the long reach of Washington and as a way to regiment New Hampshire voters, the tactic might be turned against Johnson.

Given that Johnson was viewed by most as being miles ahead of McCarthy, it was difficult to stimulate much interest in doing the hard work of contacting voters, getting pledge cards signed, or even attending many of the organizational meetings. To drum up interest Governor King and occasionally Bernard Boutin began to stump for the Johnson effort.

As early as January 12, I had found it necessary to respond to statements by Governor King. In a January 11 press conference King had asserted that there was strong support for President Johnson in New Hampshire because it was the "patriotic" thing to do in the midst of a war. "This sounds corny to some people, but I think New Hampshire voters are patriotic," King said when asked what he thought McCarthy's chances were in the New Hampshire primary. In a press release responding to King's remarks I asked if Governor King "finds it unpatriotic to support Senator McCarthy?" noting that members of the McCarthy committee had campaigned for John F. Kennedy in 1960 and Lyndon Johnson in 1964. "We are now fighting for Eugene McCarthy. Does the governor find this unpatriotic?"

Senator McCarthy responded to the same theme when speaking in Athens, Georgia, January 24 when he said, "The administration's tendency to equate loyalty to its policies with loyalty to the country is dangerous and self-serving. The Johnson administration's efforts to discourage dissent at home in order to bring false unity has not been successful." "An effort to quell dissent," McCarthy stated, "is dangerous because it obscures the real military and political causes of this stalemated war, self-serving because it seeks to give doubtful policies undeserved immunity from democratic debate, and it tries to use American armed forces as a shield for our policy makers against their critics."

"It is proof not of weakness but of democratic vitality that our people reject the contention that debate must end and we must all rally to the struggle regardless of its causes, objectives and consequences. There are differences between one war and another and between one issue and another. The essence of intelligent policy-making is to discriminate among these according to their policy effects upon our country's interests and values. I intend to do what I can in this election year to make these distinctions clear." (*Atlanta Constitution,* January 24, 1968) Instead of attempting to clarify these distinctions, the Johnson administration itself and through its surrogates at the state level sought to cloud the differences and to compel a form of unquestioning loyalty.

Governor King, speaking January 30 before a group of Sullivan County Democrats, urged that McCarthy be rejected and that they unite solidly behind President Johnson. "How would President Johnson face the parents of our Vietnam veterans should we pull out? To dishonor our commitment would be to dishonor the memory of those who have given their lives in Vietnam. What people anywhere in the world would believe in our will to protect them against communist aggression if we show that we back down when the going gets tough? The honor of America and safety of the Free World are at stake in this election. Despite a campaign of vilification and abuse that is without precedent in our history President Johnson has continued to lead. In spite of faint hearts and carping critics President Johnson is keeping faith to our commitments in Southeast Asia." (*Valley News,* January 31, 1968, p. 1)

Attending the meeting were a number of McCarthy supporters, including Sandra Hoeh who immediately called me. I was meeting with Studds in Concord and composed a response to King that we either called into the wire services or dropped under their office doors. The same day the media carried the story of the King speech they also carried our rebuttal. I charged that King "is clearly frightened," and noted that King was speaking before a meeting of Sullivan County Democrats for the first time in his six years in office and was doing so "not only to line up LBJ support but to pose as a foreign policy expert." "In the process," I charged, "Governor King has willfully and irresponsibly distorted and slandered the position of Sen. Eugene J. McCarthy and the thousands of loyal citizens of New Hampshire who agree with him. For six years he (King) has failed to address a Democratic meeting in Sullivan County, which is additional evidence that the Governor is obediently jumping through hoops held by LBJ." (*Claremont Eagle,* January 31, 1968) The *Claremont Eagle* had headlined the story on King's speech, "Gov. King Rides 'Shotgun' for LBJ at Newport," while carrying on the same page the Concord datelined response from me headlined, "McCarthy Aide Declares King 'Is Frightened!'"

At the same meeting Harry Makris, executive director of the Democratic State Committee, distributed the Johnson write-in campaign kits, gave instructions, and then, with the governor, was forced to respond to questions. The most embarrassing was asked by one of the "dozen or two doves in the audience of 70" (*Claremont Eagle,* January 31, 1968) concerning whether state committee funds were being used to advance Johnson's candidacy. Makris said, "Money spent on the Johnson drive was raised separately from state committee funds and donors had clearly earmarked their contributions to be used for LBJ." (*Valley News,* January 31, 1968)

The Newport meeting set a pattern that kept the LBJ campaign at least neutralized if not actually on the defensive in each of these organizing sessions. The media coverage carried both sides of the story, often in the same article, and the LBJ organizers faced increasingly severe questioning as time went on.

In his frustration Governor King began to escalate his rhetoric. Speaking in Dover before another gathering of Democrats, King said, "Our President is under violent personal attack and because he is the champion of the free world. That means the time has come for every true Democrat to stand up and be counted—or from now on, to be counted out. On this field we accept battle. His friends are our friends. His enemies are our enemies and we meet all comers—inside and out. The battle begins here and we will carry it forward to a great victory next fall." (*Manchester Union Leader*, January 14, 1968, p. 1)

When asked in a radio interview if he agreed with Governor King's conclusion, U.S. Senator Tom McIntyre, co-chair with King of the New Hampshire LBJ committee, said, "Oh, no, I think John went a little far there." I picked up the comment and issued a press release that said, "Senator McIntyre repudiated the unprecedented way in which Governor King threatened New Hampshire Democrats. . . . We thank the Senator for disassociating himself from the Governor's remarks and this aspect of intimidation and distortion which has characterized the Johnson campaign in New Hampshire. New Hampshire's Democrats now await an apology from John King himself." (McCarthy press release, February 17, 1968)

As with McIntyre, other Democrats were beginning to resent the tactics of the Johnson campaign and the vaguely veiled threats coming from King and others who were aggressively supporting the write-in effort. Symbolic of the effort to line up the Democratic Party beyond the write-in effort was the pledge card, the same pledge card that was the "top priority project" of the write-in organizing effort. The effort, the way it was being represented, and what it began to symbolize produced a major campaign opportunity for the McCarthy campaign.

As Governor King's speeches became more intense the dissension inside the Johnson campaign heightened. Vigorous support of the president's political future was one thing; quite another was accomplishing that by driving from the party the very people who had made it possible for a Democrat to sit in the governor's chair for the first time in forty years and for a Democrat to represent the state in Washington for the first time in twenty years.

My telephone began ringing more frequently with reports of disgruntled Johnson supporters. The first to agree to meet with me was Harold "Scotty" Scott, a former McIntyre campaign aide who had agreed to help with various organizational tasks in the Johnson effort. He had been convinced by Makris and Boutin that the LBJ organizational drive focusing on the pledge cards would produce a broader based, better organized statewide Democratic Party. Scott saw this as a way of improving Democratic candidates' chances of being elected to local as well as statewide offices.

In our first meeting, one between old friends, Scott indicated that Boutin would not tolerate anything but complete loyalty and allegiance to the campaign plan he had drafted and to the position that President Johnson's war policies were correct. He also reported that most aspects of the organizational effort were seriously lagging and that Boutin had instructed both King and McIntyre to step up their attacks of the McCarthy supporters. The campaign, he said, was not attracting volunteers. The headquarters was virtually deserted except for those employed by the Democratic State Committee or attached to either the staff of the governor or the senator.

Scott continued to perform for the LBJ committee but with increasing disillusionment over the campaign's inability to respond effectively and over the heavy-handedness of Boutin and King. During our meetings over coffee, I assured him that the ability of the McCarthy campaign to respond quickly to Johnson campaign charges and to turn those charges back on the Johnson leadership was having an important impact. Even with Governor King as a traveling main event, the LBJ effort was constantly defending itself. By the middle of February, the Johnson campaign was in considerable disarray while the McCarthy effort was "feeding" successfully and growing into a serious political challenge.

LINING UP THE "HATCHED" EMPLOYEES

As the campaign progressed and the style of the Johnson write-in became evident, a network of information gatherers grew. Many of the New Hampshire based reporters were young and sympathetic to McCarthy's effort. An excellent rapport existed between them, the McCarthy press office, and Studds and myself. While the Johnson spokespeople were often unavailable or unwilling to comment other than through press releases, McCarthy leaders, principally Studds and me, had shown our helpfulness to the reporters from the moment of the New Hampshire release of McCarthy's entry in the primary. The reporters developed a habit of calling us for a response to a statement or charge from the Johnson camp so that both items could be carried together. I came to expect a telephone call from the UPI office between 6:00 and 7:00 each morning for a response to a charge or reaction to a wire service state or national story. The reporters were making good news and reputations for themselves, and I was generating media attention for the McCarthy campaign. Coupled with the growing network of local volunteers and campaign supporters, the web of information gathering that was accessible to the McCarthy campaign was virtually total. Tips were relayed to the reporters for them to investigate, and the reporters would tip the McCarthy leaders on things that they had gathered.

A local Johnson campaign chair, Portsmouth City Councilor John Splaine, participated in an hour-long discussion of campaign issues at the University of New Hampshire. Joining Splaine in the discussion and representing the McCarthy campaign was Sandford Gottlieb, executive director of SANE, who was in New Hampshire to support the McCarthy effort. The discussion was recorded for eventual use by the student radio station. Splaine, with unusual frankness bordering on naiveté, was critical of activities of the Johnson New Hampshire campaign. In the course of the discussion he said:

> I have seen things done as a member of the Johnson Committee, as a city councilman in Portsmouth, that are absolutely unbelievable as far as the way I view how things could run.
>
> Let me give you one example.
>
> We have various people that are "Hatched," I think . . . they're under the Hatch Act; they can't politically campaign. So obviously the McCarthy people attacked that we are using these people, and we are. I'll tell you why.
>
> In attempting to get people to work for any cause—McCarthy, Nixon, or Johnson, it is extremely difficult in the real world unless there is something in it for them. Now, ideally, we ought to destroy this concept, I agree.

> But we were having real problems in getting people to do things in Portsmouth.
>
> So one day Bernie Boutin came down and sat down in the Meadowbrook and called up a few of the boys that were Hatched, a member of the public utilities commission, and they suggested that they had better start doing something. I mean this is just one of the examples of what goes on in the real world.
>
> (*Boston Globe*, February 22, 1968)

Almost as soon as the words were out of Splaine's mouth, Studds and I received a call from a Durham supporter relating the tale and the fact that the remark was on tape. Within hours we had a copy of the tape and had it transcribed. Through our press secretary Bill Gallagher, whose friend William Cardoso was the *Boston Globe* reporter in New Hampshire, the tip was relayed. To give greater credibility to the issue, I suggested that Cardoso inquire on his own about the allegation of Boutin's arm twisting. When he had established the facts and developed the story by contacting Boutin as well as Splaine, then the McCarthy campaign would respond to the discovery with appropriate outrage.

Cardoso found his editors were extremely interested in the allegations of Splaine and urged him to pursue it fully. First, Cardoso confirmed that the remarks had been made by checking with witnesses at the discussion. Second, he tried to track down Splaine who when found said he understood the severity of the charge but then began to backtrack. Cardoso's account read:

> Later Tuesday, Splaine was personally confronted during the Winter meeting of the N.H. Municipal Association . . . and was asked to identify the Hatch Act persons involved.
>
> He said he could not because he possessed no factual knowledge. He said he was not at the Sheraton-Meadowbrook at the time he placed Boutin there and added: "I don't even think it took place."
>
> He said he was informed originally during the course of "casual conversation" but could not remember who told him, or when, or how, or under what circumstances. "You're putting me where I don't even know I was told," he said.
>
> He also asked of the reporter, "Don't you think this sort of stuff takes place every day?"
>
> The reporter replied that he was not in a position to know. . . .
>
> While Splaine was being interviewed, Boutin stood not 50 feet away. Between them were some 100 municipal officials. . . .
>
> The excerpt (of the tape) was read to Boutin. He denied it categorically. "It is unfactual in its entirety," he said. "It simply is just not true."
>
> Boutin said that the Johnson campaign includes some 2000 volunteer workers but that "not one of them is a Hatch Act person."

> He said also his most recent visit to the Sheraton-Meadowbrook occurred Feb. 13 and the occasion was to address a meeting of "S.B.A. people" (Small Business Administration). He said the most recent previous visit there took place more than a month before and did not include "calling up a few of the boys that were Hatched."
>
> Boutin added that he met Splaine for the first time Tuesday night.
>
> (*Boston Globe*, February 22, 1968, p. 1)

With each twist and turn of the story, Cardoso reported back to either Gallagher or to Studds and me. The Johnson campaign squirmed in the press for almost a full week as various aspects of the story were investigated and then reported.

Following Cardoso's February 22 story, I issued a press release in which I "called for an investigation of possible intimidation of federal employees and abuse of the federal Hatch Act prohibiting federal employees from participating in partisan politics." The release went on to request an investigation of the matter by the national Fair Campaign Practices Committee and contained a letter directed to the executive director of the committee, Samuel T. Archibald.

In the release I said, "The alleged intimidation of federal employees was made public Thursday, February 22 by William Cardoso in the Morning Edition of the *Boston Globe*. . . ." In my letter to Archibald I said, "We have at this time no special knowledge as to whether these actions have actually occurred. However, if the alleged statement represents a true situation, such conduct would reflect a very grave violation of the true letter of the law and also the spirit of fair play in American democracy."

The issue continued as a lead story over the weekend. Mr. Archibald replied by letter dated February 26 that the Fair Campaign Practices Committee would look into the matter in its usual way—"to request an immediate answer to a charge of unfair campaign tactics. After all information has been collected, the Committee publicizes the facts concerning campaign practices." (Letter to Hoeh, February 26, 1968)

Boutin responded by letter dated March 4 in which he said:

> Please allow me to say at the outset that there is not the remotest bit of truth to the allegation that I, personally, or anyone else connected with the campaign for President Johnson, have directly or indirectly involved any individuals subject to the Federal Hatch Act or similar Statutes of the State of New Hampshire. No one has been able to point to one single instance or one example that would in any way give substance to this very unfair and untruthful charge.
>
> Mr. Splaine's statement was based, as he acknowledged, on hearsay and following the article which appeared in the *Boston Globe*, made a statement, a copy of which is attached, acknowledging that his statement was made in error. . . .

Statement of John Splaine:

> Statements made concerning a meeting in Portsmouth of Hatched Employees were in error, and were based upon misinformation given me by a McCarthy supporter. I have no knowledge of any meeting held and have since checked the facts and find that there was in fact no meeting held.

The issue slowly died to be replaced by others, but the substance as well as the means registered positively as other, though not as well substantiated, stories of Johnson campaign tactics came to the McCarthy headquarters. Splaine, himself, in a debate with Allard Lowenstein at the University of New Hampshire February 19 revealed his further disillusionment with the Johnson effort. Splaine agreed with all of Lowenstein's deprecatory statements about the present administration. He disagreed only on the remedy, saying that to vote for McCarthy is futile. "My battle is not with McCarthy, but with realities." He insisted that political candidates are prechosen by the power structure and that to try to buck the present establishment by backing McCarthy serves only to split the Democratic Party.

"Splaine spoke scathingly of the people around President Johnson, enumerating all of New Hampshire's representatives in Washington as 'Superhawks', declaring that President Johnson had done pretty well considering the people he has around him." (*Portsmouth Herald,* January 20, 1968)

Governor King's interpretation of patriotism and the Splaine allegations prompted one conservative Manchester Democrat, former Democratic National Committee member and current state senator, Henry P. Sullivan, to issue a release blasting the Johnson campaign leadership and then to write the following letter to me:

> As a Democrat who believes that the re-election of Lyndon B. Johnson is in the best interest of our County and the free world, I filed as a delegate candidate favorable to his renomination as the standard bearer of our party in the November election.
>
> In order to place in proper perspective my position toward those Democrats who support a candidate other than President Johnson, I issued a statement that was carried in the press by other news media. . . .
>
> As indicated in my announcement, I did not at that time, nor do I now question the *patriotism* or the *democracy* of our fellow Democrats who are supporting someone other than President Johnson.
>
> I do not consider those Democrats who have filed in behalf of Senator Eugene McCarthy as my "enemies'; neither do I consider them "unpatriotic." For example: Attorneys Cliff Ross, Eugene Daniell and Bartram Branch have distinguished records while in the uniform of their County in time of war. I am certain that there are many others within the McCarthy group and other groups who have distinguished records of service to their Country and the free world.

> It would be my hope that when the delegates assembled, nominate the candidate to carry the standard of our party in November, all of us will work for a Democratic victory in our State and Nation. . . .
>
> (Letter to Hoeh, February 12, 1968)

King's charges, Boutin management, and awkward public relations served to isolate the Johnson campaign not only from the opposition but from its workers and supporters.

FOREIGN EVENTS—DOMESTIC EVENTS

A series of foreign and domestic events that occurred during the campaign had a marked influence on McCarthy's effort. The manner in which a candidate and a campaign respond to an event reveal a great deal about both. Part of the testing process that the quest for the nomination contains is the unexpected. Being able to maintain a candidacy and to keep in touch with the theme of a campaign during moments of stress, especially stress that results from events outside the scope of the campaign plan, is the true test. Of all the unpredictable events that are possible, ones which involve threats to the national security are the most difficult to manage.

In those situations a nonincumbent candidate is party neither to the full facts nor to any role in the actual event. An incumbent president holds the foreign policy authority and, if politically adept, has the capacity to unify the nation behind him and destroy dissent. In the post-World War II tradition of a bipartisan foreign policy, the institutions of government and the public had supported the concept of a united front against threats or even perceptions of threats to the nation's interests, security, and the balance of power. President Johnson had been successful in rallying the nation around his interpretation of the threat of the Tonkin Gulf incident and had received the approval of the U.S. Senate for broad powers to protect U.S. security in Southeast Asia. The capacity to interpret an incident and to marshal the nation behind a policy and in that way to isolate disagreement had become an awesome power. A power that, given the volatile situation in Vietnam with American "boys" lodged in the jungles and American forces deployed heavily in the area, gave the president the almost single-handed capacity to interpret any extraordinary event as one that must be faced by a unified government if the nation is to survive.

This power was well understood by Senator McCarthy and others. To a considerable extent it was the growth of this virtually unquestioned power that Senator McCarthy sought to challenge. To others, such as Senator Robert F. Kennedy, it was the power to demolish opposition during such unforeseen events that kept him from becoming an opponent. Senator McCarthy saw himself as a means to focus dissension, to raise issues such as the imbalance in the tripartite federal government, and to test the resiliency of American democratic processes. To consider being nominated for the presidency was a fantasy that McCarthy would not entertain.

According to the authors of *An American Melodrama,* it was the first of the unexpected incidents that kept Robert Kennedy from becoming a candidate during the early January period when McCarthy's campaign appeared to be in the doldrums.

> . . . that night in New York, January 19, he did come very close to making up his mind to go. At dinner with his brother-in-law Stephen Smith, chief manager of the family finances, and young Carter Burden, from his New York office, he turned to Smith and said laconically, "I think I'm going to cost you a lot of money this year!"
>
> On Sunday, in a television discussion, he edged closer toward an open break with the Administration on Vietnam. He denounced the policy of insisting on "unconditional surrender" and called for a bombing halt and a negotiated peace. Then something happened. He had always been afraid that if he did run he could be destroyed by some utterly unforeseeable, uncontrollable act of fate. With his family's history, it was an understandable preoccupation. What happened between the dinner with Smith and Sperling's breakfast was something very remote indeed. It was the seizure by the North Koreans of the U.S. electronic espionage vessel *Pueblo.* In logic, there was not perhaps much reason why the *Pueblo* incident should have made Robert Kennedy change his mind. But the next day he made it plain to Allard Lowenstein that it did. For it was a reminder of other uncontrollable things that might happen, and that could put it in Lyndon Johnson's power to destroy him.
>
> (Lewis Chester, Godfrey Hodgson, and Bruce Page, *An American Melodrama, The Presidential Campaign of 1968,* New York: The Viking Press, 1969, p. 109)

Senator McCarthy arrived in New Hampshire for his first campaign visit while the *Pueblo* incident was still in full bloom. The president had activated additional reserves, placed U.S. forces on alert, and was contemplating his retaliatory options. In his first New Hampshire press conference, McCarthy faced a number of questions concerning the *Pueblo* incident that were difficult to answer given that his primary reason for coming to New Hampshire was to challenge the administration's military policy. He defined the *Pueblo* as a "limited crises," thought the president's call up of reserves was "precipitous," felt that the crisis was not of the order of the Berlin or Cuban missile crises, and that before he could respond fully he needed additional facts. (*Concord Daily Monitor,* January 26, 1968)

The president's *Pueblo* statement ended with a call for national unity. "I am confident that the American people will exhibit in this crisis, as they have in other crises, determination and unity." (*New York Times,* January 27, 1968) But given an increasing skepticism in the wake of the Senate Committee on Foreign Relations' allegations concerning the facts behind the Gulf of Tonkin incident, and the secret identity and uncertain mission of the *Pueblo,* the incident rapidly faded as a major campaign concern.

The administration seemed as willing as the public to quietly persist but to basically let the issues be resolved in time, as had been their experience with most of the incidents of the Cold War era. To engage in some form of Asian filibustering was not the national mood, especially considering the general feeling of frustration about Vietnam.

The second foreign event did become a determining factor in the New Hampshire campaign. Sunday morning, January 31, people awoke to read and hear that a coordinated, full-scale offensive by the Viet Cong and the North Vietnamese was underway in South Vietnam. Unlike earlier attacks, the National Liberation Front had managed to penetrate the defensives of a dozen major South Vietnamese cities and were even then battling U.S. Marines on the grounds of the U.S. Embassy in Saigon. The Tet Offensive had been launched. Suddenly to all of the questions that had been raised in the streets and on the campuses, in the meetings and teach-ins, and by the growing critics of U.S. policy in Vietnam was added the tone of reality. "Were those with most influence on the President (and the President himself) regarding Vietnam wrong—men such as Rusk, Rostow, Ambassador Ellsworth Bunker, and General William Westmoreland in Saigon? Before Tet broke out they had drawn together elaborate charts and statistics to prove that the huge United States commitment indeed was paying off. If it were paying off, how in the world could the enemy, even considering his heavy losses, mount so great a simultaneous attack on so many cities. The hawks and doves would dispute long after Tet who was really the loser, but it clearly had brought sobering new doubts about the United States' Vietnam strategy. . . ." (Richard T. Stout, *People, The Story of the Grass-roots Movement that Found Eugene McCarthy and Is Transforming Our Politics Today,* New York: Harper and Row, 1970, p. 25)

The vivid images of battle in full color appeared night after night as a part of the current events of the evening news broadcast. The weekly news magazines carried gruesome cover pictures and multiple page layouts showing the fighting in Saigon, Hue, and other supposedly safe and secure cities. As the casualties mounted so did the questions. For the hawk who had been urging perseverance, the question was, what would it take to win if winning was possible? For the doves there was a certain redemption, but still the question remained of how would the nation react. Would the redemption be momentary and then followed by a reaction against the doubters? Would new isolationism and possible unity behind a revived national resolve to win regardless of the cost occur? Or was the cost already too high and the errors too great?

In New Hampshire Tet shocked all of the birds—hawks, doves, owls, and ostriches. Even the *Manchester Union Leader* could not find in its rhetorical catalog a means to explain the debacle of the Tet Offensive. While still determined to support a national resolve to "beat the Communists," Loeb was torn between defending President Johnson and his support for the nomination and election of Richard M. Nixon. On the New Hampshire streets and where people gathered the quickly spoken "Let's win the war or get out," was replaced by a more thoughtful uncertainty and frustration at having been misled by Saigon and by Washington.

In the confusion that followed Tet the administration reappraised its policies. The first was a rumbling concerning a request from General Westmoreland for an additional 250,000 more troops to be sent to Vietnam. This number, he had assured the administration, would be sufficient to secure South Vietnam and drive the NLF out.

To pay for the war and to attempt to offset the impact of four years of "guns and butter" spending, the administration discussed seeking congressional authorization for a 10 percent surtax to be imposed on each taxpayer. With inflation taking a serious bite from workers' take home pay, skepticism about the cost of the war, cynicism about the Administration's domestic programs, and uncertainty about the future, a possible tax increase could not have been proposed at a worse political time.

While there were other external issues and events that influenced New Hampshire voters during the ten-week campaign, it was the general feeling of powerlessness and frustration encompassed by the Pueblo incident, the Tet Offensive, the possible call-up of 250,000 more troops, and the 10 percent tax surcharge that fueled the political fires in New Hampshire. To each either Senator McCarthy or the campaign organization responded in an attempt to link McCarthy's challenge to the possibility of a new direction and the reestablishment of credibility and purpose within the national government.

In her manuscript Barbara Underwood summarized the flow of events that assaulted the senses of the New Hampshire voters by recounting the headlines of the *Concord Daily Monitor*:

> Despite the January 1968 headline in the *Concord Monitor* calling the New Year's cease fire "bloodiest ever," there was a feeling in New Hampshire that the war in Vietnam would be won by the United States and the South Vietnamese. On January 3rd, there was the headline "Senator McCarthy Tosses Hat in New Hampshire Primary." On the 5th Eugene Daniell sought a "hearing on a RFK Write-In Test . . ." and on January 6th, Dr. Benjamin "Spock was Indicted by Jury." By the end of the week, on January 7th, the headlines were back to the fighting in Vietnam where "Cong Seize, Lose Provincial Capital Outside of Saigon. . . ."
>
> On the tenth of the month of January, "Draft Calls were predicted for 40,000 men a month." Pentagon sources said that the 39,000 man draft call announced for March is a sign of things to come for spring and summer. An additional 40,000 men would be called up on April, May and June. On the 15th of the month there were two pictures on the front page of the *Concord Monitor*. One was of the Senate Majority Leader Mike Mansfield, urging a bombing halt in Vietnam; the other was of a small Vietnamese boy saying goodbye to a duck while leaving a village twenty miles south of Da Nang, to be escorted to a safer location. The headlines January 17th read, "LBJ Faces Nation Tonight" with his formula for balancing the financial demands of the Vietnam war against the need to curb crime in the streets and to rehabilitate riot-breeding city slums. Two days later, "Miss Kitt Denounces Viet War; Upsets Lady Bird's Luncheon." The Negro singer Eartha Kitt said U.S. youth are rebelling because of the Vietnamese war. Young men don't want to be sent off to get shot in a war

they don't understand, she said, so they rebel in the streets and take pot." On January 20th, there was a front page picture in the *Monitor* of Harvard University historian Arthur Schlesinger with the caption, "Raps Viet Policy." And on the editorial page a political cartoon by William Mauldin showing Bobby Kennedy posed as a Hamlet trying to decide what to do.

On January 24th, the "U.S. Applies Diplomatic Leverage in a bid to Recover Spy Ship, Crew." The USS Pueblo had been seized. The "President Orders Air Reserves Onto Active Duty Status" on January 25th, while "Moscow Turns Deaf Ear to Washington's Request for Aid in Freeing Pueblo."

. . . On January 27th a feature article appeared on the first page, something rarely done by that newspaper. "Dust off Your Cymbals" it read "and Stop Up Your Ears—Tomorrow Night is New Year's Eve–Chinese New Year's Eve. Now Ending is the Year of the Goat. Just Ahead is the Year of the Monkey." Tet was coming to Vietnam. . . . Many in the military did join in celebration of Tet, and while they danced in festive mood, the Viet Cong guerrillas from the north launched a massive attack. . . .

Headline after headline spelled out the disasters of the Tet offensive. . . . Sections of Saigon and Hue, and ancient citadel of the Vietnamese lay in total ruin. Americans who felt the war in Vietnam would be won, now watched as stone by stone the citadel of Hue was smashed. They turned to themselves and asked, "What on earth are we doing there." Are we destroying a nation to save it?

. . . Suddenly one picture, taken by an AP photographer Eddie Adams, imprinted itself on the mind of those Americans who were trying to figure out the war and what our involvement in Vietnam meant. Running in most major newspapers, it showed the face of a Viet Cong officer being executed the moment the bullet was entering his head. The man was shot without delay or formality, no judge, no jury. The caption beneath the photo read, "South Vietnamese Police Chief Brig. General Nguyen Hgoc Loan executes a Viet Cong officer with a single shot in Saigon's Cholon Section on February 1, 1968. Carrying a pistol and wearing civilian clothes, the Viet Cong guerilla was captured near An Quang Pagoda, identified as an officer and taken to the police chief."

The South Vietnamese Police Chief's image came too close to a Nazi Gestapo SS Agent. In Manchester, Eugene Sidore, who had arranged the Sidore lecture series in memory of his father, looked at the picture and something went "click" inside him. He made up his mind. Up to that point he had not been particularly interested in Eugene McCarthy. He had even gone to great lengths trying to keep the press and TV cameras out of the hall where McCarthy was lecturing. Now Sidore became a McCarthy supporter.

Credibility had always been LBJ's weakest point among the youth of the nation. But slowly the not-so-young were beginning to be concerned about the credibility of what was being reported on the situation in

> Vietnam. Senator McCarthy was asked what effect he thought the Tet offensive would have on his campaign. He said it would take about three weeks to sink in and then he expected that he would benefit from it.
>
> (Underwood, op. cit., pp. 77–80)

The authors of *An American Melodrama* wrote that twenty-four hours after the Tet Offensive began, "Robert Kennedy realized that he had made what one of his friends called 'the mistake of his life'." (p. 109)

> In the long perspective of his decision whether or not to challenge Lyndon Johnson, the events of January were only one episode. But it brought into play all the complex thrusts and strains, for and against, that held him immobile, in paralyzed equilibrium, for so long. (p. 109)

Robert F. Kennedy had locked himself in a box of vacillation and indecision standing constantly in awe of the power that had once been so close to him. He and his friends and political advisors in New York, Washington, and New Hampshire would have to watch to see what would happen in New Hampshire knowing well that it might be too late regardless of the fate of the obscure senator from Minnesota.

ACTIVITIES OF THE OUTSIDERS

New Hampshire would have to be the battleground for those who were concerned about the administration's policies in Vietnam. To this battleground were attracted all manner of individuals and organizations whose intent was to help. As well meaning and selflessly motivated as these persons were, few had any understanding of the dynamics of New Hampshire politics. Many were intensely motivated to use the New Hampshire contest as a means of presenting their particular perspective on the war policy whether that be in moral, economic, political, ethical, or other grounds. The urge to intensify the contest in spite of the calm of McCarthy began to strike New Hampshire with the potential of a tidal wave.

Russell Hemenway, executive director of the National Committee for an Effective Congress, was an early example of this external interest in New Hampshire. He differed slightly from some of the others in that he had been a long-time supporter of Senator McCarthy, and Senator McCarthy had assisted him in his fund-raising efforts for NCEC. Hemenway had had extensive experience running and advising on various political campaigns. He felt that if McCarthy had a chance of success it would come from proper campaign organization, management, and support. Shortly after McCarthy announced in December, Hemenway began using his organization and its key and sympathetic financial supporters to develop elements of an effective campaign.

I had not been sure as to where Hemenway fit in the national McCarthy effort. Blair Clark had tipped me off about Hemenway. Clark said Hemenway could be helpful but to be cautious of any dealings that involved Howard Stein, who was a financial wonder of the Dreyfus Funds. Clark was, apparently, not clear as to what Stein was up to nor what the nature or the relationship between Stein and Hemenway would mean for the national management of the campaign. In my early conversations with Hemenway about Stein, Hemenway had said that Stein was interested in coming to New Hampshire, bringing with him a coterie of individuals who had had extensive media and campaign management experience. He asked me to locate a house near Concord that Stein could rent and use as his base of operations.

When Clark heard of the extent of Stein's interest in the campaign, he cautioned against moving in that direction. I dragged my feet on trying to find the house. At one point I checked Clark's perception of the Hemenway-Stein interest with McCarthy who confirmed the wait-and-see attitude.

Hemenway would not be put off. He recognized that he had made a mistake in commissioning the Harris data analysis of New Hampshire and let that issue slide out of sight, but he continued to see an important role for Stein and the talent and resources he could command. Although the word from Clark and McCarthy to Hemenway was to proceed with caution in any relationships with Stein, Hemenway persisted. Clark was concerned that Stein, a total novice in the political world, would seek to overwhelm the efforts of the fledgling organizations that were growing to support McCarthy in New Hampshire and elsewhere. Clark had developed considerable confidence in the judgment of both Studds and me to care for McCarthy's New Hampshire interests. He was under the impression that what Hemenway was really after was a connection with a wealthy new source of support for his organization and that he was using the vehicle of the McCarthy campaign as a means of initiating Stein to the allure of national politics. While there was considerable truth to Clark's concern, to us the specter of transplanted, high-powered New York advertising and marketing people coming to New Hampshire to take over the operation of the campaign was a potential disaster. On the other hand, we were unsure of the capacity of the national campaign to properly support the New Hampshire effort with money, personnel, and media. As late as January 26, Clark had not been able to find anyone to assign as a manager for the New Hampshire effort. Studds and I were not about to let opportunities to support the New Hampshire candidacy slip from their hands because of some worries at the national campaign level.

With Hemenway and Stein on their January 26 visit to New Hampshire was Julian Koenig, a partner in the then "hot" advertising firm of Pappert, Koenig, and Lois. The firm had developed a considerable reputation handling Robert Kennedy's senatorial campaign media program and was the firm that held the Dreyfus Fund advertising account.

Hemenway said that Koenig was in the Stein entourage accompanying McCarthy on his first campaign visit and that he wanted Studds and me to meet with Koenig to go over some advertising layout that he wanted used in the New Hampshire campaign. Not having seen anything of the sort being proposed from the Washington headquarters, we agreed to meet briefly with Koenig immediately following McCarthy's address at St. Anselm College. Blair Clark again advised caution, but said little could be lost by having the meeting.

Koenig opened a portfolio and spread a series of ad layouts on the table. Studds and I gasped as politely as possible as we saw the embodiment of what we had feared might happen if the campaign were directed from outside. The war might be the central and all-pervasive issue in New York City, but in New Hampshire Johnson administration credibility, heavy-handedness, and Texas overbearing characteristics were of greater political salience. Before us were ads directed totally toward the war using sketches, quotes, photos, and copy that stopped only slightly short of accusing the administration and its accomplice, the United States, of burning babies. The public tolerance for such charges would be very low if not totally absent in New Hampshire. Furthermore we felt that the advertising would not be consistent with the image of restraint and quiet assurance that McCarthy was beginning to project successfully.

With us in the meeting were several others, including the campaign's New Hampshire treasurer, John Holland, who was shocked to the extent that he could not critically assess the work. Fortunately, Mervin Weston, the Manchester based advertising firm executive, did attend and was able to convey to Koenig and Hemenway that New Hampshire responds to a much softer sell than is necessary in media-saturated New York City.

Hemenway, Koenig, and Stein retreated back to New York where they all three continued to work on ways to help with the New Hampshire McCarthy effort. But from then on they held greater respect for the yokels in the field and would coordinate all subsequent efforts through Studds, Holland, Weston, and me.

Much as with Hemenway and his NCEC contacts, Sandford Gottlieb, national director of SANE, had been one of those engaged in the early search for a national candidate to challenge President Johnson. His organization had devoted its staff and resources to exposing the policy contradictions of the administration's war policy, the domestic impact of that policy, and exploring alternative consequences of changing the policy. Their methods had been to support the campus teach-in movement, stimulate and organize community colloquia on the war, support prominent speakers on tour discussing the war, and to publish and mail tracts on the war. Over the years, SANE had developed a network of local committees and contacts sympathetic to its position on disarmament and nuclear arms limitation. As the war grew and the public became more concerned, SANE marshaled these grass roots contacts into a means of promoting a national debate on the administration's policies.

In New Hampshire, Gottlieb, like Hemenway a Dartmouth graduate, had developed this network through the liberal elements of the Protestant church, principally the Society of Friends and the Unitarian Church. The orientation of SANE was nonpartisan, and, as Gottlieb organized in New Hampshire, he found his most fruitful support among the progressively oriented Yankee Republicans in the smaller communities. This presented us with a special problem. As much as Gottlieb might have wished to support the McCarthy effort, his organizational base required that he remain nonpartisan and that the activities SANE sponsored also retain a certain distance from the particular interests of a specific candidate or party. Unfortunately, as both Studds and I realized, virtually any antiwar activity in New Hampshire would be linked by segments of the press, principally the *Manchester Union Leader*, with the efforts of the McCarthy campaign. If these efforts were not in accord with the way the McCarthy campaign was to develop, then serious embarrassment would result. The damage to the McCarthy campaign could come from a number of directions but principally from the Johnson campaign. Guilt by association, a revered New Hampshire campaign tactic, would result.

SANE's New Hampshire contacts wanted to stoke the fires of a major debate on the Vietnam issue as a background to the campaign. By working directly with Gottlieb, I was able to keep SANE's New Hampshire mission within either productive bounds or sufficiently disassociated from the McCarthy candidacy so as to prevent damage.

Gottlieb himself joined the New Hampshire speaking circuit on a schedule that was partially coordinated by the McCarthy campaign. As the campaign developed, it was clear to Studds and me that it would be useful to coordinate campaign schedules between the special interest groups and the activities of the campaign. In this way audience conflicts were minimized and unproductive associations avoided. We wanted to maintain a separation between campaign activities and special group schedules in order to strengthen the impact of the criticism and to avoid having all antiwar commentary tied to the political motives attributable to McCarthy's candidacy.

Gottlieb was also connected with a New York based coalition of peace activists organized as the National Committee of Clergy and Laymen Concerned About Vietnam. Its leadership included John C. Bennett, president of Union Theological Seminary; Dr. Eugene Carson Blake, general secretary of the World Council of Churches; Dr. Robert McAffee Brown, Stanford professor; Father Daniel Campion, editor, *America;* Bishop Daniel Corrigan, Episcopal Church; Dr. Dana McLean Greeley, president of the Unitarian Universalist Association of America; Rabbi Abraham Heschel, Jewish Theological Seminary; Bishop John Wesley Lord, Methodist Bishop of Washington, D.C.; and Father John B. Sheerin, C.S.P., editor of *Catholic World,* who represented others active from most denominations and laymen's groups. Gottlieb reported to me that the Clergy and Laymen Concerned were preparing a mailing piece to be sent to all residential addresses in New Hampshire. The piece, he said, would be a responsible, antiwar publication that would summarize the positions of respected critics, in a bipartisan/nonpartisan presentation.

Studds and I were concerned. The McCarthy antiadministration campaign was still in its fledgling stage, and we were not sure how even a mailing sponsored by religious leaders would be received. Gottlieb understood our concern. But he said the project had gone too far to delay now. It had been conceived before McCarthy entered the New Hampshire primary and was directed toward opening public discussion, whether that discussion focused on the primary election or was an expression of broad community concerns.

The twelve-page pamphlet arrived late in January. A complex, graphically cluttered tract, filled with photographs of prominent critics of U.S. policy in Vietnam with quotations taken from the public statements of each, it asked the questions "Who's Right? Who's Wrong?—on Vietnam." Juxtaposed against the villains—Johnson, Rusk, and Westmoreland were the faces of the foremost U.S. critics of the war.

It was a document packed with arguments against the continuation of U.S. policy extensively supported by quotations and accounts of the cost of the war in human and monetary terms. Each quotation on its own would have made an effective political flyer or newspaper advertisement, but in the format of the pamphlet the total was incomprehensible. The mailing flooded New Hampshire but was imperceptible in the tide of the campaign. We were relieved that if the waters had been stirred by the mailing the impact was neutral if not, perhaps, slightly favorable to their efforts.

We immediately made clear through Gottlieb and others associated with Clergy and Laymen Concerned that if they wished to have greater impact for the time and money they might have to spend in the future, it would be more productive to support McCarthy's candidacy—either as an organization or individually. An expensive mailing of the sort they used that did not propose an ultimate action on the part of the recipient was like feeding a vacuum. It was not enough to cry as the pamphlet did, "Stop it, Mr. President. In the name of God stop it!"—a plea signed by more than twenty-five hundred American clergymen. Not to suggest a way to "stop it" left those who took the time to read the densely packed twelve pages with only a deeper sense of frustration.

There were other groups who sought out Studds and me with suggestions as to how they might contribute on their own to the antiwar effort embodied in the New Hampshire presidential primary. We responded, urging that they contribute to the priorities of the campaign as we had outlined in their plan. Raise money, send volunteer workers, and forward their suggestions for campaign materials, but do not carry on individual, independent efforts, no matter how carefully conceived and selflessly motivated. With the exception of the independent speaking program sponsored by SANE, there would be no other separate mailings or activities other than those that flowed through the Concord headquarters of the McCarthy campaign or where authorized by the state leadership of the campaign.

Bringing the numerous individuals and organizations wishing to support the antiwar cause behind the activities of the McCarthy New Hampshire effort was a risky and complicated task. Studds and I were able to accomplish this largely because we were able to convince those offering help that their own objectives would be best served through a coordinated effort within the McCarthy candidacy. Without exception Studds and I found that the objective of changing the administration's Vietnam policy was more important to the offering group than either maintaining a particular identity or receiving exclusive credit for the contribution.

CHAPTER 8

New Hampshire Becomes the National Campaign

SUPPORTING McCARTHY IN NEW HAMPSHIRE

Studds and my concept as to how the New Hampshire effort would be supported was not matched by the performance of the national McCarthy organization. A fledgling New Hampshire committee was matched by an even less capable situation at the national level. Gerry Studds recalled:

> We became used, very quickly, to the fact that there will be nothing but chaos on the Washington end of the telephone. You would speak to somebody different every day. We kept begging to have someone put in charge of New Hampshire in Washington so that we would have a regular, steady reliable person to speak to, but it was always somebody different. And that was just unsatisfactory from the very beginning but we learned to expect it and, therefore, to live with it to do our best to do things up here without anything down there.
> (Studds transcript, p. 22)

After a particularly frustrating series of telephone calls to Washington in which each was answered by a different person who before speaking to Studds or me, insisted on getting the headquarters telephone number and address, Studds said, "Goddammit! Write that number, address, and our names on a piece of paper, mimeograph it, circulate it to every person in that headquarters, then paste it on the wall—we are trying to run a campaign up here for the presidency of the United States and it's about time the Washington headquarters realized that."

What Studds and I expected was top priority attention from the national office—attention to those aspects of the campaign that we had made clear we would not be able to manage. As we said repeatedly, New Hampshire provides the stage and the audience. The New Hampshire McCarthy Committee could organize the audience, but the production would have to be developed and financed from outside.

The dribbling of help that was evident did not reassure us, especially after the first McCarthy visit late in January. Russell Hemenway's efforts first with Harry Harris' data analysis and then with Julian Koenig's advertising campaign had not been what we had had in mind. A good poll would have been welcome as a substitute for Harris' effort, and an advertising theme that was in touch with New Hampshire habits would have been warmly received. One piece of help that did prove valuable came from one Tom Collins, a New York-based solicitation writer. As with many others Collins had volunteered to help in the McCarthy campaign.

Collins called me on January 5 saying that he would draft a support solicitation letter which could be the basis of the first statewide-mailing. Collins' draft was two pages, single spaced. I was of the opinion that a three- or four-paragraph letter capable of being read in a glance would be best. The letter would be accompanied by a brochure that would convey the McCarthy message. In our conversation, Collins said that his experience with solicitation letters was that the longer letter would be read and would engage the reader if anything was to be read at all. Accepting his judgment, Studds and I edited the draft, returned our suggestions to Collins and a final draft returned quickly.

In order to expand the organizational base in New Hampshire, Studds and I asked Collins to prepare a form for a reply card that might be returned if the receiver wanted to help in the campaign. Collins' draft of the return mailing card read:

> You can count on my vote for Senator Eugene McCarthy for the Democratic presidential nomination in the March primary election.
>
> ( ) I also want to help in the campaign. Tell me what I can do.
> ( ) Enclosed is my campaign contribution of $ ________.
> Name ______________________________
> Address ____________________________
> MAKE CHECKS PAYABLE TO ______________

The final approved draft of the Democrat and Independent versions of the letter and the return card were given to Merv Weston, head of the New Hampshire-based advertising firm, Weston Associates, for printing. The national office was not ready to take on such a printing job, but it did promise to provide the campaign brochure.

What did not appear to be moving was the preparation of other essential campaign materials. We found that the campaign that had been initiated and, to a considerable extent, funded through New York City and the Coalition for a Democratic Alternative was now shifting to Washington. In the shift few of those who, with Lowenstein, had created CDA and the national CCD was being included in the shift. A natural tension between the two organizations, the CDA and the CCD, and the new national McCarthy headquarters seemed to paralyze the effort to develop a full-scale national effort capable of supporting what we needed in the field.

A sophisticated and well-funded organization had grown in New York City under the leadership of Harold Ickes, Jr., wealthy son of the former secretary of the interior under Franklin D. Roosevelt, and Sarah Kovener, a prominent New York political activist. In addition to having established a formidable political force around efforts that predated McCarthy's entry, they controlled much of the substantial financial resources potentially available to the national campaign. Blair Clark was concerned about constructing a national campaign organization totally from those whose political base and interests were not tied directly to his leadership of the national organization. Since he would not operate the national campaign within the rubric of a coalition of political committees at the state level, he cut himself off from the personnel and resources of the CDA. While correct for a campaign that had the time to mature, Clark's choice opened him up to serious criticism.

On the one side there were people in the primary states like Studds and me who desperately needed funds, staff support, and decisions that could only be derived from the national headquarters. On the other side was the fact that Clark had to build his own national campaign staff from scratch—a difficult and time-consuming task, especially when undertaken in the midst of a full-scale national campaign. In addition, few individuals with experience in national campaigns were willing to join Clark's staff.

As a result, Clark was caught between an intransigent but well-financed and well-staffed New York based CDA operation and the entrenched office staff of Senator McCarthy. Neither was willing to relinquish either money or prerogatives to the struggling national office. Because of this confusion and delay, Clark fell victim to the vacuum. A uniquely confederated campaign emerged. The CDA leadership that had become detached from the campaign and intensely critical of Clark' s leadership began to release some of its personnel for both national and New Hampshire duty. However, they would release funds or New York based talent only for those projects they approved and they held close control over the actual expenditure, delivery of the product, and occasionally even the distribution. The senator's senatorial office staff, headed by Jerry Eller and personal secretary Jean Stack, conceded little except as directed by the senator himself.

For most of the month of January, Studds and I had maintained frequent contact with Clark in our effort to staff, fund, and begin advertising the New Hampshire effort. Clark had been reluctant to commit himself to more than the minimum support. When he finally conceded to the confederation of the campaign, New Hampshire began to receive supplies and Clark could commit specific support.

Some money began to come directly to the New Hampshire fiscal agent John Holland from the New York organization. With greater frequency I began receiving calls from New York offering volunteers and specific assistance. Studds and I were delighted that at last the New Hampshire effort was receiving proper attention. We felt that the time was too short to permit bickering, refused to pick sides except that of Senator McCarthy, and tried to avail ourselves of all appropriate resources. What we would not concede was our influence over the direction of the campaign in New Hampshire and contact with New Hampshire supporters of the effort.

Of particular urgency at this stage in the campaign were those activities that required preparation and production lead time. Working with Merv Weston, Studds and I had begun to outline pieces of the media campaign that were essential if the campaign was to succeed. Our first effort was to have Weston option as many billboards as were available in key communities.

Next he reserved as much of the better radio time and television time available on New Hampshire stations as possible. With each time or space reservation there was a production lead time and usually a time when cash must be produced in order to hold a space reservation. On the word of Clark, Weston was willing to use his agency's credit to hold the critical time openings.

Production presented Studds and me with an additional problem. The national office had not developed a logo, color scheme, or other aspects of a unified campaign image. No official photograph had been available. Selecting campaign slogans can be among the most frustrating tasks faced in a campaign. Seemingly endless hours are spent by mature adults sitting around in meetings or in offices listing possible slogans that will capture the essence of a candidacy in a phrase. Studds and I expected this task would be performed nationally either in Washington or New York. Slogan, billboard layout, and related graphics would come well set and packaged for use not only in New Hampshire but across the nation.

However, as the deadline for the billboard space neared, we realized a slogan had to be selected, colors and graphics determined, and billboard paper printed, or the space would carry another's advertiser's message while being paid for by the McCarthy campaign. Without the usual protracted consideration, Studds and I decided on the phrase ". . . there is an alternative . . . McCarthy for President" run without a photograph. Using the same slogan and graphics, stationery for the New Hampshire campaign was also printed.

What the experience represented was a slow migration of the national campaign to New Hampshire. Through January, New Hampshire—from the standpoint of Studds and myself—was competing for attention at the national level. As the month progressed, and especially in the period of reaction to the first McCarthy campaign visit, New Hampshire began to occupy the top priority position. Slowly in New York, Boston, Washington, and across the nation, those close to the candidacy or sensitive to the issues being tested saw that if McCarthy failed in New Hampshire their efforts would likewise fail or suffer serious setbacks. Clark, the various coalitions, the national office, and others began to realize that the total protest effort of 1968 rested on New Hampshire and that neither the resources nor the personnel existed to support a national campaign until the political bridge of New Hampshire had been crossed. The first concession to this conclusion was the arrival of a young former Harvard Divinity School student named Sam Brown.

HEADQUARTERS ORGANIZATION

Sam Brown had been working as a volunteer coordinator through the New York based CDA. He had actively sought to put flesh on his earlier promise that the nation's student population would respond to the opportunity of the McCarthy campaign. Brown had sent Dan Dodds and several others to New Hampshire to help but now, with Clark's blessing and also a leave from the placated CDA, Brown himself arrived in New Hampshire early in February.

Brown took charge of the volunteer activity. Dan Dodds, whom Brown had sent to recruit volunteers on New Hampshire campuses, had been assigned by Studds and me to other tasks. Dodds, Eric Schnapper, John Barbieri, and Dianne Dumanoski were the only persons able to work full-time. Sam Brown was the first of the national staff to come to New Hampshire, and he provided the first link with the New York and Washington bases of the national campaign. While not the manager we still needed, Brown, then twenty-three, could generate a sustaining flow of volunteers. His campus contacts were numerous. Articulate, engaging, with humor and constant energy, Sam Brown slipped quickly into one of the several vacuums that had grown larger as the campaign increased in size.

He established himself behind a desk in the front portion of the headquarters. With a telephone as a permanent auditory appendage, he began first, by contacting campus political leaders, to begin the steady flow of volunteers to New Hampshire, and second, to report back to New York and Washington that help was really needed in New Hampshire.

Within a week of Brown's arrival I received a call from Curtis Gans. Gans had found his way from Lowenstein's CCD back into the McCarthy campaign. Blair Clark could not find a substitute for what Gans had acquired as background during the weeks he had traveled across the country gathering support for a potential McCarthy candidacy. Gans was assigned to the nonprimary states desk in the national headquarters. On occasion I would catch Gans during the frustration of telephone calls to the national headquarters. Each call would begin, "When are you coming back to New Hampshire?" Gans would then relate his current assignments, caucus schedules, and duties of the nonprimary states. I would respond by saying that Gans wouldn't have to worry much about the nonprimary states if things didn't go well in New Hampshire.

In my conversations with Blair Clark, I urged him to send Gans to New Hampshire as the manager we desperately needed. Clark said Gans was needed in Washington and that he would find someone else. Studds and I were left to stumble through our personal schedules at Dartmouth and St. Paul's School, attending to campaign business in the evenings and on the weekends. In spite of this haphazard management we had been able to accomplish a measure of organization both in the Concord state headquarters and in the field.

Sandy Hoeh and Eric Schnapper had assumed the major responsibility for preparing Senator McCarthy's campaign schedules. They worked closely with the local organizations in the cities and towns with a priority for a McCarthy visit. Dan

Dodds was asked to explore the possibility of conducting a door-to-door canvass of voters. Dianne Dumanoski assumed responsibility for finding lodging for both short- and long-term volunteers. John Barbieri, between trips to New Haven to fight with the Selective Service Board, was in charge of the mailing operation, including collecting additional voter checklists and preparing the mailing labels. Ben and Rosann Stavis, both graduate students in New York, arrived by bus February 15 and found immediate assignments organizing materials for distribution and seeing that essential campaign items such as press releases were mimeographed and distributed.

To the departmentalization of the campaign was added an office manager, Pat Reilly from New York City, who had been an office worker in the CDA headquarters. Her month of experience in that job made her a valuable addition to the campaign.

Originally the campaign had occupied the small glass-walled office and display space of the old electric supply store. Behind a partition that separated the display area was a storage space approximately one-third the size of the front display area. When the Stavises arrived, their first job was to clean the space, find office equipment, and organize an annex to the now crowded front part of the headquarters. Rosann, as Pat Reilly's assistant office manager, assumed control of the new territory. A home economics graduate student, Rosann had a particular interest in efficient space organization.

A corner was set aside for a coffee machine with places marked for cups, sugar, cream, and wastepaper. In another corner was the mimeograph machine. The paper for the machine was neatly stacked, a large wastebasket was nearby and marked "Mimeograph Waste Only," and a shelf set nearby with ink, stencils, pads, and related mimeographing supplies. A space that had been dark and grimy was brightened with posters, signs, and an order that became contagious. There would be no piles of trash, lost supplies, damaged materials, or work environment confusion in this headquarters as long as Rosann had breath and energy.

The mailing label preparation activity, which had once occupied most of the open space in the front office, was moved back with Rosann and Ben behind the partition and then to the basement. As each activity of the campaign grew and specific assignments were made, new space had to be found. In the front space, the Concord McCarthy Committee maintained a corner. There was a reception desk, Pat Reilly's office manager's desk, Sam Brown's volunteer area, a press area, the glass-walled office that Studds and I kept, a place for secretarial work, a materials display table near the door, and a small alcove arranged with a sofa and one or two casual chairs.

The only basement access was by a narrow stairway at the rear of the back office leading to a space with not more than seven feet of headroom—a space that could only be called a firetrap. A generation of electric supply business litter made the place almost explosive. Within several days it was cleaned, bulbs found for the empty sockets, folding tables and chairs rented, and fire extinguishers nailed to each of the supporting posts.

In addition to an assembly-line arrangement of the work space and carefully marked storage areas for the labels, lists, and finished worked on the mailing, there were warning signs against smoking, fire, hitting one's head on low objects, and directions to the nearest wastebaskets. Nothing was left to chance. There was a sign

David C. Hoeh Collection—Georgetown University Collection

David C. Hoeh Collection—Georgetown University Collection

top McCarthy kicks off his New Hampshire campaign outside the Nashua City Hall in front of the memorial to John F. Kennedy who began his campaign for the White House at the same place one day and eight years earlier.

left Senator McCarthy with David Hoeh in the Concord Headquarters during the January 25th campaign visit.

bottom Media phalanx leads the way on a Nashua sidewalk during the first campaign day. With McCarthy are Gerry Studds and David Hoeh.

previous page Senator Eugene McCarthy—1968.

David C. Hoeh Collection—Georgetown University Collection

David C. Hoeh Collection—Georgetown University Collection

David C. Hoeh Collection—Georgetown University Collection

David C. Hoeh Collection—Georgetown University Collection

top Senator McCarthy with Sy Hersh, his press aide, greeting a worker leaving a Manchester factory during the first New Hampshire campaign visit.

middle Winter calls for a special campaign in New Hampshire. Senator McCarthy visiting a classroom as he frequently did during the campaign.

bottom Senator McCarthy speaking at the University of New Hampshire.

David C. Hoeh Collection—Georgetown University Collection

left After speaking to a large Concord audience, Senator McCarthy joins a hockey game during his second campaign visit.

below Senator McCarthy being escorted to the podium.

Collection of Charles Brereton

Bill Phinney, Photographer

Bill Phinney, Photographer

David C. Hoeh Collection—Georgetown University Collection

top One of the many campaign receptions, this in the home of Maria Carrier.

middle and bottom Greeting New Hampshire voters at work and in homes.

David C. Hoeh Collection—Georgetown University Collection

David C. Hoeh Collection—Georgetown University Collection

top Off the plane to a warm Keene airport welcome during the second campaign trip.

left Student volunteers canvas door-to-door discussing campaign issues. A young McCarthy campaign aide wears the hat identifying her as a "McCarthy Girl."

below McCarthy campaigns in a New Hampshire social club.

David C. Hoeh Collection—Georgetown University Collection

Not Worth the Life or Limb of a Single American

Former Commandant
U.S. Marine Corps (1960–1963)
(Condemns-Decries)
U.S. Involvement in Vietnam

"I don't believe that all of Southeast Asia, as related to the present and future safety and security of this country, is worth the life or limb of a single American."
–May 16, 1966

"I do not believe that what we are told are the reasons for being in Vietnam are valid and provable reasons."
–Dec. 18, 1967

General David M. Shoup

- 41 1/2 Year Veteran–U.S. Armed Forces
- Joint Chiefs of Staff 1960–1963
- Hero Battle of Tarawa
- Congressional Medal of Honor (1943)

Hear Him Tonight on These Stations

WKBK –Manchester
WMOU –Berlin
–Nashua
–Concord
WDCR –Hanover

–Portsmouth
–Rochester
–Dover
–Keene
–Laconia
–Claremont

David C. Hoeh Collection—Georgetown University Collection

top One of the many flyers local committees circulated to announce special events.

bottom The work of campaigning—managing.

David C. Hoeh Collection—Georgetown University Collection

McCarthy Staff Photo

The work of campaigning—preparing mailings and working in the basement of the State Headquarters in Concord.

What's happened to this country since 1963?

John F. Kennedy got his country moving. Now the fabric of that great achievement is unravelling.

All around us we can see that the last five years have brought decay to replace progress, despair to replace hope, and failure in war to replace success in the pursuit of peace.

In 1963, the economy was booming and taxes were being lowered. Now, prices are rising, the Kennedy boom is slowing down, and we are being asked to raise taxes.

In 1963, our great cities were relatively tranquil. Now, the streets of our cities are scarred by lawlessness, violence, and desperate fear. Now, the President has projected year after year of continuing violence.

In 1963, the deep concerns of American young people were the Peace Corps and civil rights. Now there are demonstrations and draft protests.

In 1963, we were at peace, just as we had been at peace for the eight previous years under Eisenhower. Now, we are at war.

Gene McCarthy stood shoulder to shoulder with Kennedy in the Senate, and he will stand head and shoulders above Johnson as President. There is one candidate who can get this country moving again, and carry on the tradition John F. Kennedy began.

That man is Gene McCarthy.

McCarthy for President

McCarthy for President Committee 815 17th Street, N.W., Washiongton, D.C. 20006 BLAIR CLARK, Campaign Mgr.
3 Pleasant Street Extension Concord, New Hampshire 03301 John S. Holland, Fiscal Agent

right A campaign flyer which asked the question on many voters' minds.

below Handout prepared for election day March 12th.

VOTE MARCH 12 FOR

Senator Eugene J.

McCarthy for President

INDEPENDENTS: Ask for the Democratic ballot and vote for Senator McCarthy.

David C. Hoeh Collection—Georgetown University Collection

David C. Hoeh Collection—Georgetown University Collection

Celebrities came to New Hampshire to campaign.

top Rod Serling—made radio commercials and met voters.

bottom Tony Randall—surrounded by fans at a New Hampshire shopping center.

David C. Hoeh Collection—Georgetown University Collection

David C. Hoeh Collection—Georgetown University Collection

top Robert Ryan—joining in street campaigning.

bottom Paul Newman—lent his star quality to the campaign and returned several times to draw attention to the McCarthy message.

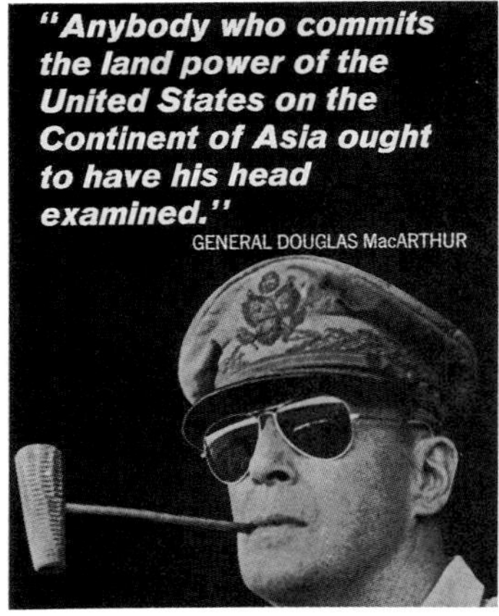

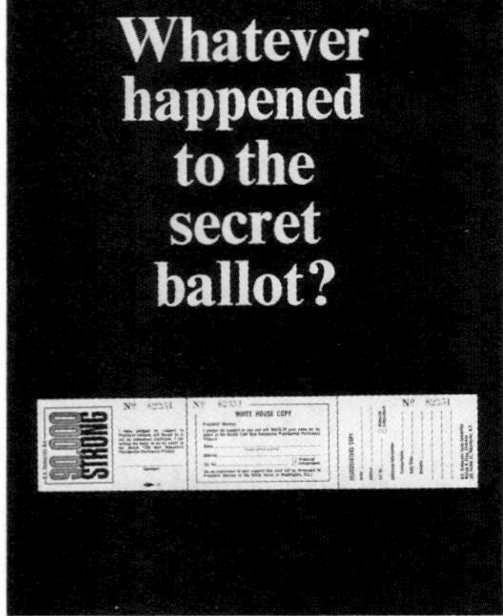

The front covers of seven of the one sheet campaign flyers used widely in the campaign by the door-to-door student canvassers. The Pope Paul VI flyer was not used.

right An example of the text used on flyers—this one described the "Shrinking Dollar–Growing War."

The Bigger the War the Smaller Your Dollar

Eugene McCarthy for President

- From 1961 to 1965, America enjoyed unprecedented prosperity. The economy grew without interruption. Unemployment fell. And prices held steady.
- But then came war — an ever-widening war — a war whose effects the Administration ignored by not taking the necessary steps to control inflation.
- What was the result?
- The first economic casualty of the Vietnam War was the value of your dollar. Inflation became the uninvited guest in the American household . . . putting the burden of war on those who could least afford it.
- Prices have jumped nearly 10% since early 1965 — the price of food, the price of a home, the price of health.
- Inflation ate up over two-thirds of the 13% increase in Social Security benefits, even before the benefits went into effect.
- Housewives know inflation has swallowed over half of most workers' pay raises since the Administration expanded the war.
- And as the dollar shrinks at home, it is steadily weakened abroad.
- The mounting cost of the Vietnam War has drained the nation's gold supply. The balance of payments deficit has leaped to nearly $4 billion.
- Not since the Great Depression has international confidence in the dollar sunk so low.
- In the wake of the devaluation of the British pound, the value of the dollar itself is now questioned.

You can put an end to the shrinking dollar. You can bring America back to its senses.

vote march 12th

McCarthy for President

New Hampshire McCarthy for President Committee
3 Pleasant Street Extension Concord, New Hampshire 03301 Attorney John S. Holland, Fiscal Agent

Collection of Charles Brereton

above The media covers a McCarthy speech—the campaign attracts attention.

below A McCarthy press conference late in the campaign as David Hoeh, John Holland, Jack Parr, and Walter Cronkite look on.

right The Senator McCarthy that New Hampshire voters came to know.
Collection of Charles Brereton

David C. Hoeh Collection—Georgetown University Collection

Bill Phinney, Photographer

Election night—March 12—Bedford, New Hampshire. McCarthy acknowledges his campaign workers and the election results—next Wisconsin!

or instruction specifying the advised action or caution for practically anything that might happen in that dungeon. Often more than fifty people would be working along the tables, typing labels, sorting lists, preparing canvassing cards, and stuffing and sealing mailings. What litter that developed in the work was quickly swept into the trash boxes and emptied. Nothing was lost or misplaced in the flow of the work. Without the quiet efficiency of Rosann, chaos, if not disaster, would have occurred.

Eventually the headquarters expanded into vacant space in the adjoining building to the east. Another part of the electric supply store—the warehouse—with a tall ceiling but little else functioned as the canvassing control center, volunteer reception and assignment center, and materials storage space. The Rosann influence spread to this domain where signs directed volunteers to shelves for storing their typewriters and sleeping bags, to toilets, and to a reception table where they would sign in and receive their work assignments.

In all, a marvelous order prevailed in the headquarters which kept each activity of the campaign defined. This physical as well as functional definition accentuated the multiplicity of campaign activities, the value of each to the campaign, and the relationship of the activities to each other. By this fact it became easy to absorb volunteers with limited time and experience. Each could be given a meaningful task or assignment quickly. Each could sense their place in the activity and contribution to the campaign no matter how brief their visit to the campaign. The volunteers enjoyed the work, how they were treated, and their fellow volunteers, and would struggle to return as often as they could during the campaign.

Even though the campaign had successfully evolved a strong organizational and management base through the Concord headquarters, it still lacked the oversight of a full-time manager and the sophistication of a well-supported national campaign. Studds and I were continually frustrated in our dealings with the Washington headquarters.

What was happening was typical of late starting campaigns. If McCarthy had set himself to run for the presidency a year or more before 1968 he, like other determined candidates, would have assembled an appropriate staff, considered strategies, melded a concept of his campaign with graphic images, photographs, and personnel. But not having anticipated his candidacy in this way, everything became a struggle against time, personalities, schedules, and deadlines. To get the desperately needed photos for brochures, movie footage for television commercials, and image photos for posters, the McCarthy campaign either contacted freelance photographers who had followed McCarthy on earlier travels or commissioned them to follow him now. In New Hampshire, Bill Gallagher used his camera more than his typewriter to build a file of photographs.

Some of the delay was the result of the basic lack of lead time in the campaign; another was McCarthy himself. He had decided on the particular conceptual frame he wanted his campaign to project. The image, as experience recounted, was almost identical with what Studds and I felt was appropriate for New Hampshire. To ensure that this image was accurate and not narrowed or distorted, McCarthy himself or Jerry Eller or Mrs. McCarthy insisted that they review both text and layout before printing or distribution. While commendable in theory the national organization was neither staffed nor properly supplied with production elements to produce drafts of materials for McCarthy's review. For a time, as a result, I found the CDA was the best source of posters, reprints of articles and clippings on McCarthy, and some flyers. While this material did not have McCarthy's stamp of approval on it, it did convey the message. When the CDA and Clark resolved their dispute, CDA staff moved to Washington and began producing additional material. Its methods remained similarly independent. The result was that often material produced and shipped to New Hampshire conveyed the CDA's image of what the campaign should be rather than what McCarthy or Studds and I felt was appropriate.

A series of one-sheet flyers was printed, each with a distinct message, usually a quote from a prominent national or international leader, followed on the reverse with other quotations and McCarthy's response. Of the two most controversial, one carried a photograph of General Douglas MacArthur, braided hat, dark glasses, and corncob pipe with the quotation, "Anybody who commits the land power of the United States on the Continent of Asia ought to have his head examined." The other carried a photograph of Pope Paul VI seated on the papal throne with his hand raised in blessing with the quotation, "We cry in God' s name STOP. . . ." On the reverse were quotations from Pope Paul, Cardinal Richard Cushing of Boston, and Bishop Fulton J. Sheen under the title "Religious Leaders Speak Out on Vietnam."

I felt that the MacArthur campaign piece could be used selectively in New Hampshire but the Pope Paul VI flyer seemed to be questionable under the best of circumstances. Shortly after the materials arrived in New Hampshire I received a call from Senator McCarthy, then campaigning in the Midwest. He had heard about the two pieces and wanted my description of them and reaction. When I finished reading and describing the Pope Paul flyer McCarthy said, "Don't use it." That night the several boxes were sealed with tape and early the next morning taken to the Concord city landfill and buried under that day's city refuse. A campaign worker watched to make sure the boxes were not broken open but buried intact and completely. The MacArthur flyer was used after McCarthy accepted my advice on how it might be effective. I kept one copy of the Pope Paul VI flyer in my files.

The ultimate irony of the difficulty between Washington perception and New Hampshire materials needs came when the long awaited brochure arrived. The carefully developed text had been attractively laid out in a graphically appealing format. There McCarthy was shown meeting voters, in formal poses, with his family, in uniform as a baseball player, with President John F. Kennedy, and in a five-and-one-half-inch by fourteen-inch fold at the bottom of the brochure meeting New Hampshire voters before the Kennedy memorial bust in front of the Nashua city hall on his first day of campaigning. With the brochure was to be the two-page letter and the return mail card, all stuffed into a number ten envelope. When the brochure arrived I took two sheets of paper, a three-inch by five-inch card, folded it together, and stuffed an envelope for weighing. I found the package was one and one-half ounces in weight. What was expected to be a one-ounce first class mailing now would double in cost or have to be changed.

It was too late to print a new brochure or to change other aspects of the mailing. What we found was the weight of the mailing could be reduced below the one-ounce limit by tearing off the New Hampshire photo flap. The next several days were occupied by volunteers tearing off that part of the brochure.

Now that Sam Brown had arrived and Studds and I had poured out our particular frustrations with Washington and the national campaign to him, some changes began. Brown had not only Clark's ear but also the confidence of the CDA leaders in New York. He affirmed our concern and urged that Clark quickly assign someone to manage New Hampshire who could connect back effectively to both New York and Washington. Clark released Curtis Gans from his nonprimary states desk. By February 20 Gans was in New Hampshire to assume the long-vacant position as manager.

Gans realized that the campaign could not meet its objectives unless it was properly staffed with long-term volunteers and unless communication time was significantly reduced. To accomplish both of these requirements meant all essential campaign activities would have to be based in New Hampshire and that, where full-time staff were not available in New Hampshire, they would have to be imported from outside of the state. The migration he immediately stimulated stripped both the Washington and New York offices of the key desk assignments along with a group of willing volunteers capable of assuming management of most of the local headquarters.

From New York came Fred Willman and Arthur Herzog, both writers who were assigned to manage the Lebanon and Salem headquarters, respectively. Jessica Tuchman, daughter of the noted author Barbara Tuchman, arrived to help Gans. Sandra Silverman, whom Studds tagged "Susie Silverfish" when his only contact with her had been in the frustration of New Hampshire to Washington telephone calls, came to schedule special events.

There were many others, some based in Concord, but most assigned to staff headquarters in each of the cities, especially the major effort that was developing in Manchester. Among this later group was Ann Hart, daughter of Senator Philip Hart of Michigan, who became a legend for her efforts. Eventually this migration would include as campaign workers Harold Ickes, Seymour Hersh, and Richard Goodwin.

With the exception of two campaign activities, scheduling, and fund-raising, all else was managed from the Concord headquarters. From Gans' arrival to the end of the campaign, almost the total national McCarthy effort emanated from New Hampshire. Scheduling of Senator McCarthy in New Hampshire was managed by Sandra Hoeh from our Hanover home. Campaign financing operated wherever money could be raised. The principal sources continued to be New York, although long-time friends of McCarthy started mailing sizable checks directly to New Hampshire during the last weeks of January and early February.

The combination of circumstances, the migration of staff, a flow of volunteers, and a good headquarters location helped build an impressive headquarters for the management and support of a campaign that was beginning to exceed even our expectations. Studds and I could attend to those policy and strategy aspects of the campaign that would keep it "New Hampshire" in its orientation while not having to worry about whether specific details were receiving attention.

Once an activity was set and its outline accepted, little but an occasional check or response to a question was necessary. A group largely inexperienced in political campaigning picked up the ethos of the effort with minimal direction and few mistakes. Describing their view of the headquarters and the campaign, Ben Stavis wrote:

> We walked into the headquarters about 10:00 A.M., suitcases in hand. . . .
>
> We were quickly put to work. We shoveled rubbish from a side room, taped extension cords to the ceilings to support light bulbs, and carried pails of water to the basement to serve as fire extinguishers. A large wooden spool that had once held heavy wire was set on end to become a table for a borrowed coffee maker. Posters were put up to cover holes in the walls. Tables were placed over holes in the floors. We then began to stack cartons of literature and sort piles of posters. The campaign existed in the national press and on television, but it had barely begun in New Hampshire.
>
> Rosann and I thought we might be able to coordinate some of the office work, do some of the envelope stuffing—that sort of thing. We expected to stay for a week or two, on the assumption that the campaign would have many effective workers from the Senator's staff and from New Hampshire.
>
> (Ben Stavis, *We Were the Campaign: New Hampshire to Chicago for McCarthy,* Boston: Beacon Press, 1969, p. 3)

But after a trip to Rochester, New Hampshire, to copy names from checklists in the cold, the Stavises realized how much the campaign needed help, and they stayed with the campaign through to its Chicago convention end. Their distinction between "staff" and "volunteer" illustrates how the headquarters melded individuals into the campaign assigning them duties according to how much time they would be able to spend in New Hampshire.

> I should clarify what the word "staff" meant at that time in New Hampshire. A staff member was essentially anyone who worked during the week. He prepared materials to be used on weekends, then supervised the people who came on weekends. To be on the staff one only had to come to the office during the week, even part of the week. If he arrived on Thursday, he would know enough about procedures on Friday to supervise people who came in on the weekends, so he was a staff member. The concept of staff involved no financial distinction. The full-time workers thought it likely that if the campaign got money they would be fed; but that would come only when the wallets grew thin and the stomachs empty.
>
> (Stavis, op. cit., p. 4)
>
> The counterpart to staff was volunteer. Of course everyone was a volunteer in the strict sense, but in New Hampshire volunteer meant part-time worker. Volunteers were college students who came to work for the weekend. On weekends, the office quickly became cluttered with sleeping bags, portable

> typewriters, textbooks, and term papers in various stages of completion. The most important item of logistical support was a record player and hardrock records. Each weekend meant a new set of records. After a week of the Beatles, Country Joe and the Fish came as a welcome change in office environment. By the weekend, everyone was overjoyed at having the Grateful Dead for a week.
>
> (Stavis, ibid., p. 7)

Rosann, of course, made sure there was never much "clutter" for very long. If something began to pile up she would find a place for it and print a sign saying that was where the items belonged. In addition to the written orientation every new arrival was required to read, there was also an orientation tour of the headquarters. The new arrivals were shown what was happening, where, why, and then shown where to put things and how to begin working.

SCHEDULING

Of the many essential activities of a political campaign nothing is quite as demanding, complex, or vital to the success of the venture as is scheduling the activities of the candidate. A campaign schedule requires a unique blending of the political ethos of the jurisdiction, an assessment of the abilities, strengths and weaknesses of the candidate, a keen sense of the opportunities available from combining place and personality, and the potential of either the scheduling organization or the local organization to make a schedule work.

Ideally the person who schedules a candidate should know and understand thoroughly both the candidate and the political terrain to be visited, although understanding the candidate side should receive priority. Unless the person who coordinates a candidate's schedule is familiar with when the candidate works best, under what conditions, what time of the day, and during which situations, scheduling becomes a game played against totally unknown odds. Consequently most major national candidates carefully regulate how and by whom they are scheduled. The schedule becomes an extension of the candidate's personality—a precise recognition of personal strengths, perceptions of how to effectively present one's self, what issues can be illustrated or avoided through candidate activity, and how the candidate evaluates the probabilities for favorable reactions to the campaign.

In addition to the personal determinants of the candidate are the expectations and traditions of the campaign locale. If carefully examined, each locale has its traditional means and manners for receiving its candidate guests. In the process of determining what to do, who to see, and how to present a candidacy, the candidate needs to avoid becoming the property of individuals or groups who seek either recognition or identity for their own purposes at the expense of the political objectives of the candidate or the candidate's organization. Ideally the candidate's schedule should be as inclusive of the characteristics of a locale as possible without conveying hypocrisy or generating conflict. The candidate is largely at the mercy of one's local contact and that person's ability to recognize what are meaningful campaign events and how to avoid needless conflicts.

Since scheduling is a complex art form priorities must be established. The first priority, in most situations, is attention to the campaign abilities of the candidate. Second are the requirements of the campaign strategy, and third, the predilections of the locale. There must, of course, be a certain synthesis between the three in order to produce the desired effects, but the strategy of the campaign has to be the principal guide.

Studds and I began our scheduling for McCarthy using the twelve-day time and place strategy we had presented to McCarthy in late December 1967. The strategy was based on the expectation that McCarthy could make an impact on the Democratic voters concentrated in the state's cities and larger towns during visits not to exceed the twelve-day period. The strategy would represent over three quarters of the total Democratic primary turnout and include every single daily paper (9) and the three major weeklies in the state. The days were allocated as follows:

New Hampshire Democratic Primary
12-Day Schedule
Senator Eugene J. McCarthy

Time	City	% Vote Statewide	% Vote 1st C. D.	% Vote 2nd C. D.
3½ Days	Manchester	27.3	44.8	
	Goffstown	1.4	2.3	
		28.7	47.1	
1½ Days	Nashua	9.9		25.7
½ Day	Portsmouth	1.5	2.4	
	New Market	1.0	1.7	
		2.5	4.1	
½ Day	Hookset	0.6	1.0	
	Allenstown	0.9	1.4	
	Pembroke	1.2	2.1	
		2.7	4.5	
1 Day	Berlin	6.3		15.7
	Gorham	0.6		1.5
	Northumberland	0.6		1.5
		7.5		18.7
1 Day	Pelham	0.8	1.2	
	Salem	2.2	3.6	
	Derry	0.8	1.4	
	Hudson	1.6	2.7	
		5.4	8.9	

1 Day	Laconia	2.0	3.3	
	Franklin	1.2		3.0
	Concord	1.7		4.4
		4.9	3.3	7.4
1 Day	Rochester	2.0	3.3	
	Somersworth	3.0	4.9	
	Dover	2.2	3.6	
		7.2	11.8	
1 Day	Hanover	0.7		1.7
	Lebanon	0.8		2.1
	Claremont	2.0		5.0
	Newport	0.8		2.1
		4.3		10.9
1 Day	Keene	1.5		3.9
	Jaffrey	0.4		1.0
	Greenville	0.6		1.6
	Milford	0.8		2.1
	Wilton	0.4		1.1
		3.7		9.7
		76.8	79.7	72.4

An important variable in any political campaign is the capacity to amplify the candidate's message through media attention to a visit, persons and groups contacted during that visit, and what the candidate had to say when in the locality. Consequently of prime importance to the campaign strategy is whether a campaign day will have more than local impact. Studds and I had been careful to note the New Hampshire media in our campaign planning.

Scheduling McCarthy in New Hampshire required attention to at least three situations of equal importance. The first was the senator's availability. Conflicting demands on his time as a senator, as a candidate needed in other states, and for possible international travel, made it difficult to set on the calendar the full schedule of twelve days. Second, the better schedules are built around either events that are independent of a campaign but can be used by the candidate or by creating events at times when people are able to attend. This, of course, means that in a state like New Hampshire, where the population centers are dispersed, the best events on a given day are usually in different communities. Travel time, dead time for a campaign, must be limited if possible or used to some advantage in the campaign. The third situation to be observed in scheduling is to create the excitement of momentum. A campaign, and especially a campaign in the New Hampshire primary, is an incremental happening. The two great mythical attributes of charisma and momentum are either discovered or lost in New Hampshire, and both are the product of the chemistry of the campaign.

Studds and I had to find someone who could schedule the senator and who could also work closely with us. To date there had been no evidence that the senator or the national campaign had staff that they would send to New Hampshire to carry out the scheduling chore. Sandy Hoeh was willing, she knew New Hampshire and its political community, and was familiar with the requirements of a good schedule. The only liability was that she lived in Hanover, had a young family, and would not be able to work from the Concord headquarters. With distance the only liability, a WATS telephone line was installed in our dining room, a calendar posted on the dining room wall, priority places explained to her, and both Senator McCarthy's office and Blair Clark's home and answering service posted with the calendar. Sandy was in business.

Sandy now stood between the national campaign, the senator's Washington office, and the state and local campaign in New Hampshire. These four organizations each would play an important role in the scheduling activity.

Studds and I had assumed that the national campaign and the senator's congressional office staff would be working as one or at least closely together. As Sandy tried to fix dates on the New Hampshire campaign calendar, she found that often more than physical distance between Capitol Hill and the national headquarters in downtown Washington separated the activities. Eventually she found that McCarthy would work through both Clark and McCarthy's personal secretary in his Capitol Hill office, Jean Stack. It depended on who was available at the time McCarthy was ready to discuss his schedule. Most frequently that person was his secretary. Following the campaign Sandy recorded her scheduling problems in an interview.

> There were a couple of problems. The first was that we rarely had enough warning, absolute dates. . . .
>
> Originally Blair Clark had promised, he said we'll give you these dates and you'll work with them. But it was more a matter of the Senator coming up and then they'd decide when he'd come again, how long. So this made it difficult.
>
> The other thing was not having a national advance person, which really turned out in some cases, to be disastrous.
>
> (Sandra Hoeh, Oral History Transcript, p. 4)

Instead of the promised series of definite campaign dates for McCarthy in New Hampshire, Sandy found herself in the middle of a series of negotiations. McCarthy was negotiating with Clark and the campaign with a trip to France and possibly South Vietnam in mind. Sandy was negotiating with Clark for definite dates from which she could build a schedule. The local committees were negotiating with Sandy over when McCarthy would visit their area and what he would do when he arrived.

A lead time of at least a week and preferably more was desirable, but because Clark had been unable to grasp full control of the campaign, the diverse and federated nature of the campaign extended into the domain of the schedule as well. Clark would give Sandy a series of dates. She would notify the local committees of them. They would suggest activities, and Sandy would begin sorting these according to the expected time of arrival, length of the visit, and options for his arrival. When she had a preliminary draft of the schedule ready, she would attempt to check it with staff in the national headquarters or with Clark himself. At this point the flow became confusing. What she had thought were firm dates often were approximate dates. Until definite times for travel to New Hampshire had been set by the senator himself, this was essentially a proposal.

Blair Clark had not been able to get the definite time commitments he had hoped to have because of the competition for the senator's time—some expected and some not. Instead of saying that this would be the case and that those scheduling the senator in New Hampshire would have to work within a floating series of time slots in their scheduling, he continued to assert that he would produce definite dates for the twelve days.

After some serious gnashing of teeth and a lost temper or two as dates and times changed, Sandy and the local organizations began to learn that a good schedule was a flexible schedule, one that could be changed, expanded, or contracted without losing the appearance of being professionally developed and planned in advance.

A part of the scheduling lesson came during the first campaign day when Studds and I found that we were advancing the senator's activity as little as fifteen minutes ahead of him. We learned that it was possible to make adjustments in the schedule with such short notice if our contacts were firm and understood why the schedule had to be adjusted. To accomplish such changes on a regular basis required initiating local workers ahead of time—something that, in the early stages of the campaign, was difficult to do. Further, neither of us realized that such quick adjustments would be necessary once we had organized a proper scheduling and advance function in the campaign.

Early in the campaign I had circulated a memorandum outlining what might be included in a campaign schedule under the title "A Day of Campaigning":

> Note: The following are items that should be considered by you when planning for a visit to your area by Senator Eugene J. McCarthy. This list is not inclusive.
>
> Please add those particular events that are of special importance in your community.
>
> - Visit local newspaper offices.
> - Schedule short local radio and TV interviews if possible.
> - Coffee parties, open house parties, evening socials, etc.
> - Communion breakfasts, other similar gatherings.
> - Tours of factories, handshaking at factory gates during shift changes.
> - Visits to places where Democrats gather—clubs, etc.
> - Super markets, shopping centers, etc.
> - Opportunities for speeches before local audiences regardless of political composition—preferably Democrats and Independents.
> - Headquarters openings, receptions, etc.
> - Special community events.
>
> With the closing admonition: "Don't forget to invite the Independents."
>
> (Hoeh memo, January 7, 1968)

While this list of items to include in a schedule was relevant in any season, campaigning in New Hampshire in the winter requires an even more demanding scheduling requirement. New Hampshire's usual campaign season is during the summer and fall leading to the September primary and November general elections. During those months there are numerous outdoor gatherings and events such as fairs, old home days, festivals, and sports events that lend themselves to campaigning.

In the winter an event must compete with uncertain weather conditions and the cold. To substitute for the fact that people were not often out during the winter, the campaign had to go where the people were when they did go out, or go to their homes, or use ways of reaching people in their homes. Other than scheduling activities that would be amplified by the media, the schedule had to emphasize taking the candidate to where people worked, shopped, and went to school. Practically every other option would have to be a specially planned campaign event.

During the winter of a presidential primary New Hampshire public schools extend invitations to candidates to address assemblies and to meet with classes. In the larger cities the candidates often accept these invitations to speak because few other opportunities to address groups exist, and if press coverage is allowed, the candidate has the chance to show his mettle in a different setting. Without press coverage such speeches were considered a good civic gesture to be done if nothing else could be found to fill that slot in a candidate's schedule.

Studds and I perceived an additional benefit from scheduling McCarthy before school groups. As educators, we knew young people often were better informed and more concerned about contemporary issues than were their preoccupied parents. We also felt since most other means of reaching parents as voters were limited during the winter, a message from a youngster returning home after having heard Senator McCarthy speak or having asked him a question would probably be the subject of that evening's dinner table discussion.

To buttress our decision to accept invitations to speak in the schools and include these in McCarthy's schedule, I recalled that former Democratic National committee chair, John Bailey of Connecticut, contended the most accurate poll that can be conducted close to an election was that of high school students. During his years of political activity he had found that high school students accurately reflect the vote of their parents on election day. New Hampshire high schools often conduct polls before elections, and the results receive considerable local newspaper attention. Studds and I wanted McCarthy to do well in these polls.

FEBRUARY 6, 7, AND 8 SCHEDULE: A CASE STUDY

After a considerable struggle Sandy was able to get a definite commitment from both Blair Clark and Senator McCarthy's office—he would campaign in New Hampshire on February 6, 7, and 8. A three-day schedule would test the capacity of the New Hampshire organization and give the senator a chance to demonstrate whether his candidacy could tap a response in New Hampshire.

Since his first visit had been in the south central part of the state, Studds and I felt he should begin this trip in the west and move back across to the center where he could generate statewide media, swing northeast to the city of Laconia, and leave from there. We also hoped McCarthy could fly directly to New Hampshire and be welcomed there by the local group rather than landing in Boston.

In her account Barbara Underwood described how part of the schedule was developed:

> Mrs. David Hoeh handled the Senator's schedule from Hanover. It fell to her to make the necessary judgments as to the best way to juggle the requests for the Senator's time and at the same time use the candidate most effectively. As a guide she could use the figures drawn up by Gerry Studds indicating the number of days McCarthy should spend in each city. But his figures still did not solve the problem of whether it would be better to have McCarthy's next speech scheduled for Concord or Dartmouth College in Hanover.
>
> The Senator had spoken at the University of New Hampshire and at St. Anselm's. It seemed only natural that next they should try to schedule him to speak at Dartmouth. There would be an audience, the press would get a further chance to evaluate him under optimum conditions; it would provide the opportunity to recruit future volunteers from among the ranks of students and professors.
>
> (Underwood, op. cit., p. 17)

At least once during each visit Studds and I wanted McCarthy scheduled to address a large group. This would be almost his only opportunity to discuss the issues of his candidacy in his own way and in a widely accepted format. There would, of course, be numerous other chances for brief talks and press sessions, but it was the major address that would attract media attention beyond that of strictly a local or statewide nature.

Barbara Underwood recalled how Concord argued its case:

> But from Concord there were telephone calls clamoring for the Senator to appear there, as Concord had only one full day of campaigning allotted to it. A strong organization had been started but it needed the Senator's appearance to keep up the momentum. Too many people needed another chance to evaluate him. Competition was strong from the liberal Republican candidate, George Romney, who seemed to be operating a smooth and successful campaign out of home headquarters. The most impressive thing about Romney was that he was willing to stand up and answer the voter's questions in a sincere and direct way. . . . The Concord committee was handicapped by the lack of time to have a series of home gatherings, but they could schedule one big meeting, where everyone would attend at the same time. The traditional place for such a political gathering was the Concord Community Center.

> Understandably, both David and Sandra Hoeh had visions of a McCarthy speech at the Concord Community Center turning into an utter fiasco. They visualized the press attending a speech by the Senator to which no audience appeared. It was a horrible specter.
>
> Concord, said David Hoeh, was known in Democratic circles as a political graveyard. No one ever came out in an evening to hear a candidate speak, particularly in February, if it's cold and the roads are icy and dangerous.
>
> (Underwood, op. cit., p. 17)

The Concord Committee argued that Concord residents tended to be political activists who could be attracted to any political event. The Vietnam War issue, they contended, was beginning to cross party lines, and McCarthy was beginning to appear as the most effective spokesperson against the administration's policies.

> Sandra Hoeh nervously, and with some misgivings relented and scheduled the Senator for February 6th, Concord Community Center, 7:30 P.M.
>
> (Underwood, op. cit., p. 18)

Where local committees were well organized and willing to accept risks in their schedule, negotiations such as that which Barbara Underwood described were frequent. The Concord committee had organizational depth and political experience which meant that it would not suggest activities the committee members themselves were uncertain about or were not willing to work exceptionally hard to make a success. In other communities, the local McCarthy organizations frequently had much less experience, depth, or understanding of their own local situation.

Sandy Hoeh knew where the McCarthy organization had local depth and where it did not, and she attempted to protect the schedule as best she could from weak efforts. Unfortunately a totally effective scheduling effort depends upon extensive advance work, checking and double-checking, to ensure that every element of the schedule fits and will work as expected. Eric Schnapper and Sandy's telephones were not sufficient to substitute for the inexperience of some new local organizations or the difficult communications between New Hampshire and Washington. McCarthy's three-day schedule was a classic case illustrating the point.

Arrival

McCarthy was scheduled to fly through New York City connecting with a flight to Keene's municipal airport, arriving early in the evening. He would then be driven to Claremont. I called the Keene McCarthy committee to see if it could arrange a press conference for McCarthy at the airport. If it had the time and inclination, I suggested that the committee might also want to arrange an airport welcome for McCarthy. Airport welcomes or campaign "whistle stops" at airports have not been particularly notable for their success in New Hampshire. People will step out of their stores or homes to welcome prominent figures in the downtown of a city but few will take the time to attend an airport rally.

I was not optimistic about attracting a crowd in Keene but felt that the Keene committee, perhaps the best organized in the state, should have the chance to do something directly for McCarthy since he was not scheduled to be in Keene until a later campaign tour.

As part of the scheduling job, Sandy booked reservations in a motel outside Claremont for the senator and those traveling with him. His morning schedule was typical of what was possible in a small New Hampshire city during a morning. The local committee had worked closely with Sandy and its community contacts to complete as effective a campaign morning as possible. Because of other demands on his time and with assurances from the Claremont workers, Eric Schnapper did not advance this portion of the schedule. Instead, Bill Gallagher, a Claremont native and the campaign's New Hampshire press secretary, checked out the schedule for Sandy.

Schedule: Tuesday, February 6, 1968

Time	Place	Function
6:40 A.M.	Claremont	Greet workers outside Joy Mfg. Co.
8:00 A.M.	Claremont	Breakfast at Pleasant Restaurant
9:00 A.M.	Claremont	Tour Claremont Paper Co.
9:30 A.M.	Claremont	*Claremont Eagle* (newspaper)
10:00 A.M.	Claremont	WTSV radio interview
10:30 A.M.	Claremont	Coffee at home of M/M John Meloney, 95 Winter Street
11:00 A.M.	Claremont	Tour Main Street
Noon	Claremont	Address Claremont Rotary, Moody Hotel
1:00 P.M.	Claremont	Drive to Newport

A note at the bottom of the schedule said, "Press Bus Starts in Claremont." A bus had been hired by the campaign to provide reporters with transportation when McCarthy was campaigning.

Having made an exceptional effort to avoid incidents such as the Manchester shift change mistake during McCarthy's first visit, we had every reason to expect that the schedule for this visit would move as planned. McCarthy arrived in Keene to one of the largest airport gatherings in recent memory. The Keene McCarthy committee had worked for days preparing signs, placards, and slogans, recruiting people to come to the airport. The airplane touched down in a light snow shower, taxied to the gate, a crowd of national reporters disembarked, and then a startled McCarthy to a cheering throng. The press conference in the small terminal building went well with the senator responding to questions, commenting on his surprise at the reception, and making several radio tapes that were played throughout the area the next day.

I then drove McCarthy to his hotel. Arriving there, we had the first-tip off that things might not go as well in Claremont as had been expected. Sandy Hoeh described the events:

> We knew that the national press was coming. No one told me that the national press like to have their own rooms. So we put them into rooms together and they were very nice about it, but some of the Senator's people were quite upset.
> (S. Hoeh, op. cit., p. 4)

There was even some confusion concerning the senator's reservations. The owner of the Four A's Motel, a Claremont resident of French-Canadian descent, spoke limited English. When the herd of press, the senator, and McCarthy's aide Jerry Eller appeared out of the snow and dark in his lobby to be registered and assigned their rooms, the man lost his ability to cope. Jerry Eller, with images of the Manchester plant gate swimming in his head, did not help calm the situation.

Eventually I had Dennis Donahue, the driver of the car from Keene, distract Eller; I was able to get the proprietor calmed down and back to the complicated task of registering the crowd—probably more business than his motel had ever experienced in so few minutes. Now after 9:00 P.M., I found that McCarthy had not eaten. Finding a place to eat that late in the evening in a small New Hampshire city is difficult. My memory of Claremont from earlier visits led the entourage of hungry reporters, the senator, and staff to Christopher's Restaurant. This was New Hampshire and in spite of Eller's fears, reporters, candidate, and campaigners settled into the restaurant's booths for a hearty and relaxed meal. McCarthy was at his best having been happily received by the restaurant staff. He joked with the reporters, told several tales about his recent experiences in Washington, and thoroughly enjoyed the time.

Disaster struck early the next morning. Sandy Hoeh recalled:

> The next morning he went to a factory gate, which someone supposedly had advanced, but he got there a few minutes late and missed almost everyone. With him were the national press.
>
> Then he went to a hotel to eat breakfast and no one told us that the hotel did not usually serve breakfast. The hotel management said they did serve but did not make clear that it was not a part of the regular operation.
>
> They then went to a restaurant to meet people who were supposed to be there for breakfast but the place was empty.
>
> I remember getting a telephone call in the middle of the morning from Sy Hersh, who said the morning had been a disaster. I had only three hours of sleep and the call absolutely shattered me. I called David [Hoeh] and said get someone else, it's not going to work. He said, oh yes it will. And things did begin to improve. . . .
>
> . . . I kept saying, the Kennedys wouldn't go anyplace without national advance, it was the only campaign I could compare with from what I'd heard. Up here people who knew the kind of thing you advance, what you

> look for, there had to be split second timing (which had not been learned by the local schedulers or those who had checked the schedule).
>
> I don't know who was responsible for the advancing, but I was after that first morning. I remember shaking, I was too tired to even take a nap and I rushed over to Newport by 2:00. But by that night things went well again.
>
> By then no one was upset, as a matter of fact, I think they were trying to be nice to me. They all acted like nothing was the matter. But I knew that he [Senator McCarthy] had been upset, because I got a call from Washington. So I knew someone had called Washington.
>
> . . . After that we used Eric Schnapper and he did have split second timing. He was just great.
>
> (S. Hoeh, op. cit., p. 5)

Toward the middle of the morning things began to go closer to what was expected. McCarthy's habit of running ahead of the schedule continued to raise problems. But the interviews went well as did the coffee at the Meloney home. The one hour allotted for a Main Street tour turned out to be too much time. There were few people on the streets or in the shops, and Claremont is not a large city.

The major event turned out to be the address at the Claremont Rotary Club. Again the advance work that should have uncovered a preference and, perhaps, have avoided an incident had not been done. Instead of the predictable debacle that was driving Jerry Eller frantic with fears that all the media that would come from New Hampshire concerning his senator would be the mistakes, Tom Wicker wrote the first story about the campaign in New Hampshire that received national attention. Under his column heading, "In the Nation: Luncheon at the Rotary Club," Wicker wrote:

> Claremont, N.H.—This is an apt state for Senator Eugene McCarthy's kind of campaigning. Not far from here, along one of the narrow roads that thread New Hampshire's hills, an old, white clapboard house has been restored and painted and a witty weekend resident has placed a sign out front that reads: "The Old Values."
>
> That is the kind of rebuke that Gene McCarthy might make to those who talk glibly about getting back to an earlier simpler way of life that New England somehow is supposed to exemplify. In this postcard state with its frozen lakes and huts of fishermen standing blackly on the ice, it is too easy to believe that there really are old values to which we all go back. It is something about the farms, the hills, the white churches in their serenity.
>
> The Birch-White Hills
>
> In fact, most of the old villages with their church steeples and their beautifully proportioned white houses and their empty red brick mills are angling for tourists and skiers these days, and the garish supermarkets and sprawling motels with their bleak parking lots lie on the land like a pox; the birch-white hills, tinged with the faint rays of sunlight on winter leaves, rise above polluted streams, intrusive highways and the creeping urban litter of the twentieth century.

Still men have to believe something and no doubt that was why there seemed to be a special quality at the luncheon of the Rotary Club of Claremont in the Hotel Moody here the other day. Beneath the four glass chandeliers and the stained class panels of the windows, the Rotarians had gathered to hear Senator McCarthy, who is running for President in the New Hampshire Democratic primary.

The first thing that happened was that President Rodney Brock ordered the television cameras out of the room. He explained that his club was non-political, that Senator McCarthy had come to discuss public affairs, not politics, and that he was not going to have the club meeting exploited either for television or politics.

A solidly built man, with a quick, nervous smile and sparse, sandy hair, President Brock encountered enough argument to make his chin tremble with tension. But he stood by his simple defiance of the television networks, which is something no President of the United States ever has been known to do, and in the end the cameras were packed up and taken out.

After that, the club sang, "L'il Liza Jane" and "Smile, and the World Smiles With You" conducted its regular business, and settled back to hear McCarthy. Apparently untroubled by the absence of television, before which most politicians bow and scrape like valets, the Senator spoke in his relaxed manner and with his corrosive wit ("We don't declare war any more, we declare national defense") and gave the Rotarians—if not much of a show, by Ronald Reagan standards—a clear picture of himself.

It was a picture of a man who had set out to discuss what he called "two or three questions of vital importance" and who was deeply in earnest about the need for the nation to "turn aside from the war in order to attend to the most pressing problems at home"—which he defined as the rebellion of Negroes against any longer being "a kind of colonial people in our country."

He was unemotional, undramatic and nothing about his speech or his manner was hoked up for cheap applause or enthusiasm. He even treated his audience as though it would understand his points and allusions, and respond sensibly to his ideas. He said what he had to say, with some eloquence but no particular flourish, and then he sat down.

Self, Not an Image

It is possible that Rodney Brock was legally off base in turning out the cameras, and it is possible that Gene McCarthy is wrong in his stand on the war. Some might question Brock's judgment and others challenge McCarthy's motives, but during luncheon at the Rotary Club nobody could accuse either of showing an image rather than a self.

That is probably not good politics; all the pros will tell you that. But in an age when the image is the idol, the old values are inspected by avid tourists, and the flagrant falsities and pretensions of American life deride verity, two men stubbornly being themselves must be worth something.

(*New York Times,* February 8, 1968)

Every newspaper that carried the *New York Times* news service and many that did not published Wicker's column. Somehow through the haze of scheduling problems, conflicts, and even a substantial incident at the expense of television, a setting, accidental in fact, had been created that illustrated the strengths of two individuals.

Once away from Claremont the scheduling problems began to disappear. Jerry Eller regained his composure, Senator McCarthy chortled over the difficulties of the often pretentious television crews, and stopped for one of the more delightful visits a candidate can have if the editor of Newport's weekly newspaper, Edward DeCourcy, brightens to him. By early afternoon Sandra's telephone carried a distinctly different message from that she had heard in the morning. The remainder of the day's schedule read:

1:30 P.M.	Newport	WCNL Radio interview
2:15 P.M.	Newport	Tour Door Woolen Co.
3:10 P.M.	Newport	Meet Newport High School faculty
3:35 P.M.	Newport	*Argus Champion* (meet Editor DeCourcey—tour plant)
4:00 P.M.	Newport	Tour Main Street
4:45 P.M.	Newport	Drive to Concord
5:45 P.M.	Concord	Arrive New Hampshire Highway Hotel
7:30 P.M.	Concord	Address at Concord Community Center

The Newport to Concord portion of the schedule had been carefully timed. The schedule clicked, the reporters saw that the New Hampshire McCarthy organization could create an effective schedule, and by the time the entourage arrived in Concord, there was a frequently expressed feeling that it had been a good day.

Later that evening when I met privately with McCarthy to apologize for the problems in Claremont and to discuss future campaign plans, I asked McCarthy if he could find someone to travel with him when in New Hampshire who could be more sensitive to the feelings of volunteers when problems developed. While Studds and I and others realized that problems might occur and that damage could result from the problems, the campaign did not have sufficient personnel with proper experience to check everything as it should be checked at this stage. McCarthy said he understood and would bring Charlie Callanan from his office as his traveling staff in the future.

Studds and I had gained the senator's respect early on, and as the campaign continued this confidence grew to be of considerable importance to the success of the campaign. When Sandy Hoeh reported to Washington the contents of the three-day schedule a few days before McCarthy was scheduled to arrive, his office stated that it did not see a reason for including as many school speaking times as there were in the draft. His office wanted most of the times eliminated and replaced with something else. When I heard about the request to cancel the schools, I said I would not and I would explain their importance to McCarthy. Sandy did not change the schedule, but printed it for distribution to the press as she had originally developed it.

On the day that McCarthy was scheduled to arrive in Keene, I was called to New York City to review changes Koenig had made in the advertising program he was suggesting for the campaign. On my return to New Hampshire I joined the same flight from New York as the senator was taking to Keene. Sitting next to McCarthy I brought up the subject of the schedule and the changes that had been suggested by McCarthy's staff. I explained the problem we had finding things of value to do on weekdays, noted that each school visit would be little more than thirty minutes, and then reviewed the reasons for going to the schools at all. McCarthy listened, then said, "Okay, we'll do them."

When McCarthy concluded his three-day visit he said he would be back for another three days, on February 13, 14, and 15, several days at the end of the month, and then a few days just before the primary. He added that he might even add a few more days if his own activities and those elsewhere in the campaign would permit.

As the campaign developed the scheduling activity became larger and more sophisticated. There would not be another time like the morning of February 6 in Claremont. While McCarthy's habit of completing activities ahead of the time allowed in a schedule presented problems along the way, the drivers or traveling staff began to develop ways of coping with the newfound time. They would add something quickly or change the route slightly to include a brief visit to a small town, a campaign headquarters, or shopping area. As I had suggested during the earliest meetings of the campaign, the local committees developed a "shelf" of potential campaign activities from which they could draw a schedule for a visit by Senator McCarthy on short notice. The Salem headquarters would put together a three-hour schedule, including a headquarters full of people, with less than two hours' notice on the last day of the campaign.

As the campaign progressed each schedule reflected the expanding organizational base and the increased recognition of the candidate. As McCarthy became better known, as his reputation and credibility as a candidate grew, the early risks such as those taken when setting McCarthy's Concord speech, were no longer hazards. The local organization guaranteed a crowd. The alchemy of scheduling events that could fail and that didn't, in which the candidate sent his audiences away impressed, built a momentum. This surprised the media and assured even larger audiences. Each favorably impressed person who saw McCarthy became a not-so-passive endorsement.

The strategy of the twelve-day schedule outlined the places where it was important for McCarthy to visit and the approximate time that he should spend at each place. After that it was the scheduling operation of the campaign, headed by Sandy Hoeh in New Hampshire, that pieced together a day of activities.

The scheduler has the choice of either building a schedule from one or two strong events filled in with less useful activities in one area or having the candidate chase prime events in widely separated locales. The remaining two days of McCarthy's February 6, 7, and 8 schedule reflected the problem of filling time, responding to opportunities, broadening the impact of the campaign, and finding a place from which to depart without retracing previously covered ground.

Schedule: Wednesday, February 7, 1968

Time	Place	Function
7:00 A.M.	Concord	Greet workers outside factories
7:20 A.M.	Concord	Greet workers outside Rumford Press
8:05 A.M.	Concord	Breakfast, McKenzie's Restaurant, Main Street
8:30 A.M.	Concord	Address assembly and Q/A at Concord High School
9:00 A.M.	Concord	Tour *Concord Daily Monitor* building and informal press conference
9:30 A.M.	Concord	Coffee with residents of JFK apartments (housing for the elderly)
10:15 A.M.	Concord	Address St. Paul's School and Q/A period
11:15 A.M.	Concord	Greeted by Mayor Gove at City Hall and introduction to city employees
1:00 P.M.	Manchester	Address at Central High School
1:35 P.M.	Manchester	Tour Cott Beverage Co.
3:15 P.M.	Manchester	Coffee at home of M/M Robert Eschoo, 1015 Chestnut Street
4:00 P.M.	Manchester	Tour shopping center
4:30 P.M.	Manchester	Drive to Concord
6:30 P.M.	Concord	Dinner in Concord
8:30 P.M.	Concord	Drive to Laconia
10:00 P.M.	Laconia	Laconia Tavern

Studds and I felt that each campaign visit should have at least part of its schedule in Manchester. As the largest city and the hub of Hillsborough County with its heavy Democratic voter registration, McCarthy had to do well in the county if he was to succeed statewide. Unfortunately the local campaign organization was weak. From the beginning many of those attracted to McCarthy lived outside the city or had had little previous campaign experience. Their contacts were limited, and their understanding of the political dynamics of the city was less than adequate to crack the community's tough political shell.

While we remained determined to have McCarthy campaign in Manchester once each visit, to do so always strained the best efforts of the state campaign and a shy local committee. In contrast, as shown by the density of the February 7

Concord schedule, a well-connected, hardworking, politically sophisticated local McCarthy committee made campaigning in Concord a pleasure not only for McCarthy but for those leading and scheduling his campaign.

The Laconia committee possessed much of the same ability as the Concord people. Somewhat younger and broader based in the community, the Laconia committee's youth and enthusiasm made the city an attractive campaign stop and one that would be used on a number of occasions when an activity was needed for some of those who came later to campaign for McCarthy.

The schedule for the third day, February 8, illustrated the committee's effectiveness.

Schedule: Thursday, February 8, 1968

Time	Place	Function
6:30 A.M.	Laconia	Greet workers outside Scott-Williams Mfg. Co.
7:30 A.M.	Laconia	Address Laconia Chamber of Commerce breakfast [an obligatory performance for all presidential candidates]
9:00 A.M.	Laconia	WLNH radio interview
9:30 A.M.	Laconia	McCarthy for President Headquarters
9:45 A.M.	Laconia	WEMJ radio interview
10:30 A.M.	Laconia	Coffee at home of M/M Ron O'Callahan, 42 Gilford Street
11:30 A.M.	Laconia	Leave Laconia for Lebanon
12:30 P.M.	Lebanon	Address Rotary, Landers Restaurant
1:45 P.M.	Lebanon	Main Street tour
2:15 P.M.	Lebanon	*Valley News* interview
3:10 P.M.	Lebanon	Leave Lebanon Airport for Boston

Because it was possible for McCarthy to leave New Hampshire from the Lebanon Airport and connect with a flight to Washington, the Lebanon schedule was added, which took advantage of a press producing speech before the Rotary Club and McCarthy's first campaigning in New Hampshire's "North Country." To do this meant that McCarthy had to be driven more than sixty miles across New Hampshire, over a winding, low speed road—not that comfortable an experience during the beginning of New Hampshire's frost heave season.

To overcome some of the communications problems between New Hampshire and the national campaign, Grace Bassett, a friend of the McCarthy family, came to New Hampshire to help Sandy Hoeh with the next schedule and also to organize activities for Mrs. McCarthy. An effective political organizer in her own right, Abigail McCarthy agreed to help in her husband's campaign by coming to New Hampshire. Her role in previous campaigns had been largely as a behind-the-scenes organizer and only occasionally as an active campaigner. Now that their family was older—the youngest was twelve-year-old Margaret—Mrs. McCarthy and Mary, a Radcliffe sophomore, were scheduled for a visit on February 14 and 15. With this added to the senator's visit on February 13, 14, and 15, the scheduling task doubled.

The same preparation was needed for Mrs. McCarthy as was required for Senator McCarthy, including advancing, transportation, and provisions for reporters. With Grace Bassett in New Hampshire, date and schedule confirmation through Washington greatly improved. Sandy Hoeh's frustration at "not having enough advance notice of the dates [of a campaign visit] and then [being given] a date and a couple of days later [being expected to have] a full schedule with exact times and telephone numbers and addresses" was reduced. Grace Bassett knew the exact route to getting definite dates and schedule confirmations.

McCarthy next campaigned in New Hampshire on February 13, 14, and 15. With this visit he first used as his base a redecorated farm house on the property of the Sheraton-Wayfarer located in Bedford, just south of Manchester's city limits. I had rented this house to serve as a living quarters for Senator McCarthy and as a "command post" of sorts for that part of the campaign traveling with the senator.

In outline, McCarthy's schedule of campaign visits by locale ran as follows:

Tuesday, February 13, 1968

Evening:	Arrive Manchester Airport
	Stay at the Wayfarer

Wednesday, February 14, 1968

Nashua:	Radio interviews, factory tours
Manchester:	Factory tours, street tour west side
Manchester:	Series of three social receptions in private homes

Thursday, February 15, 1968

Morning:	
Milford:	Newspaper interview, high school talk, factory tours
Peterborough:	Reception
Afternoon:	
Keene:	Factory and office tours, newspaper interview, radio interview, reception
Evening:	
Keene:	Speech at Keene State College
	Depart for New York City

Abigail and Mary McCarthy were scheduled together as follows, and then Mary went on her own for a part of the visit.

Abigail McCarthy and Mary A. McCarthy

Schedule: Wednesday, February 14, 1968

Morning:

Manchester:	Press conference followed by workshop with McCarthy workers in the area

Afternoon:

Nashua:	Visit a school, meet with McCarthy campaign workers, newspaper interview

Evening:

Nashua:	Attend a church supper
Manchester:	Follow Senator McCarthy at each of the three social receptions

Schedule: Thursday, February 15, 1968

Morning:

Peterborough:	Reception with Senator McCarthy

Noon:

Keene:	Press conference

Afternoon:

Keene:	Retarded Children Center tour, radio interview, newspaper interview, headquarters reception, coffee at private home, reception

Evening:

Keene:	Attend speech

Mary McCarthy campaigned on her own on the afternoon of February 15. During that time she visited Keene State College for a tour and meeting with McCarthy supporters, worked at the McCarthy literature table on the campus, was interviewed by a newspaper reporter, participated in a live call-in radio program, and then rejoined her mother at the late afternoon reception. After this initiation, Mary would campaign almost totally on her own schedule until the end of the campaign. An effective spokesperson for the issues and concerns of the campaign, she received important radio and newspaper attention wherever she visited. Eventually, Miriam Dunn of Concord was assigned to schedule Mary McCarthy exclusively.

On his departure from New Hampshire on February 15, Senator McCarthy said that he expected to add more time to his campaign. When he arrived to campaign on February 23, he had made a solid commitment to be in New Hampshire for the eight days preceding the primary in addition to the previously committed time early in March.

For the remaining time Senator McCarthy was scheduled as follows during each of his visits:

Schedule: February 23, 24, 25, 26, 1968

Thursday, February 22

Evening:	Arrive Burlington, Vermont, airport. Drive to Franconia, New Hampshire, to stay overnight

Friday, February 23

Morning:	
Berlin:	Meet with union leaders, radio interview, factory tour
Noon:	
Berlin:	Chamber of commerce luncheon
Afternoon:	
Berlin:	Meet shift change, radio interview, tour social clubs
Evening:	
Berlin:	Democratic City Committee meeting, reception

Saturday, February 24

Morning/afternoon:	Travel from Berlin to Manchester
Evening:	
Manchester:	Tour social clubs and greet volunteers

Sunday, February 25

Afternoon:	
Manchester:	Reception, skating, winter carnival
Evening:	
Nashua:	Reception

Monday, February 26

Morning:	
Manchester:	Departure for Washington

With McCarthy's return for the fourth time, his base and the focus of the campaign shifted almost exclusively to the southern portion of the state. His campaign support, primarily the press activity, now was almost exclusively based at the Sheraton-Wayfarer. Organization, operations, and related activities continued from the Concord headquarters outward to the various city and home headquarters. This now was almost a separate activity from that of scheduling and supporting the schedule of the senator. From March 2–7 Senator McCarthy's schedule took him to key Democratic vote-producing communities.

Saturday, March 2

Morning:	
Nashua:	Street campaigning and a private invited guest luncheon

Afternoon:
- Milford: Knights of Columbus reception

Evening:
- Nashua: Major address

Sunday, March 3

Morning:
- Nashua: Private: attend church

Afternoon:
- Claremont: Reception
- Hanover: Radio, newspaper interviews, press conference, cocktail reception/fund-raiser
- Hanover: Major address

March 4 was the only day during the campaign when a carefully developed schedule had to be scrapped. Senator McCarthy was called back to Washington for a critical vote on a major piece of civil rights legislation. Canceling plans that had been made considerably in advance gave Sandy Hoeh serious problems. Almost all people who arrange campaign activities know that a conflict from Washington or the weather may cause a cancellation, but when it does occur the local supporters react by saying, "Yes, I understand but why us, this day, our days of planning and hard work?" When the March 4 schedule was canceled, the McCarthy group in Hampton would not accept the fact. Sandy Hoeh recalled:

> I remember one funny thing, the Senator went back to Washington to vote on the civil rights bill and we told the people in Hampton that he wouldn't be able to be at the high school for his scheduled speech. They were furious. The fellow on the other end of the phone said that he would call the Senator directly if I did not get him here. "We were promised this." I called the Senator and got him to promise that he would come back.
>
> (S. Hoeh, op. cit., p. 8)

While a little late on his return to Hampton, an unheard of crowd exceeding four hundred persons turned out for the high school speech. McCarthy completed the remainder of the previously scheduled events in Dover.

Tuesday, March 5

Morning:
- Dover: Greet workers, tour plants, breakfast

Noon:
- Manchester: Exchange Club luncheon

Afternoon:
- Derry: Factory gate, street campaigning, newspaper interview

Evening:
- Derry: Kiwanis-Lions speech

Wednesday: March 6

Morning:	
Manchester:	College speech
Afternoon:	
Manchester:	Radio interviews and a local television interview; some open time used for media preparation
Evening:	
Manchester:	Reception

Thursday: March 7

Morning:	
Nashua:	Ward campaign visits, college address, invitational luncheon
Afternoon:	
Manchester:	Local college address, office tour, reception
Evening:	
Manchester:	Shopping night Elm Street tour, private home parties

The late afternoon and evening part of the schedule had to be canceled when McCarthy was called to an important dinner in New York City. While in New York he prepared some of the commercial material that would be used later in the New Hampshire campaign and elsewhere. To get him back on schedule as rapidly as possible and to cover part of the state that had not been visited earlier, he was met at Boston's Logan International Airport by William Johnson, a New York publisher who owned a twin-engine Beechcraft Baron. From Boston, McCarthy was flown to Berwick, Maine, the closest airport to Rochester, New Hampshire, where he resumed campaigning.

Friday, March 8

Evening:	
Rochester:	Press conference, meet mayor and chairman of Democratic City Committee
Dover:	Tour four shopping centers

Saturday, March 9

Morning:	
Franklin:	Factory tour, newspaper interview, radio interviews, shopping area tour, reception
Noon:	
Concord:	Surprise visit to state headquarters
Afternoon:	
Manchester:	Street campaigning and shopping center tour
Evening:	
Manchester:	Rally and major speech

Sunday, March 10

Morning:	
Manchester:	Brunch with local campaign workers
Nashua:	Church
Afternoon:	
Nashua:	Knights of Columbus Hall reception
Manchester:	Jewish Community Center reception
Evening:	
Manchester:	Visit convent, skating

March 10 was the end of the formal New Hampshire campaign. The next morning, Monday, March 11, Senator McCarthy traveled to Boston to tape a television program with Jack Parr, that would be shown in the evening. On his return to Manchester, I scheduled a visit to Salem, giving the local headquarters approximately two hours' notice before arriving. The press, which had not accompanied McCarthy to Boston, came down from Manchester to Salem, and a three-hour schedule that included a plant tour, headquarters reception, Main Street tour, and shopping center visit ended the campaign as a fully covered political event.

Salem was the last of the priority localities that Studds and I had identified. Instead of the twelve days we had felt were necessary to produce a result, McCarthy had devoted twenty-one days to New Hampshire during which time he visited all of the important campaign targets and several other communities of secondary importance.

Importance of McCarthy's Second Visit

Of the many days that McCarthy campaigned in New Hampshire, the second visit clearly showed how McCarthy best campaigned, how the organization could better support his efforts, and how effective McCarthy was in "feeding off" the New Hampshire political landscape.

When the schedule did not quite click on that first morning in Nashua, the press and his campaign workers saw a comfortable, composed man take advantage of the time to relax not only himself but those around him. When the schedule began to click as the day went on, Senator McCarthy responded to it with enthusiasm that was likewise contagious. His visit had attracted a cadre of top national reporters which included Harry Kelley of the Associated Press, Ned Kenworthy and Tom Wicker of the *New York Times,* and Dick Stout of *Newsweek,* Stephen Nordlinger, *Baltimore Sun,* Jack Germond of the *St. Louis Post Dispatch,* Albert Eisele of the Ridder chain, Jules Witcover of the Newhouse chain, Bill Cardoso, New Hampshire reporter for the *Boston Globe,* as well as David Schoumacher of the CBS news.

Most had accompanied McCarthy on the plane trip to Keene and were amazed to see the sizable crowd assembled to greet the candidate on this early evening stop. They had been jolted by seeing the placards in the hands of the more than one hundred people: "People before Bombs," or "McCarthy the thinking man's candidate," or "McCarthy a man for this season," or just simply, "McCarthy for President."

The brief stop in Keene, February 6, produced a photograph of the crowd waving placards, pictures of McCarthy, and a three-column story headlined, "Sen. McCarthy Shows Optimism In Hurried Campaign Stop Here." (*Keene Evening Sentinel,* February 6, 1968, p. 1) The Claremont schedule the next morning gave the *Claremont Eagle* a page-one story under a four-column photograph showing Senator McCarthy shaking hands with a Claremont paper mill employee. The story's lead paragraphs read:

> Sen. Eugene J. McCarthy, a man admittedly fighting enormous political odds, breezed through Sullivan County today on a schedule that started at 6:40 A.M. in Claremont and wasn't due to end until he will leave Newport in the late afternoon, bound for Concord.
>
> By mid-morning, when he was interviewed at the Daily Eagle offices, he was a political phenomenon in more ways than one—he was running a half-hour ahead of schedule.
>
> A tall, handsome, affable man, he appeared to be a maverick in more than his views on Vietnam. . . .
>
> "It's not only the war," he said this morning in his soft, professorial voice, "but what it's doing to us at home, especially in the problem of our cities and urban unrest.
>
> "I am campaigning because I believe that the test on these matters ought to come through the regular political processes," he continued, "not through demonstrations or by third party movements."
>
> (*Claremont Eagle,* February 6, 1968 p. 1)

The AP wired a photograph of Senator McCarthy slipping and then catching himself on the ice outside the Claremont home of Mr. and Mrs. John Meloney. The photograph appeared in a number of New Hampshire newspapers including the Dover and Nashua dailies as well as a number of newspapers outside New Hampshire that carried the AP service. In addition to Tom Wicker's column, McCarthy's comments concerning the impact of the war on the nation's domestic economic health were given good regional coverage. But the premier event that affirmed the support of McCarthy's followers was his speech in Concord and what immediately followed that event.

To ensure that McCarthy's address would be well attended, the Concord committee made a special effort. Barbara Underwood described the work in her manuscript:

> In trying to get out an audience for McCarthy's speech the Concord committee made Ward Seven and the other central Concord wards their prime target. Every registered Democratic or independent voter was called on the telephone inviting them to attend. Advertisements were placed in the newspapers and on the radio. The entire membership list of the League of Women Voters was called personally, as was the entire faculty list at St. Paul's School.

> If the people were Republicans an appeal was made to their civic pride. "Imagine how Concord, New Hampshire will look in a big picture by *Life* magazine showing rows and rows of empty seats at a speech by a member of the United States Senate," they said.
>
> Posters advertising the speech were put up wherever they were accepted; however, on Main Street most of the merchants refused to take them. McCarthy was too controversial a figure; he might be bad for business. One stroke of good fortune came at a new little Victorian-styled ice cream parlor called MacKenzie's, located on the corner of School and Main Streets. It was in the center of town. . . . The manager came from the Midwest. He was a Democrat and knew McCarthy. He was willing to put up four posters in his windows advertising the speech. The posters also invited people to come in and join the Senator for breakfast the following morning.
>
> (Underwood, op. cit., p. 23)

Eric Schnapper advanced the site and arrangements for the address carefully. Barbara Underwood recalled:

> Eric Schnapper went down to the community center to go over the arrangements. The speaker's platform, he said, should face out toward the main front door. Bleachers could be pulled out for an audience along the far right. The press should be accommodated by long tables, stretching along the length of the far left. All TV cameras should be kept on the left side. In the middle, chairs should be set up. Only 140 were to be used in case the evening was a flop.
>
> The chairs were set up so that they provided a wide aisle. "Let's see," said Schnapper. "The Senator will be staying at the Highway Hotel. Dr. Underwood, the Concord Chairman, will go over and pick him up, and bring him here as soon as the place has filled. There's a phone back here near the entrance, so he can check it out. Dr. Underwood and the Senator will pull up to the front door. We will reserve a space in front of the steps. Then Underwood and the Senator will walk up the steps together, down the aisle and the audience will stand and applaud."
>
> Schnapper made it sound all very dramatic.
>
> Gerry Studds had one suggestion. The chairs should be set back from the speaker's platform. Young people should be asked to sit up front on the floor between the speaker and the first row of chairs. The senator was at his best before a young audience, and liked to have them around. And it would look good in press photos.
>
> (Underwood, op. cit., p. 24)

The evening unfolded as Eric Schnapper had envisioned. The reporters occupied the long tables, the television crews set up to the left of the platform, and then a group of students from Concord High School took positions near the door ready to pass out campaign literature to the audience as they entered. Then the audience arrived.

> There were enough people so that all the chairs and bleachers were filled. Those who arrived late stood in the rear of the auditorium. David and Sandra Hoeh had driven down from Hanover and they smiled in relief at the turnout. Some 150 people was all that had been hoped for; instead more then 400 were showing up.
>
> (Underwood, op. cit., p. 25)

The senator arrived, joined by Marsha Macey, Concord co-chair, and David Underwood.

> A nervous sense of expectation seized the Concord McCarthy Committee. Would the audience stand for McCarthy? Would they boo or would they clap?
>
> The Concord chairman escorted the Senator, who looked tall and distinguished, down a wide aisle between scores of standing, cheering and applauding voters. Even the press noted the power of suggestion. Here was a tribute to a potential president.
>
> (Underwood, op. cit., p. 26)

Barbara Underwood recalled that McCarthy had described his campaigning to a *Time* reporter as "fighting from a low crouch. You wait for events to develop." His speech that evening demonstrated how effective a fighter he was. The story of the LBJ campaign strategy and the use of their pledge cards had broken several days earlier. There had been a series of stories either on the LBJ campaign or specifically on the pledge-card effort. McCarthy had seen these clippings and during his earlier campaigning had heard comments that gave him the sense that the use of the pledge card might backfire.

The pledge-card issue was smoldering near the surface in the campaign, but no one had quite yet been able to frame it as an issue. McCarthy began his speech with a brief summary of his reaction to New Hampshire campaigning:

> I have been campaigning two days in New Hampshire, today and one day about a week and one-half ago, and unless you're more mischievous than I have been led to believe, I've had a very good response. . . .
>
> If the response has been genuine in these two days and, if anything, it may have led me to be a little overconfident about my campaign for the nomination of the Democratic Party.
>
> (McCarthy speech transcript, p. 1)

He then went into a discussion of political parties and specifically the Democratic Party. He first chided the state for its peculiar treatment of Independent voters which was prompted by an editorial he read before coming to the community center. The editorial appeared in the *Concord Daily Monitor* and speculated on how Richard Nixon expected to win the Republican primary by attracting the Independent voter. The section of interest to McCarthy read:

Democrats can't vote in the Republican primaries. Independents can stay home in the primaries, as they have done in the past to maintain their independence of political parties, or they can choose to identify with one or the other.

Independents may participate in the New Hampshire primaries but probably not in large numbers. There is little reason to believe that those who do will vote for Nixon.

Two motives may cause Independents to join in the primaries. One is anti-war sentiment, which is more likely to cause them to vote Democratic, for Senator McCarthy.

The other is desire for a change, and that would cause them to vote Republican, but probably for the most electable Republican, Nelson Rockefeller.

(*Concord Daily Monitor,* February 6, 1968)

McCarthy picked up the theme of the dilemma of the Independent when he said:

I know some of you are Republicans, I assume that, and some of you are Independents, and that in New Hampshire, you lead rather a strange life, as Independents; once you commit yourselves, you're committed either to the party which you identify with or to the other, which is a terrible prospect, it seems to me.

If you decide to be Democrats, you ought to have some other choice than to become Republicans if you want to change. I hope we could work something out on that matter, as a matter of a new civil rights bill, I think, which we could take up.

(McCarthy, op. cit., p. 2)

With this brief analysis McCarthy touched a point of inequity in the New Hampshire primary system. Few had been much concerned about the Independent's problem before. Prior to the 1972 presidential primary season the registration law would be changed, allowing reregistration as an Independent. Of special concern to McCarthy was what had become of the institution of the American political party.

A political party is really the essential element of American politics, and it is important for us . . . in presidential election years . . . to give some thought to what a party is. We're inclined to—and I think quite properly—ridicule them and to joke about them most of the time, but there are occasions when we ought to give some thought to what their real purpose is and how they ought to function and what role they play in determining policy for the United States.

I would suggest, first, that we ought to be clear about what a political party is not. It is certainly not a club, not a kind of last-man club or something set up to ensure jobs for those who hold them by patronage or by other devices.

> It's not really a labor union or an extension of the labor movement.... It should not be looked upon as an instrument of propaganda because it has a role beyond that. It has a role to propagandize some and to educate some, but it has a practical political purpose beyond propaganda, and if that was all that I was concerned about or what you were concerned about, the Democrats here, why, we could be off with a third party movement of some kind. . . . and there are some people who seem to want to do that, in this country, with the issue of the war in Vietnam. . . . who would, as I've said, rather light bonfires on the hill, instead of coming down into the valley where the real political action. . . . and the real political fight must be carried out.
>
> A political party is not even an organization, and we Democrats knew that to be true, but it shouldn't be an organization. This is the point. It ought to be organic. It's not something to be taken over and controlled and directed, but it's something which must be alive and which must grow and which must have its own vitality.
>
> (McCarthy, op. cit., p. 3)

"A party," he noted, "is really set up to develop the issues, consider the problems of the country and to pick candidates, and then to go on from that to gain control over the government of the country, and that's not a very modest objective in these United States. . . . The important thing to keep in mind is that once you gain control, its not supposed to rule for the good of the majority but by the determination of that majority, but to rule for the good of all." The reason for this conclusion, McCarthy stated, was because the party contends that it could represent all. Here he revealed the essence of his philosophy toward the role of the political party and his view of the purpose of his campaign.

> In our party, the Democratic Party, through the years, we've been able to put together what seemed to be complete contradictions. We were the party that supposedly represented the country and also the city. We claimed that we could represent labor and also agriculture.
>
> We said that we could represent both the North and the South; we could represent the Baptists and also the Catholics who were supposed to be beyond any kind of mixing, but all of these, somehow, put together in the party, each one a kind of separate minority, each one having a position which was antagonistic in some ways, if they pursued only their self-interest . . . taken all together, this kind of majority, made up of all these different groups and different forces and different interests, could make determinations which would be good for the country as a whole.
>
> I think, really the basis upon which great things have been achieved in this the 20th century, by the Democratic Party—we were the party which gloried in dissent and in disagreement.
>
> (McCarthy, op. cit., pp. 4–5)

McCarthy then asked, "But where do we find our party today? What is the position of the Democratic Party leadership in Washington and, I might say, New Hampshire, on the matter of dissent? Well, generally, they say, 'let us have no dissent.' The cry is for unity. I think, on the record, in our party, the request for unity usually comes about the last day of the National Convention and sometimes, not until two or three weeks after. "But to be out, as Democrats," McCarthy chided, "saying in January and February, that we ought to have unity on an issue of vital moral significance, even before we've gone through any primaries, and even before we've anticipated a convention . . . is, I'd say, contrary to every tradition of the Democratic party, and really, contrary to the tradition of politics in the United States."

McCarthy then challenged his audience, "I think it all important, here in New Hampshire, that you make the first stand, Democrats, Independents, and Republicans, in so far as you can help, to stand against that suggestion and to prevent the establishment of what might develop into a wholly undesirable tradition in American politics."

Then he began "feeding" from the New Hampshire political landscape to frame an issue that illustrated what was happening to the democracy of the political party. This was what came to be known as "vintage McCarthy–1968" in the making.

> I was somewhat surprised to find out what devices the Democratic party organization here is proposing to use in order to ensure a write-in for the candidate of the party's choice—a matter of assigning numbers in triplicate so that they know who has the number and who gave it to you and, supposedly, where you go with the number.
>
> If this were to be carried out, it would seem to me, it would really tend to destroy the whole reputation that this State has in the Democratic Party for free and open primary election.
>
> This proposal, with the numbered pledges, comes closest, I think, to denying people the right of a secret ballot in a primary of any suggestion that I've seen or heard of in the country, and I hope that you will all stand boldly against it.
>
> (McCarthy, op. cit., p. 6)

The audience burst into applause with the cheerleaders being those seated at the press table. Studds and I, standing at the back of the room, grinned like the proverbial Cheshire cats knowing that not only did we have a candidate of substance but we now had an important issue that could be developed in the context of the New Hampshire political ethos.

Since McCarthy had hit a responsive chord in his audience, he did not let the subject die until he had added one of his favorite illustrative themes.

> It's more or less as though the whole Democratic Party in this country were being asked to submit to rather a kind of single identification, as though we were all to bear a particular brand and there was to be no independence of spirit, no independence of judgment, and no independence of action.

> Out in the Midwest, and I might say, also Texas, it helps some in understanding the administration in criticizing it, to have some knowledge of how cattle are handled.
>
> It creeps into the language of the administration, these figures of speech and the metaphors of the administration, things like "cut and run."
>
> Well "cut and run," if you're dealing with cattle, is a pretty good thing to do, if you're being stampeded. It's the only way you can get out, and if you're being stampeded over the cliff or into the shipping yards, why, the best thing to do is to "cut and run."
>
> We make a distinction out home, also, with reference to particular kinds of brands which, I think, ought to be explained to you.
>
> They have what you call a "hair brand" and, also a "hide brand." Now, if it's a hair brand, it doesn't really get into the hide. It grows out in one season. I hope most of you have no more than that, as Democrats, and that it will grow out before the next primary comes along, and you can vote as independent Democrats. You haven't been burned into the hide and, therefore, committed to a particular purpose or to a particular program, as it has been suggested by some of your party leaders here in New Hampshire.
>
> (McCarthy, op. cit., p. 3)

McCarthy then made the transition to the essence of his campaign and the serious concerns of those who had come to consider him. "Taken all together, of course, the issues are too important for any of us to yield to this kind of—it's not really compulsion, in the strict sense of the word, but it's a kind of pressure, a kind of move to limit the freedom of choice and the freedom of action, on the part of the electorate in this state and, beyond it, in some of the other states of the country. I think all of you know, at least, what I think are the important issues and what I'm satisfied all of you do think of as the important issues, basically, the question of the war in Vietnam."

McCarthy approached the issue of the war by not discussing the facts of the war itself but by discussing the consequences of the war. His first concern was that the issues be adequately presented and discussed "in such context that they (the people) can make a judgment on it," not simply by a debate by the U.S. Senate or a plank in the platform of the Democratic National Convention but by taking the issue directly to the people and letting them respond in the primaries. He saw little validity to the notion that "if you raise questions about a military policy, you're unpatriotic," and "that patriotism stops, somehow, at the water's edge." A concept "which we cannot accept because the obligation to be patriotic and a loyal critic of national policy applies to domestic programs; it applies to international programs; it applies to the Pentagon and to the Central Intelligence Agency and to the State Department, just as it does to the Treasury Department or the Department of Health, Education, and Welfare, or the Department of Agriculture or Labor." (McCarthy, op. cit., p. 9)

His second concern related to the consequence of the war as it distracted the nation from its "pressing domestic problems," but the issue that he was to discuss in detail that evening was what he considered of "almost equal importance and underneath, perhaps, of even more importance and that is the growing militarization of American foreign policy, the growing influence of our military establishment. . . ." An audience visibly relaxed as McCarthy continued not with strident litany of the horrors and atrocities of the war but with a carefully developed thesis of how war had grown as the consequences of post-World War II foreign policy and international strategy.

McCarthy had anticipated the mood of his audience well. There would be little tolerance for militant dissent or verbal pictures of the ugliness of war. Probably no one in the audience liked war but few would say that they would not support a war if it was necessary and just. What had brought them to hear McCarthy that evening were questions, not yet fully formed or capable of articulation, questions that revealed skepticism, uncertainty, insecurity, and even a fear that for the first time in many of their lives they were not committed to what their national government had pledged them to. McCarthy understood the nature and even the scope of this concern. He sensed that this was a new concern, something unfamiliar and personally disturbing. It tended to disrupt not only one's view toward one's government but also relations with friends, neighbors, and, even more distressingly, one's family.

To have talked about the field operations of the war, its civilian and/or military leadership, its consequence at home with specifics of draft resistance or street protest, would have made his audience uncomfortable, even hostile. What he did instead was establish a dialogue between himself and his audience. His discussion was slightly abstract, tied to times, events, and personalities not immediately but with a logical connection to current events that could be supplied by the listeners if they chose. He was reassuring with respect to his faith that the nation's political institutions could be made to work, challenged his listeners to act through these institutions, and outlined the rewards. He concluded his quiet dialogue breaking the spell only with his closing words:

> This, as I see it, is the total complex and context of issues with which we have to deal in the year 1968, and I hesitate to say that this is a most critical year, or the most critical year for American politics. There may have been times in the past in the early history of this country, or at the time of the Civil War when the decisions which were made were more significant, when the threat of some kind of deterioration and collapse of the Republic were more pressing than they are now.
>
> But I do think that this is a most important campaign because America is on the verge of becoming a great world leader. The question that we have to decide, at least in part, is whether we will give direction to that leadership by continuing a kind of militaristic policy, which now seems to be in the ascendancy, or whether we will attempt to blunt that thrust. To suggest—and—not to suggest—but to make a reality—by injecting into American politics and into American government the acceptance that this nation is not to make its record in the history of the world as a military power, but by demonstrating all of those things which we claim for ourselves. The right to life, liberty and the pursuit of happiness, and a basic belief in a non-military approach, and a basic belief in

> freedom and self determination—that these are the real strengths of America, and that these are the gifts that we have to offer the rest of the world.
>
> (McCarthy, op. cit., p. 18)

McCarthy's argument, his language, and his tone worked with his audience much like the measured beat of a large pendulum. With each swing it punctuated a point and with each point the swing of the argument or the illustration became ever so slightly more forceful. With each speech after the Concord address, McCarthy found his audience willing to accept more of the national policy critique, until toward the end of the campaign they had accepted much of his indictment and willingly heard it in stronger tones and language.

An open question session followed Senator McCarthy's address. The questions showed that McCarthy had tapped the deep concerns of his audience and would now deal with the specifics of issues that were on their minds. His answers were thoughtful yet precise and were often followed by prolonged applause as if the audience felt relief, even gratitude that there was, at last, someone believable and deserving of their attention.

The *Concord Daily Monitor* carried a letter to the editor that day which, when read afterwards, captured the spirit of the evening.

> Sir: I submit the following recipe for your readers: Take one middle-aged, lukewarm Republican—get him thinking about the war in Vietnam until he is worried sick; cause him to be vitally concerned for the survival of mankind; deny him an acceptable presidential candidate in his own party—leave him groping in a twilight zone of confusion without safe or sound leadership—Expose him to the Democratic presidential hopeful, Senator Eugene McCarthy—let simmer until March.
>
> Elaine D. Finch of Henniker
> (*Concord Daily Monitor*, February 6, 1968)

To end this extraordinary campaign day, Senator McCarthy would then play hockey for twenty minutes. Hockey is the big winter sport of school children and is especially popular among the strongly Democratic French-Canadian populations of most of New Hampshire's cities. In fact, Berlin, New Hampshire, calls itself "Hockey Town USA." Skiing tended to be the sport of the "out-of-stater" or the wealthier families. For the backbone of the working Democratic Party hockey was the sport. David Underwood told McCarthy to go home and practice, anticipating a future visit when McCarthy would have the chance to go on the ice. "It's all right," said the Senator in reply, "I'm a good player, I don't need to practice," and he didn't. (Underwood, op. cit., p. 19)

I had had enough experience with McCarthy's schedules to know that something like skating could not be confirmed ahead of time, but if the option were open then McCarthy might do it if he was in the mood. That night a Concord Old Timers game was scheduled in the local skating arena. Two of the senator's Concord supporters, Drs. Roland Hok and Anthony Bower, regularly played with the team. When asked whether McCarthy could join the game if he wished, they consulted the other team members who said yes and also said they could provide suitable equipment.

Obviously pleased by his reception during the long day of campaigning and by the reaction to his speech, Senator McCarthy would now demonstrate a further facet of his character and another one that would not be lost in its comparison to George Romney. He would not only skate but he would don the protective gear and play hockey. In fact the Old Timers team was made up of "old-timers," mostly under thirty, who had played hockey in high school and college, with a few having played semiprofessionally as well. When McCarthy came on the ice he was treated like another member of the opposition taking a turn on the ice. He beat the opponent in face-offs, was checked, skated hard, handled the puck well, and fell to the ice in the tumble of the play.

I had been delayed at the community center and when I entered the arena, McCarthy had been on the ice almost twenty minutes. Underwood grabbed me by the arm saying, "Your candidate is winded—you better get him off the ice." A fifty-one-year-old man has to be in reasonably good shape to play any hockey but to survive twenty minutes in a game was asking a lot. McCarthy responded to my wave and he left the ice, but not before the few reporters and photographers who had followed him to the arena had recorded the event.

Impact of February 6

For the reporters and for McCarthy observers outside New Hampshire, February 6 marked the first day of substantial campaigning. In the space of fourteen hours McCarthy had successfully ended any future contrasts with the style of the ex-governor of Michigan, George Romney; shown his effectiveness as a diverse campaigner capable of eliciting a favorable response on the street, at factory gates, inside the plants, from conservative service clubs, and before a sizable civic audience. He also demonstrated an ability to handle difficult and polarizing subjects in a manner that showed his insight without being confrontational.

For his New Hampshire campaigners, McCarthy had shown his ability to provide them with both the issues and the style of a potentially successful campaign. McCarthy had sensed what the political ethos of New Hampshire required. Personal sincerity, a calm, restrained, yet confident presence, a quick wit, ready smile—personified in McCarthy's tall, rather gray, presidential appearance—seemed naturally to bring people to him without harangue or hoopla. Instead of the tension that often accompanies a political campaign, McCarthy had the ability to relax and then to engage those he met. In addition, McCarthy now showed that he was willing to work very hard in New Hampshire, even play hockey at the end of a long day—not just to help out but because he wanted to and knew he could perform well.

He gave his campaign an important issue when he framed in his speech the potential threat to the voter that was implied by the Johnson campaign's pledge card. Both the twenty minutes of hockey and the brief comments on the pledge card gave the New Hampshire campaign, and especially the reporters, items that were uniquely representative of the New Hampshire campaign image and that could be used as indications of McCarthy' s energy and the political earthiness.

Those who would have liked to write McCarthy off as an "intellectual" or "aloof" or "professorial," now had to contend with an image of McCarthy shown playing a rough game of hockey. From such images reporters wrote their stories and supporters began to perk up not only in New Hampshire but across the nation.

Harry Kelly's AP story datelined Concord, N.H. led:

> At a time when presidential aspirants like to show the voters their skill at sports, Sen. Eugene McCarthy has set a new athletic standard—taking part in a rough game of ice hockey.
>
> In a yellow sweatshirt, black trousers, a red helmet and borrowed skates the Minnesota Democrat—challenging President Johnson's Vietnam war policies in primaries—skated out on the ice rink here Tuesday night to join in a game of hockey. . . .
>
> Before swinging into the hockey game—a favorite sport with New Hampshire voters—McCarthy took a shot at the regular Democratic party in New Hampshire, which has not welcomed his challenge of President Johnson. . . .
>
> The Senator took exception . . . to a card circulated in New Hampshire under the label of the Democratic state committee. . . .
>
> (*Nashua Telegraph,* February 7, 1968, p. 1)

In every story carried of the day's activities, playing hockey was an important part. The *Foster's Daily Democrat* of Dover, New Hampshire, headlined its story, "McCarthy Plays Hockey." *Newsweek* captioned its picture, "Senator McCarthy: Hawkish on Ice," and led its story with the phrase, "The Iceman Runneth." (*Newsweek*, February 19, 1968) *Time* magazine's story led, "On Thin Ice," with a picture caption which read, "Time for the Face Off." (*Time,* February 16, 1968)

The attention the press gave to McCarthy's hockey gave us the idea of trying to capitalize further on it in hockey crazy New Hampshire—especially Berlin. We wanted to buy ice scrapers in the shape of a hockey stick that we could hand out in Berlin, but we had to compromise on an ice scraper printed with a picture of a hockey player that read "McCarthy for President, he cuts the ice."

John DeGrace, who was helping in New Hampshire from the Massachusetts McCarthy organization, arranged for quick delivery of approximately ten thousand of the scrapers. These were then handed out to shoppers or at the factory gates in Berlin, with some being used in other strong hockey towns.

McCarthy's attack on the Johnson campaigns pledge card provided us with our best piece of ammunition. His remarks during the Concord speech and in subsequent press conferences started a political brushfire that could not be controlled by the New Hampshire Johnson committee. Studds and I requested that a flyer be printed that would attack the Johnson campaign's pledge card.

The flyer Weston Associates designed and printed in large numbers read, "What ever happened to the secret ballot?" It displayed a photograph of one of the serial numbered, in triplicate, pledge cards, with "You don't have to sign anything to vote for Senator Eugene McCarthy. On March 12, let Lyndon Johnson know it. McCarthy for President."

Now Studds and I had to decide what to do with the return card we had had Weston Associates prepare for a mailing that was about to leave our headquarters. Forty thousand to fifty thousand of the return cards had been printed and were at the printer awaiting completion of the remaining items in the order. The pledge-card issue had become too hot an issue in the campaign to allow the Johnson leaders to reduce its impact by saying that the McCarthy campaign also had a pledge card.

At the Sunday, February 11 meeting of the statewide McCarthy committee, I held up a proof copy of the return card and asked, "Does this look like a pledge card?" The unanimous response from the twenty or so assembled was that even though it was not at all like the Johnson pledge card, it could easily be misconstrued as a pledge card and the issue might well be lost.

Merv Weston attended the meeting and agreed that we should not take the chance. I returned the proof to Weston, and he promised to have the printer destroy every scrap associated with the printing. Since there are few secrets in politics, the Johnson campaign heard about the return card project and countercharged that the McCarthy campaign had planned to use a pledge card too. After almost ten days of cascading abuse concerning their pledge card, Senator Tom McIntyre charged that the McCarthy campaign had one too. Gerry Studds replied:

> Yesterday, in Manchester, Senator Tom McIntyre asserted that the New Hampshire campaign plans of Senator Eugene McCarthy included something akin to the intimidating system of numbered pledge cards being used by Johnson supporters in this state.
>
> No such thing is now contemplated, nor has it ever been contemplated. We once discussed the possibility of including in our statewide mailings to all Democrats and Independents a return mailer soliciting volunteer assistance and financial contributions. Even this idea was discarded some time ago.
>
> Senator McIntyre would do well to check his facts before making any more of the irresponsible statements which have begun to characterize the Johnson campaign in New Hampshire.
>
> (McCarthy press release, February 15, 1968)

THE REPORTERS AND THE PLEDGE CARD

The LBJ committee's pledge card was an issue ready-made for the press. All Senator McCarthy had to do was mention it, provide a context for the reporters to evaluate it, and then almost not mention the subject again except when asked. On February 8 the *Boston Herald* wrote an early editorial titled, "Check-Off List for LBJ," which in its lead read:

> Voting in a party primary ought to be as sacrosanct as voting in an election, with no interference, pressure or cajoling to confound the voters.
>
> That principle doesn't seem to prevail in New Hampshire, however, where the Democratic organization is baldly soliciting party members for

pledges that they will write in votes for Lyndon Baines Johnson in the March 12. . . . Sen. Eugene McCarthy . . . likens the roundup of pledges to cattle herding, although he says the gimmick may be merely a local inspiration to demonstrate loyalty to Lyndon Johnson. . . .

There is nothing illegal about the pledges, though they certainly seem presumptuous and meddling. One would think the regular Democrats would be confident of putting down Sen. McCarthy's challenge to the President without soliciting reassurance beforehand. Why should a Democrat enrolled in New Hampshire be asked directly to pledge his vote to any candidate? If a Democrat fails to sign and return his pledge or refuses to do so on principle, will he be considered disloyal to Lyndon Johnson or to the regular Democratic organization?

New Hampshire Democrats would be wise to discard their scheme of pledges to the President and to spend their energies persuading fellow Democrats that the President's pledge to the nation are worth unsubscribed write-in votes.

(*Boston Herald*, February 8, 1968)

Concord Daily Monitor columnist Jack Hubbard began stirring the pledge-card issue in New Hampshire with an approach that was pursued frequently by other reporters. He began calling both Johnson and McCarthy supporters for their reaction to the use of the pledge-card scheme. In his column dated February 8 he wrote, "The Johnson Democrat's pledge card campaign could backfire." Then he quoted state representative and McCarthy supporter, Jean Wallin, who said, "I think you are signing your right away to make a decision in the voting booth. It is the people who refuse to sign the cards. I am not saying anything will happen to those people . . . it is just the idea." (*Concord Daily Monitor*, February 8, 1968)

In a report Boutin prepared for a meeting of the LBJ campaign leaders he said that the pledge-card campaign was producing "excellent results" after the first week of operation. In the news story on his report Boutin said that large quantities of the numbered cards were being mailed to President Johnson in what Boutin called "a concrete sign of the support the President has here in New Hampshire." (*Nashua Telegraph*, February 9, 1968)

Richard W. Daly writing in the *Boston Herald-Traveler*, February 9 under the headline, "LBJ Forces Running Out of Gimmicks," said:

The teapot tempest in New Hampshire over the crude maneuver by backers of President Johnson to solicit loyalty pledges from voters illustrates once again the difficulties inherent in campaigning without a candidate. . . . Most significant, they are numbered. It is as if some aspiring Big Brother impatient for 1984 plans to pinpoint just who is faithful and who is not, lest some future postmaster ship fall into the wrong hands. . . .

(*Boston Herald-Traveler*, February 9, 1968)

John H. Fenton, New England reporter for the *New York Times*, wrote an article on February 9 that began to uncover the attitude of the Johnson campaign toward the pledge-card effort now that it was becoming controversial. Fenton reported:

> The first reaction to information kits that are being distributed among Democratic ward and town chairmen is that the White House is engaged in an arm-twisting campaign. Senator McCarthy . . . commented with a chuckle:
>
> If there is a difference of one vote between the number of pledges and the number of registered voters, then all are traitors and all must die.
>
> . . . But the cries of anguish were being heard among some rank-and-file Democrats over a three-section pledge care that each voter is asked to sign. . . .
>
> "Are we supposed to go to confession in public?" asked one Democrat who has already filed as a delegate favorable to the nomination of Mr. Johnson. . . .
>
> But Richard Weston, of Gov. King's staff at the State House, said the purpose of the numbering was to make sure that local chairmen and other coordinators distributed the cards. . . .
>
> As soon as the individual voter's name has been returned to headquarters, he will be sent an acknowledgment that his pledge is being forwarded "with thanks and deep appreciation" to the White House. The acknowledgment is signed by Governor King and by Senator Thomas J. Mclntyre. . . .
>
> A party leader in Hanover, who said he had heard about the pledge cards but had not yet received one, said:
>
> I think I am going to write in Hubert Humphrey for President, what the hell.
>
> (*New York Times*, February 9, 1968)

The *Sunday Boston Herald-Traveler* carried a major story on the New Hampshire presidential primary that included a reproduction of the serially numbered pledge card. New Hampshire newspapers began to print letters to the editor critical of the pledge card to an extent where it seemed that there was little else of interest in the campaign.

In her nationally syndicated column, Mary McGrory was also captured by the pledge-card issue when under the heading, "McCarthy Thrives On LBJ 'Pledges'," she wrote, "Sen. Eugene McCarthy said enigmatically a month ago that he expected to live off the land in New Hampshire, nobody paid much attention. But lately, thanks to an issue provided by his opposition, he has been doing just that, and thriving." She then recounted how the card was designed and that when signed, it would bring the signer "an engraved thank you from Governor King and Senator Tom McIntyre, but also a photograph of President and Mrs. Johnson standing on the steps of Air Force One."

Mary McGrory took the story back to the White House where the president's press secretary, George Christian, was asked whether Governor King had spoken as "an agent of President Johnson" when the governor had called McCarthy "an advocate of appeasement" in a counterattack on McCarthy's successful pledge-card characterization. McGrory reported that Christian "professed ignorance of the governor's remarks . . . but elsewhere in the administration, it was conceded that the pledge cards were a minor tactical error.'" Her report concluded:

> The violent reaction of the President's managers tells McCarthy that he has struck a raw nerve in opening up the question of presidential coercion. As a critic of the war, McCarthy had been tagged "a one-issue candidate." Now he is letting events speak for themselves in Vietnam, and effectively calling on the voters of New Hampshire not to let themselves be pushed around.
>
> (*Boston Globe,* February 16, 1968)

In spite of what appeared to observers as a picture of rats fleeing the sinking ship of the pledge-card campaign, Boutin persisted. Speaking in Keene, Boutin now "termed the use of the numbered pledge cards as a 'petition to President Johnson to run again'," contending "the use of the cards was consistent with the First Amendment which allows petition to the government." (*Valley News,* February 19, 1968)

On the same day Senator Tom McIntyre spoke at a kickoff session of "Pledge to Johnson Week" at a Nashua motel. Boutin, also attending, said, "Do not be fooled by the phony issue being raised by the other candidate when he proclaims we are invading the secrecy of the ballot with our pledge card campaign. The pledge card campaign was no more of an invasion of privacy than when our opponent asks his supporters to wear campaign buttons or attach bumper strips to their cars." (*Nashua Telegraph,* February 19, 1968)

Now almost totally on the defensive concerning the pledge card and what they had come to represent for many voters, the Johnson campaign faced a series of highly critical editorials that renewed the assault. The *Portsmouth Herald* said, "There is growing evidence that New Hampshire's Democratic party bosses may have overplayed their hand in their eagerness to promote write-in support for President Johnson. . . ." The editorial went on to suggest that Senator McIntyre, who the paper had supported, would do well to disassociate himself from Governor King in his attacks on Senator McCarthy. The result, they contended, was giving McCarthy "underdog status" which will "surely win him sympathy." (*Portsmouth Herald,* February 19, 1968)

The press, infatuated with the pledge-card issue, neglected some of its serious reportorial business. This lack was detected early on when a woman wrote criticizing the *Concord Daily Monitor* for not covering "the major subject of his [February 6] speech—the growth and power of the military-industrial complex. . . . Your failure to do so in reporting the Senator's talk smacks of editorializing a news item. Also, I am rapidly tiring of the tendency on your part and that of the other media of presenting McCarthy as simply anti-Johnson and anti-Vietnam without giving him credit for creativity or constructiveness. Signed: Diana Anderson." (*Concord Daily Monitor,* February 10, 1968)

By the end of February the pledge-card issue faded as the Johnson leaders shifted to an aggressive attack on McCarthy's Vietnam policies and the implications of those policies. By then even Bernard Boutin appeared to hope that the pledge cards were forgotten and for almost a two-week period they were gone as the stream of consciousness of a political campaign moved on. But on March 7, Mark Drogin, a reporter for the *Concord Daily Monitor*, made a series of telephone calls that produced one of the funnier stories of the campaign. It began when Governor King was asked how many of the cards had been sent to Washington, and he said that more than "twenty-five thousand pledge cards had been sent to the White House." He continued:

> As they come in, the New Hampshire Democrats for Johnson keep sending 'em on down. And the White House keeps mailing 'em back.
>
> If that sounds confusing, it's an improvement over Monday when the Governor's office said they weren't being mailed out, the Director of Democrats for Johnson said they had been for the past week, and the White House said it didn't know anything about it. Now it seems it does.
>
> Asst. Press Secretary Robert Fleming told the *Monitor* yesterday afternoon that "there were a few of those cards around" and that instructions are they "go back to Mr. Boutin."
>
> At the latest count, that's 25,000 little pledge cards going hither and thither.
>
> The Democrats for Johnson know about the hither but the word is yet to get around about the thither.
>
> Democratic Campaign Headquarters in Manchester . . . said Gov. King was right about the cards going out.
>
> In fact, said a young lady, "they're addressed to Mr. W. Marvin Watson . . . special assistant to the President."
>
> Could she explain why the White House was returning them?
>
> "They're mailing back all the cards?" She couldn't. Neither could John Barker, Johnson campaign aide in Manchester. He explained that, "Hmmmm, that's a surprise."
>
> Not just surprised but angry are New Hampshirites who have discovered that somebody else had been signing their names to the pledge cards.
>
> Earlier this week Eugene S. Daniell Jr. complained aloud that half the pledge cards in Franklin were forgeries and that counterfeits were cropping up all over the countryside.
>
> At least two were found in Concord yesterday.
>
> The assumption on the part of those not for Johnson . . . was that local campaigners found it easier to sit home and sign other people's names to pledge cards than to go out and solicit genuine signatures.
>
> William Craig, head of the State Democratic Committee, had replied that such might be the case in part, but he was checking it out and not overlooking the possibility that the pledge card peculiarities could have been a ploy by the McCarthy supporters.
>
> He didn't consider it a laughing matter.

A number of other persons do.

The business of pledge cards, good and bad, being mailed to here and gone, is most humorous to McCarthy Headquarters.

(*Concord Monitor*, March 8, 1968 pp. 1, 10)

The great pledge-card mystery ended with the voters entering New Hampshire voting booths March 12 without any satisfactory answer as to what actually happened to the White House portions of the cards that were signed.

McCARTHY'S LOCAL ORGANIZATION

Two factors in the organization of the McCarthy campaign were especially important to its success. The first was the existence of a large and effective local organization. The second was the involvement of large numbers of volunteers—both from inside and outside New Hampshire. To make a distinction between "local organization" and "volunteers" is difficult since all the local organizations relied on volunteers for staff and support, but in order to relate the importance of the local organization and then to, likewise, relate the effectiveness of the volunteer, a distinction is necessary. That distinction is one of saying volunteers are out-of-staters who came to work while the local organization is composed of in-staters and local residents.

In virtually every community where the McCarthy campaign was organized a separate story of that organization could be told. Each would be unique—containing its own anecdotes and reasons for success or failure. To illustrate differences in local organization three cases are selected that contain most of the positive and negative aspects of the local effort during the ten-week 1968 campaign. The three cities are Keene, Manchester, and Berlin.

Keene: Depth and Innovation

The Keene McCarthy organization was formed from a preexisting antiwar activist political group that had been seeking ways to demonstrate unhappiness with the administration's policies in Vietnam. As a political organization the group's members were largely amateurs coming to the campaign with little actual political experience but with substantial social and community service contacts within the community.

Keene, a city with a 1960 U.S. census population of 17,500, was the trading and services center of surrounding Cheshire County which contained 43,300 persons. Long the trading hub for a largely agricultural region, Keene retained a Yankee population character unlike most of New Hampshire's cities. It had become a manufacturing center only during the 1950s. The industry that had located in the Keene area produced electrical machinery, optical products, miniature ball bearings, and other products required by growing sectors of the national economy. Keene had experienced a boom of substantial proportions during a period when other New Hampshire cities were barely retaining their industries or actually losing employment opportunities. Keene became an importer of workers, managers, and related service activities.

The city and surrounding area became attractive as a residential area for those employed in or serving area manufacturing and commercial establishments. In addition, Cheshire County has long been an attractive retirement area and, with improved air transportation and highway connections to New York and Boston, it became even more appealing. Coinciding with these growth trends was an expansion of the former Keene State Teachers College into a four-year, diversified, higher education segment of the unified University of New Hampshire system.

Keene is unlike other New Hampshire cities that are affected by the influence of Concord, Manchester, and Boston. Keene has had a lengthy history of isolation within the center of New Hampshire's southwesternmost Cheshire County. To the immediate west is the city of Brattleboro, Vermont, which has served as a channel for trade and commerce to the Keene area from the north-south axis of the Connecticut River Valley, and to the south are the Massachusetts industrial cities of Fitchburg, Worcester, Athol, and Greenfield. Manchester and Nashua, the nearest New Hampshire cities, are more than fifty miles to the east over narrow, even in 1968, twisting roads. If there is a kinship between New Hampshire cities, Keene is more like Concord in its social and economic traditions than it is any other city of the state—and, perhaps, for the same reasons that Concord proved to be good political ground for Senator McCarthy, so did Keene.

Keene's new population of managers, professionals, executives, and their families provided a younger, civic minded, activist cadre that had experienced the feelings of success in both the their personal and civic lives. Civic pride, youthful political leadership, coupled with energy, and boosterism had changed Keene from a staid, even stagnant, old, Yankee New England city into a place of vitality.

Certainly not an insignificant part of the changed Keene was the leadership of the *Keene Evening Sentinel.* Its owner and publisher, James Ewing, professed a progressive editorial philosophy that was somewhere between Bull Moose Progressivism and FDR New Dealism. While maintaining an independent editorial stance, Ewing could almost always be found on the side of social activism and positive public energy.

He and his newspaper were constantly critical of the publisher of the *Manchester Union Leader,* William Loeb, and Loeb's editorial impact on the politics of New Hampshire. As the *Union Leader* is the dominant newspaper in its city, so the *Keene Evening Sentinel* is the dominant publication in Keene. The *Sentinel* served as a powerful legitimizing institution for the concerns that ultimately were reflected in the organization that would become the Keene McCarthy for President Committee.

Led by Keene State College professors John Wiseman and David Gregory, a small group of concerned Keene residents and students had begun meeting to discuss the war and how they might use the presidential primary as a means of protesting the administration war policies. Included in the group were Connie Wood and Professor David and Barbara Battenfeld.

During the late fall of 1967 they had agreed they would carry on some form of political action—whether to tie in with Eugene Daniell and his Robert Kennedy write-in campaign or to run their own teach-in community education program was the question. They had sent a representative or two to the later McCarthy organizational meetings, but at the time McCarthy announced they had not decided to become involved in the campaign. Because they had been cautious in their activities to that time in Keene, they had succeeded in expanding the credibility of their efforts while avoiding much of the polarization that such groups had experienced in other communities across the country.

The newspaper covered their activities sympathetically while maintaining a certain distance. Deciding whether or not to become involved with a candidate rather than to continue being involved with the issue of the war alone was, for them, a major decision. They were deeply skeptical of partisan politics. They had not had much experience with party politics and did not have favorable images of partisan campaigns.

Shortly after McCarthy announced that he would enter the New Hampshire presidential primary, the Keene group met and decided to back his candidacy as, principally, a means of protesting the administration's Vietnam policies. They contacted me and I met with them to discuss how they should organize their activities. They took the items of the organizing memorandum that had been presented at the January 7 meeting of the McCarthy Steering Committee and made it their own agenda. They saw that a headquarters had been designated for Keene and immediately made that their first target. They knew that in order to open the headquarters, they would need money. This led to two actions, the first being to develop a fund-raising strategy, and the second, to organize themselves so that there would be designated responsibilities.

I asked them to coordinate their activities closely with those of the state headquarters, warning that the surest way to fail would be if conflict developed between the local and state committee. While I noted that there would be very little support from the state organization except for materials, it was still imperative that a close working relationship be maintained.

The Keene committee did not presume to know much about political organization and wanted to make sure that each of their actions was in accord with what the state leadership had in mind and would approve. While amazed at the energy and speed of the Keene people, Studds and I were still a bit skeptical since neither of us had worked with any of these people previously. We hoped the committee's resolve to support McCarthy would remain in spite of what we feared might be an internal conflict between the original issue thrust of the Keene group's efforts and their recently found commitment to a political campaign.

This concern was tested early in February when I received a call from John Wiseman saying that his people had run out of things to do and wanted to begin a door-to-door canvass of Keene area voters. Studds and I had mentioned the possibility of a canvass in a December 21 memorandum to McCarthy but had not had the time to develop a plan of procedure. In fact, neither of us had had previous experience with a canvass and, to our knowledge, none had ever been conducted before as the part of a statewide campaign. In the spirit of a campaign that was being run in a "fast and loose" manner, I was given enough assurance by Wiseman to say okay to the canvassing idea.

Wiseman and the other Keene workers carefully proceeded in their planning of the canvass and again checked each of the details with us before heading into the field. I had suggested that they test the activity in a part of the city that they knew would be sympathetic so that they might gain some experience before tackling parts of the city where the reception might be less than cordial.

I also asked Wiseman to call back with a report of how the canvassing had gone, urging Wiseman to avoid confrontations or much more than a passive form of exchange at the door. Wiseman wanted something that would communicate a bit more forcefully both McCarthy's candidacy and the reasons for his candidacy. I then advised Wiseman to experiment with both, using canvassers who would be both passive and active in their door-to-door contact, then evaluate the results.

What we both overlooked was that there was no special literature for canvassing purposes. A slow production process at the Washington headquarters meant that little or no literature was available in New Hampshire for Wiseman's experiment.

Undaunted, Wiseman said they would develop and mimeograph some position flyers from McCathy's public statements. (See pages 291 and 292.) One was devoted to McCarthy's Vietnam policy and another to McCarthy's domestic policy. With minimum direction and with sensitivity to the overall purpose of the candidacy, the Keene committee was successful in not only organizing tasks that had been set out as important by the state leadership, but in also being able to expand the scope of the campaign through their initiative.

Shortly after the election on March 12, the Keene organization prepared a brief report on their activities in the form of organization and canvassing suggestions. In canvassing the bulk of the work should be done with adults willing to talk to adults rather than having students carry the canvass. With an initial success in the test using adults and also being a bit more active in the door contact, we found that the reception was encouraging. The Keene committee used some older college students in their canvass and found the results to be reassuring.

I remained skeptical about using students in the canvass outside of Keene. In other cities, less in touch with a college-aged student population than Keene, the television image of students protesting in the streets or occupying administration buildings might create hostility at the door and produce a "backlash" against McCarthy. Contrary to this assumption, the Keene canvassers found people almost relieved to have anyone, older or younger, to talk to about their concerns.

The Keene committee's canvassing experience became the basis for the eventual statewide canvass that the state campaign initiated. Their instructions and advice saved time and stimulated the state campaign to do something that might well have been passed by except for the push from Keene. Under the title, "Some Canvassing Suggestions," they advised:

Where McCarthy Stands

VIETNAM POLICY

"for an honorable, rational and political settlement to the war...."

(1) let the U.S. take the initiative by halting the bombing and thus clear the air for negotiations

(2) U.S. join with the Saigon government in seeking immediate talks with the NLF

(3) U.S. encourage negotiations by gradually withdrawing troops from certain areas and reduce its commitment to a point where the Saigon government will have to negotiate with the Viet Cong to settle the war

Reporter: "Hasn't the (Johnson) Administration sought the rational solution you suggest and offered to meet with Hanoi?"

McCarthy: "To suggest a meeting anytime anywhere is not an offer. An offer would be Let's meet next Tuesday morning in Warsaw."

Reporter: "Don't you believe that we should stop Communism?"

McCarthy: "Yes, I do — and South Vietnam is the worst possible place to try."

(John F. Kennedy said: "For the United States to intervene unilaterally and to send troops into the most difficult terrain in the world, with the Chinese able to pour in unlimited manpower, would be a hopeless solution.")

(These military leaders agree:
Gen. MacArthur — Rear Admiral True
Gen. Matthew Ridgeway — Gen. Gavin
Gen. David Shoup — Brig. Gen. Ford)

(John F. Kennedy said: "This nation must never negotiate out of fear but this nation must never fear to negotiate.")

McCarthy: "My own political survival matters less to me than the deaths of other men."

McCarthy: "We have to turn our Asian policy around...If the war stopped tommorow, we'd be five years or more getting out, but we haven't passed a point of no return."

For further information: (Keene McCarthy Headquarters 14 West St.)

Where McCarthy Stands

DOMESTIC POLICY

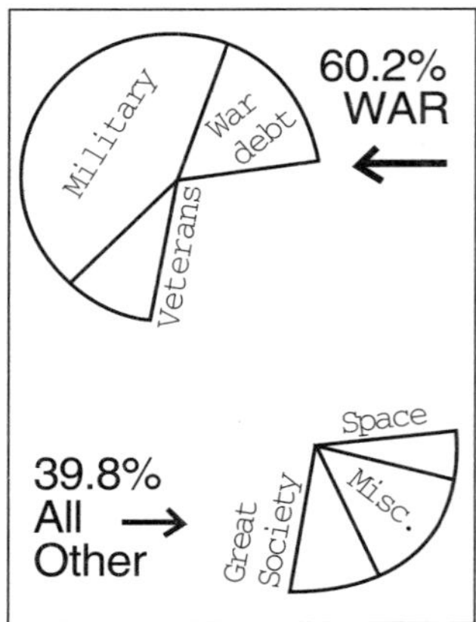

Your Present Tax Dollar

There is a crystal-clear connection between the war and each domestic crisis

RIOTS: Domestic unrest is linked to protest against Vietnam. The Black community knows that improvements in their standard of living are being scrificed to pay for the war.

INFLATION: The cost of living has increased under the tremendous strain of a daily expenditure of <u>$65 million</u> on the war. This hits hard on people with fixed incomes. You notice it in your rising food, clothing and medical bills.

HOUSING: EDUCATION: The money presently is going for war. But McCarthy believes that <u>every</u> <u>citizen</u> has a civil right to decent housing and education.

AGRICULTURE: A consistent supporter of federal legislation to provide a fair income to farmers, McCarthy has also helped develop Senate Bills to reduce farm surpluses and expand farm exports.

LABOR: If the billions now being spent in Vietnam were used on what American people need, every worker now engaged in war production could be employed in building new schools, playgrounds, housing parks and hospitals.

McCarthy: "...a solution (to Vietnam) will permit us to give necessary attention to other commitments both at home and abroad...and leave us with resources and moral energy to deal effectively with the pressing domestic problems of the United States itself."

Senator McCarthy is well qualified.
His position on these problems is based upon 20 years of experience in Congress:

- <u>Economics</u>......member of Senate Finance Committee
- <u>Agriculture</u>....member of Committee on Agriculture
- <u>Labor</u>..........Past chairman of the Farmer-Labor Party in his own state. A sponsor of many important labor bills in Congress.
- <u>Vietnam</u>........member of Senate Foreign Relations Committee

---

For further information: (Keene McCarthy Headquarters 14 West St.)

This is the most important activity—and should begin at the earliest possible moment.

1. Get the names, addresses and phone numbers typed up as quickly as possible. We took too long to do this.
2. Use cards—regardless of what other systems are suggested. The cards make neighborhood arrangements easy, telephoning easy and are excellent for keeping record of trends, comments, etc.
3. Get a map of the city, go to the city engineer's office and fill in all new streets immediately.
4. Democrats should be canvassed with great care—the bulk of the vote is here. Reach as many of them as possible with other adults but don't hesitate to use students when needed. Students should be cautioned that it is important to canvass Democrats carefully.
5. Let students handle the first canvass of all Independents. Careful records should be kept of reactions. If possible, those showing interest should be revisited by adults.
6. All canvassers should be thoroughly familiar with the Senator's Vietnam position. This is the most frequently asked question. All briefings should devote a special amount of time to this. Always give out literature which has this position spelled out.
7. When an obvious pro-McCarthy contact is made, stress the importance of voting for all of the delegates allowed. In Keene people concentrated on the preferential part of the ballot and many times did not mark the delegates at all or did not mark all of them. . . . Get sample ballots as early as possible and publicize in every available way how the ballot should be marked for McCarthy and his delegates.
8. A sound truck is very good for announcing a visit by the Senator. It is impossible to assess its effect on shopping centers, etc., at other times.

Canvassing is more important—so don't let it suffer by putting too much time and attention into sound trucks.

(Keene report, March 15, 1968)

The desire of the amateurs, like those who formed the Keene McCarthy committee, was to act professionally. Their guide and the guide of the campaign was an infrequently seen but often mentioned little booklet on campaigning known as "Larry O'Brien's Manual" written by Larry O'Brien, Kennedy campaign organizer and eventual postmaster general, shortly after the 1960 presidential election.

The booklet had been published and circulated by the Democratic National Committee as the basic guide to effective political organization. Its theory was understated among the lists of dos and don'ts of campaigning. One that was well remembered in New Hampshire was "make sure the engine in your car starts in cold weather." When there was a question in Concord, Keene, Manchester, Nashua, Portsmouth, Berlin, Salem, or any of the other headquarters or meetings, "What does Larry O'Brien's manual say?" was often heard.

On March 15 the Keene committee wrote its own manual which, if given the circulation of O'Brien's manual, might well have been its replacement. Some of their advice:

1. First meeting:
   - announce the meeting on the radio and in the newspaper and invite all interested to attend.
   - have a very definite agenda, list officers to be elected and get them elected. (do not get people together and say, "well, how shall we do this?" You never get off the ground this way and you lose half your people)
   - put through a tentative budget.

   Note: The first meeting should get the structure set up to begin functioning the following morning.
2. Have all the people who attended the first meeting raise money immediately from their intimate friends—setting a definite date within 5 or 7 days for money to be handed in.
3. Use this initial money to get a downtown headquarters open and operating as soon as possible.
4. Liaison with state headquarters.

It could be very helpful if there were permanent people in various jobs. A list of who to contact for what (canvassing, literature, student volunteers, etc.) should be given local headquarters as soon as possible.

All communications from state should go through either the chairmen of the group or the executive secretary. Having state contact members of the group individually makes for chaos.

Criticisms:

a. Having minor staffers contact local headquarters is confusing, repetitious, and very often unnecessary. Some of their directives are of the busy-work variety.
b. Patronizing attitudes of some people at state headquarters is irritating and demoralizing to older workers who are, after all, just as intelligent as they are.

(Keene report, March 15, 1968)

The structure they recommended to support the organization was headed by a chair, in their case co-chair, who they advised to "meet regularly to discuss policies and procedures." An executive secretary should serve as liaison with the state headquarters and should be available in the headquarters much of the time. Specified duties included keeping the headquarters staffed, assigning student volunteers, and directing clerical and card work. The "must" person in the scheme is the canvassing chair who "must be responsible enough to be present every single weekend" and "probably should do some canvassing himself *ahead of time*, so he knows what it is like and can *brief all volunteers. . . .*"

Ward captains should be appointed with one being male and the other female, the report advises, because "a man is needed to reach other men in the 30–65 age bracket." The ward captains should try to get as many neighborhood lieutenants as possible giving each about "10 cards." The "cards should be arranged by neighborhoods—Independents and Democrats mixed together to avoid duplicate visits to mixed households. It helps to have brief directions attached to each pack of cards, and the captains were advised to check each time the cards are returned in order to assure that they stay in order."

Other offices in the organization were the recording secretary to take minutes of every meeting, to make sure ". . . of every decision and avoid misconceptions about what the decisions were." Appointing a fund-raising chair was felt to be important although the report noted, "We got along without one, but only with luck," and the post should be held by someone "who has few qualms about asking for money."

A treasurer should "know how the records should be kept," and "no spending should be done without the Treasurer's permission." The treasurer should have a general budget to work from that has been approved at a general meeting of the committee. Completing the list of officers used by the Keene committee were a publicity chair, student housing coordinators, and a campaign day coordinator.

The publicity chair "was expected to publicize the activities of the committee" and "also stimulate or originate letters to the newspaper on aspects that are important locally." The student housing coordinator, which they noted they did not have but would have saved them "much unnecessary rushing about," was a unique addition to the list that came as the result of the influx of volunteers to New Hampshire. The Campaign Day Coordinator was the local scheduler for the visits of the candidate and should be "someone who is well established in the community...."

In addition to the Keene committee's thorough organization and campaign innovations, each of the ward captains prepared precise profiles of his or her respective wards. With these profiles the ward captain's then organized their canvassing, follow-up calls, and get-out-the-vote activities. The effectiveness of the local organization in not only carrying the statewide effort to the locality but, in fact, creating the campaign at the local level was a further example of how the McCarthy campaign federated.

Keene was a community that needed the order and assigned responsibilities of the organization it adopted. Those involved had a strong sense of the importance of their job and how much of that task rested at the local level. They also had a need to feel as equals participating in the decisions of the organization, while being willing to accept specific leadership once that leadership had been derived from the organization in accord with its objectives.

Other localities would organize in the same way in New Hampshire. Of the larger cities, Concord, Portsmouth, Nashua, and Laconia brought together their own local committees and shaped the campaign to fit their local needs. McCarthy's candidacy probably stimulated more "self-starting" local organizations than had any other previous effort. Much of this also occurred in the small towns and rural counties that had not been given organizational priority in our strategy. Where these local efforts grew they carried the total weight of the campaign, relying on occasional contacts with the state headquarters and outside volunteer aide as available. The "self-starting" phenomenon was especially important in New Hampshire and became an attribute of the campaign as it gathered strength nationally.

Manchester: Organizational Desert

From the beginning, Studds and I knew that Manchester would be exceedingly difficult to organize for Senator McCarthy. I had been involved in several political efforts in Manchester and understood its political dynamics. I had worked in John King's first campaign for governor in 1962 and had watched King fashion a winning coalition from his friends, relatives, political associates, labor contacts, social, and ethic groups. Manchester is the melting pot that never quite melted and has a club, group, church, or association for each of its many immigrant peoples. Its politics revolve around associations and their leadership.

While often playing a role in local affairs, the *Manchester Union Leader* works less as a dominant force than as a participant with others of the community's power structure. Local politics are partisan with Democrats usually holding office as a result of a high Democratic registration and the predominance of French-Canadian and Irish stock. As with other cities of similar size and having partisan electoral systems, it is difficult to extend the thread of partisanship of a national party back through to the locality. Manchester's politics tended to be issue-by-issue politics with conservative versus liberal being a more accurate way of assessing voter inclinations.

In 1968 Manchester was governed by Republican John C. Mongan. He had replaced long-term Democrat, J. T. Beniot in 1961, when he chose not to run for reelection. Mongan was reelected in 1963, was defeated by a Democrat in 1965, then reelected again in 1967. During the period no more than one Republican was elected to the fourteen-member city council. An outsider, whether a presidential candidate or a candidate for state office, will have success in Manchester to the extent that he or she is legitimized by receiving the approval of those in associational leadership. That approval comes only from what the leaders feel will be the benefit to them from such an introduction, or what damage their tie to an outsider might cause them in their constituency or community.

The latter point is where the role of the *Manchester Union Leader* is important. If the newspaper is neutral or in support of the candidate then the risk of association is minimal. If the newspaper is in opposition but the candidate stands a strong likelihood of succeeding then the tie to the winner makes it worth the risk. But in the case of someone like Eugene McCarthy, who neither looked like he could win and clearly was opposed by the newspaper and, further, cut across the loyalist vein of Manchester's strong veterans' organizations, the risk was not worth taking.

For Studds and I this meant that the traditional shortcuts to voters through power structure connections and legitimacy were almost totally closed. But Manchester was much too important in the political equation to be ignored. The nut had to be cracked and to do this would require organization, strategy, and people.

Studds and I wrestled constantly with the Manchester problem. Our first list of supporters, released at the November press conference, contained several prominent Manchester names, but not of Manchester's political/associational structure. Those who had previous political experience in Manchester and who were able to spend time on the campaign tended to be from outside the city—principally from nearby Bedford.

John Holland, who was the McCarthy campaign's treasurer, and Sylvia Chaplain, both of Bedford, had managed to get another attorney, Clifford Ross, and a businessperson, George MacLellan, involved in the campaign. Both lived in Manchester and had some previous political experience in the city. Ross was then serving as the city Democratic Party chair. Unfortunately that office tends to be outside the associational structure of the city's politics, although Ross did have some access.

Several faculty members at St. Anselm College also became involved—principally John and Jan Windhausen and William and Pat Farrell. Pat Holland, Jackie MacLellan, and Sylvia Chaplain assumed major responsibilities in the organization and scheduling activities of the campaign. Manchester was a heavily male dominated political/economic community in which women have played important roles, but where associational access remained male dominated.

When the Robert Kennedy write-in campaign ended, a number of important additions were made to the McCarthy Manchester campaign's list of volunteers. Maria Carrier, wife of a local executive, became involved first by holding a coffee party for Senator McCarthy and then worked extensively as a virtually full-time volunteer. Her husband provided clerical help, office equipment, and backup financing when immediate cash was needed to run an announcement or purchase supplies.

Because of Manchester's political importance, the local organization was constantly stressed. McCarthy would visit Manchester more than any other place. This required more time spent scheduling—in a place that was difficult to schedule at best. There were more names on the checklists to process for the mailing labels; there were more homes to canvass; there was more of practically every activity required of the campaign. The local organization was neither extensive nor especially experienced with political activity. The result was a condition of continuous frustration, tension, and unachieved priorities.

In Nashua and Keene preexisting political action groups became the McCarthy organization. In Concord, Franklin, Laconia, Portsmouth, and, to a certain extent, Lebanon and Claremont, local Democratic Party workers became the McCarthy campaign. In Berlin, Dover, Rochester, Somersworth, and several of the larger towns, a combination of local initiatives and outside volunteers created the McCarthy campaign. In none of these communities was the local organization required to assume the responsibilities that the Manchester organization faced.

Relying on the local people we had originally included as McCarthy supporters, Studds and I attempted to have the volunteers create their own organization, recruit new volunteers, and assign tasks as had the Keene, Concord, and Nashua committees. Several lightly attended meetings were held in which the scheduling, organizational, and headquarters operation priorities were discussed, but not enough people were involved to make assignments.

Hearing local cries of frustration, Studds and I began using volunteers to help with the Manchester problem. The first was a young midwesterner, Steve Landers, who had had some earlier political experience. He had arrived early in January through the Sam Brown volunteer recruiting activity. We spent an evening acquainting Landers with the Manchester situation. He was to be the full-time help that Studds and I felt the Manchester people needed in order to become effective. His first job was to find, rent, equip, and have ready for McCarthy's January 26 visit a campaign headquarters. Second, he was to assist those scheduling McCarthy's visit with the details of that schedule. He was also to facilitate the mailing label activity in Manchester.

Since the Manchester people had not structured themselves as had the Keene group, Landers had immediate difficulty finding people with particular skills, contacts, or responsibilities who would conform to the set priorities. Opening the headquarters became a complex task surpassed only by getting telephones installed, finding office equipment, and establishing a staffing schedule. All went fairly well until the ceiling collapsed in the headquarters the day before McCarthy was scheduled to visit. Needless to say, Landers had little time to check the senator's local schedule for the 26, or to do much about the preparation of mailing labels.

After the problems of January 26, Studds and I threw more volunteers at the Manchester problem without measurable improvement. We took a scarce Saturday afternoon, usually reserved for statewide campaign planning, to meet with Landers in Manchester to see what could be done to improve things. We returned to Concord with the feeling that if we had remained in Manchester much longer, we too might have caught the anomie that seemed to afflict the McCarthy effort in that city.

Occasionally, Studds and I felt that some order was beginning to evolve in the Manchester effort only to find that there had been a missed event or confused communication. By the middle of February we had basically given up on the notion that an integrated, coordinated structure was possible in Manchester. We accepted the reality of separate, even conflicting, communications allowing the state headquarters to operate in Manchester, which gave the Manchester people and assigned volunteers little sense of their own organizational entity. Eventually aspects of the campaign even spread into separate offices with little communication across the city to each other.

Accepting this situation was difficult for us because it seemed to go against the grain of our experience and what was happening elsewhere in the state. Once we reached the inevitable conclusion, it was possible to function with reasonable effectiveness within the chaos. Instead of doing as we had done with Steve Landers in the hopes of establishing a coordinated effort in Manchester, we would send a volunteer to meet with someone in Manchester to carry out a particular assignment or to aid in a specific activity without checking the person through the city headquarters.

Arleen Hynes, a close friend of Mrs. McCarthy, worked in Manchester on her own organizing project which was not easily coordinated either with Manchester or the state headquarters. Mrs. McCarthy had developed a successful activity that she and her close friends had operated quietly and effectively in each of her husband's previous campaigns. She would establish in her home what amounted to a "committee of correspondence," directed toward women's groups and church organizations—an almost totally underground activity. Mrs. McCarthy preferred a less public role but one that was uniquely effective. Barbara Underwood described Mrs. McCarthy's approach:

> The women's campaign which originated in Washington, was almost a neighborhood enterprise. Mrs. McCarthy set up an office on the top floor of her home. The house, had formerly belonged to Walter Lipmann. . . . The office that Lipmann had used to write his column was turned into a McCarthy for President headquarters. . . .

> When the McCarthys became involved in politics in Minnesota they found they were fighting the same kind of Democratic establishment they were now confronting in New Hampshire twenty years later.
>
> They had the same problems of not being able to get the voter check-lists. They had to start from scratch, finding lists from colleges, or churches, or liberal organizations, and organize coffee parties or teas. So Mrs. McCarthy proposed that the New Hampshire ladies try to obtain lists of college alumni and mail them to Washington where volunteers, not involved in a primary campaign could be writing to all the New Hampshire college alumna. . . . Letters asking for McCarthy support could be sent to both the professors at the schools and to the alumni living in the state.
>
> Using college directories was an economical and easy device for reaching and identifying large numbers of prospective voters through direct mail.
>
> (Underwood, op. cit., pp. 56, 61)

Arleen Hynes came to New Hampshire to acquaint both the state and local organizations with Mrs. McCarthy's organizing approach and to assess the chances for such an effort in New Hampshire. According to Barbara Underwood, Hynes was a writer of mystery stories, who had an interest in the peculiar activity of political intelligence gathering, but was also one who could initiate organization on her own. When she arrived I gave her a briefing and suggested that she might most profitably spend her time in Manchester attempting to unravel some of the problems the campaign was having there.

In her travels Arleen Hynes stirred up considerable activity. Her principal contribution was to bring a number of the Manchester women together to discuss how they might become effectively involved in the campaign. She described what had been organized in the McCarthy's Washington home and urged the Manchester people to help the effort by sending lists that could be used for the mailings. Tied with this effort was also her role as the coordinator of the McCarthy for President volunteers. Her objective in this effort was, as she wrote to me, "to get a state-wide list of Republicans and Independents who will agree to let their names be used on letterhead, to be used for a state-wide mailing, or as a sponsoring organization for some large tea or luncheon for Sen. McCarthy." (Letter to Hoeh, February 5, 1968)

I assigned a driver to her and gave her several contact names in Manchester in addition to her own names generated from the Washington headquarters files. At the end of her visit she filed a report of her activities and impressions. She wrote:

> In order to get suggestions for Volunteers for McCarthy met with: 4 pastors—inner city, suburban, French and Polish.
>
> Visited 2 colleges.
>
> Got some to start letters to the editor in small towns and generated offers of coffees.
>
> Two people in Manchester have definitely agreed to go on Volunteers for McCarthy stationary [sic] or will let their names be used to sponsor large gatherings: Mr. Saul Sigel, Dr. Selma Deitch, M.D.

Mr. Paul Diekman in Newbury will make some contacts up-state.

Made approximately a hundred calls, avoiding the local Democrats, since they have been contacted.

Conclusions Drawn from Trip:

Need for full time person for next 5 weeks desperate.

Hoeh and Stubbs [sic] cannot even do small essentials for adequate coverage without permanent paid *secretary* at Concord office .

Students coming into state are most welcome and needed, but permanent campaign staff person is essential.

Great need for position papers, brochures, how-to-do materials in order to get the Senator known.

They say they have no money, hope to get brochures for state-wide mailing ready. No mailings have been made.

In her summary she noted that she had spent most of her time with local "Manchesterian, non-political people" and that she felt there was a great need for information about the Senator's positions on other than "peace." Among the notes from the report was the following which summarized an outside view of the Manchester organizational problem.

Met with very discouraged small group of women Monday evening: persuaded them they could start a telephone campaign to everyone on check list. Mrs. Orcutt (with Steve, student volunteer in Manchester office) will get it going.

It should be considered since church membership lists are unavailable, that telephone book, by geographical area, be used on telephone campaign. Need to work up brief and pointed telephone approach to get best coverage.

(Letter to Hoeh, February 5, 1968)

In spite of Arleen Hynes' efforts and those of many others, Manchester remained an organizational nightmare. Discouragement seemed to follow each effort as one approach succeeded another and new volunteers followed the now disillusioned. Studds and I kept thinking the problem was one of a lack of initiative, energy, and even imagination or, perhaps, personality conflicts or even generation gaps, but the problem continued. We made several changes in headquarters management, and moved people into jobs we thought would be better suited to their experience, but usually the results were the same. What we did find was that as the workers struggled with their problems they began to understand that the lack of success was not of their own doing but a condition of the city.

To give an impression of how the Manchester organization viewed itself at an early stage, Studds and I sent the following worker list with descriptions to the state headquarters:

Steve Landers	Co-ordinator for Manchester campaign and office manager
Bob Richard	Assist Landers through March 3rd
Sylvia Chaplain (Bedford)	Handles most of scheduling for Mrs. McCarthy and the Senator in Manchester
John Holland	Fiscal Agent for N.H. Campaign
Pat Holland (Bedford)	Does a variety of things on short notice
Virginia Eshoo	Handles volunteer housing and organizes ladies
Maria Carrier	Held a coffee party and is organizing westside reception
Jan Windausen	Helps with office work and telephoning
John Windhausen	Delegate, helps with contacts at St. A's
Brenda Walsh	Works in office, occasionally rounds up high school vols.
George MacLellan	Delegate; advise on Manchester politics
Jackie MacLellan	Works in office and does telephoning
Helen White	Makes contacts for factories, sometimes helps in office
Allen Berzofsky	Handles Manchester publicity now, helps with lowdown on Manchester politics
Bill Farrell	Delegate; now a primary contact for social clubs.
Pat Farrell	Helps in all ladies projects
Paul Beauvais	Kennedy-ite, now making contacts for scheduling for Senator McCarthy
Jo Ellen Orcutt (Goffstown)	Initiator of telephone campaign
Kilton Barnard (Goffstown)	Gave advice on reaching the working people
John Coleman	Help in office
John McCarthy	
Joan Camman	Works on ladies projects
Mickey Becker	Works in office full-time, handles most clerical work

Note: This list comprises Manchester area workers whose efforts have been more than occasional, or in some other way significant.

(Report to state headquarters, early February 1968)

When Curt Gans arrived as the full-time manager of the statewide campaign and a constant flow of volunteers were coming into New Hampshire, it was possible to submerge the depressing Manchester situation in a flood of both activity and workers. The telephone contact suggestion made by Arleen Hynes and followed by Jo Ellen Orcutt became an important activity. Canvassing, largely supported and organized from state headquarters, produced a more favorable response—almost a substitute for not being able to penetrate the political/associational structure of the city.

What gave life to the Manchester campaign was assigning Ann Hart, daughter of Senator Philip Hart (Democrat of Michigan), to Manchester. To a demoralized, disillusioned, volunteer-consuming part of the campaign she brought spirit and energy. She was first given the job of assigning volunteers and serving as a clearinghouse for volunteer-supported activities. She eventually became the coordinator of the telephone bank and the calling activity that became the principal personal contact of the campaign.

With a never say-die attitude she brought political skills and sensitivity far beyond her years. When Gans, Studds, myself, or a key local person could not be found for a decision, Ann made it and the campaign moved on.

In our determination to get something going in Manchester, Studds and I became less cautious as to what or what not to do in the city. Canvassing, telephoning, special and group mailings, and special receptions became part of a strategy of trying the untried. In the last weekends of the campaign we agreed that the numerous Vietnam War veterans who had joined the campaign in protest against the war might effectively be used to bring the war issue home in a way that would startle Manchester residents. When the Vietnam Veterans Against the War asked permission to campaign for McCarthy on the street, the leaders said, okay, it's worth a try.

As the campaign closed, much of the statewide activity had shifted to Manchester. Senator McCarthy was based at the Sheraton-Wayfarer, Bedford, as were the press and travel support activities for his campaigning. While Gans remained in Concord, Studds and I spent much of our time in Manchester assisting with last-minute problems and bringing the campaign to the conclusion envisioned in our strategy.

In spite of the energy and central focus for the expending campaign resources, Manchester organizationally became little more than a series of segmented campaign activities—each with its own staff of volunteers, communications to state headquarters, and focus of activity. This was only activity possible given the community, the available local contacts, and the orientation of the candidacy.

Berlin: A Missionary in the Wilderness

In the confusion of the first weeks of the campaign, Studds and I had not been able to attend to our own Berlin problem (pronounced Burr-lin). New Hampshire's northernmost city is approximately 150 miles north of Concord with the barrier of the White Mountains between it and the larger settlements to the south. The city's 1960 population was 17,821 making it an important center of voting strength.

Berlin's principal industry had been papermaking and associated forest products industries. In recent years these industries had declined with some of the job losses being replaced by rubber products manufacturing and several other small industries.

With the decline in the wood-processing industries there had also been a population decline. There remained, however, a basic population of working class French-Canadians with a lengthy tradition of Democratic voting and strong union organization. While the language is French in Berlin, the voting orientation had been distinctly bread-and-butter basic American loyalty.

My previous political work in Berlin led me to believe that McCarthy might appeal to the concerns of the Berlin worker, but I was skeptical about how these voters would react to McCarthy's position on the war in Vietnam. Would these people hold the "my country (read president) right or wrong" view of the war and therefore see McCarthy as a disloyal even traitorous political upstart? Would they react to him as an alternative to both domestic and foreign policies that had produced both uncertainty and insecurity in their personal and political lives?

I noted that Berlin, while much like Manchester in its ethnic, economic, and social composition, had one major difference. It did not receive its news of state and national affairs through the *Manchester Union Leader.* While some copies of the *Union Leader* did find their way to Berlin, the newspapers with the largest circulation's were the *Lewiston Sun,* from nearby Lewiston, Maine, and the *Boston Globe.*

The Berlin voter tended to retain a clear focus on the basics of the bread-and-butter issues and recalled fondly the administrations of Franklin D. Roosevelt and of their neighbor to the south John F. Kennedy. In fact Kennedy had struck a responsive chord in Berlin with his 1960 presidential primary campaign. His candidacy stirred considerable political activity in the city among its younger residents. Unfortunately, with subsequent declines in the local paper industry, a number of these new and potential leaders had to seek employment in other New Hampshire cities and often outside of the state.

Seniority rules in the mills meant the younger workers were the first to be furloughed and when new prospects dimmed further those with transportable skills and sufficient English language proficiency left the city. These losses left a severely truncated population of school-aged children and adults over thirty-five. It was not particularly fertile territory for what was perceived to be Senator McCarthy's appeal. In addition, the standard of living in Berlin was relatively high. Wages in the paper industry were good as the result of union action and seniority. Berlin also had a large number of two and three or more income families. Again McCarthy's appeal might seem to be less among those reasonably satisfied with their own economic situation.

I had managed a congressional campaign in 1964 that had successfully tapped Berlin's voting strength, and I knew only a personal visit from someone familiar with the Berlin political ethos would get things going. My only contact with someone favorable to McCarthy had been Otto Olesen, a state representative from neighboring Gorham.

Olesen had been helpful, but limited time and distance made it difficult for him to either organize on behalf of McCarthy or attend the meetings Studds and I called to begin local organizing. Fully expecting to be able to visit Berlin some weekend, I let the Berlin problem rest on the "back shelf." Not until late January was I able to consider organizing Berlin seriously and realized that neither Studds nor I could afford the time to go to the city, make the contacts, and begin the organization without seriously jeopardizing other pressing aspects of the campaign. We could do nothing more at that stage than send a stranger to Berlin and hope for the best.

Our first missionary was one of the Yale Law School students who were coming to help the campaign. Eric Schnapper had recruited a number of his fellow students to come to New Hampshire for a week at a time. Subsequently dubbed the "Yalie of the Week" program, a student would arrive in Concord for a briefing late Friday or early Saturday, then travel to an assignment where the student would either relieve a returning Yalie or begin a new organizing effort. When a relief occurred the arriving and the returning students would work together before the returning student left New Hampshire for New Haven. This assured continuity in the effort, helped familiarize the new person with the details of a particular situation, and gave the campaign a permanent staffing base within the context of a constantly changing guard.

The first Yalie arrived in Berlin on Saturday, January 27. His mission was to find local people interested in McCarthy and try to form a local committee of these. After a week of introductions through Otto Olesen the volunteer reported back that there were people interested in McCarthy. However, he had not been able to either hold a meeting of these people or get anyone to come forward as the local leader for such an organizational meeting. His week was up, and with some frustration he returned to New Haven following a debriefing session in Concord on his way south.

With the election not much more than five weeks away and a date for a McCarthy visit to Berlin creeping up on the calendar, Studds and I decided to change tactics. Our next missionary would be sent north with instructions to set up a Main Street storefront headquarters, open political shop, and see if something could be made to materialize. The new Yalie was Marc Kasky, not a law student but a city planning graduate student. His experiences produced one of the classic studies of the campaign.

Like many others who came to New Hampshire during the winter of 1968, Kasky had had little involvement in political organizations. Recounting his experience, Kasky said, ". . . I don't think I'd ever been in a campaign headquarters before the New Hampshire primary. I had considered myself an Independent and had strong opposition to the war. Before going to New Hampshire I knew very little about Senator McCarthy." So little, in fact, that he recalled a conversation with Mrs. McCarthy in which he made the mistake of asking "how things were in Wisconsin" rather than in McCarthy' s home state of Minnesota. In spite of his lack of familiarity with either politics or the candidate, Kasky was willing to spend four or five days in New Hampshire to do something to protest the war. What he expected to do was to "stuff and address envelopes" a task that required little experience or political sophistication.

> I didn't feel that my lack of experience in any political campaign was any handicap because of the nature of the work I was expecting to do when I went to New Hampshire.
>
> As a matter of fact, I found out that in this particular campaign, the lack of experience quite often not only wasn't a handicap, but was many times really an asset. The typical politician who had had a great deal of experience in this type of work seemed to have more trouble with the people in New

Hampshire than he who had gone there totally inexperienced and knowing very little about the mechanics of a political campaign.

Perhaps after having worked in a number of campaigns, a worker looks at people as votes, and little more. And apparently many of the voters were taken by the approach of the young workers who looked at them as much more.

(Marc Kasky Oral History Transcript, p. 2)

Kasky expected to spend about a week in New Hampshire. He recalled:

David Hoeh asked me in New Hampshire if I wanted to go to Berlin and open up this office. He pointed to a map to Berlin, New Hampshire, which looked like it was north of the White Mountains. He told me it was completely isolated from the rest of New Hampshire but it was the third largest city, with the third largest Democratic vote. To me it looked as if it were in another state.

I didn't quite believe him. Because he didn't know who I was, he didn't know if I had any political experience. There were lots of people in New Hampshire working for the campaign. And if Berlin had been so important, I couldn't figure out why he was sending a total stranger there to open up the headquarters.

I had a question. I wasn't sure whether I'd go or not. It sounded like it would be an exciting adventure, an interesting thing to try. If I was more valuable in that way—the reason I had come there to New Hampshire was to do what they thought I could do. If they thought this was what I should do, I'd do it. I still wasn't sure if I wanted to drive 150 miles north in New Hampshire in the middle of the winter to a strange place.

(Marc Kasky, op. cit., p. 8)

What gave Kasky the push to drive that distance and to stay in Berlin beyond the one week of his planned New Hampshire visit happened the evening of his New Hampshire arrival. He heard Senator McCarthy's speech in Concord. "It was the first time I'd ever heard him. I'd read and seen news clips of him up until then and after hearing him speak, I decided that, well, I could throw in a couple of extra days."

The next morning Kasky left for Berlin with only Otto Olesen of Gorham as a contact and instructions to find and open a McCarthy headquarters. He had campaign materials he hoped would answer any questions he was asked. His intention was to read the materials immediately on arriving in Berlin so he would know a bit more about Senator McCarthy's positions and the issues of the campaign.

As he described, "Well, luckily—as things have gone for me many times in the past—I ran into great luck in Berlin and a store the first day I was there, on Main Street, and rented it immediately." Kasky then began the difficult task of creating a local organization that could give local life to the campaign.

During the first several days Kasky roamed around Berlin without either a McCarthy button or bumper sticker on his car, "trying to let people know that there was a stranger in town but not exactly explaining what [he] was there for." "[He] just sort of mentioned that [he] had just arrived in town and was looking for a place to rent, and nothing more than that. For all they knew [he] was going into business in town." What he wanted was to get to know people as an "innocent individual" before they got to know him as someone "campaigning for a politician." In that time he got to know something about the town, its political history, and who the people were who would be most useful.

His method of becoming acquainted was to visit the local coffee shops where he was quickly identified as a stranger. "They knew I was new in town and quite often they'd start a conversation with me. But probably as many times, I'd start a conversation with them and just say that I'd arrived here and was interested in learning something about Berlin."

His second way of finding himself in the city was to attend local meetings that he read about in the newspaper. From these passive efforts Kasky developed a list of thirty to forty names that he had "floating around in [his] head." He now began to know "who was friends with whom and who was against whom and who to talk to and who not to talk to."

During those first days Kasky also managed to find someone to clean out the headquarters, got a church to loan him some chairs, borrowed tables from a restaurant, and someone to paint a sign as well as the inside of the headquarters. He then made an appointment to attend the upcoming Democratic Committee meeting where he planned to introduce himself as representing Senator McCarthy.

The chair agreed to introduce him and allow him to speak for several minutes. Accepting the opportunity Kasky "just mentioned the fact that [he] had arrived in town to open up Senator McCarthy's headquarters and to make some arrangements for his visit to Berlin." He then went on to tell them how important Senator McCarthy considered the town.

He then said that if anyone had any questions or any advice for him that "I'd be more than happy to meet them, answer questions, and take any advice they had to offer." With the advantage of having met a number of those attending during his informal coffee shop visits, Kasky had a comfortable time at the meeting.

Recalling the meeting, Kasky noted on the same evening a member of the Johnson organization had "kind of breezed into town, to drop off stacks of pledge cards, and stuff like that." Kasky remained after the meeting as did the Johnson representative (Harry Makris of Nashua), waiting for people to ask questions or just visit. Kasky watched as all of the committee members went over to Makris to get their pledge cards and campaign kits. And as Kasky reported, "Many of them went outside after he [Makris] left and threw them in the trash pails," saying as they passed Kasky, "Don't worry about it; we're not being intimidated into anything like this."

Makris left Berlin that evening while Kasky made it clear that he was going to stay in Berlin throughout the campaign. The McCarthy headquarters would be open from then until the election. Kasky had extended his commitment to the campaign from his initial "few days" to five weeks in just a matter of several days after arriving in Berlin. Of this Kasky said:

> I noticed during the entire campaign (beyond New Hampshire), that the people in charge of the headquarters in a number of outlying cities quite often changed so frequently that they never really were able to establish relationships with the people. They would pass on names to the next person who came in, but it would almost kill the time that they had spent there, and in my opinion, actually make it harder for the next guy, because people don't appreciate having their names passed from stranger to stranger.
>
> (Kasky, op. cit., pp. 11–12)

Kasky viewed his local contacts as "friends" not just "people who could deliver votes," and for this reason he felt that he had to remain in Berlin for the duration of the campaign once he had successfully established the report of his early visits.

Kasky viewed his job as "never" one of "trying to win votes for McCarthy" but "just making information available and be there to answer questions . . . so that people could decide who they wanted to vote for." During the last three days of the campaign Kasky recalled that many people walked into the headquarters, saying that they had decided. "Almost like getting a load of their chest, you know. They were actually sort of proud that they had reached this decision, because they knew that they hadn't been talked into it. It had been entirely their own decision. And from the most unexpected people—you know, Republicans and Democrats, men and women would just come in and say, 'I want you to know, that I'm voting for Senator McCarthy'."

To reach this point in the campaign Kasky managed his local effort with great sensitivity and caution. To create the feeling that was reflected in those final days before the election when people stopped by the Berlin headquarters to proudly announce their decision to vote for Senator McCarthy was the culmination of Kasky's careful orchestration of every move that the McCarthy campaign made in this city. His was an effort of shaping the campaign to the social and political ethos of an isolated, tight, New England city, and a major accomplishment for a young graduate student from urban New Jersey.

Each activity of the campaign was carefully adapted to the Berlin that Kasky discovered in order to ensure that the best result would be produced. An example of his sensitivity was shown in his response to the canvassing effort that evolved during the latter weeks of the campaign, something that had not been used previously as a political instrument in Berlin.

A canvassing team arrived in Berlin about three weeks before the election. Beyond the usual briefing concerning community attitudes and background that Kasky gave those who would canvass, he went a step further:

> I realized that (before the canvas [sic] came) that was the type of thing that had not been done in New Hampshire . . . for that reason I sort of got the permission of the community to have the canvas.
>
> Even though it would have been done anyway, I figured that letting them know that it was coming and, if they had any strong objections, making them feel that it could be turned aside. . . .

> I found that this approach of letting them know that they held the veto on anything I was doing really made it possible for me to get more done than if I had told them a canvas was coming.
>
> They probably figured if I was asking for permission, how dangerous can it be and just gave me permission or cooperated in many things that I think other people might have run into problems doing.
>
> If they had said "No canvassers," I was fairly confident that there was a reasonable and rational enough case in favor of it and for that reason I was sure there would be a canvas. But let them make the decision instead of me.
>
> (Kasky, op. cit., pp. 14–15)

When it came to preparing for a visit of Senator McCarthy Kasky used the same approach. Instead of building the schedule himself from those things he thought were important to include, he relied totally on his local contacts for what should be included in the senator's visit.

> All I did was go around to people who had been in Berlin for a long time—and almost everybody was a native of the town—and ask them what they thought a candidate should do when he's in town.
>
> (Kasky, op. cit., p. 15)

When Senator McCarthy did visit Berlin "almost every place he went was at the suggestion of someone in Berlin. They must have felt that it was pretty bad to obstruct or make it difficult for me to arrange a visit that they had told me was the best thing Senator McCarthy could do."

Trying to fathom why he was able to work so comfortably within a rather tightly organized Democratic city, Kasky concluded simply, "I think they liked me. You know, they really didn't want to screw me up. They did know that I was there all alone in a heavily machine-oriented, Democratic town, knowing nothing about politics and seemed, by the mere fact that I wasn't trying to win votes, to be way off on the wrong track. 'This kid really needs help!' and for that reason they—even the Johnson supporters, quite often would say, 'Why don't you send him here instead of there? We'll take him.'"

Kasky found that his own attitude toward President Johnson helped his effort greatly. "The fact that I had never denounced Johnson, although I didn't like him, I always felt sorrier for him than I did any viciousness or hate. I felt the most convincing argument was that whether he was right or wrong, whether he made the decisions on his own or on the advice of other, was unimportant. What was important was the fact that he was unable to govern because of the way his reputation had been tainted. For this reason it was obvious I wasn't campaigning against Johnson and wasn't making personal attacks on him."

Kasky found in Berlin what Studds and I had sensed was an underlying view in New Hampshire of the war. Kasky reported that "people weren't as concerned specifically about the war" or the handling of the war as they were about the "fact that boys from their town or their friends were in Vietnam and some were being killed." He found that while "no one liked the war it was too easy to criticize the war and say it was mishandled."

That was all too obvious. What he found to be the Berlin concern to be was rather the "personality traits of the different candidates and the whole idea of honesty."

In contrast to the skepticism toward Johnson as being not quite credible, Kasky found that "McCarthy wasn't making any problems, wasn't saying how much he could do, but was merely discussing presidential politics, and for this reason they were sort of caught by his personality." He found that while the Berlin voters would want to know McCarthy's position on the war, "they usually moved on to other areas of concern to them to see his responses there."

The contention that the New Hampshire voter reacts to the presidential primary as if interviewing the next president of the United States, was supported by what Kasky found in Berlin. "They sort of looked at him as a person and tried to imagine what types of things he would do as a President." It was McCarthy's advantage that "he created a very good impression." To them, Kasky found, the image he projected "was more important than his position on larger issues—positions," they felt, "could change."

Kasky also found a way to staff his headquarters with local people. He suggested to several high school teachers that he would welcome a chance to visit their classes to discuss the presidential primary. They knew he was representing McCarthy but the way Kasky put his offer he promised to discuss "what the whole idea of the primary was" and why it had evolved in New Hampshire as well as the importance of this particular primary. He remembered "that when I had been in high school, I didn't know who was running for President, didn't know what anybody stood for and couldn't have cared less," and felt that finding out "how the kids felt" and getting into the schools was worth the effort.

When a number of the social studies teachers invited him to their classes he was surprised to find out that the "kids were really interested, and after I spoke one teacher assigned his students to get involved in a primary." The students were not instructed as to which campaign to join but simply, "Go down to some headquarters and put in an afternoon. Ask the person [at the headquarters] if he has any work to be done."

The first headquarters visited was the Nixon office because that was the first one they passed on the their way home from school. "But," as Kasky reported, "no one was there when they passed by. So about twenty of them came to the McCarthy headquarters." Immediately Kasky put them to work decorating his new storefront, handing out things, answering the telephones, and talking. Kasky's comment was, "I mean they really were needed—because I had nobody there."

The results of Kasky's visit to the high school multiplied the first twenty students to over fifty. He found that "they really wanted to read about [McCarthy] and find out about him." As a result they became exceptionally effective campaigners. As the weeks went on they would bring in their friends, even those from families supporting President Johnson, to talk with Kasky and to experience the excitement of the headquarters. The activity and attractiveness of the McCarthy headquarters tied to Kasky's relaxed, open personality was contagious. In a city that had virtually no contact with the McCarthy campaign as it developed in New Hampshire, there was, within a few short weeks after Kasky's arrival, a vibrant organization with broad local interest, with community access, and with close and sensitive ties to the city's political personality.

In all other New Hampshire cities and towns the success of the local organizing had been dependent upon local residents who guided the campaign's activities as they materialized. The success or lack thereof depended on how well connected these locals were to the politics of their locality. Kasky, a stranger, was successful in finding his way in Berlin and turning informal access into a politically effective effort because of his own engaging nature and the potential for openness that Berlin possesses as its own personality.

Kasky's reaction to the ethnic composition of Berlin reveals much about how he approached his assignment.

> You know, mention was made of the ethnic vote in Berlin and that if you could win the French Catholic vote—which is 90 percent of the city—you've got the city.
>
> But I never looked at the city as having an ethnic vote and never found it to be that way. I imagine if I had tried to look for it, I could have found it, but doing what I was—just the whole idea of meeting people rather than meeting the key people of different groups I was not looking for the people who could deliver the ethnic vote or who could deliver particular groups. For that reason I might have been in the middle of an ethnic concentration of power but I never was aware of it nor did I look for it.
>
> I was going to start with the assumption that everybody in this town was going to make up his or her own mind. Now, I realize that it is a ridiculous assumption to begin with and might not work in a lot of places, but I decided that if I was going to run the campaign—I mean no one was there to contradict me—I was going to do it that way.
>
> So I never went to any key centers of French Catholics and treated people just as people. I don't know if I hit someone who spoke to the other thousand people in his neighborhood and delivered them or not. I never indicated that I was even interested in that. I just talked to people—simple as that. It was a city of a size where it was possible to just talk to people. I probably found the "important" people but did it just a lot more informally.
>
> (Kasky, op. cit., p. 27)

Modestly Kasky concluded, "Well, I couldn't have done it any other way than I did, frankly, because as I say I had no political experience. In fact, one thing I do remember is consciously avoiding the people who I was told were strong politically. I never went to speak to them. If they came to speak to me or if I met them, I spoke to them, but I never tried to make an appointment."

Toward the end of the campaign, Kasky received a number of invitations to join local business and community leaders in their homes for dinner—events that often included others who had been invited to meet him. "It got to the point where on election night I was invited to dinner at one house at six o'clock and then someone else called and invited me to dinner also. I hadn't eaten really well so I accepted them both and spent two hours at one house and two hours at the other. That was the type of campaign it was. I felt like I was a part of the town, really."

With almost no contact with the state headquarters in Concord, Kasky effectively built the campaign in Berlin. Occasionally Studds or I would receive a plea from the north for help of one sort or another but no one with previous New Hampshire campaign experience was able to visit Berlin to help Kasky out. On his own he contacted a Yale friend and his wife urging them to come to Berlin to help him with some of the scheduling tasks that seemed more than he could handle.

Studds and I did offer Kasky various assistance mostly in the form of celebrity visitors as well as the senator and his family. Kasky resisted the former seeing such visits as violations of his personal approach to the voters—an approach that had little room for overt suggestions that people should be instructed how to vote. With the help that Kasky recruited himself from Yale, the local volunteers and the work of the canvassing crews, Kasky managed not only his local efforts but also capably developed excellent schedules for Senator McCarthy, Mrs. McCarthy, and their children. The single exception to Kasky's lack of outside aid was money.

I determined that Berlin was an exception to the contemporary rule of New Hampshire politics that few if any local workers would be paid. For years during the dark period of New Hampshire's Democratic Party local workers had been compensated for their efforts. The reason for this was that often a worker had to take a day "off work" which meant a light pay envelope. Eventually the worker began to possess the job implying that if not hired then a certain number of voters would either not find their way to the polls or would vote for the opposition.

Without a party organization capable of disciplining its workers or the rewards of holding office to encourage loyalty, the local workers gradually became minor political entrepreneurs. They would often be open to the highest bidder or take from all sides. The pattern prevailed through to the early 1960s, especially in the older French-Canadian wards where language served as something of a communications barrier. By hiring the right person it was possible for that individual to "deliver" a block of voters who had come to rely on the local workers as their source of political education.

As bilingual education grew the ability of the local worker to "deliver" votes declined. The reformers of the late 1950s and early 1960s ended the worker payment system relying on volunteers to carry the campaigns. The results at the polls seemed to improve in spite of the screeching and threats of those who had been removed from their election day dole. A few large jobs, such as identifying those who would need absentee ballots and providing them with the ballots for an election, remained paid jobs in the larger cities. In almost all situations where the paid worker had been used before, volunteers did the work of the Democratic Party and its candidates. The one exception was Berlin.

The difference between Berlin and the other cities where the compensation system had worked, was that in Berlin small payments for real work brought results. Few if any even entertained the thought of collecting a candidate's money without performing the work purchased. Berlin was too small a city for one not to be known and regarded for his or her reputation.

After not much more than two weeks of his arrival in Berlin, Kasky called to say that he had found a women who was willing to work for him in the heavily French-Canadian ward of the city. He assured me that he had checked her out thoroughly and had found that she was the right person. In fact, he reported, those who he contacted as references were astonished that he had been able to get this particular women involved. She would have to take time from her job in order to do the work she thought was necessary and needed to be paid for the lost time. I had given Kasky authority to spend campaign funds in Berlin to set up the headquarters, install the telephone, and purchase the supplies he needed but had not expected that Kasky would be successful in tapping the local cadre of political workers.

I had assumed that most of these usually hired for election work would have already been commissioned by the Johnson campaign, and had not expected that Kasky would find any of those worth using available. When he did, I authorized the expenditure immediately. Again Kasky had successfully found his way through the local cobweb to an individual who would be important to the campaign.

Perhaps some of the explanation can be found in the nature of the Johnson campaign in Berlin and its impact. Kasky recounted that the "Johnson effort was a very strange thing. All the people in the Democratic Party—members of the city Democratic Committee—felt obligated to Johnson by virtue of their position on the committee. Because the committee had done something very unorthodox, which was to endorse Johnson." This had happened before Kasky had arrived in Berlin. Since the endorsement had been what the Johnson campaign leaders had asked Berlin to do, they had done it, and, in a sense, they were absolved from further campaign responsibilities.

If they had been asked to campaign instead of endorse then they might well have generated a more effective effort. The preprimary endorsement violated the Berlin ethic of preprimary party neutrality as seriously or more so than it did in other localities. The combination of a less than popular candidate and the request to accomplish an inappropriate endorsement dissipated whatever initiative the local Democratic committee had for the campaign. As Kasky noted:

> Somehow there was never any enthusiasm. I never felt that they felt that Johnson was the man. They had some sense of loyalty to him because he was the president. . . . But they never felt like they had to campaign for Johnson against McCarthy. They sort of felt, "Johnson's the President. He can take care of himself."
>
> (Kasky, op. cit., p. 32)

As a unique form of protection Kasky was totally open and aboveboard with his campaign activities in Berlin. He made the point of describing to the Johnson people he had met informally exactly what he was doing. "For some reason," he recalled, "what I was doing never seemed to strike fear in their hearts. . . . and for that reason, they just sort of let things ride for awhile and concentrated their efforts more on the campaign for the mayor in the town than on representing President Johnson's political interests."

Although he did not frighten the Johnson supporters he did sense that there were times when the Johnson people "could have tried to stop me from doing what I was doing and very easily at any time. All they had to do was send the word out 'don't cooperate' and I might as well have closed the headquarters and left town." He felt that it was his understanding with the local political activists that they would know what he was doing at all times and until he became either secretive or "stepped out of line" they "were going to just let things ride." In the end a last-minute effort was made to "remind people that Johnson was their President and that they ought to support him, but with very little conviction."

McCARTHY'S VISIT

Kasky's two principal jobs when he left Concord for Berlin were to open a campaign headquarters and to prepare campaign schedules for Senator McCarthy. The strategy that Studds and I had worked out for the use of Senator McCarthy's time called for him to visit the Berlin area for one day. Kasky began to draft a day of activity for the senator. In the case of each schedule he developed, as with his other activities, he relied heavily on his local contacts for suggestions.

Senator McCarthy was scheduled to visit Berlin Friday, February 23. When Kasky completed the schedule it read:

10:30–10:55	Meeting with union leaders, Local 75, AFL/CIO
11:00–11:30	WMOW radio interview
11:30–12:10	Granite State Rubber Co. (meet workers)
1:00–3:15	Staff conference
3:30–3:45	Brown Co./Cascade Mill checkout gate (meet shift change)
4:00–4:30	WBRL radio interview
5:30–7:30	Private dinner
7:30–8:00	Meeting of the Democratic Town Committee
8:00–	Reception: Costello Motor Inn

With the exception of the last item, the schedule for the senator was not unusual. Kasky wanted to have an event included in the schedule that would somehow both allow Berlin people to honor Senator McCarthy and at the same time be flattering to the city. He felt that an open house or simple open reception would not quite do what he had in mind. After some thinking and talks with the Washington people scheduling Mrs. McCarthy, he found a tactic that the McCarthys had used successfully in earlier Minnesota senatorial campaigns. They had often held local receptions that were announced through formal invitations.

The formality was introduced by having the invitation printed on a panel card of engraving quality, which was then hand addressed and mailed in a first class stamped, heavy grade envelope. The formality of the invitation went also to the text which invited the recipient to meet Senator and Mrs. Eugene J. McCarthy, Friday evening, February 23, at the Costello Motor Inn. Kasky asked me to have the invitations printed, addressed, and mailed to a list of all Democrats and Independents registered in Berlin.

The invitation was received as intended. Kasky had not only chosen his tactic well but had also selected the right place for the party. He had decided to have the reception in the local hotel rather than go outside of the city to one of the motels on the tourist route. While an old structure that showed its years less than gracefully in all respects, it was the central city hotel, the gathering place of several important local clubs and service organizations. It was also within walking distance of much of the residential population of the city—something Kasky thought important.

In addition to a much larger than anticipated turnout and an extremely positive reaction to the whole event, canvassers visiting Berlin during the days remaining before the primary found, as they were welcomed at the door, that the invitation to the McCarthy reception often was in a place of honor on a sideboard or above a mantel.

"The visit," recalled Kasky, "was a tremendous success. Imagine that from the time he visited Berlin 'til the end of the campaign—which was another two and a half weeks—things steadily moved upwards. Everybody he met was impressed."

In addition to Senator McCarthy's activities, a separate schedule had been developed for Mrs. McCarthy. With the urging of Kasky, Mrs. McCarthy reluctantly shed her behind-the-scenes role and took her first tentative steps as an active campaigner. Kasky was able to entice Mrs. McCarthy to appear before the camera of a local, cable distributed, television station, visit a hospital, and engage in other activities she had successfully resisted in the past.

Throughout Kasky's work in Berlin and each of the campaign events that he shaped, the importance of the community and its people were treated with special insight. While Berlin, as a community, has a certain simplicity that is not characteristic of contemporary New Hampshire cities, it is a city that can quickly protect itself from insincerity. Another person or another approach might have succeeded for the New Hampshire McCarthy campaign in Berlin, but unquestionably it was Marc Kasky, his personality, his sincerity, and his concern for Berlin and its people which made them open not only to him but what he represented.

Kasky contends that the time, events, and candidate were unique and that the uncertainty Berlin people felt toward Washington made it possible for him to accomplish the organizing that he did. McCarthy, he felt, quietly but effectively responded to the desire of Berlin people to have a candidate they could trust and with whom they were comfortable.

The example, however, goes further than Kasky's contention that the time was unique. Such a conclusion diminishes the value of the lessons that his approach to Berlin contains even for those seeking to organize in less isolated and less open communities. In his unpretentious way Marc Kasky shaped a political event in a manner and with a style that was certainly unusual but became characteristic of the impact of the McCarthy campaign. The New Hampshire campaign evolved into a campaign of national meaning because the politically inexperienced were willing to exert the force of personal commitment.

There was nothing to sign, nothing to pledge, but what evolved was reassuring, engaging, and fun, as well as essential and alive. In Berlin, through Kasky's work, what was demonstrated with unusual clarity was what also happened in more complicated and cross-pressured New Hampshire communities.

McCarthy would carry Berlin—labor's best organized New Hampshire city and Lyndon Johnson's presumed northern bastion of support.

CHAPTER 9

Campaign Volunteers

THE KIDS

During his first visit to New Hampshire Al Lowenstein promised that the 1968 campaign would attract the wide interest of young people and they could be expected to help with the McCarthy candidacy. While both Studds and I shared this feeling, which came from our own work with college and prep school students, we were not sure that New Hampshire possessed the student resources to effectively staff a full presidential primary campaign.

In our strategy, Studds and I had encouraged the widely held view that the Johnson renomination effort might well be dominated by people and resources outside of New Hampshire. Realizing that the Johnson image of a large, powerful, even omnipotent Texan capable of submerging friends and enemies alike was not well received in New Hampshire; Bernard Boutin had promised to run the Johnson primary campaign totally with New Hampshire people and money.

His campaign plan and strategy were set, and both were heavily dependent upon the commitment of local New Hampshire Democrats. His concept of the campaign was totally dependent on the veracity of these interpersonal contacts with the "pledge card" being the medium of the reinforcing exchange.

When the pledge-card tactic failed it was already too late for Boutin to change his approach. The only notables he felt comfortable reaching for were the major governmental or political officeholders of New Hampshire—Governor King, Senator McIntyre, and Party Chairman Craig—not imports from his candidate's administration. On the other side, Studds and I knew both personnel and resources had to be imported or there would not be a meaningful campaign for McCarthy.

With great care Studds and I began to suggest that volunteers would be welcome in New Hampshire. We clearly feared that a sudden flood of outsiders was both possible and that it would destroy our efforts. On the other hand without the help it would be impossible to accomplish what was ahead in our plan. Managing the flow of outsiders became an important early task.

The first few volunteers to arrive in New Hampshire were either students who could take time away from their studies, graduate or undergraduate, or precareer adults who were between school or work of an interim activity like the Peace Corps. These, like Eric Schnapper, John Barbieri, Dan Dodds, and Dianne Dumanoski, represented a cross section of those who followed. What was not represented was a sample of volunteers who, while older, were able to leave jobs and professions to spend time with the New Hampshire campaign.

These, such as Jan Goodman who staffed the Dover headquarters, or Arthur Herzog who managed the Salem headquarters, or Fred Willman who did the same in Lebanon, or Shelia Tobias who worked in Concord, or Alan Shepard and his wife who provided important market analysis, were established in their respective careers, were in most cases at least ten years older than the students who came, and were willing to spend both their time and money to be involved in the effort.

The flow of volunteers, at least in the beginning, was less than spontaneous. A few were sent to New Hampshire, such as Dan Dodds who was directed to Concord by Sam Brown, and others who came through contacts with Lowenstein and Gans, or those involved early in the national campaign. John Teague, the Amherst College student who had been involved in the December meeting with Senator McCarthy, recruited student volunteers at Smith, Holyoke, his own college—Amherst, and the University of Massachusetts. He arranged a regular shuttle of cars to New Hampshire on weekends, which toward the end of the campaign took the form of a chartered bus.

Robert Craig wrote in his study of the primary voter's behavior that a schedule for the Dover, New Hampshire, headquarters dated January 10, 1968, read: "11:30 A.M. opened headquarters, 5 guys from Harvard arrived, 1 girl from Boston, 6 typewriters going, finished Wards 1, 2, 3, closed at 9 P.M." (Robert E. Craig, *Voting Behavior in a Presidential Primary: The New Hampshire Democratic Presidential Primary of 1968,* unpublished doctoral dissertation, University of North Carolina at Chapel Hill, 1971, p. 74) As his recollection shows there were a few student volunteers who worked at the campaign's earliest area headquarters, but with the exceptions of Dover, Keene, Nashua, and Manchester, cities near the large Massachusetts student population, the volunteers trickled to Concord and were kept there.

Beside the early arrivals sent from the national campaign, Concord area students returning home for between-semester vacations got caught in the contagion of the campaign. Eric Schnapper, who had engaged in his own advance work at Connecticut College for Women, had encouraged his friends there to come to New Hampshire to help with the campaign. One of his friends was a senior, Ann Kibling from Concord, who, when she arrived home, called Eric about his invitation. He suggested that she attend McCarthy's January 26 speech and help out with the campaign on McCarthy's first day in New Hampshire.

With her sister, a Concord High School senior, and several others from Connecticut College and Concord High School, Ann's plans for a skiing vacation evaporated as they all spent the next six days at the Concord headquarters typing address labels and sorting lists. Her parents, who had expected her to ski and didn't care much for McCarthy's politics at that time, were happy to provide meals and beds for their daughter's college friends and to watch their daughters quickly mature as workers in a campaign. Ann's reaction was, "People were always asking me why I didn't do something more important in the peace movement rather than going around marching in protest, but I never knew what else to do. I didn't know anyone in politics until Senator McCarthy came along." (Underwood, op. cit., pp. 13–14)

The week before and the week after McCarthy's January 26 New Hampshire visit was a period when college semesters ended and students began arriving in New Hampshire to work. To the delight of Studds and myself the headquarters bustled with activity. The arduous work on the mailing labels began to move, and there were always enough people around to take on the variety of tasks that had to be accomplished.

Eric Schnapper, recruiting in the area of his university, Yale; John Teague recruiting in the Amherst area; and Dan Dodds recruiting in the Boston area as well as New Hampshire had been successful in attracting enough students during the last week of January and the first week of February to build the campaign to a high level of energy.

For us it seemed that a major story of the campaign should be the contrast these volunteers provided to the current public image of irresponsible, protesting, unkempt youth. A story that, try as we would to point it out, the media refused to cover. A campaign that such writers as Evans and Novak had seen as doomed to fail did not deserve attention beyond actually covering the candidate when he was in the state.

Barbara Underwood noted:

> If Greek architecture can be divided into three periods depending on the decoration on the top of its columns, so the McCarthy campaign can be divided into three periods depending upon the decoration on the walls of its Concord headquarters.
>
> In the early period, the decoration of the walls was stark and simple, broken only by a few newspaper clippings and the sketches of children made while their mothers (local volunteers) typed or answered the telephone.
>
> In the middle period, the walls were devoted to what might be called college humor. These were then tacked up like "Strange Politics Makes Bedfellows" or in Yiddish the Avis car rental slogan, "We try harder," or in German, French, and Spanish, "No Smoking or Spitting".
>
> In the last period, the walls were covered with elaborate election charts, containing percentages and papered all available wall space with the exception of that covered by one huge picture of Paul Newman.
>
> (Underwood, op. cit., p. 1)

While students were involved in all three periods of the campaign it was not until the semester break that the tone of that involvement became something different. Before, most had been occasional local volunteers working in local headquarters doing routine tasks without either great responsibility or influence in the direction or shape of the campaign, or they were like the Eric Schnappers and Dan Dodds who could find a way to leave their university without leaving their studies. The phenomenon that Lowenstein predicted and that Studds and I began to experience was that of selfless, total commitment to a political adventure where the symbol was the war issue and, especially during the early weeks, only remotely personified by McCarthy, the candidate.

In the beginning the students were, as they had been in previous campaigns, the workers. The between semester break saw a headquarters busy with what appeared to be twenty-five or thirty nameless blurs typing, sorting, and organizing headquarters space without complaint. Their taskmasters were the Concord area local volunteers who kept track of the work flow, and the earlier volunteer arrivals such as Schnapper, Dodds, Barbieri, and Dumanoski who needed help with their own assignments.

Toward the end of the second week of the intersession break when some of those who had come earlier returned again, a murmuring came to our attention. After a week and, in some cases, even more of typing address labels from almost unreadable voting lists, it had occurred to the students that this was a peculiar way to end the war. They had come not expecting to do much more than type labels, stamp, and seal envelopes but now after a week or more of the endless drudgery they wanted to know how it fit into the concept of the campaign, and they wanted to know the importance of their contribution.

We decided to stop the work, gather everyone in the front room of the headquarters, introduce ourselves, and explain. For little more than fifteen minutes we told them about our experience in New Hampshire and how the campaign began. I then went on to discuss the strategy of the campaign and the importance of being able to mail directly to each registered Democratic and Independent voter in the state. I placed in perspective the miserable typing task and expressed regret that there was no other way to do the job. Following several questions about the campaign, McCarthy's positions, and New Hampshire politics, the crew returned to their typewriters, if not with renewed commitment, at least resigned to continue.

The brief meeting accomplished a subtle change in the attitude of the volunteers. Before they had worked without a sense of context and tended to proceed almost blindly as their individual energy and ability to concentrate allowed. After the meeting they sensed that preparing the labels was their job and as such they should become responsible for its organization and efficiency.

With the help of several of the long-term volunteers they began to organize the job into tasks that could be understood and controlled easily while at the same time being susceptible to changing personnel as volunteers came and went. Gradually as the students organized and became proficient, the local volunteers began to lose touch with the work. Their own irregular schedules and other demands on their time made it difficult for them to keep on top of the schedule and flow of work in the headquarters. In this gradual shift a sense developed that the campaign itself had come alive in the form of an organization that now responded to the campaign's tasks and requirements with the campaign's own personnel. The personnel, its student volunteers, were the phenomenon.

Like any organization that is growing the McCarthy campaign had its pains. One symptom was the difficulty the campaign had in finding things for people to do. While this might sound like a contradiction given the enormity of the task, keeping the flow of work and the flow of volunteers even was difficult throughout the campaign, especially so in the early stages.

Barbara Underwood reported, "One weekend at the end of January, David Underwood, the Concord Chairman, stopped into the headquarters and was appalled by the number of college girls who were there for one or two days and had no particular work assigned to them. Underwood was needed at the hospital but called his wife, asked her to get a baby-sitter, then go to the headquarters and start immediately organizing the students into something productive." (Underwood, op. cit., p. 4)

What she did was send several girls out on Concord's Main Street to hand out flyers announcing McCarthy's upcoming speech, while others went to a shopping center to do the same. Others were assigned to telephones and made calls inviting area residents to hear McCarthy. For this Mrs. Underwood received criticism from two sides as she recalled. "One particularly attractive girl from Smith College felt she was wasting her intelligence 'in coming all the way from Northampton and not being assigned a more useful role in the campaign'." While another complaint came from a member of the local committee she had seen on Main Street and thought "looked dreadful." Between the two criticisms was the fact that the arrival of the volunteers was not expected, and the system was not prepared to orient and absorb the sudden arrivals.

Barbara Underwood's initiative in sending kids to hand out leaflets was a good ploy for the moment but hardly the best way to use volunteer energy. No wonder, as was reported to Barbara Underwood, the girls on Main Street "were walking around looking tired, bored, and were smoking." They had neither been oriented to the campaign nor welcomed to it. They had simply been given a task to busy themselves.

Without much method Studds and I squeaked through the two-week intersession flood of volunteers, letting assignments and events evolve. To a considerable extent, while serious work was accomplished, it was more an adventure, possibly a lark, for the young men and women who came to New Hampshire those two weeks. To succeed both the leaders of the campaign and the long-term volunteers realized that special attention would have to be given to accommodating, orienting, assigning, and even, occasionally, debriefing volunteers in order to gain the full potential from the short-term visits.

One of the reasons I insisted that volunteers who expected to stay in New Hampshire for more than a day or two check in with me was my desire to provide a basic orientation to the political ethos of New Hampshire and to establish a direct line of communication with the individual. When that person then left for an assignment, either in an area headquarters or at a specific task in the state headquarters, he or she knew who to contact with any had questions. When assigned to a local office the person had the responsibility of working closely with the local committee and responding to its suggestions and recommendations. While this duel responsibility, to the state campaign and to the local campaign, created some tension it was necessary.

The surprising flock of volunteers that came to New Hampshire during late January and early February received little or no media attention. The first story to appear was written and circulated by a UPI Concord reporter and focused on seven of the college volunteers. The reporter had met these students while traveling with McCarthy during his visit to Laconia on February 8. His interviews began to pick up the reasons that prompted the visits to New Hampshire.

> "A lot of young people began campaigning for McCarthy because of the war," Christine Howells from Connecticut College for Women said. "At first he was just a symbol, but since I've been working for him I now think of him as a president."
>
> These students try to tell you that McCarthy is more than just an opponent of the war. "If people would read the speeches McCarthy has given they would realize McCarthy isn't a one issue man," Peter Sturgis of Harvard said. "He points out the symptoms, using Vietnam as his focus."
>
> . . . Susan Solenborger from Smith feels "the important thing for this nation is to have an alternative. McCarthy is a declared candidate," she added. "It would be a sicker country if McCarthy wasn't around."
>
> (*Keene Evening Sentinel*, February 9, 1968)

Because Studds and I needed people to travel with the senator during his visits and few local people could leave their jobs for the time involved in traveling across New Hampshire, we had to assign these committed but politically innocent strangers to the job. It was a peculiar position for the campaign to be in when reporters with their cars and maps followed youthful volunteers accompanying Senator McCarthy with their cars and maps headed from one New Hampshire city to another without local contacts or advance workers as their guides.

As a reporter described, ". . . in New Hampshire it's sometimes a pretty lonely business campaigning for McCarthy. The caravan of two staff cars and a reporter's car headed out of Concord for Laconia into the dark New Hampshire night, looking like a convoy heading into enemy territory." (*Keene Evening Sentinel*, February 9, 1968)

Without local people to interview on these rides the reporters came to know the students, their reasons for coming to New Hampshire, their expectations, and their backgrounds. It would be sometime later before the reporters discovered the activity in the headquarters and learned that New Hampshire was becoming a mecca of a new volunteer force in American politics.

Perhaps the reason this discovery took so long, in spite of our efforts to draw attention to it, was a coincidence in timing which found Roger Mudd with his CBS film crew in an almost deserted Concord office late in January. Mudd had come to New Hampshire to prepare a special report on the primary election and was in Concord to interview Governor King and to visit the McCarthy headquarters. He and his crew arrived at the headquarters at noon when both local and student volunteers had left for lunch. Only Eric Schnapper was in the otherwise deserted building.

Sensing that CBS was about to carry a film story of an empty headquarters, Schnapper frantically telephoned the Kibling home where a number of the volunteers were having lunch. The attempt to get the headquarters activity level up again failed as Mudd interviewed David Underwood, the Concord chair who happened by. The film crew photographed Underwood's three-year-old son drawing another picture to be added to those already on the walls. It was hardly the image of a vigorous campaign organizing to challenge the nomination of an incumbent president.

Just as suddenly as the flock of students had arrived at the beginning of their semester recess, they left. Many had stayed much beyond what they had intended. Several had missed the early classes of the next semester in order to help with McCarthy's early February three-day visit. But by February 12 only the few long-termers remained and even the ranks of these had dwindled as Eric Schnapper had to return to Yale Law School to manage some law review work, Dan Dodds had to check in with his graduate adviser in New York, and John Barbieri had to keep an appointment with his New Haven draft board.

That evening, when I joined Studds in Concord, the headquarters was almost empty. Where there had been almost two weeks of constant activity that began early and ended late each day, only a typewriter or and two clicked, and unfinished stacks of checklists remained to be scanned for mailing label addresses.

Once again the frightening sense of loneliness and despair that we had faced following the announcement of McCarthy's New Hampshire candidacy January 4 returned. Even the simplest tasks of answering a telephone, finding some notes, or sensing the next priority seemed overwhelming. For more than an hour Studds and I stumbled around our small office, roamed the empty workroom, and tried to figure out how to resolve our predicament. It was, we concluded, a national campaign, and to that moment, with the exception of a trickle of money, little national support had been there. We began calling for help—first to Blair Clark, then to the people we had come to know before McCarthy entered, Curtis Gans and Allard Lowenstein, then to those we were continually pestering for materials and assistance at national headquarters.

The tone of confidence, which had grown during the pervious weeks, was now gone. Our own feeling of desperation translated into urgent pleas for new volunteers, long-term staff people, and an assurance of adequate financial support. With our plea was a reminder that unless McCarthy succeeded in New Hampshire his campaign and the test his candidacy represented concerning the public's view of the war would be lost. The election was exactly one month from that date, February 11.

LOGISTICS AND VOLUNTEERS

While it was exceptionally uncomfortable for Studds and me, it was important for the future development of the campaign to have the break that came when the volunteers returned to their colleges and universities. It gave us and the continuing volunteers a chance to assess what could and could not be accomplished with the volunteer help, to what stage the campaign had developed, and how to respond in the management of the next flock of volunteers.

Their initiative was especially engaging and something that Studds and I found could be developed to the advantage of the campaign. With only brief instructions, the students would develop an assignment, come back to Studds and me with their findings to check their efforts, and then, with our revisions suggested, go ahead with the project. This performance was reassuring and led to the conclusion that future management of the campaign's day-to-day operations could be turned over to students as long as the students understood that when problems and questions occurred they were to check them with either Studds or me. And, further, before changing an activity in any major way, they would discuss their recommendation.

What then began to evolve within the campaign was a series of departments. The departments were almost autonomous having their own task oriented organization, their own means of communication, and their own links to other departments with which they might share an objective. The hints of this organization were there during the two-week period. Now it became important to see that the campaign took full advantage of this promise.

Besides the early assignments to Eric Schnapper to help with scheduling and advance work, and to Dan Dodds to recruit and the manage volunteers, and to John Barbieri to keep the work of the headquarters flowing there evolved the first logistical assignment. When Dianne Dumanoski arrived in Concord having left her graduate studies in English at Yale, she found herself in charge of the housing situation.

Her search for housing for herself turned up an apartment that would accommodate many of those spending an extended period of time in New Hampshire. As a result of her success and the desperate need of the campaign to be able to house arriving volunteers, Dianne's job became one of finding places for volunteers to stay. Her early efforts were concentrated in the Concord area as most of the volunteers remained with assignments in the state headquarters. Eventually her job evolved into the responsibility for housing volunteers in each of the communities where volunteers were sent.

At first Dianne's task meant finding an extra bed or couch in or near Concord were a student or two could spend a weekend. The separation of the sexes was the rule, and courtesies were easily extended from families of McCarthy supporters in the city. As the number of arrivals increased the circle of housing options was expanded to the outlying towns that were without street signs or house numbers.

A favorite story of the campaign was about one group of volunteers that Dianne sent out to Dunbarton to stay in the guest room of Virginia Colter. They followed the instructions to Mrs. Colter's house as carefully as they could in the late evening. Arriving at the house they went in the open door of the darkened house, assuming that the Colters were either asleep or out for the evening, and followed the careful instructions to their room. Not much later, the owners arrived home. Surprised to see the light in their bedroom, they walked in to find strangers. A few awkward moments passed before it was determined that the volunteers had entered the wrong house. The Colters home was a bit further down the road. Without anyone being particularly upset, apologies were made, and a laugh shared before the volunteers left for the correct destination.

As Dianne herself commented, "Despite the signs saying that 'Strange politics makes bedfellows,' sleeping arrangements for males and females were carefully segregated. All we need is for the press to report that we are all sleeping together up here and we will blow all the good we hope to achieve. Those arriving in New Hampshire who expected a 'love-in' didn't last long." Even alcohol was banned by the volunteers without a word from the leaders, even though many of the students were over New Hampshire's twenty-one-year-old drinking age.

Dianne stretched the willingness of local people to accommodate volunteer workers to the maximum. As the campaign progressed some McCarthy supporters were housing fifteen to twenty students and other volunteers in their hometowns. Hospitality had extended far beyond guest room, extra bed, or couch, and it now included carpeted floors, family rooms, and often a hallway. Doris Stanley of Nashua recalled cooking breakfast for each of the twenty who stayed one weekend in her modest home and having to step over bodies in sleeping bags to get from her bedroom to the kitchen.

Stretching the walls of homes went only so far, especially in cities like Manchester where the McCarthy locals were few and far between. In desperation Dianne began contacting churches where she had heard the pastors were sympathetic to the antiwar position of Senator McCarthy. In Manchester, Nashua, Concord, and several other cities where major volunteer campaigning was needed, church basements and activity rooms became weekend dormitories for literally hundreds of kids—a term that came to describe anyone, younger or older, student or not, who came to New Hampshire to work for Senator McCarthy.

With the exception of those who came and stayed for more than a weekend, virtually no expenses were paid. Occasionally a starving student would turn up who could not find money for a meal, and the petty cash in the headquarters would be tapped for a transfusion. In some cases those bringing cars and even a bus or two would raise money locally to sustain the volunteers during their journey. The long-term kids received an extremely modest per diem which covered the cost of meals, car operation if one were used, and housing in the case of the few who had to rent accommodations. With the exception of a few of the national staff that eventually came to work in New Hampshire and two secretaries, no other campaign workers were paid for their time.

At one time during Dianne Dumanoski's desperate efforts to find housing for expected arrivals, she urgently requested sleeping bags to help those coming without them. In her search it occurred to her that Dartmouth College had a reputation as being an outdoor-oriented institution which meant to her a large supply of sleeping bags stashed in undergraduates' rooms. She called a contact or two in Hanover and within hours a carload of sleeping bags was on its way to Concord.

Dianne's story relates how the early recruiting developed in the campaign, and that was not much different from what others were to experience later when Studds and I sought help after the semester recess exodus. She recalled, "A lot of us felt that this was the last chance within the existing political structure of government to make a change in the Johnson administration. There are a lot of kids who would take time off from school to help but they would be drafted." To which she added, "I know many students who really feel for McCarthy and what he stands for, but can't work because they have to keep up their grades." (Underwood, op. cit., p. 3)

McCarthy would comment later that his workers were the "A and B" students of the generation while Robert Kennedy had the "C" students. Without the need to compare with Kennedy, Studds and I found that our kids were among the brightest of the current college population. This was also reflected in the fact that many were able to secure releases of one sort or another from their schools in order to work in the campaign.

Beyond keeping a straight-laced, even puritanical image for the campaign, Studds and I were concerned that New Hampshire might become a haven for those wishing to escape school and especially parental authority. We feared having someone report to the press that their son or daughter had been lured away to the campaign much as a legendary circus runaway.

To avoid the possibility, we insisted that each person who arrived to work in New Hampshire register through the state headquarters or at the local headquarters. These volunteer information cards were kept in a master file at the state headquarters to be used in case of emergency and, if necessary, to demonstrate to any who asked that the campaign knew its volunteers. (See sample volunteer card on page 325.) When a volunteer returned to the state for other visits the card was pulled, the new visit recorded, and then placed in a special file of those then working in the campaign.

Although no one made the charge we feared, the file was used on several occasions to find volunteers in emergencies and also to keep track of persons who, because they returned frequently, could handle more difficult jobs. The whole process of evaluating and then assigning volunteers to jobs became thorough and sophisticated.

After the confusion of the semester recess time, Dianne Dumanoski set up the registration activity as part of her housing job. Her department in the campaign became the conduit through which requests for volunteers came not only from the state headquarters but also from the local offices. Where initially almost all volunteers would arrive in Concord and then be assigned elsewhere in the state, Dianne began to anticipate where and how many people would be needed by the local headquarters and then contacted the kids directing them to a specific local workplace. This approach was especially useful when groups of volunteers would return after an initial weekend. They could be sent directly to a community or local headquarters without having to be oriented or having to learn their assignment. In a short time these returnees had become professionals.

In addition to assignments by skills and experience, there was also a sort by appearance. There were inside jobs and outside jobs. Those who wished to work outside, that is either with the candidate or representing the campaign, had to be conservative in dress and appearance.

In that time long hair, male or female, facial hair, short skirts, or funky clothing were viewed as symbols of protest which might keep the campaign from being able to reach people beyond an immediate reaction to appearance. Those arriving with

Volunteer Information

(1) a. Name DREW SANBORN
b. School U.N.H.
c. School address 48 EDGEWOOD ROAD DURHAM
d. Home address " "
e. School telephone NONE Home telephone NONE

(2) General Availability
a. When during weekdays can he work? MORNINGS

b. When on Sunday through Thursday evenings can he work? NO

c. When on weekend can he work? NO

d. Does he have a car? Yes ✓ No ___

e. In what other cities in New Hampshire does he have friends with whom he could stay?

(3) Students-Semester Break
a. To whom and where has he been assigned, or where will he be during the break if he is not assigned?

b. When is his break? From Feb 1 to Feb 8

c. Will he have access to a car where he will be during the break? yes ✓ no ___

trimmed hair, clean faces, conservative clothing, and neat appearances were assigned the outside jobs. Those who were more casual in their appearance were assigned to the less visible jobs even, on occasion, totally out of sight.

To be "Neat and Clean for Gene" was the slogan and the fact of the campaign. Enforcement of the slogan rested with those who had come to make this "final test of the political system" and their code was stiff. If appearance or behavior did not meet the image they had set, then the alternatives were to help but stay out of sight, leave New Hampshire, or change appearances. Once the criteria had been accepted by the earliest arrivals, the rite of passage into the campaign was often more stringent than Studds and I or other local leaders would have enforced.

THE SECOND WAVE

As Barbara Underwood noted in her account, there were three periods in the evolution of the student volunteers' participation in the campaign. The first was marked by the surprise arrival of students during the semester recess and ended when they returned to their schools during the first week of February.

The second period began during the second week of February when, in response to our plea for help, a new stream of volunteers began. Important among these were

Ben and Rosann Stavis, who like others who would arrive during the second period, planned to spend more than just a weekend in New Hampshire.

In the Stavis' account of their experiences they wrote ". . . at the beginning of February, Rosann and I had a block of free time. I had just passed my oral examinations and could leave campus and studies for a while. Rosann was working on her dissertation in home economics education at New York University and could also leave New York. So on February 14th, St. Valentine's day, we took a bus to Boston and next morning, another one to Concord, New Hampshire—almost four weeks before the New Hampshire primary. We walked into the headquarters about 10:30 A.M., suitcases in hand." (Stavis, op. cit., p. 3)

A small group of McCarthy supporters from Cornell University also arrived at about the same time including Joel Feigenbaum, a graduate student in nuclear physics. When he called me to ask if he could come, the first wave of volunteers had just departed. It seemed a long way for someone to come but if he wanted to help I was in no position to refuse. With him came Shelia Tobias, a Cornell administrator, and within a week Joel's wife, a social worker, and young son also arrived.

A Wellesley senior, Belle Huang, negotiated a directed research project with a professor and was able to return for the remainder of the New Hampshire campaign after her semester break visit. She was also the president of the Wellesley student government which became a valuable source of volunteers. She, with another Wellesley student, Bobbie Kramer, and Katie Odin, a Berkeley graduate who came from Portland, Oregon, to help, worked with Dianne Dumanoski finding sleeping space, registering volunteers, and directing volunteers to local offices.

Stavis, Feigenbaum, and Dodds functioned as the guts of a small task force I set up to research how canvassing might be accomplished. The Keene experiment had just begun and some other canvassing efforts had been tried as part of the effort to reach voters with the anti-Vietnam war message. Most of these efforts, however, had been concentrated in or near academic communities such as Cambridge, Massachusetts; Berkeley, California; Ann Arbor, Michigan; or Madison, Wisconsin.

Another volunteer who came to besiege the campaign with her energy and suggestions was Arlene Popkin a graduate student in Boston. Studds quickly reacted to Arlene's aggressiveness by labeling her "Arlene Popoff." After a few days of her being on my heels at headquarters, my usually quiet manner almost came to violence. What Studds and I then worked out was that Arlene would return to Boston with a pile of the checklists and five-part label sheets she would then farm out. This preserved peace in the headquarters, and kept work flowing that otherwise would have depended on haphazard volunteer time.

Another Boston recruit was a thirty-year-old lawyer, John Grace, who had been attracted to politics and McCarthy through the activities of the Massachusetts McCarthy committee. Quiet, competent, and effective he immediately fit our description of someone who might be capable of unraveling the confusion of the Manchester effort. After a day or two with Studds and myself in Concord, we sent him to Manchester to figure out what was wrong there. In spite of his best efforts, he was unable to suggest improvements advising instead that the problems were too complex to be corrected during the few weeks that remained. His frank appraisal forced us to accept Manchester as it was and to attempt to guide the campaign so that any damage that might accrue from the situation would be minimal.

Another recruit for the Manchester campaign was a recently returned, wounded veteran of the Vietnam War, Carl Rogers. His convalescence almost complete, he arrived wanting to help. To use him as a regular volunteer seemed to not quite fit his political potential. When he arrived Studds and I discussed with him what he might do that would illustrate that the war was not opposed just by the "peaceniks" but also by the veterans who had seen their buddies die there and now felt the effort not worth the price.

Rogers concluded that he could speak on campuses to help recruit volunteers, speak before local groups and service clubs to expand the audience for opposition, or he could bring together a new organization of Vietnam Veterans Against the War—something that had already begun. On the latter point he felt an obligation to his fellow servicemen and servicewomen both still in the military and out to organize their views and to present them as part of the McCarthy candidacy. Studds and I felt that any of the three options would be helpful but that the latter, organizing antiwar opposition among Vietnam veterans, would have the greatest impact in New Hampshire and, perhaps, elsewhere. For Rogers to do this meant establishing a bit of distance between the McCarthy campaign and the activity of the Vietnam Veterans Against the War organization. While coordination was important, both sides felt it would give greater strength and credibility for the veterans to speak and act independently of the campaign.

Rogers felt that he could recruit a number of Vietnam veterans who would welcome the chance to come to New Hampshire to help end the war and that many of them would want to do more than speak occasionally. His idea was to develop a special piece of literature that stated the veterans' reasons for opposing the war and then organize to distribute this on their own. While Studds and I were concerned about having separate groups use the campaign as a vehicle for special interest advocacy, it seemed that if any group had earned the right to state a position it was the veterans. Almost regardless of what they did or said in stating their position they would be difficult to discredit or tie to the McCarthy campaign in a way that would be less than of help. In fact, we felt that even if the public reaction to the veterans' activity was negative, the fact that a significant number of the war's veterans were willing to take the time to work against the war would be unsettling to the New Hampshire voter.

While not strictly "kids" in the usual definition as applied to the campaign's volunteers, the Vietnam veterans were contemporaries of the college student but contemporaries whose experiences in Vietnam cast them differently. There was considerable kinship between the vets and the other kids but a kinship that was distinct when the vets began their efforts at antiwar public education. The public perceived that they had paid dues that others had not and deserved to be dealt with a certain respect. For this reason the Vietnam vets were able to do things that would have been poorly received, given the climate of the time, by their college student peers.

In addition to speaking and campus organizing, the veterans decided to hand their brochure out on the streets and attempt to get passersby to discuss the war with them. On weekends, during heavy shopping times, and during pleasant weather the vets occupied street corners usually accompanied by a sign that identified them as Vietnam veterans. There they politely distributed their flyers, talked with people, and urged them to support Senator McCarthy's candidacy. Dressed in their old uniforms they had a startling effect on the passersby who had had little or no direct contact with the war.

During the last three weeks of the campaign the numbers swelled from a few leaders like Carl Rogers, to forty or fifty veterans. Since Manchester was the problem city for McCarthy and the one with the largest Democratic vote, I had Rogers concentrate his fellow veterans there. On practically every corner of the city's main thoroughfare, Elm Street, there stood a veteran with a sign, flyers, and a cluster of curious questioning and listening.

John Fitzgerald, a captain, recovering from wounds received in action, was at the end of convalescent leave. He and a number of others found ways to come to New Hampshire to support the veterans' activity against the war while still either in some stage of discharge or active duty. For those with time yet to serve, coming to New Hampshire, often in uniform, to protest the war carried serious penalties if reported. Rogers' veterans seemed to melt in and out of the state when needed. Few but the leaders were identified but their impact was reenforcing to the thrust of what had been a civilian movement.

The principal leaders and organizers of the major activities of the last phase of the campaign came from the second wave of volunteers. Each department in the headquarters was staffed and often led by volunteers who had either come earlier and stayed or had arrived early in February prepared to remain. Each department tended to recruit its own staff largely from the flow of volunteers that appeared on the day when something had to be done. From the weekend volunteers came the workers who carried out the projects that were organized and planned during the week. Often students would return weekend after weekend to work.

As the source of help became reliable, those leading the various departments tended to keep track of their own volunteers and plan projects to be taken on by a reliable weekender. A highly informal hierarchy evolved which placed people in positions according to how long they had been with the campaign in New Hampshire, how long they could spend during a given visit, and how frequently they could promise to return.

In addition to the change that developed in how the campaign was managed during the second period, there was a change in the relationship of the campaign to those who had developed it earlier. Ben Stavis recounted his impressions of the second period from the perspective of a volunteer arriving, being assigned to a task, and observing the campaign from that task. His observations are important since they catch the shift that had occurred from a campaign that was attached to the locality to one that had taken its own structure and organization.

> The New Hampshire staff included very few New Hampshirites. We did hire a mature local woman to be a full-time receptionist; she could say "McCarthy" ith the proper New England nasal twang. Furthermore, she

> helped us find our way around town and the state. The local radical, a seventy-eight-year-old woman who went to world fellowship conferences all around the world, came to stuff envelopes. The Concord co-chairman has Marcie Macey, a young housewife. (The other co-chairman, a doctor, was vacationing in the Bahamas during the last weeks of the campaign.)
>
> . . . Another staff member from Concord was a boy of twelve who built tables, desks, sleeping bag lockers, and telephone tables with booths. The state chairman, David Hoeh, thirty years old and an administrator at Dartmouth College, came by from time to time with his wife Sandi [sic]. They were concerned with the media, with the Senator's schedule, and with their own relationship with the state Democratic Party. These broad responsibilities meant that neither could supervise the hourly crises in the headquarters. And since they were from Dartmouth, the staff they recruited worked in Hanover. The state headquarters, then, as it developed campaigns both in Concord and in the entire state, was dominated by outsiders.
>
> (Stavis, op. cit., p. 20)

Ben and Rosann had arrived in Concord just at the point when the transition took place from the sparse local operation of the state campaign to one of almost complete operation by the imported volunteers. In the early weeks the Concord McCarthy supporters had filled most of the state campaign jobs as their time and personal schedules would allow. Virtually no one from New Hampshire had been able to devote full time to the campaign as a volunteer. As the tasks of the statewide effort grew, the local committee members tended to recede to those local tasks that they, and only they, could accomplish. To a certain extent Stavis sensed this shift from statewide concern to local activity when he wrote:

> For the field workers the same was true to varying degrees. In most of the towns where they were deployed there were some wonderful people dedicated to Senator McCarthy and to peace.
>
> (Stavis, ibid., p. 21)

Using the example of a Portsmouth retired naval officer who had come to question the "world outlook which it [the Navy] supported," and was now a graduate student at the University of New Hampshire, Stavis noted that "people such as this man could be an inspiration to the field staff, but they could not give political guidance. They had neither the experience nor the resources in manpower or finances."

Stavis concluded, "Thus both the headquarters staff and the field staff . . . formed its work habits in an atmosphere of isolation from the local political leadership." He then contends that "we did not have in New Hampshire the opportunity to work with a strong, imaginative, resourceful local committee that could organize its own campaign and give us accurate information about the local political situation." He then noted, "I was depressed at first by this lack of local involvement but gradually realized that in New Hampshire presidential politics is a spectator sport, not a participant sport."

What Stavis missed was that the portion of the campaign that had developed earlier had been created by "a strong, imaginative, resourceful local committee," and that that committee was now occupying itself with those tasks only it could carry out. Principle among these was giving "accurate information about the local political situation." Because Stavis and others arrived in New Hampshire at a point when the transition from local management to full-time management had become almost complete, he was not included in the continual exchange that passed between the local leadership and the new managers such as Curtis Gans and Sam Brown. The simple fact that Gerry Studds' name is absent from Stavis' account of the campaign indicates that while virtually all of Stavis' time was spent in the Concord headquarters it was not necessary for Studds to relate to Stavis in ways that were important to him as he recalled his New Hampshire experience.

What Stavis did not see or understand was that what had once been a small statewide organization on behalf of McCarthy's candidacy had now become a federated campaign. When the early supporters came together in the Chaplain living room in November and December the immediate support for the McCarthy candidacy could be counted on the faces in that room. What had happened in the interim meant that for each face and each community represented there was, by the middle of February, an organization of some size and number in each of the communities and in many others.

Those who had brought together the early McCarthy Steering Committee were now fully occupied with their own local organizing and campaign activities. Even the Concord committee, which had managed the tasks of the state campaign during much of January, was now relegated to a corner of the state headquarters that was marked with one of the ubiquitous signs, "Concord McCarthy for President Committee."

Of the early New Hampshire organizing committee, only Studds and I were regularly involved in the day-to-day policy of the state campaign. John Holland, as the fiscal agent, and Merv Weston, developing the campaign's advertising, were also extensively involved but from their own offices in Manchester. While it was true that for many New Hampshire residents presidential politics is, as Stavis noted, a "spectator sport," in 1968, perhaps more than at any previous time, the McCarthy candidacy stimulated wide local participation.

As a result not only were Studds and I able to organize either storefront or home headquarters in each of their priority communities, but we were able to proceed further down the list of New Hampshire's most populous towns responding to local interest in the campaign. The outsiders were the ones with the time to spend on the campaign's local work but, though not apparent to observers like Stavis in the state headquarters, at the local level a close working relationship between the local committee and the outside volunteers was essential. Without it an outsider was almost totally adrift unless that person was Marc Kasky in Berlin. However, to every rule there seems to be an exception. The exception in 1968 was what Ben experienced from his and Rosann's desk in the northeast corner of the rear room of the old Ralph Pill Electric Supply Store.

REPORTERS DISCOVER THE STUDENTS

As determined as Studds and I had been to get the story of the flow of student volunteers told, it was not until the activity had been going for several weeks that the press finally became interested. In fact we were concerned that if the influx was not explained by the press, it might be attacked by the Johnson committee and cast in a manner that would be embarrassing to our efforts.

Once the students' positive identity had been established by the press, it would be difficult to change. I especially feared the *Manchester Union Leader*'s ability to destroy efforts they opposed by raising the activity to one of public controversy. If having students come to New Hampshire to work for McCarthy had been projected by the *Manchester Union Leader* as controversial before either the other state media or the national media had had a chance to review the activity themselves, then the old adage "were there is smoke there must be fire" might have prevailed.

Instead of students being warmly received in the communities, there might well have been a debilitating hostility. The campaign would have lost the important attributes of energy, charm, and sincerity the students brought to the campaign in the New Hampshire public's mind. To deny the campaign the numbers of students alone would have been a death blow.

With the exception of the twenty-five to thirty-five students who might be working in the Concord headquarters during peak weekend times, most of those who came to New Hampshire were dispersed to local headquarters and tasks in the communities. The reporters would usually visit the state campaign headquarters to discuss the campaign with Studds or me but would rarely see more than the ten or fifteen people who regularly worked in the front portion of the office.

On February 10 Edgar Mills of the *Christian Science Monitor* wrote under the headline "Students Back McCarthy in N.H." with a section heading that read "Student roll swells" that "Each weekend the number of participating students swells, according to Eric Schappel [sic] Yale Law School student. . . . They work at a variety of political tasks, such as typing voter file cards from checklists as the basis for later contacts with voters, manning headquarters, and the like." The article went on to note, "The flood started at the last semester break when students from Smith College and the University of New Hampshire worked in the campaign." (*Christian Science Monitor*, February 10, 1968, p. 1)

While Mills had to take Eric Schnapper's word concerning the flood, there remained an inclination on the part of the campaign to keep the "flood" and the activity of the candidate separate. During the latter weekends of the campaign, when the flood was nearing its crest, the volunteer coordinators would try to soften the rigors of a Saturday of campaigning by holding a party late in the evening in the cities where the volunteers were concentrated. No alcohol appeared nor much else in the way of party fixings, just loud music, and milling or exhausted and slumped bodies trying to sort out what their trip to New Hampshire meant and how their experiences could possibly help elect McCarthy or stop a war.

McCarthy was scheduled to campaign in Manchester, Saturday evening, February 24. With the exception of the few students who worked as traveling aides of the senator, until that evening few if any of the students had seen or met Senator McCarthy in New Hampshire. As usual a party for the volunteers was scheduled and, on this evening, it was to be in the Manchester Room of the Sheraton-Carpenter in downtown Manchester. The scheduled starting time was about 10:30 P.M., late enough so that the candidate and the reporters would be tucked away after a long campaign day.

McCarthy had traveled to Manchester from a busy day in Berlin and arrived to tour Manchester's ethnic social clubs. Before the tour began, Curtis Gans had ordered the organizers of the student party to be sure that it did not begin until after McCarthy's tour was over, and he and the press had returned to their respective accommodations. In fact he had strongly suggested that the party should not begin until after 12:00 midnight when he was quite sure all of the reporters would be out of sight.

I had been meeting with Gans when Gans issued his order. As I drove the short distance from the Sheraton-Wayfarer to the Sheraton-Carpenter, I mulled over this. I concluded that contrary to Gans' view my own was that the young people were the ones who had the greatest stake in the campaign and their commitment should not be hidden. I immediately found the person who Gans had talked to, the one organizing the student party, and said that he should continue with the preparations. The party, I said, would be held at the earlier hour. I then said that I intended to not only invite McCarthy to meet the volunteers at the party, but planned also to invite the reporters. In the time that remained and in reaction to Gans' concern, I asked the organizer of the party to ask those coming to be as respectable as possible and also to hide some of the shaggier folks in corners not easily reached by the reporters. Gans was upset with my decision to countermand his instructions but could do little except ensure that the lights in the room were turned down and the music played was less raucous than usual.

Before McCarthy began his tour of the social clubs, I suggested the visit to the party. McCarthy agreed. I then hopped on the press bus to announce the addition to the evening's schedule. When the entourage returned to the Sheraton-Carpenter there was little sign of the crowd that had assembled inside the Manchester Room. A nervous Curtis Gans had made sure that the large crowd of volunteers was not straggling outside the hotel or even in the lobby and hallway leading to the Manchester Room. McCarthy led the throng of reporters and film crews, each struggling for position or attempting to get their equipment ready to capture the event. Into a darkened room almost packed with young volunteers, McCarthy strode to the instant applause of the crowd.

One of the rare electric events of politics occurred as McCarthy was suddenly in view and reach of the several hundred who had come this far to work so hard for him. The television lights followed McCarthy through the crowd to a low platform and microphone that had been set up in a corner of the room. Gans had made sure that those closest to the door and nearest the platform were among the "neatest and cleanest for Gene."

McCarthy spoke briefly, welcoming his workers with the now famous phrase "you all look like a government in exile," which brought a roar from the crowd. He answered several question about his candidacy, the war, and other issues to which he replied with his usual skill. The crowd, the press, and Senator McCarthy were delighted. The candidate sparkled. It had been a long day, but each moment was savored as the rapport between McCarthy, his campaign, and the often cynical press blossomed.

McCarthy left for his hotel, the television lights faded, and the reporters, film crews, and volunteers made friends in the dimness of the Manchester Room. If there was a love-in during the campaign, the evening of February 24 came closest to it.

The authors of the book *An American Melodrama* wrote of earlier discussions concerning students in 1968 politics which captured the concern many felt before students, politics, media, campaign, and candidate were joined as they were in the New Hampshire campaign.

> McCarthy supplied the all-important respectability to the enterprise, the students came through with the energy. Back in November 1967, Robert Kennedy had discussed with Professor Galbraith the kind of campaign McCarthy ought to wage in New Hampshire. Kennedy was very emphatic on one specific point, urging Galbraith to tell McCarthy, "Make sure this is a grown-up enterprise. He'll have more Dartmouth under grads than he could or should use. So let him look out for that." That a campaign could be "grown-up" and yet make lavish use of student volunteers was not part of the conventional political wisdom.
>
> (Chester, Hodgson, Page, op. cit., p. 96)

With care on both the part of the students and on the part of those managing the campaign, the "grown-up enterprise" materialized. The New Hampshire leaders, like Studds and myself, had had reassuring experiences with volunteers and from this had confidence that the phenomenon would be well received. We were proud of what the young volunteers had accomplished and wanted the public to know and appreciate resourcefulness.

Like many of the more successful events of the New Hampshire campaign McCarthy's visit to the party was spontaneous. To have staged such a meeting would have been impossible. If Gans' instinct had been followed, the students might have viewed themselves as an embarrassment to the campaign and been less willing to continue. McCarthy, himself, could have vetoed the visit but he had come to trust Studds' and my judgment about campaigning in New Hampshire. He also liked the sincerity, intelligence, and energy of the young people he had met. Saturday evening, February 24, sealed the pact between candidate, issues, campaign, and an inquisitive, possibly amazed press. From then on a honeymoon continued that could not be jolted as the press attributed prodigious accomplishments to a cadre of the nation's youth. This cadre now showed effective political action against an administration and a war policy that had seemed impervious to assault or change not many weeks before.

Earlier, the *New York Times* had printed its first notice of the student involvement in New Hampshire February 18 when, in a longer story, a section heading appeared which read, "College Students Help," followed by:

> The McCarthy campaign has been bolstered, particularly on weekends, by college students from inside and outside the state who have addressed and stuffed envelopes and done other necessary chores as their contribution to the Senator's campaign against the Administration's conduct of the Vietnam war.
>
> (*New York Times,* February 18, 1968)

A few items concerning the student involvement in the campaign had appeared in the New Hampshire press. Jack Hubbard of the *Concord Daily Monitor,* a friend of mine, had written in his February 7 column:

> McCarthy had become an inspiration for the disenchanted Democrat, and the slogan (At last, Democrats have a Political Alternative) has become a battle cry for his New Hampshire organization most of whom are political novices.
>
> The McCarthy campaign perhaps has the least chance of succeeding in New Hampshire but it is by far the closest to the soil of political protest, and it represents a significant grass roots movement.
>
> The backbone of the New Hampshire McCarthy headquarters is the college student, and many of them believe McCarthy is the last bastion of opposition in the existing political structure to President Johnson.
>
> On weekends, these students trek from all over New England, pitching in with the drudge work of the campaign, typing, pasting, mailing, and answering the telephone.
>
> Last weekend, more than 90 students came from Amherst, Smith, Connecticut College for Women, Mt. Holyoke, Massachusetts Institute of Technology, Harvard, New York University, and Yale to work on the McCarthy campaign.
>
> Some of them were in Concord, while others were dispatched to storefront headquarters in Nashua, Manchester, Keene, Laconia, Lebanon, and Dover to do office work.
>
> Still others students went hunting for voter checklists in Granite State towns.
>
> The students are in contrast to the rank and file party pro that populates the "Citizens for Johnson" headquarters in Manchester, and full time campaigners working for Nixon and Romney.
>
> During the week, the McCarthy activity lulls somewhat because classes are in session.
>
> (*Concord Daily Monitor,* February 7, 1968)

The article continued with an interview with Dianne Dumanoski in which she described why she had come to New Hampshire, her background, and campaign assignment. It was a thorough review of the campaign and especially the student volunteer aspect.

However, it was not until the Manchester volunteers' party on February 24, and the feeling that came from the that and the escalating fortunes of McCarthy in New Hampshire, that the national press sensed there were more stories in the 1968 New Hampshire campaign than those tied strictly to the schedule and activities of the candidate.

The Johnson campaign now sensed an opportunity to take a crack at the volunteers coming from outside the state. In a press conference Governor King commented that the McCarthy campaign could not be considered as a serious threat because it had failed to receive broad local support. In fact, he noted, the campaign relies almost totally on college students from outside New Hampshire to support its efforts. Concerned that this charge might stir the investigative juices of the *Manchester Union Leader,* Studds and I anxiously waited to see what response might develop.

Like other tactics of the LBJ committee, King's comments seemed to backfire. A number of local people were critical of King's remarks explaining their own involvement in the campaign and defending the assistance the students were providing with their local activities. Toward the end of the campaign Governor King was quoted as having said, "It's those damned kids," when asked why McCarthy was creeping up on his candidate. In an interview published four days before the election David B. Wilson of the *Boston Globe* wrote:

> The governor was ready to concede that the student invasion has assisted McCarthy.
>
> "They're a good, clean-cut bunch," he said. "I hope they come up here and live and become good Democrats." The emphasis was on the word "good."
>
> "They have stirred up curiosity and interest, and they have very probably cut down on the President's margin," he added.
>
> (*Boston Globe,* March 8, 1968)

Even in the heat and bitterness of the last few days of the campaign, Governor King, who did not spare his language when it came to McCarthy, knew that the kids had won their way into the hearts of even many who would be voting for President Johnson on March 12. To a considerable extent we felt that the role of the volunteers had been legitimized by surviving an attack and, subsequently, by the special attention the volunteers received in the press.

Unquestionably columnist Mary McGrory became the godmother or midwife, depending upon one's view, that cast the volunteer activity into unique prominence. After her column appeared, a flood of reporters, film crews, and subsequent articles and television features developed the volunteer aspect into almost the campaign's dominant story.

Larger-than-life images of an immense "children's crusade" were marched out of New Hampshire by film and typewriter to a confused and cynical national populace.

In a time when the generations seemed irreconcilably apart, the accounts of volunteer activity from New Hampshire were refreshing if not completely reassuring.

Mary McGrory, who had been a Johnson supporter in her columns and even his ally on the war, had come to appreciate the critique of Johnson's policies by Robert Kennedy but was captured by her friend Eugene McCarthy. A skeptic, a realist, and a believer in the invincibility of an incumbent president, Miss McGrory came to New Hampshire to cover McCarthy as a friend attempting to ease the pain of his Don Quixote quest. She then visited the state headquarters and could scarcely tear herself away to write her column—a column that became among the most important of the political year. The headline read: "A Success for McCarthy: Closing the Generation Gap."

> Concord, N.H.—Sen. Eugene J. McCarthy is fighting hard here to close the wide gap between himself and President Johnson in the New Hampshire primary next Tuesday. Where he has already been visibly and dramatically successful is in closing the gap between the generations and making good on his promise to civilize dissent.
>
> It was no surprise that students from 100 colleges as far west as Michigan and as far south as Virginia should rush up here week-ends to give their all for an anti-war candidate. What is phenomenal is the reception they have been accorded by reputedly hawkish natives who are traditionally unfriendly to strangers.
>
> In all, they have knocked on 60,000 doors. They report back a "malaise with Johnson," a feeling of despair that anything can be done, and much grumbling about high taxes.
>
> Some of McCarthy's migrants wish he could speak more forcefully about the war, but they accept him as he is. They feel that his quiet, rational presentation gives the lie to the notion that he is a wild radical with an uncouth following.
>
> He is delighted with them, overwhelmed by their organization, devotion and self discipline.
>
> "My campaign may not be organized at the top," he said after a conference with an advance man who is editor of the *Yale Law Review*, "but it is certainly tightly organized at the bottom."
>
> The Concord headquarters, which is managed by Ann Hart, the dissenting daughter of Sen. Philip A. Hart of Michigan, a Johnson supporter, is now engaged in trying to hold back an expected invasion of 2,500 for the last weekend of the campaign. They can only handle a thousand.
>
> Several scores of Concord and Manchester families have offered to put up the visitors, and churches have let those with sleeping bags use the floors. St. Anselm's College in Manchester has contributed the beds of students who weekend away.
>
> Sam Brown makes no great claims for the effect of his young army. "I don't know whether we're just having a good time or we could make a difference. All

> I know is that we're the one thing McCarthy's got that nobody else in this campaign has or could get."
>
> A 17 year-old high-school dropout laboriously inscribing a stencil about a McCarthy meeting, said: "Sure, I'll tell you why I'm here. It's the only decent thing to do."
>
> (*Boston Globe,* March 5, 1968)

Mary McGrory's remarkable column stamped a permanent label of meaningfulness and legitimacy on the role of the young volunteers in the campaign. While written late and long after New Hampshire residents had become infatuated with the student effort, she did cast the activity in language that had a tremendous impact in the media. Shortly after her article appeared a steady stream of reporters and network film crews arrived at the Concord headquarters wanting to see the backroom and the basement were it was alleged the "hairys, the freaks, and the non-straights" of the campaign were laboring. To their surprise such a "chamber of horrors" did not exist. Even at their worst, those working in the basement on the mailings were neat, clean, orderly, but with straggles of beards and only slightly less than adequate skirts to face New Hampshire's cold. What they found in the Pleasant Street extension storefront was a beehive of activity, carefully departmentalized, orderly, and exceptionally neat for a campaign office. Even the ash trays, the few that existed, were emptied frequently. Whether the order came from a compulsiveness engendered by the selection process that greeted those arriving or because of the real fear of fire in the old wooden building would be hard to determine. All of the local headquarters were kept in the same constant orderliness. Each seemed to radiate energy, efficiency, and seriousness that had its only counterpoint in the humor of the occasional wall signs and the relaxed ease with which much of the campaign's drudge work was accomplished.

THE THIRD PERIOD

It took more than a series of telephone pleas from Studds and me to begin the flow of staff and volunteers to New Hampshire. A lag, of sorts, between the time that those who had come to New Hampshire and had returned to school and when they could convince others to go to New Hampshire developed. Dodds asked for help from Brown, who had not yet arrived in New Hampshire. Brown suggested that Lowenstein and others who could speak effectively about the importance of the New Hampshire McCarthy campaign be scheduled to stir interest at various campuses. In addition, Brown contacted his former National Student Association friends on many campuses stretching west from New England. The aggressive recruiting coupled with student press accounts of New Hampshire experiences, expanding national press attention to McCarthy, and the deteriorating situation in Vietnam turned the trickle of volunteers into a stream that, as Mary McGrory noted in her column, reached flood proportions.

In our campaign planning, Studds and I had expected modest volunteer help and had obligated themselves to describe tasks that volunteers could do. Our strategy targeted the cities and towns where the campaign would have to be especially effective to produce the votes needed. The priorities were set according to population and a reasonable expectation of volunteer energy.

Managing volunteers and the flow was a function of what Dianne Dumanoski could provide in the way of housing and what the canvassing operation, headed eventually by Ben Stavis and Joel Feighenbaum, could prepare in the way of materials to be circulated, maps of communities, and lists of those to be canvassed. The logistics came to determine how many volunteers could be usefully deployed. Gradually volunteers, who had come out of a certain Spartan resignation about the effort, were replaced by an increasing number who felt that the McCarthy campaign had become an important "happening" and that if they were to be a part of their times, they had to experience New Hampshire in 1968.

As Mary McGrory reported, by the last weekend of the campaign, Dianne Dumanoski could house only one thousand volunteers, and Stavis could only deploy that number in areas that had not been canvassed earlier. Reports that upwards of twenty-five hundred volunteers were planning to be in New Hampshire sent the campaign leaders in a panic. They had to stem the flow but still end up with enough volunteers to accomplish their canvassing plans for the weekend.

In a series of telephone calls to the numerous campus and community sources of volunteers, the leaders were able to discourage those coming the greatest distance and moderate the flow of those coming shorter distances. A campaign that might well have been swamped and overwhelmed in the disorder of having too many people to manage was able to protect itself.

The later arrivals came not only equipped with sleeping bags, and typewriters but also with bags of peanut butter and jelly sandwiches. Rumors of an impending "McCarthy Machine" staffed by hoards of student volunteers and fueled with peanut butter and jelly sandwiches crept from the backroom joking of the headquarters into the press. While frugal with food and housing, we found when the telephone bills arrived, the students were not short-winded in their conversations.

When asked to tally the costs of the McCarthy campaign, I replied that it was probably one of the most expensive campaigns ever run in New Hampshire. This was not because we had spent more money than had been spent before, but because of the number of volunteer hours that had been expended for McCarthy.

In one calculation I estimated that there had been over five thousand individual visits to New Hampshire and that each visit had a workday value of at least twelve hours. The per hour rate of $2 could easily be assigned to each hour producing a conservative estimate of $120,000 worth of volunteer energy. Beyond the actual worth of the work was the incalculable value of the image that was projected from New Hampshire of the students seriously at work for McCarthy. Their movement and fortunes became almost as important as the candidacy itself as portrayed in Ben Stavis' selection of the title of his book, *We Were the Campaign: New Hampshire to Chicago for McCarthy,* and Richard T. Stout's book, *People: The Story of the Grassroots Movement that Found Eugene McCarthy and Is Transforming Our Politics Today.*

What was often lost in the myth that grew larger than the reality of the volunteer involvement in New Hampshire was that an important symbiosis developed. The "kids" were not all that. Almost as many older people joined as did college undergraduates. Many of those who managed the local headquarters were outside volunteers, but volunteers like Arthur Herzog in his middle forties, or Fred Willman, in his thirties, or John Grace in his thirties.

With almost every busload of volunteers there would be a mixture of faculty, faculty spouses, and older activists from the college towns as well as students. Of equal and sometimes greater importance was the involvement of scores of local people in each of the cities and towns where the campaign developed. It was these people that created the welcoming port of entry for the volunteers. It was these people who guided the work, set the limits, oriented the newcomers, and gave the activity a sense of competence and professionalism. Without this subtle melding of locals and "kids" the effort would have failed. The volunteer would have foundered in a sea of misconceived good intentions.

When there were questions the locals were there to correct, reassure, advise, and encourage. The same was the case at the state level where Studds, Holland, Weston, me, and others were onhand to set policy, work through schedules and tactics, and help to keep the campaign in close touch with the political ethos of the state. The campaign avoided controversy because the symbiosis prevailed from beginning to end. The same feeling that produced an effective working rapport inside the campaign between volunteers and locals, migrated outside contagiously affecting the press, the politically alert, and ultimately the voting population. While there were occasional differences of opinion between the outside managers, Gans and Brown, and the inside leaders, Studds and myself, there was little if any hostility encountered by those working in the localities. It was, unquestionably, a unique and amazing social phenomenon.

CHAPTER 10

Building Momentum

PUTTING THE PIECES TOGETHER

Each campaign succeeds or fails on the basis of its ability to attract voters' interest and ultimately their votes. As a campaign proceeds, it is either effective or not in this objective because it has been able to or not able to create a sense of progress, effectiveness, excitement, movement, and momentum. Campaigns have been said to "peak" too early or "peak" too late or fail to "peak" at all. The chemistry of a campaign contains many variables which, when in certain harmony, seem to produce the attraction. The variables multiply as the campaign proceeds and their interaction, importance, and identity vary greatly from moment to moment. The totality of the campaign becomes greater than the sum of its parts. This conveys vitality that is the life of the campaign. When a campaign is less than the totality, it fails to gain the vitality, is unattractive, lacks motion, and does not achieve the effectiveness implied by the larger term "momentum."

To sort the McCarthy campaign into its constituent multiplicity of elements and to attribute to one or the other reasons for the vitality that grew into the effort would be misleading. Of great importance, of course, were the candidate, the issues, the times, the management, the workers, the strategy, the funding, the media amplification, the place, the timing, the opponents' mistakes, and many other individual, group actions and inaction, mistakes, and successes that created the momentum felt in the McCarthy candidacy during the New Hampshire winter of 1968.

There were, however, a few identifiable activities and responses that to those who worked in the campaign represented a change. The change was that after a number of weeks of uncertainty, hard work, and frustration the campaign seemed to come to life. The work was no less, nor the uncertainty, nor the frustration, but there was a spirit, a sense of accomplishment, an ability to feel attention shifting toward the McCarthy candidacy. Evidence of this shift came from the media, from the field activities, from the canvassing, and issue targeting, from the interest of celebrities, from the reaction to McCarthy public relations, and in the commitment of the candidate. In that time of change, the campaign left the managing hands of a few and became the property of the many who were working toward the election goal.

In almost all respects the campaign was no longer Studds or I or Gans and Brown, or for that matter even McCarthy. It had become greater in its pulsing energy than individual direction could contain or candidate charisma could sustain. The McCarthy campaign in New Hampshire had become what the students who came to the state in the last week sensed, a happening. Perhaps it was the first happening of the era of such events and before the term was understood.

THE REPORTERS

In spite of the best laid plans of campaign managers and political strategies, excitement in a campaign is bestowed, almost as a gift. People meeting in dining rooms and discussing candidates, issues, and campaigns cannot of themselves have much impact. It is only when the rumblings have a context and prick the ears of an inquisitive reporter or two that a heartbeat can be heard. More often than not the beat fades before long. There were four names printed on the New Hampshire ballot in 1968 and only one was that of Senator McCarthy. Also on the ballot was a place for the write-in vote. That space could have drawn the attention of other possible candidates not just Lyndon Johnson. Robert Kennedy, Hubert Humphrey, John Lindsay, or a local favorite son, Governor King or Senator McIntyre, might have been the recipient of a surprise vote.

If protest was the single objective of the 1968 presidential primary then a vote cast for almost anyone, whether listed on the ballot or not, might well have conveyed the message especially if the non-Johnson vote equaled or exceeded the number who wrote in the president's name. For a multitude of reasons such alternatives did not produce more than a scattering of votes. The contest was between the president and the senator from Minnesota, but for many weeks it was seen by the populous, through the eyes and ears of the reporters, as being no contest at all.

What Studds and I found was a certain herd instinct on the part of the reporters. This was especially noticeable when we began meeting members of the national press during the early McCarthy visits to New Hampshire. The same instinct also tended to prevail among the editors of the major national newspapers. The analogy to the herd relates effectively to the fact that within a large herd there are subgroups, families, individuals, and mavericks. The news-gathering and reporting echelons or hierarchy tend to form and follow in much the same manner. The local New Hampshire reporters, so few in number that they could hardly be labeled a herd, found the local hot spots of antiwar, anti-Johnson, pro-McCarthy sentiments, and fanned the heat into public curiosity. For most of the period between the first mentioning of Gans' October visit and McCarthy's announcement January 4, it was the state reporters for the UPI and the AP, Adolphe Bernotas and Carl Craft, who kept the possible McCarthy alternative before the New Hampshire public.

To a certain extent they were also responsible for what little national coverage the emerging New Hampshire McCarthy organization received. To them should also be added the two stringers for *Time* magazine and *Newsweek* magazine, respectively, who fed their publications weekly accounts of New Hampshire political events.

In addition to the wire service reporters, there were three other reporters, Jack Hubbard of the *Concord Daily Monitor*, Frank B. Merrick of the State News Service, and D. Frank O'Neil of the *Manchester Union Leader* who regularly reported state political activities. Hubbard and O'Neil wrote daily items and columns that appeared in their respective newspapers, while Frank Merrick's columns were carried in other daily newspapers. Merrick also wrote a summary column of New Hampshire political events that was carried in weekly newspapers.

Beyond the newspaper attention there was also the important role of the electronic media. For all intents and purposes the only electronic media capable of covering New Hampshire news were the radio stations in the three larger communities. The one television channel, WMUR-TV located in Manchester, was not financially strong enough to support continuous news coverage using video or film inputs. Its one reporter would have to drive considerable distances to cover events outside Manchester, return to the station, develop the film, write a story to accompany the film, and then read the story during the evening newscast with the film running as a background. Needless to say an event of major proportions had to be staged to justify that reporter's excursion. Most television news, therefore, was of the "rip and read" variety taken from the Teletype machines of the wire service carried by the television station.

Radio reporting was far more important. Local radio stations had often established as their competitive hallmark their respective ability to either get to the heart of a story or to add vitality to their newscasts. Using tape recordings, telephone interviews, and follow-up reports many stations had become proficient in expanding significantly the stories that they received from the wire services. It was this activity as much as any other that gave early and continuing life to the New Hampshire McCarthy campaign.

Almost all of these New Hampshire radio stations that had news departments carried the UPI wire service. As soon as a wire service story arrived, the most aggressive of the news staffs would call the quoted New Hampshire source for either a repeat of the story for taping or expanded commentary. I would often receive a 6:00 to 6:30 A.M. call from the UPI reporter who would write a story for the wire. Before 7:00 A.M. I would begin receiving telephone calls from radio news reporters for actualities. One reporter, Neal Seavey of Laconia, was particularly taken by the prospect of a McCarthy candidacy and spent considerable air time reporting the campaign's early activities with tape interviews, his own editorials, and expanded coverage of local McCarthy partisans activity. Catching the competitive urge the other Laconia stations sought to duplicate his efforts. The other aggressive radio news reporting market was Manchester. The thirst for state news items using actuality recordings to validate the account had become a fine art. Each of the stations in the major markets would cover the news in this manner to the extent permitted by staff size, news sense, and budgets.

Reporting New Hampshire events was much less a process of gleaning material from a number of significant events all competing from scarce newspaper space or air time, than it was an effort to generate news that was worthy of the space available. The McCarthy story was attractive and captured the early attention of the reporters, writers, and media news staffs. The people involved were quotable, accessible, and straightforward in their responses. For many the "homegrown" nature of the McCarthy effort was an attractive contrast to the contrived image of the New Hampshire Johnson activity.

The interest generated by the reporters from their attention to McCarthy-related stories was expanded by significant early editorial attention. The Concord, Portsmouth, Keene, and Lebanon newspapers, concerned about the direction of the administration's war policy, gave editorial attention to McCarthy campaign events. The *Manchester Union Leader* and the Dover newspaper, supporters of the war policy, also gave editorial attention. That attention, however, was not uniformly against McCarthy or the New Hampshire supporters.

While a minor herd instinct does prevail among the editors of the anti-Loeb press on certain state issues or reactions to positions taken by Loeb in his editorials, when issues separate from that, the editors tend to be quite independent in their analyses. If a herd existed, then the editors of the Portsmouth, Concord, Keene, and Lebanon newspapers were its members. The Laconia newspaper did not editorialize, and the Dover, Nashua, and Claremont newspapers were not predictable in their editorial reactions to the McCarthy activity.

Of considerable importance, however, were the local ruminations of several highly regarded weekly newspaper editors. The principals in this groups, at least those who did spend editorial lineage on the campaign, were Edward DeCourcy of the Newport *Argus Champion;* Conrad Quimby of the *Derry News;* John Ballentine of the *Somersworth Free Press;* David Hewitt of the *Hanover Gazette;* William Rotch of the *Milford Cabinet;* and the editors of the *Peterborough Transcript.*

The fact that a broad spectrum of news gathering and disseminating people in New Hampshire found the McCarthy activity to be worthy of their early attention and continued interest was exceedingly important to the success of the campaign. On its own and strictly within the confines of New Hampshire media, the campaign received better than usual coverage and editorial attention.

Since much of New Hampshire is almost entirely under the media shadow of Boston, regional media activity was also important to the McCarthy campaign. The Boston television stations, recognizing that their market extends deeply into New Hampshire, frequently cover major events there. During several of McCarthy's campaign visits, Boston television film crews followed him and carried reports of his campaigning in their news broadcasts. Perhaps as important, however, was the fact that when McCarthy campaigned in Massachusetts or when he landed at Boston's

Logan International Airport for New Hampshire campaigning, he was well covered by the Boston television stations. For them it was less expensive to catch McCarthy in an airport arrival and interview him than it was to follow him to the remote corners of New Hampshire.

The *Boston Globe,* the *Record American,* and the *Boston Herald-Traveler* as well as the Boston-based *Christian Science Monitor* maintained constant touch with the campaign. The *Monitor*'s New England political reporter, Edgar Mills, ran a circuit of the New Hampshire campaigns that meant almost a weekly article summarizing the activities for his paper. The *Globe* management had reoriented the rather bland earlier format of the paper toward a stronger editorial and reportorial image. It had been successful in absorbing much of the circulation of the *Boston Post* that had closed late in the 1950s and could now build on an economic base as a newspaper of significance. The management had sensed the political direction Massachusetts was taking and became an independent Democratic publication editorially which pleased both the old *Post* readers and the liberally inclined younger population of eastern Massachusetts.

Editorially the *Globe* was offended by the practices and opinions of the *Manchester Union Leader* and its publisher William Loeb. During labor management difficulties in Boston the *Manchester Union Leader* would increase its press runs and even prepare special editions of the newspaper for circulation in Boston. Trying to exploit the problems of other newspapers in its own market was not popular with the *Globe* management. While not taking the *Manchester Union Leader* on directly, the *Globe* management began to methodically build its circulation in those parts of the state where there were daily newspaper vacuums and among the residents of the southeastern part of the state where it would be economically important to develop an advertising market.

The *Globe* had its own New Hampshire reporter, its own Washington bureau, and a sizable and talented pool of political reporters in Boston. The staff gave the *Globe* a regional orientation that was less interested in its national image than it was in its ability to relay its message in a manner that would be accepted and consumed by its new and expanded readership.

The *Herald-Traveler,* Boston's independent Republican newspaper, was struggling to survive. The paper had failed to attract much of the old *Post* readership and with the changing political and economic orientation of Massachusetts, the *Herald-Traveler* was losing readers, advertising, and was about to lose the television station that had bolstered its economic position for many years. The *Herald-Traveler* had a sizable circulation among New Hampshire Republicans. *Herald-Traveler* reporters regularly traveled with the senator on his visits and then stayed to report campaign activities other than those surrounding the activities of the candidate.

What Studds and I had predicted in our December memorandum to McCarthy came true considerably beyond our expectations. Because there was a strong McCarthy organization in Massachusetts, McCarthy's name had been listed on the April Massachusetts presidential primary ballot, and because of the confusion in the Democratic Party as to how the president would be represented in the primary, Boston's newspapers were continually filled with McCarthy news. To a considerable extent this was a reversal of what we had expected. We had assumed that New Hampshire McCarthy activity would be reported in Massachusetts helping to build support for him in the later primary. By the time the New Hampshire primary was held, the decision in Massachusetts had already been made. Johnson's name would not appear on the ballot nor would there be a stand-in or effort to secure write-in votes. This series of events released many of the Boston political writers from having to cover Massachusetts details, and they came to New Hampshire.

Unlike the local or the regional reporters Studds and I observed, the national press performed much like a herd. They arrived in a group, moved as a group, separated only occasionally to gather news, returned to digest their information as a group, and tended to confirm their perceptions as a group. There was social, intellectual, and status reenforcement by being a part of the herd that led to preconceptions of New Hampshire politics and heavy reliance on contacts developed and shared from previous quadrennial New Hampshire visits.

In the early days of our contacts with the traveling national press, Studds and I found the situation both disillusioning and frustrating. Considerably in awe of the names we had read for years in the prominent national press, we had to struggle first to overcome our reticence and then to attempt to get the herd to shift its attention toward our own positive assessment of McCarthy's New Hampshire progress. We recognized that unless the national reporters were convinced that something was happening in New Hampshire, the campaign would have no impact outside the state. Without some recognition that the campaign was happening and that McCarthy was having an increasing impact, the money necessary to sustain the candidacy would not flow. As it was for almost two-thirds of the New Hampshire campaign, money for both New Hampshire and the national campaign was exceedingly short. For the combined reasons of money and impact, both Studds and I spent a great deal of our time accommodating reporters in hopes that somehow and at sometime before March 12 the story of what we felt was happening or had the potential of happening in New Hampshire would reach the larger national audience.

While we had had moderate success in getting attention for our efforts prior to McCarthy's entry in the New Hampshire primary, attention dropped to almost zero after the initial burst of his January 4 release. With that announcement, Studds and I expected the positive interest of the national press to continue. What happened was the reverse. Interest subsided.

Often I would make special trips from Hanover to Concord or Manchester to meet with a national reporter or occasional columnist, or for a network interview. The results were almost uniformly disappointing as either the questions or the subsequent story offered only skepticism. There was a great problem in breaking through the preconceptions that the national press tended to bring with them to New Hampshire. The skepticism came from their view of the McCarthy campaign from their normal base, Washington. There it appeared that the campaign had caused hardly a ripple. By comparison with other presidential efforts, McCarthy was poorly organized, financed, staffed, headquartered, led, and virtually without allies. It was inconceivable that such an effort could mount and manage a meaningful national candidacy much less dent the political hide of an incumbent president. Since there was so little to interest them from the Washington base of the McCarthy campaign, it was inconceivable that field operations would be any better. The reporters arrived in New Hampshire to be greeted by what was in their view a rookie leadership surrounded by unknown local volunteers and a number of pleasant but naive college kids. When they went to check the local sources they had developed during earlier New Hampshire visits, they found that these prominent political leaders were either committed to the renomination of President Johnson or had retired from the action.

There was hardly a familiar face in the McCarthy crowd. Studds and I were unknown outside of New Hampshire and untried in the view of the national press in the larger political arena we were in now. The national press skepticism became especially apparent when shortly before McCarthy's first campaign visit to New Hampshire in late January, several reporters asked to talk with us. The reporters were then traveling with Governor Romney and hoped to accomplish a bit of side scouting of the Democrats. Studds and I were asked to join the reporters for an interview at the New Hampshire Highway Hotel in Concord. When we arrived, we found that instead of the one or two reporters we had met earlier in Chicago, approximately six writers were gathered around a large table. Among the group were Jack Germond, Marianne Means, Warren Weaver, and several others, each representing a prominent, nationally recognized publication. It was obvious from the conversation that we had interrupted with our arrival that the reporters were greatly impressed with Governor Romney's organization, his New Hampshire effort, and aggressive campaign style.

They had just ordered the first round of drinks and were beginning to relax after what had been a long and strenuous campaign day. Their questions immediately began to contrast what they had experienced with Romney with what they knew of the McCarthy effort. McCarthy, they contended would never work as hard as Romney, was generally regarded as a retiring campaigner, and certainly would not permit himself to be scheduled as had Romney. Marianne Means recalled that McCarthy did not like street campaigning, handshaking, meeting with small groups, or other traditional contact forms of campaigning. She recounted that McCarthy usually resisted this form of campaigning and was going to be especially resistant given the issue orientation of his candidacy. His approach, she noted and the others agreed, would be to hold press conferences, speak before large groups, have radio and television interviews, write his views for publication, and generally project himself as a focal point for protest without becoming a personal center for the effort.

Astonished by this portrayal of our candidate, Studds and I countered. Our experience to date with McCarthy had led us to believe that he would be an effective campaigner in New Hampshire. We had not received instructions from McCarthy's senatorial office or from the national campaign headquarters concerning what to include or exclude from his New Hampshire campaign schedules.

On the contrary, Studds and I felt assured that McCarthy would do as other candidates had had to do and that was to meet New Hampshire voters where they lived, worked, shopped, recreated, and learned. We noted that radio interviews were being included but television instate did not exist nor were there many opportunities in a given campaign trip to give speeches before large audiences. Furthermore, we said, McCarthy was being scheduled to do almost all of the things Ms. Means noted he did not want to do and that if McCarthy were to be an effective campaigner in New Hampshire he would have to follow the schedule. There was simply no alternative.

The next series of questions concerned comparisons between what the reporters had experienced of the Romney organization, what they had heard from Bernard Boutin concerning the Johnson organization, and their Washington preconception of the McCarthy organization. Most had read Robert Evans' column describing the Johnson organization's plans and were as impressed by the story as was Evans. In spite of the best arguments Studds and I could muster regarding the inconsistency of the Johnson effort in relation to the political ethos of New Hampshire, the reporters remained skeptical.

Little that we said concerning our successes to date, the growth of our local organization, the attention we had received in the New Hampshire press, nor the fact that a sizable number of volunteers were already arriving from outside of New Hampshire had any impact on the cynics. The combination of a day on the campaign trail with the hustling George Romney and the establishment credibility of Bernard Boutin left Studds and me as pleasant political oddities. We were seen as good storytellers, engaging in our optimism, but hardly political realists.

From the experienced view of the hardened political writer, this was not the stuff of which election victories are made. Tight organization, managed by experienced professionals, tied closely to a carefully developed campaign strategy, and ultimately controlled by a Washington-based political elite was the image of success that the reporters carried to New Hampshire. They found reassuring examples of the model in the Romney, Nixon, and Johnson campaigns, and what they knew of the McCarthy campaign seemed to violate the basic precepts of the model.

The interview ended with the reporters drifting into their own conversations. Studds and I observed for a brief time, slowly realizing that what we had said was not being given much value in the ruminations. The reporters were orally writing their stories, composing leads, and looking for phrases that encapsulated their impressions. Occasionally one or another would slightly challenge the group's consensus but would be quickly brought to realize the weakness of the position by the others. The herd was still intact, shifting, moving, finding direction, after a day of feeding. The most Studds and I had been able to accomplish was to become acquainted.

For another month the national press remained a herd united in its skepticism and assured that a campaign that developed as the McCarthy candidacy had developed could not assault the incumbent president. McCarthy's first several visits were assessed in contrast to Romney. Scheduling and advancing problems, small crowds, and McCarthy's quiet approach were seen as confirmations of the early assessment. To the continuing irritation of people like Eric Schnapper, who was attempting improve the early advancing difficulties, the reporters kept referring to errors. On one occasion Schnapper had advanced a complicated route for a series of evening coffee parties in Manchester by carefully prerunning and timing the route several days earlier. On the evening of the parties he missed a turn he did not recognize in the dark and led his small motorcade down a dead-end street.

David Schoumacher of CBS-TV was in one of the cars that had to back up and turn around to find the correct route. This miscue became the theme of his often repeated radio and television report of the campaign's status. Being taken down a dead-end street was too much for him to resist in his analogy of the progress or non-progress he felt the campaign was making in New Hampshire. All other aspects of the schedule had gone well and McCarthy's reception had been better than anyone had expected. But the story from New Hampshire from that reporter was about the "amateurism" of the advance work. To our continuing frustration, we could not seem to break the image of the campaign the national press had brought with them. With McCarthy's second visit on February 6, 7, and 8, some of the reporters began to file stories that revealed small breaks in the herd evaluation. Tom Wicker did write his refreshing column concerning the Claremont Rotary Club's exclusion of the electronic media, but the *New York Times* news columns continued to carry only bits of reports and little that would indicate anything important was happening in New Hampshire.

E. W. Ned Kenworthy, like others among the reporters, enjoyed McCarthy's wit, use of language, and openness. He began to sense that McCarthy was beginning to get through to the New Hampshire voter and that for some, yet to be understood reason, the campaign was beginning to work. On several occasions he wrote what he was beginning to feel and the copy failed to get into the newspaper. Studds and I and the press operation of the campaign were understandably upset that the *Times* was not carrying stories that had been written that were favorable to the senator. Kenworthy would, occasionally, show us the copy he had written and telephoned to New York expecting that the coming edition would contain his report. When it didn't, and did not for several editions and for a number of reports, both the New Hampshire and the Washington headquarters were worried. It appeared as if a news block at the *Times* was somehow in operation to prevent news of the New Hampshire campaign from appearing in New York. News in the *Times* in New York meant both money and volunteers for the campaign. Without coverage the campaign slowly began to starve.

Blair Clark found, through social contacts with the *Times* editors, that McCarthy was viewed by them not as a presidential candidate but as an "issue candidate." Since in their view McCarthy was not running for the presidency but running only to raise the Vietnam War issue, he would not be accorded the coverage in the *Times* they normally allocate to a presidential candidate. In outrage that such a conclusion was possible, Clark, through many of the same prominent social and political contacts in New York, got the editors to recognize the absurdity of their conclusion. Kenworthy began to get his reports in print and the editorial page of the *Times* began to recognize the potential of the McCarthy candidacy.

What this experience demonstrated was the peculiar dynamics of the national press establishment. Studds and I found that the reporters tended to accept the established versions of the campaigns and to view skeptically accounts of the burgeoning McCarthy effort. Their reports from New Hampshire tended to be cautious, reflect the problems, and convey the image of a "David and Goliath" contest with David deprived of a weapon. When the theme changed and David was seen as being at least competent, the editors were reluctant to support their reporters' accounts. McCarthy and his amateur campaign were scoring forcefully in New Hampshire long before the editors of the major nationally regarded newspapers took much notice. The stories that were printed were buried and without editorial recognition.

While the reporters had changed their views the editors were unwilling to say that McCarthy was doing well in New Hampshire until there was a recognized, established source. If the *Times* had written editorially that McCarthy was campaigning effectively then the *Washington Post,* the *St. Louis Post Dispatch,* the *Atlanta Constitution,* the *Los Angeles Times,* and one or two other prominent publications would follow. The problem was getting the first to break from the herd. Like the reporters who would not commit themselves in their stories to the notion that the McCarthy campaign had a chance to succeed until other sources said so, the editors, reporters raised to a higher level, were not willing to put their publications out in front with a prediction that they themselves could not confirm to their satisfaction. Watching every move of the *Times* were the other press leaders. They would not say or do more than the *Times* or, conversely, the *Times* would not do or say more than they thought the other papers would support. The circle seemed impenetrable and endless to those struggling in New Hampshire to draw legitimacy from national editorial recognition.

Fortunately important secondary and independent sources of analysis exist. To a considerable extent this role is filled by the syndicated columnists. They, like the editors and the reporters, like to forecast with assurance. They like to be right and to base their conclusions on their own coveted sources. Robert Evans wrote his early negative column, which conditioned many reporters' reactions to what they experienced in New Hampshire for a considerable time. Tom Wicker began to open the circle a bit with his Claremont rotary meeting tale but in a fight for professional survival at the *Times,* Wicker had to return to Washington before he could accomplish more. Most of the other columnists tended to remain a part of the herd. The important exception was Mary McGrory whose widely read and respected columns gave both reporters and editors the source they needed to change their cautious stance. But her columns came relatively late and had the effect of confirming the work of an earlier and exceptionally important writer, Paul Wieck.

Wieck represented the independent journals of news and opinion. Wieck, basically a freelance writer, was then working for the *New Republic* and covering the presidential campaign. He had first met Studds and me at the Chicago meeting of the CCD and had kept in touch with us since that December meeting. He had caught the flavor of the McCarthy activity in its early days. Without the inhibitions of the national press and its editors, and writing for a publication that prided itself on being out in front of events, he could write and take seriously the optimism that came from those involved in the McCarthy campaign.

Wieck often traveled with the national press and sat in on daily reviews of events. However, he had found threads of credibility in those who were laboring for McCarthy that had not been detected by the others. His stories reflected this anticipation and continually placed his evaluations far ahead of his colleagues.

To a considerable degree the independent journal of opinion does serve to lead the larger press establishment. Publications like the *New Republic* have wide readership among reporters and editors. Stories often receive preliminary coverage in such publications, and through the leads that are revealed the reporters pursue subjects for their own papers. As an important investigative journalistic outlet, stories are tested that in several weeks often become the objective of widespread interest.

In terms of the herd analogy, the independent journals are much like scouts ranging across the terrain in search of new routes. They might also be considered as a picket line that tends to draw the early fire revealing how and where the enemy is deployed. In this latter analogy there is a secondary aspect that also reflects the role of the independent journal. The early fire may inflict wounds that would be fatal to the credibility of larger publications. An independent journal is expected to be at the edge and is respected according to its ability to both direct reporting toward new subjects and to shape opinion of events.

Paul Wieck performed both roles exceptionally well in 1968. He sensed and reported the flow of events and, because he had anticipated well, his evaluations and opinions gained high value as the political year unfolded.

Wieck followed McCarthy to New Hampshire during the senator's February 13, 14, and 15 visit. He carefully evaluated McCarthy's performance, the response, the status of his organization, and the competence of the opposition. When he left New Hampshire he carried an opinion of the campaign that was not widely shared by his press colleagues. Some may have agreed with him to a degree but were unwilling to put in print what they were beginning to feel—and certainly their editors were not about to tolerate such assessments. The article titled, "McCarthy: Alive and Well in New Hampshire" was written shortly after Wieck returned to Washington from New Hampshire February 15 and appeared in the edition of the *New Republic* dated March 2, 1968. Datelined Nashua, Wieck wrote:

> Here in the snow-covered hills Sen. Eugene J. McCarthy is finding his identity as a presidential candidate as he moves unhurriedly in and out of the endless and often depressing shoe factories, jokes with his supporters at coffee hours, speaks in town halls and on college campuses. He is winning friends. In return he commits more of himself each day. His wit is more incisive, his speeches stronger.
>
> (*New Republic,* March 2, 1968, p. 15)

Since this was the *New Republic*'s first major story on the New Hampshire campaign, Wieck went on to review how the Johnson managers had committed the "classic goof" with their pledge-card scheme and how the tactic had "backfired so badly it left the state's Democratic organization demoralized." But it was McCarthy's own effectiveness as a campaigner that brought Wieck to his conclusions:

> Simultaneously, (with the pledge card mistake) McCarthy's own performance began to improve. On his first trip to the state in December, he had delivered a dull, academic lecture. When he returned January 26, his supporters were at a

> low point. Then he stirred a crowd of some 700 at St. Anselm's just outside Manchester to repeated bursts of applause, and by mid-February, he had succeeded in drawing a sharp contrast between his own style and that of the pro-Johnson hierarchy. Instead of rhetorical excesses, he insisted he would "not shout at the voters of New Hampshire"(and that he hadn't found any who wanted him to.
>
> (*New Republic,* March 2, 1968, p. 15)

In this paragraph Wieck had picked up the basic difference between McCarthy and Romney's campaign style. While other reporters who had not been as close to McCarthy over the period of the campaign did not sense his effectiveness in contrast to the aggressive hustle of Romney, Wieck made it a central aspect of his analysis. He reported that he had seen McCarthy move effectively among people at their jobs, in small groups, before large audiences, and on the street. He noted that McCarthy refused to "demagogue" the issues in spite of the fact that there were clear opportunities to do so. He used the example of Bernard Boutin to illustrate McCarthy's ability to move through the thicket of interacting voter concerns to still get at the basic concerns of his campaign.

> Boutin left the federal service to return to New Hampshire and a position with Sanders Associates, a major employer in Nashua and a rapidly growing firm largely dependent on defense contracts—$125 million of its current $140 million gross, according to Pentagon figures. But many of New Hampshire's white and blue collar workers earn their paychecks from firms with defense contacts and a heated attack upon "the complex" pleasing though it might be to McCarthy's academic following, could cost hundreds, even thousands of votes.
>
> So, when the question came up at a coffee hour, he dealt with specific solutions after sizing up the Pentagon as "about the third or fourth largest nation" in the world. His solution to bring the CIA under control, as he and some of his Senate colleagues have tried to do; to put some strings on the Pentagon's sale of arms abroad, as they've also tried to do; and to take all nonmilitary procurement (he estimated this would amount to $30 billion of nearly $80 billion in Department of Defense expenditures) out of DOD, a move that could also save billions in that civilian procurement officers would be allowed to wipe out some of the endless duplication in military procurement.
>
> (*New Republic,* March 2, 1968, p. 16)

He found during his tour that New Hampshire was still "Nixon country" and that Nixon's cautious approach to the state had the "nation's first presidential primary pretty well nailed down." But in contrast, Wieck felt the "Democratic race is wide open." This conclusion was not widely shared by his fellow national reporters at the time he wrote it and even on the date of publication. He then wrote:

> To suggest, at this point, that McCarthy could win would be on the daring side of the ledger. But it no longer seems impossible. McCarthy wears well. His insistence on rational discussion is in line with New Hampshire tradition, which was summed up by Bill Cardoso of the *Boston Globe*'s bureau here: The quiet, reasoned man is always the first selectman. At the same time, he is showing no reluctance to jump on a genuine issue, such as the pledge card.
>
> This is in contrast to LBJ, who has suffered not only in New Hampshire but nationally from too much exposure. On the plane en route to New Hampshire, a young businessman who sat across the aisle from me said he is a McCarthy supporter this season. He explained that his exposure to McCarthy is "limited" but that his exposure to Johnson isn't. He predicts McCarthy will do well in his Concord suburb.
>
> (*New Republic*, March 2, 1968, p. 16)

Wieck also found a basis for his optimism in the New Hampshire McCarthy organization itself. While other reporters had tended either to dismiss the organization as amateur and inexperienced or to have neglected to consider the organization as important to the effort, Wieck wrote:

> A rapport had developed between McCarthy's supporters—as a group, they are bright, young (in their twenties and thirties), attractive and basically uncomplicated people who are thrilled just to have an alternative to LBJ—and the candidate. There is an active statewide committee of 300 backed up by a least 50 college students from inside and also outside the state. Dave Hoeh, the McCarthy chairman, believes it is as strong as any committee he has seen in his 10 years of New Hampshire politics. They have set up headquarters in 10 towns in addition to many neighborhood headquarters in private homes.
>
> (*New Republic*, March 2, 1968, p. 16)

His account of the mechanics of the McCarthy organization reinforced his analysis. He contrasted what he found in the McCarthy headquarters with the difficulties the Johnson organization was having both in its operations and in its effort to maintain control over a party membership that had long prided itself for independent behavior. Against Boutin's portrayal of a unified Democratic Party supporting the incumbent president, Wieck recounted the names of a number of local party leaders who were not only supporting McCarthy but were actively involved in the campaign. In communities where "newcomers" to politics made up the committees, Wieck reported that "they are showing indefatigable spirit," with the workers "amazed by the friendly response."

To a picture that seemed to good to be true Wieck added: "One interesting facet is the amount of Republican support McCarthy is attracting. In several towns, registered Republicans are active urging a write-in on the GOP ticket." In response to a woman who, as a registered Republican with liberal inclinations, felt she might have no choice in November, Wieck reported that McCarthy said, "That's like choosing between vulgarity and obscenity, isn't it." Wieck pointed out that there might be a November choice but in February and in New Hampshire, McCarthy was becoming an attractive alternative not just for disgruntled Democrats but also for disfranchised Republicans. The makings of something larger than a protest candidacy was implied from the conclusion.

In fairness Wieck also recounted some of the problems that had kept his press colleagues from embracing the McCarthy campaign as he did in his article. He noted the "immobilizing" effect of Robert Kennedy's "agonizing" on many potential McCarthy supporters until later in the development of the campaign. But he felt it was an important positive sign that most of Kennedy's people had become active in McCarthy's campaign. His second concern was the fact that the McCarthy campaign had had as its goal to win "only a 'psychological' victory rather than New Hampshire's 26 delegates." He wrote, "None of his supporters could bring themselves to talk about a clear-cut victory," but he concluded, "this should be corrected by McCarthy's own decision to go for broke. It could be the very thing needed to maintain momentum at this critical point in the campaign, and if it works, the timing would be brilliant."

In his final assessment before making his prediction, Wieck wrote:

> There are two additional factors working against McCarthy. One is time. As Dave Hoeh . . . put it, we're trying to do in eight to ten weeks what we should have had six months to do.
>
> The second is his major issue. McCarthy has been wise enough not to frighten the shoe factory workers by shouting "brutality" and "immorality" at them. But he is making them, in his own words, to make "a harsh historical judgment," to say to the country's leaders via the ballot box that Vietnam is costing—in lives, money and moral energy—far more than can be gained, that the decision to make a stand there is not even a good military judgment . . . that we aren't fulfilling our goal of "building a nation" but doing just the opposite and that we should summon the moral courage to negotiate for a coalition government that would included the National Liberation Front (NLF) and, if the South Vietnamese government resists this, proceed to de-escalate until they're agreeable.
>
> That is a lot to ask of a shoe worker, long abused by the jingoistic language of the cold war, conditioned to respond to all the clichés about the "threat of international communism." Nevertheless, a linotype operator in one of the plants McCarthy visited told a reporter that he plans to vote for him and added that, at the American Legion club, where he does his social drinking, they were beginning to "talk McCarthy."
>
> (*New Republic*, March 2, 1968, p. 17)

After weeks of trying to get the message through to the many reporters and news people they had talked with, Studds and I finally read the complete story as we felt it should be told. Wieck had independently found what we had felt during the six weeks since McCarthy's New Hampshire announcement. The campaign was reaching voters; McCarthy was skillfully developing his positions and his rapport with New Hampshire. The problems were being overcome, and a noticeable change from a candidacy of protest to a candidacy for the office was in the offing. It would have been enough to have left Wieck's conclusions as they were with the questions that still hung over the campaign but Wieck was willing to write and then walk to the end of his own journalistic plank.

> It would be inaccurate to say the votes for Senator McCarthy were there in mid-February. He might be lucky to get 30 or 35 percent of the vote. But the write-in votes weren't there for LBJ either. On the whole, the press appears ready to award McCarthy a major psychological victory if he gets 40 percent of the vote, which is very possible.
>
> (*New Republic,* March 2, 1968, p. 17)

Both percentages were virtually unspoken by the reporters or by McCarthy workers. The reporters were reluctant to predict what McCarthy might have or to project what he would need for the result to be considered "significant." The McCarthy leadership refused to play the numbers game with the reporters contending that virtually anything above the 3 to 5 percent figure quoted by Senator McIntyre would be enough to show the folly of Johnson's policies. If the reporters had concluded that McCarthy had 30 to 35 percent by the middle of February they were neither saying it publicly nor writing it for publication.

For Wieck to suggest that 40 percent was the figure and to go on to say that such a vote result was "possible" extended everyone's thinking. Studds and I had a feeling from the returns of our efforts that McCarthy was gaining, but we had almost no notion of what the starting point was and only a slight notion as to how large the ultimate turnout might be. Neither of us wished to be quoted saying that the campaign would rise or fall on the basis of a percentage. The significance, therefore, of Wieck's prediction was that he wrote a number and by implication attached his assessment of the reality of the McCarthy candidacy to that percentage and also committed his colleagues in the media to either agree or disagree with his prediction.

The numbers game was out in the open. Wieck had made his evaluation, picked a number, and was ready to stand by it. Since the number was much higher than Studds or I had expected, the confidence that Wieck placed in the prediction became contagious. The herd shifted direction and began to write in much the same manner as had Paul Wieck.

An excitement that had been part of the campaign from the beginning now seemed to roll across New Hampshire and outside. Mary McGrory came and wrote her frequent columns about the volunteers, the candidate, and the excitement. Robert Novak, the other half of the Evans and Novak syndicated duo, called me in my Hanover office and asked for an interview. This time instead of me driving over the rough and narrow road to Concord to meet a columnist, I said I would be happy to talk with Novak in my Dartmouth office. Novak did the driving, heard the story that we had told earlier to Evans, and this time the column read as a favorable account of the McCarthy happening. As the herd shifted it also dispersed. Reporters visited local headquarters, followed canvassers, accompanied celebrities, visited with volunteers, attended meetings, and assessed opinions of voters across the state. Beyond a political campaign the reporters found numerous human interest stories about the candidate's family, the volunteers, the local activists, and the logistics that found their way into parts of the newspaper not usually concerned with political events.

The impact of the shift and the dispersion greatly escalated the attention the campaign received. With the escalation came reenforcement, which strengthened the campaign itself. A cycle of recognition adding to credibility, adding to excitement, attracting more attention, expanding the reach of the campaign, which further increased its recognition, made a formidable media venture of national and even international significance from what had been almost a private party in New Hampshire.

Theodore White, who had all but neglected the McCarthy campaign, hurried back in an effort to catch up with the ten weeks of activity he had missed. A film crew from David Wolper Productions, the producer of White's quadrennial television account of the making of the president, scurried after anyone and anything related to the McCarthy campaign.

For the first six weeks of the New Hampshire campaign Studds and I had been surprised to find greater interest on the part of the international reporters in our activities than the national media. *London Times* reporters Lewis Chester and Bruce Page were frequent visitors. Claus Toksvig of Danish national television interviewed me on several occasions on sound film for replay in Denmark. A team of Japanese reporters visited the Concord headquarters and returned to report the election returns by wire directly to Tokyo.

In the case of the two *London Times* reporters, they saw parallels in the New Hampshire activity with its student volunteer involvement and similar antinuclear weapons protests in Great Britain. To them New Hampshire was symptomatic of a reviving youth consciousness in issues of moral and political significance. Their perceptions, drawn from a comparative view and contemporary sensitivity to young people's concerns, were ahead of and more clearly shaped than any of the national reporters.

Beyond the usual series of questions these reporters asked, Studds and I were intrigued by their accounts of similar youth-involved political efforts in Great Britain. Instead of feeling that what we were experiencing in New Hampshire was a political or even social anomaly, we sensed that we were at the beginning of a movement. The consciousness of young people was rising not just because of the war but because of a larger, international swelling of social indignation. The Old Guard was being challenged in its policies, attitudes, and behavior. What Chester and Page recounted to us was that the challenge was now coming to the United States.

While the story eventually found a context and did receive broad attention before it was too late, the delay caused a distortion that would not have been found in the writing of the English reporters. While the student volunteers were important and contributed extensively to the success of the campaign they were not the whole story. The New Hampshire campaign, as seen by the English reporters, was not a "children's crusade" but rather a broad-based political event that involved the spectrum of ages, background, and economic status. While their reports had virtually no impact on the formation of American public opinion during the campaign, their discussions helped Studds and me to perceive what was happening and to manage the campaign more effectively than might otherwise have been the case. The book *An American Melodrama* is the best total account of the 1968 campaign to be written. They were successful in capturing the subtleties and the spirit of the campaign in a way that no other domestic writers did.

FINAL PHASE OPERATIONS

Studds and I had developed the timetable for the campaign with specific dates when items would be required. Radio time had been reserved, as had billboard space, and some limited television time. Dates to begin canvassing were set as were the dates when the first direct mail would be sent. While there was always a slight margin in the schedule for delay, many of the times were fixed. When a radio reservation came due, it meant that either the copy for an advertisement was ready or the time would be lost as well as the money used to purchase the space. As the sequence of deadlines neared, Studds and I realized that little had been done in Washington to prepare the necessary materials. Often when materials did arrived they could not be used because they were not appropriate for one reason or another. Usually the problem was one of tone and content that was not consistent with how McCarthy was campaigning in New Hampshire or what Studds and I knew of the New Hampshire political ethos. These early problems were frustrating but time remained to have materials reprinted through Washington or substituted with materials developed in New Hampshire. As the critical deadlines neared the frustration turned to desperation as the communications between Washington and New Hampshire failed to improve.

When Curtis Gans arrived, he confirmed what we had been saying for more than a month. The Washington headquarters had attempted to staff and organize both primary and nonprimary state desks, and develop a number of national campaign related activities that fully involved the limited full-time and volunteer staff then available. What Gans was able to assert was that without a success in New Hampshire there would not be a meaningful McCarthy campaign after March 12. This meant that New Hampshire had to be the top priority concern of everyone in the Washington headquarters.

When Gans arrived he brought with him several of the people Studds and I had attempted to work with by mail and telephone. The first two were Sandra Silverman, who began to help with McCarthy and his family's schedules, and Jessica Tuchman, who served as Gans' administrative assistant. Within a week of Gans' arrival, almost all of the staff and functions of the national headquarters relocated to the Concord and Manchester headquarters for the duration. Instead of relying on Washington to produce radio and television materials, Gans and his staff began producing them through the Weston Agency in New Hampshire. Ad layout and materials preparation remained somewhat dispersed with preparation occurring in New York as well as New Hampshire, but the communication was direct and responded to the critical media deadlines.

Gans assumed daily headquarters management responsibilities. Most of the operating departments of the campaign were organized and staffed at least to a limited extent before Gans arrived which meant that most worked smoothly with minimum supervision. Gans completed the area headquarters staffing and made sure that each was supplied with materials and properly tied to people in the headquarters who could respond to requests for help. Studds and I retained scheduling policy, overview of materials preparation, management of staff local relations, and general supervision and press contacts concerning the New Hampshire aspects of the campaign.

CANDIDATE SUPPORT

Following McCarthy's February 13–15 tour and the favorable reaction that he and others sensed, McCarthy decided to increase the number of days he would campaign in New Hampshire. The original plan called for twelve days. On February 19, the Washington headquarters announced that McCarthy would "campaign in the New England states 14 of the last 18 days . . . this nearly doubles the time originally allotted by McCarthy . . . to the primary." (*Manchester Union Leader,* February 19, 1968) McCarthy, when making the announcement, said, "The warm response I have received thus far during three previous trips has encouraged me and convinced me of the importance of bringing the issues more fully to the people of New Hampshire." (*Claremont Eagle,* February 19, 1968) The announcement significantly bolstered the New Hampshire campaign. It was read by observers as an indication that McCarthy had escalated the showdown with Johnson in New Hampshire to his highest priority. His earlier thinking had been that Wisconsin's April 6 primary would be the real test, but the response to him in New Hampshire had been warmer and broader than anticipated.

McCarthy succeeded in his early visits for two basic reasons. His own personality and campaign style were consistent with the mood and behavior of a troubled New Hampshire electorate. He was quiet, not obtrusive, engaging, thoughtful, and attractive. He did not attempt to startle or hustle the voters as Romney seemed to, but was able to get people to join with him in thinking about and working through the nation's problems and to consider alternative policies. The contrast between McCarthy and Johnson and between his campaign and Johnson's campaign was great. His activity was relaxed, self-effacing, and refreshing in contrast to the rigid, tense, and almost anxious behavior of Johnson in Washington and his surrogates in New Hampshire.

The second basic reason was the way the campaign supported McCarthy in the field. Again the style was refreshing, open, and attractive. The gray, presidential presence of McCarthy himself was contrasted with the liveliness of the young men and women who accompanied him and the dedication of those who greeted him as his supporters at each of his campaign stops. While not part of a deliberate plan, the experience Studds and I had had with previous campaigns and especially my experiences in New Hampshire politics shaped how McCarthy could be most effective when on the campaign trail.

When McCarthy had campaigned on the main streets of Nashua, Manchester, and Concord, he had been without the immediate advancing that helps draw people's attention to the candidate. Studds, Schnapper, Dodds, or I would run ahead to a store or shop to say that McCarthy was coming and hand out a few pieces of campaign literature. This had only minimal impact. McCarthy was neither well known nor recognizable as a presidential candidate at that stage. Those persons who did turn to greet him or come out to see what was going on tended to be more interested in seeing Roger Mudd of CBS news or watching the various television film crews struggling to keep pace with McCarthy. Something was needed to introduce excitement and to get people to feel it was important to meet Senator McCarthy.

Our first inclination was to find three or four conservatively groomed and clad young men to travel and field advance, but the few who fit the description and were regularly involved in the campaign were needed as drivers and field headquarters managers. Using coeds seemed a bit risky given the caution with which we were attempting to develop the campaign, but we agreed to try it. The contrast between bright women's clothing against a snowy landscape and a gray candidate might be refreshing as well. Barbara Underwood recalled:

> David Hoeh had put in a call through to the Concord headquarters that afternoon (February 3rd) to see if any of the students there for the weekend would be available to act as McCarthy girls during the following week. He wanted about six girls to accompany McCarthy on his scheduled swing from Claremont, Newport to Concord. Hoeh asked Dan Dodds if he could find him six girls. Dan was reminded not to get them too short, or too big, or too bored, or too addicted to cigarettes. "What am I supposed to be doing," complained Dodds, "run a beauty contest." But he understood the problem, and set out to find some tall (to compliment the Senator's height) alert, smiling girls who could hand out campaign material for a few days.
>
> (Underwood, op. cit., p. 5)

Dodds had some difficulty since almost all of the students working in New Hampshire that weekend had to return for classes Monday and for the following week. Eventually he persuaded six to either cut classes for the days they would be traveling with McCarthy, or return to their colleges to make arrangements to be away for a few days. What began as a one-time assignment blossomed into an important part of the campaign.

> Chris Howells was one of the first girls to volunteer. First she had to go back to Connecticut College and pack some clothes. Eventually she persuaded her mother and the college to let her stay for the entire campaign.
>
> (Underwood, ibid., p. 5)

Of the original six young women who volunteered, at least four would adjust their academic schedules so that they could be "McCarthy girls" from the sixth of February on. Among them were Cindy Samuels, a Smith College senior; Mary Davis, Radcliffe; and other Smith students, Nicki Sauvage, Sue Solenberger, and Sara Elston who Cindy had recruited for the first volunteers to visit New Hampshire.

As McCarthy girls their job was initially to advance McCarthy's campaigning by handing out buttons, campaign literature, and announcing that he was arriving. They each wore a polystyrene straw boater with a McCarthy bumper sticker pasted to it and later would have a ribbon sash with "McCarthy for President" printed on it. When McCarthy was unknown and neither his name, candidacy, nor the office for which he was running was familiar to the people on the street, the McCarthy girls helped soften the introductions.

Another car was added to the traveling campaign for them. Within a day or so after the first assignments, the young women developed a style and spirit that was contagious. Their liveliness kept McCarthy in top form, attracted the reporters, heightened interest, and provided the campaign with what in truth amounted to a bright, smiling, courteous, and engaging face. Their presence disarmed whatever hostility there might have been and kept each event of a McCarthy schedule as a productive political moment.

I felt that it would not be enough just to meet people in their homes and on the streets. Without something more to bind the candidate to the voter the handshake and brief words would be little more than another of the many political contacts that would be made that year.

I recalled that in 1962, John King, then a candidate for governor, had traveled with a photographer. Photos were taken of the candidate with individuals he was visiting. When the prints of the photos were returned, John King would autograph and dedicate each and mail it back to those in the pictures. The recipient now had a autographed, dedicated photograph of him or herself with a man who might become the governor of the state of New Hampshire. The photos were often prominently displayed in home, office, or workstation and were objects of great pride. In spite of the fact that New Hampshire is a small state and a high proportion of the residents see, hear, and personally meet the major public officials, the photographs were still important evidence of the meeting.

I knew that it would be impossible to duplicate King's successful technique. Time and the detail work involved prevented such an undertaking. However, shortly before the campaign the Polaroid camera company had developed a new, low cost camera, the Swinger, that I thought might work. The photos were of acceptable quality, the camera was foolproof to operate, and those who were photographed with McCarthy were delighted to have an immediate print. I ordered four cameras, film, and flash bulbs in large quantity, and gave a camera to four of the McCarthy girls.

The equipment was ready for McCarthy's third visit, February 13–15. The young women became a veritable paparazzi around McCarthy, steering the people to meet McCarthy, then taking Polaroid photos that were handed immediately to the subjects. Often McCarthy was asked to autograph the still sticky print.

As with the photos taken during Governor King's first campaign, these Polaroid prints were immediately put above shoe machines, sewing machines, on the dash of lift trucks, or in other prominent places. Each person included in one of the photos now had what I wanted them to have, a personal stake in McCarthy's future.

Like the professionalism that the young women adopted with their appearance, use of the camera, and constant cheer, each of the other aspects of the candidate support effort also improved. Schedule advance work improved because there were more advance people to do the work and because those who did advance were experienced and were now working with local contacts who were likewise experienced. Prearrival advance work either by a crew of a few volunteers who ventured ahead of the candidate's arrival or by the McCarthy girls helped create the sense of anticipation that added excitement to the actual arrival of the candidate. The traveling crew now included a minimum of three cars, an advance car, the candidate's car, and a station wagon carrying the McCarthy girls with camera supplies and campaign materials. The press cars and/or a press bus usually completed the campaign caravan.

As the campaign progressed, Schnapper, usually the driver of Senator McCarthy's car and chief advanceperson, or I, who drove the senator during the final week of the campaign, reverted to a practice of sudden scheduling. Schnapper and I would see time opening in a schedule and instead of slowing down the driving between stops or delaying a departure from one stop to the next, we would call ahead to a local contact or area headquarters and say we had some additional time that could be used. The contact or the headquarters manager would then either suggest a new event, a visit, stop, or ongoing activity that could be visited, make the advancing contact immediately, and advise as to whether a stop would be productive or not.

Ultimately Schnapper or I would make the decision to add or not add to the schedule but, and more often than not such en route changes were made and turned out to be valuable events. Much like the time McCarthy skated in Concord, the shelf of possible events that could be drawn on quickly became the habit of the campaign. Studds and I had advised the local organizations to be prepared for quick scheduling, but we had little idea that McCarthy would respond as well as he did to such frequent additions to the approved format. He thrived on the spontaneous event and the unexpected opportunity. The reporters also enjoyed departures from routines. Stories concentrated less on the amateur, inexperienced aspects of the work and began to praise the effectiveness of the campaign and the professionalism of the novices. Playing fast and loose, Studds and I had concluded that the exception was the rule, and if a calculable risk might produce a benefit the risk was taken.

THE CANVASS

Once most of the voting checklists had been collected and the effort to prepare mailing labels from the checklists for all New Hampshire's registered Democrats and Independents was well underway, I had assigned Dan Dodds to begin investigating how a door-to-door canvass might be organized. My only previous experience with a canvass had been with literature drops. The materials would be prepared by the statewide campaign or by a candidate's organization and then be distributed to the cities. There members of the local committee would collate the candidate materials into packets for the door-to-door distribution. Even this level of organization and distribution was fairly new to New Hampshire and largely a product of the lessons learned in the state during the late 1950s and early 1960s by those involved in various Kennedy influenced campaigns. Such literature drops usually came during the last weekend of a campaign.

When I asked Dodds to develop an assessment of what a canvassing activity would require I expected that something a bit more personal than a literature drop would result. Dodds concluded that the checklists could serve as the basis for identifying those who would receive the material. The campaign did not want to waste its energy on either those who were not registered to vote or Republicans. To organize the canvass meant that extra copies of the voting checklists would have to be made for each of the target cities and that a map of each city found that would allow the voting lists to be keyed with streets.

Working with Ben and Rosann Stavis, Dodds began to formulate the skeleton of what the canvassing effort would involve in terms of supporting tools, materials, and manpower. What was not immediately addressed was what form the canvass would take.

Dodds had determined approximately how many units could be visited by a volunteer in a reasonable period, outdoors, in the winter. He felt that each worker would have to be equipped with their own section of the city street map and a copy of names of people to be contacted. The mailing labels would be pasted on three-inch by five-inch cards, sorted by address, packaged, and given to the volunteers for the canvass.

We felt that comments would be recorded on the cards and that a filing system would result. In those communities where the voting lists did contain addresses, these were cut and pasted on the cards as well. As with most of the mailing label preparation the work for the canvass was done in the state headquarters by the volunteers.

The canvassing priorities were the same as the campaign's other priorities as outlined by the December 21 and January 7 memoranda. The heaviest canvassing efforts would be conducted in the cities with the largest Democratic registration and then working down the list by population, we hoped to canvass as many cities and towns as time and volunteer energy would permit. The style of the canvass would dictate how much could be accomplished. If it were to be a simple literature drop, then only a few hours would be needed to cover most communities. If it were to involve finding exact households and contacting specific voters then the task would be much more complicated. Studds, Dodds, and I, and others involved in the canvass planning, concluded that something more than just handing out campaign material had to be accomplished. We agreed that some type of voter contact would be important to provide the campaign with feedback that was not coming from any other source. The major canvassing push would have to take place during the last three or four weekends of the campaign, which allowed approximately one or two weekends to experiment and then to complete the canvassing strategy.

During this time, the Keene McCarthy committee had launched its own canvassing effort. I was in frequent contact with those organizing in the Keene area, advising them to adopt essentially a passive contact. I discouraged them from their original intention, which had been to carry the issue of the war to the doorstep rather than simple support for Senator McCarthy.

Their idea for the issue-oriented canvass had come as an extension of the "Vietnam teach-in" concept. They had thought that if the war were the principal reason for McCarthy's candidacy and not his nomination, then the issue was the real concern. My advice was that most people would not be prepared to discuss world politics on their doorstep and might be offended by the stridency of the contact. I suggested that if a contact at the door was made that it should be to support McCarthy and then to respond to questions. The Keene committee adopted this advice, prepared their own canvassing literature, and reported considerable success in their efforts. I felt that Keene might be an anomaly because of its isolation from Manchester's media and its close ties with Keene State College, and was not prepared to accept the Keene test as solid evidence that such a canvass would work in the populous Democratic cities of Manchester, Nashua, Berlin, or the Seacoast region.

Several days before Dodds and I were to set the final meeting before adopting a canvassing strategy, I received a call from Dr. Al Shepard, a New York based marketing specialist. Shepard wanted to volunteer time to the campaign and wondered where he could be most useful. Shepard profiled his experience as a product researcher and marketing adviser for a number of large corporations and prominent products. He then suggested that we might need some assistance in identifying issues and strategies that would reveal McCarthy's market appeal to New Hampshire voters. I suggested that he send a brief resume ahead and if he had the time, come for a visit. He accepted the invitation and arrived just as we were about to make a final decision on how the canvass would be conducted. With Shepard was his wife who worked with him in his consulting business, and they would be joined later by a college-aged son.

Cautiously Studds and I pursued with Shepard what he might offer to the campaign. In this case, assigning Shepard, an established professional in his early fifties, the usual volunteer tasks did not appear to be a proper use of his talent. As the conversation became more relaxed and trust developed, I began discussing our plans for the canvass. Shepard indicated that the canvassing concept was much like a marketing study conducted before a new product was introduced or to evaluate the public's response to a product that had been offered. He outlined the uncertainty he sensed as being the public's reaction to both the impact of the war and the domestic consequences of the war policy. The challenge he suggested was to develop ties between the public's mood and Senator McCarthy as an acceptable alternative to President Johnson. The purpose might not be to displace the president as the Democratic Party's presidential candidate but rather to demonstrate, through voting, the public's skepticism. Shepard approached his marketing analysis from the motivational perspective of the buyer or the voter. I found his methodology convincing and asked Shepard to assist in managing the canvass.

The next meeting involved those who had been preparing for the canvass, principally John Barbieri, who had been working with Sam Brown finding volunteers; Ben Stavis, who had been preparing maps and voter contact lists; and a recently arrived Cornell nuclear physics graduate student, Joel Feighenbaum, who had begun to organize a means of analyzing the canvass returns. I reviewed the strategy I was prepared to test, which was to be a passive door-to-door contact. The canvasser would be instructed to call at the door of a listed voter, hand him or her a packet of McCarthy campaign material, and then attempt to evaluate the response.

Shepard agreed that this might be a useful approach but would probably not offer much in the way of a response. Since all were concerned that even such a low level of contact might stir hostility, we decided to prepare a careful test in a place where if the reaction was bad, news of the failure would not spread easily. Shepard agreed to work with those preparing the canvassing materials, draft instructions for those who would be making the test canvass, and conduct a training session in the technique. I advised that the test should be made in a city that had political and ethnic characteristics much like Manchester where the percentages of registered Democratic voters was high. Somersworth, located in the southeastern corner of New Hampshire, came closest to resembling Manchester. While a small city, approximately nine thousand population, it had a long tradition of strong Democratic Party loyalty, contained a sizable percentage of French-Canadians in its population, and was isolated.

I was reasonably sure that word of the test would not leak far from Somersworth since its links outward were limited, but the city would be a valid test case because the campaign had not received much attention. If the canvassers did sense a favorable response to their approach or at least not hostility, then I felt a canvassing activity statewide would be worth the risk. I was also aware that since the canvass would have to be conducted by the student volunteers, the reaction might be negative not just to McCarthy or mention of McCarthy but to the approach and even the appearance of the college-aged canvasser. As a tight little city, I felt that Somersworth would be the right place to test the reaction of the resident to the canvasser as well.

When the volunteers began arriving for the weekend, Barbieri and Brown began selecting the most experienced and best appearing of the volunteers to receive Shepard's training. Barbieri briefly described what their assignment would be and found that almost all of those he had picked were delighted to do something more than prepare mailing labels or sort campaign materials. The canvass would give them a chance to meet New Hampshire voters themselves and to express some of their own feelings about the issues in the campaign. The fifteen or so selected met with Shepard for the training session early Saturday morning. Shepard, a forceful individual, indefatigably described the dos and don'ts of the agreed upon procedure.

The canvasser was to ring a doorbell, offer a pleasant greeting and introduction, hand the packet of McCarthy material to the person at the door, and then respond to any questions that might come. If there were no questions then the canvasser was instructed to end the contact with a phrase such as "I hope you will consider voting for Senator McCarthy, March 12," and then go on to the next door. Between contacts the canvasser was instructed to note on the address card what the response had been at the door. Shepard advised the volunteers not to become involved in debates or to become trapped in lengthy or hostile exchanges. If they met hostility at the door they should end the contact as quickly and pleasantly as possible and move on.

Each canvasser was to receive a packet of address cards for approximately twenty-five to thirty households. The amount of time projected for the pack was about five hours of work. The fifteen got in their cars and headed out of Concord for Somersworth. It was February 10, a cold, gray, snowy day when most people found themselves not wanting to venture outside.

Those who had prepared for the canvass busied themselves in the headquarters. If the canvassers ran into serious problems they were to call for instructions. One of the leaders, Mike Rice, who had some earlier canvassing experience with civil rights work in Alabama, called to report that they had arrived and were not meeting hostility. What concerned him was that in the early contacts they had had difficulty determining who the person at the door was supporting.

In the dark of the late winter afternoon the canvassing volunteers straggled back to Concord. The look on their faces was unsettling. They were cold, tired, disappointed, and frustrated. They reported that it had been almost impossible to detect differences in the reactions from one contact to another or from one canvasser to another. There had been no hostility, but at the same time there was almost no recognition of McCarthy or willingness to discuss him or the issues he represented. People had accepted the campaign material courteously but the doorstep exchanges had been brief as the person who answered hurried to get back inside, out of the cold, and away from the door.

The debriefing of the canvassers revealed both positive and negative results. While the contacts had been cold and remote there had been no antagonism. I explained that New Hampshire people are apt to be shy and reluctant to reveal their own feelings. Shepard responded to this observation by suggesting that perhaps the next test should be a bit more challenging. The canvassers felt they needed something more than the campaign material and a phrase of introduction to bring a response from the person at the door. They had hoped that they would be able to discuss some of their own feelings concerning the war and related Johnson administration policies. When this did not happen their disappointment increased and with it their own sense of isolation and despair. They also felt that some local preparation for the canvass might also help encourage people to express their opinions to the canvassers and to understand why the canvass was being conducted in their community.

Shepard advised that both leading questions and precanvass preparation should be tried. He recalled that the current issue of the *Saturday Evening Post* carried a cover story written by the retired General James Gavin titled, "We Can Get Out of Vietnam." Shepard thought the Gavin article might be a means of linking McCarthy and the canvasser to a respected national figure who was critical of the administration's war policy. In preparation for the next canvassing technique try, the campaign bought about twenty copies of the magazine, and Shepard prepared modified instructions. The canvassers were scheduled to return to Somersworth for additional testing Sunday afternoon February 11.

Shepard's Sunday morning training session varied on two accounts from the one that had been held the day before. First he advised the canvassers to be somewhat more active in their contact at the door. As the lead for the contact he demonstrated how the Gavin article should be used. His instructions read:

> I'm from the McCarthy for President headquarters. This week in the *Saturday Evening Post,* General Gavin has expressed his feeling that "We Can Get Out of Vietnam." I'd be very interested in your own feelings about the war from what you have seen on television and read in the papers.
>
> INSTRUCTION: listen to the person's response
>
> Senator McCarthy feels that although we started out to help in Vietnam, since 1963, the war has become more and more an American war. It is our boys who are fighting (mostly). Why?

During this introduction, Shepard advised that the canvasser have his or her copy of the magazine folded to the lead page of the article and that the lead page be clearly in view of the person being canvassed. Following the offer to explain "Why?" the canvasser should mention as reasons summaries of Gavin's argument such as:

> Corruption in the government: Even in their own rigged election, the present government received only about 30% of the vote cast. The people do not support the government—that is why it has become an American war.
>
> Effect on United States: Over 2 billion dollars a month is being spent in Vietnam—over 70 million dollars a day. This (70 million) is more than the total fiscal budget for 1967–1968 in New Hampshire! The 2 billion a month would keep the New Hampshire government going for almost 30 years.
>
> Result? The request for a 10% tax increase (by the Johnson administration).

After suggesting aspects of the impact of the administration's policy the canvasser was advised to suggest some ways to get out of the of war. Again, rather than reference the positions of McCarthy the candidate, Shepard advised that the Gavin article be the source for ways to withdraw from Vietnam.

> How do we get out—how do we stop the waste of tax money and more important, the loss of life?
>
> General Gavin's article recommends much the same thing as Senator McCarthy.
>
> 1. Properly support our boys in Vietnam by bringing the scattered planes, ships and forces from North Vietnam and the hillsides to the cities in South Vietnam.
> 2. Cease fire on our own initiative. Maintain a holding action in the cities. We would fight back if attacked, and the forces and equipment to do it would be there. (see step #1)
> 3. Specific offer to mediate the situation. Some specific city, some particular mediator (U Thant, the Pope, etc.).

To conclude the contact Shepard advised linking the issues with the importance of the person's vote and Senator McCarthy's candidacy.

What your vote means:

51% Lyndon B. Johnson Lyndon, Johnson write-in is writing "yes, I want my taxes increased;"
"yes, I want more boys sent in to Vietnam."

51% Eugene McCarthy Congress may think twice about tax increase; people in other states encouraged to speak out; open Democratic Convention. Restore the spirit which existed before 1963—exemplified by Kennedy.

(Canvassing suggestions memorandum, DCH copy)

The second suggestion involved expanding the way the response should be recorded by the canvasser after the contact had been concluded. Instead of a three-point scale of favorable to McCarthy, favorable to Johnson, or indifferent, a five-point evaluation was advised. The five would give the canvasser a way to classify virtually all contacts and also permit the headquarters to analyze areas where additional campaigning might move voters toward voting for Senator McCarthy. The new scale read:

1. Favorable to McCarthy
2. Indifferent but leaning toward McCarthy
3. Totally indifferent
4. Indifferent but leaning toward Johnson
5. Favorable to Johnson

The long Sunday afternoon passed while the canvassers worked and the canvass organizers waited in the headquarters. Late that afternoon the canvassers returned. Their experiences had been the exact opposite of the day before. Instead of the non-response, they had been able to get conversations started that revealed not the feared hostility but deep concern about the issues that the canvassers raised. Often the canvasser was invited inside to talk and pursue the interview. While few canvassers could report that the contacts led to number 1 or "favorable to McCarthy" responses, it was clear that the war was on people's minds and that they were willing to discuss it with a stranger. There had been little or no hostility either to the contact or to the appearance of a young, quite obviously college-aged person on the doorstep. Even in working class, isolated Somersworth, the president and his administration's policies had produced concern rather than unquestioning loyalty. The canvassers were stimulated by the effort, anxious to canvass again, and genuinely surprised by the hospitality they had experienced.

The careful debriefing of each canvasser revealed little that was not positive about the experience. Shepard's advice had made it possible for the canvasser to get beyond the introduction of the day before. They found that when they did get beyond the initial minute the contact wanted to talk and appeared almost relieved that someone wanted to discuss their concerns. Occasionally a person would note that they had not been able to talk with their own children and that it was nice to once again speak in friendly tones with someone of their own children's age. The fact that the canvasser was a stranger seemed to be an asset. Many indicated that they had not talked about these things with their friends, neighbors, or relatives.

People had masked or buried their personal concerns about the state of their nation and the unsettling impact of this concern on their personal lives. The canvassers gave them a chance to reveal these concerns without threatening higher valued communications. The canvasser, obviously from out of town, would have almost no way of betraying the momentary confidence that the contact placed with the conversation. The test had produced an important new campaign tool.

Joel Feigenbaum jumped on the data the canvass had produced. He began to draft charts to serve as a record of the daily canvassing results and to project the support such an effort would require. Barbieri and Mike Rice, who had worked with the canvassers in the field, now could estimate more accurately the number of contacts that each canvasser could make during a weekend and from that project the number of canvassers that would be needed to cover the priority cities. Stavis, who prepared voter address cards, maps, and canvassing instruction packets for the tests, now had to expand his activity to cover a much larger effort.

Within a day or two of the tests, canvassing became the major volunteer activity of the campaign. Preparation for a full-scale effort would require the attention of each of the principal leaders in the test. Shepard, with Feigenbaum and me, would refine the canvassing instructions to specific details. Those first volunteers who had canvassed in Somersworth and would either be staying the week in New Hampshire or could return the next weekend became field operations supervisors. They would conduct the training and then lead their canvassing crew to the community.

Barbieri and Feigenbaum began to estimate how many volunteers would be needed to cover the priority cities. Dodds and Brown would call to the sources of volunteers and Dumanoski would work finding places for the volunteers to stay. The first flood of those scheduled to canvass arrived for the next weekend, February 17 and the flow would be steady for each weekend that followed until March 9.

To guarantee that the orientation for the canvassers was the same in Berlin as it was in Manchester and to make sure that the canvassers understood the importance of their role, the supervisors were carefully oriented to their job by both oral and written instructions. While in many ways the role of the local committees in the canvass was one of logistical support, the supervisors were instructed to check their plans with the local committee and to carefully follow their advice. From the beginning the cooperation between the local committee and the canvassing supervisors was excellent. The novelty of the activity kept everyone on their toes and offered only those who had canvassed earlier an advantage in the hierarchy. The fact that strangers had an advantage when canvassing also helped to prevent conflict from developing.

By the third weekend, February 24, the reporters had discovered the canvassing story. Film crews followed canvassers on their rounds and reporters began telling the story of the mystical relationship that had begun to develop between the canvassers and New Hampshire voters. The stories themselves often served as the means of preadvancing a canvassing visit. The area headquarters would release canvassing dates for a locality to the media with the result that the canvassers were often expected when they rang a doorbell. Residents were ready with their own welcomes and questions with the result that the canvassing showed a marked shift favoring McCarthy in the analysis of the returns. However, the success and prominence of the canvass did produce a few conflicts, which Ben Stavis recounted in his report of the campaign. He wrote:

> Our staff of graduate students was brilliant, imaginative, hard working and dedicated. But graduate students are loners by profession. They are most comfortable by themselves in a library or having tea with a colleague. They certainly do not have the skills or experience in working bureaucracies. They are not used to dividing up a job into rational (or merely convenient) chunks, to using staff effectively, to working intensively with many other people. While learning these skills, they found themselves engaged in occasional rivalry and factionalism.
>
> These problems were most apparent for the brilliant physicist on the staff (Joel Feigenbaum). A true scientist, he made tables, charts, graphs, and projections of the canvassing results. He experimented with different approaches and had no patience with those who felt the variables were too great and the data too unreliable for scientific analysis.
>
> He trained his own group of canvassing supervisors and attempted to wrest total responsibility for canvassing from John Barbieri.
>
> (Stavis, op. cit., p. 23)

When conflict did develop, Studds or I would intervene. The conflict had to be resolved as a management problem. Barbieri was assigned to the management of field operations and Feigenbaum to analysis and strategy. The separation worked as both established their own operating spaces in the headquarters and assembled supporting staff.

Another form of rivalry was less easy to control. Although Studds and I continued to be the principal sources of information on the essential policies of the campaign, the reporters had found the volunteers to be stories unto themselves. While each was instructed not to comment to the press on aspects other than their immediate job, background, and reasons for coming to New Hampshire, this was more than enough to keep a steady stream of noted reporters flowing into the Concord headquarters. Stavis, both a participant and observer of the reaction in the headquarters when reporters arrived, wrote:

> The staff rivalry was especially apparent whenever journalists such as Theodore White or David Brinkley sought interviews. Elbows became crossbars as staff members tried to rebound the questions tossed up by these famous reporters. One law student, wise to the ways of TV, bought a light blue shirt, hoping

> that Walter Cronkite would look favorably on that sign of understanding. I attracted Mr. White, but I attribute his attention not to my competitive urge or sharp elbows but to the mutual attraction of students of China.
>
> (Stavis, ibid., p. 23)

Feigenbaum carefully analyzed the data he drew from the cards turned in by the canvassers. Shepard concentrated his skills on evaluating the debriefing reports from both the canvassers and the field canvassing supervisors. Both evaluations kept the campaign in close touch with its impact and progress. Feigenbaum prepared weekly reports of the canvassing results by area. He began to detect a shift from the "3" group to the "2" and from the "2" to the "1."

The combination of press attention, additional events, and McCarthy's own effectiveness as a campaigner was being reflected in the shift. McCarthy's percentage of the vote crept from 20 to 25 percent when the 1's and 2's were taken together in the first week, to 25 to 30 percent in the second week, and 30 to 35 percent in the third week. Feigenbaum began to project election percentages that had McCarthy approaching the 50 percent figure that all had thought was impossible in the earliest days. What was of greatest concern in the optimistic analysis was the fact that the movement toward McCarthy was less vigorous in Manchester and, to a lesser extent, in Nashua as well. Both cities accounted for much of the state's Democratic primary vote. While the Keene, Concord, Portsmouth, and Laconia areas were reporting canvassing support for McCarthy exceeding 50 percent, the number of voters in those areas was far less than the likely turnout in Manchester and Nashua.

Shepard accepted Manchester as his particular challenge. In addition he evaluated the debriefing reports and formulated changes in the issues to be emphasized in the contact and the approach of the canvassers. In this way Shepard was able to monitor the flow of the issues and to adjust the details of the coming weekend's canvass to respond to a new event or issue that had either been produced during the week or was found to be important to the voter.

As the canvassing activity became large and complex, Shepard organized his own technique and issue testing group. Neither Feigenbaum nor Barbieri could respond to the many adjustments or experiments that Shepard wanted to try and still prepare for the coming weekend's flood of canvassers. As tension developed between the three, I was called in to sort things out. I encouraged Shepard to shift his operations from Concord to Manchester and to work in Manchester with his own team. I assured Shepard that I would respond to Shepard's advisories and incorporate them in the canvassing as feasible. The sparks between Shepard and the canvass managers cooled. Shepard directed his principal attention to trying to "crack" Manchester, and Feigenbaum and Barbieri could concentrate on the next canvass. The campaign was spared a serious clash of wills.

The instructions that were developed for both the canvass and for the post-canvass reports document the thoroughness of the planning and the execution of the canvass. Under the title "Information for Volunteers" the following mimeographed instructions were given to each canvasser.

Information for Volunteers

Facts about N.H. Politics—Approximate figures on voter registration give Republicans a 2 to 1 lead over Democrats, with Democrats and Independents being even at about 100,000 (very approximate number). Voting patterns, however, give Republicans 54% and Democrats 34%. The Governor, John King, is a Democrat, and the Senate seats are split between Norris Cotton (Rep) and Thomas McIntyre (Dem). King and McIntyre are very active on behalf of President Johnson.

"Independent" voter registration means that the voter has never voted in a primary before. Crossing over is not permitted, and a voter can vote in a different primary only if he changes his registration 90 days beforehand.

The primary is a two party affair. There is the selection of slate of delegates to the national party convention. These may or may not be pledged to a particular candidate. Then, there is the preferential primary, in which the voter indicates the candidate he would vote for in the election itself. In this part of the primary it is possible to write in the name of a candidate of the other party. These votes do count in the final result.

The Canvass—Part of the purpose behind the canvass is to determine the nature of support for the Senator. There will also be the effect that we have on the voters as the Senator's personal representatives. Our appearance and behavior will have as much affect as will the fact that he is interested enough about the primary to send representatives to answer their questions and solicit their opinions. We also hope to convince them that the Senator is the candidate who will best voice their concerns.

Your approach will therefore be indirect. You are to feel out the voter's opinions before pressing any of the issues (e.g. the pledge card, Vietnam, taxes and inflation, Johnson's credibility). You want to put yourself inside his frame of reference and discover how he comes to the conclusions he comes to. Be a good listener.

The pitch will vary with your own style, but bear in mind certain things.

1. Always mention the name of the person(s) on your card. We want to know if he has moved, died, etc.
2. Always identify yourself as a representative of Senator McCarthy.
3. If the Senator has been in town recently, mention the fact, ask the voter if he has seen him. If he is coming shortly, mention when and where he will be appearing, and that he would very much like to meet the person you are talking to.
4. Never ask if he is going to vote for McCarthy. Your most direct bid will be "I hope you will consider voting for McCarthy."

The following are two different approaches which you may find useful to consider:

"Hello, I am a volunteer for Senator McCarthy, who is offering the people of (town) an alternative to Lyndon Johnson." (Break for conversation of a general nature, about weather, scenery, neighborhood, etc. Mention if Senator has been or will be in town. Conversation should drift soon to Senator and issues. You can produce the least controversial piece of literature and discuss it, or ask if he knows anyone who has been sent to Vietnam.)

"Hello, I am representing Senator McCarthy, who is running for the Democratic nomination for President. I wonder if there are any questions I could answer for you, any issues you would like to discuss, if I could interest you in some literature. . . ."

Remember that you are there at their service, to answer their questions, and discuss the issues that interest them, not to press your opinions on them or pressure them into voting one way or the other. You may be asked what brings you to New Hampshire. Let them see how urgent you feel it is that everyone consider the issues carefully, and how important the New Hampshire primary is for the whole nation. Being from out of state can be turned to an advantage. Perhaps you do not have a primary in your state so you cannot express your opinion on this question except in this way. A lot of people commented favorably on the interest shown by young people in coming out to canvass.

When discussing issues be sure to state the Senator's position rather than your own adaptation of his views. If you are not familiar with these positions already, consult the pamphlet that has been prepared well before you venture onto the streets. Certain issues that will probably recur are these:

The Pledge Card—You should know that the Democratic State Committee has openly endorsed President Johnson, before the voters of the state had a chance to express their opinion. They have sent out a pledge card to all registered Democrats. These are individually numbered and it is a fair assumption that there is a master list with numbers checked off as they are returned. Voters may express resentment at coercion and the threat of reprisals, and also feel that the secrecy of the ballot is being violated.

Taxation—You all know that McCarthy is against a tax increase at this time, and that much of the taxpayers money is being used for graft and corruption in Saigon. But did you know that the war is costing every person in the U.S. $150 a year, that more is spent in Vietnam every day than goes into the N.H. General Fund every year, that N.H. taxpayers pay $2 to Vietnam for every $1 that goes into the General Fund? Your voter may not know it. Tell him.

The War—Don't get too wound up in this. You have only short time in which to deal with a question you have spent a great deal of time and thought on.

—It's not so much a question of changing horses, but of changing streams.

—McCarthy does *not* support unilateral withdrawal, but rather a negotiated peace. "Never negotiate out of fear, but never fear to negotiate."

—Present the prospect of years of war, in which thousands of young men will die needlessly, without promoting American ideals, in a land which openly regards this as America's war, that did not declare a state of national emergency until the Tet offensive, that is not yet drafting its 18 and 19 year olds. Did you know that a draft exemption in Vietnam costs $300?

Procedure—You will receive a pack of cards with addresses and a map of the area you are to cover. Number the cards before you leave so they will not get out of order. You will notice that these are marked with party affiliation, I = Independent, D = Democrat.

—You will be given a pack of literature for each house. Even if there is no one home, leave this there. Put it between screen and main doors if possible. DO NOT PUT IT IN THE MAIL BOX. IT IS ILLEGAL TO OBSTRUCT DELIVERY OF THE MAIL.

—You will make a note on each card after you leave the house, registering degree of favorability to McCarthy as follows

1. Favorable to McCarthy
2. Uncertain but possibly favorable to McCarthy
3. No opinion
4. Uncertain but possibly favorable to Johnson
5. Unfavorable to McCarthy

If there is no one at home, mark the card NA and leave literature. If the voter has moved or died note the fact on the card. Never record information in the presence of the voter.

— Do not get angry or argue with the voter.

— If a voter wishes to do volunteer work or to give money, record his wish and refer him to the nearest local contact. Do not accept money yourself.

The post-canvassing instructions not only showed the importance of reporting the results but indicated how the canvassing results would be incorporated into the planning for the get out the vote effort.

Instructions: Post-Canvassing
Addressed to: All Regional Offices

After your area has been canvassed, please follow these procedures.

SAVE ALL CARDS. Separate the cards marked ONE and TWO for purposes of listing them in triplicate. Return the ONE and TWOS to their original decks so that follow-up canvassers can visit these later.

Send two copies of the typed list (names and addresses) to the Concord Office, one addressed to "Jessica" and one addressed to "Verlin." Jessica and Verlin are organizing phone canvassing and election day activities respectively. Keep the third copy of ONES and TWOS for your own office.

Separate out all the "moved" "deceased" etc. and remove. Send these cards to the Concord Office, addressed to Verlin. Some of these will be challenged on election day.

Separate out all cards for convalescent homes, nursing homes, and the rest. Most of these people have not been contacted because an appointment is required. It will be up to the local HQ to arrange appointments with these people.

If you have many cards which have "old" or "elderly" written on them these should be separated out also. It would be helpful, if possible, to have local people go to canvass these people. They are not effectively canvassed by young people.

If you have any questions, please contact John Barbieri, your canvassing liaison at the Concord Office. Dated: February 28, 1968

What the instructions revealed was that another phase of the campaign was about to begin. As with the earlier phases, the leadership was anticipating and planning activities that would occur next in the sequence. Just as I had assigned Dodds to investigate how a canvass might be developed, Gans had assigned his assistant, Jessica Tuchman, and another former Washington headquarters staffer, Verlin Nelson, to begin preparing for the preliminaries of the election.

The canvass offered an unforeseen chance to build a get-out-the-vote effort around those who had been identified as inclined toward voting for Senator McCarthy. Since the trend was moving strongly in McCarthy's favor as analyzed by Feigenbaum, it also appeared useful, or at least worth the risk, to follow up canvassing contacts with second visits or telephone calls. Both were designed to increase the commitment of the potential McCarthy voter to him and to increase the probability that the person would actually get out and vote. Where it also appeared that the trend of the canvassing returns showed especially strong movement toward McCarthy the 3s and even 4s were recanvassed in hopes that they might be either encouraged now to support McCarthy or, in the case of the 4s (leaning toward Johnson), they might be either neutralized or shifted toward McCarthy.

The Johnson campaign had neither an alternative strategy to combat the canvassing flood nor a means of attacking it. The McCarthy campaign leaders were less concerned about an attack from the Johnson campaign than of some damaging event caused by the behavior of a volunteer. From the first weekend of canvassing to the last, the leaders anxiously waited for that telephone call reporting a drug bust, an automobile accident, some sort of violence, or virtually any other embarrassment that might sour the public's taste for the canvass. While there were minor incidents, an occasional traffic violation, or nervousness on the part of a local police force, nothing developed to the point of embarrassment. In all cases the volunteers exercised extra caution and courtesy, taking to heart the campaign's warning that they and their behavior were a direct reflection of the campaign.

After the third weekend of canvassing, Joel Feigenbaum and Sam Brown began a rather lengthy discussion as to what the final McCarthy vote would be. Feigenbaum relied on his careful evaluation of three weeks of canvassing results, the direction of the trends, and his projection for voter turnout. Brown, less willing to accept the conclusions of the scientist, thought the campaign would have difficulty in Manchester and would not develop the turnout in other parts of the state that would offset losses in Manchester. Because he had been dealing with problems in the campaign his instincts could not accept the trends that Feigenbaum reported. To resolve the discussion and get on to other things, they agreed to write the percentage each thought McCarthy would get on a slip of paper, which they sealed in an envelope. They gave the envelope to me to hold for them until after the results were in on March 12.

DIRECT MAIL

Although the canvassing activity assumed the spotlight of the campaign during the last weeks, the preparation of the mailing continued. Gans and I agreed that the laborious process of creating the mailing labels should continue as long as it was feasible and the volunteers were plentiful enough to staff the effort. But it was also agreed that when the volunteer power was needed in other aspects of the campaign, there would have to be a shift away from the mailing preparation.

About three weeks before the election, Gans saw the mailing slipping in his assessment of the priorities of the campaign. He thought the canvass would accomplish much of what the mailing had originally been conceived to do. He began to shift volunteers away from the mailing before I thought it was advisable. Gans had, on his own, concluded that, in those communities where the mailing labels had not been prepared and where the canvass showed trends toward McCarthy, it would be reasonable to blanket mail to all addresses and not be concerned about wasting mailings on Republicans.

At first I disagreed but gradually realized that it would be difficult if not impossible to produce accurate labels for all of the priority communities. Studds and I had been reviewing our strategy for the mailing in light of the canvassing returns—especially the strong returns from many of the smaller communities on our original list. These returns showed that the percentage favorable or leaning toward McCarthy was substantial. To reach more potential voters tucked away in the less populous towns, Studds and I began to extend the list of towns that would receive mailings. The only way to mail to these towns in the time that remained would be to use a commercial mailing house and blanket all addresses. Gans, Studds, and I discussed the implications of the decision and agreed that blanket mailing would have to be used. We hoped that some of the Republicans who received the McCarthy mailing would write in the senator's name on their ballot, especially since Governor Romney had withdrawn from the Republican contest.

This change was purely one of strategy and did not affect what had been going on in the basement of the Concord headquarters for more than a month. During that period the labels had been carefully typed, filed, sorted, pasted on canvassing cards, and on envelopes. The envelopes were sorted and boxed by city and zip code. The letter

Tom Collins had drafted came back from the printer toward the middle of February. Two versions had been prepared, one to be addressed to Democrats, the other to Independents. A third version and the blanket mailing had to be printed quickly.

A brochure was being prepared for the mailing by the national headquarters which arrived several days before the mailings were scheduled to be collated, stuffed, and sealed. The campaign had received a contribution of six thousand dollars in six-cent stamps that would be used to mail the letter first class. Shortly after the stuffing began I weighed one of the envelopes and found that as a unit it exceeded one ounce. Gans and I were horrified by the finding. To send the envelopes as they were would double the cost of the mailing. The weight, they found, exceeded one ounce by the weight of one sheet of paper. The volunteers spent several days tearing off the fold-out section with the picture of McCarthy's first campaign day in New Hampshire.

The mailing reached the post office and the commercial mailing house on schedule. Our original thought was to have the mailing arrive during the week before the election. For those who had been contacted by the campaign the mailing would reinforce whatever positive impact that contact had had. For those who had not been reached by the campaign, the mailing might encourage the recipient to consider learning more about McCarthy in the time remaining.

The initial mailing plan was expanded considerably. First, many more towns were added to the priority list than had been advised by Studds and I. Second, the idea of blanket mailing to parts of the state where the campaign was succeeding better than expected was an important change. Third, something that is usually tried in campaigns that have a longer development period than did the McCarthy campaign was also accomplished. A number of special group mailings were prepared when lists where available and persons willing to sign the letter to the targeted group agreed.

Preparing materials for canvassing, distribution to area headquarters, special precession drops, and other distribution ad circulation efforts also were handled by the crew consigned to the cave-like environs of the Concord headquarters basement. The space had the appearance of the galley of an ancient ship. The workers stretched along folding tables with their arms reaching for the work. In the background a stereo played the latest rock music. Stavis wrote:

> During the week, we philosophers, theologists, sinologists, lawyers, and a few people with only bachelor's degrees, all tore mailing labels, pasted them on envelopes, stuffed, sealed, stamped, and sorted by zip code. When masses of volunteers came for the weekend, we learned how to supervise. We did appropriate time and motion studies, developed executive training programs, analyzed the relationship between endurance and commitment, and moved cartons, tables, and chairs. We had seminars in folding, advanced stuffing, elementary sealing and interdisciplinary stamping. All this work was geared to the throbbing rhythm of the hardrock records.
>
> (Stavis, op. cit., pp. 7–8)

When the mistake in the weight of the mailing was discovered Stavis recalled:

> A butcher's scale revealed that it slightly over weight, and the post office would not accept that extra fraction of an ounce without extra postage. Not being able to afford that, we developed new courses in advanced unstuffing, resealing, and stamp saving.
>
> (Stavis, ibid.)

ISSUE TARGETING

Alan Shepard, who had skillfully oriented the early testing of the canvass, had shifted his attentions to Manchester at my suggestion. Shepard made a contribution to the statewide canvassing decisions but was not included in the policy advisories as the campaign continued. Once I persuaded Shepard to move his activity to Manchester, I was able to separate him from much of the mainstream of the canvassing activity and to find a crew of volunteers who were willing to work with him. In addition, I introduced Shepard to Paul Carrier, a local business owner, who offered Shepard the spare time of his office staff, use of his telephones, and office equipment to carry out Shepard's telephone canvassing tests. The office staff was paid, used to responding to specific requests, and more comfortable spending their workday on Shepard's tasks than had been many of the volunteers.

In spite of my efforts to separate Shepard's research from the operations of the canvass, he would occasionally intrude into the Manchester headquarters and begin requesting changes in the canvassing approach that he thought were justified by his findings. Shepard's orders often seemed to paralyze activity rather than propel it. Studds, Gans, and I continually had to resolve disputes about what should or should not be happening in Manchester. Eventually I was reasonably successful in getting Shepard to funnel his suggestions for changes in canvassing, telephoning, or press communications through me or Richard Goodwin who by then was based in Manchester. When we showed that we responded to Shepard's advice and implemented those aspects we felt were of value to the campaign, Shepard stopped reaching into the volunteer effort of his own.

What Shepard did was explore what was on the mind of the potential voters in the primary and then to advise strategies that would relate the campaign to these concerns. He found the voters were concerned about taxes, inflation, credibility, or a general feeling that things had become unsettled since John Kennedy's assassination. He would examine the links between subjects and compile strategies that might make the campaign reflex to the voter groups. He felt, as Studds and I had noted much earlier, that the war was a difficult issue to deal with in the context of the campaign. People wanted the war over, wanted it won or to get out, but were not comfortable with a lengthy discussion of the details. To avoid direct and unsettling confrontation with voters on the war policy with all of the conflicting emotion contained in such a confrontation, Shepard advised an oblique approach.

In Manchester, news of the Johnson administration's proposed surtax on incomes to support the federal budget was greeted with great hostility. The administration was already viewed with hostility because of the failings of the war, an increasing rate of inflation, and a general souring of credibility. The surtax proposal was the final straw. Shepard discovered that the tax proposal was mentioned most frequently by those his research group interviewed and was also an issue that canvassers had discovered was on the voters' minds. Shepard suggested that a new piece of campaign material be prepared that would tie McCarthy's opposition to the war and the continuation of the war to the voter's opposition to the tax surcharge. I sent Shepard to meet with Merv Weston, who was preparing New Hampshire campaign materials, to explain his findings.

The item that they produced was a card the same size as the Internal Revenue Service's 1040A form—the short form—of the tax return that most workers in New Hampshire file. The text of the IRS form was screened as a background for the message printed in red ink, "Will LBJ's proposed 10% tax increase put your family budget in the red?" Beneath the phrase was the suggestion printed in blue that "Your 'X' for Senator McCarthy says NO." The card helped reenforce the tax issue, demonstrate McCarthy's opposition to the tax proposal, and open the subject when McCarthy was campaigning. The card was included in the canvassing kits, some mailings, and was used in all of the cities where there was a concentration of Democratically inclined workers.

Shepard did much the same things with a number of other issues that he garnered from his research effort. Shepard spent almost three weeks in New Hampshire checking, testing, researching, and then advising campaign approaches. His influence was pronounced in the final pattern of materials, advertising, and through the telephone canvas that operated, especially in Manchester. He developed the telephone message and adjusted it almost on a daily basis. He was especially effective in tying McCarthy and his positions back to the things that were on the minds of the New Hampshire voters. To him the voters had to be motivated to vote for McCarthy, and, therefore, it was essential that the campaign reach for these concerns. Shepard worked as a consultant to the managers and, in that capacity, helped shape the themes that would bring McCarthy in closer touch with the New Hampshire voter. The sounding board he provided gave the young campaign staff the confidence to carry the campaign forward.

Because Shepard's approach was unorthodox, Gans and Weston were concerned that the direction Shepard was advising might not be correct. To check both the conclusions of Shepard and the increasingly optimistic results of the weekend canvassing, Weston advised conducting a random telephone survey of the voters. Weston's staff prepared a questionnaire, advised a telephone call selection strategy, and identified the cities in which calls should be made. The polling began during the weekend of February 24 and continued during the following week. Volunteers were assigned to the WATS lines in the headquarters to make the calls during the early evening hours. At first the results were mixed and did not seem to sustain the assumptions that either Shepard or the canvassing had revealed, but as the polling continued a pattern emerged that indicated the campaign was making the progress the canvass revealed and that it was addressing the issues that Shepard's research had identified.

The combination of the canvassing results, Shepard's research, and the inclusive results of the telephone polling, taken together, did help the managers adjust the campaign activities within the overall plan. The focus shifted from the war as the primary issue in the campaign to issues that related to the war such as the proposed tax surcharge, inflation, shifting priorities in the Johnson administration's programs, the draft, societal conflict, possible infringements of civil liberties, and administration credibility. Our early instincts about how McCarthy might be effective in New Hampshire as the focal point for a rather diffused disquiet among the New Hampshire electorate now evolved into specific subjects that the campaign could address through its mailings, advertising, and direct voter contact. McCarthy himself began to swing the pendulum of his critique across a broader arc as issues and their rhetorical illustrations were discussed.

THE CELEBRITIES

During most of the campaign there had been a number of what were described as "secondary speakers." Most of these had been scheduled independently of the McCarthy campaign by organizations concerned about the war policies. Working through church groups, local peace committees, and responding to campus invitations, a regular procession of critics had brought their backgrounds and views to New Hampshire cities and towns. Some were more closely allied with the McCarthy effort than others. Allard Lowenstein; Sandford Gottlieb, executive director of SANE; Zolton Ferency, former Democratic chair of Michigan; and several others had been involved early in the search for an alternative candidate and at one time or other had been in contact with the New Hampshire McCarthy campaign. Others, however, like David Luce, a disillusioned Agency for International Development officer in Vietnam, or several exiled Vietnamese critics of the current regime in Saigon were not connected to the campaign in any way. Their talks and the press coverage these meetings received expanded the public's information about the personal and political impact of the war and contributed to increasing the public's questions and concerns.

Occasionally during the early weeks of the campaign either Studds or I would receive calls from outside New Hampshire from organizations concerned about the war offering to send speakers to New Hampshire in cooperation with the campaign. In all cases we rejected the offers. We felt that our energies were already extended too far to manage other schedules. We also did not want to risk additional controversy. If there was to be controversy in the campaign, we felt it should come from McCarthy's own activity and be defended. Those who came to New Hampshire at the behest of other sponsoring organizations would not be the responsibility of the McCarthy campaign.

When Curtis Gans arrived to manage the campaign he brought with him from the national headquarters the person who had offered celebrity and secondary speakers, Sandra Silverman. She had been one of the few in the national headquarters that Studds and I had been able to work with by telephone. When Sandy arrived in New Hampshire she assumed responsibility for scheduling the secondary speakers and celebrities. Studds, Gans, and I had concluded that the campaign had grown to the extent that it could support this additional activity and that it could also sustain any controversy that might possibly result.

Sandy Silverman's first task was to develop campaign schedules for members of Senator McCarthy's family. Mary, the senator's second child, had just begun her freshman year at Radcliffe. She had become a part of the student group that looked for an alternative to President Johnson in 1968. As Richard Stout wrote concerning McCarthy's decision to run for the presidency:

> Though many people urged him along the way, no single person can be said to have influenced him ultimately. His decision to run was a private one. His daughter Mary had been suggesting it for months. Didn't he want to be remembered in history for some nobler act than support of Lyndon Johnson's reelection?
>
> (Stout, op. cit., p. 73)

Mary arrived for her first New Hampshire visit just before her father was to speak at the Concord Community Center, February 6. With her was a Harvard undergraduate, Stephen Cohen, who was immediately shocked by what he saw as total confusion in the Concord headquarters. They had arrived at the same time as other volunteers were arriving and the campaign leaders were preparing for the evening events. Without a person to manage the headquarters at this early stage, the volunteers who had arrived late in the afternoon were still waiting for assignments. Cohen immediately began to help get the volunteers to work and would continue helping in the campaign to its end.

Mary seemed shy and quiet, an unlikely campaigner, but her reputation as an influence on her father had preceded her. Mary spent some time with her father, worked briefly in the headquarters, and returned to Cambridge. During her short visit she did say that she wanted to help in any way she could with the campaign, but because of her schoolwork she might have to concentrate her efforts in Cambridge.

Mrs. Abigail McCarthy had been working behind the scenes in Washington, as had been her mode in previous campaigns. Now I urged her to join the campaign through both the national headquarters and her friend Mrs. Arleen Hynes. She agreed to visit and follow a schedule on February 14 and 15. To help her accept her new role as a campaigner she asked Mary to accompany her. Working with the local committees, Miriam Dunn of Concord arranged a two-day schedule that had Mrs. McCarthy and Mary visiting Manchester, Nashua, Peterborough, and Keene. In Keene, Mary decided there were some things she could try on her own. Barbara Underwood recalled:

> Mary Gregory, the wife of one of the two professors who spearheaded the McCarthy organization in Keene, asked if Mrs. McCarthy could please make a visit to a new community project. There is the New Hope Center for retarded children, she said and not one other candidate or his wife has shown interest in our center, and it really is the pride and joy of our city. There was, however, a time conflict in Abigail McCarthy's schedule, but Mary said that if her mother did not have the time to go, she would be happy to either go alone or with her mother. Mary had spent one summer at the Kennedy Foundation in Washington, tutoring retarded children, so it would be very natural for her. She also said she would substitute for her mother on an open-end radio program at the Keene station. It was the type of program where people telephoned in questions, with the answers given directly over the air.
>
> Steve Cohen reported back to Concord that Mary had been terrific on the radio, and should be scheduled for the same kind of programs throughout the state.
>
> (Underwood, op. cit., p. 66)

From that time, Mary McCarthy became one of the most important secondary campaigners for her father in New Hampshire. Sandy Silverman would schedule her to meet with community groups, McCarthy committees, to take part in radio and newspaper interviews, and to visit schools as well as act as a booster of volunteers who had not seen her father in person. Eventually, her time was in such great demand that she arranged for a leave from Radcliffe for the campaign duration. Sandy Silverman's first celebrity, Mary McCarthy, was a product of the New Hampshire experience. Mary's wit, articulate discussion of the issues, obvious personal dedication to the campaign, and self-assurance reflected the qualities of her father and expanded the trust that the voters were beginning to sense toward him.

"It's difficult to assess the exact role played by Mary McCarthy," wrote Barbara Underwood. "Probably most important was that she was there in the state of New Hampshire and gave credence to the fact that her father was a decent and intelligent man. Local people who got to know her tended to judge the Senator based on Mary's own decency and intelligence." As an example of how Mary McCarthy assisted the campaign, Barbara Underwood observed:

> She became a daily trouble shooter and confidant of the campaign workers when it seemed inappropriate for them to go to either Gene or Abigail McCarthy. For instance, after the Senator finished his campaigning in Concord, people could tell Mary that he was still throwing away his best lines. Furthermore, they wanted McCarthy to start acting as though he intended to win. "Tell your father to come out and say he is running for the presidency," they said. "People don't think he is a serious candidate."
>
> One night shortly after the final filing date for delegates, David Hoeh called a meeting at the Concord Headquarters for all delegates and alternates pledged to McCarthy. Mary came to the meeting and sat against the wall quietly observing.

> One of the delegates got up and said half jokingly, half in earnest, the he loved "Gene McCarthy, but would the Senator please look up and at least acknowledge the love and devotion that those in the audience wanted to express by their applause. Wouldn't someone please tell him not to walk on stage like he did at St. Anselm's without even glancing at the audience." Everyone looked to Mary to carry the message. She nodded and said, "Yes, I know, and he's still throwing away his best lines."
>
> (Underwood, op. cit., p. 65)

Mary did carry many messages to her candidate father but only occasionally did she carry messages back. He had set his tone for the campaign and would keep to his plans and expected the managers of the New Hampshire campaign to keep to theirs. Fortunately people understood that McCarthy did not wish to see his candidacy personalized to the extent that the issues would be lost. Therefore, each person who became involved in the campaign did so on the basis of his or her own personal decision rather than in response to some charismatic call from him as a leader. Mary, as the closest person to McCarthy during the New Hampshire campaign, conveyed the same message with her efforts. With each new experience with campaigning she blossomed from a freckled, shy, quiet, girl into a confident, assured, spokeswoman for both the issues and her father.

While Mary McCarthy was Sandy Silverman's first scheduling subject, the task that brought her to Hew Hampshire was different. Sandy Silverman expected to immediately begin scheduling a parade of notables who had been attracted to the McCarthy candidacy. We quickly but firmly advised her to be extremely careful and to clear with us each person she intended to schedule into New Hampshire. Although Studds and I were conservative in our approach to using celebrities, we understood the value of the celebrity role. A celebrity created excitement, attracted attention, and reached people who might not otherwise give thought to the campaign. I felt that McCarthy had too little time remaining to generate sufficient interest on his own to bring out a vote that would be significant. The voters we needed to get to the polls were those who, through disillusionment or disgust, had either lost the habit of voting or were in the process of losing the habit. If the interest level of the campaign could be increased then, perhaps, more of the marginal voters, many of them young and new voters, might just vote.

Sandy Silverman worked quietly arranging visits for several academic celebrities, principally John Kenneth Galbraith and others who came and went without stirring either much attention or controversy. Late in February she announced that Paul Newman had agreed to campaign in New Hampshire for McCarthy.

Newman arrived in Manchester late in the afternoon of Monday March 4. Notice of Newman's availability and arrival times were so short that Sandy Silverman had to scurry among the better organized local campaigns trying to find places for him to go and things for him to do on such short notice. Keeping in mind my concern about possible controversy, she planned a dinner in Manchester where Goodwin and I could talk with Newman about how he might be effective in New Hampshire.

Newman had admitted that he had not done this sort of thing before and needed some help with his approach. With waitresses peaking through the curtains that screened the table set for dinner, Newman, Goodwin, Mary McGrory, Sandra, and I ate a quick dinner during which Newman was briefed about McCarthy, New Hampshire, and what his visit might contribute. He then took a flight to the Lebanon airport, then to Enfield where Sandy Silverman had arranged a reception for him in a private home. Like other tests in the campaign little damage would have resulted if Newman's performance bombed in Enfield. With fingers crossed, Silverman and I waited the report of Newman's foray into the night of winter New Hampshire.

Shortly after 10:00 P.M. I received a telephone call report that all had gone exceptionally well. Newman was a bit unsure of himself at first, but after fielding a few questions effectively, he relaxed with the result that all left with a renewed feeling of the importance of the political venture they had joined. Even several of the campaign's more skeptical academic members from the Dartmouth faculty found Newman competent and engaging. Sandy Silverman began final scheduling plans for a full day of visits in Nashua, Manchester, and Dover where I felt Newman's attraction could greatly help the campaign. Newman himself returned home late Monday delighted with his evening and with a sincere feeling that he would be able to accomplish something for the campaign.

What he had accomplished was immediately revealed by the crowds he drew the next day and by the press clippings from his brief visit to Enfield. The Lebanon *Valley News* carried two photographs of Newman in Enfield. The front-page photo was captioned just as I had hope it would, "McCarthy Supporters—Paul Newman, tough-guy film star, gave Enfield area citizens a soft-sell pitch for Minnesota Senator Eugene McCarthy for president Monday night. He said U.S. needs change of policy in Vietnam." The page-three photograph was captioned, "Female Fans—Actor Paul Newman is surrounded by the distaff side during brief call at Enfield gathering Monday night." He refused to sign autographs but willingly shook hands with admiring Eugene McCarthy partisans of both sexes. The story the *Valley News* carried on his visit described how Newman experimented with his campaign style:

> Newman, who has been nominated for an Academy Award for his performance in ""Cool Hand Luke," is also a McCarthy backer and he's here in the Granite State "to do everything I can for him."
>
> When Newman finally arrived, about an hour later than scheduled, most of the crowd pushed into the front hall to watch him come in the door. And that's exactly what happened. A woman or two gasped as he walked in chewing Spearmint gum, but no one immediately uttered a greeting or even shook his hand. They were all spellbound and Newman appeared embarrassed.
>
> But he finally walked on into the house, shook some hands and threaded his way to the front of the living room to say a few words for McCarthy—very few.
>
> "I'm no public speaker," the actor began, "and in about 30 seconds you'll know why."

Newman spoke softly, thoughtfully, a far cry from the tough guy characters he's portrayed, such as Hud and Harper.

"Coming up today," Newman said, "I realized that Eugene McCarthy doesn't need me, I need Eugene McCarthy."

Newman, his face tan and his hair graying, looked at the floor and fumbled with the Spearmint package in his hand. "I don't want any more of the last four years," he said, "I've had it."

And this was his reason for coming to "New Hampshire to campaign for McCarthy." It was also the end of his few words to all for McCarthy.

Then the crowd surrounded him to ask questions and shake his hand. One young man asked for an autograph.

"That's not what I'm here for," Newman replied, "I don't want to turn this into an autograph party."

Newman would not sign a single autograph while campaigning but would sign McCarthy literature between stops that would be distributed following his visit. Instead of an autograph or a kiss, Newman adopted his own trademark. He would look a stunned admirer in the eyes and quietly say while he pinned a McCarthy button on the woman's coat, "Listen to what Senator McCarthy is saying, that is important." He would move slowly through a crowd shaking hands, pinning buttons on lapels, and reminding people that they, like himself, needed Senator McCarthy.

The schedule for March 5 read:

Nashua	
9:45–10:00 A.M.	Shopping centers
10:45–11:15	Campaign on Main Street
11:15–11:45	Nashua McCarthy Headquarters 120 Main Street
Manchester	
12:00–1:30	Manchester McCarthy Headquarters 1173 Elm Streetwalk to 839 Elm
Dover	
2:15–3:00	Factory gates
3:00–4 00	Elks Club party 123 Washington Street

The *Boston Globe* reported the visit under the headline, "Campaigner Steals Candidate's Stage." The *Globe*'s account of Newman's day began with Newman making a few calls at front doors as he once did when he was a Fuller Brush salesman and as the McCarthy canvassers were doing each weekend. As the news that he was in town spread, crowds developed along Nashua's Main Street.

Manchester was the climax. It took ten minutes and two policemen, to escort him through a milling, cheering crowd. After ten minutes, Newman had been able to move only twenty yards. He said to the cops, "I've been through this before. It's better if I get just a few feet of open space in front of me and then go out there myself. It'll be all right." Many shoves and shrieks later, Newman turned to a companion to assess his bold maneuver, "You know I was wrong." The reporter ended his account with a quote from Newman concerning why he had come to campaign for McCarthy. Newman responded, "Because McCarthy is the first guy who got off the seat of his pants and told the people what's what. Because everybody else is sitting around trying to decide which way the political winds blow. Because I sense in Sen. McCarthy a decent and ethical human being." (*Boston Globe,* March 6, 1968)

The *Manchester Union Leader* carried pictures of the crush in front of the McCarthy headquarters as Newman tried to get inside and also carried a cartoon of Newman followed by McCarthy captioned, "Who's that guy with Paul Newman?" The visit had produced more press and excitement than anything else up to that point in the campaign.

Several days after the first Newman visit, several canvassers were stopped by a state police officer in the western part of the state for speeding. Their car carried an out-of-state plate. As the trooper was writing out their ticket he said, "I'm doing this to show you that Paul Newman isn't the only one who can write autographs." Then as he handed them their warning he said, "By the way I'm a number one."

While serious candidates of presidential caliber, and especially McCarthy, disliked sharing the stage with other stars, the Newman phenomenon in New Hampshire lent celebrity status to the campaign. Although McCarthy did not meet Newman in public when he was in New Hampshire and did not want to be photographed with Newman at that time, he did not reprimand me or anyone else who planned Newman's visit. What McCarthy resisted was having the nature of his campaign changed from that of one focusing on the issues to one that personalized the effort. To him, at least at the New Hampshire stage, Newman represented what he had hoped to avoid—the hoopla of a conventional campaign. While he would not promote the idea of celebrity visits or lend himself to them, his silence allowed his managers to do what we felt was in the best interest of the campaign. Although Newman was a bit puzzled that he had not met McCarthy during his visit, he too appeared to understand the importance of separating the two images at this juncture.

In the days that followed Newman's February 4 and 5 visit, the size of McCarthy's crowds increased and were noticeably more excited and intense. By association, McCarthy had gained some of Newman's celebrity status. McCarthy's manner and style had not changed but he had become charismatic. The total pace of the campaign began to accelerate noticeably just at the crucial moment. Newman, the political novice in Enfield, had also found his own campaign pace. Before he left New Hampshire, he would meet with several other celebrities who were arriving to describe his experiences and council them on how to campaign effectively. My parting words to Newman were, "Will you come back?" To which he answered that he would like to.

Following Newman's visit Tony Randall arrived. His style was quite different. His responses to questions tended to be brittle, occasionally irritating, and defensive. He came to campaign for approximately three days but after the first day his responses caused concern. He tended to respond to the questions on the war with emotion rather than argument which was not what had brought the McCarthy campaign to its current acceptance in New Hampshire. After his first day, I asked Sandy to travel with Randall and to intercept questions that were likely to produce an inflammatory response from Randall.

During the middle of the second day of his visit, Sandy called me in the headquarters to report that on a number of occasions she had had to jump into the questioning to prevent Randall from continuing a hostile response or biting comment. She felt that it was dangerous for the campaign to allow the visit to continue. That evening Randall was told by Sandy Silverman that he had worked so hard that day that he had finished the schedule that had been planned for him. He could return to New York. To our relief, Randall left and accepted the explanation of his success.

A separate logistical activity, similar to that which supported Senator McCarthy when campaigning, had to be organized to convey the celebrities. Sandy Silverman had to organize and manage as many as three celebrities campaigning in the state or about to arrive at the same time. The heaviest flow of celebrities was during the final ten days of the campaign. During that time Paul Newman returned, and Robert Ryan, Rod Serling, and Jack Parr came to campaign. Some, like Serling and Parr, came to assist with the media campaign as well and would spend much of their time in the recording studios of Weston Associates. Each celebrity who came to New Hampshire made an endorsement tape that was added to the tapes recorded by Harry Belafonte, Robert Vaughn, Dustin Hoffman, Lauren Bacall, Jason Robards, Lee Remick, Joan Bennett, and Joanne Woodward in New York. (Stout, op. cit., p. 176)

Of the celebrities that visited, Paul Newman caused the greatest stir and was the most effective. He, as Richard Stout wrote, campaigned "tirelessly" throughout New Hampshire. "An actor no one disliked, [and] one who came across to young, and old, who radiated honesty and conviction. He had the star power that McCarthy lacked and imperceptibly was transferring a little of it to the candidate."

During his second visit Newman showed confidence in his campaigning that had been learned during his first visit. He was eager to work, would do whatever was asked of him, and wanted to be heavily scheduled. Sandy Silverman complied. A New York couple, Bill and Sandy Johnson, he a publisher with his own plane and she a former weekday serial star, were friends of Newman and agreed to fly with him and accompany him during his schedule. Sandy Silverman would brief Sandy Johnson, who would prep Newman for the campaign stops. As his confidence grew Newman became skilled at responding to the difficult questions, especially those concerning draft resistance and the administration's war policies. To the draft questions Newman responded for himself noting that he would support the decision that his then seventeen-year-old son might make, but hoped that Senator McCarthy's efforts would make that decision moot. To the questions on the war Newman would repeat McCarthy's position without the defensiveness or emotion that Randall had displayed.

Perhaps his most successful visit was the one that was planned with the greatest skepticism. Marc Kasky, firmly in control of campaign affairs in Berlin, reluctantly agreed to host Newman during the last weekend of the campaign. Kasky recalled:

> Concord was feeling guilty about how little they had done for me. They wanted to do things for me but . . . I was . . . way up north of the White Mountains. They kept offering me Paul Newman for a day to campaign in Berlin.

Silverman and I were offering a visit by Newman because we felt he would be well received in Berlin and would help in the final push before the election. We also knew that the Johnson's plane was available to shorten the trip—an advantage which was not available to the other celebrities. Kasky reacted to the offer:

> It just didn't seem like the thing that was needed for Berlin. I wasn't sure that the people in Berlin wanted Paul Newman to tell them who to vote for so I asked around to find out.
>
> The people I spoke to [asking] do you think he should come, said they didn't think it was a good idea. [They said] the people were making up their own minds, and this would make it just like any other campaign where some labor boss or the mayor comes out for a candidate. It's no longer the people's decision. It's who do you listen to? Do you listen to the mayor or the labor union council or a movie star?

Kasky concluded:

> If what we wanted to do was have them make up their own minds, this was defeating our primary purpose, so I turned Concord down a couple of times.
>
> Then, I found, many did suggest that the people of Berlin usually made up their minds by the last weekend. If Newman were to come up here the last day or two before the primary, no damage would be done. It would sort of be . . . a fitting climax to the campaign. Frankly, they just thought it would be a fairly exciting thing for Berlin to have Paul Newman there. They also thought that there might be some people who had not been contacted during the campaign and who knew very little about McCarthy who might be swayed by the visit—and many people would.
>
> The reason they figured that Paul Newman would be able to reach some people who hadn't been reached during the campaign was that there was a championship hockey game in town that final weekend. The whole town goes to the hockey game or listens to it on the radio. Most of those who go to it are those from the mills who weren't at home when the canvassers visited.
>
> A radio announcer who had dissuaded me twice from having Paul Newman come up said, "Okay, have him come that weekend and I'll arrange for him to drop the puck at the hockey game and make a speech over the loudspeaker." The radio announcer had not declared for McCarthy himself. He was just being helpful.
>
> (Kasky transcript, p. 25)

When Kasky finally called Sandy Silverman to say Newman should come he outlined a schedule that would scare most candidates much less a novice campaigner like Newman. Not giving Newman a chance to say anything but yes, Sandy Silverman got Dick Goodwin to write a brief speech for Newman to read over the hockey rink's speaker and, incidentally, the radio station covering the hockey game. Newman prepared with Goodwin's script while flying to Berlin.

> Well, Paul Newman came up to Berlin and visited a shopping center, went to the hockey game, spoke on the radio, reaching about everybody and creating a great deal of excitement in the city. Everybody loved him. He spoke very well and people all kind of looked around and started nodding to each other. "McCarthy is in this thing for real. He's not one of the—you know, a number of strange candidates enter the New Hampshire primary and they come through town one day every four years and that's all people see of them."
>
> This sort of created some feeling of permanence and determination on the part of Senator McCarthy—that he was in this seriously, he was not playing games, and that this city was very important to him.
>
> I think his visit, coming at the time that it did was very successful and might even have made the difference in the campaign.
>
> (Kasky transcript, p. 26)

A celebrity of a different sort but of no less importance was Richard Goodwin. At thirty-one years of age Goodwin abandoned his recently acquired teaching position at MIT to join the McCarthy campaign in New Hampshire. He arrived to meet Senator McCarthy in Berlin on Friday, February 3. Goodwin had become convinced that Johnson was vulnerable, and since Robert Kennedy would not be a candidate, the only game remaining was McCarthy in New Hampshire. Goodwin had been a youthful member of the Kennedy administration and was the first of Kennedy's political operatives to support McCarthy. A skillful speech writer and strategist, Goodwin had written an article for the *New Yorker* under a nom de plume outlining how Johnson might be replaced as the nominee of his party. The Tet Offensive was the final straw for Goodwin.

> An unlooked for consequence of Tet was the arrival of Dick Goodwin. Speculation at the time, suggested that Goodwin had been cunningly insinuated into the operation to oversee Kennedy's [Robert] interests. He, did, of course, but his initial motivation was uncharacteristically impulsive. At home in Boston, Goodwin read about the bombing at the temples in Hue and decided the situation demanded more of him than mere private prodding of Bobby. So he threw his typewriter into the back of his car and motored to New Hampshire.
>
> (Chester, Hodgson, Page, op. cit., p. 93)

While the *An American Melodrama* account had Goodwin arriving in Manchester, the fact was that he first met with McCarthy at his overnight stop in Franconia. The next day Goodwin joined Sy Hersh, McCarthy's traveling press secretary in Berlin, where he said, "Sy, with these two typewriters we're going to overthrow the government."

Goodwin began writing immediately. He was distressed that only a small group of the national reporters had bothered to follow McCarthy on his northern swing. He had Hersh place a series of calls to the major national newspapers and wire service editors chiding them for not covering the campaign. Goodwin told Hersh to announce that McCarthy would be making a major policy statement the next afternoon in Manchester and that if they did not wish to be scooped by their competition they had better get someone up to New Hampshire to cover the event quickly. Goodwin then sat down to write the statement.

McCarthy's invitational reception in Berlin drew a large and enthusiastic crowd, but the next afternoon in Manchester, many times the number of invitations drew a much smaller crowd to the Alpine Club in Manchester. McCarthy departed from his norm and read Goodwin's speech. Copies of the speech had been prepared for release once McCarthy began speaking. For the first time in the campaign a McCarthy address received lengthy coverage in the major publications across the nation. The reporters had the text, could mark it for their stories, and filed large parts of it with their publications. It seemed to reveal that McCarthy was peeling back his gloves. The fight was on as he said:

> In 1963, we were told that we were winning the war. In 1964 we were told we were winning the war. In 1964, we were told the corner was being turned. In 1965, we were told the enemy was being brought to its knees. In 1966, in 1967, and now again in 1968, we hear the same hollow claims of programs and victory. For the fact is that the enemy is bolder than ever, while we must steadily enlarge our own commitment. The Democratic Party in 1964 promised "no wider war." Yet the war is getting wider every month. Only a few months ago we were told that sixty-five percent of the population was secure. Now we know that even the American Embassy is not secure.
>
> (Chester, Hodgson, Page, ibid., p. 93)

Goodwin brought more than a talented typewriter to the campaign. He brought the experience of one who had been involved in a successful national candidacy and one who understood the dynamics of national politics. His perspective bolstered our efforts. Goodwin knew how to attract the attention of the national press to the campaign and also how to encourage celebrities, like Paul Newman, to come to New Hampshire and help Gene. While few if any of his speeches were subsequently read by McCarthy after the Alpine Club success, Goodwin was there to help shape the reporters' reactions to McCarthy's own speaking style. Goodwin became an important advisor in the crucial last days of the campaign.

Dick Goodwin had joined the campaign. This word passed in front of the eyes of the reporters like the revelations of a tea leaf reader. The meaning was unmistakable if unconfirmed. The fact that a prominent Kennedy loyalist had come to help in New Hampshire must mean that there was at least indirect support from the Kennedy clan for McCarthy. That speculation alone helped to legitimize McCarthy and seemed to reduce the speculation that McCarthy was really just a stalking horse for Kennedy.

ADVERTISING AND CAMPAIGN MATERIALS

Mervin Weston had been given the go ahead to prepare a media program for the McCarthy campaign by Blair Clark. Through a memorandum that had been developed through conversations with Clark and me, Weston outlined a media strategy and plan which also carried costs for each of the items. The memorandum read:

I. Media Strategy

We are planning a short but strong campaign peaking in the final days before the primary. Radio minutes, newspapers and outdoor [signs] will provide continuity, television and radio ID's, the crescendo.

The campaign uses radio minutes, TV minutes, direct mail and large space newspaper ads to build an awareness and understanding of Senator McCarthy's position on Vietnam and present administration policies; television and radio ID's and small space newspaper ads to provide maximum "noise" during the final days of the campaign.

In all media placement we are depending upon continuing news of the Vietnam War to increase the relevance and impact of our messages. In the broadcast media particular attention will be paid to scheduling announcements in news adjacencies.

II. Media Plan

1. Duration: Four weeks starting Tuesday, February 11 and ending Monday March 11 (Tuesday, March 12 for morning newspapers).
2. Media Cost: $59,652 Media costs have been reduced by 15% where media are commissionable.
3. Media

A) Radio ($17,000)

This is the basic medium. We are planning 175:60's and 50:10's on each of 25 stations during the four weeks. We will attempt to place announcements adjacent to news broadcasts for maximum impact and concentrate in the 6–9 A.M. and 3–6 P.M. time periods for greatest reach. The schedule will build to maximum weight during the final days of the campaign (see flow chart)

Radio costs assume local rates (50% of national). If rates are higher, the per-station schedule can be reduced in the six multi-station markets.

B) Newspapers

Dailies ($8,661)

We are planning four 1750 line ads in each of the nine New Hampshire dailies. This one-a-week schedule will be staggered for the different newspapers to minimize reader duplication. The final ads will be scheduled for Monday, March 11 in evening editions and Tuesday, March 12 (Primary Day) in morning editions. (If copy suggests a larger number of smaller space units these can be substituted for one or two of the 1750 line ads.)

The local "political rate" has been used for our costing. In some cases the national rate is lower, so contracts will be noted "request lowest available rate."

Weeklies ($3,646)

During the final week of the campaign one 1750 line ad in each of New Hampshire's 25 weekly newspapers will be scheduled.

C) Television ($13,525)

Boston television will he used during the final week to peak the campaign.

We will schedule 10 prime time ID's; 5 early fringe minutes and 5 afternoon minutes during the last half of the final week. The schedule will use all three Boston stations but will be concentrated on WBZ which has the best New Hampshire coverage. The prime ID's will he placed preceding high-rated programs. The fringe minutes will be purchased following the early evening news. The afternoon minutes will also be news adjacencies.

In addition to this spot schedule, two afternoon women oriented half hour programs are planned. These would feature the Senator discussing his candidacy with groups of local ladies.

D) Outdoor ($2,035)

Twenty-seven 24-sheet poster will be used for the month. These will be located in nine key areas.

E) Direct Mail ($14,885)

Two mailings will be made to the entire list of Democrat (89,000) and Independents (120,000). Because of husband and wife duplication, this will be an estimated total of 150,000. The first mailing will be done early in the campaign; the second, in the last week.

With the proposed media strategy and plan a flowchart was attached that projected each element across the campaign calendar (see page 392).

The media plan proposed what seemed to be the essential elements of the overall campaign strategy that could be funded and would take advantage of the media

NEW HAMPSHIRE CAMPAIGN
MEDIA SCHEDULING

FLOW CHART

	WEEK 1	WEEK 2	WEEK 3	WEEK 4
	FEB. 13 14 15 16 17 18 19	20 21 22 23 24 25 26 27	28 29 MAR. 1 2 3 4 5 6	7 8 9 10 11 12
Radio ($17,000) 25 Stations 125 :60's 50 :10's	- - - - - 25 - - - - - -	- - - - 25 - - - - - - -	- - - - 50 - - - - - - 7 8 10	10 10 10 10 20 10 10 20
	Buying policy: seek news broadcast adjacencies 6-9 AM, 3-6PM			
Newspapers ($8,561) A. 9 dailies 4 1,750 line ads	- - - - - 1 - - - - - - -	- - - - - 1 - - - - - - -	- - - - - 1 - - - - - - - -	- - - - - - - - - - 1 - -
	Scheduling: Stagger insertion dates in markets because of overlap. Last ad should run on Monday the 11th in evening papers and Tuesday the 12th in morning papers.			
B. 25 weeklies (3,646) 1 1,750 line ad				- - - - - - X - - - - - -
TV ($13,525) 3 Boston stations	Buying policy: prime 10's preceding high rated programs. Early fringe :60's following early news. Afternoon :60's following news.			
5 early eve. :60's				1 1 1 2
5 afternoon :60's			1	1 1 2
10 prime ID's				2 3 5
2 daytime 1/2 hour programs			- - - - - X - - - - - - -	- - - - - - X - - - - -
Outdoor ($2,035) 27 24-sheet posters	- - - - - - - - - - - - -	- - - - - - - - - - - - - -	- - - - - - - - - - - - - - -	- - - - - - - - - - - -
Direct Mail ($14,885) 2 mailings of 150,000	- - - - - - X - - - - - -			- - - - - - X - - - - -

Total Cost $59,652

options available in New Hampshire. Clark and I accepted the plan and Weston Associates immediately began acquiring options for time. Reserving time or space from New Hampshire radio stations or newspapers was not difficult. If necessary, radio stations reduced program time to insert advertising and newspapers will print more pages. Premium placement in some New Hampshire newspapers was reserved ahead. The *Manchester Union Leader* sold space on its front page; other papers did not.

Television scheduling was less flexible. Channel 8 from Poland Springs, Maine, broadcasting from Mt. Washington, and Channel 9 broadcasting from Manchester, were reasonable and covered a useful portion of the New Hampshire market. Channel 6 from Plattsburg, New York, penetrated western New Hampshire and was also used for political advertising occasionally in New Hampshire. The Republican candidates, Romney and Nixon, had booked much of the better television space for the New Hampshire aimed stations. Boston television, while predominant in the New Hampshire market, was exceptionally expensive for the time alone disregarding the high cost of preparing effective television advertising. The original plan called for "final" week use of Boston television. In all but the instance of direct mailing and billboard advertising the media plan and budget specified time or space acquisition, not preparation or production of the actual media inserts.

The first item in the plan that opened was the billboard space. Weston Associates was able to acquire most of the billboards they had advised in the "nine key" areas of the state. In order for the copy to be ready when the billboards were available an early decision on logo design, colors, and copy was necessary. I hoped that a photograph of McCarthy might also be included with the billboard layout but after a week or more of trying to secure a photo that could express what the campaign meant, Weston and I gave up the idea of using a photo. We selected the colors, deep blue and light blue, from the buttons left over from McCarthy's 1964 senatorial campaign in Minnesota. The slogan we chose read, "There is an alternative—McCarthy for President." Weston rushed the layout with the slogan into production immediately. By the time the billboard space was available the poster sheets were ready.

The billboards were the first media evidence that there was a McCarthy campaign in New Hampshire. The same slogan, logo type, and colors were used to prepare stationery, envelopes, and other printed necessities of the campaign. The stationery carried a photograph that had been selected from a number taken when McCarthy visited New Hampshire in December.

Most major campaigns are planned well before the period of the actual campaign. During that preparation period an extensive resource of photographs, film footage, draft advertising copy, advertising, and materials layouts are developed. When the campaign begins this file is used to fill space in a way that has been carefully considered.

The file materials that the McCarthy senatorial staff maintained related almost entirely to issues and scenes of concern to his Minnesota constituency. His family had been photographed with farmers, in meetings, and with appealing backgrounds but not New Hampshire backgrounds. Much of the material was dated and had not been used since McCarthy's last senatorial candidacy in 1964. Whenever Weston or anyone else went to prepare advertising materials for McCarthy, he or she had to begin from scratch.

Some of the earliest photographs used to prepare New Hampshire materials were provided by the freelance photographer, Burton Berinsky, who had followed McCarthy to New Hampshire during his first December 1967 visit. Another source were the file photos taken by the *Concord Daily Monitor*'s staff photographer, George Cooper. During the early weeks of the New Hampshire campaign and right up to the end McCarthy would have to take time from his schedules or have time included in those schedules for him to record advertising copy, prepare television materials, or work through photographic sessions.

In addition to the void in visual material on McCarthy there was also very little that had been recorded. Realizing that there was not enough time to prepare, edit, and then have McCarthy produce a media resource and that McCarthy was best when he was spontaneous, Russell Hemenway arranged for a sound film crew to follow Senator McCarthy during much of his early campaigning. In addition, arrangements were made to acquire some film that had been taken by the television network crews that were also following McCarthy. Gradually a foundation of new film, recordings, and photographs built up that provided the basis for most of the printed material and electronic media that was used in the New Hampshire Campaign.

Studds, Weston, and I managed the mailing portion of the media plan. The volunteers prepared the labels. Studds and I, working from Tom Collins' draft, prepared the letter for the mailing, and Weston had the letter printed. On February 9, Weston reported his progress to me regarding the status of mailing programs.

> We have now processed 3 mailing programs—and this memo will cover what has been done, and what has to be done.
>
> 1. Mailing to solicit funds from colleges
>   Being printed:
>   1,500 letters—one page two colors.
>   1,000 #6 3/4 envelopes one color. This has a business reply indicia which means each return will cost you $.08.
>   Outside envelopes being supplied by headquarters.
> 2. Mailing to Democratic Party members
>   Being printed:
>   60,000 Letters two colors first sheet, one color second sheet.

The next item was included in the February 9 memorandum from Merv Weston but was subsequently scratched. The "business reply cards" were destroyed to the last copy.

> 60,000 business reply cards—one color two sides. This has a business reply indicia, which means each return will cost you $.08.
> 60, 000 number 9 envelopes
> 60,000 folders out of New York

3. Mailing to Independents
Being printed:
80,000 letters, two color first sheet, one color second sheet.

The next item, like the reply cards for the Democrats, was also scratched from the plan and the cards that had been printed were destroyed.

80,000 business reply cards—Same card as for Democrats.
80,000 number 9 envelopes
80, 000 folders, out of New York

4. Mailing procedures
The mailings to Manchester, Nashua, Concord, and Portsmouth go third class, bulk rate of $.036 each.
All other mailings will go first class, at $.06 each.
Voter breakdown in the 4 third class cities are as follows:

	Democrats	Independents
Manchester	25,500	8,200
Nashua	8,500	11,100
Concord	1,675	5,428
Portsmouth	1,164	4,750
	36,839	29,478

Concluding his memorandum, Merv Weston advised:

Total number of Democrats and Independents is 66,317. We guesstimate a shrinkage of 25% because of homes with two adults registered in the same party. We are therefore printing 49,737 (or 50m) third class envelopes for this purpose. The remaining 90m envelopes will be printed with a first class indicia.

Both mailings will have to be stuffed and sealed. The letters are being folded by the printer in a special way so that the second sheet slips into the first sheet, so it will be picked up as a two page letter. This collating of both sheets must be done by hand i.e. volunteers.

The third class mailing must be addressed with zip code, sorted and tied into zip coded packages, with both address sides faced out, top and bottom.

On first class mailing, zip codes are not necessary, but preferred. They can go out in bulk, but for expediency, have them broken down into cities and towns.

Checks have to accompany deliveries to the post office. The #9 envelopes that will be delivered to you are practically free, so don't get mad if they are not perfect. Some of them will stick together in one spot—simply break them open. A few may tear. Discard them. We have supplied an overage.

(Memo to Hoeh, c.c. to Studds, February 9, 1968)

The envelopes did stick and without the extra patience and energy of the volunteers they would have delayed the mailing. More than a "few" had to be "discarded."

Materials for Distribution

Most of the campaign materials used in New Hampshire were prepared and printed either in Washington or New York. The first generation of these materials was composed almost entirely of one-sheet flyers developed from text and file photos available in Washington. The first of these to appear in New Hampshire hit an important theme of the 1968 McCarthy campaign, "What's happened to this country since 1963?" The blue-printed flyer carried a photograph of Eugene McCarthy with President John F. Kennedy, and read:

> John F. Kennedy got this country moving. Now the fabric of that great achievement is unraveling.
>
> All around us we can see that the last five years have brought decay to replace progress, despair to replace hope, and failure in war to replace success in the pursuit of peace.
>
> In 1963, the economy was booming and taxes were being lowered. Now, prices are rising, the Kennedy boom is slowing down, and we are being asked to raise taxes.
>
> In 1963, our great cities were relatively tranquil. Now, the streets of our cities are scarred by lawlessness violence, and desperate fear. Now, the President has projected year after year of continuing violence.
>
> In 1963, the deep concerns of American young people were the peace corps and civil rights. Now there are demonstrations and draft protests.
>
> In 1963, we were at peace, just as we had been at peace for the eight previous years under Eisenhower. Now, we are at war.
>
> Gene McCarthy stood shoulder to shoulder with Kennedy in the Senate, and he will stand head and shoulders above Johnson as President. There is one candidate who can get this country moving again, and carry on the traditions John F. Kennedy began.
>
> That man is Gene McCarthy.
>
> (McCarthy New Hampshire flyer, DCH file copy)

Shortly after that flyer appeared, the New Hampshire campaign prepared one of the few flyers generated entirely in New Hampshire. It carried a copy of the Johnson campaign's pledge card and read, "What ever happened to the secret ballot?" and then a picture of McCarthy with the message, "You don't have to sign anything to vote for Senator Eugene McCarthy on March 12, let Johnson know it. McCarthy for President." A duplicate of this flyer was prepared in Washington for New Hampshire except that it used black ink in reverse and was printed on both sides. Both the Kennedy flyer and the pledge-card flyer were used throughout the campaign and were included in the packet of materials delivered by the canvassers.

Another in the first phase series was a simple black reverse printed sheet with a formal photograph of McCarthy which read, "McCarthy for President" in large type with the quotation, "This can again be an America of confidence," below and adjacent to the photograph. On the back side under the heading "The Spirit of America," excerpts of a McCarthy speech read:

> John Kennedy set free the spirit of America. The honest optimism was released. Quiet courage and civility became the mark of American government, and new programs of promise and of dedication were presented: the Peace Corps, the Alliance for Progress, the promise of equal rights for all Americans and not just the promise, but the beginning of the achievement of that promise.
>
> All the world looked to the United States with new hope, for here was youth and confidence and an openness to the future. Here was a country not being held by the dead hand of the past, nor frightened by the violent hand of the future which was grasping at the world. This was the spirit of 1963.
>
> What is the spirit of 1967? What is the mood of America and of the world toward America today?
>
> It is a joyless spirit—a mood of frustration, of anxiety, of uncertainty.
>
> In place of the enthusiasm of the Peace Corps among the young people of America, we have protests and demonstrations.
>
> In place of the enthusiasm of the Alliance for Progress, we have distrust and disappointment.
>
> Instead of the language of promise and of hope, we have in politics today a new vocabulary in which the critical word is war: war on poverty, war on ignorance, war on crime, war on pollution. None of these problems can be solved by war but only by persistent, dedicated, and thoughtful attention.
>
> The message from the administration today is a message of apprehension, a message of fear, yes—even a message of fear of fear.
>
> This is not the real spirit of America. I do not believe that it is. This is a time to test the mood and spirit: To offer in place of doubt—trust. In place of expediency—right judgment.
>
> In place of ghettos, let us have neighborhoods and communities. In place of incredibility—integrity.
>
> Let us sort out the music from the sounds and again respond to the trumpet and the steady drum.
>
> (McCarthy flyer, DCH file copy)

The flyers were designed to give McCarthy identity, tie him to the lost spirit of the Kennedy era, and to introduce McCarthy to a public that did not know him. To aid in this process of introduction and legitimacy, Sandy Silverman prepared a weekly flyer called, *Newsbriefs from McCarthy for President.* The four-page, tabloid-sized newsprint was complied from national news clippings of press reaction to McCarthy's candidacy and issues illustrating the importance of his candidacy. The publication was composed entirely of clippings pasted and reproduced from the original newspaper type. A batch of *Newsbriefs* would arrive at the end of each week in time to be used as the wrapper for the packet of canvassing materials to be distributed the coming weekend.

The second generation of printed materials became more specific to New Hampshire and to the issues on the minds of the spectrum of voters eligible to vote on March 12. The second-generation flyers were aimed at particular constituencies within the Democratic Party voters of New Hampshire. Among the first of these was one addressed to New Hampshire union members. The photograph on the face showed McCarthy shaking the hand of a worker arriving at his factory in the darkness of a New Hampshire winter morning. On the reverse under the heading "Sure, George Meany tells you to vote for LBJ—but. . . ." the flyer compared McCarthy's voting record on issues of concern to organized labor as opposed to Lyndon Johnson's record on the same issues. Following the summary of the issues and voting records was a quotation under the heading, "For twenty years Gene has been an unflinching defender of the rights of labor!"

> In 1908, the AFL conference headed by Samuel Gompers declared: "We now call upon the workers of our common country to stand faithfully by our friends oppose and defeat our enemies whether they be candidate for president, for congress or other office, whether executive, legislative or judicial."
>
> What was true 60 years ago is still true today!
>
> (McCarthy labor flyer, DCH file copy)

Another flyer of the same generation titled "Shrinking dollar—growing war" showed a 1964 dollar at full size with a toy-sized battle-dressed soldier in contrast. The next panel showed a 1966 dollar crumpled and smaller with a photograph of the soldier growing in size. The third panel labeled, 1968, showed a miniature dollar and head of the same soldier now filling more than half the panel. The text on the reverse, titled, "The Bigger the War the Smaller Your Dollar," contrasted the economic situation of the United States during the period 1961–1965 with the impact of the war in the years since 1965. From "unprecedented prosperity" the war had produced "inflation" of "10%" shrinking Social Security benefits, a gold drain, and trade deficits that had already set off uncertainty in the dollar not seen since the "Great Depression." The flyer concluded, "Vote March 12th—McCarthy for President." (McCarthy inflation flyer, DCH file copy)

Most of the flyers produced in Washington during this period were aimed for use in the New Hampshire primary. They either carried the date of the election or issues of concern to New Hampshire voters. One flyer was produced, however, that was used in other states at the same time. With a photo of McCarthy backed by people shown waving a McCarthy for President poster on a stick, the text read, "McCarthy for President—Let Us Begin Anew. . . ." On the reverse McCarthy was shown photographed in his senatorial office with bookshelves behind him, looking toward a window. The draperies, woven with a presidential-looking eagle, softened the light cast across his face and three-piece suit. Other photos in the same setting would be used later in the campaign. The text, "McCarthy is the Man," summarized McCarthy's career under the headings, "Courage and Integrity, Leadership and Achievement, and Time to Act." The latter read:

> America in 1968 is a deeply troubled nation. We need new hope, new leadership, and we need it now.
>
> Eugene McCarthy and the Democratic Party can provide that leadership . . . in the spirit of Adlai Stevenson and John F. Kennedy. Let us begin anew.
>
> Help stop the War in Vietnam!
>
> We reject the notion that the people's choice will be turned down by the Democratic National Convention.
>
> Eugene McCarthy for President.
>
> (McCarthy flyer, DCH file copy)

The Washington headquarters also reprinted recent articles about McCarthy that had appeared in the major national magazines. The most widely distributed was reprinted from the February 6 issue of *Look* magazine, by McCarthy, titled, "Why I'm Battling LBJ." There was a reprint from the Catholic Church's weekly publication, *Our Sunday Visitor*, titled, "The many lives of Abigail McCarthy," which also contained a photograph of the McCarthys' three oldest children. An eighteen-page mimeographed publication prepared from speech excepts and biographical material was assembled for New Hampshire and other states titled, "McCarthy for President—His Record and His Message for America."

Following McCarthy's second campaign tour of New Hampshire beginning on February 6, enough photographs of McCarthy campaigning in New Hampshire had been taken to produce a campaign flyer. The first of these was titled, "McCarthy Speaks to New Hampshire," and used a tabloid format. A series of high-quality photographs, printed on offset paper rather than newsprint, gave the flyer an attractiveness not typically seen in political printing. Beside or beneath each photograph was a text paragraph on the issue represented by the photo. The photos were largely of New Hampshire people and places, and clearly represented McCarthy as a candidate in New Hampshire. An engaging, mature, thoughtful, sensitive, and hard-working presidential candidate, with his positions, was projected by the publication. It arrived as the result of our nagging. We had complained to Sandy Silverman, then preparing printed materials in Washington for the New Hampshire campaign, that most of the materials received for New Hampshire either had too much text and too few photographs or were not specific to McCarthy the candidate in New Hampshire. When it arrived, I called Sandy Silverman to congratulate her on producing a piece that was precisely in keeping with the theme Studds and I had conceived many weeks earlier. For several weeks afterward, the "McCarthy Speaks to New Hampshire" piece would be the wrapper for the packet of materials used by the canvassers.

A number of the local committees prepared campaign items specific to their own communities or to announce local activities. Many of these contained quotations from McCarthy and other notables concerning current issues that the local committees felt were of special concern to their area. Occasionally an issue would develop locally that would not be responded to quickly through the state or national offices, so the local committee would find the appropriate response from existing materials, print, and distribute the answer. The federated nature of the campaign continued to the end. Usually the response would be cleared through the Concord headquarters before being printed to be sure that the response was consistent with what was happening in the campaign elsewhere.

The only major publication and mailing effort outside that authorized and paid for by the McCarthy campaign came from the National Committee of Clergy and Laymen Concerned About Vietnam. Its six-page, tabloid-sized mailer was sent to two hundred thousand New Hampshire homes on March 1. Intended as a nonpartisan, voter education mailer when Governor Romney was still a candidate, the organizers of the mailing now aimed it by press release at Democrats, Independents, and Republicans urging them to vote for or to write-in McCarthy as the only candidate with a clearly stated position opposing current U.S. policy in Vietnam. An expensive effort that ultimately may have aided McCarthy, it scarcely stirred the political air during the time that it was arriving.

The final generation of printed materials for the campaign evolved in response to what was felt to be the successes and questions produced by the campaign. The final mailing would be a tabloid-sized, newsprint, two-color flyer. It would be sent to those names on the labels prepared by the volunteers and blanket mailed in the larger communities that showed a strong trend for McCarthy as the result of the canvassing. The front had a photograph of Senator McCarthy in a factory surrounded by workers, one with his finger blurred in motion as he emphasized his point. The title read, "Senator McCarthy Answers the Three Questions Most Frequently Asked by New Hampshire Voters." Opening the flyer the reader found the three questions with an appropriate matching photograph to the left and the answers to the right. Question 1: "'Why are you running for President?" (photograph: McCarthy with President John F. Kennedy). The answer:

> I hope to restore the principles and the sense of hope which guided the Democratic Party during the administration of John F. Kennedy. In 1963, the country was booming; our cities were tranquil; we were at peace, and we felt that our problems were being solved. America was respected and admired around the world. Today our cities are filled with misery and lawlessness. Our prestige is getting lower every day. Our great problems at home—the need for better schools and parks, for decent housing and clean air—are not being solved.
>
> We must concentrate our energies on the huge, unsolved problems of American society. In this way we can, perhaps, restore the sense of idealism and high purpose which we knew under John F. Kennedy. The issue is not merely Vietnam or riots. If you share my feeling that there is something wrong with the direction of American society today, then I ask your support. We cannot chart a new direction until we also have new leadership.

The second question, "Do you think it is possible to achieve peace with honor in Vietnam without sacrificing the interests of the country?" had next to it a photograph of McCarthy seated in a New Hampshire living room discussing his concerns with a group of women. The answer:

> Yes I do, but not if we follow the policies of the last five years. After all those policies are a proven failure. Every year the Administration has promised a quick victory, and every year it has increased the size of the war. The fact is that we are now involved in an endless, ever increasing war which our present leadership seems unable to end, either on the battlefield or at the conference table. If we continue what we are doing, then thousands more Americans will die, and yet the war will be no closer to an end than it is today.
>
> It seems clear to me, therefore that we need a change. Most Americans do not want withdrawal and defeat. Most Americans do want an honorable settlement at the conference table. That is what I want, and what I will try to achieve if I am elected. I think we should make some effort to achieve that peace. Thus it is necessary to take advantage of one of the many opportunities to begin negotiations—opportunities which have been pointed out by many world leaders such as Pope Paul and Americans such as Sen. George Aiken. It is necessary to devise a workable political compromise which will allow all the people of South Vietnam to share in choosing their government. No one can guarantee that new approaches will work. However we do know the old ones have failed. As you go to the polls, ask yourself if you think we are doing a skillful and effective job in Vietnam.

The final question, "Why do you oppose the President's proposal to increase taxes by ten percent?" had next to it a photograph of McCarthy talking with a jovial policeman with the background of Newport, New Hampshire's main street. The answer completed the summary of McCarthy's New Hampshire campaign and led to the back page and a reprint of the marked ballot including delegate and alternate delegate candidates as the voters would find it on election day. McCarthy responded to the question:

> I believe the tax increase will not only take badly needed income from millions of Americans, but will hurt rather than help the economy. The purpose of a tax increase is to slow down an economy which is growing too fast. Our economy is growing more slowly and higher taxes would only increase dangers of a recession. In addition, an across-the-board increase—as the President had proposed—would hit lower income families most severely. It seems to me that housewives and older people have a difficult enough time keeping up with today's rising prices. I don't think we should add to their burden by imposing taxes which are likely to become a drag on the entire economy and thus diminish the total wealth of the nation.

In addition to the ballot that ended the flyer, there was a message addressed specifically to Independents. It was a reminder that they too had a stake in the outcome of the New Hampshire presidential primary: "Independents. Vote for McCarthy or You May Have No Choice in November."

> Independence means freedom of choice. Yet New Hampshire Independents may lose their freedom of choice in November if they fail to vote March 12th. There is only one candidate in either party who promises to restore the spirit of John F. Kennedy, and get America moving again. There is only one candidate who promises to bring an honorable peace. That candidate is Eugene McCarthy. If you believe there is a need to change the direction of the nation and its leadership, vote McCarthy, March 12th.
>
> Be sure to ask for the DEMOCRATIC BALLOT
>
> (McCarthy flyer, DCH file copy)

The last major printed piece of the campaign proved to be controversial within the campaign itself. Besides direct mail, another way to reach the dispersed voters of New Hampshire was to insert campaign material within the editions of the regular newspapers. A special supplement was prepared by a group of volunteer writers, editors, and photographers based in New York. Merv Weston arranged for the supplement to be inserted in the March 3 edition of the *New Hampshire Sunday News* and March 4 edition of the *Manchester Union Leader*, the March 5 or 6 editions of the *Nashua Telegraph, Concord Daily Monitor, Claremont Eagle, Laconia Citizen, Keene Evening Sentinel, Valley News, Foster's Daily Democrat, Portsmouth Herald*, and the weekly *Berlin Reporter* and *Northland News*.

The insert orders from Weston Associates, dated February 26, said the bundles of supplements would arrive the day before the edition that would carry the insert. While this media device had not been mentioned in the original plan for the campaign, the insert cost of $8,896.96 (Weston invoices) was made possible when the budget for media was substantially expanded during the last weeks of the campaign.

McCarthy insisted that all copy and materials used in the campaign should be cleared through his senatorial office. Because of the necessities of the campaign a number of items used in New Hampshire were not specifically cleared through the Washington office but were reviewed carefully by me, Studds, and/or Gans before printing and distribution. The supplement was prepared and printed in New York. The text was cleared through Washington but the photographs were not. A number of the photos used were from McCarthy office files, which had been used in his earlier campaigns or earlier in the New Hampshire campaign. The exception was the photograph that had been selected for the cover. It showed Senator McCarthy reaching across a work table in a New Hampshire factory to shake the hand of a plump, older worker. It was a sensitive and friendly event capturing a moment of contact between a person who had obviously spent most of her life working in a factory and a presidential candidate who cared enough to come and visit her in her place of work.

When the first copies of the supplement were received from the printer, one was sent to McCarthy's senatorial office. There Mrs. McCarthy saw it and reacted negatively toward the cover photograph. To her the outstretched, bare to the shoulder, heavy arm of the older women worker was unattractive. She felt that such an unflattering photo might hurt her husband's candidacy. This reaction filtered quickly back to Curt Gans in New Hampshire, with a specific instruction that the insert was not to be used. Gans was about to call the newspapers that had instructions concerning the supplement telling them to cancel the order when I arrived.

I took one look at the supplement and said that it was excellent. The front photo, I said, "was a picture of the real Miss New Hampshire—the one that spends her life working in the mills." I told Gans not to place the cancellation calls. Such calls, I said, this late in the campaign would be an embarrassment, certainly greater than any problems that the supplement might cause as it now stood. Gans responded that he was in charge of these activities and that he had been instructed by McCarthy's senatorial office to keep the supplement from circulating. I said I would call McCarthy immediately to give the senator my thoughts on the matter directly.

McCarthy was not in his office when I called, but I left a detailed message for McCarthy with the person taking my call. A short time later I received a return call from McCarthy's staff saying that the senator okayed the supplement's distribution. The piece circulated as scheduled. Shortly after it was received I conducted an informal survey of the area headquarters to see if there had been any response to the supplement. All reported that the supplement had been well received and without negative comment. In fact, some felt it was among the most effective items used in the campaign.

For election day itself, a three-inch by seven-inch handout card to be used at the polls was printed. On it was a campaign photo of McCarthy, advice to Independents about asking for the Democratic ballot, and on the back the segment of the primary ballot showing Eugene J. McCarthy's name and the phrase, "Vote for all McCarthy Delegates and all McCarthy Alternates." This card was used in cities where tradition held that something be handed to the voter as he or she was entering the polls. Most were distributed in Manchester. The reminder card was the last item printed for the campaign.

Newspaper Advertising

To begin building momentum for the campaign, the newspaper advertising schedule and budget proposed by Merv Weston was implemented. The changes came in the size and number of the ads, which increased as the campaign came to its end and the budget expanded. The Pappert, Koenig, and Lois advertising agency of New York City, which had been brought into the campaign by Russell Hemenway, developed some of the advertising materials for New Hampshire from the drafts that had been proposed during Keonig's January 26 visit to New Hampshire. Modified material from these early efforts began to appear late in the campaign. Much of the early advertising responded to issues developing in New Hampshire.

Working with Weston's modest initial budget, the first newspaper ads began appearing on February 20 with a large, six-column by eleven-inch, ad which appeared in New Hampshire daily newspapers. The ad reproduced the Johnson campaign's pledge card and text advising that the voters didn't have to sign anything to vote for Senator McCarthy. The large ad was followed on alternate days by a two-column by three-inch identification ad which read, "Don't Sign Anything! Vote Eugene McCarthy for President."

The next week's series began with an ad of the large size followed by the alternate day sequence of the small identification ad. The theme of the large ad, which was what had happened to America in the years since John F. Kennedy's presidency, was amplified by the small ad which read, "Let's get America moving again! McCarthy for President." In the final days before the election the ad size and sequence increased, but the identification ads remained, reenforcing the statement of the larger ads.

One of the most effective of the smaller ads came from a slogan developed by the New York agency, "New Hampshire can bring America back to its senses. McCarthy for President." During the time that the McCarthy advertising appeared, the Johnson campaign responded by repeating one ad which carried a drawing of Johnson, the slogan, "A Strong Man in a Tough Job," and the line, "to vote for President Johnson you must WRITE-IN his name on your ballot."

The March 6 McCarthy ad read, "This time let's elect a President we can believe. McCarthy for President," with the quotation:

> And as far as I'm concerned, I want to be very cautious and careful and use it only as a last resort when I start dropping bombs around that are likely to involve American boys in a war in Asia with 700 million Chinese . . . so, just for the moment, I have not thought that we were ready, our American boys, to do the fighting for Asian boys. And what I've been trying to do with the situation that I found was to get the boys in Vietnam to do their own fighting with our advice and our equipment, and that's the course we're following. So, we're not going North and drop bombs at this stage of the game. . . ."
>
> Lyndon Johnson
> September 28, 1964
> Campaign Speech in Manchester, N.H.

Each of the following ads pursued major themes of the campaign to date. The ad that appeared on March 8 contained a photograph of the New Hampshire statehouse with the title, "In the next seventy-two hours more money will be spent in Vietnam than the state of New Hampshire spends all year." The explanatory text read:

> 32 billion dollars a year is enough money to eliminate poverty in America, but also to build all the roads, schools, colleges, hospitals, and houses we need. And we'd still have enough left over to invest in underdeveloped countries so we don't have more Vietnams in the future, and maybe enough for a tax cut after that. In 1952, General Eisenhower promised peace with honor in Korea. He was elected, and he delivered. Senator McCarthy can do the same. An honorable man can bring an honorable peace.

A photograph of McCarthy and the line, "McCarthy for President," completed the ad. (*Concord Daily Monitor*, March 8, 1968)

In the same edition of the *Concord Daily Monitor*, there appeared the first advertisement from several special groups that had raised their own advertising money to make appeals for McCarthy. The ad was addressed to "Republicans" and was placed by the organizer of the Republicans for McCarthy Committee, Mrs. Barbara Underwood, in newspapers where an independent Republican vote was found to exist. Concord, Keene, Lebanon, and Laconia were the cities selected for the ad. The ad contained the segment of the Republican presidential primary ballot that listed the candidate names, nine names in total, and showed, written in on the ballot, "Senator McCarthy." The text read, "Republicans—You can vote for Senator McCarthy. Write in his name on your Republican ballot."

The advertising that appeared during the last three press days of the New Hampshire campaign used three formats for what were seen as different political markets. The Monday, March 11 ad for McCarthy in the *Concord Daily Monitor*, a market with a large Independent voter population, contained a photo of the Statue of Liberty and the same text as was used on the back of the final mailing piece which challenged Independents to vote in the primary or lose their freedom of choice in the November election.

The March 11 edition of the *Manchester Union Leader* contained ten separate advertisements for McCarthy and a reminder that McCarthy would be speaking that evening. On page two, the New Hampshire McCarthy Committee placed its ad offering transportation and baby-sitting service for McCarthy voters. Also on the page was an ad placed by a private citizen who signed his ad, "a concerned non-New Hampshire Democrat, W. Hirsch, 9601 Wilshire Blvd., Beverly Hills, California." It read:

> An Open Letter to New Hampshire Democrats
>
> The presence of Senator Eugene McCarthy on the primary ballot provides an opportunity for New Hampshire Democrats to directly register their concern or approval of the State of the Union.
>
> Perhaps when the history of the 1968 campaign is written it will record that only the New Hampshire and Wisconsin Democrats had a clear-cut possibility to affirm their position as to the main issues.
>
> At this point in the campaign what is being decided is not a contest between two candidates but an answer to the question: "Has this administration handled the problems of the Vietnam War, civil rights, balance of payment, crime, foreign aid, draft, etc., to your satisfaction?"
>
> Do you have confidence in the administration's progress report and predictions of future success in solving today's problems?
>
> IF YOU ARE NOT SATISFIED, YOUR ONLY CHANCE TO BE HEARD IS BY A VOTE FOR SENATOR EUGENE McCARTHY
>
> The American dream was born in New England and Tuesday the future of that dream will once more be at stake.

The eyes of all thinking Americans who do not have the privilege of voting in this election will be on the outcome. If the New Hampshire Democrats within the confines of their polling booths show their historic courage and by their action say that things are not right, then perhaps the start of a meaningful change in direction will have been effected through a traditional electoral process.

(*Manchester Union Leader*, March 11, 1968, p. 2)

On page three of the same edition, an ad appeared as the statement of forty-four "New Hampshire Artists, Writers, Musicians and Craftsmen," supporting Senator McCarthy for president. Their message:

Because we believe . . . That he is a man of integrity, courage and reason.

That he is a man who offers an honorable and feasible solution to America's third war. That he is a man who understands the issues we face.

That he is dedicated to redirecting our energies toward pressing domestic problems.

That he is putting his political future on the line for the sake of his beliefs.

We support Senator Eugene J. McCarthy for President. . . .

A formal, waist-up photograph of McCarthy looking directly from the advertisement was included.

On the same page was another privately sponsored advertisement which filled the other part of the lower portion of the page. It read:

An Open Letter to All Fellow Democrats:

Our country is in deep crisis, as well as in Vietnam.

Our vote this Tuesday is too serious to be decided by partisan politics as usual.

WE URGE ALL FELLOW DEMOCRATS TO VOTE FOR THE CANDIDATE OF YOUR OWN CHOICE! Disregard any numbered pledge cards, with their "arm twisting" copies to Washington, as an invasion of privacy of your secret ballot; reject any unfair, last minute attacks against a genuine Democrat and distinguished American, Senator McCarthy.

In this time of crisis, make your vote count for the candidate YOU believe best for our country. When YOU decide for yourself, to vote for Senator. McCarthy, or to write in Johnson, choose the man YOU think can best UNITE ALL AMERICANS, to meet these real needs of our country;

— To protect the lives of our boys, while negotiating with determination, for an honorable end to this endless war, instead of escalating in desperation.

— To defend family budgets against more increases in taxes and prices.

— To ensure an open Democratic Convention.

— To restore the spirit of President Kennedy, and to rebuild new hope and confidence in America.
(Signed)
Joe Myers, Chairman,
Manchester Democratic City Committee, 1956–1965

G. Allen Foster, Chairman,
Plymouth Democratic Town Committee
Exec. Secty., Democratic State Committee of New Hampshire, 1960
(*Manchester Union Leader*, March 11, 1968, p. 3)

This advertisement grew out of the work that Al Shepard was doing in his effort to develop support for McCarthy in the Manchester area. Shepard discovered that the former city Democratic chair, Joe Myers, was deeply disturbed by the behavior of the Democratic State Committee in its support of President Johnson's renomination. He took special umbrage to the use of the pledge card and to the preprimary endorsement tactics being used by the Democratic State Committee. He felt that the basic political ethos of New Hampshire primary politics had been violated with the preprimary endorsement of one "genuine Democrat" over another. Shepard suggested that he develop a statement that reflected his feelings that could be run as an advertisement.

The leaders of the New Hampshire RFK in '68 Committee placed a half-page ad that appeared on page six of the *Manchester Union Leader* which read, "At the Request of Robert F. Kennedy, we urge that you *do not* write in the name of Robert F. Kennedy on the March 12th Presidential Primary Ballot. Vote Eugene J. McCarthy for President." Then included in the ad was the complete list of delegate and alternative delegate candidates for the two congressional districts. Across from the RFK ad, on page seven, was a two-thirds page ad signed by Governor John W. King and Senator Tom McIntyre which read:

We urge you . . .

SUPPORT OUR FIGHTING MEN

We know the communists in Vietnam are watching the New Hampshire Primary to see if we at home have the same determination as our soldiers in Vietnam.

To vote for weakness and indecision would not be in the best interest of our nation.

We urge you to support our fighting men in Vietnam. Write-in President Johnson on your ballot on Tuesday.

The presidential preference portion of the ballot was included with the printed names blurred and "President Johnson" written in the space provided.

To avoid the crowding of political advertising that appeared on the news pages of the edition, and to take advantage of the high readership that the sports sections receive, a group of twenty New Hampshire college students, all enrolled in military officer programs, placed an effective ad. Titled, "Don't Call Us Draft Dodgers," it read:

> The undersigned New Hampshire college students all receive commissions as officers in the United States Army this June. We believe in our country. We will all serve. Some of us may die.
>
> But we strongly oppose the war in Vietnam. We think it is tragic for Vietnam and for the United States.
>
> America has its own problems to solve. Our cities face crisis after crisis while we use our resources to conduct a senseless war thousands of miles away.
>
> We are concerned for America.
>
> We ask New Hampshire voters to show our country the way toward the solution of our problems. VOTE FOR McCARTHY
>
> This ad is paid for by the undersigned future officers, who believe in America.

The most important advertisement of the last two days was the one placed in the most prominent position for sale in the various New Hampshire daily newspapers. The *Manchester Union Leader,* the only newspaper in New Hampshire to sell advertising space on its front page, carried the ad there in a space approximating two-fifths of the page. A serene, presidential-like photograph of McCarthy in profile, arms folded, looking toward the curtained window of his senatorial office, shrouded with the eagle-embossed drapes, was to the left of the ad with the title, "Profile of Courage." The text:

> With the courage to come before the people of New Hampshire and debate the critical issues of our time, Eugene McCarthy brings a fresh approach to securing a swift and honorable peace in Vietnam. He has challenged the national priorities which put improved education and the discontent in our cities at the bottom of the national agenda. He has proposed economic policies designed to restore the Kennedy boom—a growing economy with stable prices.
>
> The issue is leadership. If you are not satisfied with our present course as a nation—if you want to return to the principles which got America moving under President Kennedy then, Eugene McCarthy is your only alternative. He, and he alone has come to New Hampshire to give you a choice. That's not only courage. That's what the democratic process is all about.
>
> McCARTHY FOR PRESIDENT

The ad developed as a comparative effort among Goodwin, Weston, and Gans, with assistance from those in New York who had been working on the campaign. It effectively countered the Johnson advertisement that shared the adjacent front-page space in the *Manchester Union Leader.* The smaller Johnson ad was the standard format that had been used in the main brochure for Johnson with a sketch and the slogan, "A Strong Man in a Tough Job." The high readability and sophistication of the McCarthy advertisement captured the tone of the McCarthy campaign and the importance of the New Hampshire result. It solicited from the voter a demonstration of courage comparable to that which McCarthy had shown by becoming a candidate.

Radio Advertising

As advised by Merv Weston, radio would be the basic medium of the media campaign. Of the $59,652 media cost budget, Weston had allocated $17,000 to radio time and production. A highly flexible medium and one that was especially suited to New Hampshire communications habits, radio was inexpensive, easily programmed, and had an almost instantaneous lead time. A message could be changed with a telephone call. The average price per spot advertisement was approximately five thousand dollars which, given the proposed Weston radio advertising budget, would pay for thirty-four hundred spot announcements. Weston planned to use mostly thirty- and sixty-second messages but, occasionally, he programmed ten second announcements.

When the media plan was proposed, Weston and I expected that most of the radio production work would be completed either in New York or Washington. The ads, we expected, would illustrate the issues of McCarthy's candidacy and broaden his appeal to the voters. The exception to this would, of course, be the spot announcements of New Hampshire speeches or campaigning. These would be prepared by Weston using the facilities of his agency and radio specialist, David Grumblatt. When the time arrived for the first flight of radio commercials to be forwarded to the stations, nothing had been received from either Washington or New York. Inquiries produced assurances that radio material was being prepared in New York that could be useful in New Hampshire but that some production had been delayed.

Curtis Gans arrived to manage the New Hampshire campaign at almost the same time as the radio advertising schedule was to begin. He immediately was in touch with Merv Weston concerning the radio material and would work on almost a daily basis with the agency orchestrating the radio advertising effort. His first chore was to get something usable for the time that had been scheduled and was about to begin. The first series of recordings was developed from material Gans and Grumblatt wrote, extracted from McCarthy's New Hampshire speeches, and recorded in New Hampshire. This first experience led to the formation of a New Hampshire based radio and newspaper advertising writing and production operation. Several graduate students were assigned to work at the Weston Associates office writing and researching copy to be used in the radio effort.

While the radio messages had been scheduled to begin on February 13, budget problems and delays in production of expected radio tapes from New York pushed the start beyond the planned date. The first placement orders were written on February 15 to begin on February 21. The first tape contained messages that had been developed by Gans and Grumblatt, two one-minute messages and four thirty-second messages. These were scheduled to run from February 21–27 during "drive times" only. The delay meant that the Johnson campaign messages began before the McCarthy ads. A flight of nine messages that were used intermittently during the remainder of the campaign dwelt on the "Strong Man in a Tough Job" theme using citizen messages as endorsements for the President Johnson write-in effort. Grumblatt called me suggesting that I come to their studio to hear the ads. I heard:

Cut 1: (Announcer) Listen!

. . . what do you think would happen to this country if right in the middle of a war we up and changed our mind. Now he knows that surrender in Vietnam would be selling the whole country down the river. He knows that turning our back and running is exactly what every communist in the world would love to see. And believe me they'll chase us just as far as we run. But he's not going to let that happen. I was in Vietnam and I really believe . . .

(Announcer, voice over: You are listening to John Martine of Kingston. The man he's talking about is Lyndon Johnson President of the United States—a strong man in a tough job—the toughest job in the world. On March 12th you will have an opportunity to endorse this man by writing in his name on your ballot in the New Hampshire residential preference primary.)

. . . and that is why I'm writing in the name of President Johnson.

Cut 2: (Announcer) Listen!

I know he's right and sometimes what I see on TV makes me ashamed. I see these draft card burners and peace marchers—they're nothing but surrender marchers in my eyes—more than ever when I see all these things I knows he's right. If there was a better way or even a faster way in Vietnam or any other place . . .

(Announcer, voice over: You are listening to Nancy Lorden of Manchester. The man she is talking about is Lyndon Johnson, President of the United States—a strong man in a tough job—the toughest job in the world. On March 12th you will have an opportunity to endorse this man by writing in his name on your ballot in the New Hampshire presidential preference primary.)

. . . and believe me I'm writing in the name of President Johnson.

Cut 3: (Announcer) Listen!

. . . backbone or all-out determination but whatever it is he's not about to throw his hands up in despair and surrender to the communists in Vietnam or anywhere else in the world. He knows that the whole world is watching to see if we are going to turn tail and run for home . . .

(Announcer, voice over: You are listening to William Knightly of Salem . . .)

. . . we've never given up yet and we shouldn't start now . . .

(Announcer, voice over: The man he is talking about is Lyndon Johnson, a strong man in a tough job—the toughest job in the world. On March 12th you will have an opportunity to endorse this man by writing in his name on your ballot in the New Hampshire presidential preference primary.)

. . . what we say come hell or high water and that's why I'm writing in the name of President Johnson.

When I came to cut four, the voice and the name used did not match. I recognized the voice:

Cut 4: (Announcer) Listen!

. . . I don't think any man has ever worked harder for his country and I don't think any man has ever faced more difficult times. I think he's doing a fantastic job and I'm proud he's standing firm and refusing to surrender in Vietnam. One of these days when the history books are written I'm sure people will realize that he, perhaps, more than anyone else knew exactly what has to be done to preserve this country. . .

(Announcer, voice over: You are listening to John O'Connell of Keene. The man he is talking about is Lyndon Johnson, a strong man in a tough job . . .)

. . . I'm for him all the way, and I want the world to know that this country still has the stuff that made it great—and that's why I'm writing in the name of President Johnson.

The voice was familiar to me as being that of Charles McMahon, Senator McIntrye's in-state representative, not that of John O'Connell, a Keene school teacher. I got a volunteer to call O'Connell to ask whether he knew that his name was being used in a Johnson advertisement. O'Connell stumbled a bit, said he would call back later, and hung up his telephone. Studds, Gans, and I then played cat and mouse for several days, threatening to release the misrepresentation as the Johnson campaigners struggled to cover up their error. O'Connell said eventually that it was not his voice but was his feeling. McMahon said he made the tape as a convenience for O'Connell so he would not have to drive from Keene to Manchester to make the recording himself. While not a major flap it did upset the Johnson campaign plan further—a campaign that was already reeling from the impact of the pledge-card gaff.

The other five Johnson messages pursued the same themes as had the first four. Johnson would not "knuckle under to the peace-niks, fuzzy thinkers, dreamers, draft card burners, and Communists" but was doing his best in spite of the "criticism" and the "terrific pressure" to accomplish peace in Vietnam. One praised his "sticking with men like General Westmoreland and not listening to those peace-at-any price fuzzy thinkers . . ." while another said he's "not about to pull out and surrender because he knows as we all should know, that could never mean peace." The war, Johnson's leadership of the war, and the possible consequences of getting out of Vietnam were the only themes pursued in the Johnson messages. There was no attempt to defend the administration against charges of domestic neglect or economic uncertainty that were the substance of the broader issue spectrum of the McCarthy messages.

The first Johnson messages were heard on February 17 and continued with increasing frequency through to March 12. The six McCarthy ads, hurriedly assembled, began on February 21 with the following sequence:

Cut 1: (30 sec.)

(Announcer) Whatever happened to the secret ballot?

Do you want to abandon your right to examine all of the issues between now and March 12th?

What does Lyndon Johnson have in the cards for you?

Will the New Hampshire primary be just a formality?
Senator Eugene McCarthy offers a choice not an echo.
There is an alternative—McCarthy can get America moving again.
Vote Senator Eugene McCarthy for President.

Cut 2: (30 sec.)

(Announcer) Senator Eugene McCarthy has come to New Hampshire because people are concerned. Concerned about higher taxes and rising prices, concerned about riots in the cities and the unending land war in Asia. Concerned because our national leadership is unable to meet these problems. Concerned because it wasn't like this five years ago.

Eugene McCarthy is a proven leader in the tradition of Franklin D. Roosevelt and John F. Kennedy. He is a man who thinks clearly and speaks honestly.

Senator McCarthy can get America moving again.

McCarthy for President.

Cut 3: (30 sec.)

(Announcer) Let's get America moving again.

Senator Eugene McCarthy has come to New Hampshire as a serious candidate and a concerned candidate. Concerned because New Hampshire people are concerned.

You don't have to sign anything to vote for McCarthy.

Help bring America back to its senses. Vote Eugene McCarthy for President.

Cut 4: (60 sec.)

(Senator McCarthy speaking excerpt from a New Hampshire speech)

. . . there are a number of reasons, of course, for my coming to New Hampshire. I want to come here, principally, to talk about the issues which I think are of concern to the country . . .

(Announcer) This is Senator Eugene McCarthy speaking in New Hampshire.

. . . there is kind of a special challenge in coming to New Hampshire, to, really, test oneself against what's supposed to be the harshest political judgment in America, and also to find out whether the people of New Hampshire really are what they have been said to be. Some of your Democratic leaders have said that you're all so well organized and disciplined now that there really is no point in my coming in, that the people of New Hampshire will vote pretty much as their party leaders tell them to vote. I doubt that this is true but in any case, this is one of the matters I hope to test along the primary trail.

(Announcer) Will the New Hampshire primary be just a formality?

Senator Eugene McCarthy offers a choice not an echo. There is an alternative—McCarthy for President.

Cut 5: (30 sec.)

(Senator McCarthy speaking)

. . . we are involved, this nation, in what has become a major war, and most of you know what the cost of that war has been and know that those costs are continuing. (Announcer: voice over: There is an honorable alternative to the continuing drain of men and materials that endless escalation has imposed upon us in Vietnam. Senator McCarthy will not turn away from our responsibilities in Asia but he will explore every avenue to begin meaningful negotiations for peace.

There is an alternative. McCarthy for President.

Unlike the Johnson advertising, the McCarthy messages could and did contain material taken from McCarthy's speeches or specially recorded messages from the candidate. To have used Johnson material directly would have meant some tacit approval of the write-in activity on the part of the president. The final McCarthy cut in the first flight of radio advertising excerpted a passage from another McCarthy New Hampshire speech. Like other aspects of the media preparation for McCarthy, the bank of audiotapes available to create the messages did not exist, but the few tapes that had been made of McCarthy's New Hampshire speeches were available during the weeks when the radio material was prepared. As the campaign went on, the recorded resources grew and the effective McCarthy, the extemporaneous McCarthy, became the basis for much of his own audio and visual material. The sixth cut drew on the scanty recordings that existed early in February 1968.

Cut 6: (60 sec.)

(Senator McCarthy speaking) We are involved, this nation, in what has become a major war—and most of you know what the cost of that war has been and know that those costs are continuing. . . .

(Announcer, voice over) There is an honorable alternative to the continuing drain of men and materials that endless escalation has imposed upon us in Vietnam. Senator McCarthy will not turn away from our responsibilities in Asia but he will explore every avenue to begin meaningful negotiations for peace. There is an alternative—McCarthy for President.

(McCarthy continuing) . . . it has long since past the point in which it can be morally justified, but their conclusion is that the war is not morally justified and, therefore, it must be questioned; it must be challenged, and it must be opposed. And this becomes a basic demand, I think, of patriotism rather than an action which can in anyway be labeled as unpatriotic or as un-American.

Added to the small radio advertising team that Gans and Weston had assembled were Bill and Kay Nee, of Fridley, Minnesota. The Nees had, as they said, "handled Senator McCarthy's campaign for the Senate in 1958 and again in 1964." They "specialized in political advertising" and had also "handled" a number of other statewide and regional political advertising campaigns. (Nee transcript, p. 1) Senator

McCarthy trusted the Nees from their earlier work for him and asked them to assist in his presidential effort. The other New York and Washington work had not met with McCarthy's approval. He was concerned that his candidacy would become strident and uncomfortably noisy on the one issue of the war. He resisted the pressure to use materials that focused exclusively on the war and its horrors, preferring material that represented the war as symptomatic of a broader policy failure affecting the institutions of American society and perceptions of national purpose.

When the Nees first joined the campaign they worked in the Washington headquarters attempting, as they said, "to try and set a pattern through the New Hampshire campaign." There first efforts were to "review and re-do literature and some of the advertising," and then "to produce radio and television materials on a standby basis." They had arrived in the campaign at the point where money to complete the modest media plan that Weston had advised did not appear to be available. The Nees recalled:

> At that time, [early February] it was thought that the New Hampshire campaign would not have sufficient funding to use broadcast medial which would include television and radio. But we did go ahead and produce the materials for this use in the hope that money would be available.
>
> (Nee transcript, p. 1)

Some of this "standby" work did arrive in New Hampshire and was included in the second flight of radio ads circulated by Weston Associates. The Nees arrived for the last ten days of the campaign to assist Gans and Grumblatt with the radio work, especially, and with some television. Using the Weston Associates studio, the Nees' resource of audio material made earlier in Washington, and equipment they had brought and assembled in their hotel suite, a major radio advertising operation developed.

Weston Associates bought as much radio spot advertising time as seemed feasible while Gans, Grumblatt, the graduate student volunteer writers, and the Nees turned out ad copy and recorded cassettes for distribution to the twenty-five radio stations used in the campaign. During the final week, Rod Serling spent several days as the announcer recording messages and introducing endorsements from other celebrities.

The frequency increased from thirty-five spot announcements per station per week during the period of February 21–27, to a schedule of twenty-eight sixty-second spots and seventy thirty-second spots to be played between February 28 and 5:00 P.M., March 12. The frequency per station per day was ordered as two sixty-second spots and five thirty-second spots per station. The messages shipped with the order mailed on February 26 "killed" the preceding tapes and substituted new material. In the final three days a third flight of messages to be used up to the election were substituted for those shipped with the original February 26 order. The final advertising was developed over the last weekend before the election. The campaign bought additional time to run the single new message, which was "New Hampshire voters, think how good you will feel when you wake up on Wednesday morning March 13th and hear that Senator Eugene McCarthy has won the New Hampshire Presidential Primary. Vote Senator Eugene McCarthy for President." (DCH recollection) Like the "Profile in Courage" newspaper advertisement used during the last three days, the radio message was the capstone of the campaign.

The total spent for radio advertising time, as nearly as can be tabulated from the remaining invoices, was approximately $23,000. Another $3,000 to $5,000 was probably spent on radio message production and distribution. Like other aspects of the New Hampshire McCarthy campaign, the radio advertising effort was a product of the creative energy of the people who created then managed the department. Curtis Gans was the principal link between the other aspects of the campaign and the radio programming. Assisting with message ideas and celebrity contacts were Dick Goodwin and, as an emphasis advisor, Al Shepard. David Grumblatt, Weston Associates radio specialist, went beyond simply assembling the taped messages to stimulating the creative process through his own understanding of the potential for this medium. The depth, breadth, and intensity of the McCarthy radio campaign kept the Johnson campaign reeling.

Television Programming

With almost nothing available to fund the radio and newspaper campaigns projected to begin during February, use of television was abandoned. Weston had originally budgeted $13,646 for television to be used during the final week of the campaign. The plan was to:

> . . . schedule 10 prime time ID's; 5 early fringe minutes and 5 afternoon minutes during the last half of the final week. The schedule will use all three Boston stations but will be concentrated on which has the best New Hampshire coverage. The prime ID's will be placed preceding high rated programs. The fringe minutes will be purchased following the early evening news. The afternoon minutes will also be news adjacencies.
>
> In addition to this spot schedule, two afternoon women oriented half hour programs are planned. These would feature the Senator discussing his candidacy with groups of local women.
>
> (Weston media memo, p. 2)

For each minute of broadcast, a production cost exceeding $1,000 was expected to make the messages effective, professional, and credible. Without the resources to produce such programming in New Hampshire nor a budget to underwrite the cost of the time much less the cost of production, nothing was done to develop a television package.

Bill and Kay Nee had prepared a standby package of television messages to fill Weston's plan, and these they brought with them when they came to New Hampshire. Senator McCarthy videotaped several messages as well which dwelt on the major themes he had developed through the New Hampshire campaign. Coinciding with the arrival of Bill and Kay Nee in New Hampshire the McCarthy campaign found its own financial "angel." From having hardly the resources to buy radio advertising time the campaign found that it could not only accomplish the radio program but could also expand its television effort. It was, however, too late to develop sophisticated television material or to begin the programming before the final week of the campaign.

A plan of ten-second IDs, sixty-second announcements, and five-minute programs was quickly developed from the standby materials and Senator McCarthy's videotaped messages. Merv Weston was able to buy time on the three Boston television stations and two New Hampshire stations for the shorter announcements. When the option to develop two one-half-hour programs came, Weston ran into a problem. He sought to reserve time for the two programs on WBZ-TV. The times he wanted were early evening several days before the election and election eve. WBZ was reluctant to sell the time to Weston for the near-prime half-hour periods he had selected. He had no difficulty reserving the time slots on New Hampshire stations but found that the Boston station did not want to sacrifice network programming for a political production of interest to a small portion of its market. When word of this refusal got back to New York, Blair Clark and Howard Stein, the source of the funds, contacted the programming executives of the National Broadcasting System, told them of their problem, and a few telephone calls later, the New Hampshire McCarthy campaign had its preelection television time. The program would be aired March 11 on WBZ-TV between 7:30 and 8:00 P.M. and between 8:00 and 8:30 P.M. on Channel 8, WMTW-TV broadcasting from Poland Springs, Maine, via Mt. Washington, New Hampshire.

The first of the two one-half-hour programs was produced by Bill and Kay Nee in a Boston studio, with Senator McCarthy discussing his campaign with a group of the volunteers who had worked in his New Hampshire campaign. The objective of the program was to capture visually some of the wide interest that had been generated by the students who had worked in New Hampshire and to use their enthusiasm as a foil for McCarthy's own sincerity and concern. The program was an engaging dialogue that ranged across the major issues of the campaign and closed with McCarthy turning toward the camera with a closing statement.

The second program was taped in Boston on the morning of March 11, the day it was to be shown. Jack Parr, the recently retired "Tonight Show" host, had been quietly managing the television station he owned in Maine when his daughter, Randy, a student at Radcliffe College, became involved in the New Hampshire campaign. She had become one of the weekend volunteers and a regular among the anonymous workers in the back room and basement of the Concord headquarters. Her accounts of the campaign and concern about U.S. Vietnam policy had motivated her father to offer to breach his retirement to help McCarthy. Working with Bill and Kay Nee, Dick Goodwin conceived of the idea of using something like Jack Parr's old "Tonight Show" interview format as the setting for the election evening program.

Parr agreed to be the host and the McCarthy campaign had an entertainment event as well as a campaign-concluding political program. A somewhat rusty Jack Parr attempted an interview of Senator McCarthy much as he had done each late evening for almost a decade. Senator McCarthy, more relaxed than Parr, responded to the questions Parr offered, questions that Goodwin had developed from Al Shepard's motivational research. Why was McCarthy running? Why had he entered the New Hampshire primary? What were his differences with the Johnson administration? What were his concerns about the impact of the war on domestic affairs? Then Parr asked questions he hoped would probe McCarthy as a personality and as an elected official.

Toward the middle of the program McCarthy rose from his chair and walked a few steps to the corner of a desk that had been placed away from the chairs Parr and he had occupied during the interview. He perched on a corner of the desk, settled slightly, and began talking directly through the camera. In the ten or fifteen minutes available, Senator McCarthy explained his candidacy, what the next day's vote could mean, how he would change policy, and what kind of a president he would be. It was an exceptionally effective media moment. The "cool" candidate had met the "cool" medium. McCarthy projected through the camera into the living room as a striking contrast to the harshness of Johnson or the tenseness of Richard Nixon—the two most prominent figures then on television.

McCarthy, the television candidate was in harmony with McCarthy the "profile" newspaper advertisement and McCarthy the "bring America back to its senses" radio message. Jubilant, McCarthy left the taping session to complete the last day of his New Hampshire campaign.

FINANCING THE CAMPAIGN

Studds and I had made clear from the beginning that funds to support the effort we had proposed for Senator McCarthy in the New Hampshire presidential primary could not be raised entirely within the state. The New Hampshire political reality is that money for campaigns is limited under the best of circumstances and money to support the primary candidacies of presidential candidates is rarely if ever derived totally from the New Hampshire populace.

The Johnson campaign sought to fund its activities with locally raised money and felt it could do so since the continuation of Johnson in office meant continued employment for some and potential rewards for others. It was also a part of the New Hampshire McCarthy strategy to make it embarrassing for the Johnson committee to import campaign money or to use money that had been raised to support activities of the New Hampshire Democratic Party. To a considerable extent the McCarthy strategy worked. The Johnson New Hampshire war chest was clearly limited. Not until very late in the campaign did the Johnson committee begin to spend extensively for radio, newspaper, and television advertising.

The financing pattern of the McCarthy campaign fell into three distinct periods. The first was the period prior to and just shortly after Senator McCarthy's announcement of his New Hampshire candidacy. The first contributions listing from the campaign read:

Rebecca Z. Solomon, 65 Middlebrook Road, Hartford, Conn.	250.00
Robert L. Finley, Tamworth, N.H.	100.00
David G. Underwood, 29 Rumford Street, Concord, N.H.	100.00
Elinore M. Adams, Box 101, E. Concord, N.H.	10.00
George M. Marrow, P.0. Box 797, Brattleboro, Vt.	20.00
Gerhard Lenski, 404 Westwood Drive, Chapel Hill, N.C.	25.00
John Stevens, Watkins Hill, Walpole, N.H.	2.00
Mary Scott-Craig, 2 Chase Road, Hanover, N.H.	10.00
Norman R. Torrey, Jaffrey Ctr., N.H.	10.00

(Ref. N.H. McCarthy for President Committee contributions report, DCH file copy)

This fund of $527 was the total resource of the campaign until the second week of January 1968. All previous activities of the New Hampshire McCarthy Committee, including mailing, travel, and telephone calls, were paid for by the individuals involved—principally, me and Gerry Studds. Studds used his own personal checking account to write deposits for telephone installation, headquarters rental, furniture rental, and some of the early equipment rentals needed to open the Concord headquarters. Once McCarthy had announced his entry in the New Hampshire primary, that first $527 in John Holland's account for the campaign was quickly expended.

Studds, Holland, and I had agreed that we would not permit the campaign to spend or commit to spend more than we were sure could be raised or was on hand to pay the campaign's obligations. Studds ventured out on a limb with his checking account as a minor violation of this principle, but he had reasonable assurance from Holland and through Holland to the national campaign manager, Blair Clark, that he would not be stuck. There was, however, a delay between the time that money was needed to begin New Hampshire activities and the time money began to arrive for Jack Holland's account. Until this delay developed, Studds and I were under the impression that sufficient money was available from national sources to fund our estimated needs and certainly enough to begin the principal phase of the campaign. Allard Lowenstein had referred repeatedly to substantial funds already pledged to an alternative candidacy if only Senator McCarthy would run.

When it came time to pay the early New Hampshire bills, it was the personal fortunes of two individuals that supported the early New Hampshire activity. Martin Peretz, Harvard professor and Singer Sewing machine heir, and Blair Clark, Clark thread heir, each sent a check for five thousand dollars to Jack Holland. Clark's check came through the national office of the McCarthy campaign and was listed as such on the contributions report filed in New Hampshire. Shortly after those two checks were received, Ann Reynolds of Springfield, Vermont, and Mabel B. Harrison of Hanover, New Hampshire, sent checks of one thousand dollars each. The second phase, the middle, of the campaign financing activity was underway.

During Blair Clark's visit to New Hampshire on January 2 and 3, he met with Merv Weston to review Weston's outline of what he considered to be the essential media components of the coming campaign. From this discussion Weston drafted his first advertising budget which totaled $43,007. This figure would continue to increase as the campaign progressed and had already grown to $50,500 by the time I submitted an overall budget for the campaign to Blair Clark on January 18. Obviously, the $50,000 figure that Studds and I had suggested in our December 22 memorandum as being the amount required to fund a McCarthy candidacy in New Hampshire had been exceeded by the advertising budget alone.

In a memorandum I prepared and submitted to the New Hampshire McCarthy Steering Committee and Blair Clark, I projected the financial needs of the campaign.

1. Media budget (attached to the original memo) $50,500.00

2. Headquarters: costs include rent, heat (where necessary), activity related advertising, telephones, signs, personnel (limited), transportation, and covering of some costs or volunteers.

Concord-State	3,000.00	
Nashua	2,400.00	
Manchester	2,600.00	
Keene	1,000.00	
Laconia	1,000.00	
Lebanon-Hanover	1,500.00	
Dover	1,000.00	
Portsmouth	750.00	
Berlin	1,500.00	
Home headquarters: up to 45 H.H. at $50 per spot	2,250.00	
	17,000.00	17,000.00

3. Personnel:

Scheduling	1,000.00	
Advance	2,000.00	
Press	1,500.00	
Overall	2,000.00	
Volunteer coordination	1,000.00	
Contingencies	2,500.00	
	10,000.00	10,000.00

4. Transportation 2,500.00

5. Television (all should be programmed out of Boston) ???

6. All other items that will come-up that I can't think of at this moment. 2,500.00

Total: $82,500.00

Note: The headquarters costs are higher than we had expected. We are having difficulty finding store-front locations and probably will not be able to open and support as many as are listed. We do not allocate budget to headquarters but urge them to raise as much locally as is possible. We will then supplement if they are in desperate need.

The staff situation remains critical. We need full time people to carry the daily load. We are making some progress but need the bodies as well as the money.

(DCH budget memo, January 18, 1968)

Clark accepted the budget from me, Holland monitored the obligations according to the budget plan, and much of the middle phase of the campaign followed the expenditure pattern advised in the memo.

One of the early mailings was to approximately fifteen hundred contacts that I had developed or presumed might contribute to the campaign in New Hampshire. The mailing went to the state's college faculties and others that the steering committee thought would contribute to the campaign, and began a modest but steady flow of money back to Holland and stimulated some local fund-raising initiatives as well.

A Dartmouth history professor, David Roberts, began organizing the Dartmouth College faculty to contribute regularly to the McCarthy campaign. He recruited colleagues in other departments who would help him and each payday would remind his contacts to hit the momentarily "flush" faculty for a contribution to the campaign. He then would bring his collection to my office, pouring it like tribute across my desk. With the bills, checks, and change, Roberts provided a careful account of the amount and the contributor names for my records. In addition, Roberts organized a fund-raising cocktail reception for Senator McCarthy when he visited Hanover and led in raising local funds to support the Lebanon-Hanover area McCarthy headquarters. Robert Craig of the University of New Hampshire's political science department and Robert Simpson of the physics department did the same in the Durham-Dover area. Their fund raising supported much of the cost of the Dover area headquarters and regularly tapped the faculty resource of the university.

In Keene, David and Mary Gregory, and John Wiseman and his wife, working with a joint Keene State College and local citizen committee, raised funds to support their local activities entirely. Other committees submitted budget requests to Jack Holland and myself. Most would raise at least a part of their needs locally but did not like to proceed without some assurance that their planning was realistic and would be approved by the statewide campaign leadership.

January 18, David Morin of Hampton sent his local budget to me:

Mr. Hoeh:
Tentative proposed budget for Hampton area:

Rental of trailer headquarters (half price)	$100
Advertising	500

Postage		500
Paper, envelopes, etc.		150
Telephone		50
Lights		25
Heat		25
Miscellaneous		150
	Total:	1,500

Sound feasible? With adequate funds, we are optimistic that we can do a job in this area. Do we have your approval?

Please send us as soon as possible literature, buttons, bumper stickers, large signs and posters for the headquarters, etc.

We plan to have our committee organized by next week, and will attempt to get pictures and a blurb in the five local papers that service this area.

Will inform you on our progress.

Sincerely, Dave Morin

Our slogan in this area will have to be along the line: "Be proud to be an American. Vote McCarthy!" (Democrats are virtually nonexistent.)

(Letter in DCH file)

Although a steady flow of contributions was regularly received at the McCarthy headquarters in Concord, the amounts did not keep pace with the proposed budget much less an emerging expenditure pattern that was projected to exceed the budget. Many contributions came spontaneously from McCarthy sympathizers across the country from states such as North Dakota, North Carolina, Illinois, Georgia, California, Washington, Ohio, and Florida, included with New York, Washington, D.C., Pennsylvania, Maryland, Virginia, and the New England states. Some state McCarthy committees, either with no primary or later primary elections, raised and forwarded money to New Hampshire for the campaign. The National Campus Concerned Democrats sent $1,000 and a New Jersey coalition supporting McCarthy made a special trip to New Hampshire to give me a check for $5,000.

In spite of the good intentions and hard work, the flow of funds was not sufficiently reliable to commit aspects of the media plan as each came due. The campaign period, ten weeks, meant that little time could be devoted to fund raising and without funds valuable time would be lost. The campaign faced this dilemma early in February. The first sizable checks had either been expended or committed by that time and the flow of funds from Washington had almost stopped. Clark could not supply the New Hampshire campaign with the money to begin the radio and newspaper campaigns, to pay for mailings, to reserve television time, to open headquarters, or to supply the campaign paraphernalia. For the first two weeks of February it looked as if the campaign might die of starvation.

Volunteers made the money go further, but no one involved in New Hampshire was willing to or financially capable of assuming the debt to go forward. Weston Associates had extended its own credit to the limit. A clear desperation began to pass over the leadership of the campaign both in New Hampshire and Washington. McCarthy had not stirred sufficient attention in the national media to attract major contributions.

Two struggles were going on among those attempting to manage the campaign outside New Hampshire. The first concerned a dispute between the powerful and well-financed Coalition for a Democratic Alternative of New York City and Blair Clark. The CDA had developed a strong, broad-based political organization during the period of the search for an alternate candidate. The leaders, Harold Ickes, the thirtyish son of the late secretary of the interior under President Roosevelt, and Sarah Kovner, also thirtyish and with a record of effectiveness in New York City liberal Democratic causes, had worked closely with Allard Lowenstein in his alternative search effort.

The role they had assumed was to offer a war chest and a ready-to-go political organization to the person accepting Lowenstein's invitation to run. When McCarthy announced his candidacy he did not immediately accept the CDA's offer. Instead McCarthy asked Blair Clark to manage his campaign. Clark set about building his own campaign team. Like Lowenstein who was set adrift by McCarthy after the Chicago CCD meeting, the CDA leadership found itself unable to get inside the McCarthy campaign. To draw Clark and McCarthy's attention, the New York CDA virtually cut the campaign off from its resources.

The second struggle was between Clark and Hemenway concerning another potential source of campaign funds. Hemenway, with the support of his organization, the National Committee for an Effective Congress, and its principal backer, Maurice Rosenblatt, was also trying to build a campaign organization and funding base for McCarthy. While doing this he had discovered that Howard Stein, director of the Dreyfus Fund, was attracted to McCarthy and McCarthy's analysis of the impact of the administration's war policies on the domestic economy. Under Hemenway tutelage, Stein became a willing student of national politics. Stein, a cautious investor, was reluctant to release his money or his contacts to Hemenway or anyone else without having some substantial role in the decisions as to how these resources were to be used. A political novice, Stein saw the McCarthy campaign as his chance to pursue the equivalent of an executive work-study experience.

Hemenway brought Stein with him to New Hampshire during McCarthy's first campaign visit. Several days after the visit, I received a call from Hemenway saying that Stein would like to help with the campaign and asking me to find a house that Stein might rent for the duration of the campaign. I called Clark to check on this offer. Clark advised me to let him handle Stein and to delay responding to Hemenway. To cover both sides I asked Barbara Underwood if she could find out whether someone near Concord might have a house available for Stein to use. Early in February, Stein himself called me to ask how my search for a house was coming to which I replied that I had not been able to find anything available but cold and drafty summer seasonal housing. Stein said he had arranged to bring several professional people with him who could provide major assistance to the senator. That was not altogether reassuring since the one thing that the New Hampshire McCarthy Steering Committee and I feared was having our role in the campaign overridden by supposedly expert outsiders. We felt that we had the pulse on the McCarthy potential under our own fingers and that the beat might be lost if too heavy a hand were to rest on it. Stein urged me to keep looking and said that he would call again in several days.

Again I contacted Blair Clark. Clark instructed me not to have further conversations with Stein and not to make arrangements for him to become involved in the New Hampshire activity. Several weeks passed with no contact with either Hemenway or Stein. Clark feared that Stein would move in on the campaign in a way that would sidetrack his efforts to build the national campaign organization. Both Clark and Jerry Eller, McCarthy's administrative assistant, feared that Stein's New York City style and desire to become extensively involved in the campaign might set off a series of negative reactions that would disrupt the fragile New Hampshire venture and their own efforts to regulate McCarthy's candidacy. The impasse continued. Hemenway tried his best to keep communications open between Stein and McCarthy but was not able to resolve things until the New Hampshire and national campaigns practically died from a lack of money.

Early in the third week of February, I received a series of telephone calls. Hemenway called to say that Stein would be calling again; I called Clark to find out what I should do, and Clark said that I should listen and work out something with Stein that suited my needs in New Hampshire. I, feeling a bit like I was walking on eggs, accepted Stein's call, agreed to discuss the campaign's financial situation with him, but promised nothing else. I assured Stein that the New Hampshire aspects of the campaign were progressing well but what I needed was help paying bills and getting things moving in both New York and Washington. Stein said he would come to New Hampshire, find his own place to stay, and help as he could—quite a different posture from that I had sensed in earlier conversations.

What I learned later was that Elliot Janeway, a friend of the McCarthys, had called Abigail McCarthy and suggested that Howard Stein really should be used and that he could help. Through Abigail McCarthy, Senator McCarthy suggested that Clark open the campaign to Stein but do so on a basis agreeable to Clark. Clark, by this time, acutely felt the pressure to get money for New Hampshire, the national office, and to meet media reservation demands in the other primary states. (Underwood, op. cit., p. 17) Stein, his wife, and several friends came to New Hampshire, took a suite at the Sheraton-Wayfarer and began quietly helping, much like the many other volunteers.

Clark went through a similar experience with the leadership of the CDA. An agreement was worked out where Harold Ickes and Sarah Kovner would have important roles in the campaign and especially in the leadership of the McCarthy effort in the New York presidential primary. Ickes came to New Hampshire to help Gans. The CDA opened its war chest. John Holland received a check for $9,700 and the CDA printed much of the material used by the campaign in the closing weeks. Through CDA contacts the celebrity visits to New Hampshire were arranged as was the aircraft that Bill and Sandy Johnson made available to fly both the celebrities and McCarthy. A number of the volunteers who came to New Hampshire to spend a week or more managing the area headquarters and assisting with important organizational tasks came from the ranks of the CDA as well. The value of the CDA contribution was at least double and probably triple the $9,700 that was received by Holland in a check.

Howard Stein's arrival in New Hampshire began the third and final phase of financing the campaign. A soft-spoken man with analytical talents, Stein came as one who respected what had already been accomplished by the New Hampshire campaign. When Studds and I met Stein, he assured us that he admired what we had accomplished to date and wanted to assist in ways that we thought might produce a McCarthy victory. Both of us relaxed as Stein made clear that what he wanted was to find his niche in the campaign and to contribute from that place as much as he could. I noted that my principal concerns were about money and that for some unknown reasons the national campaign had been slow in supporting the activities I felt were essential to the success of the campaign. Stein said that he felt he could help with the money problem if I could specify what was needed, how much it would cost, and what priority the items had in the scheme of the campaign. Several days before I had prepared an inventory of the campaign activities and the probable cost of each. I reached inside my coat for the list and began explaining each item to Stein.

The outstanding balance was approximately $70,000. On the list were items such as printing, mailing, postage, radio time, extra billboard space, newspaper advertising, television programming, headquarters costs, hotel/motel bills, telephone installations, and several other major items. Stein thoughtfully listened then took the list and checked a number of the items. When he had finished he said, "Okay, I'll take care of these. You get Clark to pay for the others." The items Stein had checked were the principal media items, radio, television, mailing costs, postage, and some aspects of the headquarters operation such as the telephone costs. His total exceeded half the value of the list or more than $35,000. Stein said that, in addition to what he had checked on my list, he had gathered approximately $6,000 worth of first-class stamps and these would be sent to the headquarters immediately. The items remaining on my list that Stein said Blair Clark should fund were materials, campaign support, and operations expenses. These had been included in the original budget for the campaign and had remained the same throughout. What Stein assumed were items that had either been added to the plan or substantially expanded as McCarthy showed increasing strength in New Hampshire.

The brief, approximately one-half-hour meeting ended with Stein asking me to make a photocopy of the list and agreeing to tell me of his progress regularly. I suggested that Stein meet with Merv Weston as soon as possible to work out the details of the space, time, and production orders that Stein now had assumed. After Stein left the table Studds and I sat stunned, once again, by the turn of events of their campaign. A few moments earlier, we had wondered whether even a minimal program of the campaign would be accomplished. We had come to the meeting with Stein feeling as if we were referees in a bankruptcy hearing and left with not only the venture in tact but with almost all of our "wish list" funded.

I called Clark in Washington immediately and reported the details of the conversation. Clark was obviously uncomfortable with the result but agreed that the only other option would be to scale the campaign back significantly and jeopardize McCarthy's chances. He did not appreciate being put on the spot by Stein concerning who would fund what, but Clark accepted, recognizing that he had lost a certain freedom of action in his own situation as the result. I recognized this loss as well but felt that unless McCarthy did well in New Hampshire there would be little after New Hampshire to manage.

Stein recruited several of his friends to assist him in his role of media financier and producer. Among these was a Boston shoe manufacturer, Arnold Hiatt. Hiatt had become involved with the McCarthy campaign as one of a group of wealthy Boston area liberals who had taken on much of the financial responsibility for the Massachusetts campaign. Hiatt had more experience with politics than Stein, and between them they became a competent and important addition to the New Hampshire leadership.

Gans' arrival in New Hampshire on February 16 was also an important aspect of the final phase of the campaign's financial management. Before Gans came to New Hampshire, Holland and I had controlled the spending of the campaign, not committing more than we had on hand or could expect to receive on short notice from Blair Clark. Gans, on the other hand, arrived with what appeared to be a "blank check" to obligate the campaign directly through Clark and the Washington headquarters. This capacity seemed to extend only to those aspects of the campaign that involved the local headquarters staffing, supply, and support. Gans did this with the tacit approval of Blair Clark and without much contact with either Holland or myself.

Consequently, at the same time that Clark was losing a bit of his overall national campaign management authority to Stein, Studds, Holland, and I were losing much of our oversight authority concerning the expenditures of the New Hampshire campaign. Gans went ahead assuming that he had a clear mandate from Clark to do so with the only restraint being an occasional check from Holland or myself when an item passed in front of us by accident or for our approval. The campaign, modestly conceived, and until the final weeks, modestly funded, became expensive in the final stage.

Stein and Hiatt controlled the funding and production of the final media push including newspaper advertising and radio messages, but especially the heavy, for New Hampshire politics, television programming. They worked directly with Merv Weston and his agency staff. The content of the messages and the theme of the advertising received clearance through McCarthy, Gans, and me in most instances, but for all intents and purposes the Stein-Hiatt activity was another of the separate departments that evolved in the campaign.

Gans' headquarters preelection strategy, get-out-the-vote planning, and vote collection effort grew to the point where it also was a separate department largely detached from the earlier management pattern of the campaign. Studds found it impossible to keep track of what was going on in the headquarters given the limited time he could devote to the campaign from his teaching at St. Paul's School. Gradually he drifted out of the activity as Gans filled the headquarters with his own personnel—people who did not know Studds nor his earlier role in the campaign. I kept closer tabs on Gans and his activities, involved Studds as much as I could, but also found that the distance between Hanover and Concord left me in a weakened position. I stopped my daily commuting from Hanover when early one morning I found myself driving in the left lane of the road on a return to Hanover. The last ten days I spent totally with the campaign in Concord or Manchester.

Contributions

The role of the small contributors and fund-raisers was also significant. David Roberts' fund-raising effort in Hanover produced more that $1,000 through more than fifty individual contributions. Approximately 160 individual contributions were directly received by the New Hampshire campaign. The total sum received and recorded by John Holland was $98,808.39. Of this amount $33,756 came to Holland from the national headquarters of the McCarthy campaign and $30,700 came to him from the New York based CDA. The remaining $34,352.12 came from individual contributors ranging from $1 to $300 each. Seven contributions between $500 and $1,500 were received as were five checks above $1,000 to $5,000 not including the early checks from Blair Clark and Martin Peretz.

Expenditures

An exact listing of all expenditures of the New Hampshire campaign does not exist. The records of the fiscal agent, John Holland, include only those disbursements he handled. He received and spent the $98,803.39 in contributions and transfers and had a debt in unpaid bills as accounted March 26, 1968, of $18,284.80. That figure, as Holland noted in his report, did not include "bills for telephone service and rented autos" which he had not yet received. (Unpaid bills statement, DCH file) The telephone bill, when finally received, was more than $8,000 and the car rental bill exceeded $2,000, totaling $127,093.19 as the amount that Holland recorded. Not included were the costs of supporting the New Hampshire campaign at the national level, nor the printing that was done in New York, nor the obligations that Howard Stein accepted and paid himself or through the national headquarters.

No accounts were gathered from the operation of the local committees nor were contributor records compiled for these committees. A conservative estimate of the monetary cost of the campaign would be between $225,000 and $250,000. To this figure it would be reasonable to add the equally conservative value of the volunteer time, $250,000, for a total value of close to $500,000. This would be a sum considerably more than either Studds or I estimated when we outlined the campaign in December.

Ultimately it was the money that made it possible to build the essential momentum of the final weeks of the campaign. Without Stein, the CDA, Blair Clark's promise to assume the debt that should result, and the media purchased in the final ten days, the sense of a building climax would not have resulted. The campaign might well have withered badly and been forced to retreat to protect itself from a debt that Studds, Holland, and I could feel breathing on us. Because of the energy of the volunteers and the skillful work of their taskmasters, the impact of the dollar contributed to the campaign grew by a considerable proportion, but ultimately there could be no substitute. Money to support the final push was essential and arrived just in time.

CHAPTER 11

The McCarthy Machine

CAMPAIGN IMPACT

A few days after the New Hampshire presidential primary vote, an advertisement appeared in the *New York Times,* sponsored by the CDA, soliciting funds for the "McCarthy Machine." A full-page ad, the heading read, "McCarthy's Machine Needs Money." A picture showed twelve serious-looking student-aged men and women, coats in hand with a caption, "The Machine." The text of the ad read:

> Senator Eugene McCarthy is backed by the most improbable political machine in American history.
>
> It works for nothing, runs on peanut butter sandwiches and soft drinks, and spends the night in sleeping bags or empty warehouses.
>
> You can't buy a machine like this, even with the of offer of money . . .
>
> And you can't con them either, with a lot of overblown promises.
>
> They're looking for a new kind of leadership for our country and they believe that Senator McCarthy is the only one who can provide it.
>
> That's why they went out and rang every doorbell in the state of New Hampshire. . . .
>
> Unless every person reading this ad sends a few dollars, McCarthy's mightiest weapon will be stilled.
>
> And the battle will have to be fought by a lone man with a limited staff.
>
> If you've already given, thank you. And ask you to please give again.
>
> If you've never given, there's no better time than now.
>
> $1 from you will feed one student for one day.
>
> $10 will provide 20 students with lunch.

> $50 will feed 25 students for two days or 10 students for 5 days.
> And there's also the cost of transportation. . . .
>
> (*New York Times* ad, DCH copy)

By the last ten days the "McCarthy Machine" was in high gear and ready for the critical final days during which all its progress might be lost. A slip, a national crisis, or an international incident might shift the voters attention from an insurgent candidacy back to support for the president. The latter two were outside the control of the New Hampshire campaign but the first, a slip that could cost voter support, was in the back of every mind. It was going to be a close election. The canvass said it, the leaders felt it, and those in the media, much to their disbelief, now recognized it.

As the tide turned in favor of Senator McCarthy, the Johnson campaign leaders fought back. By the middle of February, their pledge card had become a serious liability. Their hope that the card would serve as a party unifying device without having to face divisive issues had stumbled. Their remaining alternative was to attack McCarthy's positions. Until this time, the strategy of the Johnson campaign had been to ignore McCarthy, minimize his possible appeal, deny that loyal New Hampshire Democrats would support his insurgency, and refuse to concede more than a small portion of the vote to him. Senator McIntyre's early prediction that McCarthy would not get more than 3 to 5 percent of the vote and not more than three thousand to five thousand votes total remained the Johnson campaign "party" line well into February. A vote total better than McIntyre's projection would, by their own definition, have to be considered significant.

To McIntyre, preserving the unity of the New Hampshire Democratic Party was as important if not more important than delivering the state to Johnson in the presidential primary. For years prior to his election to the U.S. Senate in 1962, Tom McIntyre and his spouse Myrtle, had struggled to revive the Democratic Party as a meaningful political force in New Hampshire. They had seen what divisive presidential primary fights could do to that unity, and they hoped to prevent that split from occurring in 1968. But Tom McIntyre was only one-fourth of the leadership of the Johnson effort.

State Democratic chair William Craig, and Johnson renomination Chairs, Bernard L. Boutin and John W. King shared the leadership. These three felt their futures were best assured by renominating Johnson. McIntyre recognized that many of his most loyal supporters and hardest campaigners were now supporting the McCarthy effort. This was not the case with Governor King, whose base of political support in New Hampshire was distinct from that of McIntyre.

King derived his core support from the conservative Democrats of Manchester, his hometown, while McIntyre did less well in Manchester but was strong among the more liberal Democrats scattered in the smaller cities and towns. From the beginning, McIntyre had been concerned about the impact of a challenge to Johnson on his base of support. He had been in touch with Sandy and me and the others mentioned in the early McCarthy activity press reports. He had attempted to assure those he talked with that he hoped the contest would not produce lasting damage and, that for one, he would not support direct attacks upon the McCarthy organizers by the Johnson committee. However, Tom McIntyre worked in Washington and was not in New Hampshire to moderate the harder line being taken by his colleagues in the Johnson leadership.

By February 19 McIntyre felt it was necessary to comment on his concerns. The story, widely circulated in New Hampshire, read "McIntyre Admits Party Disunity."

> The Democratic party is having its "troubles internally" during the current dispute between supporters of President Johnson and Minnesota Sen. Eugene McCarthy, Sen. Thomas McIntyre said Friday.
>
> "But when it's all over," he added in an interview, "I want no recriminations and I certainly will strive for that, because as a candidate, when you stand up there with a Democratic banner, you need every Democrat you can get."
>
> McIntyre . . . was asked by an interviewer "about our own Democratic governor who has indicated" to voters that they'd "better get in step or get out."
>
> "Oh, no," McIntyre said, "I think John [King] went a little far there."
>
> McIntyre said it is important to recognize the fact that some people "in their right to dissent within our party have taken up the banner on behalf of the senator from Minnesota" and also important that "they understand when this is all over that we Democrats in New Hampshire are going to be like the Democrats in the national platform."
>
> King had said in Dover earlier this week that McCarthy is a "spokesman for the forces of appeasement" and that the Minnesota senator is advocating a "policy of surrender which would destroy everything we have been fighting for."
>
> The governor praised Johnson, saying he's under violent personal attack because he is the "champion of the free world." He added that "this is a time for every Democrat to stand up and be counted or from now on to be counted out. On this field, we accept battle. His friends are our friends. His enemies are our enemies and we meet all comers—inside and out."
>
> (*Foster's Daily Democrat*, February 19, 1968)

McIntyre, of course, had another concern that was not shared by Boutin, Craig, or King. He, as a U.S. senator, belonged to the select club of the Senate, and as a member his relationship with other members might well be jeopardized by the manner in which he conducted himself during the campaign. For him to attack McCarthy as Governor King was attacking McCarthy, questioning the senator's loyalty, and pledging political retribution for dissent, would violate a norm of the senate and could threaten McIntyre's effectiveness in that body.

The Johnson leaders had received an analysis of the probable voters in the New Hampshire presidential primary from Oliver Quayle and Associates, public opinion pollsters, that showed first that the voter was essentially a "hawk" toward Vietnam policy, and second, that these same voters did not know McCarthy's stand on Vietnam issues. Quayle's advice to the Johnson leaders was to step up their attacks on McCarthy as an advocate of peace and also to get McCarthy to define his peace plans precisely. The combination of strategies, Quayle suggested, would solidify support behind a write-in effort and at the same time drive McCarthy into a corner as his true position became generally known.

Quayle's advice unified the Johnson leaders. What was missing in Quayle's advice was that there is a difference between questioning a policy position and questioning one's political and national loyalty. King went for the jugular and concentrated exclusively on the question of political and national loyalty. McIntyre, when he joined in active campaigning, sought to draw McCarthy out on policy differences.

Unfortunately King had jumped the gun with his Dover speech and by the time McIntyre arrived in New Hampshire to begin campaigning for Johnson much of the damage had already been done. Instead of a coordinated and sustained policy attack on the McCarthy campaign, McIntyre had to separate himself from the position King had taken. Now, in addition to the split that had developed in the Democratic Party between the Johnson and McCarthy supporters, there was a split within the Johnson camp between its leaders, King and McIntyre—a split that would be especially troublesome to the Johnson campaign as the election approached.

From the beginning when the Democratic State Committee was asked to endorse the Johnson renomination, the McCarthy leaders had sought to have the machinery of the New Hampshire Democratic Party remain neutral. When this tactic failed the leaders saw political advantage in reminding voters that the basic ethos of New Hampshire primary politics was being violated by the endorsement. When Governor King launched his attacks on the loyalty of the McCarthy supporters they felt it was time to again remind the public of the trampled ethos of primary election neutrality.

William Craig, Democratic Party chair, called a special meeting of the Democratic State Committee for Tuesday evening, February 20. The announced purpose of the meeting was to select a replacement for the retiring New Hampshire member of the Democratic National Committee, Roland Vallee. When I heard that the meeting was scheduled, I sent the following letter dated February 18, 1968, to each member of the Democratic State Committee.

> Dear Democratic State Committee Member:
>
> Those of us who are supporting the presidential candidacy of Senator Eugene McCarthy have been deeply upset by the conversion of the Democratic State Committee into a campaign committee for President Johnson.
>
> A primary exists for the purpose of permitting the people to determine who the Party's candidate will be. This elementary fact has been ignored by some of our party's leadership—and the people have been told who their candidate will be. Under pressure from the White House—and by some who are eager to please the White House—our State Committee has been disrupted. To convert it into an active campaign organization for a candidate in a primary election is a perversion of the legitimate role of the committee, destructive to the growth of the Democratic Party in New Hampshire, and a distortion of the primary process.

In addition, the use of numbered pledge cards—in an effort publicly to commit voters—is unprecedented and indefensible. It constitutes a brand of intimidation and coercion which is an offense to the Party rank and file.

We are particularly shocked by the open threat of Governor King—namely that New Hampshire Democrats had better stand up and be counted or from now on be counted out. This kind of talk is simply unacceptable in a Party which bears the name, "Democratic."

We think it reasonable to ask that our State Committee reconsider its extraordinary behavior while there is still time—and before we set a precedent which could haunt us for years to come. Therefore we ask:

1) that all Johnson literature and materials bearing the imprint of the State Committee be recalled;

2) that those members of the Party supporting Mr. Johnson establish a campaign organization constituted as it properly should be—totally apart from the State Committee;

3) that the State Committee officially go on record—as Senator McIntyre has already done—as repudiating the ultimatum delivered to the members of our Party by the Governor;

4) that an audit of the State Committee books be conducted by a Certified Public Accountant for the purpose of determining receipts and expenditures of funds for State Committee purposes;

5) that a complete record of the Staff Coordinator's time be reported separating activities and sources of compensation while working on the Johnson campaign;

6) that a complete report be made regarding efforts to pay off the State Committee's $21,000 debt.

The future of our party subsequent to the March 12th primary requires that favorable action be taken on the above requests. We anticipate that hard work will be required to elect a Democratic Senator, Governor, Executive Council, and State Senate. We want to join in this task within a State Committee restored to the organizational integrity of the recent past.

Sincerely,
David C. Hoeh
Campaign Director
McCarthy for President Committee

Sandra Hoeh, a member of the state committee, introduced the motion to reconsider the earlier action of endorsing Johnson's renomination, which prompted debate. Of the two dozen members of the seventy-member state committee attending, approximately six or seven were either McCarthy supporters or concerned about the precedent that the earlier action had set. Craig did not allow the motion to come to a vote, ruling instead that the motion was "out of order." The basis for his ruling was parliamentary procedure which he said, "Forbids such a motion if it comes more than a day after the original endorsement." (*Valley News*, February 21, 1968). This action caused the McCarthy supporters to react, alleging that it was clear now that they had been, as Governor King had promised, "counted out" of the New Hampshire Democratic Party. Craig refused to recognize or ruled "out of order" subsequent motions to recall the Johnson campaign materials and to account for the expenditures of the Democratic State Committee. My comment after the meeting was that "the Democratic party has been baled and shipped to Johnson." (*Manchester Union Leader*, February 21, 1968 pp. 1, 34)

The meeting produced at least two new supporters for the McCarthy effort from the leaders of the state committee, including, Robert Proulx, chair of the Grafton County Democratic Committee, who had previously supported the endorsement of Johnson's renomination. A number of others were deeply disturbed by the behavior of Craig and Boutin toward friends who had shared the earlier battles of the Democratic Party.

The net effect of the confrontation was positive for the McCarthy leadership. It illustrated to what extent the Johnson leaders would go to deliver New Hampshire to Johnson, splitting both friends and political sensitivities. It also demonstrated again that the McCarthy supporters in New Hampshire were far from a splinter of the Democratic Party but were sufficiently strong so that their questions had to be dealt with through parliamentary rulings rather than votes. The *Manchester Union Leader* picked up the dispute in an editorial titled, "'Pedigreed' Democrats," with an editorial cartoon. The editorial read:

> Whatever else might be said of the heated controversy currently raging within the Democratic State Committee it should be stated, for the record, that it is completely unnecessary and need not have grown to such proportions.
>
> In any fair contest, President Johnson figures to run roughshod over Minnesota Sen. Eugene McCarthy, whose voice of appeasement falls on deaf ears in a state whose motto is "Live Free or Die."
>
> What concerns us, and should concern all Democrats, is the unbridled arrogance of those who, despite LBJ's insuperable advantage, nevertheless feel the need to "stack the deck" and to run roughshod over all who disagree with them. Apparently they care not a whit about the party disunity their actions are fostering.
>
> State Chairman William H. Craig of Manchester, who threw the parliamentary book at McCarthy backers at Tuesday night's State Committee meeting in the Queen City, won at best a technical victory. But it could prove to be a costly victory indeed over the long haul.
>
> As far as parliamentary procedure goes, Craig was correct in ruling out of order several indirect attempts to overturn the State Committee's official endorsement of President Johnson. Craig said he would entertain only a specific motion to "reconsider" the previous action of the committee.
>
> However, it is the Democratic State Committee itself that is out of order in endorsing LBJ and violating the neutrality that all Democrats have a right to expect it will adhere to faithfully.

> This newspaper opposes the candidacy of Sen. McCarthy with every fiber of its being, but we cannot help but sense and sympathize with the feeling of outrage of McCarthy's supporters when they the State Committee attempt to transform the Democratic Party into an exclusive club where only "pedigreed" candidates and their supporters are welcome.
>
> (*Manchester Union Leader,* February 22, 1968)

The editorial was merely a minor break in the pattern of editorial attack which the *Manchester Union Leader* aimed at the McCarthy campaign, but it did revive in the final weeks of the campaign the issues of fairness and party neutrality. After the February 18 meeting, the Johnson campaign seemed to lose its remaining momentum.

Symptomatic of what the Johnson campaign was encountering was reflected in an Art Buchwald column that appeared February 22. He wrote, "A few weeks ago David Brinkley reported that a scientist had programmed all the pertinent military information about the U.S. and North Vietnam and fed it into a computer, raising the question: 'When will the war be won and which side will win?' The computer answered that the U.S. had won the war two years ago." (*New York Post,* February 22, 1968)

As the Johnson fortunes faded, the Johnson campaign meetings became more and more unpleasant. Boutin would not tolerate disagreement within the organization any more than Governor King would outside. In the last days only those who had to attended the meetings, while the others drifted to the sides and away from the hostility. On election night several of the major Johnson workers would spend the evening at the McCarthy headquarters to wait for the returns, disillusioned by the Johnson leaders and disgusted by the direction the campaign had taken.

McCARTHY ADDS CAMPAIGN DAYS

An early indication that McCarthy might draw support from other than traditional Democratic cities came during his February 15 tour from Manchester west to Keene. A mid-stop was planned for the historical society building in the quaint town center of Peterborough. A lively local committee, headed by the community druggist, had asked that McCarthy schedule a stop in the town sometime during the campaign. A low priority community on our list, Peterborough was the traditional center of southeastern New Hampshire Republicanism.

The most that anyone outside Peterborough expected for Senator McCarthy was, optimistically, fifty folks and these mostly McCarthy committee members, friends, and family. When McCarthy arrived he was greeted by a cheering crowd of several hundred people waving placards, wearing buttons, and overflowing the modest hall of the historical society. Former long-term Republican congressman Perkins Bass had asked the local McCarthy committee if he might introduce McCarthy to the gathering. Delighted by this unexpected interest, the committee accepted the offer. Bass introduced McCarthy with praise for his record in the U.S. Congress and appreciation for his campaign. When McCarthy left Peterborough after a visit of not much more than one-half hour, he left a community captured by his candidacy and himself taken by the enthusiasm the town's people had shown.

Shortly after McCarthy returned to Washington, he announced he would increase his campaign schedule in New Hampshire. He was obviously reassured by the welcome he had received and felt that he could best focus the attack on the stumbling Johnson campaign himself. He could think of no better way to support his candidacy than by doing very well in the primary voting.

The extended schedule meant that more of the larger towns could be included in McCarthy's appearance schedule. Instead of campaigning only in the cities and a few of the larger towns, McCarthy's could visit many of the five regional centers, such as Peterborough, that contained an important but usually unreached—at least by Democratic candidates—constituency. In a February 28 press release, the New Hampshire headquarters announced the senator's campaign schedule for March 2–7. McCarthy's earlier successes and the demise of the Romney candidacy left McCarthy as the only campaign of interest in New Hampshire. The press bus rented by the campaign for the duration was now filled with an excited crowd of reporters and media people. An entourage of cars followed him on every move he made from his headquarters. For the final ten days of the campaign, the campaign's principal locus shifted from Concord to the Sheraton-Wayfarer located just outside of Manchester.

Anticipating that Manchester would become the base for McCarthy, I rented a cottage on the grounds of the Wayfarer that had been renovated by the Dunfey family as a special activity space. I expected that it would serve both as a living quarters for Senator and Mrs. McCarthy and as a subheadquarters for the staff supporting his campaigning. Within hours of the senator's arrival at the cottage, campaign activity exceeded capacity and the campaign began renting rooms in a wing of the main motel.

To keep the Manchester and Concord campaign centers in close touch I arranged for a tie line to be installed in the cottage. Such a telephone line is activated simply by lifting the receiver at either end. The telephone rings automatically. The first night McCarthy stayed in the cottage, someone working late in the Concord headquarters accidentally lifted the tie line receiver, awakening McCarthy in Manchester. The next morning McCarthy quietly asked to have the line disconnected or at least to have the ring stopped.

By this time, Richard Goodwin had moved his press operation into several connecting rooms in the motel. One room became a communications center and duplication office. The tie line was installed there along with a WATS line and several regular telephones. A mimeograph machine was set up in the bathroom, the bedroom furniture moved out, and tables, chairs, and typewriters moved in. Another telephone line was installed in Goodwin's room for his use. Across the hall, Sy Hersh, McCarthy's press secretary, had his room. The next was that of Mary Lou Oates, another press aide. Both had migrated with much of the national campaign from Washington. Before long most of the rooms in that wing of the motel building would be occupied by McCarthy staff, jammed with volunteers, or housing celebrities like Rod Serling, Tony Randall, and Paul Newman.

Within a few days the motel manager realized that part of his building was unusable except by those associated with or sympathetic to the campaign. This definition expanded to included the press who enjoyed the around-the-clock activity and did not object to the constant sound of typewriters, mimeograph machines, and late hour hallway conversation.

Within forty-eight hours of McCarthy's arrival in New Hampshire for the five-day schedule, March 2–7, almost all of the campaign's activity that either supported McCarthy in the field or was part of the candidate-related press activity was located at the Wayfarer. A New Hampshire campaign press office stayed in Concord as did other aspects of the campaign, including the volunteer support, canvass management, mailing preparation, celebrity scheduling, and election-day planning. The two headquarters worked closely on those activities that required coordination but much of the campaign was now on predetermined tracks, allowing only slight modification.

The national press, now in awe of the McCarthy activity, seemed to become part of the campaign. With little to cover except McCarthy, they spent the days traveling with him and the off hours watching the volunteers, finding new stories, and even helping with some of the tasks. The campaign had become professional almost before the reporters' skeptical eyes.

McCarthy's campaigning was now amplified by wider press attention, the enthusiasm of the local committees, and the excitement that presidential campaigning lends to a New Hampshire winter. It began to build, that elusive commodity essential to a successful campaign, charisma. Now when McCarthy arrived in a community, people came out of their shops to meet him, went out of their way to shake his hand, and crowds even gathered anticipating a visit. McCarthy began to reach New Hampshire taciturn voters in a way that had not been seen since Estes Kefauver's campaigns of the 1950s.

On Saturday, March 2, McCarthy campaigned in Nashua's heavily Democratic ward 3 and along Main Street, then lunched with a group of supporters at a popular family restaurant. That afternoon the McCarthy entourage traveled west to Milford for a Knights of Columbus reception and some shopping area handshaking. That evening McCarthy spoke to a packed house at the Bishop Guertin High School. A placard-waving crowd greeted him when he arrived, and a cheering foot-stomping audience responded to each of his best lines. The reporters picked up the enthusiasm as the spotlight shifted to McCarthy:

> The Minnesota Senator during a door-to-door campaign tour of Nashua . . . , asked for the independent vote. (McCarthy) said, "Governor Romney's decision not to campaign any further in this state eliminates choice in the Republican primary.
>
> Because of the urgencies of the issues facing the nation today, I want to formally request the support of those independent voters in New Hampshire who were planning to vote for Gov. George Romney in endorsement of his stand against the Vietnam war."
>
> A clothing merchant, Samuel J. Tobias, grasped the candidate's hand on Main Street. "I'm switching my vote from Johnson to you," he said.
>
> Tobias later told newsmen he had been impressed with McCarthy's manner during a Rotary Club speech and said he had signed "one of those L.B.J.

> pledge cards. But I think I'll write the President—tell him to deduct one card," he said.
>
> McCarthy encountered Mr. and Mrs. Willis K. Shirley and Mrs. Shirley stuck out her hand, "I'm for you," she said.
>
> "We're Democrats," Shirley said, "We voted for Johnson. I'm not satisfied with the way things are going in the country. And I'm very dissatisfied with this war."
>
> Asked whether he thought about the controversial pledge cards, Shirley said, "hate to say it, but I think that's dirty politics. This is a free country, I don't think we should be regimented."
>
> (*Boston Globe,* March 3, 1968)

The same edition of the *Boston Globe* carried a page-one story headlined, "Is 'The Establishment' deserting LBJ?"

> There are growing signs that such may be the case, and they are being taken seriously by administration officials, particularly those who must strike a balance between policy and politics on the war.
>
> Last week, George B. Kistiakowsky, Harvard University chemistry professor and science adviser to three Presidents, quietly severed all connections with the Pentagon in protest over Vietnam policy.
>
> No routine academic dissenter, Kistiakowsky is known as the establishment scientist. . . .
>
> (*Boston Globe,* March 3, 1968, p. 1)

Among the serious lines the *Globe* also carried a McCarthy hockey story:

> Senator Eugene J. McCarthy, once the high-scoring captain of the St. John's University hockey team, doubted last week that he would exhibit his skating form for Massachusetts voters.
>
> But the Boston setting reminded him, he said of a game he played decades ago against fellow Minnesotan Frank Brimsek, who went on to become a popular Bruins goalie and the NHL's "Mr. Zero."
>
> "I had one clear shot against Brimsek," said McCarthy, "but before I got it off, I was tripped from behind. I've never stopped wondering whether I could have beaten him."
>
> (*Boston Globe,* March 3, 1968)

The *Boston Globe,* with its important New Hampshire circulation, was becoming almost a campaign piece for McCarthy. The Sunday March 3 edition was the first to show what the wide news and editorial support might lend to McCarthy's New Hampshire effort. The Monday edition kept up the fire with an editorial page column written by Christopher Lydon discussing the continuing "row" within the ADA, prompted by the earlier McCarthy endorsement. Like the pledge cards and the changing of the "establishment" guard, the ADA victory by the McCarthy majority was not allowed to die in the McCarthy-favorable press.

After attending church on March 3, McCarthy joined a reception in his honor at the Moody Hotel in Claremont. Sundays are home and family days in New Hampshire and difficult times for campaigning. However, the reception attracted a warm crowd. That evening McCarthy spoke at Dartmouth College as I had promised he would. Nowhere outside of a college campus would it have been possible to attract a crowd on a winter Sunday evening in New Hampshire.

David Roberts and Lee Baldwin, co-chairs of the Hanover McCarthy committee, arranged four busy hours of activity for McCarthy, beginning with a 4:00 P.M. press conference, followed by thirty minutes of special radio interviews for the local reporters, and then a 5:00 to 6:00 P.M. fund-raising cocktail party in the faculty lounge of the Dartmouth College's Hopkins Center. McCarthy took the next hour and forty-five minutes to dine in his room and go over his notes for the evening speech. With him during this time were Gerry Studds, David Schoumacher, a CBS reporter, and myself.

McCarthy opened his briefcase taking out a large folder of papers which he slowly shuffled through and at the same time asked me what I thought that evening's student audience might want to hear. I felt it was time again to discuss the war and relate it to student concerns and international consequences. Using these two themes I suggested McCarthy could reach the skeptical students, while revealing his own analytical breadth to a cautious faculty. I had advised McCarthy that Dartmouth student audiences tended to be reserved in their reaction. If he could stir them to interrupt his speech with applause it would be a significant response but not to expect other than attentive listening.

McCarthy, with the editor of the *Daily Dartmouth,* came on stage before a packed Webster Hall. The applause was courteous, no shouting, no standing, no signs, just more than fifteen hundred people clapping. McCarthy was introduced and began his speech.The speech contained McCarthy's best illustrations and rhetorical allusions floating out across the silent hall like a breeze in a sound absorbing room—no response, no reaction, no clapping, almost not a sound. The only noise in the hall came from the outside when a few late arrivals found the door closed. The hall was filled to capacity and no more could be allowed inside.

His speech ranged across the arguments of his candidacy and criticism of the administration's polices and behavior toward these concerns. Inserted in his frequently used arguments were sections that had been prepared by Sy Hersh on the problems of the cities McCarthy and I thought might be of particular interest to the largely urban originated Dartmouth audience:

> "This priority is not being recognized by the present administration. The time, as the President's Riot Commission tells us, is short if we are to prevent more bloodshed. I believe that this nation can stem future riots and bloodshed—we have the potential, we have the intellect, and we have the will.

"But we cannot solve any problems if we persist in wasting manpower, money and moral energy in the war in Vietnam."

McCarthy noted two years ago Johnson said the United States could fight the war in Vietnam and the war on poverty at home. But "the President's recent budget message was nothing more than a signal of surrender, a sign of abandonment of the War on Poverty and the special needs of America.

"The people of this nation and the Congress have not had a chance to pass objective judgment on this war. As our military component has grown so has our commitment to South East Asia. And no place along the line did anyone pass a reasoned judgment on what was happening in South East Asia."

He said in 1966 most members of the Senate Foreign Relations Committee, including himself, "decided this country was involved in an effort in which we could not succeed."

"I'm a messenger bringing this message and it's not a popular one. In ancient history, such messengers were usually the first ones executed. I may be in that same situation," he said with a laugh.

(*Valley News,* March 4, 1968, p. 1)

McCarthy quietly brought his speech to an end as he frequently did, with a series of poetic allusions, similar to those with which he concluded his speech before the CCD in Chicago the previous December.

The message from the Administration today is a message of apprehension, a message of fear, yes—even a message of fear of fear.

This is not the real spirit of America. I do not believe that it is. This is a time to test the mood and spirit:

To offer in place of doubt—trust.

In place of expediency—right judgment.

In place of ghettos, let us have neighborhoods and communities.

In place of incredibility—integrity.

In place of murmuring, let us have clear speech; let us again hear America singing.

In place of disunity, let us have dedication of purpose.

In place of near despair, let us have hope.

This is the promise of greatness which was stated for us by Adlai Stevenson and which has brought to form and positive action in the words and actions of John Kennedy.

Let us pick up again these lost strands and weave them again into the fabric of America.

Let us sort out the music from the sounds and again respond to the trumpet and the steady drum.

(*Valley News,* March 4, 1968, p. 2)

As McCarthy ended and returned to his chair on the stage, the audience rose almost as if it were one person. Their silence during the forty-minute speech, as if bottled, was expelled in a sudden rush of extended standing applause. Hands beat against each other as if the action might reinforce their own convictions, so effectively pronounced by the speaker, and at the same time somehow vent their own individual frustration with the course of national events.

When at last the applause subsided, the student moderator called for questions. The first to rise was an army lieutenant, in uniform. The lieutenant asked whether McCarthy had received any military support during his campaign. McCarthy's reply was that it was interesting "who was willing and free to speak out," and that some retired military officers had expressed views which paralleled his own. The lieutenant went on, "Well, I just want you to know I drove two and a half hours to get up here from Fort Devens, Massachusetts, to show my support for your campaign." The lieutenant received a standing ovation from about half those in the hall. (*Valley News,* March 4, 1968, p. 1)

A series of questions followed concerning McCarthy's position on the war, how he proposed to end it, and what might be the effect on the U.S. economy of ending the military effort. On this latter point he said, "This is the first time in our nation's history war has not stimulated economic growth. Economic transition from war to peace is the least of our worries." He then received several questions about the Selective Service law, draft resistance, and conscientious objection policies. To these McCarthy advised, "Act according to your conscience," and stated that he favored a policy of "selective conscience objection." McCarthy satisfied his listeners with his responses to these questions without suggesting that the students ignore the Selective Service laws or promising unconditional amnesty to those who had broken the law.

It was on this last point that McCarthy spoke with considerable courage. He reviewed his own feeling of qualified support for the notion of war in national self-defense and the idea that a nation so threatened might compel citizens to engage in defense. He then distinguished this view from what was then occurring in the United States to support the unjustified war in Vietnam. He closed by suggesting that when the war concluded a policy of amnesty should be proposed for those who have been jailed or exiled because of their objection to the war.

His answers to the questions had brought repeated applause, even cheering, and several standing ovations. That evening Dartmouth students discovered the McCarthy campaign and would join it for its last days in New Hampshire and then follow it in large numbers as McCarthy campaigned in the other primary states.

On March 4, McCarthy was scheduled to begin a day of campaigning in the Seacoast region with a 9:00 A.M. interview on Portsmouth's radio station WBRX. Late Sunday evening he received a call from his senate staff saying that a cloture vote was expected Monday and that his vote might be required to close debate. The measure being discussed was an important civil rights bill. In spite of assured passage, it was important for McCarthy to be in Washington and voting. He left Boston at 8:50 A.M. A carefully organized schedule of campaigning in an important part of the state had to be scrapped on extremely short notice.

The morning schedule of interviews, street campaigning, meetings with local officials, travel to a speech at Phillips Exeter Academy, and several coffee receptions was relatively easy to cancel, but McCarthy had been scheduled to speak before an areawide audience that evening at a Hampton high school. The organizers refused to accept a cancellation.

Sandy Hoeh and Sandy Silverman were the first to catch the reaction when they made the cancellation calls. Next came calls to me from David Morin, Hampton area McCarthy chair, and others on Morin's program committee. The first instructions about the cancellation were to do just that, cancel McCarthy's Monday schedule. When the pressure from Hampton began to build I tried to get them to accept a celebrity substitute. This was not acceptable. Morin began calling McCarthy's Washington office urging that the senator's schedule be changed to have him return to New Hampshire in time for the Hampton speech. Morin had called the airlines, he knew what flights were available from Washington to Boston, and promised to pick McCarthy up in Boston and drive him to Hampton in time for the originally scheduled speech. I confirmed the importance of the Hampton appearance.

In the midst of these machinations, McCarthy missed the bell call for the cloture vote. He had been on the senate floor once, had returned to his office to conduct some business, and had expected to be called by his staff for the actual vote. Someone missed the cue, and when it was discovered McCarthy rushed to the senate, but arrived a minute or so after the roll call had closed. At about the same time, the senator's office confirmed that he would return to New Hampshire for the Hampton speech and would complete the original schedule for that evening.

Missing the cloture vote gave the Johnson leaders a chance to attack McCarthy for the first time since the campaign had begun. The first volley came from state Democratic chair William Craig who claimed that McCarthy "ran out on his responsibility as a senator when he failed to vote on cloture. . . ." The story had been widely covered by the national press since McCarthy had broken off from a previously announced campaign schedule to travel to Washington. When he missed the vote McCarthy explained that he was "one minute too late" and the backers of cloture already had the required two-thirds vote they needed. "If they had needed my vote," he said, "they would have waited until I arrived before calling for the senate vote on the issue." (*Portsmouth Herald*, March 6, 1968) Not willing to accept this explanation Craig charged:

> . . . McCarthy . . . is putting political aspirations before the hopes of the millions of Americans to whom this vote meant a promise as important as freedom itself.
>
> McCarthy's inaction in the Senate this week represents a terribly warped sense of value and priorities such as has seldom been displayed in American political history. . . .

Craig then suggested the voters "express their displeasure with Sen. McCarthy's irresponsible behavior by writing in President Johnson's name on the ballot." (*Portsmouth Herald*, March 6, 1968) The governor and Merrimack County

Democratic chair, Melvin Bolden, also attacked McCarthy for failing to cast a cloture vote. It was the beginning of a shift in the Johnson campaign strategy from ignoring McCarthy to one of directly attacking his positions and actions.

McCarthy arrived thirty to forty minutes late for the Hampton speech but an enthusiastic crowd greeted him in the packed auditorium of Hampton's Winnicunnut High School. Hampton's leading Democratic citizen, Bill Dunfey, commented afterwards that he had never seen such a response to a candidate, Republican or Democrat, in this conservative community.

What McCarthy had missed, when it was necessary to cancel his Portsmouth schedule, was an endorsement editorial timed by the editor to immediately follow his visit to the port city. Titled: "How to Vote Against the War," the editors captured a sentiment that would be repeated often in other editorials and among the voters in the seven days remaining before the election:

> Despair over our ever-deepening involvement in Vietnam is settling upon the country like an unshakable pall, and although the gloomy atmosphere is punctuated by the noise of those imbued with the spirit of protest, a general sense of hopelessness and helplessness still abides—and it continues to spread.
>
> The citizen who beholds the complicity of his country in a war which he doesn't understand, which he can find no good reason to condone, which frightens him because of its ugly implications of destructiveness and depravity, is sorely moved to seek some kind of reconcilement between his conscience and what is said to be the national interest, but the two don't correspond.
>
> From such painful introspection comes the conclusion that surely the war is wrong and that something ought to be done to bring it to a halt. But then that familiar feeling of impotence intrudes upon the private mind and leads the troubled citizen to ask: what contribution can I make to the purpose?
>
> Actually, the individual citizen can contribute a great deal, and he doesn't have to embarrass himself in the process by marching in a picket line or engaging in any other kind of unseemly display. He need only perform the ordinary duty of citizenship by considering the effect of his voting power.
>
> In New Hampshire a special opportunity of timely expression has been provided in this connection through the presidential primary. Although the war does not come into focus as a blunt question on the ballot, the effect is the same nevertheless—because the way a person votes can be intended, and made to register, as the way he feels about the war in Vietnam.
>
> Cynics may argue that it makes no difference, that no matter how many people vote in the New Hampshire primary, or how they vote, nothing in the total result will have the slightest bearing on the future course of world events. And the fact must be faced that if such a proposition had to be refuted with documented proof it would be hard to put aside. But certain things must be taken on faith, and it is such a thing that shapes our belief in this particular New Hampshire primary as an effective instrument of public expression regarding the war.

> Never was this more true than on the Democratic side of the ballot where voters of that party can directly declare their disapproval of President Johnson's war policy by backing Sen. Eugene McCarthy.
>
> While the prevailing opinion seems valid enough that Sen. McCarthy's chances of ultimate political success must be viewed with skepticism, that does not dilute the value of his candidacy a single bit. There are no illusions that, in this primary, New Hampshire Democrats are about to point a new face toward the presidency, so that has nothing to do with our recommendation for support of McCarthy. What's at issue is the war, and nothing else—and the Democratic voters of New Hampshire could have a lot to say about that if they respond to it in the right way.
>
> A strong outpouring of support for Sen. McCarthy is important, therefore—and we urge it.
>
> (*Portsmouth Herald*, March 5, 1968)

While the editorial was reassuring, what happened on March 5 in Derry was not. One of New Hampshire's larger and more rapidly growing towns, Derry is east of Manchester and in its media and economic shadow. The afternoon schedule had McCarthy campaigning at a factory gate and on Main Street, being interviewed by Conrad Quimby, the favorable editor of the local weekly newspaper and then speaking to an evening meeting of the Kiwanis-Lions Club. Quimby had tried since coming to the town to spark a liberal interest within a *Manchester Union Leader* dominated and conservative populace. He felt he had been making progress in this effort and was pleased when the local McCarthy supporters arranged the senator's visit.

Following his speech McCarthy received a nicely framed certificate honoring his visit which was inscribed in the appropriate place, "Senator Joseph E. McCarthy." When Studds and I saw the inscription we looked at each other and recalled that at one time we had thought McCarthy might do well in Manchester and its satellite towns if only people would recall the fond feelings of the *Manchester Union Leader* toward the late Wisconsin senator. Perhaps they should revive that thought and begin introducing McCarthy as "E. Joseph" instead of "Eugene J."

On March 6 McCarthy campaigned exclusively in Manchester. His schedule included a morning speech before the locally derived student body of the New Hampshire College of Accounting, an afternoon plant tour of the Pandora Sweater factory guided by Eugene Sidore (no problems this time at the factory gate as there had been on McCarthy's first visit January 26), a local radio interview, a local television interview late afternoon preparation time for radio commercials, and then an evening reception at the Sheraton-Carpenter in downtown Manchester.

Robert Lowell, the noted poet, arrived during the week to speak for McCarthy and join him in his campaigning. Lowell found the factory tours of great interest, especially when the visits took the entourage through Manchester's venerable Amoskeag Millyard. Once the largest corporation in the world, Amoskeag developed a diversified manufacturing complex that had stretched for a mile along both sides of the Merrimack River and drew its energy from that river's Amoskeag Falls. The corporation failed in the Great Depression leaving thousands of Manchester families without work and a city without an economic base. The city never quite regained either its economic power or its self-confidence. The buildings remained as a fossil of a previous age. Smaller corporations, principally textile, shoes, bottling, storage, and electronics, occupied the low-cost space of the old buildings.

Through these buildings McCarthy, with the poet Robert Lowell at his side, walked, shaking hands, greeting workers at their machines, benches, and workstations. Around them was the ever-present history of a workplace that went back four or five generations—a workplace that had shaped the lives of countless individuals.

What excited Lowell's imagination the most were the old elevators in some of the buildings. These elevators rise on tracks that guide the peaked roof of the carriage up through the hinged doors that are the floor above. Lowell felt like he was ascending to heaven through Dante's levels as the carriage silently pushed up from one floor to the next. On each floor the riders saw another group of workers busy at another series of tasks. Without question this was a different campaign. It had its own traveling poet who gave special sight to what is often viewed as a cynical, impersonal, and occasionally crass contemporary activity—the political campaign.

McCarthy campaigned on March 7 in Nashua during the morning, attending a brunch that involved persons from wards 1, 2, 3, 8, and 9, which had been pegged by local leaders and the canvass as being particularly important. A noon address followed at Rivier College, a Catholic school for women where Mrs. McCarthy's earlier visit had stirred considerable interest in the campaign among both the students and the faculty. McCarthy then lunched with local committee members in a prominent downtown restaurant before leaving New Hampshire to catch an early afternoon flight to Washington.

McCarthy's announced schedule for Thursday, March 7, had him returning to Manchester to street campaign, visit the telephone company offices, and attend a series of receptions in private homes. Instead McCarthy had been invited as a special guest to attend the Radio and Television Correspondents dinner at the Shoreham Hotel in Washington, D.C. It seemed more important for him to attend that gathering now that his campaign was receiving national attention than to keep the prearranged New Hampshire schedule. Some events were canceled and others, such as the evening receptions, had a celebrity substitute for the senator. He remained in Washington until 3:40 P.M. Friday, March 8 when he boarded a flight for his return to Boston.

Scheduling had now become the principal activity of the campaign team. Sandy Hoeh, Sandy Silverman, many of the local committee leaders, and I spent a great deal of time building or adjusting schedules. To help tighten the schedule, Bill Johnson, the New York publisher, kept his twin-engine Beechcraft Baron available in New Hampshire. On March 8, I had arranged with Johnson to meet McCarthy at Logan Airport, fly him to Berwick, Maine, the airfield closest to Rochester, New Hampshire, where an evening schedule could begin. To lose a crowded Friday shopping night just before the final weekend of the campaign was something I felt the campaign could not afford.

In the early campaign planning, I could identify only a few contacts in the Rochester, Somersworth, and Dover area and none that would serve as a focal point for a local McCarthy organization. Dover, five miles from the university town of Durham, became a special project of university faculty and students. Eventually a strong joint Dover-Durham committee developed which then spread to neighboring Somersworth and Rochester.

On March 8, Johnson piloted his plane out of the congested night air space of Boston toward the isolated airport in Berwick. With him, in addition to McCarthy, were McCarthy's traveling aide, Charles Callanan, and myself. Somewhat later than scheduled, we landed. A caravan of three cars were waiting, and within a few moments we were off on the fifteen- to twenty-minute ride to Rochester. The first stop was Mayor John Shaw's city hall office. There McCarthy was greeted by the crusty figure of the mayor and his sidekick, Henry Paradise, chair of the Rochester City Democratic Committee. Without an identifiable local McCarthy organization in Rochester, the McCarthy campaign had stumbled upon an old political organization now revived to help McCarthy's candidacy. Shaw and McCarthy exchanged quips with the press looking on, Shaw wished McCarthy well, then McCarthy shook hands with the crowd that had been attracted to the city hall. The brief visit concluded, the caravan headed to Dover, about six miles to the southeast.

Easily accessible from Rochester, and a number of smaller Maine and New Hampshire towns, Dover was a regional shopping community. It was Friday, the traditional New England shopping night. The local McCarthy committee had organized a shopping center schedule which included stationing greeting committees at each of the four centers. Before McCarthy arrived, the supporters handed out balloons, buttons, brochures, waved placards, passed out coffee, and scoured the stores to gather a lively, welcoming crowd. When the caravan arrived at the first center, Siegel's, a large crowd was in place and McCarthy was given a warm welcome as he circulated, shaking hands, and then stopped to make a few brief remarks. The scene was repeated at each of the three other stops, and at the last he toured the old textile mill that had been converted into Sawyer Mills Factory Outlet. By 9:00 P.M. the entourage was on the road back to the Wayfarer satisfied with both the schedule and the reception.

Instant scheduling, schedule changing, and schedule additions had developed to a fine art that last weekend of the campaign. By the end of Friday, March 8, almost all of the target cities and larger towns had been visited at least once. Virtually all of the usual activities that could be included in a schedule had been included.

On the last weekend, we concentrated on things and places that could be done or reached easily from Manchester. No one wanted to spend much time traveling. The only exception was the schedule for Saturday morning, March 9. Franklin, New Hampshire's smallest city, is a bit off the campaign route and had not been visited earlier. Eugene Daniell, the former RFK committee organizer, had shifted his energies to McCarthy and during the intervening weeks had generated considerable local McCarthy interest. He had continually urged that a visit to Franklin be scheduled, but, until almost the last days, this had not been possible.

Daniell and his McCarthy committee developed a tight morning of campaigning. Saturday morning is not a particularly good time to visit, but in Franklin the local textile mill, J. P. Stevens, worked and McCarthy began a handshaking tour at 9:00 A.M. Then followed the usual newspaper interview, two radio interviews, and a handshaking tour of the downtown shopping centers, and shops. McCarthy moved quickly through the thin Saturday shoppers, through the stores, and was ready for the reception in the Franklin Savings Bank's community room almost twenty minutes before the scheduled 11:25 A.M. time. To extend the time a bit more Daniell led McCarthy to several side street shops and to the subarea office of the *Concord Daily Monitor.*

While visiting in the office, a call came through from the *Monitor*'s Concord office saying that the Johnson committee had just issued a press release charging that McCarthy had promised to grant unconditional amnesty to all draft evaders. The verbal account of the release indicated that the source of the charge had been McCarthy's speech in Hanover that previous Sunday. McCarthy issued a brief denial alleging that the charge was a serious distortion of his response to the amnesty question he had fielded from the Dartmouth audience.

A friendly crowd welcomed McCarthy in the community room. He spoke, answered questions both from the local citizens and the press, shared in the refreshments, and appeared anxious to leave although there would be more than two hours between his Franklin stop and the next scheduled event, street campaigning in Manchester. Anticipating that some time would be opening in the schedule and that, on the return to Manchester, we would be passing through Concord, I called ahead to the Concord headquarters to say I would bring McCarthy in for a quick visit. McCarthy had not been to the headquarters since his first campaign visit to New Hampshire on January 26. He had not seen the organization or the activity that had so impressed the reporters. I felt it would be good not only for the workers to be visited by the candidate but for McCarthy to see what had happened on his behalf during the weeks since January 26. Just before leaving Franklin, I suggested the schedule change to McCarthy, who agreed, and without notifying the press of the change, drove McCarthy to Concord. The press bus went back to Manchester to join McCarthy for the next stop on the announced schedule.

The advance warning gave the Concord crew, led by Curt Gans and Sam Brown, time to call some of the local committee members to have them come to the headquarters and also time to promote additional order in a frantic but amazingly orderly space. I had promised to drive slowly over the fifteen-mile road between Franklin and Concord to allow Gans the time to assemble the welcome. When I arrived at the door of the Pleasant Street extension storefront a small crowd was waiting. McCarthy stepped inside and was obviously taken by the transformation. What had been a drab, hastily decorated front room was now a tightly arranged series of desks with people busily working at telephones, typewriters, recording data on charts, discussing canvassing details with newly arrived volunteers, or straightening the campaign literature on display near the door.

McCarthy slowly wandered from section to section in the headquarters eventually even reaching to the depths of the notorious basement. At each stop he responded to the volunteers' questions, friendly encouragement, and explanations of their respective tasks. Both McCarthy and the hard-working volunteers were buoyed by the forty-five-minute visit. Most of the volunteers had not met McCarthy before. To them he had become almost an imaginary figure to whom they had become attached through his words and the sense that he shared their concerns.

New Hampshire's winter weather produces its own surprises which, when adverse, are a special hurdle facing political campaign managers. An aspect that few recall, however, is that New Hampshire winters sometimes offer a few brilliantly clear, sunny, and even springlike days. For McCarthy's first campaign day, January 26, a snowstorm passed over the state the previous evening which then cleared for one of those sparkling, coats-unbuttoned days. With each schedule went the presumption that the weather might cause a delay or a cancellation. Flights from Washington to Boston or from New York to New Hampshire airports, and especially the latter, are risky during the winter. Once McCarthy arrived either in Boston or New Hampshire, weather would not be a factor. The importance of the winter recreation industry to New Hampshire and clear roads to the state's industry and commerce dictates that for all but a short time during the height of a storm New Hampshire's main roads are not only passable but usually clear to the pavement.

If there is such a thing as luck in a campaign, then weather is its most important attribute in a New Hampshire presidential primary campaign. From the first day Studds and I commented on the phenomenon of "McCarthy weather." When the Senator was in New Hampshire the weather was always near perfect for his campaigning.

The one weather-induced phenomenon that McCarthy sensed as he traveled New Hampshire's secondary roads was the frost heave that inflates the surface of many roads into something resembling a roller coaster. The warming weather of late February melts the snow water which seeps under the less well constructed, sloped, and drained older roads. Alternating freezes and thaws produce large hills and valleys in what during other seasons of the year are smooth roads. McCarthy's reaction to the frost heaves was that they were not what the natives called them, but indications of the ground swell being produced by his campaign. Because of the relative mildness of the winter, the ground swells were more frequent and more intense than usual.

Saturday, March 9 produced the best of the McCarthy weather. The day began cold and overcast when McCarthy toured Franklin. By the time he reached Concord the sky had cleared. A warm sun shown, and people were beginning to come outside sensing in the warmth and brilliance a hint of spring. McCarthy was scheduled to campaign in Manchester's shopping centers and to street campaign from 2:00 to 4:30 P.M.

He began with a walking tour of the main commercial district of Manchester's westside Kelley Street. The usual crew moved ahead of the senator preannouncing his campaigning. Following McCarthy was the largest contingent of reporters and cameramen that had yet been attracted to the campaign. The excitement of such a crowd slowed traffic and drew people out of the stores, but the weather was just as important. The Kelley Street tour, scheduled for not more than thirty minutes took at least forty-five minutes. Stops at four shopping centers where volunteers had gone on ahead to attract a crowd produced the same outpouring, but it was along Manchester's Elm Street that it seemed that the campaign had reached its peak. The bright, late afternoon sun, warm and refreshing, turned McCarthy's street campaign into a parade.

As McCarthy campaigned south along Elm Street shoppers and shopkeepers tumbled out on the street to see what was going on. McCarthy shook hundreds of hands as friendly faces and words of encouragement came from those now lining the sidewalk. It was a day to be outside and many had lingered at corners, taken a seat on a bench, or just strolled in the sun. It seemed as McCarthy passed among them that finally something was beginning to happen in Manchester. McCarthy was no longer a stranger. People sought out his handshake and congratulated him on his candidacy. It was an unexpected afternoon for candidate, campaign, and reporters. A perfect ending for a campaign that had been thought to be totally without prospect, possibility of recognition, or potential for impact—especially in New Hampshire's most conservative political community, Manchester.

CONCLUDING THE CAMPAIGN

Traditionally New Hampshire campaigns end with some large gathering on one evening of the final weekend. Studds and I had kept that option in mind throughout the campaign but had been reluctant to risk scheduling such an event. We were concerned about attracting a crowd, conflict with other events, and problems with the weather. As McCarthy's prospects improved, Studds and I decided to plan a speech for Saturday evening, March 9, in Manchester. The traditional site for campaign concluding rallies is the National Guard Armory.

When I inquired about its availability for the date I wanted, I found that the Democratic State Committee had reserved the time. The press had speculated for some time that President Johnson might make a surprise, last-minute visit to New Hampshire just before the primary election. To preserve this option the Democratic State Committee reserved the armory and could hold it to a point where others would be prevented from planning events in the building for the optioned times.

We chose the ballroom of the Sheraton-Carpenter Hotel in downtown Manchester. The capacity could exceed five hundred, and there was an audio-connected room nearby that could handle an overflow crowd. Further, the room had a lengthy history of hosting important New Hampshire political events including several visits by John F. Kennedy and the famous Lyndon Johnson speech of his 1964 campaign.

Since celebrities would be in the state during the final weekend of the campaign, it seemed reasonable to use some in the program of the evening. Robert Ryan had campaigned for several days and agreed to perform as well as introduce Senator McCarthy. Sandy Silverman tentatively scheduled several others for the program. As the time for the meeting approached, McCarthy made it clear that he wanted a simple program and especially a simple introduction. One aspect of his presidential campaign that McCarthy had come to dislike was the lengthy introduction by some prominent person. Not infrequently the introduction distorted the tone and spirit of

McCarthy's speech. For Studds and myself this was the perfect setting for an emotional cap to the campaign. McCarthy would be introduced as simply, "The next president of the United States."

To accomplish this meant adjusting the program significantly. There could only be one star and that had to be McCarthy. Anyone else would be a distraction from the emotional high point of the introduction. This meant that Sandy Silverman and I had to cancel several invitations to participate that had already been issued to visiting celebrities, and then we had to downgrade Robert Ryan's role.

After McCarthy completed his downtown Manchester street campaigning, I drove him to his rooms at the Wayfarer and then went to meet Robert Ryan who was dining with his Dartmouth undergraduate son. Ryan had already selected several passages from a poem he intended to read as his participation in the evening program. He saw them as important reflections on his own attitude toward the Vietnam War and the importance of McCarthy's candidacy. I said I agreed the passages were appropriate but that the scope of the program had been changed. Ryan would introduce McCarthy using no more than a variation on the phrase, "It is my privilege to introduce to you the next president of the United States, Senator Eugene J. McCarthy."

Since this would be the concluding event of the campaign, the Concord headquarters had worked for a considerable part of the week in an attempt to generate the Saturday night crowd. McCarthy committees within driving range of Manchester were contacted, volunteers had leafleted as McCarthy campaigned and radio messages announced the rally played throughout the day. The volunteers working that weekend had been invited to the speech but were asked to fill the nearby Manchester Room leaving the ballroom open for New Hampshire people.

The report at 7:45 was that the ballroom was more than half full already and a steady stream was filling the remaining spaces. When I picked up McCarthy at 8:30 the last report was that the ballroom was jammed. The Manchester Room was also packed and the lobby leading to both was a mass of milling supporters all trying to squeeze into one room or the other. The crowd estimates exceeded two thousand. Getting McCarthy into the ballroom and behind the stage began to appear to be a problem. A fundamental role of scheduling, even in those pre-Secret Service days, was to scout for two entrances and two exits for each room. The only way to the stage was through the lobby, then along a corridor that paralleled the main floor of the ballroom.

An immediate stir rippled through the crowd as McCarthy appeared at the door. As he quickly moved through the crowd to the entrance to the corridor, an enthusiastic lobby crowd surged toward him. Ryan waited just off stage at the end of the corridor. McCarthy and Ryan chatted a moment. Robert Ryan was introduced, and with a phrase from the poem he had intended to read, Robert Ryan presented McCarthy as agreed. As Ryan spoke the words the audience rose as one from their chairs and cheered. It was the hoped for climax.

The cheering continued for several moments while McCarthy stood alone on the stage vainly trying to calm the crowd so that he could speak. His address summarized his campaign but reached for new themes that had come from the experiences of the past weeks in New Hampshire. He said his campaign had become "a movement of all the people of America. Even some members of the Senate are joining. Politicians are sometimes slow to move. This is a people's movement and now they have begun to join." (*Sunday Herald-Traveler,* March 10, 1968, p. 1) The *Herald-Traveler*'s account of the speech read:

> McCarthy said it was "distressing to witness the decline in American prestige since 1963. Not because it is nice to be popular but because that decline is the most serious threat to our ultimate security."
>
> McCarthy said John F. Kennedy was elected "partly on the basis of his pledge to restore American prestige around the world. And he succeeded. Yet the harsh fact of the matter is that our prestige today is lower than it was in 1960; and that the achievements of 1961, 1962 and 1963 have been steadily eroded."
>
> McCarthy described as "the saddest of all" a situation under which the President of the United States "cannot ride through the streets of the great cities of South America, with the exception of Mexico City, or even through Europe for fear of hostile demonstrations. Yet every President—Roosevelt Truman, Eisenhower and Kennedy—was greeted with enthusiasm and acclaim in those same continents."
>
> McCarthy concluded:
>
> "We are in danger of becoming an international outcast—a giant to be feared and dealt with, and the object of suspicion and resentment in other lands. No country, not even the United States, can afford callous disregard for the sentiments of the world. To do so is to follow a most shortsighted and dangerous course. And we will pay a mounting price, for prestige and respect mean influence. And our influence is eroded."
>
> (*Sunday Herald-Traveler,* March 10, 1968, pp. 1–44)

His speech was devoted almost entirely to foreign policy concerns. He had taken the "high road" and not responded to the charges from the Johnson campaign or references back to issues that had earlier shaped his campaign. This was the chance to summarize and then to give meaning to the Tuesday election and the thrust of his candidacy after New Hampshire. In the course of the campaign he had addressed war, domestic issues, civil rights and civil liberties concerns, and now concluded with a broad foreign policy statement. Regardless of what he had to say that evening, those in the crowd had assembled to praise their candidate. His speech called for them to rise toward deeper issues. He would not jibe them with a recollection of anecdotes of the past six weeks or engage them in a mutually reenforcing congratulatory exercise. He reached out once again to the intelligence of those in his audience. They listened, emphasized with their applause, and reaffirmed their resolve with a cheering, standing, stamping ovation when he finished. In almost all respects the campaign in New Hampshire was over for Senator McCarthy. For those who had assembled, the tasks of getting the vote to the polls would now begin with added vigor.

With McCarthy scheduled to be in New Hampshire until election day, the campaign continued to use his time although the climax was reached Saturday evening.

On Sunday morning those from New Hampshire who had worked on the state and local committees gathered at the Wayfarer for a brunch with their candidate. After Studds and I gave a brief pep talk, Senator McCarthy thanked the group for its efforts. His thanks were couched in language that left little doubt as who should take pride in the effort. Rather than thanking the workers for efforts on specifically his behalf, he retained the posture that it was a people's movement and that he was simply the personification of the issues rather than the wellspring.

The source of any success that the campaign might achieve came, as McCarthy asserted, much less from his actual candidacy than it did from the willingness of people like those assembled to become involved on behalf of their own concerns. Regardless of the results of Tuesday's election, and McCarthy was most encouraged by the predictions, the emphasis should remain more upon the accomplishments of the many who had turned their concern into political organization than upon the candidate.

It was, unquestionably, a unique and, in some ways, confusing posture for a candidate to take. McCarthy still had not accepted the notion that his candidacy was more than an effort to focus attention on issues. McCarthy had become a candidate December 21 to permit a test in the presidential primaries on the issues in dispute. He had not announced his candidacy with the expectation of being elected. Now that the New Hampshire campaign seemed close to success, a transmutation was underway. For the first time during the campaign, Senator McCarthy had been introduced as the "next president of the United States" to a New Hampshire audience. The audience had now come to believe it was possible to go all of the way, and, to a degree still discomforting to McCarthy, he himself had begun to recognize the change as well. He did, however, still understand that it was then and would continue to be the ground swell of the public, organized in campaigns, committees, and as delegates, that might make such a result possible. Keeping the distinction between himself as a charismatic leader and himself as a focal point for action was an important attribute of McCarthy's success.

The thanks that McCarthy felt should be extended to the workers in the campaign was less thanks from him than from each individual to themselves. To him the campaign success came from his sense in the personal pride that each individual should have for making the commitment to join in the protest and then in the personal pride each should sense from the result. Given this, thanks from McCarthy or thanks from anyone from those outside the effort for the fact that the effort had occurred would be a misrepresentation of what had and was happening. To McCarthy the movement was the totality of hundreds even thousands of individual decisions to seek a change. Once an individual had made that decision and had become involved in the campaign, the credit was his or hers alone and not something that could be amplified by a pat on the shoulder from the candidate who himself had responded to his own concern.

After the brunch, McCarthy and his family went to private church services in Nashua. McCarthy disliked press coverage of his religious observances and did not want the location of the church he was attending released to the press. He was personally offended by Lyndon Johnson's practice of attending several services of differing denominations on a given Sunday and then, as was occasionally reported, driving by several other churches as the services were letting out. To McCarthy his religion was personal and private, but for the sake of the campaign and a press corps that had nothing to do on a Sunday morning, the church McCarthy and his family attended in Nashua was quietly leaked to the reporters.

As with previous Nashua visits, the local committee had scheduled a semiprivate luncheon at a popular family restaurant in the downtown. McCarthy had now become a familiar figure. Without intruding on those dining, local workers would take McCarthy to meet people in the restaurant they knew and while circulating in this way McCarthy received friendly greetings and words of encouragement.

Between 2:00 and 3:15 P.M., McCarthy joined a reception in his honor at the Nashua Knights of Columbus Hall which concluded the Nashua campaign. At 4:00 P.M. he arrived at a packed house reception at the Manchester Jewish Community Center where his brief remarks drew sustained applause. He remained in the hall long enough to shake hands with most in the audience. With his speech of the previous evening, the brunch in the morning, and now a reception, the campaign seemed much less a political activity than some form of a "progressive" social party. Sunday's receptions had the tone of victory parties. Campaign stories and anecdotes were already becoming legends as McCarthy workers and supporters related their experiences and recalled the bleak early days in January and early February.

Soon McCarthy would be gone from New Hampshire and on to other states and other primaries. These receptions were the last chance to share with him the experiences and relationships that had grown from the campaign. After Tuesday, March 12, most sensed that the fleeting moments would have passed and things would not be quite the same again. The reality of New Hampshire political life would return as well as the dismal season that New England is during March and April's muddy, cold, damp, and gray days.

The end of a campaign is a strange time. There are a few spots to be visited here and there, and a few requests for visits that could not be filled earlier seem somehow to find a space in the waning hours of the effort. For sometime there had been a request in the Manchester headquarters to have McCarthy meet with a group of Manchester nuns. Sunday evening was the time. After dinner, McCarthy and I, who had been driving McCarthy's campaign car for several days, slipped away to visit the convent where approximately thirty-five nuns had assembled to hear him talk. McCarthy enjoyed clerical audiences since he could draw on his considerable knowledge of the differences in the religious orders and their traditions within the Roman Catholic church.

In spite of his best efforts to crack the rather stony faces of the nuns, he was able to cause only a minor stir here and there. Then followed questions that revealed a sharp split within the convent between the older politically conservative nuns and the younger politically liberal nuns. It became an experience that McCarthy thoroughly enjoyed as he responded to both shades of political questioning and sought to reenforce the sentiments of the liberal members.

Monday morning I drove McCarthy, Richard Goodwin, and Jack Parr to Boston where McCarthy and Parr taped the election eve program. On the return I arranged one of the "instant scheduling" visits for McCarthy in an important community that had been missed during the campaign, Salem.

Arthur Herzog, the New York City writer who managed the Salem office, pulled from his "shelf" of possible campaign activities a schedule that included several plant tours, a hastily organized reception of local supporters in the headquarters, a main street walking tour, and a visit to a nearby shopping center. Since this had not been a scheduled campaign day, the news reporters were resting in Manchester until the activities of the next day, March 12. Herzog called Manchester, told the press office that McCarthy would be campaigning in Salem, and within moments a full crew of reporters and miscellaneous headquarters personnel were on the press bus heading for Salem.

Later as McCarthy left the last store in the shopping center with the reporters pressing at all sides, an elderly women approached him with an air that seemed hostile. She began, "My grandson is fighting in Vietnam." It seemed that this would be the moment when McCarthy would be assaulted for his lack of patriotism and commitment to "our boys" fighting abroad. Instead she said, "I don't know why he's there and I want him home as soon as possible. Senator McCarthy I'm going to vote for you tomorrow and get the rest of my family to do the same." A better ending could not have been staged.

During the return drive to Manchester, McCarthy relaxed obviously savoring the final coup of the morning and his personal satisfaction with his performance during the earlier television taping session. He would now wait at the Wayfarer for the election results, working privately, meeting with reporters, and visiting with supporters.

ELECTION DAY ORGANIZATION

Gans and I began developing the election day plans. The first task was to assign one of the volunteers the job of evaluating what was needed to ensure that the McCarthy vote got to the polls. For this task Richard Norling, a Yale undergraduate student, was selected. Rich developed a letter that was approved by us and sent to the local McCarthy committee chairs on February 22. The memorandum read:

> Tuesday, March 12, is fast approaching, and it is time to give some thought to preparations for activities on election day itself. Our main activities will include providing McCarthy poll watchers, rides to the polls, and volunteers to get out the McCarthy vote.
>
> We are asking you to appoint one person (it could be yourself) to coordinate election day activities for your local area. This person should plan to spend some time each day getting local volunteers to work for McCarthy on election day, and should be able to spend election day at your local headquarters coordinating these volunteers.
>
> Enclosed is a list of cities and towns with a large number of registered Democrats in your area. Your election day coordinator should be responsible for recruiting and coordinating volunteers in these cities and towns. Obviously, the largest towns are most important, and should be organized first.
>
> Here are some things your election day coordinator should start on right away:

- Call city or town clerks to obtain opening and closing times and addresses of polling places for each city ward or town. Keep a copy of this information for yourself, and please also send me a copy as soon as you get it.
- Find a person in each city ward or town to coordinate drivers on election day This job can best be handled from a name in each area. The only necessity is a telephone, and somebody who will answer it on Monday and Tuesday, March 11 and 12th. Ads containing these telephone numbers will be placed in newspapers prior to the election.
- Find drivers to take people to vote. An approximate guideline for the number of drivers you will need in each city ward or town is one for every 400 registered Democrats—your own local experience may suggest a different number of drivers. You should also try to have a few extra drivers on hand at your headquarters to help out in areas that need extra drivers.
- Find poll watchers for each polling place.
- Obtain maps for drivers. The location of the polling place and the driver coordinator's home should be marked on each map. If canvassing is being done in your area, copies of the maps provided to canvassers can be made.
- Find a volunteer lawyer to be available to your headquarters in case of election procedure complaints on election day.
- Stockpile election day supplies, and set them away in a special place reserved for election day. Suggestions: a 3 × 5 note pad for each driver coordinator and several for your headquarters, 2 posters for the sides of each car you plan to have, crepe paper and masking tape for decorating cars, enough McCarthy buttons for election day workers, and enough McCarthy literature to put a small stack in each car on election day.
- As you get volunteers for election day activities, please send me their names, addresses, telephone numbers, and where and what they have volunteered to do. Also keep a copy for yourself. The week before the election, I will send out instruction sheets to the volunteer workers; they will also receive thank you notes after the election. Your volunteer workers should be on duty all the time polling places are open. You may want to set up shifts for volunteers who can work only part of the day.

Please try to keep me continually informed on your progress in acquiring an election day organization. I shall try to keep in frequent contact with you by telephone.

Your estimates of the number of drivers, poll watchers, and volunteers to distribute literature outside polling places or to turn out the McCarthy vote are important. We expect to have out of-state volunteers to fill in gaps where you are unable to obtain your own local volunteers. However, local volunteers are much more effective because they know a large number of voters, know their way around town, etc. In addition, the job of assigning out-of-town volunteers where they are needed most will probably be a large one. For all these reasons, it is extremely important for you to do as much as you possibly can to build your own election day organization.

I expect to be in the Concord Headquarters at the following times:

Feb. 26–27 Monday evening through Tuesday afternoon.

Mar. 1–5 Friday evening through Tuesday afternoon.

Mar. 7–12 Thursday evening through Tuesday evening.

If my help is required at other times, I may be able to make myself available. [Rich would return to New Haven to keep up with his classes as much as he could during the other times.]

Please appoint an election day coordinator as soon as possible. I shall contact you next Monday evening (February 26th).

Sincerely yours,

Richard Norling

Attached to the letter was a listing titled, "Election Day Assignment Regions." A note on the list stated, "Numbers in parentheses are the number of registered Democrats in each town or city."

The strategy Studds and I had developed early in the campaign had now been refined into a series of target cities and towns clustered around area headquarters. In addition to the preparations Norling outlined in his February 22 letter, area committee chairs and election day activity coordinators were asked to attend a meeting at the Concord headquarters, Sunday evening, March 3. There Gans and I reviewed preparations for election day, adding several aspects that had not been covered in Norling's earlier letter. The most important of these additions was the suggestion that each area headquarters organize telephone or canvassing recontact procedures to remind those who had been canvassed to vote. The basis for this recontact was to be the canvasser's card and the notation on that card indicating whether the person contacted was a "1," "2," or "3" respondent to the canvass. Those "favorable to McCarthy (the "1" voter) and those "leaning toward McCarthy" (the "2" voter) would be called or recanvassed to remind them to vote. The "3" voters would also be contacted in hopes of convincing them to vote for McCarthy. This recontact would be made especially in the case of those who had been canvassed early in the campaign. The recent escalation in the campaign and McCarthy's extensive press attention were presumed to be having a sufficient effect on the "3" voter to justify the recontact.

The recontact activity was not intricately organized in the outlying areas. Only those area committees with sufficient volunteers to devote to the effort were able to do much more than the minimum suggested in Norling's initial letter. For Manchester, an extensive recontacting operation was established. Al Shepard had continued his market and motivational analysis of the Manchester voter and was producing a series of new and, he hoped, convincing arguments that could be used in canvassing and telephoning that might improve McCarthy's vote. Shepard worked his small crew through the office of Maria Carrier's husband, using his telephones and occasionally his office staff when they were not otherwise occupied.

Curtis Gans ordered telephones for a telephone bank to be set up in vacant space above an Elm Street store in Manchester. Ann Hart, Senator Philip Hart's daughter, was given the responsibility for staffing and managing the telephoning. The bank went into operation during the week of March 3.

To gather election results and to report any voting irregularities, Gans had installed ten or fifteen new lines and telephones in the Concord headquarters. His previous election experience had been in large cities where it is often difficult to get the returns quickly and one form of voting irregularity or another is possible. What Gans did not understand was that in New Hampshire almost all of the election machinery is controlled by the majority, the Republican Party. With Republicans in control "stealing" the election for Lyndon Johnson would not be in their best interests. They would want to report as many McCarthy votes as possible in order to reduce Johnson's political credibility.

As for reporting the results, the news-gathering services, principally AP, UPI, and the television networks, had pooled polling place coverage and all relied upon the volunteer services of the New Hampshire League of Women Voters to report town and city ward returns. The "pool" vote report was centrally collected then distributed to each wire service and network. The service was efficient, accurate, and complete as well as being considerably ahead of anything that could be collected by the McCarthy campaign organization. With more than four hundred voting districts to cover, only the pool could do the job. Gans' extra telephones would be silent most of the evening.

What the election day activity depended on the most was the competence of the respective local organizations. People experienced with the political campaigns and the vote production of their respective communities were the key to reaching the McCarthy vote. The canvassing results gave the basis for knowing where McCarthy was strong or weak. In the strong districts, the local committees organized to pull voters concentrated their planning where the work would produce the best returns.

As the demands on the local organizations for candidate and celebrity schedules ended and the canvassing activity reached its final peak during the weekend of March 9 and 10, election day preparations became the highest priority concern. In addition to the advertising blitz on the radio, television, and through the newspapers, a number of local committees distributed printed reminders to vote and last-minute appeals to vote for Senator McCarthy. Strong local organizations supported a number of simultaneous activities during the final weekend.

The local committees that were less well organized assumed only the highest priority tasks as directed from the state headquarters. As had been the case throughout the campaign, the managers had tried to offer a shelf of activities that would stimulate the weaker and more recently formed area organizations as well as challenging the strong, well-developed, early committees.

Only one separate activity was allowed to develop with the sanction of the campaign and its support. That was the efforts of the Vietnam Veterans Against the War. Members spoke separately to separate audiences. They campaigned in their own way on street corners with leaflets and placards. They organized and conducted their own press conferences, presenting their own view of the issues. During the last weekend of the campaign they escalated their efforts considerably. They held a press conference on Saturday, March 9, announcing that their members would be posted on street corners in a number of New Hampshire cities to answer questions about the war and to urge support for Senator McCarthy's candidacy.

THE RED HERRING CHARGE AND NEW HAMPSHIRE POLITICS

Legends of New Hampshire politics and especially Manchester politics are filled with tales of how last-minute charges changed the results of close elections. Almost a political fossil in the way the city frequently reacts to the last-minute charge, Manchester acted as if it were still in the age of the "yellow journalists" and the issue distorters of the late nineteenth century rather than in the age of multimedia news and skepticism. A charge need not be made through public media to be given credibility. It might simply be a rumor circulated in a few crucial places and spread rapidly in the ethnic communities of the city during the last hours of a campaign. Manchester was a divided city physically, socially, ethnically, and economically. The physical barrier is the Merrimack River which separates the city's predominantly French-Canadian west side from the commercial district and the Irish, Yankee, Greek, and upper-income communities of the east side.

A long history of social, economic, religious, and especially ethnic conflict had built numerous unseen barriers between neighborhoods, parishes, social clubs, and even financial institutions and professional organizations. Each had created its own communications networks and response mechanisms. The most sophisticated of these was the network within the French-Canadian community. The church, parochial schools, and the French language had kept the French community a tight, provincial, and socially regulated entity for generations.

Only since the advent of television in the post-World War II period had the tightness of that community begun to crack. The first cracks began to appear in the late 1950s and widened in the 1960s as the younger members of the community sought education, jobs, and status outside the traditional community. The second factor was a change in the educational emphasis of the parochial schools. Up to the late 1950s French was taught as the primary language. In the 1960s English became the primary language with French language education remaining an important part of the curriculum. The shift slowly began to provide the language facility that made it possible for the young people to succeed in post-secondary education. The language barrier had kept the French-Canadian communities in the United States closely tied internally and to their source of culture and heritage, French Canada, and the French-Canadian Catholic Church.

Achievement outside of the community, and especially economic and academic achievement, was not viewed as a particularly desirable objective. The exception was for a few to return to Canada for education in the law or priesthood or as medical doctors. To do this was a mark of exceptional ability and received the respect of the community. The rest joined the industrial work force. Few were comfortable in political activity although the French-Canadians were predominantly registered as Democrats.

In a city like Manchester, which was once dominated politically by the Republican Yankees and then for several generations by the Irish, the French-Canadians were usually at the bottom of the socioeconomic/political ladder. As the French-Canadian population grew beyond the 50 percent mark, an inevitable conflict developed between the two principal ethnic populations—the politically skilled Irish and the culturally isolated French-Canadians.

In Manchester city politics, an eventual accommodation was achieved between the two groups that centered on politically sensitive jobs. If the police chief was Irish his deputy would be French, and the fire chief would be French and his deputy Irish. The scheme carried into the political jobs in the postal service, city boards and commissions, and into the board of mayor and alderman.

Politics outside of Manchester was quite another thing. In order for a Democrat to win one of the three statewide electoral offices (governor or the two U.S. Senate seats) that candidate would have to carry Manchester by a substantial margin. From 1912 until 1962, only once had the Democratic Party been successful in electing one of its candidates to statewide office. That happened in 1932 when former Governor Fred Brown was elected to the U.S. Senate. In order to reduce what would normally be expected to be a substantial Democratic plurality from Manchester, leaders of New Hampshire's Republican Party had learned to play the Manchester political instrument with great precision. Accommodation reached within the city did not extend to statewide offices.

The first line of battle for those who sought to play the Manchester political instrument was in the selection of candidates before the state primary. Often the Democratic ticket was loaded with unknown candidates with ethnically recognizable names. For the most part these were "straw candidates" who had entered or been encouraged to enter solely to reduce the vote for the one candidate with the highest potential for seriously challenging the incumbent Republican.

If by chance a strong candidate did slip through the maze of the nominating primary then several other tactics were still available, principally the "red herring charge" and the "backfire" issue. By generating a plausible rumor and then spreading it judiciously within the communications network of one ethnic community or the other just before an election, it was possible to change the Manchester vote enough to defeat the Democrat and elect the Republican. The rumor had to be reasonably credible, spread through credible channels, spread so late that it would be impossible to answer, and usually carry some emotional tone such as an ethnic slur or some damned-if-you answer or damned-if-you-don't aspect.

As the New Hampshire Democratic Party revived during the late 1950s and early 1960s its principal fear was the rumor instrument of Manchester. The last few hours before each election required special vigilance on the part of candidate organizations in order to head off and to neutralize the last moment charge. William Loeb of the *Manchester Union Leader* had so successfully played the Manchester instrument in his favor that since 1950 no candidate had succeeded to the governorship of the state of New Hampshire that had not taken Loeb's pledge, asserting that he would veto any sales or income tax legislation. Even a slight equivocation on the part of a candidate toward the "broad-based tax issue" was enough for Loeb to set in motion the machinery to ensure that the candidate would not secure a sufficient margin in Manchester to win statewide. In fact Bernard Boutin, now the Johnson committee chair, had lost his 1958 bid for election when he did not secure a sufficient plurality of Manchester votes to overcome the Republican strength outside the Democratic cities. Loeb alleged that Boutin was a "broad-based taxer" and, in spite of Boutin's fervent denials, Loeb's view stuck, especially in Manchester.

As the final days of the presidential primary neared, the Johnson campaign was searching for a way to reach the voters that were slipping rapidly toward McCarthy. It knew the Manchester political ethos and felt it could play the instrument to Johnson's benefit if the right issue could be found. Oliver Quayle's polling revealed what could be viewed as a conflict in perception between the New Hampshire voters' issue profile and the position that they attributed to Senator McCarthy. The profile revealed that the voters held "hawk" views toward the Vietnam War solution and yet seemed to be moving toward Senator McCarthy in their support. To counter this trend, the Johnson campaign shifted from ignoring McCarthy to challenging McCarthy to make clear his position on the war. Governor King escalated the attack during the last weeks of February but made the mistake of not only challenging McCarthy to make his position clear on the war, but also charging those supporting McCarthy with disloyalty.

Unable to gain much attention for these charges, especially since Senator McCarthy was not in the least hesitant to explain his approach toward Vietnam both in his speeches and in response to questions, the Johnson leaders shifted their efforts somewhat. The first was to recognize that McCarthy had gained considerable strength in New Hampshire. Boutin began backtracking from McIntyre's early prediction that McCarthy would have to get more than three thousand to five thousand votes in order for the result to be considered significant. Boutin now said McCarthy would have to get more than 30 percent of the vote and would on the eve of the election say that all he, Boutin, was interested in was securing more than 50 percent of the vote for President Johnson. Everyone had conceded the convention delegates to Johnson.

Second, Boutin's organization had been scouring the record of the McCarthy campaign to find an error, inconsistency, misstatement, or issue position that it could use to its advantage in the final hours. Its strategy to hit McCarthy hard on his war position was failing. What the McCarthy leaders had found was that the New Hampshire voters found McCarthy credible and were willing to support him even though when asked their own position of the war the answer was that of a hawk. When given the alternative, win-the-war or get out, the respondents took the win-the-war position. What seemed to be happening was that even the hawks were attributing to McCarthy their own view of how to end the war because they found McCarthy reassuring as an alternative to present policies and Johnson's personality. They had become supporters of McCarthy in considerable numbers. This was a baffling phenomenon to the Johnson campaign leadership. Its approach, at least as led by Governor King, was to turn up the heat.

THE JOHNSON CAMPAIGN FIGHTS BACK

The first evidence of the increased heat came with the first run of newspaper advertisements placed for the final weekend and an introductory blast from Governor King. The governor charged that Senator McCarthy was perpetrating a massive hoax on the voters of New Hampshire by claiming friendship and support for the late President John F. Kennedy. King charged that McCarthy had "tried to scuttle President Kennedy's nomination at the 1960 Democratic National Convention," and that since then McCarthy was the "biggest thorn in President Kennedy's side." (*Portsmouth Herald*, March 6, 1968, p. 3)

The second attack came through a newspaper advertisement that echoed the same theme but added, "Sen. McCarthy promises an 'alternative' but he refuses to give one significant detail of his alternatives. Because of this he has not gained the support of a single member of the U.S. Senate. Don't vote for indecision and wispy promises. . . ." Both King and McIntyre signed the advertisement which appeared in a number of New Hampshire newspapers toward the end of the week before the election (*Manchester Union Leader*, March 8, 1968, p. 11)

While King tended to reach for the jugular of McCarthy's issues, McIntyre represented McCarthy as being "vague and oftentimes contradictory in his statements." McIntyre would read excerpts from McCarthy endorsements as reported in the newspapers and charge that McCarthy's statements were "poor substitutes for positive and definitive polices." McCarthy, McIntyre contended, was simply "exploiting the frustration so many Americans feel about Vietnam." (*Valley News*, March 5, 1968)

King, on the other hand, ended the final full week of the campaign with the charge that any significant vote for McCarthy in the presidential primary would be "greeted with cheers in Hanoi."

> King's comments, made during a press conference at the capitol, were obviously inspired in part by a McCarthy charge on Wednesday that supporters of President Johnson were using tactics like those employed in the 1950s by the late Senator Joseph R. McCarthy of Wisconsin, the Republican red-hunter.
>
> "That's political poppycock," said King. "He (McCarthy) is using smear tactics himself."
>
> King's harshest comments were directed to McCarthy's position calling for an early end to hostilities in Southeast Asia.
>
> King said: "The question to be answered is, shall we continue to resist naked Communist aggression with all the resources at our command, or will we say the price is too high, the going is too rough. We are ready to negotiate on terms laid down by Ho Chi Minh.
>
> "That is why the people most interested in this election are Ho Chi Minh and his Communist friends. They will be scrutinizing the returns for signs of a weakening of American will."
>
> King was asked if he thought his attacks on McCarthy might not be a bit strong. "I have always used the hard-sell approach," said King. "I am a hard-sell person, I guess."

King concluded the press conference by revising his predictions for the election.

> His earlier estimate that McCarthy would receive only 12 to 18 percent of the Democratic vote was revised with the Governor stating that McCarthy "could get as much as 25 percent."
>
> (*Boston Herald-Traveler*, March 7, 1968)

Within several days a major controversy began to brew that would splinter the Johnson campaign as it entered the final weekend of the campaign. Governor King had been intemperate in his remarks before, but now the comments revived images of red-baiting by demanding the sort of unquestioning, unthinking loyalty that Joseph McCarthy had demanded during his scourge of the 1950s.

In one of his famous front-page editorials, William Loeb wrote under the heading, "Don't help Hanoi! (for Democrats Only)":

> This newspaper believes it is hard to find anything more stupid than the activities of the Democratic Party leadership in New Hampshire with their pledge cards for Lyndon Johnson.
>
> If we were a Democratic voter and the Democratic leadership attempted to put something like that over on us, we would surely be tempted to tell the Democratic leadership what they could do with their pledge cards.
>
> However, it is easy, in a situation such as this, to become so angry that you lose your sense of perspective. The Democratic voters of New Hampshire should not forget that the eyes of not only the whole nation, but of Hanoi, too, will be focused on how they vote on March 12.
>
> The people in the rest of the nation and the world don't know about the feud over the pledge cards. If they see a large vote for McCarthy because the Democratic voters are angered by those pledge cards, they will regard the vote, not as a repudiation of the Democratic leadership in New Hampshire, but rather, as a rejection of President Johnson and his commitment to the defense of Vietnam in the face of Communist aggression.
>
> *So don't get so angry that you throw the baby out with the bath water. We* plead with the Democratic voters of New Hampshire to settle the score with the Democratic Leadership in some other fashion, at another time.
>
> What is important in this primary is for New Hampshire to give a clear indication to the nation that we do believe in our state's motto, "Live Free or Die," and that we do not favor turning tail and running away from the enemy in Vietnam.
>
> A big vote for McCarthy in New Hampshire because of anger over the pledge cards will lead the rest of the nation into thinking that New Hampshire has abandoned its state motto and that the appeasement sentiment of Sen. McCarthy, which history proves always led to bigger and more costly wars, is the popular position.
>
> This would be a national tragedy.
>
> The newspaper urges New Hampshire Democrats to please think of the main issue at stake. Wait until after March 12 to kick the Democratic leadership in the shins for the asinine idea of the pledge cards.
>
> DON'T HELP HANOI
>
> (*Manchester Union Leader,* March 6, 1968, p. 1)

Governor King apparently had drawn his theme for the press conference that followed from his reading of Loeb's editorial, at least the part that related to defending Vietnam against Communist aggression.

Other news accounts of the press conference were widely and prominently carried in the New Hampshire press. During the thirty minutes of informal briefing that King devoted to his views on the McCarthy and Johnson campaigns, he maintained that the contest was more than just one between two candidates but "it is a measure of the will and resolve of the people of New Hampshire." (*Foster's Daily Democrat,* March 7, 1968) He predicted a three to one victory for Johnson over McCarthy and estimated that from forty thousand to forty-five thousand Democrats would turn out to vote.

He did concede that McCarthy might get as much as "25 per cent of the vote" but if he did then "I will be disappointed with the voters of New Hampshire." To justify the possible increase in the McCarthy vote, King commented that "if President Johnson had been campaigning in New Hampshire himself, the Democrats would get him at least a 7 to 1 margin." (*Foster's Daily Democrat,* March 7, 1968)

In response to King's comments, McCarthy held a press conference at the Wayfarer headquarters where he played several of the radio tapes sponsored by the Johnson campaign that urged against voting for "fuzzy thinking and surrender" and called for a vote on March 12 in "support of our fighting men." He also showed as further examples of the Johnson committee's campaign style copies of recent newspaper advertisements that repeated the same themes. (*Valley News,* March 7, 1968)

"In my twenty years in Congress," McCarthy said, "I have never been the target of such charges from fellow Democrats." He then went on to compare the statements that King had made and that McIntyre had endorsed to those made in the 1950s by the "more irresponsible" Republicans, like an earlier Senator McCarthy, the late Joseph R. McCarthy of Wisconsin. He added that the same charges could be aimed at his fellow members of the U.S. Senate Foreign Relations Committee such as the Democratic leader, Mike Mansfield, and Vermont's Republican Senator George D. Aiken. In fact McCarthy noted, "The Senate Foreign Relations Committee was lined up about 2 to 1 against the administration's conduct of the war." (*Valley News,* March 7, 1968)

McCarthy charged the New Hampshire Johnson campaign leaders with following secretary of state Dean Rusk and other administration figures in trying to "prevent free discussion in the United States. There might be people who could resent it some, and I hope so," McCarthy added. It was McCarthy's feeling that the tactics to which he objected could be controlled by the White House and the Democratic National Committee if they wished. Earlier McCarthy had called upon the White House to repudiate the tactics of Johnson's campaign managers in New Hampshire but there had been no response.

Concluding the press conference McCarthy denied advocating surrender and said that he felt his campaign had encouraged voters to ask hard questions about the war. In fact, the reaction of the Johnson leaders in the final days seemed to McCarthy to be an indication that he had "thrown a scare" into their campaign and that their tactics would "generate resentment among New Hampshire Democrats bringing more votes." Faced with what the reporters felt was still a less than optimistic position in the polls which showed Johnson winning easily, McCarthy responded that "it was too early to yield to the polls." (*Valley News,* March 7, 1968) As at the beginning, McCarthy was not prepared to concede to the findings of the pollsters.

Governor King's attack and McCarthy's measured response gave the press the chance to shape the public view of the last charges of the campaign. To the reporters and their editors, King's attempts to snuff out the McCarthy challenge by tactics reminiscent of those of Joe McCarthy sparked their intense interest at a critical moment in the campaign.

Now with the Johnson surrogates apparently unleashed to attack McCarthy at will in a manner that struck a certain horror of the past in editors' minds, the full power of the press shifted perceptibly behind McCarthy. McCarthy stories moved from inside pages to the front page. It was as if the Johnson leaders, and especially Governor King, had handed the "David" in this contest the rock to slay themselves—"Goliath." It became the combined function of McCarthy and the press to shape that weapon into something that might actually slay Goliath.

The *Portsmouth Herald* led the editorial attack:

> Arrogance and Deception—Editorial Opinion
>
> New Hampshire's Democratic party leaders have shown a boundless capacity for insulting the intelligence of their political brethren; now they seem bent upon a campaign aimed at impugning their loyalty as well.
>
> First there was that arrogant business about the pledge cards. The party's hierarchy triggered understandable resentment among the rank-and-file with this coercive device, and the effort to obtain such pledges has since been all but abandoned.
>
> The pledges were sought, of course as a means of "lining up the troops" so to speak, for a President Johnson write-in movement. Those who signed were made to feel that they were irrevocably committed, while any abstainers were left to wonder about their future standing with the party.
>
> In fact, Gov. John W. King, one of the principal promoters of the pledge cards even went so far as to threaten the laggards. Democrats who didn't join up with Johnson could later expect to be "counted out," he warned.
>
> Such talk obviously didn't give much credit to the mentality of Democrats, nor did it take into account the fierceness of their independence. By and large, they reacted with predictable hostility at such a brazen attempt to regiment them, and the pledge card venture thus collapsed its own dead weight.
>
> It's a hardheaded hierarchy that presumes to direct the thinking of New Hampshire Democrats, however, and the mischief goes on.
>
> The latest sample of it is even more shocking than what's gone before, since it constitutes an attack upon the patriotism of Democrats who don't happen to agree with the party leaders as regards President Johnson and the extent of American involvement in Vietnam.

U.S. Senator Tom McIntyre and Gov. King are the principals, if not the perpetrators of this particular outrage, for it is they who lend their names to a large, page-deep newspaper advertisement which clearly seeks to trick the reader into believing that a vote for President Johnson is somehow essential to showing "support for our fighting men in Vietnam."

In other words, according to the rationale of the ad, the voter who doesn't cast his lot with Johnson might be doing his country a disservice. The same reasoning applies, and the doubts that go with it, to any critic of the war.

It is particularly appropriate that the advertisement was placed with the *Manchester Union Leader*, since the language of it is strictly the language of Loeb.

The ad, incidentally, lists the Democratic State Committee as the sponsor of record. This means that it probably was paid for out of regular party funds. Hence, all Democrats are made to share the responsibility for it whether they agree with the ad or not. Furthermore, a lot of party contributors of adverse persuasion probably have been charged with the cost.

Interest now forms around the question of how disdainful Democrats will respond to the ad after they realize the ruthless manner in which their right to think differently has been trampled down. Theirs is just cause for violent protest against the excesses of the party's leadership, and it will be surprising indeed if the rebellious clamor doesn't make itself heard from one end of the state to the other.

(*Portsmouth Herald*, March 8, 1968, p. 4)

The *Concord Daily Monitor* published two editorials restating similar themes. The first, titled "Dirty Pool," written by the newspaper's general manager Thomas W. Gerber, read:

The activities of New Hampshire's Democratic machine politicians in the presidential primary campaign are little short of revolting.

Their actions and statements are a disservice to their candidate, President Johnson, an insult to the state's Democratic voters and a violation of the democratic process.

The three who are responsible are Gov. King, Sen. Thomas J. McIntyre and Bernard Boutin of Nashua, one time Small Business Administrator.

Their activities hark back to the darkest days of American politics—big city bossism and the era of the smear and the innuendo characterized by the late Sen. Joseph R. McCarthy (R. Wis.).

The tragedy of these tactics is that they are invoked at a time when there is an aching need for the injection of ethics, responsibility and statesmanship in the operation of the American system .

The word "politics" still has a derogatory tone. Arm-twisting tactics implied threats of retribution, and the dictatorial denial of the right to dissent only sour further the public's attitude toward the honorable pursuit of public service.

> New Hampshire's Democratic bosses began their bulldozer operation in November.
>
> On a snowy Sunday, they rammed through a meeting of the Democratic State Committee a resolution backing President Johnson in the primary campaign.
>
> State committees of both political parties traditionally have refused to take sides in primary contests. This is because state committees are supposed to represent rank-and-file Democrats or Republicans who support a particular candidate.
>
> Then came the numbered pledge card bit.
>
> While we are confident the original intent was not to twist arms—a "you support us or else" tactic—that is just the way it came across.
>
> In the public view, names of loyal Democrats could be associated with numbers, and thus checked upon. The distinct impression was that if you didn't sign, the bosses would get even.
>
> But by far the most disgusting aspect of the Democratic campaign has been the statements of King and McIntyre against the President's opponent, Sen. Eugene J. McCarthy (D. Minn.).
>
> What they say is that a vote for Sen. McCarthy is a vote for Ho Chi Minh, communist premier of North Vietnam. This is a smear. It suggests that to disagree is treason.
>
> We hope President Johnson can stay aloof, or even disassociate himself, from such irresponsibility.—T.W.G.

The second editorial, written by the assistant editor, George W. Wilson, titled "Short Memories, Convenient Ethics," was especially pointed since it was aimed at the politically vulnerable Senator McIntyre and Governor King. Support from the *Concord Daily Monitor* and the independently minded Concord voters had been particularly important in both their 1966 elections and both would need that support again to succeed in future electoral contests. Wilson wrote:

> Gov. King and Sen. McIntyre, as chairmen of the campaign to corral write-in votes for President Johnson, have stooped to reprehensible smears to discourage votes for Minnesota Senator Eugene McCarthy.
>
> In advertisements and public statements, the two have suggested it would be unpatriotic not to support President Johnson when the nation is at war, that a vote for McCarthy "will be greeted with great cheers in Hanoi."
>
> King and McIntyre suggest that the normal Democratic process of criticizing U.S. policies should be suspended when the nation is at war.
>
> They say "the communists in Vietnam are watching the New Hampshire primary to see if we at home have the same determination as our soldiers in Vietnam."
>
> Writing-in President Johnson's name is equated with "supporting our fighting men in Vietnam."

With this nonsense, they invoke the flag and primitive chauvinism to line Democrats up behind the President.

Has it occurred to King and McIntyre that the very purpose of elections is to test the policies of the incumbent officeholder or administration? That Senator McCarthy's dissent and presence in New Hampshire is in the finest tradition of American government?

If they disagree with McCarthy, let them discuss the weaknesses in his proposals, let them emphasize the differences between the President's Vietnam policies and the Senator's views.

Statements by King and McIntyre violate "good taste, fair campaign procedures and are a direct insult to voters of New Hampshire."

They seem to feel that anyone who disagrees with them is "un-American."

Those sentiments, shared by King and McIntyre, were voiced in September 1966 by Hugh Bownes of Laconia, who now is a Superior Court Judge but then was a national committeeman for the N. H. Democratic Party.

He made the comments in response to signs erected by retired Brig. Gen. Harrison Thyng that said: "Think American, Vote Thyng for U.S. Senate."

Thyng's injured opponent? Senator Thomas J. McIntyre—G.W.W.

(*Concord Daily Monitor*, March 8, 1968)

McIntyre Criticizes Johnson Campaign Tactics

The editorial barrage and the consequences of Governor King's attack began stirring the conscience of several prominent, liberal, and fair-minded supporters of President Johnson. The protest began to take shape when McIntyre arrived in New Hampshire to join in the final weekend push for the President Johnson write-in. His first stop was Claremont where he restated the themes that King had set earlier in the week but without sharing King's rhetoric. Further he referred to "political Disneyland" noting that in his mind Senator McCarthy had not made his alternative policies clear. He did not, however, share the view that McCarthy had called for "surrender" and noted that he felt the use of the word "surrender" was unfortunate. (*Claremont Eagle*, March 9, 1968, pp. 1–2)

By the time McIntrye reached West Lebanon in his campaign tour on March 9, he was carefully separating himself from the King characterizations and the advertisements that had been run with his name during that week. Under a headline that read, "Wording of Some Ads Regretted by McIntyre," the senator was quoted as saying he was "sorry about the way certain advertisements pushing for a large write-in have been worded." The *Valley News* had editorialized against the Johnson campaign tactics in the same edition carrying McIntyre's interview. He stated that it had not been his intent to "question the patriotism of Senator McCarthy" adding that "he sits right behind me in the Senate and I've never known a nicer, more gentlemanly man. And I'd never question his patriotism." (*Valley News*, March 9, 1968, p. 1)

Either before or shortly after his interview in West Lebanon, McIntyre received notice that five candidates for delegate favorable to the nomination of President Johnson had signed a statement repudiating Governor King's remarks and would be releasing the statement that afternoon. All five were prominent in Democratic politics and had been vigorous supporters of McIntyre in his recent campaigns. Their advance notice to McIntyre of their action gave him time to disassociate himself from King's language.

Datelined Hanover, the statement hit the afternoon New Hampshire newspapers with great impact. The *Concord Daily Monitor* headlined the news, "LBJ Delegates Repudiate King for Statements," and led the story:

> The hard sell Presidential primary pitch of Gov. King was repudiated last night by five Johnson delegates who said they could not claim the President "has cornered the patriotism market."
>
> In a prepared statement sighed by five delegates from Lebanon and Hanover, King's contention that a vote for Sen. Eugene McCarthy, D. Minn., would be a vote for "surrender" was rejected.

The statement was signed by Mrs. Jean Hennessey, Hanover, former head of the Democratic State Platform Committee; Robert H. Guest, Hanover, a member of the Democratic State Executive Committee; Robert C. Elliot, Lebanon, former Democratic town chair; Herbert Hill, ex-state chair and former history professor at Dartmouth; and Richard Sterling, a professor of government at Dartmouth. In their statement they said:

> As delegate candidates favorable to the renomination of Lyndon B. Johnson, we wish to make clear that we do not claim he has cornered the patriotism market.

They noted their support for the President in his domestic programs, in foreign policy areas including the handling of the "Pueblo" incident, and in his "continuing to seek valid negotiations in Vietnam. They concluded by saying:

> We make clear, however, that in our opinion, those who vote for Sen. McCarthy, will not be voting for "surrender," but for the second best candidate.
>
> In addition, we believe that all New Hampshire citizens who vote Tuesday in accord with their reason and conscience contribute importantly to the democratic process.
>
> (*Concord Daily Monitor*, March 9, 1968 pp. 1, 14)

The *Concord Daily Monitor* account of the statement written by Jack Hubbard went on to note that "the statement by the five delegates was mild compared to the private comments":

> "I think the governor has gone way overboard this time," said one highly disgruntled delegate, whose name was withheld.
>
> "Some of us were around when Nixon did this to Stevenson. And we don't like it. . . ."

"It is all over, this feeling," said a spokesman.

"This is no Hanover syndrome. Everybody I know agrees that McCarthy is a good Democrat. Talking about withdrawal is a difference in judgment, not in patriotism."

"The governor is way over his head in foreign policy."

"I don't think the governor has recognized that he has gone too far," said one person.

"When it comes out in advertising from the Johnson committee it makes everybody look like they are supporting this view, and I don't think it is the view that they support."

"There are a lot of people who feel very uncomfortable about the position they have been put into by Gov. King," said a delegate.

"There are a lot of people voting for Johnson who feel very uncomfortable about the war and wish there was a way out of it."

"And they feel very uncomfortable about hurling names at McCarthy, there is no question about it."

Hubbard concluded his report noting that the White House and officials at Citizens for Johnson headquarters had no comment on the statement from the delegates. (*Concord Daily Monitor*, March 9, 1968, pp. 1, 14)

The *Portsmouth Herald* took the opportunity to hammer away at Governor King again through an editorial titled, "Disgraceful Political Tactics," noting that it is "customary to make allowance for a certain amount of deviltry in politics," and that within the bounds of usual political exchange, it is acceptable to promote a candidate while attacking the record, issues, "flaws and shortcomings" of the opponent:

> But these Johnson-minded Democrats are not content to go by the usual rules. They turn their backs altogether on the real issues in the process of inventing trumped-up arguments deliberately calculated to trade upon fear and confusion.
>
> Until today we thought we had seen the worst of it when Sen. Tom McIntyre and his coconspirator, Gov. John W. King, joined in placing a newspaper advertisement which presumed to show that a vote for President Johnson, because of his war policy, was proof of one's patriotism.
>
> Readers of the ad were led to believe that since the war in Vietnam was in the national interest, and since President Johnson was devoted to continuing the war it naturally followed that voting for Johnson was also in the national interest.
>
> Further, the inference was made that failure to support the President was tantamount to "letting the boys down" in Vietnam.
>
> This, of course, was a vicious and cynical repudiation of the whole idea of fair play in politics, since it was born of utter flimflammery.
>
> That Sen. McIntyre would lend his name to such evil tactics was especially reprehensible since he has had so much experience defending himself against the same kind of chicanery.

> As for Gov. King, he seems oblivious to any restraints that decency would impose. And he remains so, for the governor struck again only today with a further statement designed to put the national loyalty of voters in question if they dare to make a political choice other than President Johnson.
>
> According to Gov. King, a "significant vote" for Sen. McCarthy in next week's primary would be "greeted with cheers in Hanoi." He said such an ill-omened event would be interpreted as "a sign that the American people are ready to quit."
>
> What gives Gov. King such strong feelings about this forthcoming political decision? Considering that he never was very active before in advancing the interests of the party which favored him with the governorship, the matter of his present passion arouses interest. There must be something in it for him if President Johnson's good name survives the primary.
>
> Could it be that he hopes by his efforts to clinch that federal judgeship in Concord which is supposed to be awaiting him? If so, it's a rotten bargain when the people of the state have to be deceived as part of the price.
>
> (*Portsmouth Herald,* March 9, 1968)

The combination of the editorial assault and the statement of repudiation by the five Hanover/Lebanon Johnson delegate candidates had a considerable impact upon Senator McIntyre. His statement of disagreement with Governor King's characterization of the McCarthy candidacy and consequences of voting for McCarthy was widely carried in the newspapers and radio news broadcasts that dominated Saturday afternoon.

Senator McIntyre was now in a most precarious position. To disagree with King and the approach that King, Boutin, and Craig had taken in the campaign meant damaging President Johnson's chances in the election. At the same time many of McIntyre's most vigorous supporters, which included both Johnson and McCarthy supporters, objected to the tactics being employed. Further to lend his name to irresponsible attacks on a fellow senator or to engage in such activities could only damage his standing and effectiveness in the senate. McIntyre had tried to clear himself of this dilemma by standing on the side of decency and the preservation of the Democratic Party organization in New Hampshire that he had helped to build and that had supported his candidacy. The *New Hampshire Sunday News* knew how best to damage his record, especially in Manchester where McIntyre had trailed King in both the election of 1962 and 1966.

> Sen. Eugene J. McCarthy's campaign to wrest the presidential nomination from President Johnson got a startling boost this weekend from Sen. Thomas J. McIntyre of Laconia.
>
> For Gov. John W. King it appeared to be a deliberate slap in the face.
>
> King and McIntyre are co-chairmen of the movement to drum up write-ins for LBJ at next Tuesday's presidential primary.
>
> In remarks Friday McIntyre defended McCarthy against a series of attacks by the governor—whom he did not name—in which Mr. King has

> been warning that votes for McCarthy will be greeted with cheers by Hanoi, the Communist capital of North Vietnam. King's assertion coincided with the editorial view of both the *Manchester Union Leader* and the *N.H. Sunday News.*
>
> King, in these attacks has been joined by a number of other Johnson leaders, notably State Democratic Chairman William Craig, who has sponsored a series of ads saying "the Communists in Vietnam are watching the New Hampshire primary."
>
> McIntyre called such warnings "unfair" and a grave injustice to the Minnesota senator.
>
> Less surprisingly yesterday, McIntyre was joined in defense of McCarthy by U.S. Sen. Robert R. Kennedy. He called the attacks "baseless" and said they would dangerously increase "the terrible stains and divisions" of U.S. political life.
>
> Like McCarthy, Kennedy is a bitter critic of administration war policy and an advocate of "de-escalation" in Vietnam. Some McCarthy critics have looked upon the Minnesota Senator as a "stalking horse" candidate, with Kennedy scheduled later to emerge as the major Democratic opponent of President Johnson for this year's nomination.
>
> McIntyre, however, has recently paraded himself as a "hawk" and strong backer of the Johnson war policy, although in his campaign last year against Gen. Harrison Thyng he took a pronouncedly "dovish" line against Thyng's proposals to deal bellicosly with the Communists. . . .
>
> (*New Hampshire Sunday News,* March 10, 1968, pp. 1, 33)

In addition to the first-page "news" story the *New Hampshire Sunday News* carried, the edition also contained two editorials. The first titled "McCarthyisms" led, "New Hampshire Democratic leaders, especially Gov. John W. King, are to be congratulated for getting out their shillelaghs last week to give the peacenik's candidate, Senator Eugene McCarthy, a vigorous belaboring." It went on the congratulate the Johnson leaders for "borrowing" the editor's description of McCarthy as "The Hanoi Candidate." The editorial countered that the "howls of anguish from the McCarthy camp prove the effectiveness of this attack. We have even the delicious spectacle of a McCarthy lamenting that he's the victim of McCarthyism!"

The second editorial attacked Senator McIntyre for his "boost" to Senator McCarthy's "flagging New Hampshire campaign." The title "Mac the Knife" cast McIntyre as stabbing the Johnson campaign in the back by criticizing King's characterizations of McCarthy. The editorial contended:

> We would be the last to suggest that McCarthy is less patriotic than McIntyre.
>
> The fact is nobody in New Hampshire—certainly not Governor King or Mr. Craig—has impugned McCarthy's loyalty.
>
> It is his judgment which is being questioned.—Neville Chamberlain at Munich acted out of the highest regard for his country's welfare—"peace in our

time." But his tactics, like those of McCarthy, were those of appeasement and surrender.

Hitler was overjoyed, just as will be Ho Chi Minh if McCarthy gets a good vote on Tuesday. Indeed the Communists must already be delighted at the boost given their cause by President Johnson's New Hampshire co-chairman!

Bad blood between McIntyre and Gov. King long had been rumored. They are reported to be rivals for the federal judgeship which LBJ will shortly bestow in this district. This latest bit of back-stabbing by McIntyre will not close any rifts but it should greatly assist President Johnson in making up his mind on the judgeship.

(*New Hampshire Sunday News,* March 10, 1968)

McIntyre Recants

When Senator McCarthy returned to the Wayfarer after his campaign visits that Sunday afternoon, he accidentally encountered Senator McIntyre arriving for a Johnson campaign sponsored event at the same motor inn. McCarthy thanked McIntyre for his statements of moderation and courage in speaking out against the remarks of Governor King. McIntyre mumbled a response, appeared a bit stunned by the encounter, and hurried off to the reception.

Those watching were puzzled by the exchange and especially by Senator McIntyre's reaction. (DCH recollection) What they would soon learn was that McIntyre had just come from a meeting arranged by Bernard Boutin to get his co-chair back on the track of the campaign. From subsequent accounts of the meeting Boutin, using the full force of his ties with the White House, insisted that Senator McIntyre clarify his earlier statements and reaffirm his full support for not only President Johnson but also for the campaign and its leadership.

The next morning the *Manchester Union Leader* carried a story headlined, "McIntyre Drops Defense of McCarthy" with a subhead, "Does Complete About-Face, Joins Gov. King"

U.S. Sen. Tom McIntyre of Laconia, reportedly under heavy pressure from the regular Democratic establishment, last night abandoned his defense of Minnesota Sen. Eugene J. McCarthy against charges by Gov. John W. King that votes for McCarthy "will be greeted with cheers in Hanoi."

McIntyre's clarifying press release read:

Let me make it clear! Gov. King and I are united in our support of President Johnson. Gov. King said that Hanoi is watching the New Hampshire primary. I say that is the truth. Gov. King said that a significant vote for Sen. McCarthy will be greeted with cheers in Hanoi. I agree 100%—that is unfortunately true. Gov. King says that McCarthy's charge that we are using foul techniques in this campaign "is a smoke screen." I agree with Gov. King.

> Gov. King and I have said repeatedly in this campaign that we support President Johnson's stand in Vietnam. We support our fighting men in Vietnam. We say, Gov. King and I, that the people of New Hampshire can best show their support of our troops in Vietnam by writing in the name of President Johnson on Tuesday. We ask that the people of New Hampshire join us.
>
> (*Manchester Union Leader*, March 1, 1968, p. 1)

In response to what the *Manchester Union Leader* reported as "heavy pressure from the regular establishment here and in Washington," McIntyre not only issued this statement, which was released at about the time McIntyre had the chance meeting with McCarthy, but sealed his renewed resolve by making a radio commercial tape that would be aired during the brief hours remaining before the election. It would be McIntyre who would be the vehicle for the famous, especially in Manchester, last-minute charge.

McIntyre's Recording: The Red Herring

A week had passed since Senator McCarthy had spoken before the student audience at Dartmouth College. On Saturday morning, March 9, McCarthy was campaigning in Franklin. A radio station Teletype carried a report of a charge coming from the Johnson campaign that referenced McCarthy's response to the question he had answered in Hanover concerning amnesty. The Teletype report stated something to the affect that McCarthy had promised blanket amnesty to all draft dodgers, resisters, and deserters of the Vietnam period. I, then traveling with McCarthy, called the press office at the Wayfarer to get them to monitor the release and also to review the tape of McCarthy's Hanover speech. To me this appeared to be the last-minute charge that had been expected as the campaign neared its climax.

Later that afternoon the McCarthy press office issued a statement concerning the charge which noted that the statement attributed to McCarthy had been taken out of context, was distorted, and that the correct reading was as transcribed from the tape of the senator's speech. Since Saturday is a dead news day in New Hampshire, the only mention either the Johnson charge or the McCarthy rebuttal received was over the radio. The matter seemed to have gone the way of many charges during the campaign when it did not appear with any prominence in New Hampshire's only Sunday newspaper.

That evening, however, I received a tip from one of my contacts at a Manchester radio station that Senator McIntyre had recorded a political advertisement that was scheduled to run at a saturation rate on Monday and Tuesday. The summary of the message was similar to that which had been picked up Saturday, except that packaged as a radio message, running heavily during the final hours of the campaign, the impact, especially in Manchester, could be devastating.

I relayed my information immediately to Richard Goodwin and explained to Goodwin the potential impact of such a last-minute accusation on the voter. It was a charge that could not be satisfactorily answered in the time that remained, and further, McCarthy's answer, as transcribed from the tape, did lend at least a half-truth substantiation to the charge.

By the time I found out where the tape had been recorded it was after midnight. Goodwin said it was imperative that either the tape be held up or that a copy of the exact text be secured. He hoped that copies had not been made or the message transmitted to other stations and that the release might be delayed if someone could gain access to it. The station where the tape had been recorded was closed and off the air.

Goodwin sent two members of the campaign to case the station to see whether it might be possible to get in, but the two returned reporting that an electric company crew was changing the transformer outside the station. I called Merv Weston to find out who operated the station and whether Weston thought the operator would be willing to let me inside to listen to the tape. Sometime after 2:00 A.M. I roused the station manager who agreed to meet me at the station to let me hear the recording. With another campaigner, we met the manager at about 2:30 A.M., and found that the tape was already in a cassette. The best we could do was get an accurate transcription of the recording. The manager also showed us the booking schedule for the tape. The heaviest plays were for Manchester, Nashua, and Berlin.

The substance of McIntyre's message was that McCarthy had promised blanket amnesty to all Vietnam draft dodgers and deserters. He contended that such an action would undermine the moral fiber of the nation. To vote for McCarthy, McIntyre contended, would be to turn a back on the boys fighting in Vietnam and could do nothing more than please Hanoi. By implication, a vote for McCarthy would be tantamount to endorsing treason if not actually an act of treason.

I was stunned by the nature of the charge, the distortion of McCarthy's response, and by its potential impact during the last hours of the campaign. I told Goodwin that I felt the message would have a considerable impact in Manchester and might also be damaging in Nashua and some of the Seacoast cities. I advised that the campaign take steps to stop the message from being aired. It seemed to me to be sufficiently inaccurate as to be libelous and the threat of such legal action might be enough to keep stations from accepting the message for transmission.

While I explored this option with Sy Hersh and John Holland, Goodwin reacted differently. The likelihood of stopping the message seemed remote to him and perhaps the consequences of letting the message go would be more destructive to Johnson's candidacy nationally than blocking it in New Hampshire would be helpful to McCarthy.

As the sun rose on the last full day of the campaign, Monday, March 11th, Goodwin had worked out a strategy. Hersh would call an early morning press conference. Next a statement, which would put McIntyre's tactic in the proper cast, was written for McCarthy and he was briefed concerning what had been learned during the evening. I felt the McIntyre message should be stopped in order to keep it from cutting down the margin that had been so carefully built over the weeks for McCarthy. I had even come to feel that McCarthy might do well in Manchester, especially after his reception of the weekend. To let McIntyre's message play without a rebuttal—and no rebuttal was possible—would produce irreparable damage to McCarthy's New Hampshire vote.

Goodwin, on the other hand, saw in the charge the essence of how Johnson would continue his national campaign. If the tactics embodied in King's characterizations and McIntyre's last-minute message succeeded, then the Johnson managers would reproduce the fear motive, the patriotic image, and the characterization of dissent in each subsequent contest. To Goodwin, what might cut into some of McCarthy's New Hampshire vote would be seen through the eyes of outraged reporters, editors, columnists, and television anchor persons as a severe threat to treasured traditions of free speech, free press, and civil dissent. Johnson might survive the New Hampshire primary through this stratagem, but the image of a newly repressive political ethos would destroy his chances in other states, especially the next primary in Wisconsin. It was with this response in mind that McCarthy convened the early morning press conference.

With restrained outrage in his tone, McCarthy gave the reporters transcripts of the McIntyre message, read it, then read the statement that had been prepared as his reaction. The message was clear and needed little amplification. What McIntyre represented in his statement was White House ordered and White House approved. This would be just the beginning of a campaign strategy that would be used across the nation unless it was immediately and convincingly shown for what it was. The reporters needed no further prompting. The proof was at hand of what they had seen and felt during the past week. A national reaction against the Johnson campaign tactics and characterizations was growing and regardless of whether McCarthy succeeded or failed in New Hampshire, his service had been to reveal the nature of the Johnson candidacy and the willingness of its managers to repress dissent, limit debate, and cast aspersions as to the motives of those questioning administration policies.

A full-blown image of a national politics shaped according to the model of the Texas unit rule caucus system and the unquestioning loyalty that Lyndon Johnson demanded was now clearly presented to the nation. This would be a difficult if not impossible image to shake. Richard Goodwin knew this would be a consequence and had the experience to draw this from what might have been simply another in a long history of the infamous last-minute, "red-herring" charges of a close New Hampshire political contest.

REPORTERS FIND McCARTHY CAMPAIGN IRRESISTIBLE

When the Johnson campaign leaders began increasing their attacks on the McCarthy campaign the reporters' instincts led them to conclude that all was not as the Johnson camp had predicted earlier in the campaign. Robert Novak drove to Hanover to interview me and wrote a new column predicting difficulty for President Johnson. Theodore White, who had ignored New Hampshire this presidential primary season and lost complete interest when Romney abandoned his campaign, scurried back for interviews during the last week and weekend. A David Wolper film crew, taking footage for the television presentation of White's next making of the president book arrived for the last weekend and comically scouted McCarthy's every move. It was the crew's last chance to catch glimpses of an event they had almost completely missed.

CBS news had withdrawn its major election night coverage when Governor Romney withdrew. As reports of a narrowing contest in the Democratic primary filtered out of New Hampshire, CBS struggled to recover its position. Walter Cronkite arrived for the final weekend, traveled with McCarthy, and grappled in his own mind with what was happening. He had just recently changed his own position from one of support for U.S. policy in Vietnam to one of serious doubt. Reflecting on a conversation he had with Cronkite, McCarthy said, "Walter still doesn't quite understand what is happening as a result of the administration's policy. He still thinks that we should be able to win if we would only use our machines more effectively." (DCH recollection)

But what was of greatest importance to the campaign was the attention the high-circulation New Hampshire newspapers, the *Boston Globe,* and the *Boston Herald-Traveler,* gave to the campaign. Both newspapers sent reporters to New Hampshire to cover specific activities while relying heavily on correspondents to fill in with accounts when their reporters were not in the state.

For much of the final week the *Globe*'s political editor, Robert Healy, directed his newspaper's coverage of the campaign. Each day the *Globe*'s interest mounted until those editions that were circulated widely in New Hampshire appeared as virtual campaign sheets for McCarthy. The headline of the *Globe*'s morning edition on Saturday, March 9, read, "McCarthy Drive in New Hampshire Now Has Party Leaders Worried." A series of major stories on the campaign dominated the front page and the news pages inside the edition.

As if challenged to top the Saturday coverage, the Sunday edition's front page carried two major McCarthy stories. The first headlined, "'Hanoi Jibe Splits Democrats," subheaded, "LBJ Boosters in N.H. Defend McCarthy," had a picture of Senator McIntyre with a caption quote from him ". . . a great injustice." A five-column by five-inch story followed discussing McIntyre's comments, the LBJ delegate candidates protest, and the status of McCarthy's campaign during that final weekend. A second story, headlined "Veterans Backing McCarthy in N.H.," contained a picture of the press conference held by the veterans supporting McCarthy's position on the war in Vietnam. In the photograph were retired Brigadier General William W. Ford, and air force veteran of Vietnam, Colonel Charles Vaughn, and army captain John Fitzgerald. Fitzgerald, an infantry officer from Holyoke, Massachusetts, Bronze Star hero and Purple Heart recipient, charged Governor King with "trying to slur us. What he is trying to do is make anyone who questions the effectiveness of our current policy in Vietnam seem to be in some way to be a sympathizer with communism; I certainly am not." (*Boston Globe,* March 10, 1968, pp. 1, 19)

Also on the front page was a "tease" quote from Mary McGrory's page-eighteen column which read, "McCarthy Now Figure of 1st Magnitude." Turning to page eighteen the reader found a full page of photographs surrounding Miss McGrory's column which was headlined, "'All Is Changed, Changed Utterly' . . . by Army of Students." The photographs showed students arriving at the Manchester headquarters, working at telephones and typewriters, handing out materials on the street, and two photographs of Ann Hart directing activities at headquarters.

Her story:

Manchester, N.H.—The only way to describe what is happening here is to quote Yeats: "All is changed, changed utterly."

Sen. Eugene J. McCarthy whose antiwar challenge a week ago was a joke at the White House, has become a political figure of the first magnitude both at home and abroad.

An insignificant primary, complacently contemplated as an organizational exercise by the forces of the President, has become an unpredictable event of worldwide importance.

Two definable elements have contributed to the incredible ferment here: One is the brutal excess of the Johnson camp, which was repudiated by members of his own party in the state and in the Senate, where dove candidates were appalled at the prospect of "pro-communist" smears in their own campaigns.

The other is the invasion of a mighty army of college students who have suddenly discovered a use for people over 30—voting for McCarthy.

Their presence on street corners and village greens in a hundred towns and cities has contributed immeasurable exuberance and manpower to the McCarthy effort, and bodes ill for Lyndon Johnson in future primaries. All McCarthy will have to do is to knock on university doors to unleash a river of free labor that could change the face of American politics.

No one knows what effect the national uproar over the Johnson tactics or the massing of student legions all dedicated to the overthrow of Lyndon Johnson, will have on the Hawkish and uncommunicative voters of the Granite State.

But what is happening is that violet-eyed damsels from Smith are pinning McCarthy buttons on tattered millworkers and Ph.D.'s from Cornell, shaven and shorn for world peace, are deferentially bowing to middle-aged Manchester housewives and importuning them to consider a change of commander-in-chief.

Some of the best young minds in the country are sitting in the cellar of Manchester, Nashua, and points north, pouring over precinct lists, drawing up baby-sitting rosters for summa cum laudes of the Ivy League.

The spin-off is incalculable. Will grownups, grateful to the senator for gentling their young and saving them from the New Left begin to consider his candidacy?

A kind of reconciliation process between the generations had begun to occur. McCarthy is leading the children back into the political process. Thus into willy-nilly communication with their elders.

The immediate political repercussion occurred when rumors began to circulate that Sen. Robert F. Kennedy, as a result of the New Hampshire ferment, was reconsidering his refusal to run in 1968.

A tremor ran through the under-21 staff at the McCarthy headquarters, and the cry went up and down the corridors of the Wayfarer Hotel "Where's Goodwin?"

Richard Goodwin resurfaced several hours later, having been making television tapes for McCarthy, and the young pioneer politicos breathed easier.

During pauses in their endless errands, they contemplated their future loyalties. Some dismissed the Kennedy initiative.

Said a Mount Holyoke sophomore who was passing out literature on a McCarthy's Vietnam views on a Manchester street corner: "We don't care what he does. He wasn't there when we needed him."

"He's a moral slob," said a Cornell senior, sending out voter cards in the headquarters. "In our crowd, we're circulating a 'Dump Kennedy in '72' letter."

Matt Zwerling, a third-year Yale law student who drives McCarthy's daughters on their rounds, said "I'll stay with McCarthy until he lets me go. He was there when it counted."

Some of the scholars are beguiled by the thought that Kennedy might have a better chance than McCarthy, and since their lives are focused on stopping Johnson and the war, think they would change. Most of the students came to the issue, not to the man, but he is, they say, "growing on us."

Among those who have come to know McCarthy is this mild, round-eyed young researcher, Stephen Cohen, a Ph.D. candidate at Harvard. He shook his head when he heard that Kennedy might change his mind.

"I think now that the most beautiful thing that could happen to this country would be if Senator McCarthy would become President. I think America would be a better place if he would share with it his personal qualities."

No one knows how much of what is happening here is irretrievable. But what is plain is that the youthful elite is giving the country a second chance. If the country doesn't take it, they consider resistance, or as they say, "Jail or Canada."

Whatever else happens on Tuesday, Sen. McCarthy has taken the place of Robert Kennedy as the symbol of hope and change among America's bright children.

The question is whether Lyndon Johnson can put the Democratic Party back into the LBJ bottle. The top is off here.

(*Boston Globe,* March 10, 1968, p. 18)

Not to be outdone by its sister Boston newspaper, the Sunday edition of the *Boston Herald-Traveler* carried an equal amount of lineage on McCarthy's increasing New Hampshire strength. Its front-page headlines read, "206,000 more GIs Sought for Viet: Westmoreland Bid Splits Administration; Would Also Thrust Into Laos, Cambodia," and "GIs Kill 129 at Da Nang." The McCarthy story and picture, "Everything's Going McCarthy's Way" (*Boston Herald-Traveler,* March 10, 1968, p. 1)—was the one spot of optimism on a front page that also had the caption for Tom Wicker's column that read, "The Mood of the Country: 'A creeping Disaster . . .'."

Even the *New York Times,* which had been reluctant to cover McCarthy as a serious candidate, carried three important items on McCarthy's candidacy and the New Hampshire primary in its Sunday edition. The front-page story headlined, "Big New

Hampshire Edge Seen for Johnson, Nixon," discussed the rising fortunes of McCarthy and the unknown affect of a write-in campaign being organized for Nelson Rockefeller against Richard Nixon. (*New York Times,* March 10, 1968, p. 1) An op ed column titled, "McCarthy rides on Student Power," discussed the growth of the student volunteer activity in New Hampshire and contained a quote from Bernard L. Boutin, the Johnson New Hampshire campaign manager. He said, "McCarthy's whole operation is a carpetbag operation. You can import 10,000 people and end up with 5,000 votes." The columnist went on to note: "True, but if McCarthy could get 5,000 votes as a result of the student volunteers, he might win this election. 'Winning' to the McCarthy camp means getting 30 percent of the Democratic vote. There are 89,000 registered Democrats, of whom not more than 50,000 are expected to vote. Therefore, 'winning' would be 15,000." (*New York Times,* March 10, 1968)

The Coalition for a Democratic Alternative ran a full page advertisement challenging U.S. Vietnam policy and calling for contributions to the Coalition for use in the McCarthy campaign. This was the one of a series of striking advertisements that the Coalition sponsored in their fund raising effort. The response to these ads was exceptional. (*New York Times,* March 10, 1968, p. E9)

As if to make amends for their lack of attention earlier, the editors of the *New York Times* wrote:

A Man for This Season

> Senator Eugene McCarthy's campaign is steadily gaining in strength and significance. His showing in the precinct and ward conventions in Minnesota last week was unexpectedly strong. President Johnson's refusal to run in person or through a proxy candidate in Massachusetts defaults that state's votes to Mr. McCarthy for the first ballot at the Democratic National Convention. These developments have heightened interest in Tuesday's primary in New Hampshire.
>
> Every serious political campaign represents an interaction between the candidate and the issues. Senator McCarthy, comparatively little known on the national scene, is tapping a sizable vein of antiwar sentiment. He is winning support because he is willing to talk sensibly and calmly about Vietnam, the subject that is most on the minds of the electorate, and is willing to submit his beliefs to the judgment of the voters.
>
> The McCarthy campaign appears novel because so many Americans have become accustomed to political campaigns in which issues are ruthlessly subordinated to personalities. It is rare and refreshing for a man to be more concerned with his ideas than his image. Mr. McCarthy is not merchandising himself as if he were a popular singer or new brand of detergent; he is not seeking support because he has an attractive wife or children or dog or any other irrelevancy.
>
> What is remarkable, however, is that so many of Senator McCarthy's own supporters who agree with him on the Vietnam issue are so ready to complain about what they regard as his deficiencies as a campaigner. It is as if having made up their minds on the subject of Vietnam, they only want a

spokesman who will ventilate their emotions by shouting slogans and making fiery attacks.

But surely the Vietnam debate is already too envenomed by passion and rancor. What is needed is a man who will, in Adlai Stevenson's phrase, "talk sense to the American people"—and that means talking sensibly and calmly and treating audiences as adults capable of comprehending complexity. That is what Senator McCarthy is doing and what he deserves great credit for doing. If he underplays his points and occasionally trails off into vague inconsequence, that is—or ought to be—preferable to the more usual escalations into bombast and simple-mindedness. A man of wit and of learning and of decent respect for the opinions of others, he is a man for this season of emotionalism.

Politics is normally defined as the art of the possible. It is the purpose of the idealist in politics such as Senator McCarthy to expand the boundaries of what is thought possible. Regardless of the outcome in New Hampshire or in the later primaries in Wisconsin and California, Senator McCarthy has no reasonable chance of winning the Democratic nomination—as he himself has recognized from the outset. But a series of McCarthy victories or near-victories in the primaries and state conventions could conceivably alter President Johnson's perception of public attitudes toward the war and therefore his management of the conflict.

Like any man who has ever run for political office, President Johnson has a healthy respect for the ballot box. An outpouring of McCarthy support may convince him of the deepening public conviction that the war cannot be won in the terms in which he is trying to win it. A Johnson change of viewpoint on the war is not probable, but it is more clearly within the realm of the possible than it was before Eugene McCarthy began to campaign.

Senator McCarthy has succeeded in making a negotiated settlement in Vietnam a more credible alternative simply by campaigning for such a settlement. He has removed the issue of the war from the sideshows of controversy to the main tent of politics where the two great parties contend. For all citizens, but particularly for students and young people, he has provided constructive political leadership in a hard, confused time. For that service alone he commands the respect and gratitude of all who cherish democracy.

(*New York Times,* March 10, 1968)

The Monday editions continued the attention with concluding stories and, in the case of the *Boston Globe* and the *Boston Herald-Traveler,* editorial endorsements of McCarthy. The New Hampshire editors who had become especially interested in the McCarthy-Johnson contest added final comments. The *Manchester Union Leader,* torn between supporting Johnson and the war in Vietnam and securing the Republican nomination and ultimately the presidency for Richard Nixon, was unable to ride both horses. It advised voting for Nixon and made the suggestion that Democrats write-in Nixon's name on their ballot if they were totally frustrated with the behavior of the Democrats.

McCarthy, on the other hand, received vigorous endorsement editorials in the *Concord Daily Monitor, Portsmouth Herald, Valley News,* and *Keene Sentinel.* The *Claremont Eagle* supported Johnson and the other three daily newspapers did not take a position. The previous week a number of the weekly newspapers editorialized in support of McCarthy in their last edition before the Tuesday primary.

McCarthy's heavy weekend speaking schedule and the response he had received while campaigning highlighted the coverage through to election morning. The television networks carried lengthy segments on the primary which contained film footage of McCarthy's crowd-attracting, handshaking tour of Manchester's Elm Street Saturday afternoon.

The McCarthy campaign managers and volunteers thought the time lines were about to cross. To Joel Feigenbaum, tabulating each weekend's canvassing results, it seemed to be happening a bit early. He would have liked another week, another weekend of canvassing, to predict that McCarthy would get at least 50 percent of the total vote. For him and those who sensed that the campaign was developing well, another week would have had the campaign momentum line and the time line of the election date cross at the peak, the climax of the effort.

To others it appeared as if the final weekend had accomplished a climax that was near the peak. Certainly the media peak was reached during the weekend of March 9. Campaign events, response to the campaign, and campaign coverage coincided to produce the reaction reflected in the media that weekend and through to election morning March 12.

PREDICTING THE OUTCOME: WHAT WILL BE SIGNIFICANT?

The numbers game had been a favorite topic of the reporters throughout the campaign. Now in the final hour they each had to pick a number, a percentage, that each candidate would have to achieve in order for the results to be significant. For Lyndon Johnson the figure had to be above 50 percent and to be a decisive victory at least 60 percent would be expected. For McCarthy the subheadline of a March 11 *Boston Herald-Traveler* story summed up the problem: "And the Experts Are Still Baffled."

I had been quoted as anticipating about one-third of the vote for McCarthy when the McCarthy candidacy was first being mentioned. I quickly opted for Senator McIntyre's "5,000 votes" or "5 to 10 percent of the total vote." Throughout the campaign I, and all others, refused to be trapped by the numbers questions of the reporters. McCarthy refused the bait himself by answering that he expected to "win" the New Hampshire primary but refused to define the word "win"—something that the reporters felt they must define as something less than the 50 percent plus one vote.

The Johnson campaign leaders began their campaign with the assumption that almost all true New Hampshire Democrats would be voting for the president—"90,000 Strong" was the theme. To concede even a few votes to McCarthy was upsetting and a position that made it difficult for Bernard Boutin, especially, to adjust to the reality of the growing support for McCarthy.

On February 18 the *New York Times* reported: "Neither the New Hampshire Senator nor the Governor seemed unduly concerned . . . about the possibility of Mr. McCarthy's staging an upset—the official party estimate is that the Minnesota Senator will be lucky to get 12 percent of the vote."

Boutin commented in an interview on February 26:

> "If we're free of snow storms or sub zero weather, I would guess we'll get a vote of somewhere in the area of 50,000 to 55,000, and I think more than that is still conceivable."
>
> How many of those votes would be for President Johnson? "What we're looking for is a substantial majority. We're out to better the record of 1964 when the President got something in the order of 29,000 and I would hope we could roll up 60, 70 or more percent."
>
> Does Boutin think a Johnson winning margin of two to one enough to have Johnson look good in New Hampshire? Boutin replied, "I wouldn't couch it in those terms. I say the President should do as well or better than he did in 1964 when he had everything going for him . . . no opposition . . . and he got around 29,000 votes."
>
> "Now, I'd say anything 25,000 and up is a very clear victory."
>
> (*Foster's Daily Democrat,* February 26, 1968)

Governor King predicted a Democratic vote of "42,000" with Senator McCarthy receiving "between 12,000 and 18,000 votes." (*Manchester Union Leader,* February 26, 1968) The *Boston Globe* reported the findings of a *Time* magazine poll of New Hampshire voting that gave "President Johnson 62 percent, Sen. McCarthy 11 percent, and Robert Kennedy 9 percent." (*Boston Globe*, March 4, 1968) A *Newsweek* article in the March 4 edition reported, "A poll by the state's biggest paper, the arch conservative *Manchester Union Leader*, projected a 6-to-1 Johnson victory over McCarthy, whose name will actually appear on the March 12 ballot. More disheartening to the insurgent forces is a survey conducted by a McCarthy-prone University of New Hampshire political science professor: it gave LBJ 49 per cent of the vote, Sen. Robert Kennedy 21 percent and the Minnesota senator only 9 to 10 points." (*Newsweek,* March 4, 1968, p. 22)

When Evans and Novak looked at the New Hampshire situation again just before the election they wrote, "So unpredictable is the size of the voter turnout and the number who will actually write in the President's name, that scientific pollsters cannot guess the outcome. But contrary to early boasts by the Democratic regulars here that McCarthy would be held to 10 percent, his total is likely to exceed 25 percent and conceivably could climb to 40 percent—enough to give him momentum for next month's Wisconsin primary." (*Boston Globe,* March 7, 1968)

To add to the fun, the results of New Hampshire high school polls began to trickle into the newspapers. Remembering that the former Democratic National Committee chair, John Bailey, held much stock in such polls, the results were encouraging:

> . . . In a mock primary election held yesterday at Concord High School, on the Democratic ballot, Sen. Eugene McCarthy, D. Minn., easily topped the list polling 184 votes while President Johnson, whose name did not appear on the ballot, received 37 write-in votes.
>
> A total of 542 students, 48 percent of the student body, turned out to take part in the mock election.
>
> (*Concord Daily Monitor,* March 8, 1968, p. 1)

This was an indication of the impact that Senator McCarthy had made on the New Hampshire populace. Concord was an important city for him and contained an independent voting population. If his candidacy had been this attractive the returns in similar communities on election day would be encouraging.

With a headline, "McCarthy Drive Snowballs Through New Hampshire," the *Boston Herald-Traveler* concluded, "If McCarthy pulls more than 25 or 30 percent of the vote he is a 'winner'." (*Boston Herald-Traveler,* March 10, 1968, p. 44) Such concluding analyses began to frighten Bernard Boutin and he raised his expectations of what McCarthy would need in order to be termed a "significant" vote:

> Neither the Johnson people nor McCarthy is making any broad predictions. Bernard Boutin . . . added last week that if McCarthy does not get 40 percent of the vote his campaign will be a failure.
>
> But what will be interpreted as a dramatic win by most in New Hampshire is roughly 35 percent to 37 percent of the vote. With this McCarthy could capture all of the 24 delegate votes to the Democratic convention in Chicago in August.
>
> (*Boston Globe,* March 10, 1968, p. 21)

In this item was the first mention of delegates. Most, except this writer, Robert Healy, the *Globe*'s political editor, had conceded the delegates to Johnson. This was certainly the case among the McCarthy leadership. Boutin's struggle to escalate his prediction of the McCarthy percentage was reported by the *New York Times:*

> Two months ago leading New Hampshire Democrats gave Senator McCarthy less than 15 percent of the vote. Two weeks ago a top Johnson administration strategist raised this to 30. With five days to go, the Johnson campaign director, Bernard Boutin, said it would be "a disgrace if McCarthy gets less than 40 per cent," based on his spending and campaigning.
>
> McCarthy backers said they would be well satisfied if the Minnesota Senator got 25 percent of the vote.
>
> (*New York Times,* March 10, 1968, p. 1)

During the final week an advance staff for the NBC coverage of the election had been preparing a background book on the 1968 New Hampshire primary for David Brinkley and Chet Huntley. Part of that assignment was to determine the percentages above which a "significant" result could be ascertained. Into the mysterious crystal ball they used to produce their calculation went numerous interviews, some spot polling, the wisdom of such pundits as Richard Scammon, former director of the U.S. Bureau of the Census, and the expectations of the candidates' managers. The McCarthy managers set 25 percent as their figure hoping the network would not set its mark much above 30 percent.

Boutin scrambled to get the network to accept his threshold for McCarthy as being 40 percent. Late Monday afternoon, March 11, NBC's conclusion was set and rumored about the halls of the Wayfarer. Anything above 35 percent for McCarthy was determined by the network as being "significant." Given what the canvassing results had shown, the McCarthy managers protested like Cheshire cats. NBC had placed the figure a bit higher than the McCarthy campaign had wanted but not unreasonably so. For Johnson the NBC threshold was 50 percent. No delegate count prediction was included nor a projection of a vote total in the Democratic primary. Now that NBC had come to its conclusion, the election could be held.

NEW HAMPSHIRE VOTES

On March 11, when McCarthy returned to the Wayfarer from the television taping session in Boston Monday afternoon, he relaxed, met with Robert Lowell, dined, and then, with those who had worked with him during the New Hampshire campaign, watched the early evening broadcast. All complimented him on his performance that he himself appeared to enjoy. The remainder of the evening he spent between his own quarters and strolling through the Wayfarer talking with reporters and friends.

Gans began winding up the election day machinery from the Concord headquarters. Studds and I made a number of telephone checks with our contacts around the state to find out what the status of the election day preparations was and to offer answers to last-minute questions. The press activity at the Wayfarer, which had been humming almost around-the-clock for the last ten days, was now silent as the workers began to feel the exhaustion of little sleep, tension, and almost no other contacts but the campaign and each other. Relations had been remarkably smooth considering the pressure.

For the first time in more than ten weeks there seemed to be little to do. The local organizations now had the full responsibility to get-out-the-vote and to watch the election process. March 12 was town meeting day. In each town the citizens would gather to vote for local officials, discuss budgets for the coming year, and deal with the items placed on the warrant for the town meeting. Unlike the cities, with their representative councils and regularly scheduled legislative meetings, the annual town meeting is usually the only time during the year when a New Hampshire town can do legislative business. Regardless of the weather, the turnout in the small towns is high for this important annual event.

For the state's fourteen cities, the day is much less important. The only attraction for the voters is the presidential primary, and occasionally some other local item may be contained with the primary ballot. Turnout is more closely modulated by weather than in the smaller towns on presidential primary election days.

Like a gray blanket being pulled silently over the landscape, the sky darkened toward the afternoon of March 11 and snow was predicted for that evening and much of the next day. When asked by the reporters whether McCarthy would be helped or hurt by what they described as "bad weather," I replied that throughout the campaign the weather had cooperated fully with McCarthy. There was no reason to think there would be any change. "Whatever the weather it would be McCarthy weather," I stated optimistically. By midnight a full storm was blowing outside and the temperature was falling.

Before tucking in for the night, most waited for the first returns from New Hampshire's smallest towns. One or two would decide it was worth the trouble to get the attention of being the first to vote. This year it would be Waterville Valley. An isolated enclave tucked back in a remote valley surrounded by the White Mountain National Forest, Waterville Valley had found a new life during the previous two years when former Olympic skier, Tommy Cochran, began developing a major ski facility. To boost this development, the eighteen registered voters of Waterville Valley gathered in their town hall before midnight, March 11. Just after midnight they each selected their party's ballot, voted, and immediately tallied the result with the attention of the television cameras, reporters, and lights.

The first returns trickled back to Manchester. Richard Nixon won all eight Republican votes. On the Democratic Party side there were eight votes for McCarthy, two write-in votes for Robert Kennedy (most assuredly cast by Tom Cochran and his wife, close friends of Robert Kennedy), and not a single vote for Lyndon B. Johnson. With that omen, most campaign workers and reporters straggled off to sleep.

When the dawn, although not the sun, emerged that morning, the radio and morning newspapers had the early returns to report. It was certainly a surprise since Waterville Valley, before Tom Cochran's development, had been a Republican stronghold. In 1968 there was a change. Not only were there Democrats in Waterville Valley but Democrats willing to support persons other than the president, in spite of the fact that much of the early development at Waterville Valley had been financed by loans from the Economic Development Act of 1965 which President Johnson had urged Congress to enact.

Two activities occupied the McCarthy workers on election day. The first was to get out the McCarthy vote. The second was to get ready to tabulate that vote once the polls had closed. At the state headquarters in Concord and the campaign headquarters at the Wayfarer, tally sheets, name cards, and tote boards were carefully lettered and arranged for those who would later come to watch the returns. Someone had had credential stickers printed that would be distributed to the campaign workers to ensure that they would be allowed into the rooms where the excitement would be the greatest. How these would be distributed no one had quite figured out, but each of the principals involved in the campaign was given a pack to hand out to those they recognized when the crowd arrived that evening.

NBC had reserved the convention hall of the Wayfarer and had been spending the week building sets, erecting computerized tally boards, installing numerous telephone lines, and Teletypes, and setting up tally tables with adding machines to aggregate the vote. David Brinkley and Chet Huntley had arrived a day or so before. Their evening news broadcast originated from the Wayfarer studio the previous evening. The highest status symbol a McCarthy campaigner could possess in these final hours of the campaign was an NBC numbered badge that would allow the wearer access to the convention hall.

CBS, once again interested in the New Hampshire result, had set up a mini-studio in a downtown Manchester hotel where Walter Cronkite would report, "That's the way it is." ABC relied on the primitive facilities of its network affiliate, Channel 9, as its base. Volunteers from the New Hampshire League of Women Voters and university students had been organized to collect the vote at each polling place and report to the wire service pool which then relayed the tallies to their network, newspaper, and radio station subscribers. NBC had commissioned Richard Scammon and Oliver Quayle to select sample precincts for early analysis and projection purposes. Since, with only a few exceptions, New Hampshire voted by paper ballot, the results would take some time to tally. Also, since there were a number of local issues to be voted upon at the town meetings, and town meeting polls do not usually close until the warrant for the meeting has been completed, some towns would not have their presidential vote tallies completed until late in the evening. With all of the local issues, presidential candidates and write-in candidates on both the Democratic and Republican ballot, and numerous candidates for delegate and alternative delegate to the national conventions, completing a vote tally for even the small towns was a demanding and time-consuming task. The ballot that faced each voter was the size of a newspaper page.

McCarthy spent the day with friends, chatting with reporters, and being photographed watching volunteers prepare placards, posters, and trimmings for the evening. He was relaxed, seemed confident that the returns would be favorable, and visibly enjoyed witnessing the final burst of energy that was concluding the campaign. The same thoroughness that had become a campaign trademark carried through the preparations for the image of what had been accomplished in New Hampshire and how it would be projected from the McCarthy headquarters that evening. That image had to summarize and exemplify what the New Hampshire vote should signify in terms of the McCarthy candidacy and the McCarthy position on the issues.

What had become an exceptionally exciting political event for the reporters, the volunteers, the professionals, and an important part of the New Hampshire electorate now had to be encapsulated for transmission outside New Hampshire. To do this, the McCarthy campaign rented the largest meeting room left in the city—an expandable banquet room at the Wayfarer, set up a stage, and decorated the stage with tally boards and a large McCarthy for President banner. The television networks set up their cameras, special telephones and tables were set aside for the reporters, and radio connections and tape recording equipment were installed. With all the electronic equipment, the stage, the backdrop, and other paraphernalia, even a few people standing in the remaining space would look like a crowd.

As the day wore on, Senator McCarthy made a few visits around Manchester to see polling places and to sense what was happening. When he returned to his cottage he found that the living room had been transformed by Harold Stein and his wife. The Steins had ordered fruit, hors d'oeuvres, cold cuts, and a bar. With the Steins were Arnold Hiatt and his wife; Robert Lowell; John Cogley, editor of the *Center* magazine; Dick Goodwin; and others who had come to witness the finale.

Outside the weather remained marginal. The snow slackened but the wind increased and it was cold. The hint of spring that had brought the outpouring on Saturday as McCarthy street campaigned in Manchester was only a memory. Each local McCarthy committee and headquarters kept close track of the voting. In the afternoon they began calling those names on the canvassing cards that were identified as number "1" and "2," favorable to or leaning to Senator McCarthy. If time and volunteer power allowed, the "3" names were also called in hopes that the last-minute Johnson campaign charges and steady McCarthy response might have motivated them toward voting for McCarthy.

To make getting to the polls more convenient for the voters, rides and babysitting were offered. Radio and newspaper ads carried headquarters' telephone numbers for voting help. As the final plug to the voter an advertisement appeared both on the radio and in newspapers:

> How will you feel tomorrow morning?
>
> Just stop and think for a minute.
> How would you feel if you woke up
> tomorrow to find that Eugene
> McCarthy had won the Democratic primary?
> Wouldn't you feel that suddenly there
> was new hope for America—that perhaps
> we might break out of the dreary circle
> of rising discontent and continuing
> stagnation? Wouldn't you be proud that
> New Hampshire had changed the entire
> political picture of the nation—
> and restored vitality to the democratic
> process? And, wouldn't you be pleased
> that the independence of New Hampshire
> voters had enabled a lone man of conviction
> to triumph over huge odds and all the
> prophets? You can make Wednesday that
> kind of morning . . . by voting for
> Eugene McCarthy.
> McCarthy for President.
>
> (*Manchester Union Leader*, March 12, 1968)

With the ad was a photograph of the smiling face of McCarthy that had become the principal photograph used by the campaign.

With almost no information about what was happening during the day, except some turnout figures from the cities' ballot box totals, McCarthy workers busied themselves, as in a vacuum, throughout the day. In spite of the weather, the turnout of voters selecting the Democratic ballot appeared to be ahead of the projected fifty thousand to fifty-five thousand total. Spot checks of voters by NBC at selected polling places and reports from McCarthy workers suggested that the McCarthy vote was holding about as had been projected from the canvassing results analysis of Joel Feigenbaum.

The city polling places closed at 8:00 P.M. Portsmouth, voting by machine, reported first.

Ward	McCarthy	Johnson
1	157	44
2	122	68
3	115	38
4	119	48
5	43	46
6	43	24
	599	268

(N.H. Manual for the General Court No. 41, 1969, p. 464)

The port city, location of the two important military installations, had voted more than two to one for McCarthy. The excitement produced by this first serious return rippled through the Wayfarer. The polls in many districts were now closed, and those who had worked throughout the day getting voters to the polls began gathering at the Wayfarer listening for news of results and watching the updates reported by the television networks.

Few people stayed in any one place long, preferring instead to walk anxiously from one part of the sprawling motel to another. From the McCarthy headquarters wing in the motel, to the McCarthy reception room, to the press room, across the covered bridge to the NBC studio in the convention hall, then outside to McCarthy's cottage fifty yards from the convention hall, became a route a number of the campaign leaders followed. The best information seemed to be coming to the NBC center, but as campaign workers arrived from their cities and towns, their tales of the day's activity often told more of what the result might be.

During the early evening the Johnson-McCarthy vote hovered close to even at 48 and 49 percent. What no one seemed to know was where the returns had come from and what districts were still outstanding. Telephone reports and workers arriving with their won district tallies gave a better account of where the vote had been reported.

Surprise after surprise in the results kept the crowd on edge of hysteria. Shortly after 10:00 P.M., some of the large Manchester wards began reporting. The McCarthy percentage began to recede from the high point of 48 percent. The Johnson percentage seemed to hold but was still below the critical 50 percent that most agreed an incumbent president must achieve.

At 10:30 P.M. someone standing in the NBC center caught the rumor that even though McCarthy's vote percentage was beginning to recede as the totals built, he was still holding almost all of the delegate positions. The network was beginning to project that McCarthy might win all of the delegates and certainly would hold at least eighteen of the twenty-four delegate slots. His percentage in the presidential preference section of the ballot would probably be between 40 and 45 percent—well above the 35 percent that NBC had set as assuring a "significant" result. While mildly disappointed that they had not achieved the 50 percent plateau, the fact that McCarthy was solidly above 40 percent and had a good chance of electing a majority of the delegates was enough to release the full celebrating energy of the crush of volunteers.

In the turmoil, two other events further excited the gathering. Those arriving from the polling places reported something that had not been assimilated by the network. McCarthy had received a significant write-in vote on the ballots of Republican voters—especially in communities like Concord, Peterborough, Hanover, and others with disaffected Romney supporters and liberals disguised as Republicans for state primary election purposes. This information led McCarthy leaders to immediately call for a careful tabulation of all of these votes. Occasionally local vote counters neglect the write-in votes as being too erratic or diffused to be worth listing.

The second moment of surprise came when Marc Kasky, almost forgotten during the last days of the campaign, called in the results from Berlin.

Ward	McCarthy	Johnson
1	404	429
2	401	361
3	358	294
4	473	440
	1,636	1,524

(N.H. Manual for the General Court No. 41, 1969, p. 452)

McCarthy had carried Berlin!

Quite late in the evening a number of those who had been supporting President Johnson drifted, like the snow that evening, into the Wayfarer with their congratulations and tales of the other camp during the campaign. According to one, as Bernard Boutin watched the percentages shift on the tote boards they had set up in the ballroom of the Sheraton Carpenter, he said, "I've got to call Marvin Watson at the White House with the results very soon but I'm going to wait until Berlin comes in. That should easily put the President over the fifty percent mark." (DCH recollection) Shortly after the Berlin vote did come in, a dejected Boutin had to make that call and report the bitter news to his political associate, Marvin Watson, who would then give it to the President.

At about 10:30 P.M. McCarthy slipped out of his cottage to drive into Manchester for an interview with Walter Cronkite. McCarthy enjoyed Cronkite's manner and the fact that he had come to New Hampshire during the past weekend to see what was happening himself. McCarthy was also amazed that NBC would go to such elaborate lengths to cover the voting but not really cover the campaign. As a personal tweak at NBC's extravagance, he let CBS and Cronkite have the first interview. He returned to the cottage in time to be summoned for a live interview with David

Brinkley and Chet Huntley for the 11:00 P.M. news. With Blair Clark, Studds, me, and several others, he plowed a path through the snow from his cottage to the rear of the convention center, arriving minutes before the live broadcast was to begin.

Introducing McCarthy, David Brinkley said that McCarthy had scored a stunning upset not only in the preferential vote but by the election of delegates as well. McCarthy summarized his own reaction to the results and the meaning he felt it conveyed. To Brinkley's question as to whether he had talked to Robert Kennedy, he said that he "had talked with Robert Lowell," which McCarthy felt was at least as important that evening as having received a congratulatory telephone call from Senator Robert Kennedy.

As the concluding rite of the campaign, McCarthy then strode across the covered bridge into the Bedford room where his supporters, workers, and the curious waited for their hero. Amidst cheers that erupted with the slightest provocation, McCarthy thanked all for their help, urged them to continue, and expressed the possibility that what had started in New Hampshire now would go all the way to the Chicago convention and, perhaps, even beyond. In the few hours of that evening, McCarthy had become a serious presidential contender, and everyone in the room sensed the importance of the change

Eventually McCarthy returned to the cottage where he was interviewed, recorded, and photographed. The crowd at the Wayfarer slowly began to break up but would not do so completely until sunrise March 13.

During the evening almost nothing had been heard from the headquarters in Concord. Realizing that many of those who had worked the longest and the hardest had decided to spend the evening in Concord where they had dedicated themselves to the campaign, Studds and I drove north from Bedford. When we arrived we found Gans, Brown, Stavis, Norling, Dodds, Feigenbaum, Silverman, Barbieri, Dumanoski, Tuchman, and the others who had taken on the responsibilities of the headquarters.

As I stepped through the door, Sam Brown and Joel Feigenbaum, jumped up from their chairs together. "Do you have the envelope?" they asked. I reached into the coat pocket of the dark blue suit I had worn out in the campaign, extracted the envelope and tore it open. Inside were two slips with the vote percentage that Brown and Feigenbaum had each written and signed several weeks before: Brown's percentage nineteen, Feigenbaum's percentage forty-two. The nuclear physicist won the five-dollar bet and had hit the final McCarthy percentage of the Democratic vote exactly. With the addition of the Republican write-in votes for Senator McCarthy and for President Johnson, the total vote percentage was forty-eight for each person. McCarthy had 518 fewer actual votes than Johnson. The total number of votes cast in the Democratic primary exceeded sixty thousand.

The champagne was gone and the celebration was almost over. On the wall was a list of the winning delegates, and on the faces of those who had worked for McCarthy was a mixture of deep satisfaction and bone-deep exhaustion. The scraps of paper on which were recorded the voting district results littered the headquarters in a way that would have normally driven Rosann Stavis to distraction. But this was the end. Tomorrow it would be on to Wisconsin.

Appendix

1968 CANDIDATE TALLY

	Total Vote	% of Total Vote	% of Tabulated Vote**
DEMOCRATIC: (4)		60,519	55,470
Lyndon Johnson	27,520*	45.5	49.6
Eugene McCarthy	23,269#	38.4	41.9
Richard Nixon	2,532*	4.2	4.6
Robert Kennedy	606*	1.0	1.1
Paul Fisher	506*	.8	.9
Nelson Rockefeller	249*	.4	.4
George Wallace	201*	.3	.4
John Crommelin	186	.3	.3
Richard Lee	170	.3	.3
Jacob Gordon	77		
Others	154	.3	.3
	55,470		

* Write-in

The McCarthy total is inaccurately listed as 23,263 in the Manual.
(Brereton, Charles. *First in the Nation*. Portsmouth, N.H.: Peter E. Randall, 1987.)

** The total vote is the number who participated in either the Democratic or Republican primary. The tabulated vote is what was tallied for the candidates. The discrepancy in these figures is attributed to the fact that a number of people would vote in the delegate selection part of the primary—but not the presidential preference poll; or their vote was a write-in not counted for Others. The tabulated vote percentage is used in listing the election results.

	Total Vote	% of Total Vote	% of Tabulated Vote**
REPUBLICAN: (9)		108,273	103,938
Richard Nixon	80,666	74.5	77.6
Nelson Rockefeller	11,241*	10.4	10.8
Eugene McCarthy	5,511*	5.1	5.3
Lyndon Johnson	1,778*	1.6	1.7
George Romney	1,743	1.6	1.7
Willis Stone	527	.5	.5
Harold Stassen	429	.4	.4
Paul Fisher	374*	.3	.4
Ronald Reagan	362*	.3	.3
Herbert Hoover	247	.2	.2
David Watumull	161	.1	.2
William Evans	151	.1	.1
Elmer Coy	73		
Don DuMont	39		
Others	636	.6	.6
	103,938		

* Write-in

** The total vote is the number who participated in either the Democratic or Republican primary. The tabulated vote is what was tallied for the candidates. The discrepancy in these figures is attributed to the fact that a number of people would vote in the delegate selection part of the primary—but not the presidential preference poll; or their vote was a write-in not counted for Others. The tabulated vote percentage is used in listing the election results.

Source: *Manual for the General Court.* Volume 41

SUMMARY JOHNSON/McCARTHY VOTE TOTAL

Johnson/ McCarthy Democratic & Republican Vote	Democratic Vote	Republican Write-in Vote	Total Vote	Total Vote Johnson/ McCarthy % of Democratic Vote Cast	Johnson/ McCarthy % of Total Democratic Vote Republican Write-in Cast
				(60,519)	(67,808)
Lyndon Johnson	27,520	1,778	29,298	48.4%	43.2%
Eugene McCarthy	23,269	5,511	28,780	47.6%	42.4%
Difference					
For Johnson	4,251		518		
For McCarthy		3,733			

1968 DEMOCRATIC PRESIDENTIAL PRIMARY RESULTS BY COUNTY

County	% Johnson	% LBJ Total	% McC	% McC Total	PARTICIPATION % County Total	% Total Rep. & Dem. Participation	% Dem. of Total
Belknap	+ 47.0 (949)	3.5	42.5 (858)	3.6	3.6 (2,020)	46.1	27.1 (2,279)
Carroll	44.0 (292)	1.1	+ 45.7 (303)	1.2	1.2 (663)	52.2	12.6 (766)
Cheshire	+ 45.9 (1,220)	4.4	45.5 (1,210)	5.1	4.8 (2,657)	41.3	27.9 (2,868)
Coos	45.6 (2,231)	8.1	+ 48.5 (2,373)	10.1	8.9 (4,889)	52.4	52.4 (5,697)
Grafton	36.5 (1,093)	4.0	+ 54.7 (1,639)	7.0	5.4 (2,998)	47.0	25.9 (3,355)
Hillsborough	+ 56.8 (12,791)	46.4	34.1 (7,684)	34.0	40.6 (22,535)	47.0	48.7 (24,105)
Merrimack	+ 48.0 (2,503)	9.1	43.0 (2,242)	9.5	9.4 (5,214)	47.6	28.3 (5,667)
Rockingham	41.0 (3,155)	11.5	+ 50.3 (3,866)	16.5	13.9 (7,692)	51.7	27.0 (8,501)
Strafford	45.4 (2,076)	7.5	+ 48.9 (2,235)	9.5	8.3 (4,574)	34.2	39.8 (4,865)
Sullivan	+ 54.7 (1,210)	4.4	38.9 (859)	3.5	4.0 (2,211)	43.2	35.1 (2,416)
Totals	49.6 (27,520)	100.0	42.0 (23,269)	100.0	100.0 (55,454)	46.4 (168,792)	35.9 (60,519)

+ Winner

1968 REPUBLICAN VOTE FOR McCARTHY AND JOHNSON BY COUNTY

County	% Johnson	% McCarthy	LBJ/McCarthy % of Total Co. Rep. Vote
Belknap	17.0 (65)	83.0 (318)	6.2 (6,143)
Carroll	25.4 (53)	74.6 (156)	3.9 (5,329)
Cheshire	21.0 (109)	79.0 (409)	7.0 (7,430)
Coos	41.0 (166)	59.0 (238)	7.8 (5,173)
Grafton	19.9 (129)	80.1 (521)	6.8 (9,601)
Hillsborough	28.1 (466)	71.9 (1,192)	6.5 (25,434)
Merrimack	19.8 (223)	80.1 (899)	7.8 (14,355)
Rockingham	24.4 (347)	75.6 (10,78)	6.2 (22,994)
Strafford	16.9 (88)	83.1 (436)	7.1 (7,350)
Sullivan	33.3 (132)	66.7 (264)	8.9 (4,464)
	24.4 (1,778)	75.6 (5,511)	6.7 (108,273)

TARGET LARGE CITY/TOWN RESULTS, 1968 PRESIDENTIAL PRIMARY

Community	% LBJ	% LBJ Total	% McC	% McC Total	% Comm.	Participation: % Dem. Vote of Total Reg.	Participation: % of Total Dem. Vote
Manchester	+ 69.0 (7,591)	45.9	31.0 (3,412)	29.5	40.6 (12,351)	27.7 (46,921)	21.5 (13,031)
Nashua	+ 59.3 (2,585)	15.6	40.7 (1,776)	15.3	14.9 (4,527)	21.1 (22,579)	7.9 (4,765)
Berlin	48.3 (1,524)	9.1	+51.7 (1,636)	14.2	10.8 (3,282)	36.2 (10,398)	6.2 (3,768)
Somersworth	+ 57.5 (600)	4.0	42.5 (444)	3.8	3.6 (1,103)	21.2 (5,612)	2.0 (1,189)
Claremont	+ 62.1 (673)	4.1	37.9 (411)	3.5	3.7 (1,131)	16.6 (7,266)	2.0 (1,207)
Dover	+ 52.0 (676)	4.1	48.0 (625)	5.4	4.5 (1,352)	11.4 (12,256)	2.3 (1,400)
Rochester	49.0 (394)	2.3	+51.0 (410)	3.5	3.7 (870)	16.6 (9,205)	2.0 (930)
Laconia	+ 60.5 (527)	3.2	39.4 (344)	3.0	3.2 (963)	11.8 (8,504)	1.6 (999)
Concord	46.1 (606)	3.4	+ 53.9 (707)	6.2	4.6 (1,392)	8.9 (15,736)	2.3 (1,399)
Keene	+ 53.3 (470)	2.8	46.7 (411)	3.6	3.2 (979)	10.5 (9,472)	1.6 (992)
Portsmouth	30.9 (268)	2.0	+ 69.1 (599)	5.2	3.0 (924)	12.6 (8,586)	1.8 (1,080)
Salem	43.5 (597)	3.5	+ 56.5 (776)	6.7	5.0 (1,520)	39.5 (8,345)	2.7 (1,633)
	58.8 (16,511)	100.0	41.2 (11,551)	100.0	100.0 (30,394)	19.7 (164,880)	53.5 (32,393)
	% Total Vote LBJ		**% Total Vote Mc.**		**% Total Dem. Vote**	**Total Reg. Voters**	**Dem. Total Vote**
	60 (27,520)		49.7 (23,263)		50.2 (60,519)	16.7 (363,503)	100.0 (60,519)

+ Winner

1968 DEMOCRATIC PRESIDENTIAL PRIMARY RESULTS BY SIZE OF VOTING DISTRICT

Size of Voting District (pre-1968 Dem. Registration)	% Districts McCarthy Won	% Districts Johnson Won	% Ties	% McCarthy Vote	% Johnson Vote	% Sub-total	% of Total McCarthy Vote	% of Total Johnson Vote	% of Total Primary Vote
Districts under 100**	58.6	36.4	5.0	48.7	41.0	100	10.4	7.4	9.0
(N=140)	(82)	(51)	(7)	(2,428)	(2,043)	(4,985)	(2,428)	(2,043)	(4,985)
Towns: 100–199	65.2	34.8	—	48.2	41.5	100	11.5	8.4	10.2
(N=46)	(30)	(16)	(0)	(2,681)	(2,307)	(5,563)	(2,681)	(2,307)	(5,563)
Wards: 100–199	69.2	23.0	7.7	52.8	38.9	100	3.5	2.2	2.8
(N=13)	(9)	(3)	(1)	(815)	(600)	(1,544)	(815)	(600)	(1,544)
All Districts: 100–199	66.1	32.2	1.7	49.2	40.9	100	15.0	10.6	13.0
(N=59)	(39)	(19)	(1)	(3,496)	(2,907)	(7,107)	(3,496)	(2,907)	(7,107)
Towns: 200–499	56.0	44.0	—	49.4	42.2	100	11.8	8.5	10.2
(N=25)	(14)	(11)	(0)	(2,735)	(2,336)	(5,536)	(2,735)	(2,336)	(5,536)
Wards: 200–499	44.0	56.0	—	45.3	48.8	100	9.6	8.8	9.1
(N=25)	(11)	(14)	(0)	(2,242)	(2,417)	(4,951)	(2,242)	(2,417)	(4,951)
All Districts:200–499	50.0	50.0	—	47.5	45.3	100	21.4	17.3	19.3
(N=50)	(25)	(25)	(0)	(4,977)	(4,753)	(10,487)	(4,977)	(4,753)	(10,487)
Towns: 500–999	38.5	61.5	—	45.1	46.2	100	12.0	10.4	11.4
(N=13)	(5)	(8)	(0)	(2,799)	(2,866)	(6,207)	(2,799)	(2,866)	(6,207)
Wards: 500–999	16.7	83.3	—	41.9	53.4	100	13.0	14.0	13.2
(N=18)	(3)	(15)	(0)	(3,021)	(3,855)	(7,215)	(3,021)	(3,855)	(7,215)
All Districts: 500–999	25.8	74.2	—	43.4	50.1	100	13.0	24.4	24.6
(N=31)	(8)	(23)	(0)	(5,820)	(6,721)	(13,422)	(5,820)	(6,721)	(13,422)
Towns (3) and **Wards** (19):	13.6	86.4	—	33.7	57.0	100	28.1	40.3	35.7
1,000–3,100 (N=22)	(3)	(19)	(0)	(6,548)	(11,096)	(19,453)	(6,548)	(11,096)	(19,453)
Grand Totals 100%	52.0	45.4	2.7	42.0	49.6	100	100	100	100
(302)	(157)	(137)	(8)	(23,269)	(27,520)	(55,454)	(23,269)	(27,520)	(55,454)

** including 3 city wards under 100. (2 Concord; 1 Portsmouth)

DELEGATE SELECTION, 1ST C.D. ELECTED DELEGATE VOTE, 1968 DEMOCRATIC PRESIDENTIAL PRIMARY

Name	Residence	Candidate Allegiance	Vote
1) McIntyre (senator)*	Laconia	LBJ	10,315
2) King (governor)	Manchester	LBJ	9,630
3) Morin	Hampton	McCarthy	8,994
4) Ross	Manchester	McCarthy	8,929
5) Craig	Manchester	LBJ	8,888
6) Farrell	Manchester	McCarthy	8,852
7) McEachern	Portsmouth	McCarthy	8,840
8) Beauvais	Manchester	McCarthy	8,729
9) Carrier	Manchester	McCarthy	8,722
10) Holland	Bedford	McCarthy	8,716
11) MacLellan	Manchester	McCarthy	8,694
12) O'Callaghan	Laconia	McCarthy	8,675
13) Blanchard	Portsmouth	McCarthy	8,572
14) McKay	Hudson	McCarthy	8,419
15) Dishman	Durham	McCarthy	8,395
16) Sullivan	Manchester	LBJ	7,965

* 12 to be elected
Results: 3 LBJ, 9 McCarthy delegates elected

DELEGATE SELECTION, 2ND C.D. ELECTED DELEGATE VOTE, 1968 DEMOCRATIC PRESIDENTIAL PRIMARY

Name	Residence	Candidate Allegiance	Vote
1) Bouchard*	Nashua	McCarthy	7,684
2) Kennedy	Keene	McCarthy	7,555
3) Boutin	Nashua	LBJ	7,421
4) Daniell	Franklin	McCarthy	7,322
5) Oleson	Gorham	McCarthy	7,240
6) Wallin	Nashua	McCarthy	7,108
7) Meloney	Claremont	McCarthy	7,108
8) Whelton	Nashua	McCarthy	7,033
9) Hoeh, D.	Hanover	McCarthy	6,967
10) Marrow	Chesterfield	McCarthy	6,952
11) Proulx	Ashland	McCarthy	6,905
12) Studds	Concord	McCarthy	6,895
13) Underwood	Concord	McCarthy	6,768
14) Winn	Nashua	LBJ	6,366

* 12 to be elected
Results: 1 LBJ, 11 McCarthy delegates elected

ALTERNATE DELEGATE SELECTION, 1ST C.D. ELECTED ALTERNATE DELEGATE VOTE, 1968 DEMOCRATIC PRESIDENTIAL PRIMARY

Name	Residence	Candidate Allegiance	Vote
1) Tobin*	Manchester	LBJ	9,881
2) Bergeron	Manchester	LBJ	9,607
3) Raiche	Manchester	LBJ	9,579
4) Preston	Hampton	LBJ	9,476
5) LaFleur	Manchester	LBJ	9,336
6) Levesque	Rochester	LBJ	9,293
7) LaCrois	Rochester	LBJ	9,146
8) Normandin	Laconia	LBJ	9,089
9) Belair	Salem	LBJ	8,763
10) DesJardins, H.	Rollinsford	LBJ	8,708
11) DesJardin, G.	Manchester	McCarthy	8,617
12) Sanders, Jr.	Hampton	LBJ	8,552
13) Abbot, Jr.	Jackson	LBJ	8,476
14) Nardi	Manchester	LBJ	8,450
15) Barnard	Goffstown	McCarthy	8,295

* 12 to be elected

Results: 11 LBJ, 1 McCarthy alternate delegate elected

ALTERNATE DELEGATE SELECTION, 2ND C.D. ELECTED ALTERNATE DELEGATE VOTE, 1968 DEMOCRATIC PRESIDENTIAL PRIMARY

Name	Residence	Candidate Allegiance	Vote
1) McCarthy*	Gorham	McCarthy	7,027
2) Philbrick	Milford	LBJ	6,862
3) Boggis	Nashua	McCarthy	6,861
4) Stanley	Nashua	McCarthy	6,768
5) Taylor	Nashua	McCarthy	6,725
6) Makris	Nashua	LBJ	6,687
7) York	Concord	LBJ	6,569
8) Wood	Keene	McCarthy	6,568
9) Hoeh, S.	Hanover	McCarthy	6,482
10) Richardson	Fitzwilliam	McCarthy	6,462
11) Morse	Nashua	McCarthy	6,461
12) Eberhart	Concord	McCarthy	6,451
13) Sheridan	Concord	McCarthy	6,447
14) Coniaris	Hollis	McCarthy	6,442

*12 to be elected
Results: 3 LBJ, 9 McCarthy alternate delegates elected

Bibliography

Adler, Bill (ed.). *The McCarthy Wit* (Greenwich, Conn.: Fawcett Publications, 1969).

Beman, Lamar T. *The Direct Primary* (New York: The H.W. Wilson Co., 1926).

Binstock, Robert H. *A Report on Politics in Manchester, New Hampshire* (Cambridge, Mass.: Joint Center for Urban Studies of Technology and Harvard University, 1961).

Brereton, Charles. *First in the Nation* (Portsmouth, N.H.: Peter E. Randall, 1987).

Cash, Kevin. *Who the Hell Is William Loeb?* (Manchester, N.H.: Amoskeag Press, 1975).

Chester, Lewis; Hodgson, Godfrey; and Page, Bruce. *An American Melodrama: The Presidential Campaign of 1968* (New York: Viking Press, 1969).

Churchill, Winston. *Coniston* (New York: The Macmillan Company, 1906).

Churchill, Winston. *Mr. Crewe's Career* (New York: The Macmillan Company, 1908).

Craig, Robert E. *Voting Behavior in a Presidential Primary: The New Hampshire Democratic Presidential Primary of 1968* (unpublished doctoral dissertation, University of North Carolina, Chapel Hill, 1971).

Davis, James W. *Presidential Primaries: Road to the White House* (New York: Crowell, 1967).

Dunfey, William L. *A Short History of the Democratic Party in New Hampshire* (unpublished master's thesis, University of New Hampshire, Durham, 1954).

Eisele, Albert. *Almost to the Presidency: A Biography of Two American Politicians* (Blue Earth, Minn.: The Piper Company, 1972).

Eisenmenger, Robert W. *The Dynamics of Growth in New England Economy 1870–1964* (New England Research Series), (Wesleyan, 1966).

English, David, et. al. *Divided They Stand* (Englewood Cliffs, N.J.: Prentice Hall, 1969).

———. *The Presidential Nominating Convention 1968* (Washington, D.C.: Congressional Quarterly Service, 1968).

Gorman, Joseph Bruce. *Kefauver* (Fair Lawn, N.J.: Oxford University Press, 1971).

Herzog, Arthur. *McCarthy for President* (New York: Viking Press, 1969).

Larner, Jeremy. *Nobody Knows: Reflections on the McCarthy Campaign of 1968* (New York: Macmillan, 1970).

Lockard, Duane. *New England State Politics* (Princeton, N.J.: Princeton University Press, 1959).

McCarthy, Eugene J. *America Is Hard to See* (New York: Holt, Rinehart and Winston, 1967).

McCarthy, Eugene J. *The Limits of Power* (New York: Holt, Rinehart and Winston, 1967).

McCarthy, Eugene J. *The Year of the People* (New York: Doubleday and Company, 1969).

Merriam, C. E. *Primary Elections: A Study of the History and Tendencies of Primary Election Legislation* (Chicago: University of Chicago Press, 1908).

Merriam, C. E., and Overacker, L. *Primary Elections* (Chicago: University of Chicago Press, 1928).

O'Brien, Lawrence F. *The Democratic Campaign Manual* (Washington, D.C.: Democratic National Committee, 1964).

Parris, Judith H. *The Convention Problem, Issues in Reform of Presidential Nominating Procedures* (Washington, D.C.: The Brookings Institution, 1972).

Perry, James M. *The New Politics* (London: Weidenfeld & Nicholson, 1968).

Pierce, Neal R. *The People's President* (New York: Simon & Schuster, 1968).

Stavis, Ben. *We Were the Campaign: New Hampshire to Chicago for McCarthy* (Boston: Beacon Press, 1969).

Stout, Richard T. *People, The Story of the Grass-roots Movement that Found Eugene McCarthy and Is Transforming Our Politics Today* (New York: Harper and Row, 1970).

Underwood, Barbara. *St. Crispin's Day, Gene McCarthy in the New Hampshire Primary* (unpublished manuscript, Concord, N.H., 1970).

Veblin, Eric P. *The* Manchester Union Leader *in New Hampshire Elections* (Hanover, N.H.: University Press of Northern New England, 1975).

———. *Newspaper Impact in Election Campaigns: The Case of Two New England States* (university Microfilm, 1970 Yale thesis, New Haven, 1969).

Viorst, Milton. *Fire in the Streets* (New York: Simon & Schuster, 1979).

White, Theodore H. *The Making of the President 1968* (New York: Atheneum, 1969).

Index

Cisqua

Elemental Gelade III / Mayumi Azuma

Elemental Gelade Volume 3

Created by Mayumi Azuma

Translation - Alethea and Athena Nibley
English Adaptation - Jordan Capell
Copy Editor - Stephanie Duchin
Retouch and Lettering - Star Print Brokers
Production Artist - Kimie Kim
Graphic Designer - James Lee

Editor - Troy Lewter
Digital Imaging Manager - Chris Buford
Pre-Production Supervisor - Erika Terriquez
Art Director - Anne Marie Horne
Production Manager - Elisabeth Brizzi
Managing Editor - Vy Nguyen
VP of Production - Ron Klamert
Editor-in-Chief - Rob Tokar
Publisher - Mike Kiley
President and C.O.O. - John Parker
C.E.O. and Chief Creative Officer - Stuart Levy

A TOKYOPOP® Manga

TOKYOPOP Inc.
5900 Wilshire Blvd. Suite 2000
Los Angeles, CA 90036

E-mail: info@TOKYOPOP.com
Come visit us online at www.TOKYOPOP.com

ISBN: 978-1-59816-600-2

First TOKYOPOP printing: March 2007

10 9 8 7 6 5 4 3 2 1

Printed in the USA

Volume 3

by
Mayumi Azuma

HAMBURG // LONDON // LOS ANGELES // TOKYO

Story So Far

FOLLOWING A ROUTINE RAID, SKY PIRATE COUD VAN GIRUET DISCOVERS A MOST UNUSUAL BOUNTY--A BEAUTIFUL GIRL IN A BOX NAMED REN WHO SHE SAYS SHE NEEDS TO GO TO A PLACE CALLED EDEL GARDEN. BUT BEFORE COUD CAN MAKE SENSE OF IT ALL, A GROUP CALLED ARC AILE ARRIVES, STATING THAT THE GIRL IS IN FACT AN EDEL RAID (A LIVING WEAPON WHO REACTS WITH A HUMAN TO BECOME A FIGHTING MACHINE), AND THAT THEY WISH TO BUY HER. COU IS OUTRAGED THAT THEY WOULD TREAT HER LIKE PROPERTY, AND REFUSES TO LET THEM HAVE HER. A BATTLE BREAKS OUT, AND REN BONDS WITH COUD, BECOMING HIS WEAPON DURING THE FIGHT. REN IS SO TOUCHED BY COUD'S RESOLVE TO HELP HER, THAT SHE DECIDES TO BECOME HIS PERSONAL EDEL RAID.

DURING HIS ATTEMPT TO ESCAPE WITH REN, COUD'S ESCAPE POD IS SHOT DOWN...BUT NOT BEFORE REN'S GRAPPLING HOOK MANAGES TO BRING DOWN ARC AILE'S PLANE AS WELL. COUD, REN AND THE THREE MEMBERS OF ARC AILE ARE THEN LEFT TO WANDER THE FOREST BELOW WITH NO FOOD OR MONEY. CISQUA (LEADER OF THE ARC AILE TEAM) DECIDES TO FOLLOW COUD AND REN, MUCH TO COUD'S ANNOYANCE. THEY SOON REALIZE THAT EVEN THOUGH THEIR DIFFERENCES MAY BE MANY, THEIR COMMON DESIRE TO PROTECT REN MAY BE ENOUGH TO KEEP THEM FROM KILLING ONE ANOTHER--WHICH IS A GOOD THING, BECAUSE PROTECTING REN IS DEFINITELY A FULL-TIME JOB...A FACT MADE PAINFULLY CLEAR WHEN SHE IS KIDNAPPED BY A BLACK MARKET EDEL RAID DEALER NAMED BEAZON, AND THEN LATER HUNTED BY WOLX HOUND, AN EDEL RAID HUNTER. EVEN THOUGH COUD AND CISQUA ARE ABLE TO STOP WOLX FROM KIDNAPPING REN, THEY AREN'T ABLE TO KEEP KUEA (ARC AILE AGENT ROWEN'S EDEL RAID) OUT OF HIS CLUTCHES. NOW, AS WOLX PREPARES TO SELL KUEA AND HIS OTHER EDEL RAID BOOTY, COUD AND THE AGENTS OF ARC AILE MUST RACE AGAINST THE CLOCK TO STOP HIM...

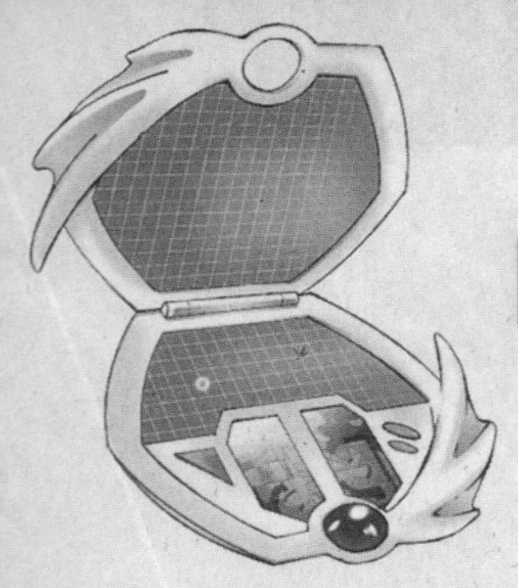

Contents

ゴト
ゴト
THAT HURT!!
ぎゅっ
OW!!

GOOD EVENING, TILEL.
YOU'RE TEN MINUTES EARLY.
I GUESS OU MUST MEAN USINESS.
WE'VE BEEN HERE FOR THIRTY MINUTES, ALREADY.
Yeah!

Re-No: 9

Edel Raid Hunter—Unexpected Move in the Dead of Night

BY THE WAY...

...WHAT HAPPENED TO THAT MOTOR-CYCLE YOU'RE SO PROUD OF?
!!!!!

CAN IT BE? DID THE GREAT HUNTER WOLX...
...GET INTO AN ACCI-DENT?
GASP!
WHATEVER COULD HAVE HAPPENED?
HE DOESN'T WANNA TALK ABOUT IT!

THE BIKE'S FINE.
DON'T LISTEN TO THE MEAN LADY, BABY. ONCE I GET THE MONEY, I'LL GET YOU PROPERLY FIXED...!
....

ENOUGH ABOUT THAT.
LET'S TALK BUSI-NESS.

I CAUGHT SOME UNEXPECTED PREY.
WHEN WE LAST SPOKE, YOU ONLY HAD ONE.
I HAVE THREE IN ALL.
TWO OF THEM ARE EDEL RAIDS FROM ARC AILE.

THREE AT ONCE, EH? HEH HEH...

I SHOULD'VE EXPECTED NO LESS FROM THE GREAT WOLX HOUND.

EDEL RAIDS TO YOU ARE WHAT *RABBITS* ARE TO *HUNTING DOGS.*

NEITHER WILL EVER *ESCAPE* YOUR *FANGS.*

HMPH.

I DON'T NEED YOUR FLATTERY.

YOU, WHO WORK UNDER THE PALE LUNAR GLOW OF THE MOON!
YOU, THE NEFARIOUS VILLAINS WHO PLAN AND SCHEME IN THE SHADOWS OF NIGHT!
GOD MAY ALLOW IT...
...BUT ARC AILE WON'T!!
WELL BLOW ME DOWN...
SHE ACTUALLY SOUNDS KINDA COOL!

ARC AILE?! WHAT'S THE MEANING OF THIS?!
I HOPED YOU'D COME.
MY INSTINCTS WERE CORRECT!
YOU WERE HIDING IN THIS TOWN UNTIL IT WAS TIME FOR THE TRANSACTION!
BUT YET, MY KEEN INTELLECT AND MASTER DETECTIVE SKILLS HAVE FOILED YOU!
WOLX?
BUT BECAUSE THE EDEL RAIDS THAT WERE SEALED WITH THE SEALING CHARMS DON'T SHOW UP ON RADAR...
...I COULDN'T FIND YOU.
I KNEW...
I *KNEW* THIS IS WHERE YOU WOULD TRY TO *SEAL* THE *DEAL*.

BUT WHAT ARE YOU GOING TO DO?

FIGHT ME?

CISQUA!!

YOU DON'T EVEN *HAVE* A PARTNER, DO YOU?

OF COURSE NOT!!!
THAT'S MY PLAN!!
MY GOODNESS... THIS HAS BECOME QUITE THE HASSLE.
RELAX. IT'LL BE OVER BEFORE YOU KNOW IT.
PSST...! I'LL TAKE CARE OF THE HUNTER!
COU, YOU GO ALONG THE CRUMBLED WALL TO THE OTHER SIDE AND HELP KUEA AND THE OTHERS.
SURE, I'LL JUST GO TO THE OTHER SIDE AND--
WHAT?! YOU WANT ME TO DO IT?!
YOU OWE US.
YOU OWE US FOR WHAT HAPPENED AT ELÉ BLANCA!
FINE, FINE!
BUT AFTER THIS, WE'RE EVEN!

COU?
UGH!
PWETTY PWEASE?
I SAID I'LL DO IT! SEESH...!
Our hearts are beating merrily...
...we make the vow!!
With a bewitching sigh...

YOU'LL REGRET YOU EVER CAME HERE!!
I MAY NOT HAVE MY EDEL RAID...
...BUT I'M FAR FROM HELPLESS!!
THOSE THINGS WON'T WORK.
SPARE ME. THIS MAY WORK AGAINST STREET PUNKS...
...BUT DO YOU REALLY THINK THOSE TOYS CAN MATCH THE POWER OF A PLEASURE EQUIPPED WITH AN EDEL RAID?!

TELL ME SOMETHING I DON'T KNOW!
HE'S RIGHT! I **CAN'T** BEAT A PLEASURE AND HIS EDEL RAID!

BUT...ROWEN'S NOT HERE, SO I DON'T REALLY HAVE A CHOICE!
I HAVE TO BREAK THE BOND BETWEEN THE EDEL RAID AND THE PLEASURE!

BUT FIRST...
WHAT'S WRONG?!
SCARED?!
...I NEED TO ANALYZE THAT EDEL RAID'S POWER...!

PATHETIC. YOUR EFFORTS ARE FUTILE.

THIS IS EASY!

IT'S STARTING TO COME TOGETHER...
THAT EDEL RAID STRESSES DEFENSE OVER ATTACKS...!

IT WAS THE SAME BACK IN THE VILLAGE...

HER ATTACKS LOOK FLASHY, BUT SHE MISSES HER TARGET QUITE A BIT!

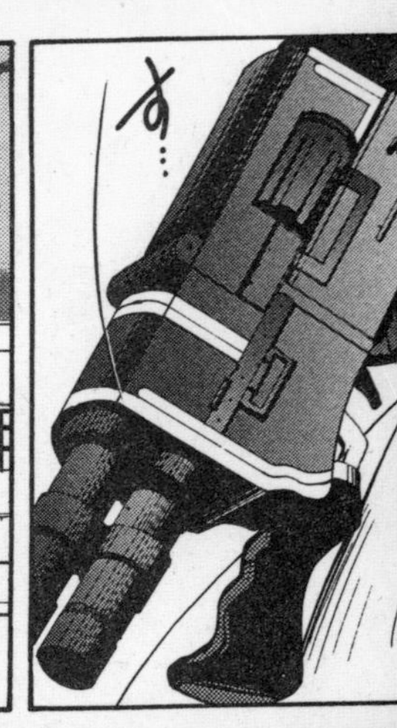
す…

OH?

CISQUA...

JUST WHAT ARE YOU TRYING TO PULL?
WOW! I'M IMPRESSED!
YOU'VE DEFLECTED EVERY ONE OF MY BULLETS. YOU MUST BE SOME KIND OF FIGHTER, HUH?

HOW-EVER...
...UNDER THIS CAPE, I'M HIDING SOMETHING EVEN BIGGER.
SOMETHING SO BIG...IT COULD ANNIHILATE THIS ENTIRE NEIGHBOR-HOOD.

SHE'S BLUFFING!
REALLY?
LET'S SEE IT.

CLACK
OKAY... BUT DON'T SAY I DIDN'T WARN YOU...!
EXCUSE ME WHILE...

...I WHIP THIS OUT!

TARGET LOCKED !!
LAUNCH IN THREE!!
IT'S OKAY! I'LL PROTECT YOU!
TWO!!
Without fail, I will protect you intuitively!
The boulders intuitively offer a prayer!
ONE!!

LAUNCH!!
We hunt each other under beloved darkness and sing a song of good fortune...
Let us scatter away those changeable and treacherous!

WHOOAAA!!
DANG! EVERYTHING SHE DOES IS SO FLASHY!
NOW'S OUR CHANCE TO FREE THE OTHERS!
BUT HOW?
I THINK YOU JUST HAVE TO TAKE THE SEAL OFF, LIKE YOU DID WITH ME.
OH YEAH...
?

WHAT'S GOING ON?
REN, LOOK OUT!!
WHAT ARE YOU DOING?!

CISQUA MUST HAVE TOLD HIM TO COME HELP US.
OH, MAN...

WHAT A SURPRISE. ANOTHER EDEL RAID.

WELL, WELL...

I THOUGHT I KNEW ABOUT EVERY KIND OF EDEL RAID.
What are you staring at?
I'VE NEVER SEEN ONE LIKE THAT BEFORE!

NOOOO!!
LOOK OUT, COU!!

GYAAAHH!!
HEY...
PLEASE BE CAREFUL WITH THAT ONE.
I WOULDN'T WANT YOU TO BREAK IT.

ガアアア

WELL, HELLO AGAIN.
FOR A MINUTE I THOUGHT YOU WERE GOING TO DEMOLISH THE ENTIRE NEIGHBORHOOD.

HEE HEE! NONE OF YOUR ATTACKS WILL EVEN REACH WOLX...
...BECAUSE I WON'T LET THEM!

HAAH!

VEIL CLIFF!!

TRY AS YOU MIGHT--I WON'T LET YOU HIT HIM!!

I WAS RIGHT! HIS EDEL RAID HAS DEFENSIVE SUPERIORITY...!
SHE'S A DJINN DEFENDER!

THE DEFENSIVE MECHANISM ACTIVATED BY THE SONG AUTOMATICALLY CREATES A WALL TO STOP ANY ATTACK IF THE PLEASURE IS IN DANGER.
Look out!
TWELVE SOLID IRON SHIELDS PROTECT THE PLEASURE--EVEN AGAINST MISSILES!
AUTO GUARD!!

BUT...

TSK... SOME PEOPLE NEVER LEARN.
VELL CLIFF!!

WHAT?! SHE'S GONE?!
DAMN!!
Tch! THE MISSILES WERE A DECOY!!
TILEL!!
TURN OFF THE AUTOMATIC SHIELD!!!
BUT...
SHE'S--

WAAHHH!!
SON OF A--
WELL, WELL... IS THAT SHOCK I SEE ON YOUR FACE? HMPH. WHILE AUTOMATIC DEFENSES ARE INCREDIBLY HANDY...
...THEY CAN STILL BE OUTSMARTED.

ザザッ

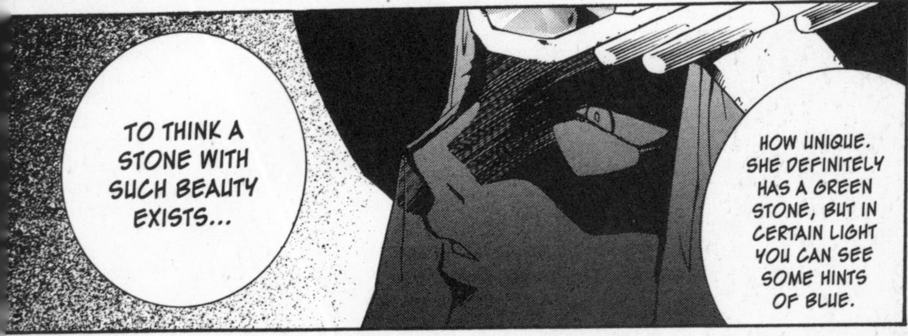
HOW UNIQUE. SHE DEFINITELY HAS A GREEN STONE, BUT IN CERTAIN LIGHT YOU CAN SEE SOME HINTS OF BLUE.
TO THINK A STONE WITH SUCH BEAUTY EXISTS...

SHE MUST BE A PRETTY HIGH-LEVEL EDEL RAID.
HER PLEASURE, ON THE OTHER HAND...
...HAS NO IDEA WHAT HE'S DOING. WHY DOES THIS SIMPLETON...

...HAVE SUCH A MAGNIFICENT WEAPON?

WHAT'S SHE DOING?
SHE'S JUST WATCHING REN...
HER BODYGUARD ISN'T EVEN TRYING TO WIN!

RAAAGH!!

ズ
ウウ
ズズ
GREEN STONE...
WIND...
SPEED AND PRECISION...
SUCH SPEED... SUCH PRECISION...
IT'S LIKE THE WIND ITSELF.
—?!
?!!!
METHERLENCE--IN SHORT. THOSE WHO ARE SUBJECT TO SLEEP. FEEDING OFF OF DEEP, SWEET SLUMBER, ONCE AWAKENED, THEIR JEWELS, REFLECTING VIOLET-JADE AND GREEN-BLUE, BECOME A SHARP SWORD LIKE A PEACOCK'S FEATHER...

IF THE LEGEND IS TRUE...

...THEN THAT EDEL RAID...

UNH...
W-WOLX ...?

YAAY! MY INTEL-LECT PRE-VAILS AGAIN! ♡
LET ME SPELL THIS OUT FOR YOU...
...I FIRED MY MISSILES, AND YOUR AUTOMATIC DEFENSES REACTED.

AND WHY WOULDN'T THEY? MISSILES ARE POWERFUL, RIGHT?
SO ALL TWELVE OF YOUR DEFENSIVE WALLS WENT UP.

IT MUST HAVE BEEN HARD TO SEE AROUND THEM, HUH?
IN FACT... I BET YOU COULD HARDLY SEE ME MOVING AT ALL, CORRECT?
ESPECIALLY WITH ALL THE SMOKE AND FLAMES IN THE WAY...

YOU WERE COMPLETELY UNGUARDED ON THE LEFT, RIGHT AND FROM BEHIND! ♡
SO... THE GUNS WERE... A TRICK?
YEP! I NEEDED TO SEE WHAT SHE WOULD DO...
I NEEDED TO FIND A WAY AROUND IT!
I DOUBT SHE HAS ENOUGH ENERGY LEFT TO REACT AGAIN.
AND I'M NOT AN EDEL RAID... SO YOUR SEALING CHARM WON'T WORK ON ME.

CISQUAAA!!

GUNNH!!
ALL THAT MAY BE TRUE...
...BUT LIKE I TOLD THE BLOND KID, I HAVE NO INTENTION OF RELYING ON TILEL ALONE.
THE SEALING CHARM IS ONLY ONE WAY TO SUBDUE AN EDEL RAID.
BUT YOU SHOULD KNOW...
...I SHOW NO MERCY--NOT EVEN TO WOMEN AND CHILDREN.

UH-HUH.

THAT WORKS FOR ME.

ぎゅっ

I AM CISQUA OF ARC AILE!! WE ARE THE SWORN PROTECTORS OF EDEL RAIDS!
I CHALLENGE YOU TO A FAIR FIGHT!

UMPFF ...!

YOU CAN'T, ROWEN! NOT IN YOUR CONDITION!

K-KUEA WAS T-TAKEN...
SHE'S MY RESPON-SIBILITY...
...AS WELL AS CISQUA!

ROWEN!! NO!!

Re-No: 10
Edel Raid Hunter–Rose-Colored Dawn

QUIET, TILEL! I DON'T NEED YOU...!
WOLX...

ONCE I'VE DEFEATED HER, I'LL HAVE THE BROKER GET ME A BETTER SHIELD ANYWAY.
COCKY INGRATE !!
YOU DARE TO TREAT HER LIKE THAT AFTER WORKING HER SO HARD?!
JERK!!

GUH ...!

COLD-HEARTED BASTARD!!

!!!

WELL, THEN... IF *THAT'S* HOW YOU WANT DINNER SERVED... THEN I'LL GIVE IT TO YOU *PIPIN' HOT!!*
OOOKAY...
I GUESS THAT WHOLE "NO MERCY TO WOMEN" THING WAS MORE THAN MACHO CHEST POUNDING...
INTERESTING. I ALWAYS THOUGHT ARC AILE WAS A BUNCH OF COWARDS...
...BUT I UESS THERE ARE SOME EXCEPTIONS AFTER ALL!

SO?!

WHY DO YOU DO IT?!

!!
...ALWAYS GET IN THE WAY OF MY WORK!!
YOU GUARDIANS ...
UNH ...
CISQUA!!
UAAHHH!!

JUST THE SIGHT OF YOU MAKES ME SICK!
HUP...!
W-WE... GET IN THE WAY OF Y-YOUR WORK?
GOOD.
FOOLS.
OH? AND WHY IS THAT?
BECAUSE OUR MISSION...
...IS TO PROTECT EDEL RAIDS FROM PEOPLE LIKE YOU!

THEY'RE TOOLS-- NOTHING MORE.
A DISTANT COUSIN OF THE GARDEN SHEAR, AT BEST.
COCKY LITTLE--!!
YOU SAY YOU WANT ONLY TO PROTECT THEM...
...BUT THAT'S NOTHING BUT A FILTHY LIE!!
JUST MORE OF YOUR SELF-SERVING ARROGANCE!!

OOOH...

YET EVEN YOU, WHO ARE SWORN TO PROTECT THEM...

...USE THEM AS WEAPONS!

HEY!!
WHAT IS WITH YOU?!
CHALLO!!

ARC AILE ISN'T LIKE THAT!
WE'RE DOING IT TO *HELP* OUR *FELLOW MAN!*

WHATEVER GETS YOU THROUGH THE DAY, HONEY.
HOWEVER... IN THE COURSE OF YOUR NOBLE GRANDSTANDING, YOU SEEM TO HAVE FORGOTTEN SOMETHING...

IN THE END, *YOU'RE* JUST *TOOLS* FOR THE PROTECTION OF SOCIETY.

SO, WITHOUT HUMANS... EDEL RAIDS DON'T EXIST.
BUT... WITHOUT ME...
...YOU DON'T EXIST.

IS THAT SO ...?!
ガッ
ガッ

WHO'S THE ARROGANT ONE NOW?!
YOU REALLY THINK YOU'RE THAT SUPERI-OR?!
THINK?! I KNOW I AM!!
AN UNUSED TOOL DOES NOTHING BUT RUST!
IT'S THEIR WISH TO BE USED!!

I KNEW IT ...!
ONLY A HUMAN...
...COULD HAVE SUCH AN EGO!!
WOLX!

IT'S WEIRD...
HE SEEMS DIFFERENT...

AH...!!

I GOT CARRIED AWAY AND KEPT USING VEIL CLIFF...
THAT MUST BE WHY HE'S MORE WORN OUT THAN USUAL.

AND THE BLEEDING ON HIS RIGHT ARM HAS GOTTEN WORSE.

IT'S MY FAULT...

IF ONLY I HAD BEEN A BETTER SHIELD...

IF ONLY I WAS STRONGER...

SNIFF...

HEEEY!!
WAAAAH!!

OUCH.
That's gonna leave a mark...

COU... ARE YOU OKAY?

WHAT A CREEP!
I JUST KNOW SHE'S TOYING WITH US!

DANG IT!
LET'S BRING HER CRASHING DOWN-- LIKE WE DID AT THE FORTRESS!
WE CAN'T.

REN?
WHAT...
...DID YOU JUST SAY?
WE CAN'T BEAT HER, GOU.

CISQUA!!

STOP IT!!

YOU CAN'T GO ON LIKE THIS!!

WHEN I'M DONE HERE...
CISQUA...
...WE ARE SO THERE--MY TREAT!

YOU GUARDIANS CAN'T BEAT ME!!
IT'S NO USE!!
YOU TALK A BIG GAME...
...BUT IN REALITY, I THINK YOU'VE REACHED YOUR LIMIT!!
WHA--?!
CISQUA?!

HE'S ALMOST REACHED HIS LIMIT PHYSICALLY AND MENTALLY.

THE BLEEDING HASN'T STOPPED ON HIS DOMINANT ARM. HE CAN BARELY RAISE IT.

HE PROBABLY DOESN'T WANT TO PROLONG THE BATTLE ANY FURTHER.

IN THAT CASE, IF I GIVE THE SMALLEST OPENING...

...HE'LL FINISH ME.

BUT WHEN YOU KNOW THE ATTACK IS COMING...
...IT'S JUST SO EASY TO EVADE!
NO!!

I AM NOWHERE NEAR MY BREAKING POINT!!

WOLX!!
HUFF...
Y-YOU... TH-THINK YOU'VE W-WON...?
!!

NO.

I KNOW I'VE WON.

NO WAY! YOU SAID NO WEAPONS!

CALL IT BEING PRE-PARED.

Where'd she get that?

HE WAS RIGHT. I WAS NEAR MY BREAKING POINT.

BESIDES, I DON'T WANT TO GET HIT ANYMORE.

IT'S OVER.

TILEL?

IF ONLY I WAS A STRONGER SHIELD...
IF ONLY I COULD HAVE PROTECTED YOU...

THEN, MAYBE ...

...JUST **MAYBE**... I COULD HAVE SAVED YOU.

IF NOTHING COULD REACH HIM...

LET'S REACT ONE LAST TIME.
LET'S CRUSH ARC AILE!
ONE LAST TIME...
I'LL DO BETTER...
I PROMISE!!

WHAT'S SHE DOING?!

COU! LOOK OUT!

GAAH!!

HMPH.

THIS GUY IS WEAK.

NOTHING?
ゴト
NO...
ゴト

I'VE LEARNED SOME-THING VERY IMPORTANT.
I MUST TELL HIM RIGHT AWAY!

LET ME ASK YOU SOME-THING, WOLX...

WHAT DO YOU SEE?
DO YOU SEE A GIRL WHO WILL LAY DOWN HER LIFE TO PROTECT YOU?
OR DO YOU SEE A TOOL?

ENOUGH.
DON'T PUSH YOURSELF, TILEL.
I... NEED YOU FOR OUR NEXT JOB.

IT SEEMS THE BROKER GOT AWAY.
YEAH... BUT NOT BEFORE SHE BEAT THE CRAP OUT OF ME!

THANKS TO YOU, I LOST MY BEST CUSTOMER.
LOOKS LIKE ARC AILE HAS MANAGED TO GET IN THE WAY AGAIN.

I HAVE AN IDEA...
WE, ARC AILE, WILL BECOME OUR NEW BEST CUSTOMERS!

WHAT?

HERE IS MY PROPOSAL...
...YOU CONTINUE HUNTING AS YOU HAVE UNTIL NOW...
...AND THE OCIETY WILL AKE THE EDEL RAIDS INTO UR CARE AND PAY YOU A REWARD FOR INDING THEM.

THIS WAY WE BOTH WIN!
CISQUA?

HEH HEH...

YOU'RE A STRANGE ONE.
YOU ACTUALLY WANT TO MAKE A DEAL WITH AN EDEL RAID HUNTER LIKE ME?

JUST KNOW...

...I DON'T COME CHEAP.

COOL! I'LL LET MY BOSSES KNOW!

WAIT ...!
WHAT?
I WASN'T ABLE TO THANK YOU BEFORE...
...FOR CHOOSING THESE CLOTHES FOR ME.
SO THANK YOU.
WELL... IT REALLY WOULD LOOK BETTER WITH A BLACK RIBBON!
YOU CAN'T RELY ON THAT LOSER YOU HANG WITH TO HAVE ANY FASHION SENSE.
HEY!
LISTEN ...
...IT WOULD BE STRANGE FOR ME TO TELL YOU TO BE CAREFUL...
...BUT IT LOOKS LIKE THE BROKER HAS HER EYE ON YOU.
YOU SHOULD BE ON GUARD FROM NOW ON.
....

THIS BIKE..
?
ギクッ
IT'S THE BIKE COU BROKE.
WAIT!! REN!!
SHHHHHH!!
S-SHE'S..
SHE'S JUST A LITTLE C-CONFUSED! HEH HEH!
GULP ...!
WE BLEW ALL THE MONEY WE HAD PAYING TO FIX THE BIKE.
SO I GUESS WE'RE BROKE AGAIN.

WAS HE RIGHT?

ARE HUMANS THAT SUPERIOR?

ちら

WOLX?

I'M SORRY..

I'M SORRY I'M SO USELESS...

I WON'T BE DEALING WITH ARC AILE ANYMORE. THEY'VE GOT SOME KIND OF JINX.

I HAVE TO HURRY AND FIND MY NEXT PREY. I NEED TO GET THE BIKE FIXED PROPERLY.

TILEL?

DOES IT HURT?
NO... IT'S NOTHING.
I PROMISE TO DO BETTER NEXT TIME.
MEAN-WHILE.
ROWEN, WHO WAS SUPPOSED TO BE COMING TO HELP...
HUH?
ISQUA...? BOSS...?

I SEE... A SHICHIKO-HOJU.

NICE WORK
I'LL BE SURE TO INFORM THE PRESIDENT.
YOU ARE DISMISSED.
YES, SIR.

I'LL TELL HIM...
HEH... HEH HEH...

FIRST OF ALL, IF I WERE TO BE SO NAIVE AS TO JUST TELL THE PRESIDENT ABOUT A SHICHIKO-HOJU...
...HE WOULD JUST GO AND GET HER HIMSELF. IT IS HIM WE'RE TALKING ABOUT, AFTER ALL.

BUT... IF I GET THE SHICHIKO-HOJU FIRST...
...EVEN THE PRESIDENT WILL HAVE NO CHOICE BUT TO ACKNOWLEDGE MY CAPABILITIES.
THEN I'D BE TREATED THE WAY I DESERVE TO BE!

Re-No: 11

The Newly-Opened Road, En Saguwan–Beginning Milestone

INN
ふあぁ
EVERY-ONE'S GONE.
I WONDER IF THEY WENT DOWNSTAIRS TO EAT OR SOMETHING.
I AGREE.
IT REALLY WOULD BE BEST TO GIVE REN OVER TO HEADQUARTERS AS SOON AS POSSIBLE.
!!!!

BUT THAT WOULD MEAN BETRAYING COU AND REN.
SHE'S RIGHT, BOSS.
WE SAID WE'RE TAKING REN TO EDEL GAR--
UH... EDEL WHAT-NOW?
NOTHING ...!
UHH...
IT'S TRUE THAT AT FIRST WE MEANT TO LOOK INTO EDEL GARDEN...
...BUT IT'S BEEN MORE THAN TWO WEEKS SINCE WE CAME TO TAKE REN INTO OUR CUSTODY, AND YOU AND I ARE BOTH BEAT UP PRETTY BADLY.
IT'S IMPOSSIBLE TO PREDICT WHAT MIGHT HAPPEN NEXT.
WE NEED TO GET HER TO HEADQUARTERS SO SHE'LL BE SAFE.

CAN YOU CONTACT HEAD-QUARTERS, SUN?

IT WOULD BE IMPOSSIBLE TO CONTACT THEM DIRECTLY FROM HERE.

BUT IF YOU LEAVE THIS TOWN AND HEAD NORTH, THERE'S A LARGER TOWN.

THERE'S AN ARC AILE BRANCH OFFICE THERE.

THERE'S A BUS THAT GOES THERE.

You'd ave to walk a ays, to the bus stop, hough.

……

WHATEVER OTHER REASONS THERE MAY BE, WE MEMBERS OF ARC AILE MUST FULFILL OUR MISSION!
IF WE GET CARRIED AWAY BY OUR EMOTIONS, WE WON'T GET OUR JOB DONE!
...!
THAT'S TRUE, BUT...

...BECAUSE WE HAD TO PAY FOR REPAIRS FOR A STUPID BIKE, WE ARE NOW COMPLETELY BROKE!!!
WE CAN'T PAY THE INN CHARGES, OR THE BILL FOR EVERYTHING KUEA ATE!! WE GOT ZILCH!!!
うわーん
SO, SUNWELD... CAN YOU PLEASE LOAN US SOME MONEY?!
....
WE SAVED CHALLO.
THAT'S WORTH SOMETHING, ISN'T IT?
IT BETTER BE!
CISQUA ...

BAR
BAR

to MANFE
to RASFE
THERE IT IS!
I FOUND THE BUS STOP!
THERE'S NOBODY HERE.
ハァ
ハァ
ハァ
THIS CAN'T BE RIGHT...
THIS DOESN'T LOOK GOOD.
Cou, what's a bus?
A bus is...
WHAT'S THE MATTER, ROWEN?
IT LOOKS LIKE WE'LL HAVE TO WAIT FOUR HOURS FOR THE NEXT BUS!
11:20
8:45
15:25
18:00
A ticket is required to
Please buy a ticket in
entrainment.
An entrainment charge

What?!
FOUR HOURS?!
Man!
OUT HERE IN THE MIDDLE OF NOWHERE?!
THE INSTANT I HEARD FOUR HOURS, I GOT HUNGRY.

SO WHY ARE WE...
... RESPON-SIBLE FOR CATCHING LUNCH?!
GOOD LUCK, BOYS!
HEY ...
WHERE'S REN?
Eeeeep! A bug!
Man, you're annoying.

はっ…
OOPS!
S-SORRY...!
WHY DO I FEEL LIKE I JUST SAW SOMETHING...
...I SHOULDN'T HAVE?
ドキ
ドキ
S-SORRY TO BOTHER YOU...!
THE WATER...
...IS NICE AND COLD.

UM...

SHE SPOKE TO ME! I CAN'T BELIEVE IT!

I'm touched!!!

THIS IS THE SECOND TIME THAT SHE'S SPOKEN TO ME AT ALL!

BRR!

FEELS NICE, THOUGH.

UM...

YES?

I GET IT.

THE WORDS I FIRED AT ROWEN WHEN HE WAS DOWN...
"IF WE GET CARRIED AWAY WITH EMOTIONS, WE WON'T GET OUR WORK DONE!"

THEY WERE A WARNING TO MYSELF.

I CAME TO TAKE REN INTO CUSTODY.
THAT IS MY JOB.
I SHOULDN'T HARBOR UNNEEDED EMOTIONS.

WE BARELY KNOW EACH OTHER.
WE'RE NOT FRIENDS.
I SHOULDN'T EVEN CONSIDER THINGS LIKE THAT.

I KNOW THIS...
... BUT ...

...REN'S HAND...
IT'S THE SAME AS MINE.
HER PALM, HER FINGERS...
THE WARMTH OF ITS TOUCH...

NO... HERS IS MORE SLENDER.

IT SEEMS LIKE IT WOULD BREAK IF I HELD ON TOO TIGHTLY.

IF REN WASN'T AN EDEL RAID...

OR IF SHE WASN'T A SHICHIKO-HOJU...

AND IF I WASN'T IN ARC AILE...

THEN MAYBE...

JUST MAYBE...

...WE COULD BE FRIENDS.

I'M SORRY!!
I KEEP SLIPPING!!

COU TOLD ME NOT TO LET MY GUARD DOWN AROUND YOU.

YOU'RE SUSPICIOUS, HE SAYS.
HE WOULD SAY THAT.
COU!
That slanderous little twerp!

YOU CAME LOOKING FOR ME JUST NOW, DIDN'T YOU?
YOU TAKE YOUR JOB VERY SERIOUSLY, DON'T YOU?

REN ...
I AM A MEMBER OF ARC AILE.
IT'S MY JOB TO PROTECT YOU.

PROTECT ME?
WHY?

FOR MONEY?
EEEP!!

ER, THAT'S NOT THE ONLY REASON...!

FOR A PROMOTION, THEN?
EEEEP!!
ドキィーッ

UM...
fidget
fidget
YEEEAH... THAT *MIGHT* BE PART OF IT, TOO...
... BUT ...

!!!!!

じー

じー

OKAY!!! I GIVE!!! JUST STOP LOOKING AT ME WITH THOSE COW EYES!!!
YOU FIGURED ME OUT, OKAY?!!

I HAVE A PROMOTION RIDING ON THIS MISSION WITH YOU, REN.
THAT PROMOTION WOULD GREATLY INCREASE MY PAY.
SO WHAT COU SAID ABOUT ME BEING AFTER MONEY WASN'T *ENTIRELY* UNTRUE.
IT'S NATURAL THAT WOLX WOULD CCUSE ME OF BEING THE SAME AS HIM.
SO?
ARE WE REALLY JUST *TOOLS* TO YOU?
WHEN I STARTED AT ARC AILE... YES, I THOUGHT THAT WAY.
BUT AFTER COMING INTO CONTACT WITH KUEA, CHALLO AND OTHER EDEL RAIDS I'VE MET ON MISSIONS...

...I REALIZED SOMETHING...

...THEY'RE JUST LIKE ME.

WE HAVE MORE IN COMMON THAN I FIRST REALIZED.

KUEA COMPLAINS ALL THE TIME...

...CHALLO TEASES PEOPLE...

...JUST LIKE HUMANS.

JUST LIKE *ME.*

I USED TO *HATE* HUMANS.

I THOUGHT HUMANS ONLY SAW US EDEL RAIDS AS TOOLS...

BUT THAT'S WHAT I THOUGHT.

...THAT IS, UNTIL I MET COU.

BUT WHEN I HELD YOUR HAND JUST NOW... I REALIZED SOMETHING...

YOUR PALM...
...YOUR FINGERS...
...AND THE WARMTH I FELT WHEN I TOUCHED IT.
REN...
...EVEN IF YOUR GOAL IS MONEY, EVEN IF IT'S A PROMOTION, EVEN IF THE PROTECTION SOCIETY'S DIGNITY IS AT STAKE...
...I WATCHED YOU FIGHT WOLX TO SAVE US.

NOW *I* HAVE A FAVOR TO ASK *YOU.*

THE BUS IS HERE.
CAMPING OUT WAS KIND OF FUN, HUH?
HEY, REN? WHAT WERE YOU DOING ALONE WITH CISQUA EARLIER?

NOTHING.

I REALIZED SOMETHING, THOUGH...

YOU AND CISQUA ARE VERY MUCH ALIKE.

TAKE ME TO EDEL GARDEN.

AFTER WE GET THERE, YOU CAN DO WHATEVER YOU WANT WITH ME.

BUT IF YOU DON'T TAKE GOOD CARE OF ME UNTIL THEN, YOU WON'T BE PROMOTED.
I GET THE POINT, ALREADY!!
YiPe!

BUT...
...WHY DO YOU WANT TO GO TO EDEL GARDEN SO BADLY?

I CAN'T TELL YOU.
さらり
DANG... I THOUGHT SHE WAS OPENING UP TO ME!

YOU SEEM PRETTY HAPPY, BOSS. DID SOMETHING GOOD HAPPEN?
HEH HEH...
I'LL FILL YOU IN LATER.
OOOOOOHHHH!!
HEY! IT'S THE OCEAN!

I CAN SEE THE TOWN, TOO!
THAT PLACE IS HUGE! I'M SURE SOMEONE THERE WILL KNOW HOW TO GET TO EDEL GARDEN.

Razfe Ankul

ザッ

HEADQUARTERS INFORMED US YOU'D BE COMING.

THE ARC AILE RAZFE ANKUL BRANCH HAS ALREADY MADE PREPARATIONS TO ESCORT THE EDEL RAID REVERIE METHERLENCE TO HEADQUARTERS.

THIS WAY, PLEASE.

ESCORT?!

HEAD-QUARTERS?!

WHAT THE *HECK* ARE YOU *TALKING ABOUT?!*

CISQUA, THAT BACK STABBING LITTLE...!
I SHOULD HAVE KNOWN BETTER THAN TO TRUST HER!
I CAN'T BELIEVE...
...SHE TRICKED US!

Re-No: 12

Milliard Trey Betting Grounds –Place Your Bets

HELLO, COMMISSIONER FAULK.
IT'S BEEN A LONG TIME.
Commissioner Faulk-- Head of all Guardians in the Society for the Complete Protection of Edel Raids

YOU'VE WORKED HARD ON THIS MISSION, CISQUA.
BUT STILL, I MUST ASK--WHAT IS THE MEANING OF THIS?
AFTER WE CONFIRMED HER WHEREABOUTS, YOUR ORDERS WERE CLEAR.
TAKE REVERIE METHERLENCE INTO CUSTODY AND RETURN HER TO HEAD-QUARTERS.

SO, WHY ARE YOU IN RAZFE ANKUL?

HEADQUARTERS RECEIVED A MESSAGE THAT KUEA AND AN UNCONFIRMED EDEL RAID WERE HEADING TOWARD THIS BRANCH OFFICE.
FOR NOW, WE'RE SAYING THAT OUR MESSAGE FROM HEADQUARTERS GOT TO THIS OFFICE LATE.
WE MANAGED TO AVOID BLOWBACK SO FAR.

BUT THE MISSION YOU ACCEPTED WAS A SERIOUS ONE!
YOU WERE WELL AWARE OF THAT!
YOU ALSO KNOW HOW **DANGEROUS** REVERIE METHERLENCE CAN BE!!

WELL?! WHAT SAY YOU?!
EXPLAIN YOURSELF, CISQUA!!
UM...
WELL?!
WE TOOK A VOTE...
...AND WE ALL DECIDED WE WANTED TO GO SIGHT-SEEING.

YOU THINK THAT'S AN EXCUSE?!
WHAT CAN I SAY? WE NEEDED A LITTLE TIME TO RECOVER FROM OUR ARDUOUS JOURNEY.

AND, MIGHT I ADD...

WE HAVEN'T HEALED NEARLY ENOUGH...
...SO WE'D LIKE TO TAKE A MONTH OFF.
WHEN OUR VACATION IS OVER, I WILL ESCORT REVERIE METHERLENCE TO HEADQUARTERS.

WHAT?! YOU IDIOT!!
WHY ON EARTH WOULD I ALLOW SUCH A THING?!

COMMIS-SIONER, PLEASE CALM DOWN.

CISQUA...

YOU UNDERSTAND THAT YOU ARE IN THE MIDDLE OF AN IMPORTANT MISSION, CORRECT?

YES, I DO.

AND YOU DO REALIZE HOW VALUABLE AN EDEL RAID REVERIÉ METHERLENCE IS, RIGHT?

BUT IT IS A MISSION THAT WAS ENTRUSTED TO US...

...AND NOBODY ELSE.

Aide Cruz--
Aide to the Head of all Guardians in Arc Aile.

SO PLEASE...

...LET ***US*** BE THE ONES TO ESCORT HER TO HEADQUARTERS.

WILL *ONE MONTH* WILL BE SUFFICIENT?
!!
CRUZ!!
ばんッ
YOU WILL ESCORT HER TO HEAD-QUARTERS AS SOON AS YOUR VACATION HAS ENDED, CORRECT?
YES, SIR!
GOOD.
I WILL INFORM THE COMMIS-SIONER.
WHA--?!
YOU DON'T ACTUALLY *BELIEVE* THIS NONSENSE, DO YOU?
AIDE CRUZ ...?
DON'T WORRY. I KNOW WHAT KIND OF KIDS YOU ARE.
THAT'S WHY I'LL TRUST YOU.

BUT REMEMBER-- ALTHOUGH YOU MAY BE ON VACATION, YOU ARE STILL ***GUARDIANS.***

YOU MUST NEVER FORGET THAT IT IS ARC AILE'S MISSION TO PROTECT EDEL RAIDS.

BESIDES, THOSE KIDS WILL BE ALL RIGHT.

I GUARANTEE IT.

I HOPE YOU'RE RIGHT-- FOR ***ALL*** OUR ***SAKES!***

GOT IT! I UNTIED THE KNOT!
REN! LET'S GET OUT OF HERE!
BUT...
WHAT? YOU DON'T THINK I CAN FIND MY WAY OUT?
AFTER ALL, I'M AN SKY PIRATE, FOR GOODNESS SAKES!
GET DOWN...! SOMEONE'S COMING...!

ガばッ
GOTCHA! DON'T MAKE A SOUND!
NOBODY HAS TO GET HURT!
Ahem.
CISQUA?!
NEVER MIND. JUST PLEASE LET GO OF ME.
S- SORRY...!
UM, WHAT ARE YOU DOING, COU?
HEY... WHY ARE YOU DRESSED LIKE THAT?
MORE IMPORTANTLY, WHAT ARE YOU GOING TO DO WITH REN?!

NOTHING
BUT... I THOUGHT YOU WERE GOING TO ESCORT ME TO EDEL GARDEN?
AND I'M DRESSED LIKE THIS BECAUSE I'M ON VACATION.
WHERE DO YOU THINK WE'RE GOING FOR THAT VACATION?
BESIDES...
...I MADE A PROMISE TO YOU, REN.
RIGHT?
WHAT PROMISE?
WHY DO YOU CARE?
LET'S GO. ROWEN AND KUEA ARE WAITING IN THE HALL.
HEY! WHAT DO YOU MEAN, PROMISE?!
Ren, are you okay?
HEY!!

WHAT?!
COMMISSIONER FAULK ALLOWED THIS?!
OF COURSE THE COMMISSIONER WOULDN'T ALLOW IT.
IT WAS AIDE CRUZ.
AIDE CRUZ IS A KIND MAN WHO UNDERSTANDS PEOPLE.
ON THE OTHER HAND...
...COMMISSIONER FAULK WAS NAGGING AND COMPLAINING AS USUAL.
Eh?
Ha ha ha!
AAACHOO!!
HAVE YOU CAUGHT A COLD?
NNNN?
ずずー
SAY... MAYBE YOU COULD USE SOME TIME OFF YOURSELF.

CISQUA...
THERE IT IS.
THAT'S THE CATHEDRAL I WAS TELLING YOU ABOUT EARLIER.

IN RAZFE ANKUL, JUST OUTSIDE THE CITY, THERE ARE THE CRUMBLING REMAINS OF A CATHEDRAL.
YOU'LL SEE A BLACK-CLOAKED MAN STANDING AT THE ENTRANCE. GIVE HIM THE FOLLOWING SECRET PASSWORD...
..."IF YOU CALL THE GODDESS, THE OPPORTUNITY WILL COME."
"THE LORD WILL RESOUND ON THE EARTH SHE LOOKS DOWN UPON."
THE MAN WILL THEN GUIDE YOU INTO THE CATHEDRAL AND TO A HIDDEN DOOR. PASS THROUGH IT AND CLIMB DOWN THE STAIRS TO THE UNDERGROUND.

SURE IS DARK IN HERE.
EVERY WEEKEND IN THAT UNDERGROUND CHAMBER...
REN, WATCH YOUR STEP!
OW!!
...THE GAMES BEGIN.

THIS IS THE HOME OF GREAT JOY AND DEEP SORROW-- MILLIARD TREY!!!!

GOOD EVENING, LADIES AND GENTLEMEN!
ボッ
WELCOME TO MILLIARD TREY!

WHAT WILL OUR FIGHTERS BE BETTING TONIGHT?!
PRIDE, FAME, FORTUNE-- OR THEIR OWN LIMBS?!
DON'T YOU DARE MISS IT!

I CAN'T BELIEVE THIS PLACE EXISTS...!
WHOA! BOSS, LOOK AT THAT!
THEY'RE FIGHTING WITH EDEL RAIDS!
WE HAVE TO PROTECT THEM!
SHHHH!!
BUTTON YOUR LIP!
Sorry...!
HAVE YOU FORGOTTEN *WHY* WE *CAME HERE?!*
There's food everywhere. ♡

EDEL GARDEN
VOLCYONE
RAZFE
SANKUL
NO, I HAVEN'T FORGOTTEN.
PROBLEM IS, WE CAN'T AFFORD PASSAGE FOR EVERY-ONE.
ACCORDING TO THE MAP...
...TO GET TO EDEL GARDEN FROM THIS TOWN, WE HAVE TO GO BY SEA TO THE VOLCYONE CONTINENT, RIGHT?
WE SHOULD HAVE HAD THE COMMIS-SIONER SEND US SOME MONEY.
NO! HE MUSTN'T FIND OUT THAT WE LOST ALL THE DOUGH HE GAVE US IN THE FIRST PLACE!
SO... WE'LL BE ON THESE FIGHTS!
I'D RATHER NOT GO INTO--
WHOOOA!!
IT'S TRUE!! THERE ARE GIRLS HERE WHO REALLY DO WEAR BUNNY EARS!!
DID YOU HEAR WHAT I SAID?! BUNNY EARS!!!

Yahoo!
SWEET, SWEET BUNNY EARS!!!
IT'S JUST LIKE RAGDOLL SAID!
COU!! MELLOW OUT!!

I CAN'T HELP IT!
WHEN WE CAME HERE SEVEN YEARS AGO, THEY MADE ME STAY WITH THE SHIP.

WE'RE LUCKY COU REMEMBERED HOW TO GET HERE.
TRUE...

...BUT IT'S BAD THAT THEY'RE USING EDEL RAIDS FOR GAMBLING.
PLUS, THEY'RE DOING IT IN AN AREA UNDER ARC AILE'S JURISDICTION. DOES THE BRANCH OFFICE KNOW ABOUT THIS?
I DOUBT IT. THESE EDEL RAIDS ARE ALL UNDERGROUND SO THEY WOULDN'T SHOW UP ON ANY RADAR.

I'M JUST GLAD WE CAME HERE OUT OF UNIFORM.
OTHER-WISE, THEY WOULD'VE NEVER LET US IN.

NOT LIKE IT WOULD MATTER. COU WILL BE FIGHTING FOR US, ANYWAY.

What?!

WHY ME?!

THIS IS A GOOD OPPORTUNITY FOR US TO GET USED TO REACTING.
SO LET'S DO IT.
WHAT...?
REN...?
WE CAN'T GO TO EDEL GARDEN WITHOUT MONEY.
YEAH ...
I GUESS.
BUT WE DON'T KNOW HOW THE BETTING WORKS.
HOW DO YOU EVEN ENTER?
DO YOU KNOW, COU?
I NEVER MADE IT PAST THE BUNNY EARS.
OOF!

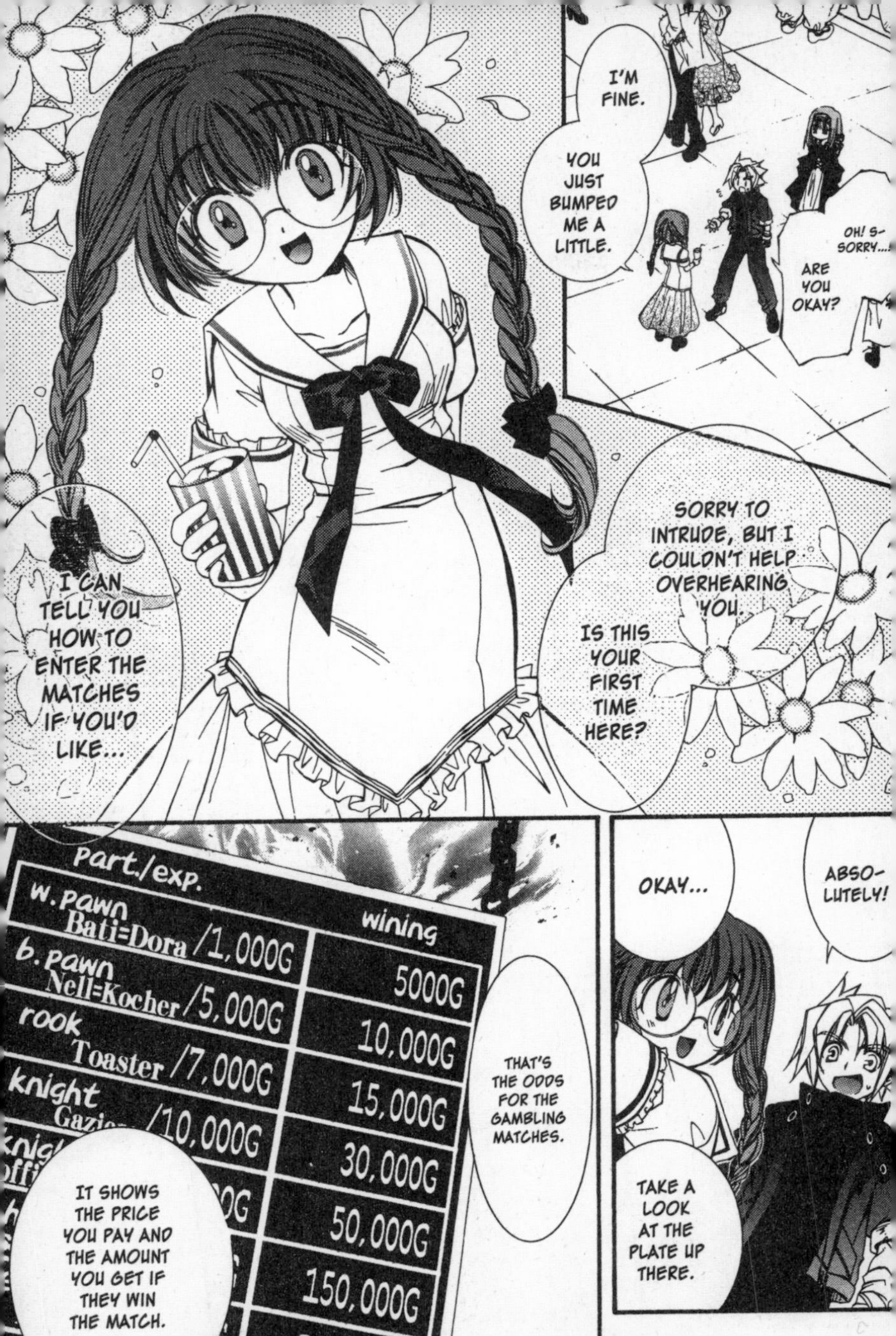

OH! S-SORRY...
ARE YOU OKAY?
I'M FINE.
YOU JUST BUMPED ME A LITTLE.
SORRY TO INTRUDE, BUT I COULDN'T HELP OVERHEARING YOU.
IS THIS YOUR FIRST TIME HERE?
I CAN TELL YOU HOW TO ENTER THE MATCHES IF YOU'D LIKE...
ABSO-LUTELY!
OKAY...
TAKE A LOOK AT THE PLATE UP THERE.
THAT'S THE ODDS FOR THE GAMBLING MATCHES.
IT SHOWS THE PRICE YOU PAY AND THE AMOUNT YOU GET IF THEY WIN THE MATCH.
Part./exp.
wining
w.pawn Bati=Dora /1,000G
5000G
b.pawn Nell=Kocher /5,000G
10,000G
rook Toaster /7,000G
15,000G
knight /10,000G
30,000G
50,000G
150,000G

THE AMOUNTS ARE ALL DIFF-ERENT.

THE PROMOTERS HAVE ORGANIZED EIGHT DIFFERENT RANKS OF FIGHTERS.

DEPENDING ON THE RANK, THE FEE REQUIRED TO ENTER--AS WELL AS THE PRIZE MONEY--FLUCTUATES.

YOU'RE FREE TO CHOOSE ...

...HOW MUCH YOU PAY AND WHAT CLASS OF FIGHTER YOU GO UP AGAINST.

BUT ONCE YOU'VE FOUGHT A RANK AND WON, THEN YOU CAN'T REENTER IN THAT RANK.

WHAT ELSE... OH! YOU'RE ALLOWED TO USE WEAPONS...

...SO YOU CAN PARTICIPATE WITH EDEL RAIDS.

WHEN MY BUDDIES CAME HERE BEFORE, THEY DIDN'T SAY ANYTHING ABOUT EDEL RAIDS.

COME TO THINK OF IT, I HAD NEVER EVEN HEARD OF EDEL RAIDS UNTIL I MET REN.

IT WAS THREE YEARS AGO THAT THEY STARTED USING EDEL RAIDS.
I saw them for the first time here, as well.
THREE YEARS AGO, EH?
NO WONDER. WE CAME HERE WAY BEFORE THAT.

LET'S ENTER.
CISQUA, GIVE ME MONEY.
"GIVE ME MONEY," HE SAYS.
JUST WAIT A SECOND ...!

WE GOT SIX THOUSAND FROM SUNWELD.
ADMISSION PRICE WAS THREE HUNDRED EACH. THAT'S FIFTEEN HUNDRED, TOTAL.
SO WE HAVE FORTY-FIVE HUNDRED LEFT.

t./exp.
awn ati Dora /1,000G
awn Nell Kocher /5,000G
ook Toaster /7,00
/10,0

LOOKS LIKE YOU HAVE TO ENTER AT THE LOWEST RANK.
I CAN'T BELIEVE YOU CAME HERE WITH-OUT ANY MONEY!
WELL, WE'RE JUST HERE FOR A LITTLE PREVIEW TODAY.
HEH HEH...

ENTERING AT THE RANK OF WHITE PAWN...
...COUD VAN GIRUET!!
LET'S DO THIS, REN!!
I'M A LITTLE SLEEPY, BUT IT'S ALL RIGHT.
GOOD LUCK, COU!
HE'S SO NOT COOL.
THERE ARE THREE WAYS...
...GIVE UP, GET KNOCKED OUT, OR GET KNOCKED OUT OF THE RING.
COOL...! HE'S A PLEASURE!
SO HOW DO YOU LOSE IN THESE GAMBLING MATCHES?

SO YOU'RE A PLEASURE, EH?
I SEE YOU'VE GOT A GOOD ONE.
Rank: White Pawn
Bati Dora
Expense: 1,000
Prize: 5,000
IF I BEAT YOU, I GET FIVE THOUSAND, RIGHT?
WELL ...
... THAT'S *IF* YOU WIN.
HEH ...
LET'S DO IT!!!

Money left in Cisqua's wallet...3500.

Money left in Cisqua's wallet...2500.
1000G
YOU'RE MAKING ME POOR, COU!!
......
OUT OF BOUNDS!
CHALLENGER IS DEFEATED!
I JUST LET MY GUARD DOWN!
A TEENSY LAPSE OF DEFENSE--THAT'S ALL!
One more time...
Money left in Cisqua's wallet...1500.
1000G
......
WHAT THE HELL, MAN?!!
OUT OF BOUNDS!
CHALLENGER IS DEFEATED!
Wow...
THAT WAS WEIRD.
......
Money left...

HEY ...

...LET'S TRY JUST ONE MORE TIME...

ARE YOU NUTS?!! AT THIS RATE, I'LL BE LUCKY IF I WALK AWAY WITH MY SHIRT!!!

YOU SUCK-- END OF STORY!!!

THIS CALLS FOR SOME...

... SPECIAL TRAINING!!

EEEEEEK?!

T-TRAINING?
SERI-OUSLY?
TOMORROW, YOUR SPARTAN TRAINING COMMENCES!
SO BE READY!
WHAT IS THIS ONE?
THE GAME FOR THE THIRD HIGHEST RANK IS STARTING. IT'S WHAT EVERYONE IS HERE FOR TONIGHT.
THEY SAY THAT THE BISHOP-RANKED CLASS FIGHTER RASATI IS UNDEFEATED.
EVEN I COME HERE BECAUSE I WANT TO SEE RASATI! ♡
RASATI?
IS RASATI AN EDEL RAID PLEASURE?

ENTERING
AT BISHOP
RANK--FERO
DA STEELO!!

THIS IS IT, FOLKS!!
THIS IS THE MOMENT YOU'VE ALL BEEN WAITING FOR!!

THE PRIDE OF MILLIARD TREY, THE UNDEFEATED YOUNG TIGER-- RASATI TIGRES!
WILL TONIGHT'S WAGER BE BLACK OR WHITE--OR GREAT JOY AND DEEP SORROW?!
SO YOU'RE THE MIGHTY, UNDEFEATED RASATI, HUH? I THOUGHT YOU'D BE SOME KINDA MONSTER OR SOMETHIN'...
...BUT YOU'RE JUST A SCRAWNY LITTLE THUMBSUCKER!
Rank: Bishop
Rasati Tigres
Expense: 50,000
Prize: 150,000
YOUR LUCKY STREAK ENDS NOW!!

HOLY--!! HE'S FAST!!
UMPFF!!

GOOD-NIGHT.

武

HE HAS AN EDEL RAID, BUT SHE STILL MANAGED TO TAKE HIM OUT IN ONE HIT!
Zzzz...
AND SHE'S NOT EVEN A PLEASURE!
WOW...
NOT TO MENTION ...
...RASATI'S A WOMAN?!
To Be Continued in Volume 4

In The Next Volume of

WHEN COUD SPIES ON RASATI IN ORDER TO LEARN SOME OF HER SECRETS, HE UNCOVERS MORE THAN HE BARGAINED FOR WHEN HE DISCOVERS THAT RASATI IS FIGHTING TO EARN THE FREEDOM OF BOTH HER AND HER SISTER. THIS PLACES COUD IN A PICKLE OF A MORAL DILEMMA...SHOULD HE FIGHT RASATI WITH EVERYTHING HE HAS AND TRY TO EARN THE CASH HE AND HIS FRIENDS SO DESPERATELY NEED? OR SHOULD HE THROW THE MATCH SO RASATI AND HER SISTER CAN FINALLY BE FREE?

FIND OUT WHAT HE DECIDES IN THE NEXT ACTION-PACKED VOLUME!

The name Cisqua isn't her real name, but something like a codename given to her by Arc Aile.
Inside Cisqua's hat and cape, there are indeed pockets into a fourth dimension. What does she keep in them, and how much...?
Cisqua
A member of the Protection Society, she is passionate about her work, honest and honorable... or she was supposed to be. Before I knew it, she became a character who would do anything for money or her promotion. Along with Ren-chan, she is a heroine of this story, but she's not very lady-like, is she? And also she's physically strong. Cisqua's the strongest (when it comes to bad luck, that is)!
The model for Cisqua is an original character of mine that I drew when I was in middle and high school. That character also wore a big hat and looked like a boy. She is also modeled after a fiendish, red-hooded character* I was allowed to draw when I worked on a certain famous fighting game.
The things she does are nonsensical, but she's fun to draw. But when Cisqua gets too wild...Cou starts to fade into the background. Work hard, Cou!!
*Most likely B.B.Hood from Dark Stalkers.
"Trade Smile
qua's expressions change
ne most frequently. She
kes bad faces often, too.
Because Cisqua isn't an Edel Raid Pleasure, she fights with guns, knives, missiles and hand-to-hand.
Uraaaaahhh!!!
Cisqua's gun. By converting it, she can use it as a launcher, a shotgun, or a machine gun.
She packs a punch with her small frame.

Arc Aile's symbol mark. It's the image of wings protecting a jewel.

Arc Aile (Edel Raid Conservation Aile) refers to "the wings that protect Edel Raids."

Rowen

Cisqua's good junior officer. He's kind and honest, but he's a pushover and a bit dull. He's always being pushed around by Cisqua and Kuea.

He's older than Cisqua, but he entered the Academy after she did, so he is her junior. Row is the son of a rich family and was raised in great comfort, so why would he join Arc Aile...? It hasn't shown up in the story yet, but Row keeps a journal (or more like notes). It seems that things he didn't know about the world until now, Cisqua's secrets, etc. may or may not be written in it. Maybe being with Cisqua makes everyday exciting...

Row, like Cisqua, is modeled after an original character I drew a long time ago.

Row is relatively muscular for how he looks. (No, well, I like to draw muscles.)

Rowen doesn't make many seriou expressions, so this looks like a different person, doesn't it? He's supposed to be handsome, but... No, but he is handsome... right? Rather, his panicked face better fits his personality. He inherited this expression from a character I drew for another project. I like this expression.

Cou told him he's such a fuddy-duddy, so I want to write a romance story with him. But with Kuea...it's probably impossible.

Kullweet Envatilia

Kuea's an Edel Raid from the Protection Society. In the early stages of planning, she was supposed to be in charge of sex appeal...but now, of the five main characters, she's the most manly. And she's a brute, too! (no, a beast?) It's all right. It's more about food appeal than sex appeal with Kuea. She's always biting at Cisqua. Cisqua must look pretty tasty.

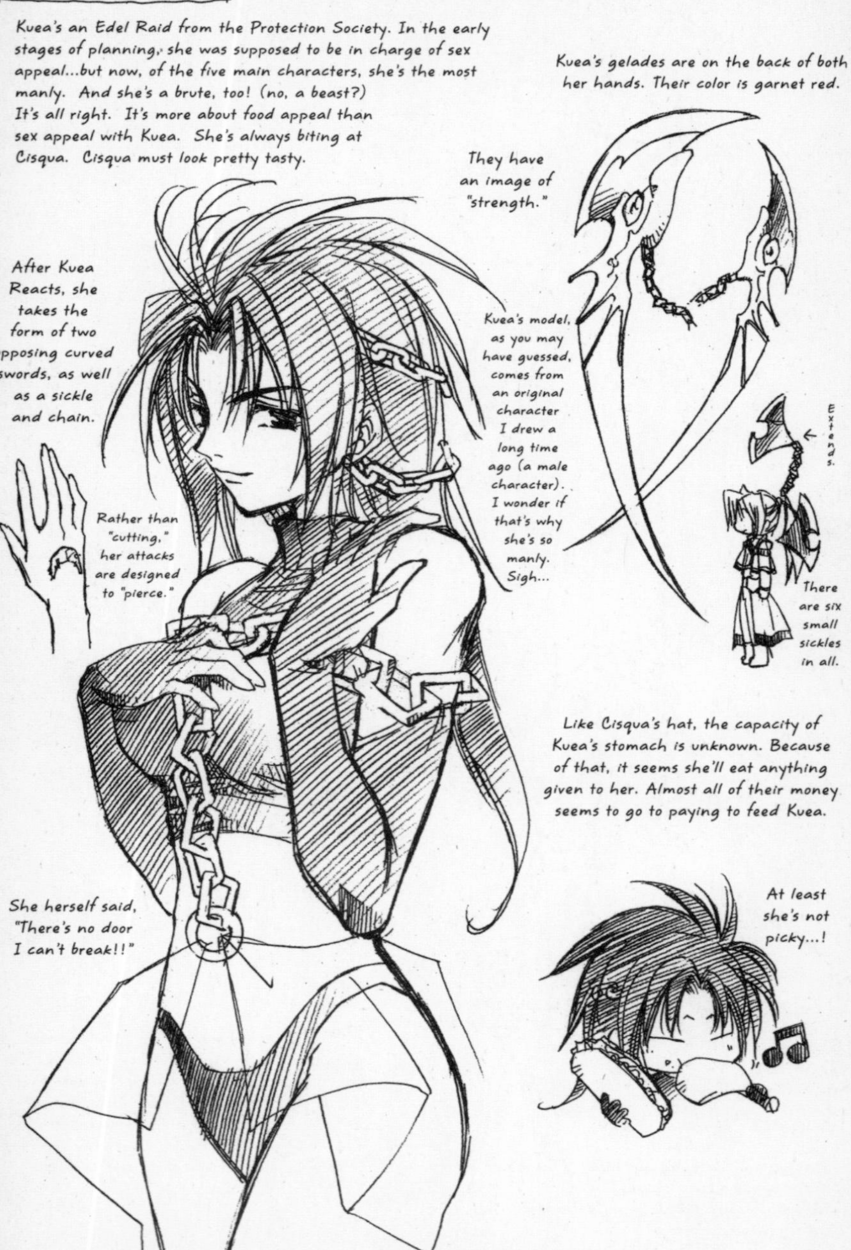

At Elé Blanca

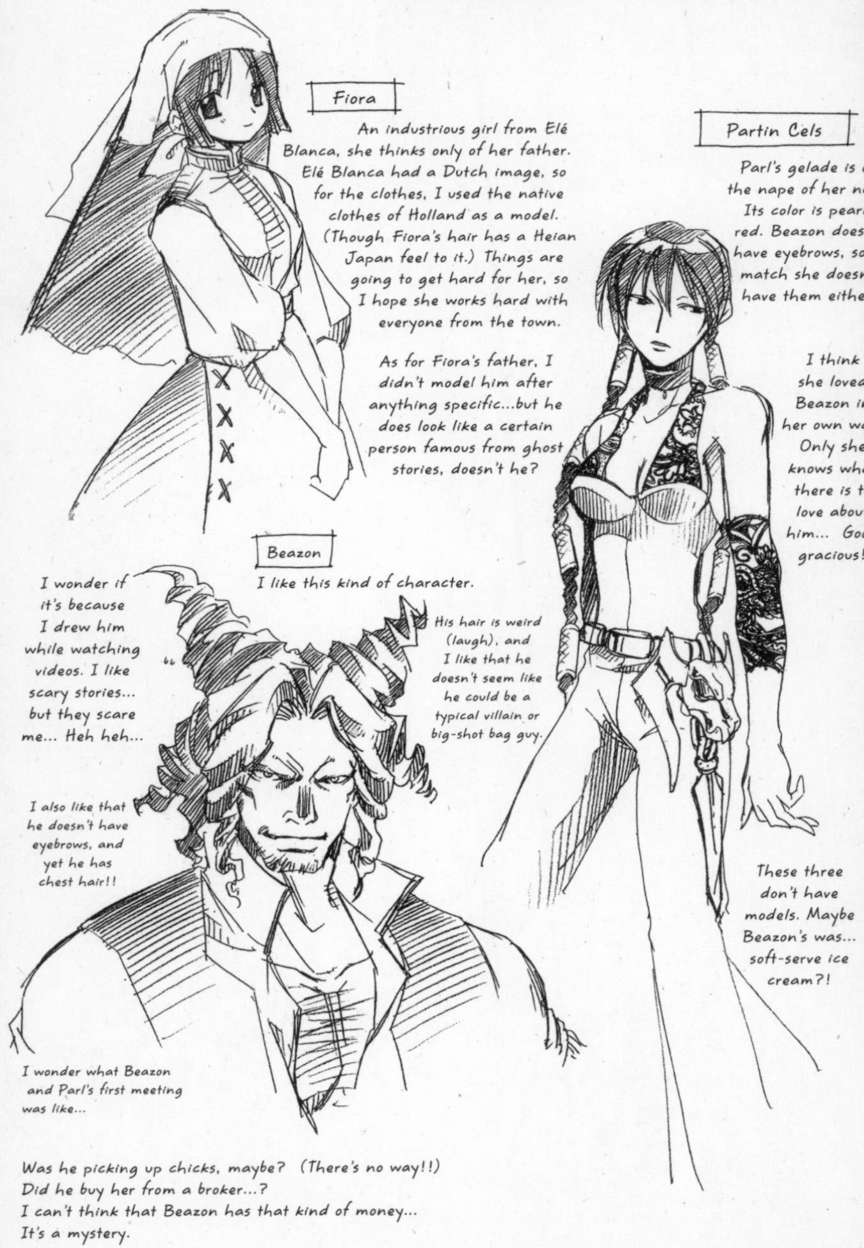

Was he picking up chicks, maybe? (There's no way!!)
Did he buy her from a broker...?
I can't think that Beazon has that kind of money...
It's a mystery.

Steady Beat
2
Fool's Gold
1
Fruits Basket
Natsuki Takaya
16
Ultra Cute
2
Little Queen
Yeon-Joo Kim
1
Someday's Dreamers
Story: Norie Yamada
Art: Kumichi Yoshizuki
2
Buy these and other
Shojo
manga from
TOKYOPOP
at your local retailer.
Steady Beat © Rivkah and TOKYOPOP Inc. Fool's Gold © Amy Hadley and TOKYOPOP Inc.
Ultra Cute © Nami Akimoto. Little Queen © YEON-JOO KIM, DAIWON C.I. Inc.
Someday's Dreamer: Spellbound © NORIE YAMADA/KUMICHI YOSHIZUKI.

Shojo showers bring April Flowers!
Shojo manga that doesn't miss a beat.
DRAMACON
TOKYOPOP
2
Created by Svetlana Chmakova
Dramacon © Svetlana Chmakova and TOKYOPOP Inc.

TERRORISM,
CORRUPTION
& SCHOOLGIRLS WITH GUNS!
ROSE HIP ZERO™
BY TOHRU FUJISAWA
VOL. 1 & 2 AVAILABLE NOW!
Appearances can be deceiving.
There is trouble in Tokyo as a
mysterious terrorist organization
called ALICE plots against the
police department. Just as
Division Four is tasked to bring
these men to justice, they are
given a "secret weapon" who
happens to be a young girl with
a mysterious past. She may loo
innocent, but she walks softly
and carries a big gun.
FROM THE
NOTORIOU
TOHRU FUJISAWA
CREATOR
OF GTO!!
ACTION
OT
OLDER TEEN
AGE 16+
© Tohru Fujisawa / KODANSHA LTD.

tactics™
Geeky ghost-hunters unite!
Kantarou, a folklore scholar
living in the Taisho period,
is always broke and always
late on his deadlines. But
Kantarou moonlights as an
exorcist solving the problems
of ghosts and demons,
all with the help of Haruka,
the legendary super-sexy
demon-eating tengu!
The manga
that influenced
the popular
anime!
COMEDY
T
TEEN
AGE 13+
© SAKURA KINOSHITA and
KAZUKO HIGASHIYAMA / MAG Garden.

STOP!

This is the back of the book.
You wouldn't want to spoil a great ending!

This book is printed "manga-style," in the authentic Japanese right-to-left format. Since none of the artwork has been flipped or altered, readers get to experience the story just as the creator intended. You've been asking for it, so TOKYOPOP® delivered: authentic, hot-off-the-press, and far more fun!

DIRECTIONS

If this is your first time reading manga-style, here's a quick guide to help you understand how it works.

It's easy... just start in the top right panel and follow the numbers. Have fun, and look for more 100% authentic manga from TOKYOPOP®!